SAGE | 50 YEARS

Global Marketing Research

Global Marketing Research

V. Kumar
Regents' Professor, Georgia State University

⑤SAGE | Response Business Books
www.sagepublications.com
Los Angeles • London • New Delhi • Singapore • Washington DC

First published in 2015 by

SAGE Response
B1/I-1 Mohan Cooperative Industrial Area
Mathura Road, New Delhi 110 044, India
www.sagepub.in

SAGE Publications Inc
2455 Teller Road
Thousand Oaks, California 91320, USA

SAGE Publications Ltd
1 Oliver's Yard, 55 City Road
London EC1Y 1SP, United Kingdom

SAGE Publications Asia-Pacific Pte Ltd
3 Church Street
#10-04 Samsung Hub
Singapore 049483

Published by Vivek Mehra for SAGE Publications India Pvt Ltd, typeset in 10/12 pts Stone Serif by RECTO Graphics, Delhi, and printed at Chaman Enterprises, New Delhi.

Library of Congress Cataloging-in-Publication Data Available

ISBN: 978-93-515-0750-5 (PB)

The SAGE Team: Sachin Sharma, Vandana Gupta, Nand Kumar Jha, and Rajinder Kaur

Dedicated with love

To my parents, S. Viswanathan and Pattammal Viswanathan,
my uncle, N. Kannan,
To my parents-in-law, Dr Lalitha Ramamurthy and Mr Ramamurthy, and
To the rest of my family, Aparna, Prita, Anita, Rohan, and Ryan.

Thank you for choosing a SAGE product!
If you have any comment, observation or feedback,
I would like to personally hear from you.
Please write to me at **contactceo@sagepub.in**

Vivek Mehra, Managing Director and CEO,
SAGE Publications India Pvt Ltd, New Delhi

Bulk Sales

SAGE India offers special discounts
for purchase of books in bulk.
We also make available special imprints
and excerpts from our books on demand.

For orders and enquiries, write to us at

Marketing Department
SAGE Publications India Pvt Ltd
B1/I-1, Mohan Cooperative Industrial Area
Mathura Road, Post Bag 7
New Delhi 110044, India

E-mail us at **marketing@sagepub.in**

Get to know more about SAGE

Be invited to SAGE events, get on our mailing list.
Write today to **marketing@sagepub.in**

BRIEF CONTENTS

Preface xvii
Organization of the Book xxi
About the Author xxix
Acknowledgments xxxi

SECTION I	INTRODUCTION TO MARKETING RESEARCH FOR THE EMERGING AND DEVELOPED MARKETS
1	The Nature and Scope of Global Marketing Research 3
2	Marketing Research in the Global Environment 41
3	Global Marketing Research Process 66

SECTION II	DESIGNING AND ADMINISTERING THE RESEARCH PROCESS
4	Preliminary Stages of the Research Process 95
5	Secondary Data Research 117
6	Marketing Research on the Internet 137
7	Primary Data Research 155
8	Qualitative and Observational Research 180
9	Survey Research 205
10	Scale Development 228
11	Questionnaire Design 250
12	Sampling 272

SECTION III	DATA ANALYSIS AND REPORTING THE RESULTS
13	Simple Data Analysis 303
14	Advanced Data Analysis 322
15	Multivariate Data Analysis 346
16	Presenting the Results 366

SECTION IV	MARKETING RESEARCH APPROACHES ACROSS THE GLOBAL MARKETS
17	Asia-Pacific 375
18	Europe 400
19	Latin America 419
20	Middle East and Africa 441
21	North America 463

SECTION V	FUTURE DIRECTIONS IN GLOBAL MARKETING RESEARCH
22	The Future of Global Marketing Research 481
	CASE STUDIES
Case I	Starbucks—Going to the Source 493
Case II	Tesla's Trademark Troubles 498
Case III	Segmenting Indian Households 505
Case IV	Subaru—A Problem of Plenty 506
Case V	Millennials at Work 512

Index   I-1

DETAILED CONTENTS

Preface xvii
Organization of the Book xxi
About the Author xxix
Acknowledgments xxxi

SECTION I	INTRODUCTION TO MARKETING RESEARCH FOR THE EMERGING AND DEVELOPED MARKETS

CHAPTER 1	THE NATURE AND SCOPE OF GLOBAL MARKETING RESEARCH 3

Introduction 3

Global Marketing Research: Is It a Valid Concept? 7

What's Different About Global Marketing Research? 8

Culture 16

Culture Classification Model 21

Alternative Types of Global Marketing Research 22

Importance of Comparability 24

Classification of Global Marketing Research 25

Challenges to Research 29

Marketing Researcher of the 21st Century 30

Ethics in Research 37

Global Marketing Research in Practice 38

CHAPTER 2	MARKETING RESEARCH IN THE GLOBAL ENVIRONMENT 41

Introduction 41

Role of Research in Global Marketing Strategy Formulation 41

Issues Specific to Global Marketing Research 43

Complexity of Global Marketing Research 46

Cost 48

Equivalence 49

Personnel 51

Information on the Global Marketing Research Industry 52

Research Activities of Some Top Firms 52

Approaches to Global Marketing Research 59

Selecting the Research Firm 61

Coordination of Pan-Global Research Studies 61

Global Marketing Research in Practice 64

Summary 64

CHAPTER 3	GLOBAL MARKETING RESEARCH PROCESS 66

Introduction 66

Research Objective 66

Problem or Opportunity Analysis 68

Decision Alternatives 68

Research Users 69

Information Requirement 69

Unit of Analysis 71

Data Availability 73

Research Design 74

Issues in Primary Data
Collection 75

Qualitative Methods 75

Surveys and Instrument Design 76

Sampling 77

Data Analysis 77

Interpretation and Presentation 78

Need for Global Marketing
Research 78

Global Marketing Research in
Practice 90

SECTION II   DESIGNING AND ADMINISTERING THE RESEARCH PROCESS

CHAPTER 4   PRELIMINARY STAGES OF THE RESEARCH PROCESS   95

Introduction 95

Information Requirements for
Global Marketing Decisions 95

Market Orientation 96

Strategic Orientation 103

Problem Orientation 107

Unit of Analysis 108

Global Marketing Research in
Practice 110

Summary 115

CHAPTER 5   SECONDARY DATA RESEARCH   117

Introduction 117

Sources of Secondary Data 117

Syndicated Data Sources 121

Electronic Point of Sale (EPoS)
Scanning 126

Uses of Secondary Data 127

Advantages of Secondary Data 129

Disadvantages of Secondary
Data 129

Problems in Collecting Secondary
Data 130

Evaluating the Value of
Research 131

Guidelines for Effective Online
Secondary Data Research 133

Global Marketing Research in
Practice 134

Summary 135

CHAPTER 6   MARKETING RESEARCH ON THE INTERNET   137

Introduction 137

Current Trends in Internet 139

Secondary Research on the
Internet 143

Primary Research on the
Internet 146

Social Media 149

Leveraging Big Data 151

Global Marketing Research in
Practice 153

Summary 154

CHAPTER 7	**PRIMARY DATA RESEARCH 155**	

Introduction   155

Types of Primary Research   159

Issues in Primary Data Collection   167

Types of Primary Sources   168

Problems with Collection of Primary Data   171

Advantages and Disadvantages of Primary Data Collection   175

Establishing Equivalence in International Marketing Research   175

Global Marketing Research in Practice   178

Summary   178

CHAPTER 8	**QUALITATIVE AND OBSERVATIONAL RESEARCH 180**	

Introduction   180

Need for Qualitative Research   180

Types of Qualitative Research   181

Types of Observational Methods   187

Advantages and Disadvantages of Qualitative and Observational Research   189

Frequency and Ease of Use   191

Cultural Influences   191

Biases in Qualitative and Observational Research   192

Landmark Developments   193

Global Marketing Research in Practice   203

Summary   203

CHAPTER 9	**SURVEY RESEARCH 205**	

Introduction   205

Types of Surveys   205

Advantages and Disadvantages of Survey Methods   216

Frequency and Ease of Use   220

Requirements   221

Applicability   222

Cultural Influences   222

Problems Specific to Developing Countries   223

Sources of Bias in Surveys   223

New Approaches to Survey Research   225

Global Marketing Research in Practice   225

Summary 226

CHAPTER 10	**SCALE DEVELOPMENT 228**	

Introduction   228

Attitudes   228

Measurement and Scaling   229

Measurement of Equivalence   238

Accuracy of Attitude Measurement   240

Types of Scales   231

Scales in Cross-National Research   236

Global or Pan-Cultural Scales   237

Psychophysiological Approaches to Scale Development   243

Cultural Issues   246

Global Marketing Research in Practice   247

Summary   248

CHAPTER 11 **QUESTIONNAIRE DESIGN   250**

Introduction   250

Questionnaire Development   252

Cultural Issues   262

Construct Equivalence   263

Guidelines for Online Questionnaire Design   266

Global Marketing Research in Practice   269

Summary   270

CHAPTER 12 **SAMPLING   272**

Introduction   272

Statistical Basis for Sampling   272

The Sampling Process   273

Types of Sampling   275

Determining the Sample Size   286

Sampling Equivalence   294

Cultural Issues   294

Modifications Required for Developing Countries   295

Global Marketing Research in Practice   296

Summary   299

SECTION III **DATA ANALYSIS AND REPORTING THE RESULTS**

CHAPTER 13 **SIMPLE DATA ANALYSIS   303**

Introduction   303

Data Preparation   303

Data Analysis   306

Statistical Techniques   307

Summary   321

CHAPTER 14 **ADVANCED DATA ANALYSIS   322**

Introduction   322

Analysis of Variance   322

Correlation Analysis   327

Regression Analysis   331

Pooled Time-Series Cross-Sectional Analysis   335

Genetic Algorithms   338

Hierarchical Bayes Models   340

Summary   342

CHAPTER 15 | **MULTIVARIATE DATA ANALYSIS   346**

Introduction   346

Interdependence Techniques   346

Dependence Techniques   358

Summary 364

CHAPTER 16 | **PRESENTING THE RESULTS   366**

Introduction   366

Written Report   366

Oral Presentation   368

Validity, Reliability, and Generalizability in Presentations   368

Integrating Advances in Communication Technology   369

Summary 372

SECTION IV   MARKETING RESEARCH APPROACHES ACROSS THE GLOBAL MARKETS

CHAPTER 17 | **ASIA-PACIFIC   375**

Introduction   375

Regional Characteristics   375

Culture   377

Seasonality and Holidays   378

Language and Translation Issues   380

Secondary Sources of Information   380

Australia   381

China   383

India   388

Japan   394

Summary   399

CHAPTER 18 | **EUROPE   400**

Introduction   400

Regional Characteristics   400

European Statistical Sources   403

Europe—One Economy?   404

Culture   405

Seasonality and Holidays   406

Language Issues   406

Mailing Lists   408

Computerized Information and Services   408

France   409

Germany   411

Great Britain   414

Summary   418

CHAPTER 19 | **LATIN AMERICA   419**

Introduction   419

Conducting Research in Latin America   419

Argentina   429

Bolivia   432

Brazil   435

The Mercosur   427

Latin American Relations with Asia   428

Venezuela   437

Summary   440

CHAPTER 20 | **MIDDLE EAST AND AFRICA   441**

Introduction   441

Conducting Market Research in the Middle East and North Africa   441

The Gulf Cooperation Council   452

Saudi Arabia   453

Conducting Market Research in Sub-Saharan Africa   456

South Africa   460

Summary   462

CHAPTER 21 | **NORTH AMERICA   463**

Introduction   463

Conducting Market Research in North America   463

North American Free Trade Agreement   464

The United States of America   467

Mexico   470

Canada   473

Summary   477

SECTION V | **FUTURE DIRECTIONS IN GLOBAL MARKETING RESEARCH**

CHAPTER 22 | **THE FUTURE OF GLOBAL MARKETING RESEARCH   481**

Introduction   481

Global Marketing Research: The Road Ahead   482

CASE STUDIES

CASE I | **STARBUCKS—GOING TO THE SOURCE   495**

Brewing Success   495

Hola Colombia!   498

Why Colombia Now?   498

The Go-To-Market Strategy   499

Questions for Discussion   499

Sources   499

CASE II | **TESLA'S TRADEMARK TROUBLES   500**

Revving It Up   500

Marketing Approach   501

Competitive Landscape   502

Betting Big on Research & Development (R&D)   503

To The "T"   503

Civil Code Versus Common Law   504

Legal Changes to the Rescue   505

Questions for Discussion   505

Sources   506

CASE III	**SEGMENTING INDIAN HOUSEHOLDS 507**
	Questions for Discussion 508
	Source 508

CASE IV	**SUBARU—A PROBLEM OF PLENTY 509**

	The Power of Niche Marketing 509	The Way Forward 512
	Awards Galore 511	Questions for Discussion 513
	Too Big for Comfort 511	Sources 513

CASE V	**MILLENNIALS AT WORK 514**

	The Face of the Millennials 514	Watching the Expenses 516
	Millennials and Education 514	Questions for Discussion 517
	Millennials and Employment 515	Sources 517
	Optimistic About Work 515	

Index   I-1

PREFACE

The increase in international trade and the emergence of global corporations resulting from the increased globalization of business have had a major impact on all facets of business, including marketing research. The increase in global competition, coupled with the formation of regional trading blocs such as the European Community and the North American Free Trade Agreement (NAFTA), has spurred the growth of global corporations and the need for global marketing research. This need is also accentuated by the tumultuous economic scenarios present in countries around the world. These global developments have spurred companies to consider all country markets as possible contenders to expand into and stabilize their financial performance. Such a scenario calls for collecting information relating to international markets, and monitoring trends in these markets, as well as to conduct research to determine the appropriate strategies that will be most effective in international markets.

The increasingly global scope of market research can be attributed to the rapid pace of globalization of markets, trade, communication, and transportation. Having access to a myriad of products from across the globe, consumers find themselves facing a wide range of options while businesses are subject to increasing competition, saturated domestic markets, and pressures to control costs. The other side of the coin presents a world of opportunity for small businesses and multinationals to establish their presence in foreign markets, build coalitions, and maintain a rapid rate of growth and profitability. The designing, branding, advertising, and positioning of a global product needs to address market requirements of varied economies and cultures.

All these realities point to the need for timely and accurate marketing research to guide global business decision making. Researchers not only need to familiarize themselves with the latest technological advancements that can facilitate and expedite global research, they have to keep abreast of an increasingly fast paced, rigorous, and competitive environment, while being sensitive to economic, cultural, political, and legal implications of undertaking market research in the international arena. This idea is clearly evident from the prevalence of and business significance of social media in the global marketplace. With consumers now more interconnected than ever before through the power of social media, marketing has gone truly global. The emergence of such consumer-managed communications has given rise to an exchange of product comparisons and consumer experiences, with results often indicating a precedence of other consumers' product evaluations over traditional company-driven marketing communication. This marketplace development now brings a series of marketing challenges that companies will have to counter in order to create or retain their place among their competitors.

The purpose of writing this book is to provide a practical, detailed, and well-documented guide that takes students, academics, and market researchers through all phases of developing and conducting global marketing research. This book not only accounts for the recent developments in the scope and extent of global marketing research, but also examines advances in both quantitative and qualitative research techniques, and the impact of the Internet on research in the global environment.

The trend of providing a comprehensive coverage of all the relevant topics will be continued in this edition also. This includes coverage of all phases involved in designing and executing global marketing research—from analyzing the nature and scope of the research to the preliminary stages, gathering data, designing the questionnaires, sampling, and presenting the data. Numerous country-specific examples and case studies will add to the understanding of the concepts laid out in the book. Coverage is also being provided by the book's website, including a list of readings, sample datasets for analysis, and links to academic and business websites for additional information.

The content of this book is focused to include the revolutionary changes to the field of global marketing which is a result of rapid globalization, technological innovations, and increased adoption of a consumer-centric approach to marketing. The overarching objective of this book is to provide the most current and relevant information about the global marketing research industry and outline the necessary techniques that can guide researchers in their work.

OBJECTIVES

The book is positioned to serve as a complete guide to modern global marketing research techniques involved in the collection, analysis, and interpretation of information on a global scale. The strength of this book is in the positioning, content, and coverage of the relevant topics. The book uses up-to-date examples of marketing research in practice relevant to the global marketing context to heighten the understanding of the facts and principles presented in the text. The wealth of information provided in this book is in terms of practical characteristics of major individual country markets and pragmatic approach adopted in dealing with the issues in global marketing research. This book will also be relevant and appealing to practitioners of global marketing research, executives in multinational corporations overseeing international operations, and many small business enterprises interested in entering foreign markets. Specifically, this book aims to:

1. Highlight the significance and necessity of global marketing research.
2. Bring out the differences in domestic and global marketing research.
3. Provide a comprehensive understanding of the global marketing research process.
4. Develop an in-depth knowledge of the issues that govern the conduct of global marketing research.
5. Offer numerous examples and applications of how to conduct global marketing research in various regions.

6. Track the use of Internet, social media, and other advances in marketing research and illustrate their applications in global marketing research.
7. Provide a clear and comprehensive treatment of simple and advanced data analysis topics for global marketing research.

The book is organized in a manner that will give the readers the feel of conducting global marketing research. Section I is the introductory section consisting of three chapters and provides an overview of global marketing research. Further, the steps involved in conducting global marketing research are described in detail.

SECTION I: INTRODUCTION TO MARKETING RESEARCH FOR THE EMERGING AND DEVELOPED MARKETS

Chapter 1

Companies are constantly looking to expand into new country markets. How do they decide on the choice of market(s) to enter? What strategies would they adopt with respect to key functions such as marketing, advertising, branding, distribution, and selling? Will they always be guaranteed success in the new markets? And to increase their chances of success, what market information would they need? These and many more global marketing research issues are addressed in the first chapter.

Specifically, the first chapter introduces the concept of global marketing research and discusses the growth and development of global marketing research over time. Particularly, it addresses the changes and advancements made in global research over the past decade. In addition to discussing the nature and scope of global marketing research, the challenges in conducting global marketing research are discussed in detail. This book also includes information on the latest trends in marketing, including the penetration of the Internet, digital communications, mobile marketing, and social media. How these revolutionary changes in the global marketplace are used effectively in conducting market research on a global scale is discussed with the help of current examples. The chapter also contains new examples that demonstrate the importance of national and cultural differences, data comparability, and the dimension of power distance for further explaining the nature and scope of global market research. The ethics in research as discussed in the chapter are extended to online research and the subsequent ethical challenges associated with it as well.

Chapter 2

Once companies have decided on expanding into new country markets, how do they decide on their target markets? What mode of entry would they have to adopt? When should they enter the market? How must they allocate their marketing resources? These are the next level of information that companies need to guide them in the international expansion process. This chapter explores the role of research in global marketing strategy formulation that will aid companies in this process.

The issues unique to global marketing research, such as the complexity of research design, problems related to the use of secondary data, the high cost of collecting primary data, and the problems associated with conducting and coordinating research in different countries, among others, are discussed in this chapter.

While maintaining the relevance of the topics discussed, such as the complexity of conducting global market research in the present age, all efforts have been made to provide the latest information on cost comparability. This chapter also includes information about the global marketing research industry, the demand for global research, the changing needs of the multinational clients, and the major commercial market research agencies. Discussion is made on the world market for market research, where, how much, and what type of research is done worldwide. Further, the sources from which global marketing research industry expect future business growth and from which directions can the industry expects to face future challenges, have also been presented.

This chapter features the most up-to-date profile of the top global research companies with information from the latest issues of relevant magazines such as the American Marketing Association's *Marketing News*, as well as individual company websites. The chapter also incorporates the latest developments in the field, such as cell-phone-based measurement systems, portable people meters, and using social media to collect data as well as implement social-media-based campaigns.

Chapter 3

Seeking information about new markets can be a lengthy and intensive process. How should researchers identify the relevant issues to research on? What information will be needed and how will they go about acquiring it? How must they design the study? How must they analyze and interpret the data? Insights on these topics will result in a relevant and meaningful study.

Specifically, this chapter deals with issues of global marketing research design. The global marketing research process is introduced and explained in this chapter. Tactical issues such as the type of information for each task, the level of analysis, the type of decisions to be made, and the unit of analysis to be determined are addressed in this chapter. This chapter also provides a detailed description of the organizational structure required for conducting marketing research. The pros and cons of centralized and decentralized structures are also discussed in detail in this chapter.

Along with the discussion of the design process of global marketing research, the chapter elaborates on the challenges facing global marketers in today's world. Topics include the growing market complexity that necessitates applied market knowledge, the blurring of categories that calls for coordinated planning and research, the shortened product development cycles that highlights the importance of higher quality, and the feature overload that requires more benefits research. The chapter also includes other topics such as the unit of analysis in global research, including the definition of urban in various countries.

SECTION II: DESIGNING AND ADMINISTERING THE RESEARCH PROCESS

Section II talks about the issues related to global marketing research—aspects such as the *what* and *how* of conducting global marketing research. This section consists of nine chapters and deals with issues such as data sources (primary and secondary data), modes of information collection (survey-based and non-survey-based techniques), instrument design inclusive of questionnaire design, sampling techniques, measurement, and scaling procedures, and data collection methods.

Chapter 4

When considering new country markets, how can companies identify (dis)similarities across countries? What mode of entry would be most appropriate, and why? What should their strategic orientation toward the proposed market entry be? Should they standardize their offerings from their existing markets, or adapt it to match the new market? These are some of the questions that companies would need an answer to in the preliminary stages of global marketing research.

This chapter includes information on the latest research in the globalization process, such as the mode of entry decisions in global markets and the efficient methods of forecasting using multinational diffusion models. Using variables derived from market research in the multinational, multicultural context, marketers can gain insights into the potential adoption rates of products in global markets through diffusion studies and can predict how markets will react to products and marketing strategies.

Chapter 5

Secondary data is often relied upon when collecting information about country markets. How do researchers go about collecting secondary data? What are the sources of secondary data? What is secondary data typically used for? What are the pros and cons of collecting secondary data? What are the issues in considering secondary data for analysis and interpretation?

This chapter focuses on secondary data sources by identifying the various sources of international data. Further, the availability of data regarding the general environment of the target market, data on social, cultural, political, legal, and economic factors, and data for assessing country-specific information are discussed in great detail in this chapter.

Even though traditional forms of secondary research are still relevant, in reality, many firms have resorted to Web-based methods for collecting secondary data. Internet information suppliers are able to offer more selective, dynamic, and up-to-date information to a larger number of users while saving on publishing, distribution, and other costs. However, the abundance of information available on the Internet can cause confusion and sometimes lead to conflicting or contradictory information on the same topics. Along with discussing the various sources of global research data available on the Web, this chapter provides guidelines for conducting effective online secondary data research.

Chapter 6

The Internet is constantly reshaping personal lives and the business world. In this scenario, how can companies make use of the Internet to collect data? What are the popular sources of collecting secondary data? Can companies use the Internet for collecting primary data, and if so, how? With the prevalence of big data, how can researchers make use of it through Internet and technology? These are some of the issues that this chapter discusses.

Beginning with a discussion of the current trends in Internet usage, including average weekly hours of Internet usage worldwide, the top online languages, and the nature of Internet searches performed by global users, this chapter incorporates other relevant topics that reflect the present-day market trends as well. Some of these are social media proliferation, voice-over-Internet Protocol and online video, online retailing, satellite industry, and digital music industry. Other topics of discussion covered in this chapter include the online methods used by various research firms, including online panels, focus groups, interviews, ethnography projects, and options for computer-aided interviewing.

Chapter 7

Often, the immediate and unique needs of a researcher require collecting primary data. In this regard, how do researchers approach primary data collection? What types of primary data exist, and how can they be used? How can researchers design experiments to help them in drawing conclusions about specific phenomena? What issues will researchers have to contend with regarding primary data? These are some of the topics that this chapter focuses on.

This chapter also discusses the importance of establishing data equivalence to create comparability of data from one country to another. The EMIC–ETIC dilemma in primary data collection is discussed and the possible sources of cultural bias in research design, communication, and interpretation are discussed. Some recent developments in primary research in the global arena such as Online International Omnibus surveys are discussed as well.

Chapter 8

Seldom is enough known about a marketing problem for the researcher to proceed directly to formulating the research question and structuring the design for the study. In such cases, how does a researcher undertake the data collection efforts? What are the types of qualitative data and observational methods available to the researcher? What are the pros and cons of using these approaches? What are the cultural connotations that need to be countered when adopting this approach? This chapter addresses these topics regarding qualitative data and observational methods.

This chapter reviews both survey and non-survey techniques of data collection. The non-survey techniques, including observational data, protocols, projective techniques, in-depth interview, and focus group techniques, are discussed, and the advantages and disadvantages of non-survey techniques and survey techniques are explained. Along with the discussions on traditional qualitative and observational research methods, some landmark developments relating to measuring minds in the 21st century are elaborated. These include the latest neuroscientific methods and the use of magnetic resonance imaging (MRI) and electromyography techniques to test the physiological and emotional responses elicited by particular ads. We have also discussed the Zaltman Metaphor Elicitation Technique (ZMET) which uses images and metaphors to reveal how consumers think and feel about brands or other research topics.

Chapter 9

Surveys are a popular way of collecting primary data. What are the types of survey methods available and how can researchers identify the appropriate type for their study? What are the pros and cons of each type? What are the cultural issues that could play out through these methods? These and other topics in survey technique are addressed in this chapter. Further, this chapter devotes considerable attention to potential sources of bias in survey research methods and offers suggestions to overcome these biases.

Chapters 10–12

Chapters 10, 11, and 12 discuss the development of scales, questionnaire design, and sampling issues, respectively. To make the right decisions, researchers have to understand the prevailing attitudes by asking the right questions to the right audience.

Chapter 10 addresses various measurement and scaling techniques and the limitations of these procedures. This chapter, in addition to the traditional methods of scale development and attitude measurement, discusses certain psychophysiological approaches that reveal involuntary physiological responses intended to provide insights into the real attitude of participants to a particular product or attribute in question. Some of them are the galvanic skin response (GSR) or heart rate, pupillary dilation or facial musculature (corrugator or zygomatic muscles).

Chapter 11 discusses the issues involved in developing questionnaires for global marketing research. It also includes a discussion on guidelines for online questionnaire design.

Chapter 12 discusses the sampling techniques in global marketing research. Problems in identifying an efficient sampling procedure for the purpose of global marketing research are discussed in detail. Concepts such as probability and non-probability sampling designs, estimation of sample size, and evaluation of traditional and Bayesian approaches are also addressed. Along with the discussion on various types of sampling designs and the sampling process, this chapter includes a comparison of online and offline sampling techniques.

SECTION III: DATA ANALYSIS AND REPORTING THE RESULTS

Having collected the data, Section III talks about the issues related to analyzing the data and presenting the same. This section consist of four chapters, each outlining the importance and relevance of various tools of analyzing the data, when to use which technique, and how to present them effectively.

Chapters 13–15

The collected data is rarely in a format conducive to analysis and meaningful results. So how can researchers prepare the data for analysis? What analytical and statistical tools can be employed to understand the data?

Chapter 13 discusses topics associated with data preparation, data analysis, and statistical techniques. The chapter also incorporates the introduction of new and advanced techniques currently employed in data analysis, such as pooled cross-sectional time series analysis, Genetic Algorithms, and Hierarchical Bayes Linear Regression.

Chapter 14 deals with issues related to analysis of variance and with the interpretation of experimental results. This chapter also provides an introduction to Regression Analysis with a description of the simple linear regression model. Examples are provided for better understanding of each of these techniques.

Chapter 15 deals extensively with the various multivariate techniques of data analysis. A description of each technique followed by an example of its application is the pattern adopted in this chapter. The major multivariate techniques discussed in this chapter include multiple regression analysis, discriminant analysis, canonical analysis, factor analysis, cluster analysis, conjoint analysis, and multidimensional scaling.

Chapter 16

Too often, researchers focus on research techniques and ignore the importance of good communication. In this regard, how do researchers effectively present the results? Chapter 16 discusses the techniques in oral and written presentation of results. This chapter also presents the advances in communication technology, and the presentation of research results to make them more effective, exciting, and comprehensible.

SECTION IV: MARKETING RESEARCH APPROACHES ACROSS THE GLOBAL MARKETS

This section talks about different regions, such as Asia Pacific, Europe, Latin America, the Middle East and Africa, and North America, their peculiarities, and the important factors to bear in mind while conducting research in those regions. This section consists of five chapters, each outlining the important information about conducting research in that region.

Chapters 17–21

Chapters 17–21 concentrate on discussing marketing research issues related to Asia Pacific, Europe, Latin America, the Middle East and Africa, and North America. Issues pertaining to each of these nations are dealt with individually in each of these chapters. Information on sources of secondary data, issues related to sociocultural, economic, and political environment, the marketing research industry, costs of conducting marketing research, and issues related to sampling and questionnaire designs are provided and discussed in detail in these chapters. These chapters also include the latest information relating to Internet penetration, social media prevalence, and the adoption of mobile communication technologies in these regions. Further, the various issues and challenges to be mindful of while carrying out research in these regions are also enumerated.

SECTION V: FUTURE DIRECTIONS IN GLOBAL MARKETING RESEARCH

This section talks about the future of global marketing research as envisioned by the author. It also includes cases for illustrating the applications and challenges involved in global marketing research.

Chapter 22

Chapter 22 discusses the future of global marketing research as envisioned by the author. Consumers are no longer passive recipients of advertising and commercial information, but actively involved in various stages of the product life cycle right from design to demise. Therefore, marketers have to be constantly in tune with customer preferences and desires. This chapter presents some guidelines for current and future marketers in the light of the developments in wireless communications and digital marketing. This chapter also discusses some of the techniques being developed in data collection, especially in the context of radio audience measurement, which will have implications for research in other industries as well.

V. Kumar is a Regents' Professor, Richard and Susan Lenny Distinguished Chair and Professor in Marketing, and the Executive Director of the Center for Excellence in Brand and Customer Management, and the Director of the PhD Program in Marketing at the J. Mack Robinson College of Business, Georgia State University. He is also the first person outside of China to be named Chang Jiang Scholar, Huazhong University of Science and Technology, Wuhan, China, and Lee Kong Chian Fellow, Singapore Management University, Singapore.

Dr Kumar has been recognized with twelve *lifetime achievement awards* in Marketing Strategy, Inter-organizational Issues, Retailing, Business-to-Business Marketing, and Marketing Research from the American Marketing Association and other professional organizations, including the Paul D. Converse Award. Other awards that he has received include the Donald R. Lehmann Award, MSI/Paul H. Root Award, Harold H. Maynard Award, Davidson Award, the Sheth Foundation/Journal of Marketing for the Best Paper Award for contributing a Long-term Impact in marketing, the Robert Buzzell Award from the Marketing Science Institute, and the Gary L. Lilien ISMS-MSI Practice Prize Award. He has published over 200 articles in many scholarly journals in marketing including the *Harvard Business Review, Sloan Management Review, Journal of Marketing, Journal of Marketing Research, Marketing Science,* and *Management Science, and Operations Research.* His books include *Managing Customers for Profit, Customer Relationship Management (CRM), Customer Lifetime Value, Marketing Research, Statistical Methods in CRM,* and *International Marketing Research.* He has won several awards for his research publications in scholarly journals. He has also had the privilege and the honor of being named as the Editor-in-Chief of the *Journal of Marketing,* the number-one-ranked academic journal in the field of marketing.

Dr Kumar teaches a variety of courses including Database Marketing, e-Marketing, Customer Relationship Management, New Product Management, Marketing Models, International Marketing Strategy, International Marketing Research, and Multivariate Methods in Business. He has spent a significant amount of time living and traveling around the world and has taught in MBA programs in Australia, France, India, Spain, Holland, and Hong Kong. He has lectured extensively on marketing-related topics at various universities in the United States, France, Spain, Germany, China, Israel, the Netherlands, Finland, Belgium, the United Kingdom, Sweden, Australia, Brazil, Turkey, Mexico, India, and South Africa. He has also conducted numerous executive development seminars in North America, South America, Europe, Asia, Africa, and Australia.

Dr Kumar spends his *free* time visiting business leaders to identify challenging problems to solve. He plays tennis and basketball to relieve his stress arising out of being in academics. Finally, Dr Kumar has been chosen as a *Legend in Marketing* where his work is being published in a 10-volume encyclopedia with commentaries from scholars worldwide.

More information about Dr Kumar's involvement in teaching and research is available at www.drvkumar.com. He can be reached at the following e-mail address: vk@gsu.edu.

ACKNOWLEDGMENTS

I wish to express my sincere thanks to Tamer Cavusgil, Keith Cox, Raj Echambadi, Jaishankar Ganesh, Les Johnson, Philip Kotler, Robert Leone, Werner Reinartz, Seenu Srinivasan, and Bart Weitz for their valuable comments on previous drafts. I am also appreciative of all the industry executives of international marketing research firms for their helpful interactions and insights.

I am also thankful to Anita Iyer, Prakash Ravichander, and Divyapriya Muthukumaran for their assistance in abstracting information from various sources. Special thanks goes to Bharath Rajan for coordinating the activities in the creation of this book.

I am thankful to Dr Srini. R. Srinivasan, Chairperson, PhD Center, Vivekanand Education Society's Institute of Management Studies and Research (VESIMSR), Professor (Dr) Tanima Ray, Indian Institute of Social Welfare and Business Management (IISWBM), Kolkata, and Dr Uma Chandrasekaran, School of Management, Pondicherry University, Pondicherry, for the suggestions and comments provided as reviewers.

I am deeply indebted to the commissioning and editorial teams at SAGE Publications India for their assistance and support in the creation of this book.

Section I

Introduction to Marketing Research for the Emerging and Developed Markets

1   The Nature and Scope of Global Marketing Research   3

2   Marketing Research in the Global Environment   41

3   Global Marketing Research Process   66

1

The Nature and Scope of Global Marketing Research

INTRODUCTION

The world is extremely interconnected today. Can you remember how it was just a decade back? There was no trace of smart phones in our daily lives, Google was a private company, and Facebook and Twitter did not even exist. The innovations made by the communication and information systems technology industry have allowed for an efficient relay of messages between companies engaged in trade, irrespective of their location. The lack of barriers in communication has helped the international trade tremendously in the last decade or so. In the post-recession era, while the growth of the developed economies slowed down, emerging markets remained resilient. Markets like China, India, and Africa showed potential even in tough times and are serving to be prospective markets for small as well as big businesses. A lot of businesses have tried to capitalize on the growth of these developing nations by means of expansion. Expanding into unfamiliar markets increases the risk for a company. Also, expansion helps companies beat their competition. In all, increase in competition, saturating domestic markets, and cost pressures are further accelerating the globalization of businesses in almost all industries.

Technology has been a life changer during the last decade. Today, technology companies are among the top 10 in the list of global brands. Internet has enabled people to engage in e-commerce to buy or sell goods and services without hesitation. The impact of the globalization of businesses is so profound that we witness it while walking across streets in any country; the growing presence of KFC in China is one such example. Although globalization has been a huge advantage for companies, it also has brought them face-to-face with the complexities involved with marketing products to different sets of audience. For a company, this means more information about the different target audience to be able to cater to each one individually. Consider the following scenarios:

- Cisco had no presence in India before 2005 but opened a second headquarters in Bangalore to take advantage of opportunities in India and other neighboring locations such as Dubai.[1] In such a venture, how do they begin the internationalization process? What are the factors that they look out for in selecting the market(s) to enter?

---

[1] Vikram Mahidhar, Craig Giffi, and Ajit Kimbal, with Ryan Alvanos, "Rethinking Emerging Market Strategies," *Deloitte Review*, no. 4, 2009.

- To advertise their hair care products, Helene Curtis observed that middle-class British women wash their hair frequently, Spanish women less so, and Japanese women avoid over-washing for fear of losing protective oils.[2] In this light, how do they plan their advertising and distribution strategies for each of the regions they operate in?
- When KFC entered Japan in 1970, they learned that the Japanese viewed fast food as artificial and unhealthy. To build trust in the brand, their advertising campaign included depicting Colonel Sanders' beginnings in Kentucky to convey Southern hospitality, tradition, and authentic home-cooked food.[3] How does KFC go about studying its brand image in the various global markets?
- Campbell Soup Company lost an estimated $30 million when they introduced condensed soups in small-sized cans in England. The reason for the failure—consumers did not realize that water had to be added. Could the company have known about this before the product launch in England?

Exhibit 1.1 illustrates the difficulties faced by a giant retailer when trying to enter an international market. Venturing into unfamiliar markets brings in additional burden on managers to stay afloat in their business. Proper information and thorough knowledge of the international market go a long way in avoiding pitfalls in the future. It has been proven that export companies that train their executives in international businesses tend to do better than export companies that do not.[4] The complexity of the international marketplace, the extreme national differences, and lack of knowledge of foreign markets add to the importance of global marketing research.[5] Before making market entry, product positioning or marketing mix decisions, accurate information about the market size, market needs, and competition must be available. Research helps avoid costly mistakes of poor strategies or lost opportunities, in addition to enabling the process of product development in foreign markets. It has been observed that the field of global marketing research has made substantial progress both in the development of conceptual frameworks for the studies conducted and in the empirical testing of concepts and theories.[6]

Marketing research has been defined by the American Marketing Association as "the function that links an organization to its market through information." This information is used to identify and define marketing opportunities and problems, generate, refine, and evaluate marketing actions, monitor marketing performance, and improve the understanding of marketing as a process. Marketing research specifies the information required to address these issues, designs the method for collecting information, manages and implements the data collection process, interprets the results, and communicates the findings and their implications. Marketing research can be thought of as application of scientific disciplines to the collection

---

[2] Philip Kotler and Kevin Keller, *Marketing Management* (Upper Saddle River, NJ: Prentice Hall, 2011), 14th edition, p. 611.

[3] Philip Kotler, Kevin Keller Lane, Abraham Koshy, and Mithileshwar Jha, *Marketing Management: A South Asian Perspective* (Boston, MA: Pearson Education, 2013), p. 546.

[4] Adapted from Eugene H. Fram and Riad Ajami, "Globalization of Markets and Shopping Stress: Cross-Country Comparisons," *Business Horizons* 37 (1994): 17–23.

[5] Anthony C. Koh, "An Evaluation of International Marketing Research Planning in United States Export Firms," *Journal of Global Marketing* 3 (1991): 7–25.

[6] Preet S. Aulakh and Masaaki Kotabe, "An Assessment of Theoretical and Methodological Development in International Marketing: 1980–1990," *Journal of International Marketing* 1, no. 2 (1993): 5–28.

Exhibit 1.1

Issues Faced by Wal-Mart in India[7]

Wal-Mart, the world's leading employer and one of the largest publicly traded companies, has been known for its well-managed operations and great value for customers for a long time. Providing customers with low prices for goods every day, it has managed to remain a success story for years now. India, one of the fastest growing economies in the world, was the next target for Wal-Mart.

In 2006, the company announced a joint venture with an Indian counterpart—Bharti Enterprises. Entering the Indian market posed a lot of challenges for Wal-Mart. With the level of efficiency in operations and supply chain management along with sustained growth and exceptional experience, one would think that entering India would be an easy task for the giant retailer; however, reality was far from it. Indian market conditions posed a whole new set of challenges for the giant retailer.

First, Wal-Mart could not remain a stand-alone brand as foreign companies were not allowed to directly enter the retail sector in India. So, Bharti Wal-Mart was opened under the name Best Price Modern Wholesale. Second, the controversy relating to lobbying in the Congress, which is considered bribery in India, severely dented its image. Third, the supply chain and logistics proved to be one of the biggest challenges for Wal-Mart in India. India lacks proper facilities such as refrigeration trucks, efficient storage, and maintenance, thereby losing about a third of its produce each year to spoilage. From bad road conditions to government-imposed middlemen, maintaining an everyday low price is going to be a tough task for Wal-Mart.

However, the company has been working to resolve these issues it faces in India. It is like starting all over again for Wal-Mart. They need innovative techniques to surpass this hurdle in India.

of market data for use in making marketing decisions.[8] It is the means by which marketers obtain consumer and trade responses to their marketing activities. It is a critical marketing function and a useful managerial tool and can be viewed as the management's attempt to bring science to marketing.

Any one or more of the abovementioned activities conducted in one or more foreign country can be considered as global marketing research. Traditionally, global marketing research has been defined as "research conducted to assist decision making in more than one country."[9] At the simplest level, global marketing research involves research studies in a single market outside the firm's domestic market. More elaborate and complex are multi-country research programs, which often concern both establishing intercountry priorities and optimizing the intra-country marketing approaches. Global marketing research can, therefore, be defined as "market research conducted either simultaneously or sequentially to facilitate marketing decisions in more than one country."

Global marketing research obtains significance as companies expand their operations into foreign markets, which presents the need for current and accurate market information. In

---

[7] Adapted from Amol Sharma and Biman Mukherji, "Bad Roads, Red Tape, Burly Thugs Slow Wal-Mart's Passage in India," *Wall Street Journal*, January 11, 2013, p. 12

[8] Alvin A. Achenbaum, "The Future Challenge to Market Research," *Marketing Research* 5, no. 2 (1993).

[9] Susan P. Douglas and C. Samuel Craig, *International Marketing Research* (Eaglewood Cliffs, NJ: Prentice Hall, 1983), pp. 24–25.

this regard, global marketing research can be viewed as a confluence of international marketing and marketing research functions. From this perspective, it would be easy to see that while international marketing focuses on catering products and services as demanded by the international consumers, marketing research focuses on gathering, analyzing, and presenting information regarding the needs and wants of international consumers that would facilitate the international marketing tasks.

If so, then is conducting research for the New York market the same as conducting research for the New Delhi market? The answer to this is an obvious "no," and it is here that marketing research for domestic markets differs from that of international markets. While the fundamental research processes and methods adopted for research will be similar for New York and New Delhi, the research regarding international markets has two key additional features. First, efforts have to be taken to communicate the research issues between the two cultures. That is, the research questions pertaining to New York will have to be communicated to the New Delhi market, without any *information loss/change* in the process. Second, the answers from the New Delhi market will have to be translated to the American milieu so as to enable comparison and understanding in terms of the New York market.

In other words, global marketing research is the result of international marketing initiatives by companies and the marketing research process that ultimately aids in decision-making within a firm. Global marketing research process helps companies to manage global marketing decisions in several ways that include: (a) determining the level of presence in international markets, (b) ascertaining the attractive and conducive markets to enter, (c) identifying the form of operation in international markets, (d) developing the product offerings and the international marketing plan that is well suited with the specific market(s), and (e) deciding on the long-term international marketing strategy to stay in/grow in/exit the international markets. From this perspective, this book will predominantly focus on multi-country marketing research, whose purpose is to help in solving multi-country marketing problems, as opposed to a purely national marketing problem. Figure 1.1 illustrates the concept of global marketing research and its role in making global marketing decisions.

The following section gives a brief overview of global marketing research and stresses on the importance of research in formulating marketing strategies on a global level. The purpose of this chapter is to motivate the reader regarding the necessity and usefulness of global

FIGURE 1.1
GLOBAL MARKETING RESEARCH AT WORK

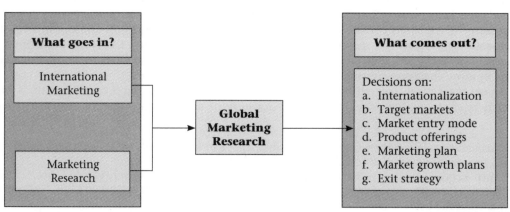

marketing research. What is global marketing research? Is such a concept valid? If so, how is it different from domestic marketing research? After establishing the need for global marketing research, the discussion will focus on the different types of global marketing research and how it helps in the international marketing decision-making process.

GLOBAL MARKETING RESEARCH: IS IT A VALID CONCEPT?[10]

Critics of global marketing research challenge the very concept in itself. They argue that all marketing research is basically national and there is no such thing called *global marketing research*. However, the recent growth of international business should convince the critics of the potential of international marketing, and thereby the need for in-depth understanding of the markets and establishing local connection with the customers. Global marketing research is essential for businesses today more than even before.

Some researchers also argue that the very nature of conducting marketing research in any location is basically the same. This is the reason why some believe that if you can handle research in one country, you can handle it anywhere and there is no local knowledge or expertise needed, their point being that the basic techniques of conducting research remain the same everywhere. Marketing products on international soil need some level of local understanding. Similarly, conducting research on an international ground would need some degree of local knowledge. While the basic techniques might be the same, without knowledge of the domestic market, the researcher is bound to miss out important nuances that may be critical to that region.

A business involved in international marketing has to take decisions such as priorities of markets, distribution strategies, allocation of resources between countries, etc. Global marketing research provides guidance to the manager of the company to take these decisions. The purpose of global marketing research is to provide information that will serve as a basis for decisions of this type. While some of the information obtained will only be of national relevance, an international (or multinational or multi-country) survey is distinguished from a national survey, or a collection of national surveys, by the fact that it is undertaken to aid an international marketing decision. With the increasing reach of international marketing, the need for timely and accurate marketing research to guide the decision-making process is essential.

Global marketing research can be said to be a valid concept so long as the market surveys carried out affect decisions concerning more than one country. After all, it is only logical that where marketing strategy is conceived on a multinational basis, marketing research should follow suit. It just does not make sense to base an international marketing program on marketing research fragmented on a country-by-country basis. Exhibit 1.2 presents some key questions that global marketing researchers must consider.

---

[10] This section adapted from P. D. Barnard, "International Research Is Different: The Case for Centralized Control", presented in ESOMAR Seminar on International Marketing Research: "Does It Provide What the User Needs?," Brussels, 1976.

Exhibit 1.2

Global Marketing Research: What to Look Out for?[11]

Global marketing research initiatives can be a daunting exercise when there is no clear agenda or plan. A good place to start would be to gather information on questions that will help the management narrow the possibilities for global marketing activities. Some of the possible questions worth considering include:

- Do opportunities exist in foreign markets for the firm's products and services?
- Which foreign markets warrant detailed investigation?
- What are the major economic, political, legal, and other environmental facts and trends in each of the potential countries?
- What mode of entry does the company plan to adopt to enter the foreign market?
- What is the market potential in these countries?
- Who are the firm's present and potential customers abroad?
- What is the nature of competition in the foreign markets?
- What kind of marketing strategy should the firm adopt?

WHAT'S DIFFERENT ABOUT GLOBAL MARKETING RESEARCH?

The process of global marketing research is not very different from that of domestic marketing research. Disciplines that apply to domestic research are applicable for international research also.[12] However, the major differences between global marketing research and domestic—single-country—research are: (a) that international research involves national differences between countries arising out of different political, legal, economic, social, and cultural differences, and (b) the problem of comparability of research results that arise due to these differences in international research, while this is not the case in single-country research. For instance, the color *red* is considered a sign of luck in China, but it may be interpreted as a warning signal in many other nationalities. Exhibit 1.3 highlights the various idiosyncrasies prevalent around the world. These idiosyncrasies provide a flavor of the cultural traits present in various countries that have to be accounted for while researching international markets. The presence of such varied traits worldwide, therefore, makes a strong case for global marketing research to be a valid concept.

---

[11] David A. Aaker, V. Kumar, George S. Day, and Robert P. Leone, *Marketing Research* (New York, NY: John Wiley and Sons, 2013), 11th edition.

[12] Author's interview with Research International.

Exhibit 1.3

Idiosyncrasies of Select Regions[13]

Asia	Europe	Latin America	Middle East
• The Chinese have a habit of telling a person whatever they believe the listener wants to hear, whether or not it is true. This plays an important role while conducting surveys. • Surveys in China, when approved by authorities, lead to higher response rates, implying a strong presence of bureaucracy. • Chinese respondents are cooperative and eager to try new products. They are also more patient when compared to their Hong Kong counterparts. • Indians only deal favorably with those they know and trust—even at the expense of lucrative deals. • The Japanese's purchasing behavior is centered more on the vendors selling the product than on the product itself. This denotes brand loyalty and the importance placed on quality and reliability. • They prefer the use of title and first names to be avoided. • They are an extremely group oriented and community-based people.	• Despite the excellent telecommunication network, it is normal for a Swede to not reciprocate calls. • The French believe in status and often do not mingle between groups. They believe that one is born into a class. • The French value their personal time at home and often are unreceptive to questions being posed. • Germans respect time and are considered one of the most punctual. • In Germany, people are private and tend to keep their opinions to themselves. Seniors should be greeted first before any others present. • While the Germans prefer one-to-one talk to telephonic conversations, the British take more to telephone calls than to direct marketing programs.	• Most Argentines maintain little physical distance while speaking to others and tend to broach personal issues pertaining to family. They are frank in voicing their opinions, but take extreme care in being diplomatic. • Business in Brazil is personal. They have a relaxed approach to life and business. • Most Latin Americans are uncomfortable talking over telephone or responding to mail and prefer one-to-one interviews. They prefer the respondent fees in kind rather than in cash. • Latin Americans have a great difficulty in saying "no" for an answer. Likewise, asking favors is common in Latin America. It is advisable to say "I shall try" rather than a firm "no." • Measuring purchasing power of consumers in Latin America with income level may not reveal the true picture. This is so because the actual number of consumers who have income that are willing to spend on foreign products is much lower than expected.	• In the Middle East, direct eye contact for too long is considered offensive. Likewise, private conversations and whispering while in a group is considered rude. • It is best not to admire the possessions of an Arab host. They feel obligated to give the items to you. • In a recent AMER World Research survey, the new generation of Arab respondents were found to be conservative in their clothing styles, considered family and marriage to be strong institutions, and believed that while women should get more prominence, the family takes precedence. • Nonverbal communication is complicated in Saudi Arabia as most Arabs express themselves using different gestures. • Islamic etiquette recommends that one waits for the other to withdraw their hand first, during a handshake. Also, use of the right hand is preferred.

[13] Adapted and updated from V. Kumar, "International Marketing Research," in *The Handbook of Marketing Research: Uses, Misuses, and Future Advances*, eds Rajiv Grover and Marco Vriens (Thousand Oaks, CA: SAGE Publications, 2006); http://www.kwintessential.co.uk/. (Retrieved on May 10, 2014).

Importance of National Differences

Every country has its own similarities and differences as compared to other countries. As an international researcher, it is important to be aware of these similarities and differences. A domestic researcher may be concerned only with one country, but an international researcher has to deal with a number of countries that may differ considerably in a number of important ways.

1. When operating in foreign countries, companies may be accorded an *alien status* that may cause additional difficulty for the researcher in assessing and forecasting the international business climate. Such a status means that the company can be seen as an exploiter and could possibly receive unfair treatment from the political/legal authorities. For instance, the Indian government gave Coca-Cola the choice of either revealing their secret formula or leaving the country. They chose to leave. However, when they were welcomed back into the country, Coke faced constant interference from political activists.[14]
2. The demographic data obtained from the Census Bureau and private vendors in the US are highly reliable; however, the quality of statistics generated in some other countries is extremely poor. It is very difficult for the researcher to keep up with the changing census geographies and area definitions as they are constantly changing according to the whims of the national governments or social service organizations.
3. Some developing nations are not as equipped and advanced as the developed ones. For instance, in the top 20 countries with regard to the number of Internet users, as on June 2012, India ranked third (137 million). However, in terms of Internet penetration, it finished last from among the same list (only 11.4%). Compare this penetration rate with other developed countries that occupy the first three ranks—such as UK (83.6%), Germany (83.0%), and Korea (82.5%)—and the difference is stark. This is important for researchers to consider in evaluating international markets.[15]
4. There exists a language barrier as these differences are too obvious in some of the regions. For instance, communicating in Papua New Guinea can be an issue with nearly 750 languages, each distinct and unintelligible, being spoken there.[16] Language differences also make it necessary for a questionnaire to be translated into the foreign language and translated back to English to detect differences in meaning.

The main factors that affect the way in which people from different cultures behave are:

Cultural Differences

Culture refers to widely shared norms or patterns of behavior within a large group of people. Culture determines the behavior of consumers in terms of their purchase behavior.

---

[14] Philip R. Cateora and John L. Graham, *International Marketing* (New York, NY: Irwin/McGraw-Hill, 1999), 10th edition, p. 11.

[15] "The Top 20 Countries with the Highest Number of Internet Users (2012)," http://www.internetworldstats.com/top20.htm (Retrieved on July 30, 2013).

[16] Bernard Kong, "Papua New Guinea: A Land of Extreme Contrasts," *Trade and Culture*, May/July, 1997, p. 40.

For instance, in Indonesian culture, people believe in collectivism, while countries like the US are highly individual-driven. The family structure and hierarchy also determines the decision-making authority. There are differences within a single nation as well. For example, despite being politically united, Canada is divided culturally between its French and English legacies. As a result, successful marketing strategies that worked with the French Canadians could very well end in a failure among the remaining Canadians. Consumers' attitudes and behavior toward certain products and services too are shaped by culture. Consider the refrigerator market in Europe, for instance. While Northern Europeans want large refrigerators with freezers at the bottom because they shop only once a week in supermarkets, Southern Europeans prefer smaller refrigerators with freezers on the top, as they shop at open-air markets almost daily. And Britons, who consume large quantities of frozen food, prefer units with 60 % freezer space. Given these variations in product expectation and usage, companies like Electrolux cannot possibly think of standardizing their offerings across Europe. This also explains the crowded marketplace with several manufacturers vying to get a piece of the market by catering to the minute variations in product choice. Contrast this with the vastly different refrigerator market in the US that is largely standardized across the country with freezers on top, very few differences in unit sizes, and dominated by a few manufacturers holding a major share of the market.[17]

Racial Differences

Differences in cultures mean differences in physical features as well. Consider Japan and the US. In Japan almost everyone is Japanese, whereas the US has a strong mix of people belonging to various cultures and races. In fact, the 2010 American Community Survey estimated the number of foreign born in the US to be nearly 40 million, or 13 % of the total population.[18] For companies that sell personal care products (for example) in the US and across the world, these differences are crucial as the needs and expectations of people from one country will likely be different from those in the others, owing to inherent differences in skin/hair types.

Climatic Differences

Climatic conditions dictate the use of certain products in certain parts of the world. This difference in climates in different parts of the world depicts some of the most exciting differences between geographical regions. For example, Bosch-Siemens had to alter their washing machines in Europe. Reason—the sun does not shine regularly in Germany or in Scandinavia, and, therefore, machines must operate a spin cycle range between 1,000–1,600 RPM so that the clothes come out dry. In Italy and Spain, on the other hand, it is sufficient for machines to have a spin cycle of 500 RPM because of the abundant sunshine.[19] Depending on such differences, companies will have to alter their global communication messages accordingly.

---

[17] Cateora and Graham, *International Marketing*, 10th edition, p. 343.

[18] "The Foreign-Born Population in the United States: 2010," May 2012, published by the American Community Survey, US Department of Commerce, Economics and Statistics Administration, US Census Bureau.

[19] Scot Stevens and Dan Davis, "Battle of the Brands," *Appliance*, February 1997, p. B21.

Economic Differences

The levels of wealth and income also affect consumer behavior in different countries. Despite the continuing changes to the economic patterns of countries, stark differences do remain. For instance, the 2007 Human Development Report published by the United Nations Development Program finds that the poorest 40% of the world's population accounts for 5% of global income, while the richest 20% accounts for nearly 75% of world income. The marketing implications of this economic disparity are many. For example, the presence of electricity around the world presents a compelling fact. An estimated 79% of the people in the 50 poorest nations have no access to electricity. The total number of individuals without electric power estimated at 1.5 billion (25% of the world's population) is concentrated mostly in Africa and southern Asia.[20] In light of this, consider the sale of electrical products such as electric can openers and electric paper shredders around the world. Not only are these products unattainable and unusable in less affluent countries, but spending on them would also be a waste of disposable income that could be spent more meaningfully on other essentials such as food, clothing, and shelter.[21]

In view of these income differences, marketers and researchers have traditionally focused only on the *cash-rich* section of the population in their pursuit toward establishing a viable market. However, recent studies have shown that a viable market is possible even in the lower economic strata. It has been shown that the *Fortune at the Bottom of the Pyramid* can be *discovered* by companies when they rethink their strategies on pricing, quality, sustainability, and profits. Specifically, by (a) creating increased buying power, (b) fostering consumer aspirations, (c) developing local solutions, and (d) improving access to products and services, companies can stake out a viable market even in the low-income segment of the market.[22]

Religious Differences

Certain religions have laid down very specific behavioral patterns. For instance, religion plays a key role in Africa, and it is evidenced by the marketing slogans across the region. "Service of God Beauty Parlor" or "No phones to heaven" illustrate the religious priorities of people clearly. A classic example is the recall of Nike shoes. The leading shoe brand agreed to recall a line of shoes with a logo that a Muslim group found offensive. The logo that was intended to represent flames or heat rising off the shoes inadvertently resembled the word *Allah* in Arabic script. Launched to be sold under different names such as *Air Bakin'*, *Air Melt*, *Air Grill*, and *Air B-Que*, the line of shoes was eventually recalled from Saudi Arabia, Kuwait, Malaysia, Indonesia, and Turkey and diverted to *less sensitive* markets.[23] Also, Middle Eastern countries prohibit the consumption of alcohol. This national rule must be respected or the offender may be imprisoned or even publicly flogged. Further, not long ago, Saudi Arabia banned Barbie dolls declaring it as a threat to morality, their concern being the clothes of the dolls were offensive to Islam.

---

[20] Nathanial Gronewold, "One-Quarter of World's Population Lacks Electricity," *Scientific American*, November 24, 2009.

[21] Cateora and Graham, *International Marketing*, 10th edition, p. 89.

[22] C. K. Prahalad and Stuart L. Hart, "The Fortune at the Bottom of the Pyramid," *strategy+business*, issue 26, 2002.

[23] Jeff Harrington, "Nike Recalls Disputed Logo," *Cincinnati Enquirer*, June 25, 1997.

Historical Differences

Historical differences help explain facts concerning each country, playing of cricket in England being one such example. Such differences that have evolved over time have a deep impact on consumer behavior. For instance, while drinking Scotch whiskey is considered prestigious and trendy in Italy, it is not so in Scotland.

Differences in Consumption Patterns

There are vast differences in consumption patterns between regions. For example, there is a vast difference in the consumption of beverage around the world. The per capita consumption of soft drinks per year in the US is the highest at 760 eight-ounce servings. The Mexicans drink 674 servings, Brazilians 315, Russians 149, and the Chinese just 39.[24] For soft drink manufacturers having presence worldwide, this information is crucial in determining the sales and marketing efforts of their offerings.

Differences in Marketing Conditions

Researchers need to know the ground realities in foreign markets to understand the different nuances of marketing products and services. As ubiquitous as they have become, the prevailing market conditions and the strategies implemented to market mobile phones are varied and ever-changing. Grameenphone marketed cell phones to 35,000 villages in Bangladesh by hiring women as agents who leased phone time to other villagers, one call at a time. This approach effectively tackled the issues of low levels of disposable income and poor mobile penetration in Bangladesh.[25] Nokia sent its entry-level staff from the marketing, sales, and engineering departments to spend one week in people's homes in rural China, Thailand, and Kenya to observe how they use phones. The inputs from these observations went into the development of low-priced phones with just the right functionality, ultimately securing them a larger share of the African and Asian markets.[26] Similarly, Nokia customized its 6100 series phone for all major markets. For Asia, developers included rudimentary voice recognition in the devices to counter the issues with keyboards and raised the ring volume to make it audible on crowded Asian streets.

From a research perspective, conditions to interview respondents are also different around the world. For instance, if the research is being conducted in Hong Kong, people will have to be interviewed through the grill in their front doors because they will not let strangers into their houses. Likewise, the Japanese are not keen on being contacted over the telephone. The rich in Latin America are difficult to interview because they are difficult to contact and approach. Researchers will have to make note of such small differences in different cultures.

---

[24] "U.S. Soft Drink Consumption on the Decline," *Reuters*, August 24, 2009.

[25] Vijay Mahajan, Marcos V. Pratini De Moraes, and Jerry Wind, "The Invisible Global Market," *Marketing Management*, Winter 2000, pp. 31–35.

[26] Clayton Christensen, Stephen Wunker, and Hari Nair, "Innovation Vs. Poverty," *Forbes*, October 13, 2008.

Differences in Actual and Potential Target Groups

In countries like England and Germany, it is possible to do national samples. Small towns and villages can be included because distances are not very great. In Spain, interviews can be conducted only in cities with population of over 100,000 people, as the cost of interviewing people in small towns and villages is prohibitively high.[27] Similarly, in India, a significant proportion of people are illiterate in the rural regions. Hence, self-administered survey is out of question for these set of consumers.

Differences in Consumer Language

Consumers in every country interact differently. While there are differences in the languages consumers speak in different countries, an international market researcher needs to pay close attention to the language spoken by different age groups in every country. The median age in markets like India and China is about 25, while in markets like Japan, Germany, and Italy, it is around 43 years. Therefore, the younger generation within and across market(s) have a language of their own, and these are the target consumers for products categories such as clothing, consumer electronics, appliances, and automobiles, among others. So, as a researcher, it is important to know the language that each segment of consumers speaks in order to understand these fine distinctions and test them in the survey.

In addition, the global marketing researcher may also have to deal with the following:

- Language differences
- Differences in the way that products or services are used
- Differences in the criteria for assessing products or services
- Differences in market research facilities
- Differences in market research capabilities
- Differences in the way domestic consumers respond to survey questions

The abovementioned differences are reflected in the results of multi-country research, just as differences between sexes, age or social class groups are reflected in the results of single-country research. The nature of these differences mentioned above does not just impact the results of the study alone. These tend to have a considerable impact even in the initial phase of the study. It is important to incorporate these nuances at the planning and development stage of the multi-country survey to get an accurate picture of the market, and thereby reliable results.

While many researchers comment on national differences, the importance of their relevance at the planning stage of international research is frequently not realized. However, it is very easy for a marketing researcher to ignore the differences and get trapped by some of the pitfalls of obtaining marketing intelligence in a foreign country. Exhibit 1.4 describes some of the key pitfalls in global marketing research.

---

[27] Author's interview with Research International.

Exhibit 1.4

A Practitioner's View of the Key Pitfalls in Conducting International Research[28]

The key pitfalls to avoid when conducting a global marketing research project are:

1. *Selecting a domestic research company to do your international research.* Only a handful of domestic research companies are both dedicated to and expert in international research. It is important that international projects be coordinated by a team whose sensitivity and knowledge of foreign markets will ensure a well-executed study. Emphasis should be placed on selecting a research company with a solid reputation and extensive experience in the design, coordination, and analysis of global research.
2. *Rigidly standardizing methodologies across countries.* Attempting to be consistent with a methodological approach across countries is desirable, but, among other things, two key questions need to be asked in order to determine whether a particular methodology will yield the best results: (a) Does the culture lend itself to that methodology? For example, relationships in Latin America are based on personal contact. Hence, when conducting business-to-business (B2B) surveys, personal interviews, though expensive, are more efficient than telephone interviews. (b) Does the local infrastructure hinder the use of that methodology? For example, telephone surveys are very common in the US, but in Russia, the telephone system is notoriously inefficient.
3. *Interviewing in English around the world.* When conducting B2B research, even if the executives in the foreign country speak English, interviewing in English might result in inaccurate responses. Are the subjects able to comprehend the questions accurately and fully, or are there nuances to the questions that are not being understood? Are their answers to open-ended questions without detail and richness due to their apprehension about responding in a nonnative language? Moreover, has their attention been diverted to a consideration of accents (theirs and/or the interviewer's) rather than the research questions at hand? Hence, even though translating the questionnaire may be costly and time-consuming, it results in more accurate responses.
4. *Setting inappropriate sampling requirements.* Several country-specific variables influence the selection of appropriate sampling procedures in multi-country marketing research. For example, although random sampling is statistically the most reliable technique to use, it may be impractical in a given foreign market. Reasons may include the fact that in many of the less developed countries, the literacy rate is very low. Hence, when sampling for surveys that require the respondent to be literate, random sampling might not work.
5. *Lack of consideration given to language.* Translations into the appropriate local languages need to be checked carefully. When possible, a quality control procedure of *back-translation* should be followed. The prime consideration is to ensure translations of the questionnaire so that there is equivalent meaning and relevance in all the countries where the project is being conducted.

---

[28] Adapted from Daphne Chandler, "8 Common Pitfalls of International Research," *The Council of American Survey Research Organizations Journal* (1992): 81.

6. *Lack of systematic international communication procedures.* One of the biggest problems of international research is communicating clearly with the local research companies. Do they understand the objectives of the study? Do they understand the sampling criteria? And do they understand what is expected from them? All too often, assumptions are made concerning the above issues that lead to major problems in the study's execution.

7. *Misinterpreting multi-country data across countries.* Analysis of the study's data must focus on the international market from which the data was gathered. Survey comparisons across countries should be made with the understanding of how the particular countries may differ on many key factors, including local market conditions, the maturity of the market, and the local competitive framework for the study category.

8. *Not understanding international differences in conducting qualitative research.* When conducting qualitative research such as focus groups, group discussions, and in-depth interviews, the researcher must be aware of the importance of culture in the discussion process. Not all societies encourage frank and open exchange and disagreement among individuals. Status consciousness may result in situations in which the opinion of one is reflected by all other participants. Disagreement may be seen as impolite or certain topics may be taboo. Also, in some countries such as parts of Asia, mixed sex and age groups do not yield good information in a consumer group discussion. Younger people, for example, often defer to the opinions of older people. If groups cannot be separated by age and sex, one-to-one interviews should be done.

CULTURE[29]

All countries are known to be rich in their cultural values and consumers tend to express these cultural differences, knowingly or unknowingly, in their behavior. One can witness differences in cultures and cultural values, language, and the level of trust among strangers while conducting research. There have been enough faux pas in the past as a result of disregard of cultural differences. These mistakes can be appalling, as illustrated by the following:

- *Product*: Nokia's recently launched Nokia Lumia is a great example of this. The brand faced some strong criticism when the translation of its brand name in Spanish meant *prostitute*.[30]
- *Price*: An American firm was negotiating with a Japanese buyer for an acceptable price for its product. After a detailed presentation, the American firm offered their price, which was followed by silence from the Japanese. Thinking that the Japanese were going to reject the offer, the American firm lowered the price. This was followed by more silence. The Americans then said they would lower their price one last time, which would be their final price. After a brief silence, the Japanese accepted this offer. It was later learnt

---

[29] Richard L. Sandhusan, *Global Marketing* (Hauppage, NY: Barron's Educational Series, 1994), pp. 100–101.

[30] "Why Nokia Is Being Mocked in Spain," *Olive Press*, November 19, 2011, http://www.theolivepress.es/spain-news/2011/11/19/nokia-lumia-prostitute-spain/(Retrieved on July 2, 2013).

that it was Japanese custom to consider a proposal silently before making a decision. The Americans lost a lot of profit by not interpreting the cultural signals correctly.[31]

- *Place*: A US cake mix manufacturer launched their range of products in Japan that resulted in a major failure. The company had relied on an American frame of reference by assuming all Japanese homes had ovens.[32]
- *Promotion*: The Scandinavian vacuum cleaner manufacturer did not realize the blunder they were making when they launched their product in the American market with the slogan "Nothing sucks like an Electrolux."[33]

The comprehension of the definition and scope of global marketing research are critical, as the cultural differences distinguish global marketing research from domestic research. In the world of marketing, culture is defined "as the values, attitudes, beliefs, artifacts and other meaningful symbols represented in the pattern of life adopted by people that help them interpret, evaluate and communicate as members of a society."[34] Culture drives people to react to situations the way they do, and a market researcher should have a clear understanding of this in a given situation. Culture is developed and followed not just by an individual; it is a collective behavior of the society and it impacts all members of that society who have been conditioned by similar education and life experiences. Culture is a learned behavior, not inherited. The term can be applied to groups of individuals in a country, society, profession, or social organization.[35] Culture is also an important factor in determining how information processing occurs.[36] For instance, retailers in West Africa prefer face-to-face meetings over e-mails or telephone conversations. Trust is important for businessmen from the Middle East. Hence, they tend to believe in forming relationships before making a deal.

Hofstede identifies five dimensions of culture, namely, power distance, individualism versus collectivism, masculinity versus femininity, uncertainty avoidance, and long-term orientation.[37] Each of these dimensions helps to explain the differences between various countries.

Power Distance

This dimension primarily deals with the notion that not all members of a society are equal. The power distance dimension can be defined as the extent to which less powerful members of a society accept and expect that power is distributed unequally. Cultures endorsing high

---

[31] "Cultural Awareness—International Business Communication," 2011, http://www.cba.uni.edu/buscomm/InternationalBusComm/blunders.htm (Retrieved on January 20, 2014).

[32] Gary A. Knight, "International Marketing Blunders by American Firms in Japan: Some Lessons for Management," *Journal of International Marketing* 3, no. 4 (1995): 107–129.

[33] "Top 10 Translation Blunders of International Marketing, PR and Branding," July 27, 2010, message posted to http://www.utalkmarketing.com/Pages/Article.aspx?ArticleID=18456 (Retrieved on May 1, 2014).

[34] Geert Hoefstede, *Culture's Consequences: International Differences in Work-Related Values* (Beverly Hills, CA: SAGE Publications, 1998), pp. 42–43.

[35] Marieke de Mooij, *Global Marketing and Advertising—Understanding Cultural Paradoxes* (Thousand Oaks, CA: SAGE Publications, 1998), pp. 42–43.

[36] Edward T. Hall, *Beyond Culture* (Garden City, NY: Anchor Press/Doubleday, 1976).

[37] de Mooij, *Global Marketing and Advertising*, pp. 42–43.

power distance index tend to be more autocratic. Exercising authority by powerful people and acceptance of this authority by the less powerful comes naturally. Japan can be considered as an example of a culture with a very high power distance index. The Japanese recognize and accept hierarchy in their personal and professional lives.

China is another country which is said to believe that inequality among members of society is acceptable. In many other cultures like the US, where the power distance index is very low, authority is not easily accepted, and in fact, the term has a negative connotation. Low power distance index countries tend to relate to one another more as equals, and subordinates expressing their views is not considered rude or out of line. These differences impact the way decisions are made, and hence, impact the manner in which various groups are targeted for marketing a specific product. When a manufacturer from a low power distance index country decides to launch a product in a country with a high power distance index, the marketer needs to be extra careful about the communication style while interacting with the domestic team at base.

Individualism Versus Collectivism

Hofstede defines the contrast between individualism and collectivism as people looking after only themselves and their immediate family versus people belonging to in-groups that look after them in exchange for loyalty. Individualistic cultures place a lot of emphasis on the identity of individuals, expression of private opinions, self-actualization, individual rights, and personal achievements. Collectivistic societies stress on identities based on the group or social class to which they belong. Individualistic cultures draw a sharp distinction between private and professional lives, whereas in collectivistic societies there is very little distinction. This makes marketing very different in these cultures. Consider the case of a computer manufacturer targeting the home-computer market in Japan and the US. The Japanese are very collectivistic and do not believe in working out of homes; hence, the number of homes in Japan that have computers is very low. In contrast, the US has a tremendous market for home computers because of the tendency of a lot of people to work out their homes. Also, people from the UK are generally considered to have high individualism, while people from Mexico act more collectively.

An offshoot of this is the definition of high-context and low-context cultures, which distinguishes cultures according to the degree of context in their communication.[38] Low-context cultures place very high importance on explicit, direct, and unambiguous verbal messages. Most of the Western cultures could be classified as low-context. In contrast, communication in high-context cultures is internalized in the person. There is very little explicit communication. Most high-context communication is economical, fast, and efficient, and nonverbal communication plays a major role. The Japanese society is an example of high-context culture, where people do not appreciate verbosity and eloquence. Understanding this is very important to a global marketing researcher because the research design has to be suitably modified to give an accurate picture of the culture.

---

[38] Hall, *Beyond Culture*.

Masculinity Versus Femininity

This dimension can be defined as follows: the dominant values in a masculine society are achievement and success; the dominant values in a feminine society are caring for others and quality of life. It measures the distribution of emotional roles between male and female. Masculine cultures promote an admiration of the strong, the importance of winning, assertiveness, ambition, and power. Feminine cultures, on the other hand, advocate sympathy and caring, and place importance on the quality of life. The Scandinavian cultures, such as Sweden, Denmark and the Netherlands, are predominantly feminine cultures and give importance to sensitivity and not being devious. The US, Japan, and most countries in Latin America score very high on the masculine aspect, with Japan scoring the highest. There is a big difference between the way people in these cultures perceive winning, success, and status, and this creates an important dimension for marketing. For instance, many cultures that score high on femininity do not appreciate hard sell. Marketing researchers must bear this in mind when designing the study.

Uncertainty Avoidance

This is defined as the extent to which people feel threatened by uncertainty and ambiguity and try to avoid these situations. It measures a society's tolerance for uncertainty and ambiguity. People belonging to cultures that score very high on uncertainty avoidance tend to experience higher levels of anxiety and express their emotions more freely. Cultures that are weak in uncertainty avoidance believe in having fewer rules to define their lives and are not threatened by competition and conflict. France is an example of high uncertainty avoidance. They tend to minimize unknown situations and plan accordingly. Denmark, on the other hand, is an example of low uncertainty avoidance.

Long-Term Orientation

Long-term orientation is the extent to which a society exhibits a pragmatic, future-oriented perspective rather than a conventional historic or short-term point of view. Any culture that has long-term orientation places a lot of importance on characteristics like persistence, respect for status and position in society, thrift, and sense of shame. Most Asian countries, China in particular, score very high on this dimension. This could be contrasted with the short-term orientation of many Western countries. These cultures focus on instant gratification and pursuit of material pleasures.

Time is another variable that is culturally sensitive. One of the most important differences faced by researchers in global marketing research is the friction that occurs between parties because their understanding of time is completely out of sync.[39]

As a researcher, it is understandable to be concerned about the impact that each of these five dimensions has on the perceptions, attitudes, and ultimately consumer behavior, as these factors play an extremely important role in global marketing research. While it is critical for a

---

[39] Edward T. Hall and Mildred Reed Hall, *Understanding Cultural Differences* (Yarmouth, ME: Intercultural Press, 1990).

researcher to comprehend these aspects, it is not always possible. Researchers themselves are bound by their own culture and mindsets, which influence the way they view the research problem in different countries. This phenomenon, termed as the self-reference criterion (SRC), is explained in greater detail in Chapter 3. The classification of cultures that are identical in these dimensions will help researchers group the countries that are similar and develop identical research methodologies for these countries. Effective marketing strategies can be developed if the researcher is able to identify relevant product attributes that would impact the purchase decision. Exhibit 1.5 talks about the various cultures that make up the world and should be considered important by researchers.

Exhibit 1.5

If the World Were a Village of 100 People[40]

If someone thought of reducing the world's population to a village of precisely 100 people (all existing human ratios remaining the same) the demographics would be as shown below:

The village would have 61 Asians, 13 Africans, 12 Europeans, 9 Latin Americans, and 5 from the US and Canada.

- 50 would be male, 50 would be female
- 75 would be non-white, 25 white
- 67 would be non-Christian, 33 would be Christian
- 80 would live in substandard housing
- 16 would be unable to read or write
- 50 would be malnourished and 1 dying of starvation
- 33 would be without access to safe water supply
- 39 would lack access to improved sanitation
- 24 would not have any electricity (And of the 76 that do have electricity, most would only use it for light at night.)
- 8 people would have access to the Internet
- 1 would have college education
- 1 would have HIV
- 2 would be near birth, 1 near death
- 5 would control 32% of the entire world's wealth; all 5 would be US citizens
- 48 would live on less than $2 a day
- 20 would live on less than $1 a day
- 33 would be receiving—and attempting to live on—only 3% of the income of *the village*

---

[40] Adapted from Family Care Foundation, http://www.familycare.org/special-interest/if-the-world-were-a-village-of-100-people/(Retrieved on May 15, 2013).

CULTURE CLASSIFICATION MODEL[41]

With any business, factors like the use of time, approach to task at hand, and the role of relationships in making business decisions show a varied trend across the globe. Based on these factors, countries have been classified into six major groups: Northwestern/Central European, North American, Mediterranean European, Latin American, Traditional (includes developing countries, centrally planned and former centrally planned countries), and Middle Eastern. As we move from Northwestern/Central European regions toward the Middle Eastern areas, we observe a decrease in the importance given to the task at hand relative to that given to relationship building.

North American and Northwestern/Central European cultural groups tend to mainly focus on the task at hand. A lot of importance is given to accomplishing the task at hand as quickly and as efficiently as possible. The completion of the task takes precedence over the relationship between the two parties involved. Strict adherence to schedules and meeting times is usually practiced in these regions. This is not to say that relationships are not built at all. With tasks involving long durations, the concerned parties do have to develop a relationship, but this is still mainly a business or working relationship.

As one moves toward the eastern parts of the world, this focus on the task at hand decreases. The Mediterranean countries, for instance, show relatively more focus on relationships. They still consider the task to be extremely important but have a more flexible attitude toward time. The Mediterranean regions consist of non-Parisian French, Iberian, Italian, and Greek cultures. These cultures exhibit a concept of the *extended tribe*. In this case, negotiations with an individual or a party who is considered to be part of the clan, tribe, country, or cultural group take place with a focus on building a common bond and a strong relationship. On the other hand, the same kind of kinship is not sought with foreign people who are not considered to be part of the group. This culture also has a polychronic attitude toward time. As compared to Northwestern/Central European countries, there is more flexibility with time. Attention is simultaneously focused on many different tasks at the same time.

The importance given to relationships further increases in Latin cultures. The notion of the extended tribe is broader with Latin countries as they tend to include other Latin- or Spanish-speaking countries as part of their group. Though this group is quite capable of doing business with a focus only on the task, this is not their preferred method. They are also more willing to be inclusive and let foreigners be part of the group. If the foreign business representative demonstrates trustworthiness, credibility, and an interest in the culture and tradition of the host country, a relationship can be built over time. For building a good relationship, practices in this culture include multiple meetings, meals with local people, and spending time to learn about the host culture.

The Traditional group includes Asian countries, developing countries, and those countries that have, or recently had, a centrally planned economy. With a strong agrarian tradition, this group relies heavily on forming a network of contacts. In these cultures, relationships play a major role in business decisions. They choose to do business with people only after a relationship has been established first. Thus, to be able to successfully conduct business in these cultures, it is important to first develop a relationship with decision makers or people who can provide access to decision makers. With high focus on relationships in business, a lot of these cultures are high-context cultures with a lot of nonverbal cues as part of their communication.

---

[41] Camille Schuster and Michael Copeland, *Global Business—Planning for Sales and Negotiations* (Orlando, FL: Harcourt Brace and Company, 1996), pp. 17–27.

Middle Eastern cultures also place relationships first. A major distinction is that blood relationships take major precedence over any other kind of relationship. Family relationships and relationships with members of the same faith come first. Outsiders referred or introduced by relatives and trusted friends can also become part of the group, and such introductions are highly significant in such cultures. Once a relationship is established, persuasion becomes the least significant part of their dealings. When a relationship is well established and appropriately maintained, the constraints or parameters of a given situation are discussed, and if the objective is mutually agreeable, one side will just go along as a favor to a friend.

ALTERNATIVE TYPES OF GLOBAL MARKETING RESEARCH

Global marketing research can be conducted through descriptive research, comparative research, or theoretical research.

In descriptive research, the researcher examines in depth the attitudes and behavior of consumers in another country or culture. Comparative research, on the other hand, involves comparing attitudes and behavior in two or more countries or cultural contexts, with a view to identifying similarities and differences between them. In theoretical research, the researcher has a predetermined theory or model and it is possible to examine cross-cultural generalizability of these theories or models. Exhibit 1.6 explains consumer types and their prevalence in different nations.

Exhibit 1.6

Consumer Types Around the World[42]

The Global Consumer Survey by Roper Worldwide Inc. interviewed consumers from 35 countries and ranked 56 values by the importance they hold as guiding principles in their lives. The survey found the following six dominant values exhibited by consumers worldwide, but to varying degrees.

- *Strivers*: Largest group (12% of the population); more likely to be men; place more emphasis on material and professional goals. Found more across Asia and Russia—one-third of people in developing Asia, and one-fourth in Russia and developed Asia.
- *Devouts*: 22% of adults; include more women than men; tradition and duty are the most important. Most common in Africa, Asia, and the Middle East. Least common in Europe.
- *Altruists*: 18% of adults; larger portion of females; interested in social issues and societal welfare; older group (median age 44). More common in Latin America and Russia.
- *Intimates*: 15% of the population; personal relationships and family are the most important; as likely to be men as women. Most common in Europe and North America.
- *Fun Seekers*: 12% of the population; youngest group with a male–female ratio of 54: 46. Large percentage found in developed Asia.
- *Creatives*: Smallest group (10% worldwide); high level of interest in education, knowledge, and technology; as likely to be men as women. More common in Latin America and Western Europe.

[42] Adapted from Tom Miller, "Global Segments from 'Strivers' to 'Creatives'," *Marketing News*, July 20, 1998, p. 11.

A researcher, while conducting research to solve an international marketing problem, has the option of conducting it using a single questionnaire or one sampling and data collection method in all the countries. However, the researcher must consider carefully and evaluate if it can be done or not right at the outset of each survey. This initial decision making itself differentiates his/her job from that of a researcher dealing with a single-country research. A single-country survey usually involves the use of one set of survey techniques, a sample design applying to the whole area of the survey, and a uniform questionnaire, and produces a homogeneous set of results. A multi-country survey, on the other hand, may necessitate the use of more than one data collection technique, a number of different questionnaires, and sample designs varying from one country to another. Different languages and changing economic and cultural environments call for great amount of coordination and supervision. Also, the accurate interpretation of these results is important. The differences among countries in terms of their culture, language, and attitudes puts additional burden on the researcher while interpreting the results of these surveys.

The fundamental cultural differences among people from different parts of the world affect the way people respond to survey questions. As a researcher conducting a global marketing research, knowledge about this is paramount. For example, consumers' propensity to say "yes" to a simple "yes or no" question varies by country.[43] Similarly, their propensity to say they "like" something or "agree" to a statement tends to be different. India is a country where consumers would say "yes" more often to avoid insulting or hurting the interviewer. Researchers should pay attention to this aspect while analyzing the data collected from international countries. Once the researcher has a clear understanding of overstatement or understatement of respondents from a particular country, they can make adjustments for this in their analysis while comparing research results from multiple countries. Exhibit 1.7 given below is an example of a multi-country survey in which national differences were not taken into account.

Exhibit 1.7

Talking to the Right Audience[44]

McDonald's was involved in a dispute in South Africa over the rights to its brand name in that market. Among their claims was that South Africans can recall the McDonald's name. As part of proof in the proceedings, they conducted two surveys and showed that the majority of those sampled had heard the company's name and could recognize the logo. However, the Supreme Court judge hearing the case did not think too highly of the evidence because the surveys were conducted in *posh, white* neighborhoods when 76% of the country's population is black. In view of these sampling issues, the judge threw out the case.

---

[43] J. Puleston and M. Eggers, "So Many Variables, So Little Time: A Practical Guide on What to Worry About When Conducting Multi-Country Studies," February 12, 2013, message posted to http://rwconnect.esomar.org/2013/02/12/a-practical-guide-on-what-to-worry-about-when-conducting-multi-country-studies/(Retrieved on April 30, 2014).

[44] Adapted from "Management Brief—Johannesburgers and Fries," *Economist*, September 27, 1997, pp. 75–76.

Based on the facts discussed above, an international researcher requires substantial skill and experience in three basic areas:

- Thorough knowledge and certain level of experience about the individual countries and global environment, as well as the ability to obtain and assimilate new information depending on the encountered problem.
- The ability to relate this experience and knowledge to a specific research problem and incorporate it into the survey design.
- The ability to synthesize data from different countries and interpret the factors on which they are based so as to produce results that are meaningful and actionable both from a national and an international point of view.

Researchers operating in one country may or may not have these abilities and are certainly not required to use them in their work.

IMPORTANCE OF COMPARABILITY

There are some similarities and differences between single-country and multi-country research Some of the key differences have been discussed above. The concept of comparability is, however, unique to multi-country surveys. There is unanimous consensus among the researcher community about the intensity of the problem of comparability of results, faced when dealing with data from two or more countries.

The interpretation of results heavily depends on this aspect. If the data is not comparable, it is likely that the interpretation of results may not yield useful information. Irrespective of the purpose of the research that is conducted, the research must be structured in such a way that the results can be used to make valid comparisons between the countries covered. In other words, marketing problems such as "Which country or countries provide the best opportunities?", or "How should marketing expenditure be distributed between various countries?", or "To what extent should the product, or the pack, or the advertising be varied between one country and another?" are classic questions that a multi-country survey should be able to answer. Exhibit 1.8 provides an example to illustrate the importance comparability of data.

What does comparability of data actually mean? It means that the results can be interpreted the same way for all country involved in research and the results would have the same meaning. Comparability of data enables a researcher to infer that the variations presented in the data are genuine, and are not merely due to differences in methodology or approach. Therefore, a research coordinator involved in a multi-country study, apart from instructing people, giving orders, and demonstrating maximum precision in the definition of research requirements, has to ensure that the following differences have been accounted for:

- Availability of resources and expertise in the respective fields
- Working habits and corporate cultures
- Organizational aspects

It is easy to confuse the concept of comparability with standardization. It is often misunderstood as the exact replication of research methods with the assumption that comparability of results depends on comparability of techniques. To understand this clearly, it should be

Exhibit 1.8

Comparability of Data

This example concerns a questionnaire administered to women in seven countries. The information sought at the beginning of the questionnaire was of a very simple type: whether the respondent was married or engaged, whether she had received an engagement ring, and the type of engagement ring received. The first three questions on the questionnaire used in England were:

(1)   Are you married?   If yes, in what year were you married?
                            If no, are you engaged to be married (again)?

If married or engaged, ask:

(2)   Do you own an engagement ring or did you obtain one or more rings at the time of engagement?

If yes:

(3)   What type of ring is it/was it?
      (a)   No stones
      (b)   Single diamond only
      (c)   Several diamonds but no other stones
      (d)   Diamond(s) and other stones
      (e)   Other stones only.

This looks like a very simple list of questions, involving no difficulty of direct translation. However, if the same questions were asked in all the seven countries, results would have been meaningless due to the different interpretations of the word *engaged*. In England, to be engaged involves a formal or semiformal agreement to marry. In Spain or Italy, it means no more than to have a boyfriend. If we had used the questionnaire as it stood, we would have obtained wildly inflated results for the number of women who were engaged, and—what is even more serious—significant understatements with regard to the ownership of engagement rings in the target group. In Italy and Spain, the questions were modified as follows:

(1)   Are you thinking of getting married in the near future?

If yes:

(2)   Has your hand been asked in marriage?

This is a very simple example of the use of different questions to obtain comparable information, while the use of the same questions would have resulted in information that was not comparable.

The differences, however, did not end there. The question "Do you own an engagement ring?" would not have served any purpose in Germany, since many German women receive a plain gold band at the time of engagement which they later transfer to the other hand and use as a wedding ring. Frequently, there is an exchange of rings between the couple at the time of engagement, and hence a whole battery of questions was required to obtain information for Germany that was equivalent to that for the other six countries.

Another modification that was made was in the list of precoded ring types in Question 3 (What type of ring is it/was it?). Although pearl rings were relatively unimportant in most of the countries covered, they accounted for a high proportion of engagement rings in Japan, and a significant proportion in France. To include pearl rings as a separate category in most of the countries might have unnecessarily complicated the list. However, to exclude them in Japan or France would not only have resulted in loss of information but also in confusion arising from the list of ring types being incomplete.

known that comparability at the data collection stage is separate from comparability at the interpretation stage. In all multi-country studies, comparability at the interpretation stage is mandatory. Comparability at data collection stage, that is, comparability of techniques is something that may not be necessary and often may not even be a sensible option to go for. The differences among different countries warrant the use of different countries at the data collection phase. For instance, self-administered questionnaires are common in developed nations like the US, while in countries like India, for a lot of research studies, an interviewer asks questions and respondents answer. It is incorrect to apply the same techniques for the sake of comparability while the research necessitates a different treatment.

Marketing academicians and practitioners concur that international marketing decisions for multinational companies require the use of diverse marketing strategies. Standardized procedures in all participating countries are not necessary while conducting international marketing. Moreover, an exact replication of research techniques in all the countries under investigation is also not required. Same sampling along with same questionnaire administering techniques across a number of countries for the sake of standardization beats the purpose of conducting global marketing research.

The field of global marketing research pays special attention to ironing out differences between countries, such as differences in language or social class divisions, so as to achieve a perfect uniformity of data collection. However, multi-country research involves dealing with countries that differ not only in language, but also in economic and social structures, behavior, and attitude patterns. These differences must be taken into account in the formulation of the design of a multi-country survey. To ignore these differences in the interests of a *spurious* comparability is to commit the cardinal sin of so many researchers—both national and international—namely, to take a technique-oriented rather than a problem-oriented view of their function. In fact, the results of an international research are richer as compared to those of national research due to the differences between the countries covered as well as the necessity to allow for these differences to occur in the survey. In short, comparability of data for interpretation and inference can be achieved in spite of adopting different data collection techniques. The researcher's main concern should be the comparability of the responses that are obtained with *similar* instruments of measurement, instead of *equality* of these instruments of measurement themselves. While comparability of results is regarded as all-important, practitioners in the multi-country research field are increasingly coming to realize that techniques may have to be varied between countries to achieve their objectives.[45] Comparability, therefore, is concerned with the end, not the means.

CLASSIFICATION OF GLOBAL MARKETING RESEARCH

As established earlier, global marketing research is a valid concept. However, what classifies as global marketing research? The following section will address this question. As mentioned earlier, global marketing research encompasses the entire gamut of marketing research studies that span from single-country research at one end to more elaborate and complex multi-country research studies at the other end.

---

[45] This thought was reiterated by almost all major international marketing firms the author interviewed in both the US and Europe.

Single-Country Research

A company is sometimes faced with a situation where it needs to conduct research to assist the formulation and implementation of marketing strategies in a single foreign market. Typically, this need arises when a marketer based in country X wants to know whether the marketing strategies that work well in the domestic environment can be translated to a market in country Y. If the market of country Y has unique characteristics that require adapting the marketing mix strategies to serve the needs of the local consumers better, research will help determine the strategy.

Exhibit 1.9 points to some of the blunders made by companies in marketing their products in a foreign market. While single-country research studies present many of the problems involved in a multi-country study, and thereby qualify to be classified as international research, the focus of this book is more on multi-country research studies.

Exhibit 1.9

What Went Wrong—Big Business Blunders!![46]

Big companies sometimes tend to fall into a trap while applying multinational marketing campaigns without evaluating the impact on the local audience. Some examples of international marketing blunders are illustrated below.

In 2011, Puma, a German sports gear and apparel company, decided to launch a new shoe under its brand name in the United Arab Emirates (UAE). These shoes were produced with the colors of the national flag on it. While the intentions were fine, they did not realize that they were offending the locals by placing the colors of flag on their feet. This act was seen as *walking on their flag*. A little more understanding of the culture could have saved Puma from committing this faux pas in the UAE.

A lack of effort in understanding the local connotation of words and phrases can cause trouble in marketing. Some companies, at times, tend to translate their slogans or messages directly into the local language without paying too much attention to the meaning it derives. A famous example is that of the American beer Coors. The company's slogan "Turn It Loose" was literally translated into Spanish. While the slogan was fine in the US, the marketing campaign turned upside down when the slogan translated as "Suffer from Diarrhea" in Spanish.

Pepsi's "Come Alive with Pepsi Generation" slogan in China is another well-known blunder in the international marketing scene. The cola giant failed to realize the meaning of the translation which turned out to be "Pepsi Brings Your Ancestors Back from the Grave," hurting their marketing efforts.

Nike made a blunder while trying to capture the Chinese market. In 2004, Nike put forth an advertisement with Lebron James, the American basketball player, as the selling point. The commercial showed the basketball star defeating traditional Chinese elders, women, and a dragon. The advertisement ended up offending the traditional sentiments of the Chinese, many of whom are still close to their tradition and culture. While westerners viewed dragons as mystical creatures, many of the Chinese people considered them to be a symbol of power and luck. At the same time, a lot of respect and authority is associated with elders and women. Nike failed to understand the local traditional and cultural values and could not apply this to their marketing campaign.

---

[46] Adapted from W. Corry, "What Company Famously Advertised, 'It Won't Leak in Your Pocket and Make You Pregnant'?", April 7, 2012, http://www.themarketingblog.co.uk/2012/04/

Another example of single-country research would be the survey conducted in Greece to study the criteria involved in the selection of credit and charge cards.[47] Interviews of card users and marketing personnel at major card-issuing companies in Greece were collected. Further, a list of 15 attributes that were important in the selection of a card was compiled. The questionnaire was then prepared attempting to identify the importance attached to each of these 15 attributes by cardholders. A five-point, itemized Likert-type scale was developed and pilot-tested for the purpose. The selection of a quota sample of 151 cardholders was made randomly after accounting for factors such as the sex, income, and age of cardholders. A national media survey in Greece suggests that 62% of cardholders live in the Greater Athens area and 32% in Thessaloniki, 52% of cardholders are male, 47% are high-income earners, and 12% are low-income earners. The data was collected by personally interviewing cardholders living in Athens.

Multi-Country Research

Multi-country research studies, as the name indicates, are research conducted in more than one country market. Multi-country research studies can be further classified into three broad categories:[48]

- Similar research conducted *independently* in several countries
- Research projects conducted *sequentially* in several countries
- Research projects conducted *simultaneously* in several countries

Independent Multi-Country Research

This is possibly the most common form of global marketing research. Independent multi-country research studies occur when subsidiaries or branches of multinational companies independently conduct similar research on the same products in a number of countries. Common examples are awareness/penetration checks on international brands and the test marketing of new products. The major disadvantages of this type of international research studies are: (a) It often leads to duplication of efforts (such as questionnaire, etc.) and hence is not very efficient, and (b) since such studies are conducted in isolation, it makes comparisons of results across countries more difficult.

Despite these drawbacks, such independent multi-country studies are prevalent as most marketing research funds are obtained from local budgets. In the absence of a global marketing research manager, these budgets tend to be spent entirely independently of each other.

---

what-company-famously-advertised-it-wont-leak-in-your-pocket-and-make-you-pregnant/(Retrieved in July 2013); "3 International Marketing Blunders You Shouldn't Forget," December 5, 2012, http://www. backpackingdiplomacy.com/3-international-marketing-blunders-you-shoulding-forget/(Retrieved in July 2013).

[47] Arthur Meidan and Dimitris Davos, "Credit and Charge Card Selection Criteria in Greece," *International Journal of Bank Marketing* 12, no. 2 (1994): 36–44.

[48] Adapted from P. D. Barnard, "The Role and Implementation of International Marketing Research," presented in ESOMAR Seminar on International Marketing Research: "Does It Provide What the User Needs?," Brussels, 1976.

Often, no agreed system exists whereby research managers can inform their foreign colleagues of their activities. The position is even worse where no formal market research position exists in some, or all, of the individual subsidiaries.

An international research manager or a coordinator helps in developing a coherent framework for the research planning of the subsidiary operations. Furthermore, even if projects are being conducted independently by the member companies of an international business, a considerable degree of comparability between the findings can be achieved if the international research manager creates or encourages a research philosophy and study guidelines which are to be observed by his colleagues in the countries concerned.

Sequential Multi-Country Research

Sequential multi-country research is very attractive for many researchers in the sense that lessons can be learned in the first one or two markets to be researched and then applied to the other countries subsequently involved in the research program. This procedure is often valuable in helping to:

- Define the limits of the subject matter to be covered
- Ensure that operational problems arising with countries researched early in the program are avoided or overcome more easily elsewhere
- Ensure that key findings in the earlier studies influences the focus of later ones
- Spread the costs of conducting the research over a longer time period

Typically, in cases of a rolling launch across multiple countries, a sequential approach is used. The biggest advantage of this type of study is when the research company can plan to avoid variations in research procedure from country to country that might give rise to spurious international differences.

Simultaneous Multi-Country Research

Simultaneous multi-country research involves conducting marketing research studies in multiple country markets simultaneously, and is, perhaps, the *purest* form of global marketing research studies. It provides the toughest tests of research supplier capability and also raises in the most acute form the question of comparability. The bulk of issues discussed in this book will address this form of international research. Because simultaneous multi-country research is the most complex and involves handling unique problems, having such a form of research study as the focus will ensure that the problems that an international researcher might encounter in conducting other forms of international research are also addressed.

CHALLENGES TO RESEARCH[49]

In the day and age of the *Big Data* phenomenon, it is vital for market researchers to not get overwhelmed by the quantity of data available. It is exciting to note that 90% of data

---

[49] Achenbaum, "The Future Challenge to Market Research."

available today was created in the last two years.[50] There have been concerns expressed on aspects such as:

- The level of importance given to statistics and techniques over the interpretation of results. With the amount of data available, researchers tend to become very method-oriented by using methods to work back to the problems rather than letting the problems decide the suitable method.
- The undue importance given to data as well as the heavy reliance on computers. The amount of time spent in trying to provide insights to all of the available data is not sufficient.
- The role of a marketing researcher is not mere collection of data. Presentation of analyzed results is different form interpretation of raw data. A researcher's experience and skill should ideally add to the insights and recommendations.

The costs of collection of data, interpreting it in local context, communication with domestic teams conducting the research, and dissemination of results are some of the key challenges faced by a researcher while conducting a global marketing research study. It is the market researcher's responsibility to present the findings in a manner that can be used in the decision-making process by the managers of the company. The focus of this book is to provide the tools required for a marketing researcher to do this with an international perspective.

MARKETING RESEARCHER OF THE 21ST CENTURY[51]

The marketing researcher of the future will continue to be affected by four main factors: speed, the Internet, globalization, and data overload. Speed is becoming increasingly necessary to provide marketing intelligence and insight much more rapidly. The Internet, advancements in communication technology, and improvements in computer and computing systems among others have sped up the exchange of information. This places heavy emphasis on collecting data and getting it to the end users as quickly as possible for timely decision making. With Internet penetration extending to even the remote corners of the world, the opportunities presented in terms of data collection, administering research surveys, and even implementing marketing campaigns pose exciting times for the researchers. In terms of globalization, researchers are required to learn more about foreign markets, as well as the values and cultural differences represented in the world economy. Further, researchers must be able to add value and insight to numbers without creating confusion for the user by data overload.

The marketing researcher for the 21st century should be better trained, must work smarter, and have more varied skills than the researcher of today. Comfort with cyberspace, excellent computer skills, proficiency in statistical methods, and an ability to communicate with speed and precision are necessary traits. Exhibit 1.10 presents an example of a successful marketing campaign that has effectively used all the developments in recent times.

---

[50] C. Casseb, A. Garrido, and D. Baronni, "The Insight Innovation Exchange LatAm," May 8, 2013, message posted to http://rwconnect.esomar.org/2013/05/08/the-insight-innovation-exchange-latam/ (Retrieved on May 6, 2014).

[51] James H. Fouss, "Faster and Smarter," *Marketing Research* 8, no. 3 (1996), pp 16–17.

Exhibit 1.10

Adobe Turns Employees into Brand Ambassadors[52]

Adobe, the American multinational software company, has a strong social media presence. As of early October 2014, Adobe had over 340,000 Twitter followers, 260,000 Facebook likes, and 300,000 Google+ followers. By enabling its own employees to be brand ambassadors, Adobe has been quite innovative in its social media marketing efforts.

By assessing existing employee advocacy and taking necessary steps to encourage employees to refer them, Adobe has driven a lot of its sales through social media. For example, Adobe's employment branding leadership introduced hashtags to motivate its employees to take photos and share updates that promote the lifestyle that comes with working for Adobe. The company also mandated a *social shift* training for all its employees, conducted at different levels for different employees. From mentoring employees to use their personal social accounts to share company-related content or engage on behalf of Adobe to educating them on its key social media principles, these interactive training sessions were a clear and focused step toward brand management. In the recent past, as a result of these social media efforts, Adobe's Creative Cloud subscriptions increased by 20%.

Exhibit 1.10 reveals the latest trends in marketing, new product introduction, and consumer research in the global marketplace. The growth and increasing technological sophistication of the communication infrastructure facilitates marketing research on a much broader and diverse geographic scale. The marketing landscape has changed from the traditional broadcasting model to that of social media marketing, digital communications, online communities, and web-based interactive marketing. People with no technical interest or knowledge can now easily chat, publish, promote, discuss, and interact online with the rapid growth of web tools. For instance, by the end of 2011, a Nielsen/McKinsey study tracked over 181 million blogs around the world, up from only 36 million in 2006.[53] Other easily accessible digital tools such as Facebook, Twitter, Pinterest, RSS, Podcasting, Feedster, Flickr, etc. are also gaining popularity.

Impact of Global Internet Penetration

The global penetration of the Internet at the beginning of the 21st century is captured in Table 1.1. The global penetration has in turn resulted in rapid dissemination of information, making the consumer more powerful, more knowledgeable, and actively involved in what is going on in different parts of the world.

---

[52] Adapted from Louise Julig, "4 Ways to Turn Your Employees into Brand Ambassadors," October 21, 2014, http://www.socialmediaexaminer.com/turn-employees-brand-ambassadors/#more-70724 (Retrieved in October 2014).

[53] Nielsen Newswire, "Buzz in the Blogosphere: Millions More Bloggers and Blog Readers," 2012, http://www.nielsen.com/us/en/newswire/2012/buzz-in-the-blogosphere-millions-more-bloggers-and-blog-readers.html (Retrieved on June 10, 2013).

TABLE 1.1
WORLD INTERNET USAGE AND POPULATION STATISTICS[54]

World Regions	Population	% World Population	Internet Users as % of Total Population	Internet Users as % of Total Internet Users	Internet Users Growth 2000–2014 (%)
Africa	1,125,721,038	15.7	21.3	8.6	5,219.6
Asia	3,996,408,007	55.7	31.7	45.1	1,006.8
Europe	825,802,657	11.5	68.6	20.2	438.8
Middle East	231,062,860	3.2	44.9	3.7	3,060.9
North America	353,860,227	4.9	84.9	10.7	177.8
Latin America/ Caribbean	612,279,181	8.5	49.3	10.8	1,571.4
Oceania/ Australia	36,724,649	0.5	67.5	0.9	225.5
World Total	7,181,858,619	100.0	39.0	100.0	676.3

* Internet usage and population statistics are as of December 2013.

Era of Consumer-Generated Marketing

Consumerism and consumer-directed marketing tools have gained rapid prominence in the new era. Termed *consumer-generated marketing*, consumers are influencing the way marketers design and promote their products through online media. George Masters, an American schoolteacher and an Apple fan, created a homemade ad for his iPod Mini, which was seen by 64,000 people in the first few weeks it was online.[55] What were previously considered as *high-end production technologies* are now available to the digital generation in the form of video/audio-editing software, and design software tools to capture video, audio, and digital images. The other side of the coin is demonstrated by a spoof ad showing a terrorist driving a Volkswagen Polo in a failed suicide bombing attack.[56] All these point to the fact that consumers are in control and marketers have to find out innovative ways by which they can positively influence customers. Jim Stengel, Global Marketing Officer, Procter & Gamble (P&G), states, "We need to embrace the urgent implications of consumer control." According to Tom

---

[54] Adapted from Internet World Stats, www.internetworldstats.com (Retrieved on September 29, 2014).

[55] "Homemade iPod Mini 'Tiny Machine' Ad by George Masters Takes Internet by Storm," *Internet Patrol*, 2007, http://www.theinternetpatrol.com/homemade-ipod-mini-tiny-machine-ad-by-george-masters-takes-internet-by-storm/(Retrieved on June 10, 2013).

[56] David Smith, "Suicide Bomber Sells VW Polo—Hoax Ad Takes Internet by Storm, *Guardian*, January 22, 2005, message posted on http://www.guardian.co.uk/technology/2005/jan/23/arts.artsnews (Retrieved on May 2, 2014).

Glocer, CEO, Reuters, "Our audiences have moved on dramatically. Now they are consuming, creating, sharing and publishing their own content online."[57]

In 2005, General Mills Inc.'s Haagen-Dazs brand suffered a blow in China when bloggers circulated rumors that the company's ice cream was made in an unsanitary factory in the southern city of Shenzhen. This is despite the fact that the brand doesn't even have a plant in the city.[58] The instance of consumerism is also identified when companies do not live up to the expectations of the marketplace, as in the case of Domino's Pizza. In 2009, when two of their employees posted a prank video on the Internet, the company was severely hit with declining sales, negative publicity, and customer dissatisfaction. The company had to embark on a brand-rebuilding exercise to restore the brand's lost credibility.[59]

These examples reveal two important dimensions of the world of marketing today. On one side, the Internet has evolved as the gateway to the world for corporations and business entities. Providing a user-friendly, interactive environment, the cyberspace has become the portal for commerce, retail, and advertising. This has revolutionized the marketing industry and replaced many of the traditional marketing strategies with web and online resources. On the other hand, research has to be done in a systematic, well-planned way to incorporate the geographical, cultural, political, legal, and economic aspects of various regions.

Mobile and Social Media Marketing

Mobile marketing refers to direct marketing to mobile phones, PDAs, and tablet PCs. Rich multimedia messages sent to mobile phones utilizing the benefits of sound, images, and text are challenging conventional channels of advertising and marketing. Technologies such as SMS, Bluetooth, WLAN, Infrared, and quick response (QR) codes are being used to distribute commercial (or in some cases non-commercial) content to mobile phones. SMS media has a successful history of generating high response rates. Large-volume on-pack promotions have produced response rates ranging from 8percent to 20%. Responses from *opted-in* mobile number databases have averaged at 15%.[60]

The total number of mobile subscribers worldwide in 2013 is estimated at 6.8 billion, an increase of nearly 15% since 2011. This translates to an estimated global penetration rate of 96.2% by the end of 2013. In other words, per 100 inhabitants, nearly 96 people will have a mobile phone subscription. A breakdown of this number for the developed and developing nations reveals the intensity of penetration. The subscription per 100 inhabitants by 2013 is estimated at 128.2 for the developed nations (meaning one person will be having multiple mobile subscriptions), and 89.4 for the developing nations.[61] Such high mobile density rates

---

[57] James Cherkoff, "Collaborative Marketing," 2014, http://www.collaboratemarketing.com/about/ (Retrieved on June 10, 2013).

[58] "Mad as Hell in China's Blogosphere," *Bloomberg Businessweek Magazine*, August 13, 2006, http://www.businessweek.com/stories/2006-08-13/mad-as-hell-in-chinas-blogosphere (Retrieved on June 10, 2013).

[59] V. Kumar and Yashoda Bhagwat, "Listen to the Customer," *Marketing Research—A Magazine of Management and Applications* 22, no. 2 (2010): 14–19.

[60] A. Micheal and B. Salter, *Mobile Marketing* (New York: Taylor and Francis Group, 2006), 1st edition, p. 39.

[61] International Telecommunication Union, "Yearbook of Statistics", February 2012, http://www.itu.int/en/ITU-D/Statistics/Pages/stat/default.aspx (Retrieved on July 2, 2013).

are bound to do wonders for the burgeoning area of mobile marketing and open up several marketing challenges for researchers.

Social media marketing as a new form of marketing has gained significant momentum in the recent years. The social media platforms, broadly comprising of (a) blogs, (b) social networks, and (c) content communities, have evolved as a means for consumers to share text, images, audio, and video information with other consumers and with companies, and vice-versa. The social media portals are enabling users to find their trusted sources for everything from pie recipes to product reviews. With marketers monitoring this space closely, their activity online has only increased in recent times. For instance, according to the 2013 Online Advertising Performance Outlook, a report produced jointly by Vizu, a Nielsen company, and the Chief Marketing Officer (CMO) Council, nearly 70% of the brand marketers surveyed plan to increase their use of social media in 2013, followed closely by mobile advertising (69%) and video advertising (64%). These numbers are all up from 2012 projections, indicating a continued shift toward the channels where consumers are spending an ever-increasing amount of their time. Moreover, from a consumer standpoint, social media is a new way of interacting with friends and family. For marketers, it is encouraging to see how consumers use social media in their daily lives. Exhibit 1.11 highlights some interesting statistics on use of social media at a global level.

Exhibit 1.11

The Global Social Consumer

Social networking has made the world even smaller. Social media has greatly affected the lives of consumers; marketing too is playing a catch-up to adapt to the new setting in which a global consumer interacts and exchanges ideas. According to "State of the Media: The Social Media Report 2012," mobile is an important driver for continued growth in social media. With consumers having access to mobile devices like smartphones and tablets, they are using this media extensively on social networking websites. As per the report, from the overall time spent using social media, time spent on mobile apps and the mobile web accounts for 63% of the year-over-year (YOY) growth. Moreover, 46% of smartphone users and 16% of tablet users connect to social media through their respective mobile devices.

The impact of social media on marketing is apparent from the rise in social word-of-mouth communication. The power of word-of-mouth has increased greatly now with social media as there is no limitation on the influence and reach. Moreover, social media has made consumers very informed. It has transformed the way consumers make purchase decisions globally. Using social media to learn more about products and services and to find deals on them has become very common.

The use of social media while watching television has also increased lately. Consumers are engaging with the world to share their experiences instantly via social media on the movies and shows that they are watching. As of June 2012, more than 33% of Twitter users had actively tweeted about TV-related content. Some 44% of US tablet owners and 38% of US smartphone owners use their devices daily to access social media while watching television. A recent Nielsen survey of more than 28,000 global consumers with Internet access explored social media's global reach and impact. A couple of the findings from the survey pertained to the mode of accessing social networking sites and interacting with social media while watching TV. The following table provides the findings.[62]

	Asia-Pacific (%)	Europe (%)	Middle East and Africa (%)	Latin America (%)
Accessing Social Networking Sites via:				
Computer	93	96	91	96
Mobile Phone	59	33	48	33
Tablet	28	8	10	6
Internet-Enabled TV	9	4	9	4
Game Console	5	3	2	3
Handheld Music Player	5	2	2	2
Interacting with Social Media While Watching TV	63	52	47	38

Among the social media channels, Facebook and Twitter have been the most widely used social networking websites. Here are some interesting statistics for each in 2012.[63]

Facebook	Twitter
➤ Monthly active users now total nearly 850 million.	➤ 175 million tweets sent from Twitter.
➤ 21% of Facebook users are from Asia, which is only less than 4% of Asia's population.	➤ Average Twitter user has tweeted 307 times.
➤ 488 million users regularly use Facebook mobile.	➤ Total of 163 billion tweets since its beginning.
➤ Brazil publishes the most number of posts out of all Facebook countries. More than 800 Pages kept their Facebook walls busy with almost 86,000 posts per month.	➤ 56% of customer tweets to companies are being ignored.
➤ 23% of Facebook's users check their account five or more times daily.	➤ Top 3 countries on Twitter are the US (107 million), Brazil (33 million), and Japan (30 million).
➤ Witnessed a 41% growth in active users from Russia, South Korea, Japan, India, and Brazil.	➤ The 2012 election broke records with 31.7 million political tweets.
	➤ Election Day was by far the most tweeted event in US political history.
	➤ 32% of all Internet users are using Twitter.

---

[62] Adapted from "State of the Media: The Social Media Report, 2012," http://www.nielsen.com/content/dam/corporate/us/en/reports-downloads/2012-Reports/The-Social-Media-Report-2012.pdf. (Retrieved on May 10, 2014).

[63] Adapted from Brian Honigman, "100 Fascinating Social Media Statistics and Figures From 2012," http://www.huffingtonpost.com/brian-honigman/100-fascinating-social-me_b_2185281.html (Retrieved on November 29, 2012).

Facebook	Twitter
➤ 250 million photos are uploaded to Facebook every day.	➤ Projected to make a total of $540 million in advertising revenue by 2014.
➤ 210,000 years of music have been played on Facebook.	➤ YouTube is the most followed brand with 19 million followers.
➤ 17 billion location-tagged posts and check-ins were logged.	➤ The US's 141.8 million accounts represent 27.4% of all Twitter users.
➤ 77% of business-to-consumer (B2C) companies and 43% of B2B companies acquired customers from Facebook.	➤ 50% of Twitter users are using the social network via mobile.
	➤ 34% of marketers have generated leads using Twitter.

Impact of Technology on Business Practices

In this era of rapid globalization, with tremendous advances in technology and communications channels, managers from global corporations are changing their strategy in handling customer service (inbound and outbound calls and customer inquiries) from *call centers* to *customer contact points*. By outsourcing increasingly complex customer care needs, there can be added focus on core competencies. PBX-based technology is being replaced by sophisticated automatic call distribution systems.[64] Some of the latest technologies include:

- *Voice over Internet:* Phone calls transmitted over the web with a single telephone line handling both voice and data.
- *Text chat:* An older technology in which two or more people communicate in real time by typing messages to one another.
- *Escorted browsing:* The agent sees what the customer sees and directs him or her to specific web pages.
- *Virtual conferencing:* Real time communication in which *slide shows* are presented to people all over the globe while engaging them in interactive dialogue.

All these developments in the field of marketing demonstrate a shift from traditional marketing strategies and thereby marketing research methodologies to more sophisticated technology-based marketing.

Relevance of the Shift from Traditional to Technology-based Marketing

We will be examining in detail the implications of the shift from traditional marketing methods to technology-based marketing in the context of their effect on global marketing research. The effects on the following parameters will be highlighted in the following chapters.

---

[64] Clarence Henderson, "Globalization Revisited," Asia Pacific Management Forum, http://www.apmforum.com/columns/orientseas29.htm (Retrieved on July 2, 2013).

1. Response rate
2. Response quality
3. Accessibility to respondents
4. Cost of research
5. Time taken to complete the study (speed)
6. Larger sample size
7. Relevancy of global sample
8. Access to multilingual groups
9. Reducing biases due to:
   a. Construct equivalence
   b. Measurement equivalence
   c. Sampling equivalence

ETHICS IN RESEARCH

Ethical issues concerning the domestic marketing research apply to global marketing research as well. Researchers in many countries have voluntarily set up ethical standards that will have to be observed in marketing research. It is important for marketing researchers to adhere to certain principles irrespective of the country where the research is being done. Some of the important issues are discussed below.

- *Respondents' rights:* The first aspect is that the respondents have rights and they should be allowed to participate voluntarily in the survey with no coercion from the firm for conducting research. They need to be informed accurately of the purpose of the study, and where permitted, the sponsors' identity. There have been instances where the telemarketers call potential customers and try to sell their product in the pretext of conducting surveys. This has created general mistrust among respondents, resulting in high non-response ratios. The second aspect is ensuring respondent's safety. Taking part in the survey should not be a cause of any harm to the respondents. Also, respondents must be told about the confidentiality of their identity and details prior to conducting research. Once confidentiality or anonymity is guaranteed, it is the onus of the researcher to see to that these are fulfilled, especially if the topic of the research is socially or politically controversial.
- *Sponsors' rights:* A sponsor is the client who has commissioned with the researcher. It is a researcher's moral duty to respect the agreement and conduct research in the manner that has been agreed upon with the sponsor. Researchers have to make ensure that legitimate steps have been carried out during the data collection process and the analysis is unbiased without any consideration for the needs of the sponsor or any other agency. Companies commission many types of research, some of which are to prove or support their judgment. In this scenario, it is possible that the sponsor or representatives of the sponsoring company may try to influence the research findings. It is the researcher's ethical responsibility to ignore such influences and present the true findings.

As far as the sponsor's and the respondent's ethical obligations are concerned, each party has a moral obligation to not misuse the trust placed in them. Like researchers, sponsors should respect the agreement/contract; thereby, should not seek more deliverables than agreed upon as part of the initial screening process to conduct remaining research in-house. Moreover, sponsors should not ask researchers to tweak results to present a favorable picture. As for the respondents, once they have agreed to participate in the survey, they should provide true answers to the questions asked by the researcher.

There is a widespread implementation of data privacy laws in the European Union (EU). Some of the guidelines are that personal data will be obtained and processed fairly and lawfully and will be used only for the purpose stated at the time of data collection, and that data will also not be kept longer than required and will be protected from unauthorized access, disclosure, alteration, and destruction.[65]

The ethics pertaining to research on the Internet have become a significant area of concern in the recent years. People flock to chat rooms and message boards to share experiences or thoughts or ideas with *virtual* strangers, making their social and behavioral information easily accessible on the Net. Even when respondents choose to remain anonymous, privacy issues and the unclear distinction between public and private domains make it possible for researchers to record their online interactions without the knowledge or consent of the respondents. A sensitive, ethical judgment by individual Internet researchers is imperative if their participants' privacy and well-being are to be protected. Some of the ethical guidelines for conducting online research are[66]:

1. The researcher should take into consideration whether the purpose of the research is compatible with the purpose of the forum.
2. The members of the group under study should be appropriately informed about the researchers' presence, purpose, and identity.
3. If the researcher wishes to quote some of the individuals in a forum, they should be informed and their consent received.
4. Even though the virtual community's discourses are accessible publicly, researches should maintain a respectful sensitivity toward the psychological boundaries, vulnerabilities, and privacy of the individual members.

GLOBAL MARKETING RESEARCH IN PRACTICE

This chapter should be able to convince the reader of the importance of conducting global marketing research before making a decision to enter foreign markets. This book will use practical examples to illustrate concepts as well as the example of a hypothetical fast-food chain, Tasty Burgers, based in the US and trying to penetrate the global fast-food market. The example will specifically deal with four foreign countries, namely UK, Brazil, India, and Saudi Arabia. Each of the chapters starting from Chapter 2 will take the reader through the process of global marketing research as it is practiced.

---

[65] Simon Chadwick, "Data Privacy Legislation All the Rage in Europe," *Marketing News* 27, no. 17 (August 1993): A7.

[66] Dag Elgesem, "What Is Special About the Ethical Issues in Online Research?," September 1, 2002, http://www.nyu.edu/projects/nissenbaum/ethics_elg_full.html (Retrieved on July 2, 2013).

SUMMARY

A company aspiring to launch operations on a global scale has to take care of a lot of resources like manpower and finance. As seen in the chapter, marketing a product internationally can be quite a challenge for marketers. The national and cultural differences discussed in this chapter direct the whole concept of global marketing research. If it were not for these differences, this book, and indeed the whole concept of global marketing research, would not exist. The recent developments in terms of social media and the Internet have been included to give the reader a more holistic view of global marketing research as it is today. The chapter uses examples to explain the concepts in detail. The marketing blunders mentioned illustrate small mistakes made by some of the big brands. This proves that no matter how big a player one is, careful consideration should be given to any marketing decision before it is implemented. Various strategic decisions need to be made about the selection of markets, mode of entry, allocation of resources, and method of management. Driven by data, global marketing research provides companies a more scientific approach to maximize the benefits of going global. This chapter should have convinced the readers of the importance and uniqueness of global marketing research. It is pertinent to mention that the ethical issues do not change for global marketing research, and in this aspect it is identical to domestic marketing research.

 QUESTIONS AND PROBLEMS

1. Rashad Wallace, the owner of a mixed martial arts gymnasium in Los Angeles, California, feels that a demand exists for indoor gymnasiums in certain European countries that presently are not being served. He is considering employing a marketing research company to conduct a study to ascertain whether a market exists for the indoor facilities.
   a. What factors should Mr Wallace consider before ordering global marketing research to be conducted?
   b. What are the possible pitfalls that the marketing research company must avoid while conducting the study?
   c. After obtaining the marketing research recommendations, Mr Wallace decided not to use the information generated by the global marketing research study. Which factors could have influenced his decision not to use the research information?
2. Given the developments in recent years with mobile and social media marketing, and the increase in speed at which information passes, what are certain factors that determine whether a firm decides to conduct marketing research studies on its own versus hiring outside suppliers for their services.
3. With the decreasing knowledge gap and increasing speed at which information is passed, what continue to be the ethical dilemmas marketing researchers face when conducting field studies in different countries?
4. Robert Sanders, a software engineer, has designed a website for the online purchasing of groceries, targeted at elderly/disabled individuals. The website allows individuals with transportation difficulties to purchase their desired items and have them delivered at their doorstep. The website has been a success in Sanders' native state of California, and he is looking to expand toward the east coast. Acting as Mr Sanders' marketing

consultant, suggest a course of action to help him bring this service to other states outside of California.

5. How might the following use global marketing research? Be specific.
   a. Whole Foods, a health-driven food store, opening in Canada.
   b. The US National Football League (NFL) promoting football in Europe.
   c. A major US television network (CBS, NBC, or ABC) reviewing operations in far East.
   d. Apple Macbook Computers looking out for foreign countries for manufacturing.

2

CHAPTER _____

Marketing Research in the Global Environment

INTRODUCTION

Marketing success in international markets requires that industrial firms collect and analyze market and environmental information and formulate strategies that are appropriate to specific country markets.[1] A number of key parameters are to be considered in such strategy formulation. The nature and impact of these strategies will depend on the phase of the internationalization process. The degree of experience and the nature of operations in international markets will also need to be considered. Strategic planning by an international industrial marketing company must integrate dimensions such as industrial supplier–customer interaction, the levels of marketing perspective, and the purchase of industrial products and services. The following strategies will need to be clarified:

- Which markets and target segments will be entered?
- Which mode of entry and operation should be adopted for specific target markets?
- What should be the timing for entry when entering a number of markets (considering available company resources and competitive conditions in different countries)?
- How marketing resources must be allocated between different levels of marketing management (product/product line level, customer level, and market segment/country market level) to attain desired goals and degree of control over international operations?
- How to establish a control system to monitor performance in the target market strategic business unit (SBU), and so on?

ROLE OF RESEARCH IN GLOBAL MARKETING STRATEGY FORMULATION

Marketing strategy decisions will be based on information about market potential, customer requirements, industry and market trends, present and future competitive behavior, expected sales, market segment size and requirements, and sales and profit performance for customers, products, and territories.[2] In the marketing of industrial products, the following levels of market definition can be identified: customer level (micro-market), segment level (macro-

---

[1] Milan Jurse, "Organizing Information for Effective International Industrial Marketing Management," in *How to Do It: Managing the Process*, pp. 193–211.

[2] Michael D. Hutt and Thomas W. Speh, *Business Marketing Management* (Orlando, FL: The Dryden Press, 1994), 5th edition.

market), country level, and global level (worldwide market, being the aggregate of markets on a segment or country level).

Selection of target customers and market is one of the basic strategies of an international industrial marketer. Choice of target customers and market segments facilitate adequate allocation of resources within the supplier's present and future market portfolio. Perceived importance and risks of markets and internally acquired market knowledge influence strategic choice at the market level. Market opportunities and risks associated with operating in different countries influence market choice at the country level. Global strategies are formulated at the corporate level and necessitate determination of overall allocation of a company's resources across countries product markets and target segments. At the customer level, actual and potential customers in each market of operation should be evaluated. The market decision process for each target customer at the SBU level would involve:

1. The analysis of demand (customer's requirements)
2. The analysis of competition offerings (differentiation analysis)
3. The setting of objectives (micro-market share, volume, profit)
4. The definition of a strategy
5. Planning (marketing programs)
6. Implementation
7. Control and evaluation

Formerly, the basic role of market research was *fact-finding*, but as it is called on to furnish more and more qualitative and analytical information, its function will be the solution of problems. This calls for a transition to strategic marketing research. The market researcher should, therefore, became a source of actionable marketing information with the capability to respond promptly to information requirements of marketing managers and to perform a marketing consultancy function by advising management on actions to be taken. Two prerequisites must be fulfilled in order to enable such strategic transition of marketing research. First, market information must be treated as a vital ingredient of the firm's marketing resources and be managed and matched to marketing managers' requirements. Second, the market research department should be innovative and customer-oriented in the process of satisfying the information needs of marketers. The communication gap between managers and researchers in marketing should be bridged at the very outset if any measure of success is to be achieved at all. Exhibit 2.1 points to the formation of strategic alliances in the international marketplace.

According to the European Society for Opinion and Marketing Research (ESOMAR), global spending on marketing research topped $31 billion in 2010, with an estimated $5 billion being spent in the Asia Pacific region.[3] Further, according to Philip Barnard, chief executive of WPP's Research International,

> When you look at the remaining 65%, most research companies here and abroad would claim to do international work. And indeed they do. The real difference is whether it is something they can do through their own international subsidiaries, as we do, on through loose associations with other companies, or ad hoc partners. Perhaps it comes down to whether clients want to develop a serious strategic relationship with their suppliers, or shop around each time.

---

[3] ESOMAR, "2009 Global Market Research Report," 2009 www.esomar.org, (Retrieved on June 2, 2014).

Exhibit 2.1

General Mills Partnered with Nestlé to Create Cereal Partners Worldwide[4]

Back in the early 1990s, when one of the world's largest food companies, General Mills, wanted a share of the rapidly growing breakfast-cereal market in Europe, it joined hands with Nestlé to create Cereal Partners Worldwide.

For General Mills to enter the market from scratch would have been extremely costly. Although the cereal business uses cheap commodities as its raw materials, it is both capital- and marketing-intensive; sales volume must be high before profits begin to develop. For General Mills to reach its goal alone would have required a manufacturing base and a massive sales force. Further, Kellogg's stranglehold on supermarkets would have been difficult for an unknown to breach easily. The solution led to a joint venture with Nestlé.

The deal was mutually beneficial. General Mills provided the knowledge in cereal technology, including some of its proprietary manufacturing equipment, its stable of proven brands, and its knack for pitching these products to consumers. Nestlé provided its name on the box, access to retailers, and production capacity that could be converted to making General Mills' cereals.

ISSUES SPECIFIC TO GLOBAL MARKETING RESEARCH

Figure 2.1 represents some of the decisions that companies have to make for going international. There are several risks associated with these decisions and companies should be looking at some key indicators before they invest in the process of internationalization.

FIGURE 2.1
SAMPLE INDICATORS FOR ASSESSING RISKS AND OPPORTUNITIES[5]

Financial Risks	Market Risks	Political Risks	Other
• Understanding of countries' inflation rates, depreciation levels, foreign exchange rates, restrictions	• Important to analyze growth potential, potential sales, competition, labor costs	• One must have an understanding of stablity levels, expropriations when deciding whether or not to enter international market	• Must be aware of various restrictions including those on imports–exports, population levels, degree of ownership rights

---

[4] Philip R. Cateora and John L. Graham, *International Marketing* (New York: McGraw Hill Publications, 2007), 13th edition.

[5] Adapted from C. Samuel Craig and Susan P. Douglas, *International Marketing Research* (West Sussex: John Wiley and Sons, 2005).

Even though economies are slowing down, internationalization provides for growth, and not because of the emergence of common markets. Coca-Cola, Unilever, Mars, Shell, L'Oreal have always taken into account issues related to management across countries. Companies like BSN, Whirlpool, and Marks & Spencer are beginning to define or redefine their global marketing strategies. The major characteristics of the ways of operating and their consequences on the business can be analyzed as follows.

Globalization

As companies restructure and operate internationally, they find little choice when it comes to global marketing and advertising. Brand property analysis, portfolio management, line extension exploitation, name changes, and transfers of brands to other markets are common issues today. Niche marketing opportunities and new ways of segmenting consumers are being studied in this connection.

There is, however, a fine line between globalization and local adaptation. Marketing achievement is assessed in terms of achieving the right balance between integrated central marketing and strategic thinking and a flexible and more decentralized marketing approach adapted to national cultures. Both these approaches are needed. United Distillers and McDonald's seem carved out for this double task, but it is difficult to decide on the right approach—issues vary with industry sector, maturity of markets, or company's culture.

Major Decisions

Events such as acquisition of a brand of Italian mineral water by BSN in France, the purchase of shares in British Rail by SNCF, or the adoption of a pan-European media approach by Unilever make the task of marketers more complex and multidimensional.

Complexity

Gaining familiarity with systems, structures, and cultures radically different from one's own is a complex maneuver. The old international style, where each market was treated in a separate way, was far more simple and akin to being in the export department. Under the new style, companies have restructured, assigning their best people to coordinate international marketing, advertising, media, or research activities. Today, the international researcher's role is to help clients reduce risks by making better decisions. Clients today expect solutions, not just answers, to all problems. This is reflected in all aspects of their requests.

Fragmentation

Specialists and centralized market research departments are becoming fewer and smaller, and end users of research are becoming more involved in purchase decisions. Research agencies will need to play a different role advising clients on which research decisions to make and providing recommendations to them.

In the current recessionary climate, there is more demand for advice and less for ad hoc services. This is true more of emergent rather than traditional industries. Mature industries have developed research departments that tend to commission research from market research agencies and have specialists or experts in research within the companies, but new industries like telecommunications would rather use consultants than set up their own research departments. Even traditionally research-staffed companies like automotive or IT (information technology) industries are restructuring activities, reducing head-office staff, and dealing directly with customers.

Speed and Actionability

More time is needed to implement decisions on a larger scale or wider area; that is why information must be provided faster. A large-scale research program introduces a longer chain of decision making because decision making is delegated to higher and higher levels all the time. Complex decisions involving people take more time, but the time spent on proposals and result delivery is vastly reduced. Quick answers to complex requests are a strong advantage in a competitive bidding situation. In researching specific countries, people like local client representatives and local advertising agencies that are not vested with real control, just with critical involvement when results are produced. As the information is more extensive and complex, clients need to have a much greater degree of analysis of that information, but sometimes clients ask for shorter reports, graphically presented, for immediate use.

Global marketing research is further complicated by the fact that each country has different political, legal, cultural, and business environments. It is the responsibility of the researcher to get around these differences and determine the true market potential. Figure 2.2 lists the major environmental variables that have tremendous impact on the marketing strategy.

FIGURE 2.2
MAJOR ENVIRONMENTAL VARIABLES

Variable	Indicators	Importance
Economic	• GNP, GNP per capita, population, inflation, unemployment rate, interest rate, etc.	• Measure of economic wealth, macro-level indicator of market potential, etc.
Political	• Type of government, expert ratings of political stability, number of expropriations, etc.	• Measure of political stability and political risk, government's attitude toward business, etc.
Legal	• Import–export laws, tariffs, non-tariff barriers, taxes, copyright laws, etc.	• Measure of legal risk, protectionism, influences marketing mix strategies, etc.
Sociocultural	• Religion, language, literacy, values, work ethics, role of family, gender roles, etc.	• Measure of high/low context culture, attitude of people, differences in lifestyles
Infrastructural	• Energy costs, extent of computerization, number of telephones, fax machines, presence of mass media, etc.	• Measure of technological advancement, influences marketing mix strategies

COMPLEXITY OF GLOBAL MARKETING RESEARCH

Quality issues are far more complex for international research suppliers than for those working solely within national markets.[6] For one thing, research facilities and capabilities still vary widely from one country to another, and this will continue as new countries join the market research community. For another thing, there are multiple users within a client company often working miles apart, and understanding their differing requirements is a key element in providing decent client service. The two main problems in international research may be summed up as follows:

1. Differences in results between countries are so fascinating that superficiality and loss of quality are masked attempts.
2. Attempts to reject smuggled-in additions or to abbreviate overly long questionnaires often give rise to responses like "We had no problems when we did this in such-and-such a country...."

International research buyers cannot hope to know, in detail, the variety of standards used outside their own country. They tend to take certain standards for granted or insist that things be done in an identical manner across countries. This may prove to be costly or detrimental to the research project. Further, it is sometimes unclear as to which aspects of the research process are covered by quality standards. Fieldwork is usually covered, as is the responsibility toward informants and mutual responsibilities between clients and suppliers. But certain other key areas such as research design, data processing, qualitative analysis procedures, or executive training are often not covered. This lack of clarification becomes further complicated in international research because maintenance of standards is a responsibility that must be shared between several parties including clients at the international level, clients at the national level, coordinating suppliers, and subcontracting suppliers.

When multinational research first started, the problem was of inadequate facilities abroad and assurance of transnational comparability, but this was solved when research facilities in other countries quickly came up to the US level. As for comparability, the original concern was to try to ensure exact literal translation of original English questionnaires,[7] but the US headquarters research department could not do this—it had to be done by experienced researchers in the foreign country. Headquarters staff could not even check the translation unless they were fluent in the language and were not familiar with the original English version. Knowledge of the original would create a bias that would work against finding errors. A standard procedure was, therefore, developed of an outsider retranslating the foreign language version into English. Comparison of the retranslation with the original was clumsy and time-consuming, but it worked, and is still standard procedure.

Today, when a US manufacturer wants to study market needs and attitudes for the same product in several countries, it is possible to decentralize the project and have the company offices in each country conduct the research based on guidelines issued by headquarters.

[6] Jane Kalim, "Quality Standards: The push-me-pull you of marketing research," Seminar on *Marketing and International Research: Client Company Needs and Research Industry Skills; Can the Gap be Bridged?* (1993, March 10–12) pp. 11–26.

[7] Thomas T. Semon, "Red Tape Is Chief Problem in Multinational Research," *Marketing News* 28, no. 4 (1994, February 14): 7.

This strategy produces a set of country reports of varying quality and format that are difficult to summarize; however, centralization of the project may not be a solution, as the staff in a particular country may have valid concerns that are at variance with those of central management in the US.

Centralization of the project can add to the complexity with problems of hierarchy and authority because such a study can involve staff at headquarters, staff at foreign offices of the company, foreign survey contractors, and possibly an overall coordinator, such as a US-based survey contractor. This can result in an outstanding amount of dispute, delay, and inefficiency. The best way to overcome this problem is through organization. The headquarters research department has to draw up a very detailed schedule of tasks, responsibilities, and reporting channels and obtain the agreement of all concerned before starting the project.

Most international research problems have similar characteristics.[8] They are complex issues involving multiple interdependent and interactive variables. These problems are heavily relationship-oriented, reflect the complexity of the research environment, and are unstructured. This type of difficulty affects all international research, but particularly field research, because field researchers try to understand a problem within its context and do not confine them to investigating a narrow area in isolation.

Heavily Behavioral and Relationship Orientation

Both the organization and the elements in its environment try to exert control over each other. A firm and the groups in its environment must constantly work at effectively managing the relationships created. This process of management needs to be researched for a better understanding of how firms operate internationally and what factors differentiate successful operations from unsuccessful ones. Culture, as an important variable, must be taken into account.

Reflection of the Complexity of the Environment

The degree of competitive product market, technological and regulatory variations, and the number of relationships with multiple groups within and outside the organization reflect the degree of complexity in organizational environment. These groups control contingencies and strongly influence corporate actions and decisions. Internal and external interdependencies increase and become constraints on the firms' decision makers. There is also the possibility of multiple interest groups in the environment having goals and values that are conflicting. Cultural and ideological differences between nations also increase complexity.

Lack of Structure

Behavioral interaction is necessary to reduce uncertainty and to define the environment. Normal corporate guidelines and courses of action may not be appropriate in ambiguous

---

[8] Lorna L. Wright, Henry W. Lane, and Paul W. Beamish, "International Management Research: Lessons from the Field," *International Studies of Management and Reorganization* 18, no. 3 (1988): 55–71.

situations. Normal, well-defined research strategies may not be adequate to capture the problem. Complex, unstructured problems that involve multiple important relationships and that are behaviorally interactive cannot be studied in a quick or easy fashion. This is a challenge that researchers strive to overcome through clinical field research.

COST

The cost of conducting marketing research varies greatly, not only by country but also by service type and across various research suppliers. New clients keep entering the field of international research and many are reluctant to pay the premium fees charged by the major international networks.[9] If medium-sized companies wish to compete, they must have comparable levels of quality control. While conducting global marketing research, companies have to pay attention to differences in the way research agencies budget for various costs like fieldwork or tabulations and analyses. Also, it is better to ask for the quote in a common currency or fix the exchange rate upfront to avoid complications later.

Global Comparability

The ESOMAR conducted a Global Prices Study in 2012 that provides a basis for constructing the overall price indices. This study provides insights into the differences in pricing that exist between countries, between types of projects and over time. Table 2.1 displays the top 10 most expensive and least expensive countries for research. In order to obtain a composite index that can throw some light on the costs of countries, the Global Index was developed by combining the cheapest option for an ad hoc usage and attitude study, with a series of group discussions—both of which are widely standardized and quoted for.

It is interesting to note that along with the prices of conducting research, the available research options also tend to vary greatly between countries. For example, although online research tends to reduce the overall cost, it is not feasible or logical to conduct online research in some of the countries. Similarly, even if face-to-face research tends to be far more expensive than online research, the preference to conduct face-to-face interviews is high in developing nations like, say, India. The trend for the cost of conducting online research is negative; but, central location testing and CATI (computer-assisted telephone interviewing) costs have increased.[10]

In addition to these, the pricing of online research has been a cause of concern. Due to the criticism of fraudulent and duplicate response, researchers over time have spent resources improving the quality procedures. However, with more and more agencies offering online research and the declining prices for research, there are apprehensions about the downward price changes having an effect on work being done and the costs being incurred to maintain the high quality standards. Exhibit 2.2 provides a snapshot of the study conducted to obtain the global price index discussed in the above paragraphs.

---

[9] Kalim, "Quality Standards."

[10] Global Prices Study (2012). US Market Research – Price is no Object? Message posted to http://rwconnect.esomar.org/2012/10/11/global-prices-study-2012/

TABLE 2.1

THE TOP 10 MOST EXPENSIVE AND LEAST EXPENSIVE COUNTRIES FOR RESEARCH[11]

Countries	2012 Global Index	2012 Ranking	2010 Ranking
Top 10 Most Expensive Countries			
USA	241	1	1
Switzerland	239	2	2
Canada	229	3	10
Japan	222	4	5
UK	187	5	9
Sweden	168	6	4
Germany	165	7	6
Denmark	162	8	8
France	161	9	3
Netherlands	156	10	7
Top 10 Least Expensive Countries			
Democratic Republic of Congo	51	58	NA
Romania	50	59	46
Serbia	47	60	59
Kenya	46	61	NA
Croatia	44	62	53
Ukraine	43	63	54
Bulgaria	39	64	64
Ecuador	38	65	61
Latvia	31	66	45
Pakistan	30	67	67

EQUIVALENCE

Acceptable and consistent quality standards must be maintained in international research. At present, it is difficult for international buyers and research coordinators to determine what standards and practices are being used or can be set across countries.[12] The areas wherein quality standards can be applied are qualitative recruitment, interviewing and analysis, quantitative fieldwork, questionnaire editing, back-checking, data entry, and record keeping. There is, at present, considerable variation in the practices and standards maintained. Some suppliers apply very stringent controls and have clear policies for action in case of unsatisfactory or

---

[11] Adapted from Global Prices Study, 2012, "US Market Research—Price Is No Object?," http://rwconnect.esomar.org/2012/10/11/global-prices-study-2012/(Retrieved on May 15, 2014).

[12] Carol Coutts, 1993, "Quality Standards in International Research—A Review of Current Practices," in *Identifying the Gap*, Amsterdam, 27–47.

Exhibit 2.2

Global Prices Study 2012[13]

Study Scope

The Global Prices Study conducted in 2012 highlights the differences in the price for conducting research in various countries. The last run of this study was conducted in 2014 with approximately 1600 participants across 40 countries. The quotes for the 2012 study were provided by 633 agencies across 106 countries. The bids were submitted in response to a standardized set of projects including five consumer research projects (three quantitative, one qualitative, and one utilizing online communities), one B2B project and a set of commercial tariffs for staff time, and a presentation.

> Project 1: Usage and attitude survey on chocolate confectionary product
> Project 2: Tracking study on washing powders
> Project 3: Computer-assisted advertising pre-test
> Project 4: Four group discussions on retail banking services
> Project 5: Research communities
> Project 6: B2B survey on laptop computers

Commercial Tariffs

A day of an executive time (junior, mid- and senior) and a face-to-face presentation. There was a significant amount of similarity between the Global Index scores of 2010 and 2012 (correlation of 0.93). Even in 2010, the correlation between 2007 and 2010 price indices was 0.94. In spite of the countries having different currencies, the report is in terms of US dollars (unless specified explicitly), using the exchange rate as on June 1, 2012.

The Sample, Fieldwork, and Responses

The sample includes agency with ESOMAR membership. In countries where the numbers were low, the agency nominated by the local research association or ESOMAR representative was included in the sample. The fieldwork period was between April 3 and June 26. The report only includes quotes where a minimum of three agencies responded for at least one project, a step taken to safeguard the anonymity of the respondents as well as the companies. Protection, in terms of the anonymity of respondents and the companies, was the focus at every stage of the project, that is, from collection of data to processing of the results. Median, a measure less susceptible to outliers than mean, was used in 2010 as well as in 2012.

poor quality work. Others appear to apply very low standards or none at all. A survey was conducted to determine practices being used. It generated concern on quite a few topics, such as:

1. High incidence of use of panels for qualitative recruitment
2. Negligible amount of training for qualitative recruiters and quantitative interviewers among a minority of suppliers
3. Low levels of verification for coding and punching of quantitative data
4. Very low levels of back-checking among a minority of suppliers

---

[13] Global Prices Study (2012): US Market Research – Price is no Object? Message posted to http://rwconnect.esomar.org/2012/10/11/global-prices-study-2012/

5. Retaining data records for less than six months or not at all by a high percentage of suppliers

Areas where high standards are more consistently applied are in detailed analysis of qualitative data and comprehensive editing of quantitative data.

Achievement of quality in market research calls for attention to standards in project management and general company management. The industry as such would be well advised to use government-sponsored schemes, such as ISO 9000, to encourage good management practice. Standards vary widely among suppliers and countries. The variations are sometimes understandable and acceptable, given the type of work concerned or the conditions prevailing in a particular county. On other occasions, lapses are experienced from what are considered the most basic principles of good research.

A growing number of international data banks will be developed not just for carrying information on consumer behavior, market volumes, brand shares, and consumer profiles, but also for illustrating similarities or differences in terms of:

1. General attitudes, lifestyles, social–cultural trends
2. Attitudes about specific product fields
3. Needs, motivations, and perceived and ideal images
4. Brand or corporate images and their development
5. Response to advertising and promotion.

It is widely accepted that

1. The only way to objectify lengthy, difficult discussions on the differences and specifics of each national market is to measure the reality concerned by applying the same research techniques everywhere.
2. These techniques must be normal in order to draw relevant conclusions; for example, the allocation of very high scores and the use of superlatives do not really mean or imply the same thing in Latin as they do in Germanic countries.
3. Such systematization brings with it the benefits of scale, experience, and comparability, but high development costs will require rapid payback across as many countries as possible.

Percentages and mean scores observed in different cultural frameworks do not necessarily have the same meaning. For example, Latin people are more likely to use superlatives or extreme positions on sales. Answers to buying intention questions or attitudinal data must, therefore, be carefully interpreted.

PERSONNEL[14]

International research means a real commitment in terms of resources such as:

- Technological resources; for example, centralized CATI systems, data processing capacity.

---

[14] Katherine Passerieu, 1993, "What Changes Will Be Needed Within the Research Agency?—Radical Change, Evaluation or Head Down?" in *Identifying the Gap*, Amsterdam, pp. 49–64.

- Personnel resources; for example, operations experts (sampling experts, telephone interviewing experts, etc.), and executives with appropriate skills.
- Systems (within the company and across networks). Large-scale multinational projects and globalization tend to make us view research data as *hard data* instead of *soft data*. There may be a danger here of missing or misinterpreting an important local factor just because it was hidden behind this need for harmonization. There are also certain areas that will always be difficult to approach globally. For example, trying to achieve comparability in approach and results across the US, India, and Saudi Arabia is a Herculean task.

On the qualitative side, because research clearly focuses on people and cultures, the danger is far less important. Exploring behaviors, attitudes, and motivations is part of the objectives. Because data on the quantitative side is more concise and people have less time to spend on each single local report, information tends to be treated like facts. It is a worrisome fact that big quantitative reports with management summaries, graphics, and projections are based on research, which fundamentally deals with inconsistent, subjective, and often irrational human beings.

INFORMATION ON THE GLOBAL MARKETING RESEARCH INDUSTRY

The world's largest marketing, advertising, public opinion research conglomerates accounted for approximately 54% of global spending with total revenue of $21.5 billion in 2011, up 4.1% over 2010. The year 2011 witnessed some civil unrest and war-like conditions, and the industry's *real growth* rate of 2.0% after adjustment for inflation is impressive. More than revenue, a lot of the top 25 grew in size as a result of acquisitions. In 2013 alone, top 25 companies bought 24 research firms around the world.

The home countries for 2013's Top 25 include the US, Germany, UK, Japan, France, and Brazil. The world's top marketing research firms are increasingly spreading their wings globally. The collective revenue from operations outside their home country accounted for 55% of the total. Only three of the Top 25 do not have revenue contributions from outside their home countries. As a group, the Top 25 had 122,310 research-only full-time employees in 2013 from only 103,136 in 2010.[15]

RESEARCH ACTIVITIES OF SOME TOP FIRMS[16]

Nielsen is a global information and measurement company that studies consumers and their behavior in more than 100 countries. As of January 2011, the firm was listed on the New York Stock Exchange. Nielsen's services can be divided into Nielsen's Watch segment that includes measurement and analytical services related to TV, online, and mobile devices, and offers viewership data and analytics primarily to the media and advertising industries. Nielsen measures retail, television, online, mobile, audience, consumer neuroscience, radio, and global consumer confidence. In addition, the 2012 purchasing of Arbitron, Inc. has increased their global research revenue. Nielsen's Buy segment provides retail transactional measurement data, consumer behavior information, and analytics primarily to businesses in the consumer

---

[15] Laurence N. Gold, "2012 Global Top 25 Rankings Chart," *Marketing News*, August 23, 2012.
[16] Laurence N. Gold, "The Global Top 25 Company Profiles," *Marketing News*, August 21, 2012.

Exhibit 2.3

Top 25 Global Research Organizations[17]

Rank 2013	Rank 2012	Organization	Country	Global Research Revenue (US$)	Percentage of Global Revenue Outside Parent Country
1	1	Nielsen Holdings N.V.	US	6,045.0	47.2
–	9	Arbitron Inc.	US	476.0	1.3
2	2	Kantar*	UK	3,389.2	71.9
3	5	IMS Health Holdings Inc.	US	2,544.0	63.2
4	3	Ipsos SA	France	2,274.2	93.1
5	4	GfK SE	Germany	1,985.2	70.0
6	6	Information Resources Inc.	US	845.1	40.4
7	8	Westat Inc.	US	582.5	3.2
8	–	dunnhumby Ltd.	UK	453.7	46.5
9	7	INTAGE Holdings Inc.**	Japan	435.5	5.6
10	10	The NPD Group Inc.	US	287.7	29.7
11	11	comScore Inc.	US	286.9	29.3
12	15	J.D. Power and Associates*	US	258.3	33.1
13	13	IBOPE Group	Brazil	231.1	22.4
14	14	ICF International Inc.	US	225.3	23.7
15	13	Video Research Ltd**	Japan	204.0	–
16	19	Symphony Health Solutions	US	198.7	1.1
17	16	Macromill Inc.	Japan	184.7	10.9
18	17	Maritz Research	US	177.6	21.8
19	18	Abt SRBI Inc.	US	172.8	9.9
20	–	Decision Resources Group	US	150.3	28.1
21	20	Harris Interactive Inc.	US	139.7	38.4
22	24	ORC International	US	122.0	32.9
23	22	Mediametrie	France	106.1	14.0
24	25	Yougov plc	UK.	101.4	70.3
25	21	Lieberman Research Worldwide	US	100.3	32.2

Notes: *Estimated by Top 25 author; **For fiscal year ended March 2014.

---

[17] Adapted from Laurence N. Gold, "The 2014 AMA Gold Global Top 25 Report", *Marketing News*, August 2014.

packaged goods industry. Nielsen provides end-to-end consumer insights to help businesses grow faster.

Kantar is a consumer insights division of WPP plc, a London-based public company, consisting of 12 research business units, namely, (1) Kantar Media, (2) Millward Brown, (3) Kantar Japan, (4) Added Value, (5) Kantar Retail, (6) IMRB International, (7) Kantar Health, (8) Kantar Worldpanel, (9) Lightspeed Research, (10) Benenson Strategy Group, (11) The Futures Co., and (12) TNS. With these 12 sub-business units, Kantar provides a range of services including demand forecasting, ad testing, copy testing, shopper insights and solutions, audience measurement, data collection and processing, retailer insights, virtual shopping trends, media and marketing effectiveness, product development and innovation, and the like.

IMS Health Holdings Inc. is a global information and technology services firm that provides comprehensive services to healthcare industry clients to help measure and improve their performance. Operating in over 100 countries, IMS delivers information and insights on nearly 90% of the world's pharmaceuticals.

Ipsos is a global market research firm that is organized around six areas of specialization: advertising, marketing, media, opinion, and customer relationship management research, along with data collection and processing. Ipsos has six global brands that serve all major markets around the world. These are: (1) Ipsos ASI, (2) Ipsos Marketing, (3) Ipsos Media CT, (4) Ipsos Public Affairs, (5) Ipsos Loyalty, and (6) Ipsos Observer. Ipsos moved from Rank 5 in 2010 to Rank 4 in 2013.

GfK Group is the fifth largest marketing research organization after Nielsen, Kantar, IMS, and Ipsos, converting data into meaningful insights for its clients. It comprehensively understands how consumers live, think, and shop in more than 100 countries. It focuses on services relating to consumers, pharmaceutical, media, and services sectors. They divide these into two segments: (1) Consumer Choices provides insights on market sizing, currency, media, and sales channels; (2) Consumer Experiences understands consumers' attitudes, consumer perceptions of the world, and the way they experience it.

Types of Research

Expenditure on online research studies have been increasing each year, now accounting for more share than the traditional face-to-face approach. Online research now accounts for 22% of the total market research investment while face-to-face accounts for 11% of the total. Telephone surveys and group discussions have a share of 13% each. Quantitative research companies are 76% of the total research worldwide. Online, however, varies greatly. For instance, online services are used widely in Japan (around 40%), followed by New Zealand.

Data Collection Methods

GreenBrook Research Industry Trends Report (GRIT) Winter 2013 suggests that budgetary constraints from the client's side urged for major changes in data collection methods. Among the data collection methods that were used, online surveys (66%) were used most often by firms.[18]

---

[18] GRIT Winter 2013 Report, http://www.greenbookblog.org/grit-winter-2013/(Retrieved on May 16, 2014).

The others among the top three are CATI (13%) and face-to-face surveys (12%). In terms of qualitative research, traditional in-person focus group dominates the qualitative arena.

Employment

Finding the right set of people to hire, when entering into new markets, has been one of the biggest challenges for research firms. Some markets with little or no history of research have a shortage of talent. While there is an option of assigning the task to a foreigner, for the most part, this is an expensive affair. There is huge demand for candidates who are great researchers, part entrepreneur, and part leaders.

Research Organizations

The ESOMAR directory includes *full information* listing about the research organizations globally. One can search by country like the US, Australia, UK, multi-county, etc., by research solutions such as demographic research, advertising research, Omnibus, web panel, etc., by market sectors such as durables, consumer packaged goods, etc., or by research services such as computer-assisted personal interviewing (CAPI), CATI, online, email, etc.

Mergers and Acquisitions (M&A)

The highlight of 2011, in terms of M&A, was the acquisition of Synovate by Ipsos. This had an impact on the ranking of Ipsos in the top 25.

Television Advertisement Measurement

There has been a huge shift in content consumption by consumers in recent years. There are multiple platforms by which companies can reach their target audience. Television itself has changed in recent years, with several interactive and on-demand content applications becoming standard features. With the growing pervasiveness of the Internet, the digital media has added a new dimension to the advertising industry. While Internet continues to gain importance, advertising expenditure on TV has not reduced.[19]

Television is a powerful medium that reaches a large number of audiences around the world. With new features added to televisions such as multiple screens and picture-in-picture modes, the importance of measuring TV advertising has only increased. Further, content viewing on mobile devices is increasing and research companies are incorporating this aspect in their methodology. For instance, the research company TNS developed a software version of their people meter to measure viewing as if PCs were just another TV set. This enabled them to make online measurement compatible with standard TV metrics.

---

[19] E-Marketer, "TV Advertising Keeps Growing as Mobile Boosts Digital Video Spend Message," April 3, 2013, posted on http://www.emarketer.com/Article/TV-Advertising-Keeps-Growing-Mobile-Boosts-Digital-Video-Spend/1009780

There are several companies that provide measurement services across the globe. US television measurement is taken care of by Nielsen Media Research. Canada seeks the information for television as well as radio measurement from BBM Canada. In Australia, OzTAM, Regional Television Audience Measurement (TAM), and Nielsen Media Research Australia cover different sections of the country and provide data related to television ratings. While IBOPE handles measurement in Brazil, GfK handles it in Germany. In India, it is TAM Media Research and aMaps (Audience Measurement Analytics Limited). aMaps introduced the latest technology from Telecontrol-Switzerland while entering the market in 2005. Using the GSM network, it polls 6,000 households to provide overnight ratings. TNS handles measurement in many countries including Kazakhstan. Kantar Media provides television measurement service to Vietnam in six of its main cities.

With millions of dollars being invested in TV advertising, companies look forward to using tracking methods to learn the response of target audience in real time. This not only helps them to optimize their advertising efforts to get the desired impact, but also assists in maintaining a healthy return on media investment. Nielsen is a global provider of information and insights into what consumers watch and buy.[20]

For marketers, Nielsen measures advertising expenditure and creative content daily across all major media types at a global stage including countries like North America, Europe, Asia Pacific, Middle East, and Africa. The Nielsen ratings give the percentage of a given population group consuming a medium at a particular moment. Nielsen's launch of its automated Local People Meter (LPM) technology replaced its existing People Meter present in the market. LPM provides accurate measurements of particular local markets by reporting the full range of programming viewers watch, inclusive of channel surfing. Similarly, Arbitron's technology service is used for radio measurement in the US. Exhibit 2.4 gives a snapshot of how Nielsen's people meters are faring across the world.

While on the one hand the measurement of television advertisement is gaining significance, on the other hand, it continues to provide some specific considerations and challenges to marketers that are different across nations. Two of the more prominent differences are:

Penetration of TV

It is estimated that in 2011 there were nearly 1.3 billion households worldwide with access to television. This number is expected to reach 1.5 billion by 2016.[21] Among this, the number of households with digital TV is estimated at 675 million (up from 300 million in 2007) and analog TV at nearly 700 million. Further, the penetration of TV is not uniform across all countries. Of the 370 million digital TV households added between 2007 and 2011, 194 million were from the Asia Pacific region, with China accounting for nearly 149 million households. Global digital TV penetration reached 49% by 2011, up from only 24% in 2007. Regional penetration of television by 2011 varied from 89% in North America to 33% in Latin America. Only Spain and Finland had fully converted to digital TVs by 2011.[22]

---

[20] Nielsen Pressroom, "Nielsen Expands Digital Measurement with Pilot Program for New Content Ratings," April 30, 2013. Retrieved on June 2, 2013 from http://www.nielsen.com/us/en/pressroom/2013/nielsen-expands-digital-measurement-with-pilot-program-for-new-c.html

[21] IDATE Media, "2012 World Television Market Report," http://www.idate.org/en/News/World-Television-Market_759.html (Retrieved on June 2, 2013).

[22] Simon Murray, "The Digital TV World Factbook," June 25, 2012.

Exhibit 2.4

Nielsen's People Meters Around the World[23]

The People Meter is a box connected to the TV that records whatever is being viewed on TV. The information regarding what is being watched, the duration of watching, the programs recorded, and even the ones that are not watched and fast-forwarded are collected in the meters. Each member of the household (including children) is provided with a separate remote control containing an *I'm watching* button to discern which family member is watching a particular show.

The collected data is sent back to Nielsen each night and integrated into the various ratings that are available for up to seven days after the initial air date. The ratings, to a large extent, decide the continuity of a particular show. For instance, a 1.0 rating in the US indicates that 1% of the (approx.) 116 million estimated TV-watching households in the country were watching a program. For a show with such a rating, it is unlikely that it would be continued. The data is also broken off into different demographic ratings, and used for further marketing efforts. More importantly, these ratings perform the role of a *currency* based on which advertising time is bought by the advertisers.

Despite the wide presence of the people meters, they have not been without setbacks. For instance, the TV-ratings system in Turkey was mired in controversy in 2012 following allegations that the identities of the 2,500 households equipped by Nielsen with people meters to collect viewing data were widely leaked across the industry. Further, the local production companies and TV stations have been accused of sending viewers lavish gifts in order to distort the ratings data in their favor. Following the unreliability in measurement ratings, a new system with TNS (Nielsen's competitor) is being envisioned by the industry to gain trust among the media agencies and the advertisers.

Similarly, in July 2012, NDTV—one of India's 24-hour news channels—sued Nielsen for billions of dollars for allegedly manipulating viewership data in favor of channels that were willing to provide bribes to the officials. In the complaint, NDTV has also targeted TAM, a joint venture between Nielsen and Kantar Media Research and the sole TV viewership ratings agency in India, in monopolizing the market for TV viewership data.

More recently, leading Indian broadcasters—Sony Entertainment Group, NDTV, and Times Television Network—have sent letters to TAM about their intent of discontinuing their subscription for its data. The reasons cited: fluctuations in data, and questions regarding the credibility of the data. In TAM's defense, they contended that with over 600 channels, and the average daily time spent on TV watching being two hours, there was bound to be lot of "flirtatious viewing," and hence the fluctuations and credibility in the data. The allegations and counterpoints notwithstanding, the Indian broadcasters have taken steps to form an alternative TV viewership ratings system under the joint sectoral body, the Broadcast Audience Research Council (BARC), that came into effect in April 2015.

---

[23] Adapted from John Herrman, "Why Nielsen Ratings Are Inaccurate, and Why They'll Stay That Way," January 31, 2011, http://splitsider.com/2011/01/why-nielsen-ratings-are-inaccurate-and-why-theyll-stay-that-way/(Retrieved on May 20, 2013); Emma Hall, "TV Audience-Measurement Data in Turkey Hit by Scandal," March 1, 2012, http://adage.com/article/global-news/tv-audience-measurement-data-turkey-hit-scandal/233041/(Retrieved on May 20, 2013); Economic Times, "NDTV Sues Nielsen for Viewership Data Manipulation," July 31, 2012, http://articles.economictimes.indiatimes.com/2012-07-31/news/32961619_1_ndtv-viewership-data-television-audience-measurement (Retrieved on May 20, 2013); Gaurav Laghate, "Advertisers Bat for TAM After Broadcasters' Boycott," June 11, 2013,

Such an uneven presence and growth of TV around the world presents a unique challenge for marketers to plan their media activities and customize their communication to suit the tastes of international audiences.

According to the 2011 Nielsen Global AdView Pulse report, television advertising rose 11.9% since 2010 and increased its share among other traditional media (radio, magazines, and newspapers) from 63.5% to 65.3% in both developed and many emerging economies. The report also contended that television continues to remain as the most important and cost effective advertising medium for companies looking to reach new consumers, especially in booming emerging markets, as evidenced by Exhibit 2.5.[24]

Exhibit 2.5

Global Spend by Region in 2011[25]

Region	Percentage Change over 2010
Europe	2.9
North America	5.4
Middle East and Africa	10.4
Latin America	11.0
Asia Pacific	12.4
Global	8.8

Scheduling of Advertisements

A major challenge faced by marketers around the world pertains to the limitations imposed on the number of ads that can be shown in a specific time frame. This not only piques a marketer's creativity but could also work toward diminishing the role of advertising. Here are a few examples of restrictions placed on advertising on television from around the world.

1. In Kuwait, the government-controlled TV network allows only 32 minutes of advertising per day, in the evening.[26]

---

http://www.business-standard.com/article/companies/advertisers-bat-for-tam-after-broadcasters-boycott-113061000892_1.html (Retrieved on May 20, 2013).

[24] "Global Ad Spend Up 8.8% in Q1 2011 as Advertisers Increase TV Spend," July 5, 2011, http://www.nielsen.com/us/en/newswire/2011/global-ad-spend-up-q1-2011-as-advertisers-increase-tv-spend.html (Retrieved on May 18, 2014).

[25] Adapted from Nielsen Global AdView Pulse Report, 2011.

[26] Sree Rama Rao, "Legal Constraints," October 11, 2010, http://www.citeman.com/11067-legal-constraints.html (Retrieved on June 2, 2013).

2. The EU limits the time taken by commercial breaks to 12 minutes per hour (20%).[27]
3. Recently in India, the telecom and broadcasting watchdog, the Telecom Regulatory Authority of India, has capped advertising breaks at 12 minutes per hour, or 20% of programming per hour.[28]
4. In Ireland, commercial broadcasters must limit the time allotted to advertisements to 18% of their entire broadcast programming for the day, with a maximum of 12 minutes of advertisements per hour. However, for children's programming, the advertising cannot exceed 10 minutes per hour.[29]
5. In Germany, commercials must be spaced at least 20 minutes apart and the total time allotted to advertisements must not exceed 12 minutes per hour.[30]
6. In the Philippines, the Association of Broadcasters of the Philippines limits advertising to 18 minutes per hour.[31]

The above examples are but only a sample. Several other nations have similar regulations placed on advertisers and the number of permissible advertisements during the specified programming time frame. While such restrictions may lead to temporary fluctuations in the industry with respect to ad rates and programming schedules, the long-term effect is expected to bode well for all the stakeholders. For instance, such a regulation would pave the way for the removal of ad clutter for the consumers and make marketers produce more targeted ads for a more engaged audience.

Generally considered the most powerful of traditional media, TV ads have the capability to reach a wide audience and at a low cost per exposure. It blends together several strengths—vivid display of information, highly engaging, scalable across countries and markets, and possibility of customizing to suit the tastes of international customers—ones that are not commonly found in other forms of traditional media. Despite these benefits, they do have the tendency to create clutter among consumers when exposed to excessively. This leads to the situation wherein consumers exhibit poor ad recall. Further, the vivid display could at some times be distracting to the viewer and take the focus away from the intended message. Nevertheless, suitably developed and executed ads have the power to drive up brand equity and positively impact sales and profits.

APPROACHES TO GLOBAL MARKETING RESEARCH

Marketing research can be thought of as a reflection of the consumers' opinion. However, interpreting the results accurately costs marketers and researchers a lot of time, effort, and

---

[27] European Parliament, "Culture and Education Committee Endorses New TV Advertising Rules," November 13, 2007, http://www.europarl.europa.eu/sides/getDoc.do?language=nl&type=IM-PRESS&reference=20071112IPR12883 (Retrieved on June 19, 2013).

[28] Meenakshi Verma Ambwani, "The 20 Per Cent Conundrum," *Hindu Business Line*, June 6, 2013, http://www.thehindubusinessline.com/features/weekend-life/the-20-per-cent-conundrum/article4784932.ece (Retrieved on June 19, 2013).

[29] "BAI Rules on Advertising and Teleshopping," Broadcasting Authority of Ireland, July 2010, www.bai.ie (Retrieved on June 19, 2013).

[30] Miriam Hils, "TVINTL German Spot Checks," *Variety*, May 19, 1997, p. 30.

[31] Riza Olchondra, "ABS–CBN Supports Cap on Ad Load," Philippine Daily Inquirer, March 17, 2008, http://business.inquirer.net/money/breakingnews/view/20080317-125318/ABS-CBN-supports-cap-on-ad-load (Retrieved on June 19, 2013).

money. Hence, whether it is done in-house or by an outside agency, it has become increasingly important in the marketing mix. Given the high level of competition, complexity, and cost involved in today's markets, business decisions can no longer go by instincts and intuitions. It is important to back business decisions with sufficient market research to avoid disastrous results. Tropicana had to learn this the hard way. When they launched a redesigned packaging for the orange juice, they decided to do away with the iconic image of an orange pierced with a straw without any prior market testing. The results were dismal with sales dropping by 20%. Following the poor showing, Tropicana quickly brought back the old packaging.[32]

There is no one research approach or tool that will work in all environments. They have to be selected based on the research problem at hand. While the following chapters will provide a detailed discussion on the tools adopted in international research, this chapter will provide a brief look at the most commonly used market research tools—observational research, focus groups, surveys, and experiments.

Observational Research

Here, data is collected from the respondents from their natural settings, discreetly observing them as they go about their activities. Examples of such activities may include studying shopping behavior, using specific products in the actual setting, and consuming products, among others. Observational research can be classified into two broad categories: direct observation and contrived observation. Direct observation is often used to obtain insights into research behavior and related issues. Examples such as product selection decisions at grocery stores and packaging effectiveness fall into this category. Contrived observation can be thought of as behavioral projective tests that are designed to reveal some aspects of their underlying beliefs, attitudes, and motives. Examples of researchers observing the normal interaction between the customer and the retailer, bank, service department, or complaint department, and the quality of public performance by employees of government agencies and private institutions, are based on contrived observation.

Focus Groups

Focus-group discussions help researchers obtain possible ideas or solutions to a marketing problem from a small group of respondents (typically 6–10 people) by discussing it in the presence of a skilled mediator. The emphasis of this method is on encouraging participants to express their views on each topic and to elaborate on or react to the views of the other participants. Focus groups have a wide range of applications from social sciences to public governance, and manufacturing design to usability studies. In the field of marketing, this tool enables companies to gather vital information about product attributes, product usage, and packaging, among others. It is also helpful in test marketing a new product, to discuss, view, and/or test the new product before it is made available to the public.

---

[32] Natalie Zmuda, "Tropicana Line's Sales Plunge 20% Post-Rebranding," *Advertising Age*, April 2, 2009.

Surveys

Surveys are designed to capture a wide variety of information such as customer attitudes (as reflected by their awareness, knowledge, or perceptions about the product, its features, availability, and pricing, and various aspects of the marketing effort), customers' overall product acceptance, their perception of a person's image that will be used in determining the type of celebrity endorsements or product ambassadors, and customer lifestyles, among others. In short, surveys attempt to answer the question of the *why* of a certain phenomenon by measuring the relationship between actions and needs, desires, preferences, motives, and goals. This is usually done through the use of a survey instrument such as a questionnaire that respondents are asked to fill up.

Experiments

Experiments are research investigations in which implementation involves an active intervention by the observer beyond that required for measurement. That is, the researcher manipulates the independent/experimental variable(s) and then measures the effect of this manipulation on the dependent variable(s). Thus, this tool attempts to capture the cause-and-effect relationships by eliminating contrasting viewpoints, often uncovered during observational studies. While this tool is perhaps the most scientific compared to the other tools, it comes with several considerations that have to be fulfilled to get meaningful and accurate results. They call for the right selection of subjects, matched pairs, exposing them to different treatments, controlling for external influences, and checking for statistical significance.

SELECTING THE RESEARCH FIRM

Many companies are likely to shop around for the right choice of research firm by requesting for proposals from multiple agencies. In this regard, the obvious considerations pertain to the product area, and the understanding of the problems and nature of proposed solution(s). But deciding the right firm becomes complicated when two equally experienced companies define the problem in similar terms, propose very similar solutions, but quote very different prices. In such a situation, price should not necessarily be the deciding factor since the pricing structure reflects, to a large extent, the time spent toward the research (e.g., interviewer time, data preparation time, executive time, etc.). That is, a cheaper quote can mean less rigorous procedures (at the data verification and checking stages) or minimal executive supervision or that the company has underestimated the time needed. It is also important to realize that market research provides data to enhance and not to replace decision making. Therefore, substituting decision making with research only because it is priced lower is likely to undermine not only the entire research project but also the decision-making process.

COORDINATING PAN-GLOBAL RESEARCH STUDIES

For research projects that are coordinated from a central location, it is important that such projects be staffed with executives who have knowledge of and sensitivity to local issues. Language and mobility should be viewed as strong advantages. The strong language skills advantage exuded by the local office will be helpful in solving issues and smoothing relationships with local partners, thereby saving valuable time by not expecting the central office to sort out the issues.

It is often found that the problem in international research is not just to make sure that research colleagues in other countries carry out a research project; instead, highly specific abilities, expertise, and impressive resources must all be coordinated to achieve optimum results.[33] Further, the design of research and the compatibility of data across countries should take into account differences such as: (a) availability of resources and expertise in the field concerned, (b) working habits and corporate cultures, (c) organizational aspects, and (d) the best approach for recruiting motivating participants.

A popular practice in coordinating studies with local offices around the world is subcontracting, that is, the local office in turn subcontracts a part of the work to local contractors. The span of work subcontracted could range from something as important as securing data to something basic like desktop support in compiling the report. Providing full freedom to the local office in the choice of subcontractors can be a mixed blessing. While it would help them focus on the more important tasks at hand, it might pose considerations such as: (a) hiring a subcontractor who charges the lowest price could lead to poor quality of output, (b) loss of valuable time in briefing and getting them on-board with respect to the tasks, (c) concerns about the dedication of the subcontractor, and (d) fewer opportunities for grooming local expertise in the local offices. Therefore, it is important to know the relative strengths and weaknesses of the partners involved with respect to their cost structure, organizational setup, and manpower resources. This helps to avoid overheads and internal competition. Exhibit 2.6 emphasizes how marketing research is being used by companies to make strategic decisions.

Adapting the coordination process to client organization structures is critical. The way in which each client company is organized must be taken into account regarding decision making for marketing policies and marketing research investments. The approach and direction from the organization's headquarters can vary from *proposing* to *imposing* research programs on their national operating companies. *Proposing* is inviting national subsidiaries to adhere to or join in common research programs that are centrally designed but locally financed. The emphasis is on *convincing* and *serving* with full information being provided for the *local* situation. *Imposing* implies that all national subsidiaries participate in the exercise, unless they succeed in demonstrating the irrelevance of the specific approach concerned as applied to their home market. Budgets are likely to be managed centrally and emphasis is more on *discipline*, with local executives being provided with limited information.

The success of these approaches depends on corporate culture, history of the development of the activities in the foreign markets, level of evolution in adapting to the reality of the single European market, and so on. In some cases, national marketing and research executives will be involved right from the inception. Local support may be requested from the coordinating agency in analyzing and interpreting data and its conversion into local conclusions. The organization's headquarters may favor or finance close cooperation between its national subsidiaries and research partners, but the coordinating agency will remain responsible for standardization and comparability of techniques across borders. In other cases, national client operating companies will be informed but not at all involved in the conception or initial analysis of projects. In still other instances, local contracts will carefully avoid project information being distillated (or not) by client executives within their organization.

---

[33] Jean Quatressooz, "Coordinating International Research Projects—Easy to Say But...," in *How to Do It: Managing the Process*, pp. 233–245.

Exhibit 2.6

Use of Marketing Research[34]

One of the top multinational consumer goods company, P&G is a market leader in the US razor market. As per a recent statistical report of Harvard Business Review, P&G's Gillette brand has an 80% market share in the US. In the Indian market, the brand claims about 50% of the upscale market. To capture the lower income groups seemed promising to P&G.

In this effort, they conducted a series of ethnographic research to understand the issues concerning the product efficiency of their razor designs. They observed that a typical male in India was more price-sensitive as compared to his US counterpart. Also, shaving experience was different as he was more likely to be seated on the floor, with a small amount of still water, balancing a hand-held mirror in low light, and experiencing frequent nicks and cuts from his double-edged razor.

The profound insights were translated into a new design, Gillette Guard, catering to the whole Indian market. This product was hugely different from P&G's traditional product; 80% fewer parts, a plastic housing, and a single blade to minimize cost while preserving *good-enough* shaving performance. They introduced several features to suit the Indian shaver, by making it safer and cheaper for the Indian consumer. They had a large safety comb to reduce nicks and cuts, and an easy to rinse cartridge for better cleaning without running water. Reports revealed that around 74% of the respondents reported fewer nicks and cuts and about 75% of the research respondents claimed that they felt safer with Gillette Guard as compared to the double-edged razor.[35]

In addition to changes to the product, P&G adopted a much localized manufacturing and marketing approach. Taking cue from the insights of the research conducted earlier, P&G attempted to cater to the price-conscious consumers by means of reducing the overall cost of the product with the help of their controlled production and streamlined supply chain costs. P&G's story is a good example of a company successfully using marketing research to enter into an unknown market.

The coordinating research agency must know the client's requirements and points of view so that they can define the way in which local agencies are briefed as well as the level of complexity of the task. For example, it is good to know if the client's local operating companies will be invited or ordered to provide customers' names and addresses for a satisfaction study initialized centrally.

Finally, projects that are conducted from a central location covering markets around the world would require a sufficiently detailed report. For companies that want to a global picture of the market, the following will have to be considered in the presentation and report to provide a high level of clarity:

1. Analyses and insights regarding the differences between national markets.
2. In-depth, parallel analyses of each of the national markets covered with additional reports on transnational consolidation.
3. The elements and topics covered in the transnational analysis.

---

[34] Adapted from V. Govindrajan, "P&G Innovates on Razor-Thin Margins," Harvard Business Review Blog Network, April 16, 2012, http://blogs.hbr.org/cs/2012/04/how_pg_innovates_on_razor_thin.html (Retrieved on May 20, 2013).

[35] J. L. Nilsson, "Procter & Gamble Innovates on Thin Margins in India," June 5, 2012, http://jacoblangvad.com/2012/06/procter-gamble-innovates-in-india/(Retrieved on August 2, 2013).

The answers to these questions will influence the analysis and presentation of results and formulation of conclusions. Therefore, for an efficient and effective research project that is coordinated from a central location, elements such as (a) close cooperation with direct clients, (b) sharing of in-depth knowledge of structure of the client organization, (c) focusing on getting the right messages across, and (d) investing more time in analyzing and producing figures, conclusions, and recommendations without ignoring cultural aspects are extremely critical in the success of the study.

GLOBAL MARKETING RESEARCH IN PRACTICE

Continuing with the example of Tasty Burgers, the parent company has to first conduct a feasibility study in all of the countries where they are planning to set up operations. This will involve conducting marketing research in UK, Brazil, India, and Saudi Arabia. The company has two choices—they can look for a US-based marketing research company that can conduct research in all these countries, or they can hire independent marketing research companies in each of these countries. There are benefits and drawbacks to both these options.

By hiring one company to conduct research in all the countries, Tasty Burgers can get standardized information across all countries. This will help them compare potential sales and profit figures and work out an optimum plan to allocate resources among these countries; however, the marketing research company must be an established player in the field of international marketing. All of the national and cultural differences mentioned in the first chapter will come into play, especially in Brazil, India, and Saudi Arabia, countries vastly different from the US. Hiring a local marketing research company in these countries greatly increases the chance that these subtle differences will be brought to the notice of the management of Tasty Burgers. The flip side is lack of comparability of data across countries. There are differences in units of measurement, exchange rates, and so on, that have to be converted back to American standards for the management to decide if operating in a given country is financially viable.

There are many major research agencies with multinational operations that provide the benefit of coordinating the project from the home country and assuring the client of comparability. At the same time, these agencies also ensure that they have local staff in all these countries that are familiar with the local culture and traditions and will be in a position to provide better insight about the market. The standard practice is to ask for basic quotes from multiple research agencies, shortlist, and discuss the project with a few of them. The final selection of research suppliers by Tasty Burgers should take into account all of the different aspects of the research project.

Tasty Burgers should also decide the hierarchy within the company. The external research agency should be made accountable to a specific individual or a committee within Tasty Burgers. This will help avoid duplication of effort for both Tasty Burgers and the external agency.

SUMMARY

This chapter gives an overview of the process of global marketing research focusing on the issues that are specific to global marketing research. It emphasizes the vast difference between domestic and global marketing research. The problems that are faced by researchers in data collection and other stages bear testimony to this fact. In addition, this chapter also provides general information and statistics on the global marketing research industry. It is observed that nearly half of the revenue earned by the top 25 marketing research firms comes from global marketing research.[36] In the past, there has also been a move for top marketing research firms to form strategic alliances to gain entry into the global market. There has been a steady growth in the global marketing research expenditure by firms all over the world.

QUESTIONS AND PROBLEMS

1. When conducting marketing research in foreign countries, what are the critical elements/issues that must be addressed?
2. What are the main elements that make global marketing research a complex study?
3. What are the steps to be taken in coordinating global marketing research?
4. Sketch a marketing plan for Nuturama, a health-focused US-based fast food chain, to market their products in France.

---

[36] Gold, "2012 Global Top 25 Rankings Chart."

3

Global Marketing Research Process

INTRODUCTION

The global marketing research process provides a systematic, planned approach to the research project and ensures that all aspects of the research project are consistent with one another.[1] Research studies evolve through a series of steps, each representing the answer to a key question. Some of the questions that the firm or the researcher should ask include the following:

1. *Why* should research be done?
2. *What* research should be done?
3. *What* are the firm's long-term goals on globalization?
4. *Is it worth* doing the research?
5. *What* information is needed?
6. *How* should the necessary information be obtained?
7. *How* should the research study be designed?
8. *How* can the data be analyzed and interpreted?

The objective of this chapter is to take the reader through the process of global marketing research and explain the logic behind the sequence of steps as depicted in Exhibit 3.1.

RESEARCH OBJECTIVE

The first step in the research process is to decide why the research should be done—the research purpose. At this stage, most research problems are poorly defined, only partially understood, and do not have a lot of decision alternatives. It is in the best interest of the firm and the researcher to be sure that the research purpose is fully understood. The research purpose comprises a shared understanding (between the manager and the researcher) of the following:

1. Problems or opportunities to be studied.
   - Which problems or opportunities are anticipated?
   - What is the scope of the problems and the possible reasons?

---

[1] This section draws heavily from *Marketing Research* by Aaker et al. (2012).

Exhibit 3.1

Global Marketing Research Process

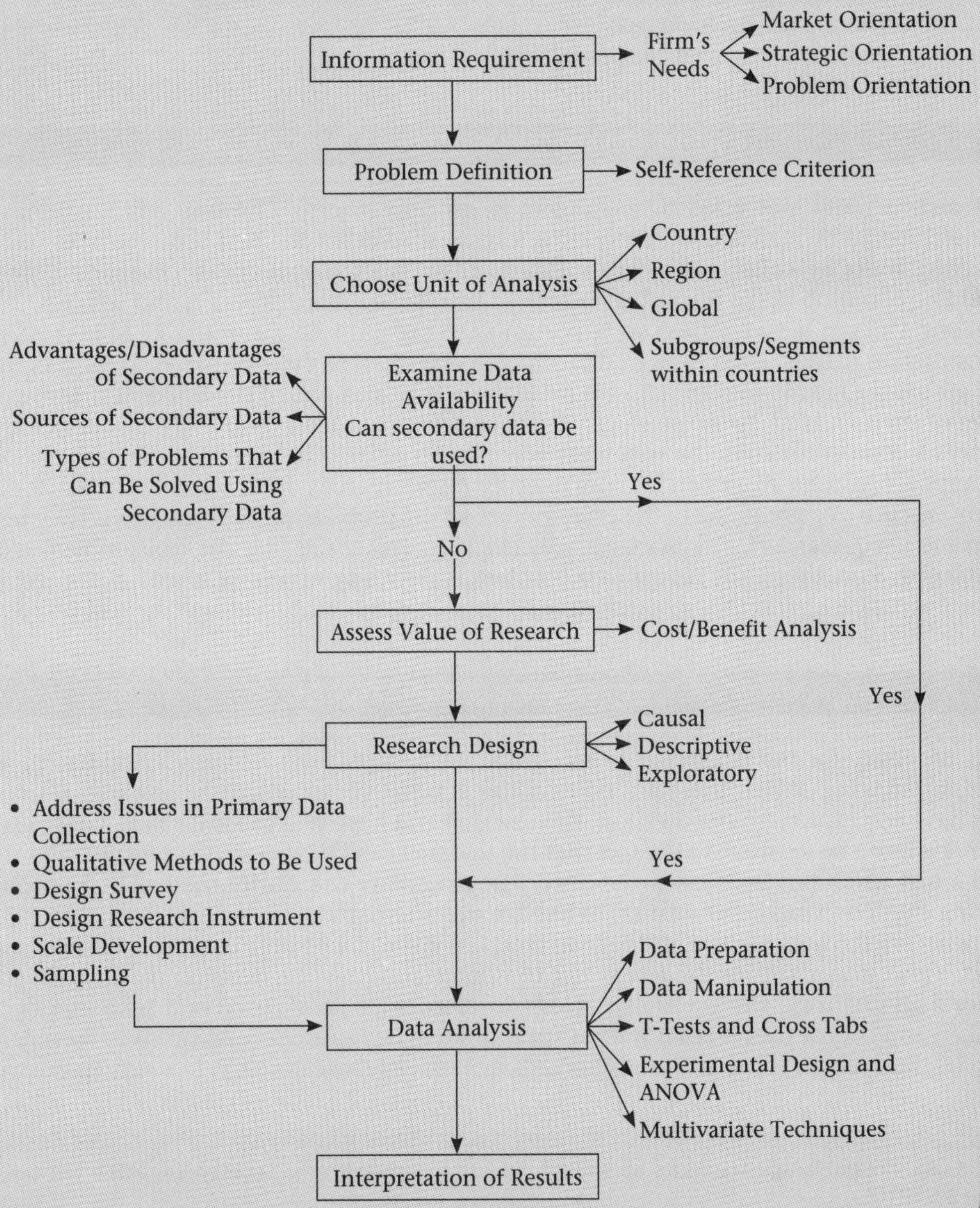

Information Requirement → Firm's Needs

- Market Orientation
- Strategic Orientation
- Problem Orientation

Problem Definition → Self-Reference Criterion

Choose Unit of Analysis

- Country
- Region
- Global
- Subgroups/Segments within countries

Examine Data Availability
Can secondary data be used?

- Advantages/Disadvantages of Secondary Data
- Sources of Secondary Data
- Types of Problems That Can Be Solved Using Secondary Data

Yes

No

Assess Value of Research → Cost/Benefit Analysis

Yes

Research Design

- Causal
- Descriptive
- Exploratory

Yes

- Address Issues in Primary Data Collection
- Qualitative Methods to Be Used
- Design Survey
- Design Research Instrument
- Scale Development
- Sampling

Data Analysis

- Data Preparation
- Data Manipulation
- T-Tests and Cross Tabs
- Experimental Design and ANOVA
- Multivariate Techniques

Interpretation of Results

2. Decision alternatives to be evaluated.
   - What are the alternatives being studied?
   - What are the criteria for choosing among alternatives?
   - What is the timing or importance of the decision?

3. Users of the research results.
   - Who are the decision makers?
   - Are there any covert purposes?

PROBLEM OR OPPORTUNITY ANALYSIS

Research is often motivated by a problem or an opportunity. The firm commissioning the research could be planning on entering a foreign market for the first time, such as Starbucks entering India by collaborating with Tata Coffee, Asia's largest coffee company.[2] The firm could be planning to tap into a bigger market by offering more products and services, such as DuPont. DuPont has identified an opportunity to expand into the entire $7 billion US home construction market, even though they enjoy a 70% market share of the $100 million market for air-barrier membranes (to control air leakage into and out of the buildings) through the sales of their DuPont Tyvek product.[3] There could be a sudden drop in sales in a foreign territory. A competitor could be weaning away market share. Any one of these problems could prompt a company to undertake a marketing research study. It is important that the company executives communicate the exact nature of the problem and the decisions they need to make to the researcher. The manager also needs to make sure that the real problem is being addressed. Sometimes, the recognized problem is only a symptom or a part of a larger problem. A separate exploratory research may have to be conducted to isolate the real problem.

DECISION ALTERNATIVES

It is necessary for the researcher to recognize the fact that the research study has to aid in decision making. When there are no decision alternatives or when the research results will not have any impact on the decision, the research will have no practical value. The researcher should always be sensitive to the fact that the research can be an exercise in futility and should call a halt when this becomes a certainty. The researcher can clarify the research purpose by asking the following questions: (a) What are the alternative actions being considered?, and (b) what are the possible actions that can be taken given the feasible outcomes of the research?

It is also important for the researcher to understand how the decision makers will choose among alternatives. The researcher needs to discuss all possible criteria with the decision makers and choose the one that is most appropriate. The researcher also needs to consider how crucial the decision is to the firm. In today's dynamic global economy, it is very important for

---

[2] "Tata Coffee Brings Starbucks to India," Business-standard.com, January 14, 2011 (retrieved on June 22, 2013).

[3] Conference Summary, "Excelling in Today's Multimedia World," Economist Conferences' Fourth Annual Marketing Roundtable, Landor, March 2006.

companies to time their decisions well. A delay in the decision could mean competition gets ahead and corners a huge chunk of market share.

RESEARCH USERS

It is very important for the researcher to know who the decision makers are and what they expect of the research project. This will give the researchers a better understanding of the research objective and help them develop a more realistic research proposal. Talking to all the decision makers will also help the researcher decide if the study is being conducted for covert and sometimes illegitimate reasons.

INFORMATION REQUIREMENT

The next step is to isolate the main issue that needs to be tackled and decide on the information needed to solve the problem. An example would be the efforts of P&G to introduce disposable diapers in India. There are a lot of decisions that need to be made by P&G in this scenario—how big is the market, what is the ideal price, how can the product be distributed, what promotion strategy should be adopted, etc. At this stage of the research process, the researcher should focus on the main issue—is there a market for disposable diapers in India? Many companies have failed in the international market because they have been sidetracked by small issues and have ignored the one main problem that needs to be addressed. For instance, when Coca-Cola Company launched Coke in India, they were not able to overcome the popularity of Thums Up, a local brand. To gain a foothold in the market, Coca-Cola bought out the bottling operations of Thums Up. Despite this, the market share for Coke did not improve. The company failed to take into consideration the powerful brand loyalty commanded by Thums Up and position their product accordingly. Failure to pin down the root cause for the problem can be very costly in global marketing research.

Once the key issue has been identified, it is necessary to define the research objective. The research objective is a statement, in as precise terminology as possible, of what information is needed. This helps the researcher develop hypotheses that are possible answers to the problem under consideration. The research objective also defines the scope of the research.

The research question asks what specific information is needed to achieve the purpose of the research. In the case of P&G, the research objective is to determine if there is a market for disposable diapers in India and, if so, whether it is financially viable to market this product. Some of the research questions could be:

- What is the main alternative to disposable diapers used by parents currently?
- Are parents familiar with the cost of disposable diapers?
- Are there any other brands of disposable diapers sold in India currently?
- What is the estimated market size?
- What price are the consumers are willing to pay for a disposable diaper?

While defining the problem, researchers face one major stumbling block, termed as self-reference criterion (SRC). It is the tendency of researchers to allow their own values and beliefs to bias their opinion of situations in foreign markets. Marketers of Esso, a successful brand of a gasoline in the US, when launching the brand in Japan, thought the brand name was fine in the foreign country. However, in Japan, the name phonetically means stalled car—not an appropriate image for gasoline. Similarly, the *pet* in pet milk is another example. The name has been used for decades, yet in France the word pet means, among other things, flatulence. Again, not the desired image for canned milk.[4] It is easy for an American to take the knowledge of English for granted, but to do so in a market like Japan can spell disaster for the marketing strategy. It is crucial in global marketing research that the researchers keep an open mind and try to study the problem from the point of view of the foreign market.

The next step in the process is to decide on the information required by the firm to make decisions regarding globalization. There are a number of options available to companies that want to go international. The simplest way would be to export the products to the target country. Some firms (such as Subway and McDonald's) decide to license or franchise. Some companies prefer to set up partly or wholly owned subsidiaries. Imperial Chemical Industries (ICI), Britain's largest manufacturing company and one of the world's largest chemical companies, is an excellent example of a foreign-based global company with several business units outside the home country.[5] Similarly, JCPenney has three modes of operating at a global level: (a) owning and operating JCPenney department stores as it does in Chile and Mexico, (b) licensing with local partners as it does in the Middle East, and (c) operating under a licensing agreement with a local retailer, as in Dubai.[6] The researcher should be clear about the motives of the company before designing the study.

The second category of information required will aid in making decisions concerning the strategic orientation of the company. The strategic orientation of the company helps work out the expansion plans in an international market. Some companies look upon their international operations as merely a way of dealing with excess production in their domestic market. These firms do not devise any special strategies for their international markets. Some other companies, however, cater to the specific needs of the foreign markets they operate in. They have independent marketing plans for these markets. Most big car manufacturers follow this policy. They manufacture automobiles keeping in mind the specific needs of the market.

The third category of information required helps find solutions to specific problems such as pricing policy, positioning of the product, and the promotional aspects. The researcher will do well to have a clear definition of the problem that needs to be solved. In this stage of the research process, the researcher should watch out for the pitfall of SRC, previously mentioned. If, for instance, in a developing country, a consumer were to choose a product that has been packaged in an aluminum container instead of a plastic carton, the reason could simply be that the consumer plans to use the container for storage purposes after the contents have been used. It would be erroneous for an American researcher to assume that consumers in that country are eco-friendly as the motive for this purchase. SRC causes researchers to miss out on important problems and lead to fundamental flaws in the research design.

---

[4] Sree Rama Rao "The Self-Reference Criterion and Ethnocentrism: Major Obstacles," October 16, 2009, http://www.citeman.com/7414-the-self-reference-criterion-and-ethnocentrism-major-obstacles.html#ixzz2WULz8ves (Retrieved in June 2, 2013).

[5] Jean-Pierre Jeannet and Hubert D. Hennessey, *Global Marketing Strategies* (Boston, MA: Houghton Mifflin Company, 1998), 4th edition.

[6] Alfred P. Lynch, "In Search of Global Markets," *Strategy and Leadership*, November 21, 1996, p. 40.

UNIT OF ANALYSIS

One of the most important aspects of global marketing research is deciding on the unit of analysis, which is the basic unit considered in the statistical analysis. In a global marketing research problem, it is important for a researcher to have a clear idea of the unit of analysis, at both the macro level and micro level. Macro-level units comprise of larger segments, such as countries and cities. Micro-level units may consist of firms, customers, and specific market segments. Unit of analysis would also help researchers define the geographic scope analysis. The problem could involve looking for information all over the world, in certain regions or country groupings, specific countries, or specific cities. Each of these factors is defined as a unit of analysis.

The additional problem faced by researchers in global marketing research projects is in defining a country. Depending on the research problem definition, the country can be defined as a political unit, an economic unit, an organizational unit, a cultural unit, or a linguistic unit. For instance, if the study involves understanding the spending habits of double income families in the US and the UK, the unit of analysis would be the individual households. However, if the study were interested in determining if there is any difference in the spending habits of these households in the two countries, the unit of analysis would be the countries themselves. The difference would be the data used in the two cases. In the second case, the average spending for the double income households in both the countries would be considered.

One problem that arises in global marketing research is the definition of various units of analysis. Consider an example of a cosmetic firm wanting to enter several countries simultaneously. The firm wants to target urban working women and asks the researcher to study the market potential in all these countries. This sounds simple enough until the researcher actually gets down to working on a sampling procedure. How is urban defined? Exhibit 3.2 gives the definition of urban in various countries around the world. The researcher has to find a way of obtaining equivalent data from each country while meeting the requirements of the sponsor. This is one of the areas where global marketing research differs substantially from domestic research.

Based on the definition of *urban*, the company will have to make a decision regarding how the target markets are to be grouped. If the countries are significantly different from one another with respect to the product, each has to be treated as a separate entity. The country is the most commonly used unit of analysis in international marketing. If there is a reasonable similarity, then these countries can be grouped as one region. For instance, while testing for brand awareness of Coke, research is done on a global level. Disney, the US-based entertainment company builds theme parks all over the world.

In some cases, it becomes necessary to devise different marketing plans for different market segments. When launching baby diapers worldwide, P&G discovered that Japanese mothers had different needs. Japanese mothers changed their babies so frequently, thick absorbent diapers were not necessary.[7] Instead, P&G designed thin diapers that took up less space in the Japanese homes. Similarly, PepsiCo uses a different definition of consumption across various countries. In Mexico, Venezuela, and Argentina, the consumers are asked how much of the product was consumed the day prior to the interview. In Germany and Spain, the question is

---

[7] Douglas and Craig, *International Marketing Research*, pp. 33–35.

Exhibit 3.2

Definitions of Urban, by Country[8]

Country	Definition of Urban
Albania	Towns and other industrial centers of more than 400 inhabitants.
Argentina	Populated centers with 2,000 or more inhabitants.
Belarus	Cities and urban-type localities officially designated as such, usually according to the criteria of number of inhabitants and predominance of agricultural, or number of non-agricultural workers and their families.
Canada	Places of 1,000 or more inhabitants, having a population density of 400 or more per square kilometer.
China	Cities only refer to the cities proper of those designated by the state council. In the case of cities with district establishment, the city proper refers to the whole administrative area of the district if its population density is 1,500 people per kilometer or higher; or the seat of the district government and other areas of streets under the administration of the district if the population density is less than 1,500 people per kilometer. In the case of cities without district establishment, the city proper refers to the seat of the city government and other areas of streets under the administration of the city. For the city district with the population density below 1,500 people per kilometer and the city without district establishment, if the urban construction of the district or city government seat has extended to some part of the neighboring designated town(s) or township(s), the city proper does include the whole administrative area of the town(s) or township(s).
Dominican Republic	Administrative centers of municipalities and municipal districts, some of which include suburban zones of rural character.
France	Communes containing an agglomeration of more than 2,000 inhabitants living in contiguous houses or with not more than 200 meters between houses, also communes of which the major portion of the population is part of a multi-communal agglomeration of this nature.
Greece	Urban is considered every municipal or communal department of which the largest locality has 2,000 inhabitants and over.
India	Towns (places with municipal corporation, municipal area committee, town committee, notified area committee, or cantonment board); also, all places having 5,000 or more inhabitants, a density of not less than 1,000 persons per square mile or 400 per square kilometer, pronounced urban characteristics and at least three-fourths of the adult male population employed in pursuits other than agriculture.

---

[8] Adapted from United Nations, "2009–10 Demographic Yearbook," United Nations Publications, November 2011, http://unstats.un.org/unsd/demographic/products/dyb/dybsets/2009-2010.pdf (Retrieved on May 20, 2013).

Country	Definition of Urban
Japan	City (shi) having 50,000 or more inhabitants with 60% or more of the houses located in the main built-up areas and 60% or more of the population (including their dependents) engaged in manufacturing, trade, or other urban type of business.
Kenya	Areas having a population of 2,000 or more inhabitants that have transport systems, build-up areas, industrial/manufacturing structures and other developed structures.
Malaysia	Gazetted areas with population of 10,000 and more.
Mexico	Localities of 2,500 or more inhabitants.
Norway	Localities of 200 or more inhabitants.
Switzerland	Communes of 10,000 or more inhabitants, including suburbs.
Pakistan	Places with municipal corporation, town committee, or cantonment.
Republic of Korea	For estimates: Places with 50,000 or more inhabitants. For census: the figures are composed in the basis of the minor administrative divisions such as Dongs (mostly urban areas) and Eups or Myeons (rural areas).
Thailand	Municipal areas.
Uganda	Gazettes, cities, municipalities, and towns.
United Kingdom of Great Britain and Northern Ireland	Settlements where the population is 10,000 or above.
United States of America	Agglomerations of 2,500 or more inhabitants, generally having population densities of 1,000 persons per square mile or more. Two types of urban areas: urbanized areas of 50,000 or more inhabitants and urban clusters of at least 2,500 and less than 50,000 inhabitants.

based on the number of drinks consumed in a day or a week.[9] It is possible for a company to target specific subgroups within countries. Catholic French-Canadian teenagers are, for example, members of the Catholic subculture and also the French-Canadian subculture. Due to the differences between countries and the nature of the product, companies have different market orientations. This makes it necessary for the researcher to choose the unit of analysis for conducting the study.

DATA AVAILABILITY

Once the unit of analysis has been identified, researchers need to start collecting data. Although data may not be available for all the variables that interest the researcher, data is available from private and public sources at a fraction of the cost for obtaining the primary

---

[9] Jeannet and Hennessey, *Global Marketing Strategies*.

data. Though it is not possible to list all the sources of secondary data, some sources are banks, consultants, chambers of commerce, and trade journals. The Internet has now become a powerful tool to obtain secondary data with very little investment of time and money. Secondary data are particularly useful in evaluating country or market environments, whether in making initial market entry decisions or in attempting to assess future trends and developments. The three major uses of secondary data in global marketing research can be summarized as follows:

1. Selecting countries or markets that merit in-depth investigation
2. Making an initial estimate of demand potential in the target market
3. Monitoring environmental change

However, there are some problems associated with the use of secondary data. They can be outdated and inaccurate. It may not always be possible to compare data collected from different countries. The researcher may not be able to find all the data required to complete the study. Chapter 5 explains in detail all aspects of secondary data with regard to global marketing research.

RESEARCH DESIGN

Secondary data is used to arrive at initial hypotheses about the research project. These tentative conclusions are used to conduct a cost–benefit analysis. If the study proves to be financially viable, the researcher starts working on the research design. The choice of the research approach depends on the nature of the research.[10] These types of research can be classified under three broad categories:

1. *Exploratory research:* Used when one is seeking insights into the general nature of the problem, the possible decision alternatives, and relevant variables that need to be considered.
2. *Descriptive research:* Used when an accurate snapshot of some aspect of the market environment is needed.
3. *Causal research:* Used when it is necessary to go beyond inferring that two or more variables are related and the researcher has to show that one variable causes or determines the values of other variables.

Chapter 7 focuses on primary data collection techniques and explains in detail the three types of research mentioned here.

An important aspect of this textbook is the extensive coverage of marketing research on the Internet. Global marketing research typically requires very high investment in terms of time and money. Due to the paucity of information and lack of understanding of foreign cultures, researches have to spend a lot of time and resources to gather data and analyze it. The Internet is a very cheap and extensive source of information.

Before starting on primary data collection, researchers can locate information about the region of interest and gather useful information, such as the market size and presence of local and global competition. This information might help eliminate many countries in the early

---

[10] This section adapted from V. Kumar, David A. Aaker, and George S. Day, *Essentials of Marketing Research* (New York: John Wiley and Sons, 1999), 1st edition.

stages of the research process. After potential markets have been identified, researchers can then proceed to the next stage. This will help save lot of time and resources. However, data collected from the Internet must be used with caution and only after verifying the authenticity of the information. It would also be beneficial if the Internet data were backed by secondary data from traditional sources. Chapter 6 gives a detailed account of the Internet and its uses in global marketing research. Some of the statistics presented in Chapter 6 clearly indicate that Internet is the research tool for the future—for both primary and secondary research.

ISSUES IN PRIMARY DATA COLLECTION

Primary data has to be collected to proceed with the research process. One of the issues that needs to be dealt with in global marketing research is the equivalence of data. First, it has to be ascertained whether the constructs being studied are equivalent. Second, the equivalence of the measures of the concepts being studied has to be assessed. Finally, the equivalence of the sample studied in each country or culture has to be taken into consideration. Exhibit 3.3 gives a brief description of the three types of equivalences that should be taken into account in global marketing research. These concepts are discussed in later chapters in connection with the research stages that they are applicable to.

Exhibit 3.3

Types of Equivalence

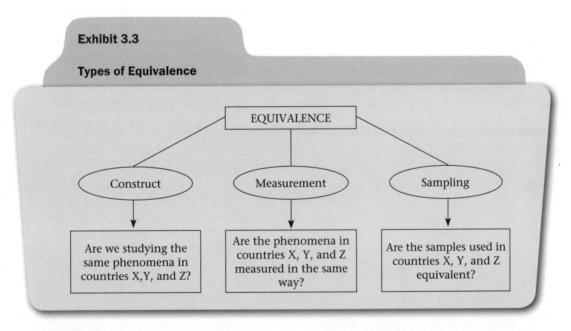

QUALITATIVE METHODS

As mentioned earlier in the chapter, exploratory research requires qualitative data collection methods, as it is unstructured and needs data that deal with feelings, attitudes, and past behavior. Qualitative methods are classified into three broad categories: observational methods, projective techniques, and interviews.

Observational techniques are based on watching how respondents behave. In most cases, the respondents are not aware that they are being watched. Sample sizes vary depending on the type of observation and the research subject. Projective techniques require the respondents to perform a specific task, like word association, sentence completion, or interpretation of an action or a picture. In the interview method, the respondent is required to verbalize his or her opinion. Qualitative and observational methods are discussed in depth in Chapter 8.

In all the types of data collection mentioned thus far, there are several sources of bias. The researcher working in a foreign country may not be completely in tune with the environment. Several national and cultural differences can come into play, as discussed in Chapter 1. Language differences make it difficult for researchers to translate their intentions verbatim in the foreign language. Chapter 7 deals specifically with collection of primary data and the problems associated with the process.

SURVEYS AND INSTRUMENT DESIGN

Surveys are a popular means of collecting primary data and are conducted using questionnaires that can be self-administered or administered by the interviewer in person or over the telephone. The first step in designing the questionnaire is to determine the information that needs to be obtained. Information collected through questionnaires can be classified under three major categories: demographic data, behavioral data, and psychographic or lifestyle data. The researcher needs to determine whether the questions should be open-ended or close-ended. It is also necessary to ensure that the translation of the questionnaire in several languages will impart the same meaning to the respondents to ensure comparability of the data.

An important aspect of questionnaire design has been the use of scales to obtain information on attitudes, preferences, and behaviors of the respondents. Scaling is the process of creating a continuum on which the objects are located according to the amount of the measured characteristic they possess. The different types of scales being used are:

- *Nominal scale:* Objects are assigned to mutually exclusive, labeled categories. That is, if one entity is assigned the same number as another, then the two entities are identical with respect to a nominal variable. Else, they are just different. Sex, geographic location, and marital status are examples of nominally scaled variables. The only arithmetic operation that can be performed on such a scale is a count of each category.
- *Ordinal scale:* Objects are ranked and arranged in a particular order with regard to some common variable. This scale provides information as to which object has more of a characteristic and which has less of it. Since, the difference between the ranks are not known, a mean cannot be drawn based on this scale. However, median and mode can be computed on such a scale.
- *Interval scale:* The numbers that are used to rank the objects also represent equal increments of the attribute being measured. This implies that ordinal scales give room for comparing differences. For example, Fahrenheit and Celsius temperatures are measured with different interval scales and have different zero points. In this type of scale, the entire range of statistical operations can be employed to analyze the resulting number, including addition and subtraction. Consequently, it is possible to compute an arithmetic mean from interval-scale measures, apart from median and mode.

- *Ratio scale:* A modified interval scale with a meaningful zero point. With this scale, it is possible to say how much greater or lesser one object is than another. This scale also gives the opportunity to compare absolute comparisons of magnitude.

For a global marketing researcher, the challenge of questionnaire design does not end with choosing the type of scale to be used. In countries where literacy levels are low, researchers need to use innovative means to convey the intentions of the survey to the respondents. Researchers also need to watch out for typical tendencies of the respondents that introduce biases in the survey. As mentioned earlier, studies have shown that Japanese tend to be neutral, and hence, the scale should be designed without a neutral point to force a response from them. On scales measuring lifestyle attributes, Latin Americans tend to overstate their responses; hence the scale should be suitably toned down. Refer to Chapter 9 for a detailed explanation of survey methods.

SAMPLING

The first step in sampling is to determine the level at which the sampling is to be conducted. That is, the key decision makers for the purchase decision of the product involved must be determined. For instance, if the survey is about marketing a cake mix, housewives should be contacted. The next step is to decide the sampling frame. In the international context, getting a list of population for the sampling frame can present a problem. Telephones are not so widespread in less developed countries and they do not have comprehensive electoral lists from which the researchers can draw a list of names. More often than not, researchers resort to non-probability sampling. The researcher then decides on the geographic level at which the sampling is done. The idea is to ensure that all heterogeneous groups in the population will be adequately represented. The various sampling techniques can be broadly classified as non-probability and probability sampling. Non-probability sampling includes convenience sampling, judgmental sampling, quota sampling, and snowball sampling. Probability sampling includes simple random sampling, stratified sampling, and cluster sampling. A detailed discussion on these techniques is provided in Chapter 12.

DATA ANALYSIS

In a multi-country research study, the first step in data analysis is preparing the data. The data needs to be coded and edited and the researcher should ensure the quality and reliability of the data. During this stage, the researcher checks for ambiguity, interviewer error, inconsistency, lack of cooperation, and ineligible responses. The main issue in coding is to ensure that data are as comparable as possible across samples to aid in multi-country analysis. Once the data has been coded and edited, the researcher has to examine the reliability of data. The researcher then conducts within-country and across-country analysis. For the purpose of analyzing data, univariate or multivariate techniques can be used. The various univariate techniques used in data analysis are cross-tabulation, t-tests, and analysis of variance (ANOVA). The different multivariate techniques are analysis of covariance, regression analysis, discriminant analysis, conjoint analysis, cluster analysis, factor analysis, and multidimensional scaling. These topics will be considered in detail in the chapters 13 and 14, dealing with simple and advanced data analysis.

INTERPRETATION AND PRESENTATION

The final stage of the research process, this is a very important step because here the researchers convey the results of the survey to the decision makers of the firm commissioned it. The researchers apply their knowledge and experience to use the information obtained during the data collection and analysis stages to arrive at conclusions that will aid the decision-making process. The presentation can be written or oral depending on the client preferences. Chapter 16 deals in detail with the finer points of presenting a research study and its results.

NEED FOR GLOBAL MARKETING RESEARCH[11]

Defining the research problem accurately is probably the most important step in any marketing research project, and even more so in global marketing research. Even the biggest of companies have made marketing blunders—all because marketing research was not conducted accurately. Exhibit 3.4 discusses Coca-Cola's classic blunder that will be used time and again to illustrate the importance of marketing research.

Gillette committed a similar blunder in the Middle East by launching their shaving products. Despite heavy promotions, there was no improvement in sales. It was only when the product failed that the company realized most men in Middle Eastern countries do not shave. The increasing importance accorded to marketing research cannot be stressed more. Some of the reasons for the high degree of importance are as follows:

Growing Market Complexity

The world of business looks different from every angle today. There are newer ways of conducting business, reaching consumers, making processes more efficient using the abundance of available data on consumer purchase transactions. All of these offer a great platform for conducting business globally. But, the interconnectedness between countries, nations, people, and businesses makes it a complex web, changing at the fastest pace one can image today. Conducting business in a truly global world has challenged marketers to come up with truly innovative techniques to combat the effects caused by this constantly evolving business environment.

The world is a much smaller place today. An event in one country can have rippling effects in not just the neighboring nations, but all around the world. For example, the eruption of a volcano in Iceland, which is a nation with only 300,000 inhabitants, caused the entire European airspace to stay shut for six days, resulting in losses of approximately $2 billion for the airline industry. Moreover, losses of billions of dollars were incurred for the makers of urgent, perishable, and high-value goods, logistics firms, and tourism operators around the globe. Adding to this, the loss of productivity for stranded employees and canceled business meetings and the impact of this relatively small event on the global economy becomes huge.[12]

---

[11] Robert F. Hartley, *Marketing Mistakes and Successes* (Hoboken: John Wiley and Sons, 1998), 7th edition, pp. 160–175.

[12] G. Seijts, M. Crossan, N. Billou, "Coping with Complexity," June 2010, http://www.iveybusinessjournal.com/topics/leadership/coping-with-complexity#.Ub80Y-fqlMg (Retrieved on June 2, 2013).

Exhibit 3.4

New Coke Fizzles Out[13]

Market share for Coke had begun dropping in the 1970s despite widespread advertising and superior distribution. The company then turned to the product itself to look for reasons for this drop in market share. There was strong evidence that taste accounted for this decline. Blind tests had been conducted and the results showed that people preferred Pepsi to Coke. As a consequence, Project Kansas was launched with the objective of scrapping the original formula. Approximately 2,000 people in 10 major markets were interviewed to find out if they would be willing to accept a different Coke. Research showed that most people were more favorable toward a sweeter, less fizzy cola that had a sticky taste due to high sugar content. Blind taste tests were conducted once again and this time around the reaction for the new Coke was overwhelming. Majority of the people subjected to this test preferred the new Coke to Pepsi.

The new Coke was launched on April 23, 1985. Word spread quickly. Within 24 hours, millions around the world were aware that the Coke formula had been changed. Early results indicated that the response to the new flavor was fantastic. Coke was selling like it had never before.

This success, however, was short-lived. Complaints started trickling in and within a month became a torrent. Media publicity added to the fervor and soon Americans began talking of an old friend who had suddenly betrayed them. Sales for the new Coke started dropping and bottlers began demanding the return of the old Coke.

Finally, on the 11th of July, within four months of introducing the new flavor, the company executives apologized to the public for withdrawing the old Coke. The message was that those who enjoyed the taste of new Coke could continue to do so and those who wanted the old Coke would get it back. The reaction was very favorable and even the Wall Street was happy.

This blunder could be blamed on improper marketing research. The decision to introduce the new flavor was based solely on the results of blind taste tests. However, the participants were not told that choosing one flavor would mean they would lose the other. Hence, the test failed to include the emotional attachment that consumers have toward the 99-year-old formula. The target segment which was represented heavily in the taste test, youth, in general, prefers sweeter flavors. The researchers missed this point. They also overlooked the fact that preference for sweet things tends to diminish with use. The taste test focused on the flavor but failed to consider the emotional appeal that the original formula held for the American public.

IBM's Global CMO study findings from 2011 report indicates that 79% of the CMOs surveyed believed the level of complexity will be high or very high over the next five years, with only 48% being prepared to cope with it.[14] In words of a telecommunications CMO in Brazil, "The empowerment of the consumer is generating more complexity. The mental model is changing. We are facing a major social transformation." The study was conducted with over 1,700 executives from 64 countries and across 19 industries. The report also brought the four most prominent challenges for CMOs in the forefront; the data explosion (71%), social media

---

[13] Adapted from Hartley, *Marketing Mistakes and Successes*, 7th edition.
[14] IBM Global CMO Study, 2011, http://www-935.ibm.com/services/us/cmo/cmostudy2011/cmo-registration.html (Retrieved on July 10, 2013).

(68%), proliferation of channels and devices (65%), and shifting consumer demographics (63%). At least 80% of CMOs rely on market research and competitive benchmarking to make strategic decisions. Also, more than 60% rely on sales, campaign analysis, and the like. While market research is still prevalent, CMOs are mining new digital data sources to discover what individual customers and citizens want. But the investment in consumer reviews, third-party rankings, online communications, or blogs are relatively still low, indicating the CMOs' current focus on understanding markets rather than understanding individuals. The abundance of data generated by consumers has resulted in data explosion. But the CMOs' lack of focus on understanding individuals can hamper the long-term prospects of their business.

Applied Market Knowledge

It is clear that the growing nature of businesses is creating more and more opportunities and challenges. An in-depth knowledge and understanding of markets as well as consumers will help companies sail through the times of complex marketing environment in the global marketplace.

In this regard, an applied knowledge about the market would help companies in designing appropriate market entry strategies. When a company chooses to go global, the choice of entry strategy is critical. This decision must reflect an estimate of the market potential, the company's level of preparedness for surviving in the new market, and the degree of marketing involvement the company can commit to. Based on these, companies can choose entry strategies that range from a low-risk–low-return entry strategy such as export to a high-risk–high-return strategy such as direct investment. Chapter 4 discusses the various modes of entry in detail. Figure 3.1 provides the various entry strategies on a continuum.

As shown in Figure 3.1, the level of involvement, risk, and financial reward increases as a company moves from market entry strategies such as licensing to joint ventures and, ultimately, various forms of investment. When a global company seeks to enter a developing country, there is an additional strategy issue to address: whether to replicate the strategy that served the company well in developed markets without significant adaptation. To the extent that the objective of entering the market is to achieve penetration, executives at global companies are well advised to consider embracing a mass-market mindset. This may well mandate an adaptation strategy.

It would also help companies in designing the appropriate communication strategy that includes advertising, promotion, and other forms of marketing communication. Marketing communication is an area where mistake are likely to occur when expanding into new markets. Often, this stems from the thought that "if the product is liked in the domestic market, then it will also be liked in the international market." Such an erroneous line of reasoning has several important implications in marketing the product. This is where an in-depth knowledge about the market will help marketers navigate the new environment successfully. Further, while designing marketing communication campaigns, it is important to keep track of the cultural differences that may make the seemingly *normal* message inappropriate. Examples of such instances include:

1. *Differences in market opportunities:* McDonald's targets the young and upwardly mobile customers in the emerging markets and is positioned as a premium restaurant, very different from their positioning in the US.

FIGURE 3.1
MARKET ENTRY STRATEGIES

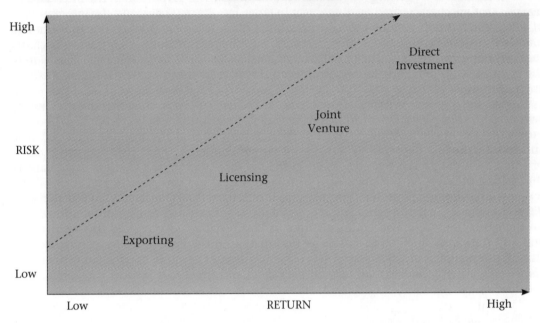

2. *Variations in meaning and connotations:* It is common wisdom that countries that speak American English and British English have differing meaning and interpretations. Usage of terms such as rug versus carpet, closet versus cupboard, elevator versus lift, soccer versus football, and cookie versus biscuit, have to be carefully selected for effective communication to obtain the desired result.

3. *Differences in decision making:* Decision making may vary between countries and family style. For instance, in collectivist societies such as Mexico and India, many purchase decisions are made for the entire family, while in individualist societies such as the US and Canada, purchase decisions are made by the individuals consuming the products.

4. *Variations in consumption patterns:* For instance, Brazil is distinctly divided into northeast and southeast regions because of the large regional differences between the two regions with respect to income, resources, culture, and lifestyle. In terms of laundry detergents' usage, it has been observed that the women in the northeast region prefer washing clothes five times a week by hand in public using detergent bars and very little detergent powders, whereas, women in the southeast region wash clothes in washing machines using detergent powders at least thrice a week. For Unilever, this regional differentiation has raised significant challenges for their popular detergent brands from penetrating into the northeast region.[15]

---

[15] Unilever in Brazil, case by INSEAD, http://faculty.insead.edu/chandon/personal_page/Documents/ Case_Unilever%20Brazil%201997-2007-corrected-w.pdf (Retrieved on July 10, 2014).

Finally, since packaging is the first interaction a customer has with the product, getting it right is extremely critical for getting helpful market knowledge. This is more so in the international markets that are characterized by differences in language, literacy rates, and the interpretation of colors and symbols, among others. Packaging is often regarded as a valuable medium in a marketer's toolkit because of its salient features. Such benefits include: (a) attractive packages that contribute positively to the impulse buying behavior, (b) securing instant recognition to the brand, and (c) providing an opportunity to innovate by using newer packaging methods and techniques.

Despite the inherent benefits of packaging, marketers still have to contend with country laws pertaining to package sizes and labeling issues to make sure it helps in the success of the product. Some of the labeling considerations prevalent around the world include: (a) clear and specific product descriptions (Brugel, a German children's cereal that featured pictures of animals on the package was displayed in the pet food section in a Chinese supermarket), (b) printing of prices on the labels (it is considered illegal to print prices on labels in Chile), (c) providing additional product information, if necessary (Brazilian law interprets the word *diet* to have medicinal properties and requires daily-recommended consumption information on the labels. Diet Coke had a difficult time in Brazil trying to get around this restriction.), and (d) printing product name and other information in the local language (China requires that all international products have their name, contents, and other specifics in Chinese). In some cases, country laws extend beyond packaging and apply to a broader category also, as provided in Exhibit 3.5.

Exhibit 3.5

France Serving Up a Quick Meal[16]

Recently, France considered banning establishments from calling themselves restaurants if meals are not made from the start by in-house chefs. Included as an amendment to the Consumer Rights Bill, this effort is aimed at putting a curb on the increasing number of restaurants that are serving ready-to-eat or microwaved meals as restaurant-quality cuisine. Through such a proposal, France would limit the right to use the term *restaurant* only to eateries where food is prepared on site using raw materials, either fresh or frozen. The exceptions to this would be for items such as bread, prepared meat products, and ice cream. When included in the Consumer Rights Bill, this proposal would not only to protect the culinary reputation that France is known for, but also help bolster a hard-hit restaurant business. In 2012, fast-food and take-away meals accounted for 54% of the French market, or €34 billion in sales, for the first time outselling traditional sit-down meals with table service.

---

[16] "French Move to Ban Industrial Food from 'Restaurants'," June 6, 2013, http://www.themalaysianinsider.com/food/article/french-move-to-ban-industrial-food-from-restaurants/(Retrieved on May 20, 2013).

Blurring of Product Categories

In order to meet the ever-growing consumer demand, marketers are introducing products for every segment of consumer. When marketers find difficulty in categorizing a product into one particular category, there arises a product which falls in multiple categories. For instance, the cereal brand Kellogg is now available in the snack aisle as well. Also, Britannia Treat Choco Decker and Unibic's upcoming Chyawanprash cookie target more than one product category in India.[17]

While there are products that fall in multiple categories, there are also examples of products that combined into one. One such example is sports and energy drinks. Initially, there was a clear demarcation of these products and messages. Energy drinks were for non-sports-related consumers for the dose of energy and caffeine, while sports-related consumers consumed sports drinks for energy and hydration during their physical workout. Clearly, the gap between the two has diminished. The market growth for this industry is fueled by the growing awareness of health-related issues among consumers who tend to have less time and energy, and are eager to fight the day-to-day fatigue with energy-boosting drinks.[18]

If we look at technology as well, there are newer categories being created as the products no longer fit any of the categories. For instance, the emergence of tablets is a great example. Tablets were created as there was the need for an ultra-portable mobile device with a larger screen display for better reading. Smartphones in parallel gained a lot of popularity. Together, tablets and smartphones have changed the way people interact and exchange thoughts and ideas with their friends and family. Now, with intense competition in smartphones as well as the tablet market, we see blurring of products. Samsung's new Galaxy Mega phone has a 6.3-inch screen while the Google Nexus tablet is 7 inches. Samsung is reported to be creating a "phablet" category soon. [19] As marketers, it is important to be informed of the current market trends to be able to take proactive actions with the brand and gain competitive advantage in the global marketplace.

Coordinated Planning and Research

To ensure a successful entry and stint in international markets, companies have to undertake a coordinated approach regarding research and planning efforts. These efforts include: (a) deciding on which country market(s) to enter and in what order, and the choice of product offerings, (b) identifying the marketing-mix, and (c) gathering knowledge about uncontrollable elements such as economy, competition, infrastructure, culture, and political/legal setup that could impact the performance of the company in that country.

Deciding on the country market(s) to enter is the critical first step. In this regard, the company's objectives, culture, resources, and product offerings must match with the country's culture and market potential. When considering countries among the emerging markets, such conditions are may pose some challenges owing to the absence of well-developed

---

[17] S. Jacob, "Companies Blur Food Category Boundaries, Position Products in Multiple Categories," February 2, 2011, http://articles.economictimes.indiatimes.com/2011-02-02/news/28425975_1_chyawanprash-kellogg-india-unibic (Retrieved on June 2, 2013).

[18] "Sport and Energy Drink Industry: Market Research Reports, Statistics and Analysis," 2013, http://www.reportlinker.com/ci02023/Sport-and-Energy-Drink.html (Retrieved on June 2, 2013).

[19] E. Pullan, "Is Bigger Always Better? The Blurring of Product Boundaries," April 12, 2013, http://www.citnow.com/is-bigger-always-better-the-blurring-of-product-boundaries/(Retrieved on June 2, 2013).

infrastructure, distribution channels, and political/legal structure. Further, when considering multiple markets to enter, the company must look for commonalities among the markets and opportunities for standardization across them. Markets that satisfy these criteria can be considered as potential markets to enter.

When companies identify more than one country to enter, deciding on the order of entry is also important. Two broad categories of strategies are available to marketers to decide on the entry strategy—the sprinkler strategy (entering all the chosen markets simultaneously), and the waterfall strategy (entering the most profitable market first, and expanding to other markets thereafter). Chapter 4 provides a more detailed discussion on the expansion strategies available to marketers.

Regarding the choice of product offerings to be made available in the new markets, a thorough analysis on the degree of standardization or adaptation has to be performed. Even products that are exemplars of standardization have taken to minor adaptations when entering foreign markets. McDonald's, for instance, had to introduce vegetarian and lamb burgers in India in an effort to adhere to the dietary and religious practices. Typically, the extent of adaptation required for the new market depends on the cultural differences in product usage and the perception of the product present between the market the product was originally developed for and the new market. The greater the cultural differences between the two markets, the greater the extent of adaptation that may be necessary.

Once the target markets are selected, it is important to determine the marketing-mix variables such as product, price, promotion and distribution. The key decision here is to determine the extent to which these variables are to be standardized or adapted, as the case may be. A misstep in evaluating the level of standardization could result in an inappropriate product for the market, apart from a drain on the profits of the company, as provided in Exhibit 3.6.

Exhibit 3.6

Euro Disney's Faux Pas[20]

Disney paid a heavy price for not considering local customs and values when they launched the Euro Disney Theme Park outside Paris in 1992. They were severely criticized for creating a mere extension of the American cultural imperialism, even failing to adopt local customs such as serving wine with meals. Other issues that they did not consider included having only open-air restaurants that did not offer any protection from the long rainy weather prevailing in Paris, and offering only a French sausage that irked people from other nationalities as to why their local sausages were not available. The company realized this mistake as noted by a senior executive, "When we first launched there was the belief that it was enough to be Disney. Now we realize that our guests need to be welcomed on the basis of their own culture and travel habits."

They eventually renamed the park as Disneyland Paris and fixed all the criticisms, including having covered seating for all restaurants, and having a wider selection of sausages and other food items catering to the multiple indigenous cultures in Europe. The result of these corrective measures and including local touches has made them Europe's biggest tourist attraction, even more popular than Eiffel Tower.

---

[20] Paulo Prada and Bruce Orwall, "A Certain 'Je Ne Sais Quoi' at Disney's New Park," *Wall Street Journal*, March 12, 2002.

Companies operating across multiple countries often face contrasting experiences with respect to economy, culture, technology, and political/legal setup. Such critical functions linked to the smooth functioning of businesses, however, turn out to be elements that businesses have little or no control over.

Over the years, world economic development has been uneven across nations. This has been more perceptible in the last decade with several countries going through crests and troughs of economic prosperity. The nature of skewed economic development among nations have been largely due to differences in balance of payments through export performance, foreign investments, and currency exchange rates, and protectionist tendencies to safeguard domestic markets through tariff barriers and non-tariff trade barriers (such as trade licenses, quotas, subsidies, embargoes, technical barriers to trade, and standards, among others).

However, in recent years, reform efforts globally have focused on making it easier to start and conduct business operations. The 2013 Annual Doing Business Report, a joint initiative by the International Finance Corporation and the World Bank, reports that 108 economies implemented 201 regulatory reforms in 2011–2012, making it easier to do business than ever before. The report also found that there has been more convergence in those that relate to the complexity and cost of regulatory processes (business start-up, property registration, construction permits, electricity connections, tax payment, and trade procedures) than in those that relate to the strength of legal institutions (contract enforcement, insolvency regimes, credit information, legal rights of borrowers and lenders, and the protection of minority shareholders).[21]

Culture is another uncontrollable factor that impacts every marketer when conducting international business operations. As discussed in Chapter 1, culture includes values, attitudes, customs, beliefs, and symbols that we all use to interact and communicate in a society. In the world of marketing too, these elements direct consumers to interact and behave in a certain manner as practiced in that particular society.

While culture per se is important to consider, marketers and researchers should pay close attention to the subcultural aspects also. Subcultural aspects refer to the beliefs, values, and customs that are exhibited by a certain cultural group that are different from other members of the same society. Subcultures can be identified on the basis of:

1. Race: Hispanics, African Americans, Asian Americans, etc.,
2. Religion: Hindus, Muslims, Christians, etc.,
3. Geography: Easterners, Westerners, urban, rural, etc.,
4. Age: Millenials, Gen-Xers, Baby Boomers, etc., and
5. Gender: male, female, LGBT, etc.

When differences within a culture can be so varied, then differences across cultures can only be even more expansive and deep-rooted. Understanding the cultural ideologies of an economy is the key to building successful businesses.[22] How well a product matches with the cultural and social beliefs of a country will define its acceptance and success. On the con-

---

[21] Doing Business (part of World Bank Group), "Doing Business 2013: Smarter Regulations for Small and Medium-Size Enterprises," co-publication of World Bank and International Finance Corporation, October 23, 2012.

[22] David K.. Tse, Lee Kam-hon, Ilan Vertinsky, and Donald A. Wehrung, "Does Culture Matter? A Cross-Cultural Study of Executives' Choice, Decisiveness, and Risk Adjustment in International Marketing," *Journal of Marketing* 52, no. 4 (1988): 81–95.

trary, wrong interpretations or ignorance about cultural or religious preferences can cause undesirable effects on the company's efforts in creating customer loyalty, as experienced by McDonald's in Mexico. To celebrate Mexico Flag Day, the company embossed placemats with the country's national emblem as part of their celebrations. However, this act upset the Mexicans who are very possessive about their national emblem. This also caught the attention of the Mexican government, and authorities confiscated the placemats as this act was seen as being disrespectful toward the country's legend.[23]

Technology plays an important role in energizing an economy's growth and performance. While this stimulation aids in innovation and creation of new trends, it also paves the way for the decline of old methods. The advent of television hurt the print media and transistor radios, and the growth of Internet added to this. Similarly, communication technologies have witnessed the growth and stagnation or decline of several methods such as telegram, pagers, and fixed telephone line, among others, that have been largely replaced by the Internet, e-mail, and mobile phones. Exhibit 3.7 captures the Indian experience of two legacy technologies—the telegram and the transistor radio.

The rise and fall of technology notwithstanding, marketers and researchers must keep a close watch on the speed at which technology is changing, the avenues for innovation that are opened as a new technology emerges, the resources allocated toward research and development (R&D) activities to promote the development of new technologies, and the role of national regulatory bodies in monitoring technologies.

Political/legal challenges can get companies mired in tussles with the foreign government over the nature of functioning. Further, the status of a *foreign company* often aggravates issues and prevents companies from arriving at a precise understanding of the foreign business climate. Wal-Mart faced a tough time in their attempts to enter the Indian market. Soon after the Indian government's announcement to allow overseas companies to own as much as 51% of supermarkets, Wal-Mart made efforts to set up shop and other business operations. However, this move by the government attracted severe opposition by political parties and the local business community who contended that this move would severely hurt the mom-and-pop businesses. Following this, the government's decision was reversed two weeks later. However, the political/legal environment can also lead to positive changes in the business climate, as observed in the case of South Africa. When South Africa announced the decision to do away with apartheid, several countries that had placed an embargo in protest of the discrimination removed the ban and resumed business and trade activities.

Further, companies operating in multiple economies simultaneously face a more complex problem—differences in government regulations between the emerging economies. For instance, government regulations pertaining to business partnerships (e.g., M&A), export fees (e.g., customs and clearance duties), and tax codes (e.g., tax laws and tax incentives) vary significantly between Brazil and China. Therefore, a company operating in these two countries will have to plan its resources and strategies accordingly.

Shortened Product Development Cycle

Companies face a lot of pressure before the release of a product. The stiff competition builds more pressure on the timing of launch of a product or service. HTC One, for example, had a delay in the launch due to sourcing issues related to camera parts. This delayed launch

---

[23] Cateora and Graham, *International Marketing*, 10th edition.

Exhibit 3.7

The Case of the Indian Telegram and the Transistor[24]

The telegram was India's first brush with technology. Soon after the world's first telegram was sent in 1844, its potential was identified by the then Governor of India, Lord Dalhousie, who commissioned a 27-mile experimental line (between Calcutta, now Kolkata, and Diamond Harbor) in 1850. Spurred by the success of the experimental line, by 1856, the network stretched 4,000 miles across British India, connecting strategically important cities of Calcutta, Agra, Bombay, Peshawar, and Madras. It played a vital role in squelching India's first major uprising against the British in 1857. But for this device, the British would not have been able to send information across in almost real time to make important decisions.

However, after a successful run spanning 163 years, the Indian telegram was sent for one last time on July 15, 2013. It is interesting to note that the last message also used a similar technology that was used to send the first successfully transmitted telegram. Government authorities cite the burgeoning mobile and Internet connectivity, even to the remote corners of India, as the reason for the decline of the telegram. While India is the last country in the world to use the telegram on such a large scale, the losses of more than $3 billion have rendered the telegram service financially unviable. However, India is not alone in phasing out this technology. In Britain, telegrams are marketed by a private company as retro greeting cards or invitations. While this service was shut down in the US in 2006, similar services are being offered in Russia, Germany, and Canada. From humble beginnings to dizzying heights and now on the verge of passing, this technology has come a full circle and will be remembered not only for its nostalgia, but also as a simple and instantaneous communication tool.

Unlike the telegram, the Indian transistor is going to get a new lease of life. With the popularity of mobile phones, mp3 players, and, more recently, the Apple products (iPods, iPads, iPhones), the utilitarian transistor had almost faded into oblivion. That is when Eveready Industries, India's largest selling brand of dry cell batteries and flashlights, decided to revive the transistors. The company is specifically eyeing towns in semi-urban and rural areas (population less than 100,000) to launch transistor sets for ₹500 (approx. $8–10). The company also expects this move to charge up its core business—the declining D-size batteries on which the transistors run. The ₹1,300-crore (approx. $250–300 million) battery category is growing at about 5%.

Though the brand has a wide reach in the semi-urban and rural markets (nearly 800,000 outlets), it is up for stiff competition from unbranded Chinese FM sets that retail at ₹150 (approx. $2.5–3) and mobile phones that have an inbuilt radio. However, what attracted Eveready to the transistor market is its size (around ₹100 crores, approx. $20–25 million) and the fact that only one branded player is currently operating in it—Philips. Eveready is planning to launch radios in a wide variety of color shades that will be available across India, all in an effort to rekindle a declining market and, hopefully, revive an old technology.

While technologies may come and go, during their lifetime they get entrenched into the culture and lifestyle of the consumers. Though both these technologies were rudimentary forms of communication, they were powerful enough to reach even the farthest corners of the country. They received the message across in time, acted as a catalyst in bringing together people, and more importantly became the only source of communication. Despite the rich history behind them, their existence is not always guaranteed.

---

[24] Adapted from Barney Henderson and Dean Nelson, "End of an Era. Stop. India Scraps the Telegram. Stop.," June 13, 2013, http://www.telegraph.co.uk/news/worldnews/asia/india/10118966/

supposedly hit the first-quarter profits of 2013.[25] A streamlined and efficient product development process is extremely important and essential. A number of things can happen as a result of delay. It directly hits the profitability as one loses sales for those many months the product wasn't launched.

With technology evolving like never before, the product development cycles are seen to reduce. This reduction in the product development cycle puts additional pressure on marketers to be ready to fully understand the market and be ready with an efficient plan for launch. About 95% of new products introduced each year fail, according to Cincinnati research agency AcuPoll.[26] With short product development cycle and the rate of success in market, research is an essential tool to avoid failure in market.

Focus on Product Features and Benefits

Creating products that fit the needs and wants of the customers is the key to success for any organization. This is even more certain in international markets where the needs, wants, and aspirations of the consumers are likely to be different from those present in the home country. Consequently, this requires a set of product offerings that are in tune with the local requirements.

Companies often have different approaches when it comes to developing products for international markets. Traditionally domestic companies that are foraying into foreign markets for the first time may be more likely to offer the same product that they are selling in the home market. Such an approach raises concerns on whether the product would find a viable market in the foreign country. Companies that have experience selling in foreign markets are likely to look out for uniqueness in each market and tailor the offerings based on that. While their products are more likely to be attuned to the local requirements than a product originally developed for a different market, they could still face issues on whether they covered all the local idiosyncrasies and did not leave anything as trivial. Finally, global companies that look at foreign markets to identify commonalities between them develop global products that appeal to consumers across countries. Even in this case, they run the risk of not covering enough of each country and could end up developing a product that does not appeal to anyone. Regardless of the approach adopted, companies have to analyze foreign markets against the following parameters: (a) market opportunities available for developing the proposed product, (b) the degree of standardization versus adaptation required for such a product, and (c) positioning of the product.

End-of-an-era.-Stop.-India-scraps-the-telegram.-Stop..html (Retrieved on May 20, 2013); Sandeep Joshi, "Dot, Dash, Full Stop: Telegram Service Ends July 15," June 12, 2013, http://www.thehindu.com/news/national/dot-dash-full-stop-telegram-service-ends-july-15/article4806921.ece (Retrieved on May 20, 2013); Purvita Chatterjee, "Eveready Tunes into Radios to Recharge Battery Sales," June 6, 2013, http://www.thehindubusinessline.com/companies/eveready-tunes-into-radios-to-recharge-battery-sales/article4788423.ece (Retrieved on May 20, 2013).

[25] L. Whitney, "HTC Profits Smacked by Delayed Launch of HTC One," April 8, 2013, http://news.cnet.com/8301-1035_3-57578378-94/htc-profits-smacked-by-delayed-launch-of-htc-one/(Retrieved on June 2, 2013).

[26] L. Burkitt and K. Bruno, "New, Improved ... and Failed," March 24, 2010, http://www.nbcnews.com/id/36005036/ns/business-forbes_com/t/new-improved-failed/#.Ub9k0efqlMg (Retrieved on June 2, 2013).

In evaluating potential markets, many companies prefer to sell first to the neighboring countries before considering distant markets. This is because the company understands the market better and has more control over the operation and cost structure. This explains the closer trade ties prevalent among the US, Canada, and Mexico, and among the European nations. In some cases, companies make judgments about markets by the *psychic distance*. That is, companies prefer to market to countries that have similar culture, laws, and language. This is the reason why American products find relatively easier entry into traditionally English-speaking markets like Canada, England, and Australia rather than non-English-speaking markets like China and Japan.

Regarding the degree of standardization or adaptation, the evidence from the marketplace and academic research has been divided. Research on standardization has found that the effects of competitive strategy and market structure variables generalize across the US, UK, Canada, and western Europe to a large extent.[27] Further, it has been found that companies would be better off standardizing their offerings only if the strength and form of the relationship between marketing-mix elements, market structure, competition, and business process in a newly entered market resemble a market that the company is already operating in. Similarly, adaptation strategy can be fruitful only if the markets are not alike.[28] Evidence from the marketplace suggests that products that focus on technological solutions, provide luxury and prestige, and offer high quality can be marketed similarly across nations. Examples of these products include Apple, Mercedes Benz, and Audi. On the other hand, it is difficult to standardize food and beverages across different nations, given the varying tastes. Examples include the Big Mac from McDonald's and Fanta that are sold as variants of the original developed in the US.

Positioning the products is critical to the success of products in the international marketplace. It enables marketers to highlight the meaningful differences between the focal brand and the competitors that are worthy to be considered by consumers during the purchase process. The aim of appropriate positioning is to create a market-focused value proposition that would appeal to the target audience. Typically, companies choose to position their products based on attributes such as form, features, quality of performance, quality standards, dependability, long life, style, and design, among others. For instance, Philips reserves their higher-end, premium medical equipment products for developed markets and promotes products with basic functionality and affordability in developing markets. Here, Philips is positioning their products based on products' features in international markets.[29] Similarly, many companies position themselves based on their nationality and their reputation for design. Examples of this include Italian design in apparel, Scandinavian design for functionality, aesthetics, and environmental consciousness, and German design for robustness.[30]

These above-discussed areas should illustrate the importance of researching a foreign market before deciding to enter it. The Coke example should remind researchers how important it is to consider all aspects to a problem and design the research methodology in a manner such that it covers all these angles.

---

[27] David M. Szymanski, Sundar G. Bharadwaj, and P. Rajan Varadarajan, "Standardization Versus Adaptation of International Marketing Strategy: An Empirical Investigation," *Journal of Marketing* 57, no. 4 (1993): 1–17.

[28] James Wills, A. Samli, and Laurence Jacobs, "Developing Global Products and Marketing Strategies: A Construct and a Research Agenda," *Journal of the Academy of Marketing Science* 19, no. 1 (1991): 1–10.

[29] Leila Abboud, "Philips Widens Marketing Push in India," *Wall Street Journal*, March 20, 2009.

[30] Philip Kotler, *Marketing Management* (Upper Saddle River: Prentice Hall, 2001), 10th edition.

GLOBAL MARKETING RESEARCH IN PRACTICE

Tasty Burgers will have to define their research problem and work with the research agency to develop the research objectives and formulate a research plan. The first step is to define the research problem. For Tasty Burgers, the objective is to enter international markets that are profitable and present good growth potential. The research question will address specific issues, such as the profit margins that can be expected from various countries, the growth potential in each of these markets, and how to address policies regarding product, pricing, and promotions in each of these markets. An important question that needs to be addressed in this stage is whether the products offered by Tasty Burgers should be standardized or whether they should be customized to suit the local tastes. Decisions should also be made as to whether Tasty Burgers will follow a standardized marketing program, that is, use the same marketing strategies that are being used in the US, or design custom strategies for each of these markets. This is called the strategic orientation of the company.

As a first step, the research agency will collect secondary data for all the markets that Tasty Burgers is interested in. Analyses of secondary data will provide information to shortlist some countries. Information required by Tasty Burgers fall into the following major categories:

- Customer information: The consumption patterns, dining-out habits, food preferences, religious sentiments which may prohibit consumers from eating certain types of food, and so on.
- Competitor information: The distribution network, pricing and promotion policies, relations with key suppliers, and so on.
- Country information: The political risk, the legal system, terms of ownership and repatriation of profits, availability of real estate and competent workforce, investment benefits such as tax breaks, and so on.

After the countries have been selected, a cost–benefit analysis is done by researchers to justify the costs incurred in conducting the research study. An estimate of profits that can be earned will be weighed against the costs of conducting the research. A decision is made to proceed with the research only if the benefits meet the required standards of Tasty Burgers.

Primary research is undertaken in all the countries that have been selected. The objective of primary research is to gather data to answer all the research questions. The method of data collection has to be decided depending on the country and culture.

Data that has been collected will then be coded and analyzed. The data analysis technique depends on the quantity and quality of data and the nature of the research problem. Results are interpreted and presented to the client, Tasty Burgers, in the format that was decided upon in the initial stages.

Each chapter in the textbook will deal with relevant sections of this example. Each of the stages mentioned above will be discussed in depth to provide readers with a thorough understanding of the global marketing research process.

SUMMARY

The idea of this chapter is to give the reader a bird's eye view of the global marketing research process. Also, the need for conducting marketing research in today's market environment is stressed upon in this chapter. Each of the stages mentioned in this chapter is explained in detail in the successive chapters. The purpose of this chapter is to act like a roadmap, giving the readers a better idea of where they stand as they progress through this textbook. The research purpose of the firm is to better define the problem and identify the possible decision alternatives that can be delved into. This is made concrete by writing down the research objective, which defines the scope of the research. The research question enumerates specific information needed to solve the problem. Secondary research helps gather data that is already available so that researchers can further their understanding of the research problem. The next step in the process is gathering primary data. There are many ways in primary research where data can be collected, such as qualitative research, observation, and surveys. The final stage in the research process is analyzing the data that has been collected and summarizing it in a manner such that it helps in decision making.

QUESTIONS AND PROBLEMS

1. Robert Smith, CEO of ComfortWear Inc., is considering expanding his clothing company outside of the United States. Smith's board of investors and leaders are apprehensive of expanding the brand internationally as they fear the demand for their products will pale in comparison to at home. What are some research questions and hypotheses that, if answered, could help them make a final decision?
2. VisionArt, Inc., a New York-based manufacturer of exotic jewelry, is interested in taking their products to a foreign market. You are hired as a marketing consultant to the company. Explain to them why it is essential to conduct a global marketing research study to ascertain the viability of entering new markets.
3. Sweet Water Creamery (SWC) is planning to launch its operations in India and parts of Southeast Asia. Does SWC need to create a new menu to be considered if it wants to develop a unique menu for each area? What type of research design is appropriate? Develop the research purpose, research questions, and hypothesis.
4. What possible problems might be encountered by a domestic research company conducting an international research study?
5. Answer the following:
    a. How is a cost–benefit analysis useful to management in deciding whether or not to conduct a marketing research study?
    b. What are the two approaches to budgeting for a market research project?
    c. For what situation is each approach most suitable?

Section II

Designing and Administering the Research Process

4 | Preliminary Stages of the Research Process   95

5 | Secondary Data Research   117

6 | Marketing Research on the Internet   137

7 | Primary Data Research   155

8 | Qualitative and Observational Research   180

9 | Survey Research   205

10 | Scale Development   228

11 | Questionnaire Design   250

12 | Sampling   272

4

Preliminary Stages of the Research Process

INTRODUCTION

Chapters 1 and 2 discussed the differences among different cultures and nationalities that make global marketing research complex and challenging. Chapter 3 discussed the process of global marketing research. This chapter focuses on the preliminary stages of the research process. Research is an integral part of any company wanting to go global. Even before the decision to enter foreign markets is made, research helps determine if internationalization is a viable option for the company. Research also helps decide which markets to enter and when and how to enter these markets. Most companies base their product launching and pricing decisions on market research. Each of these aspects of research is dealt with in detail in this chapter.

INFORMATION REQUIREMENTS FOR GLOBAL MARKETING DECISIONS

Global marketing research has often been called "comparative marketing research, with its principle focus being the systematic detection, identification, classification, measurement, and interpretation of similarities and differences among entire national systems." There are five main challenges any marketing manager faces in planning global marketing research:

1. Understanding similarities across countries so as to define a target market
2. A lack of accurate secondary information
3. The high costs of conducting research, especially when primary data is desired
4. Coordinating research across countries, which involves losing control of not only the research process but translations as well
5. Establishing comparability and equivalence in marketing research instruments

Against a background of diversity and change in the strategy and structure of international businesses, information needs are extremely varied. Three broad areas can be identified in which research inputs can be valuable: market orientation, strategic orientation, and problem orientation.[1]

---

[1] Vern Terpstra and Ravi Sarathy, "Techniques for Dealing with International Marketing Research Problems," in *International Marketing* (Orlando, FL: Dryden Press, 1994), pp. 213–218.

MARKET ORIENTATION

Companies are always faced with more questions than answers when trying to enter a new market with their product/service. A thorough understanding of the market needs via primary quantitative research and feasibility studies can be of great help to companies while launching their product/service in a foreign country. One of the more common uses of marketing research in international ventures is in the screening and identification of potential country markets for possible entry. At this initial stage of its internationalization process, a company needs to shortlist and identify one or two potential target markets to enter and decide on the mode of entry. While doing so, a company needs to understand the readiness of the market in which it plans to launch its product or service. Exhibit 4.1 points to one such example of a company that decided to not open franchises as indicated by research.

Exhibit 4.1

Mexican Restaurant Chain in Israel[2]

A casual dining Mexican restaurant was advised against opening franchises in metropolitan Tel Aviv, Israel, following a detailed research study that comprised of several phases.

First, with the help of market analysis, the company was able to get insights on the industry trends, location and facility, area characteristics, competition, customer demographics, and projected sales. Identifying the current trends in the desired market, along with in-depth analysis of the strength and weaknesses of competition, gave them an early heads-up of the issues they could face.

Moreover, on the feasibility front, it was critical to answer how many customers each franchise could potentially serve a year. This depended on the areas where the potential target audience lives. The restaurant knew that there was an economic base for the type of clientele to justify the investment they were planning to make. The feasibility study helped them come to a conclusion that there was scope for a moderately priced casual dining restaurant located in mall settings.

They then decided to carry out primary marketing research to answer questions such as: (a) Will Israeli yuppie couples frequent a restaurant when, to them, the slogan "South of the Border" means Egypt?; (b) Will their children whine for tacos in a nation where hummus is king?; (c) Can the lure of a burrito beat the Steakia restaurant next door that features *a la aish* (mixed grill) and lamb hearts? Research was carried out with the help of a local partner.

Using the results from the survey and feasibility study, it was clear that the Israelis liked the idea of an upscale casual dining Mexican restaurant. However, according to the various forecast scenarios, the market was not ready enough. Hence, the company did not move forward.

---

[2] Adapted from Quirk's Marketing Research Review, "Tacos in Tel Aviv?," September 12, 2011, Quirk's e-newsletter.

Globalization Process[3]

A key factor in determining why firms go international is the type and quality of management. A dynamic management is important when firms take their first international steps. Over the long term, success of a firm in international markets depends on the commitment, attitudes, and perceptions of the management. Researchers have shown that aggressive firms with a long-term view of the business are active in a larger number. Because international markets cannot be penetrated overnight and require vast amount of market development activity, market research, and sensitivity to foreign market factors, the issue of managerial commitment is crucial. It has also been shown that in most cases managers of global firms show a higher level of formal education and foreign language fluency than do managers of domestic firms.

However, one factor alone cannot account for success in international markets. Usually, a mixture of factors results in firms taking steps in a given direction. These factors are differentiated as proactive and reactive motivations. Proactive motivations represent stimuli to attempt strategic change and include profit advantage, technological advantage, exclusive market information, managerial urg e, tax benefits, and economies of scale. Reactive motivations could be in the form of competitive pressures, overproduction in domestic market, stable or declining sales in the domestic market, excess capacity, saturation in the domestic market, and proximity to customers and ports.

Market Selection

To provide a preliminary understanding of a market or range of markets in one or more countries, only rather limited background data is usually required. Such information would cover: (a) market size and trends, (b) market structure/segmentation, (c) names of companies operating in the market (both suppliers and buyers) with indication of their importance, (d) lists of products and prices, (e) distribution channels, and (f) media availability and rates.

Desk research, using published or other easily available sources, is normally adequate for the purpose. Not only are the statistical series of governments and international bodies becoming more numerous and relevant, but also the range of market surveys published by trade associations, chambers of commerce, financial concerns, government trade/commerce departments, the media, consultants, and so on is becoming increasingly wide. A number of commercial organizations offer such market analyses on a regular, syndicated basis at low prices.

Add to these sources the judicious use of trade directories, trade and financial press, and, possibly, information already in the firm, and it is not surprising that companies often feel capable of handling this first market orientation themselves. Market research suppliers are rarely involved at this stage. A more detailed discussion on conducting global marketing research using secondary data can be found in Chapter 5 of this book.

---

[3] Michael R. Czinkota and Illka A. Ronkainen, *International Marketing* (Orlando, FL: Dryden Press, 1998), pp. 296, 5th edition.

Mode of Entry

Entering a foreign market is not a one-step decision. Companies carry out a lot of analysis in order to narrow down on a country, place, or area where they want to expand their business. Broadly, the evaluation involves three stages, namely, (a) screening stage—where companies evaluate the macro indicators such as political stability, sociocultural factors, etc., (b) identification stage—where companies dig deeper into industry-specific information, the market size, growth opportunities, entry barriers, competitive positioning, etc., and (c) selection stage—where companies identify potential country segments based on this information.[4] To begin with, managers often have multiple objectives in mind while entering a foreign market. The constraints in terms of resource and information add to their dilemma. The plethora of options as markets makes life more difficult. It is possible to use an interactive technique, find the most preferred solution from the earlier iteration, and then again use it for further iterations, helping managers narrow down their options of countries/localities/areas depending on the objective. Managers can then use this knowledge to perform a more intense primary research on the reduced set of options. It is cost-effective and a more focused approach.

The nature of a firm's operation in a country market depends on its choice of mode of entry.[5] A mode of entry is an institutional arrangement chosen by the firm to operate in the foreign market. This decision is one of the most critical strategic decisions for the firm; it affects all the future decisions and operations of the firm in that country market. Because each mode of entry entails a concomitant level of resource commitment, it is difficult to change from one entry mode to another without considerable loss of time and money. The contingency model of decision making consists of a series of stages, as shown in Figure 4.1.

FIGURE 4.1
CONTINGENCY MODEL OF MODE OF ENTRY DECISION[6]

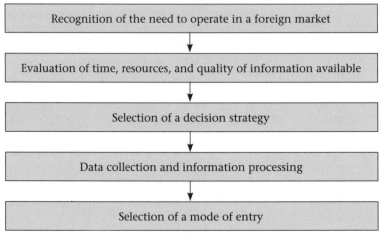

---

[4] V. Kumar, Antonie Stam, and Erich A. Joachimsthaler, "An Interactive Multi-Criteria Approach to Identifying Potential Foreign Markets," *Journal of International Marketing* 2, no. 1 (1994): 29–52.

[5] V. Kumar and Velavan Subramaniam, "A Contingency Framework for the Mode of Entry Decision," *Journal of World Business* 32, no. 1 (1997), pp. 53–72.

[6] Ibid. Reprinted by permission of JAI Press, Inc.

The first stage of the model involves recognizing the problem and defining it. In the second stage, the decision makers ask questions such as "What factors that affect the modes of entry have to be considered?" and "Where can information on these factors be obtained?." This is the stage where global marketing research comes into play. In the third stage, managers select the mode of entry with the basic information at hand. In the fourth stage, decision makers collect and process information consistent with the decision strategy they have selected. Some strategies may involve elaborate and costly information collection and processing while some may be based on simple heuristics. The final stage is the actual decision choice as to which mode of entry to use when entering a foreign market.

While there is a need for research to determine how to enter or operate in different markets, the degree of interest and commitment to international operations will determine how much time and effort the management is willing to spend in investigating foreign market potential, and the most appropriate mode of operation. Modes of entry into foreign markets can be broadly classified into four major categories: exporting, licensing (and other forms of contractual agreements), joint ventures, and wholly owned subsidiaries.[7,8]

The choice of mode of entry can be determined by: (a) the objectives of the company in the foreign market, (b) its preparedness toward taking risks, (c) the amount of capital investment at its disposal, and (d) the level of control it would like to have in the foreign market. Figure 4.2 presents the various modes of entry against the determinants of entry choice.

FIGURE 4.2

DETERMINING THE MODE OF ENTRY

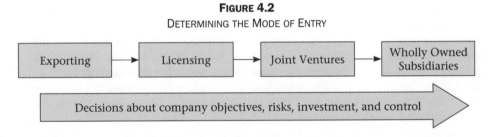

Exporting. In the initial stages of their internationalization process, companies typically export directly or indirectly. Direct exporting is when the company sets up its own export department and actively seeks and fulfills overseas orders. Indirect exporting refers to filling unsolicited orders from abroad via their domestic-based export agents. Indirect export has two key advantages: (a) There is no need to set up a dedicated export department, thereby freeing up investment that can be used for other purposes; (b) the risk is lowered as the export agents provide the services and know-how, thereby reducing the level of mistakes. Given these advantages, indirect export is typically the first step companies take when venturing into foreign markets. However, as this is a low-risk approach, the downside to this is the low return to the company. Consequently, little research is likely to be conducted in relation to international markets.

From indirect exporting, companies may choose to get involved in direct exports. This mode of exporting can be done through: (a) the setting up of a dedicated export department in the home country, (b) the appointment of overseas sales offices, (c) a traveling sales team,

[7] P. B. Barnard, "The Role and Implementation of International Marketing Research," International Marketing Research Seminar, Rotterdam, ESOMAR, 1976, pp. 67–88.

[8] Franklin R. Root, *Entry Strategies for International Markets* (Washington, DC: Lexington Books, 1983).

or (d) exclusive distributors located in foreign markets. For instance, export management companies could be used to market and/or produce the product overseas. Small- and medium-sized companies that want to develop export markets without making a substantial commitment of management or financial resources can employ such companies to gain entry into foreign markets. These intermediaries arrange the mechanics of exporting, identify markets, find potential buyers, and select distributors. Ultimately, however, as these markets develop, direct contact will need to be established with a separate sales organization for international markets. When companies undertake this form of exporting, a keen focus on foreign markets and effective market penetration is crucial. This then takes over all the complex problems of research to determine which markets to enter, and with what strategy.[9] In addition to that, a strategy to maintain the continuous exporting relationship with a country is important. Research has shown that marketing methods such as direct marketing can play a significant role in exporting. In addition to the prior experience of the company in the market and their level of preparedness, direct marketing serves as a substantial predictor of exporting on a consistent basis.

Licensing. Licensing is when the focal company (the licensor) grants permission to another company (the licensee) to use a manufacturing process, patent, trade secret, or product formulation in exchange for royalties, license fees, or any other form of compensation. This mode of entry is appealing to companies as it (a) provides incremental profitability with little initial investment, thereby boosting the return on investment; (b) enables the licensor to circumvent tariffs, quotas, and other export barriers; and (c) is relatively inexpensive to implement. However, there is a flip side to this mode. By limiting the direct participation of the licensor in the foreign country to a minimum, this mode also prevents the licensor from having control, limits the amount of returns, and could pave the way for the licensee to emerge as a competitor in the foreign market. A scenario where Coca-Cola provides the secret formula to the licensee, who in turn uses that to manufacture and sell the beverage in the foreign country, is a good example of licensing.

Two popular forms of licensing are adopted by many companies. First, companies can resort to *contract manufacturing* where they provide technical specifications to a subcontractor or local manufacturer to produce a product. While the benefit of this form lies in a faster start-up of operations, and a possible opportunity to buy out the local manufacturer if the operation becomes successful, the downside is that the company has no control in the production process and could risk losing profits. Several automobile companies use this mode to get the auto components manufactured based on specific requirements from foreign manufacturers. Second, companies can go in for *franchising*, wherein a contract between the focal company (in this case, the franchisor) and a local business (the franchisee) can be signed that allows the franchisee to operate a business developed by the franchisor in return for a fee and adherence to franchise-wide policies. Companies such as KFC and Subway have appointed franchisees around the world to field storefronts in various countries of interest.

Licensing, while apparently a low international commitment strategy, also requires research, not only to identify the most appropriate licensee, but also prior to the licensing decisions to determine whether market potential will grow rapidly. In this case, alternative forms of entry, such as joint venture or wholly owned subsidiaries, may be preferred.

---

[9] S. Tamir Cavusgil and John R. Nevin, "State-of-the-Art in Marketing," *Review of Marketing* (1981), vol. XVIII, pp. 296–301.

Franchising, the parallel to licensing in the service industry, also requires research to find potential franchises and to assess how far strategies should be adapted.

Joint Ventures. Joint ventures with local companies in a foreign country also provide a means of reducing the risks associated with foreign market entry. Here, the local partner brings expertise and familiarity with local market conditions. This mode of entry brings with it several benefits to the focal company, such as: (a) sharing of risk, (b) getting to know the new market firsthand, and (c) benefits accruing from synergies with the foreign company. Further, the presence of a local partner reduces the need for research to determine how far products or strategies should be adapted to these conditions.

In such initiatives, the local partner can advise the foreign company on several country specifics regarding economy, culture, political/legal framework, and infrastructure that play a key role in determining the success of a company in foreign markets. The emerging markets are seeing the most number of joint venture initiatives. Examples of such initiatives include the IBM–China Great Wall Computer Group joint venture, wherein IBM owns 80% of stakes, and the remaining are owned by Great Wall,[10] and the recent Indian joint venture between AirAsia and Tata Sons wherein AirAsia will hold 49% of the company.[11]

However, the downside of this mode of entry includes: (a) increased level of investment, (b) sharing of returns, and (c) conflict among partners. A recent instance of a conflict among partners is the case of Hero Motors and Honda. In 1984, Honda of Japan and Hero Cycles based in New Delhi, India, entered into a joint venture to manufacture scooters and motorcycles for the Indian market. In 2010, Honda started having ideas to enter the Indian two-wheeler market alone. Honda had realized that the Indian market had completely changed since their joint venture, more than 25 years ago.[12] Soon after, the Hero Group bought the shares held by Honda and the company split after a successful partnership.

Wholly Owned Subsidiaries. If, however, a company is willing to assume all risks associated with foreign operations, then wholly owned subsidiaries may be established. The setting up of wholly owned subsidiaries involves the foreign company setting up its own manufacturing or service facilities in the foreign market. In some cases, these may be independent country units, such as P&G's country operations for Europe and Asia-Pacific regions. Though this type of mode of entry can be expensive and would require a major commitment of managerial time and energy, it has several benefits, such as: (a) full control over operations, marketing efforts, and manufacturing, (b) returns that do not have to be shared with any other company, (c) full access to the market and other locally available resources needed for production such as labor, land, and capital, and (d) ability to economize on the costs of production by catering to the entire market.

While wholly owned subsidiaries may resolve many of the foreign company's concerns, it is not without political or other environmental factors that sometimes impede this setup. Other ways of setting up such subsidiaries may be through Greenfield operations or investment, mergers with existing companies, and acquisition of existing companies. As an alternative to

---

[10] Liu Baijia, "Great Wall, IBM in Partnership," *China Daily*, December 13, 2004.

[11] Reeba Zachariah and Rajesh Chandramouli, "AirAsia to Tie Up with Tata Sons for New Airline in India," *Times of India*, February 21, 2013.

[12] Subramaniam Sharma and Siddharth Philip, "Hero Buys Honda's $1.9 Billion Stake in India Motorbike Maker on Exports," *Bloomberg*, December 17, 2010.

Greenfield investment in new facilities, acquisition is an instantaneous—and sometimes, less expensive—approach to market entry or expansion. Although full ownership can yield the additional advantage of avoiding communication and conflict of interest problems that may arise with a joint venture or coproduction partner, acquisitions still present the demanding and challenging task of integrating the acquired company into the worldwide organization and coordinating activities.

For companies that do set up wholly owned subsidiaries, research comparable to domestic marketing research must be conducted by the local subsidiary. If, however, products and strategies are to be transferred across national boundaries, some prior research is needed to assess how far standardization will result in loss of market potential. In other cases, such as in the automobile industry, wholly owned subsidiaries consist of a complex mass of intertwined global operations. The transmissions for the Ford Fiesta were, for example, made in Bordeaux, France, the windshields in Oklahoma, the spark plugs in the UK, and the bumper plating in Cologne, Germany. Here, research to establish the global marketing plan and to determine how far programs and strategies should be standardized or adapted to different national environments is more likely to be directed from corporate or regional headquarters, based on input from local subsidiary management.

Forecasting

A market entry is almost always surrounded by a lot of uncertainty. For a company, some level of judgment and forecasting is involved in understanding the potential demand for the product/service, readiness of consumers for a particular product/service, the market condition, exchange rates, etc. A company's ability to accurately forecast the future trends, market conditions, and expected performance of a product/service in advance gives them a great competitive advantage in a new market, thereby reducing the level of uncertainty involved in the whole process. Forecasting is a key step in a new product development cycle. While this is valid for the domestic market, the level of uncertainty doubles up in an international marketing environment. There are various forecasting methods that are used in planning and control at different stages. There are qualitative and quantitative approaches to forecasting as explained below: [13]

Qualitative Approaches. These approaches are fast, cost-efficient, and flexible. Although subjective judgments and biases are a drawback of this approach, in most cases, it helps organizations get a quick feel of the situation. Some types of qualitative approaches are:

1. *Jury of executive:* These include combining the judgments of a wide group of managers from different functions of an organization about the forecast.
2. *Sales force estimates:* These include judgments from the sales force. A salesperson's knowledge of the customer or a client is comprehensive and current.
3. *The survey of customer intentions:* This is where customers are asked to make their own forecasts about the usage and buying intentions.
4. *Delphi approach:* This is similar to jury of executive, although here, the group members submit their individual forecasts, compare it with others, and get a chance to revise it, if needed. Typical three to four iterations provide a conclusive direction to the group.

---

[13] Aaker et al., *Marketing Research*, 11th edition, p. 690.

Quantitative Approaches. These methods tend to be more robust. However, they are time consuming and may require data collection in some cases. There are two broad categories:

1. *Time series extrapolation:* This involves the use of historical data to project the future results. This is a popular method in many cases. It works well for short-term forecasts where data is available to capture a clear trend, or a cyclical or seasonal pattern. The biggest disadvantage of this method is that it does not account for the sudden unexpected events such as natural disasters, collapse of an economy, etc.
2. *Causal models:* These are statistical models that involve finding the cause-and-effect relationships between a set of variables. A simple regression is an example of this.

Diffusion of Innovation

In an international setting, the diffusion process of a new product/service is different in each country. Researchers study the multinational diffusion patterns of products and technologies to understand how new products diffuse in different cultural and market environments. Research has shown that when a product or technological innovation occurs in one country, the lag countries (the ones where the product is introduced later) demonstrate a faster diffusion process of the said product or technology.[14] The world is shrinking in size. The advance in technology has enabled faster spreading of a message. In such a scenario, the introduction of a product or technology in one country is likely to have a more significant impact on the diffusion of products on the other countries adopting it later. Diffusion models have provided great assistance to companies in forecasting the sales potential of a market. Moreover, companies can chose the countries based on their analysis of the diffusion patterns.

Today, in the day and age of *big data*, forecasting techniques are getting more sophisticated. Use of existing data for forecasting purposes is gaining popularity. Techniques such as artificial neural networks are a great example of this. Using variables derived from market research in the multinational, multi-cultural context, marketers can gain insights into the potential adoption rates of products in global markets through diffusion studies and can predict how markets will react to products and marketing strategies.

STRATEGIC ORIENTATION

Whereas the market orientation phase can help a company establish priorities between both markets and countries, more detailed information is required to develop a strategy for entering or extending a presence in a selected market. Data relevant for such a strategic orientation would include: (a) market shares (estimates will often be available in published material too), (b) product awareness/penetration, (c) buying motivations, (d) barriers to change and how to overcome them, (e) brand/product images, (f) buyer attitudes and profiles, (g) competitors' weaknesses, and (h) detailed structure of the distribution system and how to take advantage of it.

---

[14] Jaishankar Ganesh, V. Kumar, and Velavan Subramaniam, "Cross-National Learning Effects in Global Diffusion Patterns: An Exploratory Investigation," *Journal of the Academy of Marketing Science* 25, no. 3 (1997): 214–228.

This more detailed market study and diagnosis generally involves primary research; that is, further data collection designed for the particular client (or group of clients). Such studies, which can follow the desk research phase or be combined with it, usually involve interviewing consumers or end users of the products or services to provide a better *feel* for the market. The interviewing may range from a few contacts with key buyers or decision takers in certain industrial sectors to simple habit and attitude studies in consumer goods markets. Information obtained to help provide a market or strategy orientation when investigating foreign markets primarily gives a picture of the total market, with limited diagnostic data to help formulate plans in marketing, sales, and distribution.

Expansion Strategy[15]

Most firms begin their operations in the domestic market. Over a period of time, some of them expand into international markets. In looking at the internationalization process, one finds that initially the vast majority of the firms are not at all interested in the international marketplace. Over time, a firm may become a partially interested exporter. Most companies that make a transition from uninterested to partially interested exporters are those that have a track record of domestic market expansion. In the next stage, the firm gradually begins to explore international markets, and the management is willing to consider the possibility of exporting. After this exploratory stage, the firm becomes an experimental exporter, usually to psychologically close countries; however, the management is still far from being committed to international marketing activities.

At the next stage, the firm evaluates the impact that exporting has had on its general activities. It is possible at this stage for the firm to be disappointed with international markets and to decide to withdraw from international activities. More often, the firm continues to exist as a small exporter. The final stage is that of export adaptation. The firm becomes an experienced exporter to a country and adjusts exports to changing exchange rates, tariffs, and other variables. The management is ready to consider the possibility of exporting to additional countries that are psychologically farther away. Revenues from exporting, which were earlier considered as surprise income, will now become a part of the budget. In these conditions, the firm can be considered as a strategic participant in the international market.

The strategies adopted by firms to enter foreign markets fall under two broad categories: the sprinkler strategy and the waterfall strategy.[16] A firm adopting the sprinkler strategy will decide on which markets it plans to enter and simultaneously enter all these markets. This is a risky method to adopt because of the high cost involved in entering a foreign market. Microsoft launched their Windows 7 software in over 100 countries simultaneously in fall 2009. Though there were some minor changes in the marketing approach, the launch was worldwide that involved several decisions on marketing, operations, and logistics.[17] This can be viewed as a sprinkler approach. Typically, this approach is adopted when companies have to make strategic product and marketing decisions to stay ahead of the competition, and timing of the product introduction is of the essence.

---

[15] Czinkota and Ronkainen, *International Marketing*, 5th edition.

[16] Shlomo Kalish, Vijay Mahajan, and Eitan Muller, "Waterfall and Sprinkler: New Product Strategies in Competitive Global Markets," *International Journal of Research in Marketing* 12 (1995): 105–119.

[17] Marc Gunther, "The World's New Economic Landscape," *Fortune*, July 26, 2010, pp. 105–106.

The waterfall strategy is a more conservative approach in which the firm follows a roll-out policy, entering the most profitable market first. Depending on the performance of the product in this market, the firm identifies the next best market for entry. This is a strategy more suited for internationalization. It has generally been observed that new products follow a certain pattern of diffusion. For instance, research has shown that after a product has been introduced and accepted in the US, the next likely market is Germany.[18] Researchers can study the pattern of product diffusion for a given category of products and decide on the roll-out strategy. This way the company has the opportunity to cut losses in any market where its products are not accepted. Companies such as Wal-Mart, Audi, Subway, and Starbucks have followed this approach. Unlike the sprinkler strategy, this approach allows the firm to carefully plan the expansion without placing any strain on their company or management resources.

Standardization and Adaptation[19]

Deciding on the level of standardization or adaptation of a product is a crucial decision when entering new markets, and this holds important implications for researchers studying such markets. Among the support for adopting a standardized approach are:

1. *Significant cost savings.* By producing standardized products, the production base is strengthened and unit costs are controlled. This enhances the more judicious use of resources, enables better planning, and provides control to the firm.
2. *Price over culture.* While cultural variations may exist, the benefits accruing from the cost advantage, price, and consistent quality will offset the advantages of producing culturally adapted products.
3. *One world, one market.* With more markets opening up for world trade, the free movement of men, money, and materials is paving way for the homogenization of tastes and preferences of people the world over. As a result, the needs and wants are trending to be similar, thereby creating the need for standardized products.

Though standardization has cost advantages associated with it, the local market characteristics may require some form of local adaptation. One of the challenges of global marketing research is to determine the extent of standardization that may be used. While the case for standardization hinges on economies of scale, the case for adaptation firmly rests on addressing the cultural variations between country markets. Some of the points that support adaptation include:

1. *Law of the land.* The legal system prevailing in foreign markets may dictate certain conditions that the firm may have to adhere to. For instance, the Brazilian law interprets the word *diet* to have medicinal properties and requires daily-recommended consumption information on the labels. For food and beverage companies that sell *diet* variants

---

[18] Jaishankar Ganesh, V. Kumar, and Velavan Subramaniam, "Learning Effect in Multinational Diffusion of Consumer Durables: An Exploratory Investigation," *Journal of the Academy of Marketing Science* 24, no. 3 (1997): 214–228.

[19] Erdner Kaynak, "Difficulties in Undertaking Marketing Research in Developing Countries," *European Research* (1978), vol. 6, pp. 251–259.

of the original product, standardizing the product with respect to labeling will not be possible.

2. *Usage patterns.* Different country markets have differing consumption patterns based on their needs, wants, and purchasing power. For instance, the popular snack food Cheetos had to launch 15-gram-size packages in China at one Yuan so that a wider segment of consumers could buy it. With respect to standardization, it raises issues regarding packaging, standard pack sizes, and stock keeping units (SKUs).

3. *Infrastructure issues.* Even if the products per se may be standardized, other support setup required to use the product may warrant adaptation. For instance, Coca-Cola had to withdraw their 2-liter bottle in Spain after they found that few Spaniards owned refrigerators that could accommodate it.

While standardization and adaptation have different points that support their usage, the extent of standardization or adaptation depends on the foreign environmental conditions existing in each of country markets. The factors that determine their level may be categorized into four major groups:

1. *Market characteristics.* The physical environment of a market, such as the climate, product use conditions, and population size, often force marketers to make the product fit local conditions. Some of the other factors that affect the extent of standardization/ adaptation are income level, exchange rate fluctuations, language, culture, and social factors.

2. *Industry conditions.* The maturity of the market determines the strategy to be followed for introducing and promoting the product. The level of competition, the level of technology, the varying prices of local substitutes, and local production costs can affect the marketing policy.

3. *Marketing institutions.* Practices in distributions systems, availability of outlets, advertising agencies, and presence or absence of mass media channels can affect the extent of standardization/adaptation.

4. *Legal restrictions.* It is necessary for companies to follow the standards issued by the local governments. Tariffs and taxes make it necessary for the companies to make price adjustments. Restrictions on advertisements affect promotion plans. Also, local governments may impose local content requirements in the production of products when operating as a wholly owned subsidiary. This might hinder the plans to have a standardized raw materials and production process.

In light of these differences, undertaking marketing research in developing countries is significantly different from the way it is conducted in developed countries. The techniques used are the same; however, the application of certain methods differs.[20]

EPRG Framework

With international business operations being conducted at increasing levels, the dynamics of operating in foreign markets are bound to be different and ever-changing. Research has shown that the ethnocentric, polycentric, regiocentric, or geocentric orientation (EPRG) framework,

---

[20] This section draws heavily from Johny K. Johansson, *Global Marketing* (New York: Irwin, 1997).

through its four types of orientations toward internationalization, can be used by companies to make informed decisions as they expand into new markets.[21] These four orientations reflect the goals and philosophies of the company and help in developing management strategies and planning procedures with regard to its international operations.

In the ethnocentric orientation, the focus of the top management firmly rests on its domestic performance and considers the revenue from foreign sales only an extension of its domestic sales. Typically, such firms have a centralized way of administration and operation. Further, the company regards their approach in the domestic market and their human resource pool to be superior to the foreign market. Firms with this outlook will enter only those foreign markets that closely resemble the domestic market in terms of product demand and acceptability. Consequently, there is no systematic research conducted overseas and there are no major modifications to products.

In the polycentric orientation, the company understands the differences between the domestic market and the various country markets. They recognize the idiosyncrasies that belong to each market, and identify the need to adapt their product offerings to suit each market. Typically, such firms have a decentralized administration. Further, the company also feels the need to include local inputs in designing and delivering the products that would accommodate the local tastes. As a result, they appoint subsidiaries in the overseas markets that operate independently. Marketing is organized on a country-to-country basis, with each country having its own unique marketing policy.

In the regiocentric and geocentric stages, the company views the world as one whole market, and seeks to create an integrated marketing approach that accommodates all the local needs and wants. In other words, such firms have an integrated administration where the development and implementation of policies are either at a regional or world level. Correspondingly, all decisions regarding product development, marketing and promotion, production, and operations occur at the global level.

PROBLEM ORIENTATION

The third category of information needs brings us to research studies designed specifically to aid the making of particular decisions. Often, such studies focus only on one or more key elements in the market mix, such as product formulation, price, advertising, package design, or promotions; however, they sometimes involve assessment, directly or indirectly, of the total market or sector through the collection of data to help in market segmentation, target group identification, and detailed brand positioning. New concept or product development work would also feature here. Problem orientation is a feature that all projects in this third category have in common. Usually, companies also face the need to employ a market research company to design and interpret a study involving the collection of primary data.

Problem Definition—Self-Reference Criterion

When researching global markets, the self-reference criterion (SRC) is an important issue to deal with. This refers to the condition where the researchers unconsciously refer to their own

---

[21] Y. Wind, S. Douglas, and H. Perlmutter, "Guidelines for Developing International Marketing Strategy," *Journal of Marketing* 37 (1973): 14–23.

culture, values, lifestyle, knowledge, and experience in understanding a phenomenon. In other words, when researchers are confronted with differing and unfamiliar cultural norms, they instinctively apply their understanding of the situation by applying their cultural understanding and experience to bring about a solution. The SRC not only impedes the ability of a researcher to define the problem in its true light, but also prevents the researcher from being aware of the cultural differences and recognizing the importance of those differences. An example of the SRC at play can be seen in Kellogg's experience in Britain. When the company launched their Pop-Tarts in Britain, they did not realize that fewer homes had toasters than in the US, and the product was too sweet for the British palette. This resulted in the failure of the product in Britain.

To eliminate the problem of SRC, the following four-step framework should be followed:[22]

1. Define the problem in terms of home-country cultural traits, habits, and norms.
2. Define the problem in terms of foreign-country cultural traits, habits, and norms.
3. Isolate the SRC influence in the problem and examine it carefully to see how it complicates the problem.
4. Redefine the problem without the SRC influence and solve for foreign market situation.

In some cases, researchers find it easier to develop research instruments specific to one country and then coordinate and compare across countries. Here, both researchers who are familiar with the country and those who are not examine the instruments and the data and draw conclusions. The second method of considering one country at a time and then comparing is preferable even though it is time-consuming. This method also poses a number of intersection problems, as researchers from different cultural backgrounds have to be in constant touch with one another.

UNIT OF ANALYSIS[23]

After preliminary research has been completed, the company will have an idea of the markets it plans to enter. The firm should then segment the market to get a better understanding of the market dynamics; however, deciding on the geographic boundaries within which to conduct research is becoming extremely complicated. For instance, the blurring of borders among the North American countries—US, Canada, and Mexico—and the creation of the North American Free Trade Agreement (NAFTA) has effectively integrated the three countries into a single market. Here, an estimated 440 million people consume nearly $16 trillion worth of goods and services annually. While this creation of regional trade bloc facilitates the coexistence of various cultures within one region, it makes it difficult for the researcher to decide on a unit of analysis.

In some cases, it becomes necessary to conduct research within specific regions in the country. Consider Belgium, which is divided neatly in half, between Flanders in the north and Wallonia in the south.[24] Flemish people use margarine and Walloons use butter. This is everyday product usage that American food retailers need to understand. Such region-specific

---

[22] James A. Lee, "Cultural Analysis in Overseas Operations," *Harvard Business Review*, March–April 1966, pp. 106–111.

[23] Ibid.

[24] Ira Sager, "The Stealth Computer—Annual Design Awards," *Business Week*, June 2, 1997, p. 103.

product usage calls for market research on a regional basis. Researchers will have to compare lifestyles of target populations in individual regions before arriving at a marketing plan. Such target populations could also be based on age, gender, region, or any other demographic variables. Exhibit 4.2 highlights the demographic changes within the US and its importance in marketing research.

Exhibit 4.2

Breadwinner Moms[25]

Findings by the Pew Research Center shows that US's working mothers are now the primary breadwinners in a record 40% of households with children, up from only 11% in 1960. The report also found that while most of these households are headed by single mothers, families with married mothers who bring in more income than their husbands are also on the rise.

Experts cite three factors as the main reasons for this structural change. First, education rates and participation of women in the labor force have increased tremendously. It is reported that women make up nearly 47% of the American workforce. Second, economic downturn and job losses, especially in industries dominated by a male workforce such as manufacturing and construction, have elevated the relative earnings of married women. Further pay hikes have occurred even among those in mid-level positions such as teachers, nurses, or administrators. Finally, falling marriage rates and increasing childbirths out of wedlock have led to an increase in single-mother households.

These findings highlight the changing role of women in American society. Further, the increase of breadwinner moms also has important implications on the family structure and family dynamics. As a result, marketers should monitor such changes and incorporate them into the product development and product positioning to make their offerings meaningful and relevant.

There is a wide gap between consumers in different countries. Alcohol consumption differs among the various European nations.[26] For instance, the annual consumption of beer is the highest in Czech Republic at 81.9 liters per capita, while it is the lowest in Norway at 40.3 liters. Similarly, Portugal features at the top of the annual wine consumption pattern at 33.1 liters per capita, while Finland consumes the least at 9.9 liters per capita.[27] In terms of tastes and preferences, the French prefer wine, the Germans prefer beer, and the Spaniards like aperitivos. In England, port is drunk after a meal, while in Portugal it is consumed before. Such differences in consumption patterns must be taken into account while conducting marketing research. In this case, it becomes necessary to conduct research using the country as the unit of research.

In some cases, it becomes necessary to target certain specific groups across countries. For instance, women in China have types of hair different from women in Africa. With respect

---

[25] Adapted from Hope Yen, "Mothers Now Top Earners in 4 in 10 US Households," *Columbus Dispatch*, May 29, 2013.

[26] Jim Williams, "Constant Questions or Constant Meanings Assessing Intercultural Motivations in Alcoholic Drinks," *Marketing and Research Today*, August 1991.

[27] The Economist, *Pocket World in Figures* (London: Profile Books, 2009).

to usage patterns, it has been observed that middle-class British women wash their hair frequently, compared to Spanish women, and Japanese women avoid over washing their hair for fear of losing the protective oils.[28] Therefore, companies producing hair care products will need to conduct research targeting women in these countries to understand the varying needs of these markets.

Information needs are also shaped by the nature of the business, with firms in the trading or raw-material/extractive industries rarely turning to commercial research suppliers at all. Manufacturing industries have made the greatest use of global marketing research, although there has been considerable growth over the past few years in research demand by companies in the services sector. For example, internationalization of several sectors of the distribution trades has led to greater interest in retailing, transportation, and logistics studies recently.

From the perspective of the research suppliers, marketing companies do not represent the entire target group for their activities. Various forms of social research have grown in importance in the past decade, but when conducted for governments or their agencies, these have largely been confined within national boundaries, for obvious reasons. Increasingly, however, information is being sought on a multi-country basis to provide a yardstick for comparison.

Many companies resist global markets because the problems associated with going global seem insurmountable. Most companies do not seem to acknowledge the fact that their international sales force and the distributors' sales force can be valuable in surmounting cultural and marketing barriers. In 1965, Webster argued that the "use of the sales people for gathering information" can be much more critical than their use for promotion".[29] Exhibit 4.3 summarizes a study on information requirements for marketing research. It has been observed that salespeople are a likely source of information about marketplace problems.[30] Most multinational companies rely on secondary information obtained by hiring outside consultants. In addition to the above problems, language barriers, absence of contacts in foreign data collecting offices, lack of knowledge of government agencies, and gathering footwork locally are other problems.

GLOBAL MARKETING RESEARCH IN PRACTICE

Now we will look at the market orientation, strategic orientation, and problem orientation of Tasty Burgers.

While considering the market orientation, it is important to look at several features, as stated in the chapter. One of the first details that should be paid attention to is the market size and number of players in the market. Many US fast-food chains like McDonald's and Pizza Hut have already established operations in numerous international locations. The researchers will first look for information on the performance of these companies and their profit figures. The advantage of being a follower as against a first-mover is that there is an opportunity to learn from the mistakes of other players.

---

[28] Aradhna Krishna and Rohini Ahluwalia, "Language Choice in Advertising to Bilinguals: Asymmetric Effects for Multinationals Versus Locals Firms," *Journal of Consumer Research* 35 (2008): 692–705.

[29] Frederick E. Webster, Jr., "The Industrial Salesman as a Source of Market Information," *Business Horizons*, 1965, 8 (1), pp. 77-82.

[30] C. Mellow, "The Best Source of Competitor Intelligence," *Sales and Marketing Management*, 1989, 141 (December), pp. 24-29.

Exhibit 4.3

Information Needs in Marketing Research[31]

Research was undertaken by Chonko, Tanner, and Smith to study the information needs of companies and sources used by them operating in an international environment. The study is based on the following assumptions:

- Because of added political and economic risks in operating abroad, accurate and timely marketing information is more important than in domestic marketing.
- Risk of unreliability of international business conducted in the US and the cost involved make companies eager to find satisfactory alternatives.
- In many cases, salespeople are a company's only link to the customer. So the sales force in any company has almost exclusive access to valuable customer data.

The research is designed to investigate what types of information are being gathered during each phase of the marketing cycle, how it is communicated to marketing offices, if salespeople are given research results, and if so, in what format. In addition, centralization and formality issues are also discussed. The methodology followed is explained below in detail.

THE SAMPLE

The sample consisted of companies who, according to *Standard and Poor's Guide to Business for Corporations*, had revenues of more than $2 million, whose industry entailed personal selling, and who listed names of executives in an international division. The last step was to enable executives to be contacted and asked for by name to ensure higher respondent success rate. No more than two corporations were chosen from any one industry so as to avoid bias. Examples were: office products, pharmaceuticals, cosmetics, home care products, computer systems, raw metals, air travel and tours, foods, insurance, etc. Only those companies originating in the US were chosen. Foreign companies, even those headquartered or operating in the US, were excluded. From 26 sample corporations, 23 usable interviews were available. Each executive was screened to test knowledge of international marketing practices of firms.

MEASURES

Phone interviews were used, though more success has been reported with personal interviews. A structured, in-depth telephone interview was used that had 10 open-ended questions, four of which had three parts each. Six types of information were gathered:

1. Types of information collected in each stage of the product life cycle.
2. Problems in gathering and using information.
3. System used to gather and relay information.
4. Role of expatriates in information gathering.
5. Types of decisions used in information gathered by the international sales force.
6. Differences in using sales forces internationally versus locally for gathering data.

---

[31] Adapted from Lawrence B. Chonko, John F. Tanner Jr. and Ellen Reid Smith (Winter 1991). "Selling and Sales Management in Action: The Sales Force Role in International marketing research and Marketing Information Systems", *Journal of Personal Selling & Sales Management*, XI (1).

RESULTS

The three types of decisions used were: sales forecasting, product design, and company/product image. 71% of companies surveyed used sales force information for sales forecasting. Only 35% used it for product design and 46% for company or product image-making.

PROBLEMS IN GATHERING AND USING INTERNATIONAL MARKET DATA

One-third of the participants reported situational problems, 40% reported sales force problems. Many felt that data may not be accurate if its use is perceived as too broad or too local to be of value. These problems could arise due to situational limitations or problems with the sales force.

INFORMATION COLLECTION AND DISSEMINATION

Companies used written questionnaires (32% of the sample), informal phone conversations (25% of the sample), and continuous communication (26% being written, telephone, and face-to-face). Periodic reports were mentioned most often (30%), but only one company used a monthly newsletter. The formats in which findings are presented include summarized data (30%), along with guidelines and suggestions (30%).

It was assumed that executives knew the best way to communicate findings to salespeople, but may be unable to implement their system. Respondents were asked what they thought was the optimal technique for communicating findings. It was felt that the frequency with which data was relayed to the marketing office could contribute to success. Daily or weekly communication (telephone and telex) contributed to more timely information and understanding. Of the companies who felt their company's information system was good, their reasons were:

- Open communications between sales force and marketers
- Regular meetings between sales force and marketers
- Continuous exchange of information
- Flexibility of system to meet changing market
- Autonomy of sales force to make independent decisions
- It is one of the best
- We are good at it all
- The sales force is our only touch with the consumers

GROWTH PHASE

Companies use their sales force for gathering information on competition and any new market requirements. Two companies felt this was the most important phase for using a sales force. The first one gathered information on service needs and satisfaction once the product was in place. The second one concentrated on customer likes and dislikes of its product and of competition. Essential market data which sales people collect during the growth phase include:

- Competitor information
- New market requirements
- Customer surveys

- Product quality and features
- Relationship of company with end consumer
- Which areas are most profitable
- Whether or not to expand
- Volume versus start-up costs to determine growth size
- Distributor survey for customer satisfaction index.

MATURITY PHASE

Few companies considered themselves mature. One felt use of sales at this point was vital because of considerable investment of capital. Another company felt that it could be an *early warning system* for competition. Essential market information which salespeople collect during the maturity phase include:

- Competitive information
- Government data on product usage
- Type of businesses using the product
- Improved means of distribution
- Customers' desire for product changes
- New customer needs
- What new products could replace mature product
- Product weaknesses

INTERNATIONAL AND DOMESTIC DIFFERENCE

When asked to elaborate on the common differences between international and domestic sales forces, respondents replied that informational differences found in foreign countries included:

- Not as much information available.
- Information being harder to obtain.
- Information being less reliable, resulting in the need for time-consuming cross-checking.
- Because of many complexities and increased competition in foreign market, there are more types of information needed.
- International sales depends more on relations, so there are more areas to monitor, and more representatives who need the information.
- Our US strategy is to copy, but increased competition internationally necessitates the need for more market information and market research for more aggressive market strategies.

Other respondents noted that the differences lie in the sales force personnel.

USING AN US EXPATRIATE

Of the respondents, eight did not use expatriates and 10 used both expatriates and foreign salespeople. The use of expatriates is not a universal process. Data indicate that many practices are in use.

CONCLUSIONS AND IMPLICATIONS

A study of US export market research reported that companies typically had information overload and that information was frequently conflicting.[32] The study under focus shows that multinational companies frequently use international salespeople as sources for both marketing intelligence and research data. It was felt that more multinational companies should consider their salespeople for product design information.

In general, salespeople play a more significant role in the market entry stage than in the domestic marketing cycle because of proximately to the markets, a position not easily attainable by marketers located outside the foreign country. The main reasons for multinational companies to rely more on international sales force than domestic sales forces for market data include:

- Foreign published data is often unreliable, necessitating primary information gathering for cross-checking.
- US management does not understand foreign customers or foreign sales techniques to make effective educated decisions on market strategy.
- International sales in many countries rely more on relations so that more information areas need monitoring and more people in the marketing and sales process need the information.
- In a volatile market, close monitoring of the market may only be possible through use of the sales force, since by the time the information was released, it would be obsolete.
- The increased complexity and competition in foreign marketing result in more information being needed to formulate successful marketing strategies.
- Too often, domestic strategy is copied, but increased competition in international markets necessitates the need for more information and marketing research by the sales force to design *aggressive* marketing strategies.

In the ultimate analysis, multinational companies believe that regular input from the international always force is needed and they benefit from the close working relationship between international salespeople and marketers.

Tasty Burgers should also be concerned about other related industries that supply materials required for the running of a fast-food chain. Because food items are generally perishable, they must identify reliable sources that are also at reasonable proximities from the outlets. Tasty Burgers would have to look for availability of trays, plates, cutlery, containers, and bags. These items, however, can be transported from distant locations if need arises.

Another important aspect is the availability of suitable locations in all these countries. The outlets must be located at places that are frequented by a lot of people, and yet, the real estate prices should not eat into the profits. The company should also consider the product modifications and the pricing required to corner a fair market share.

A decision has to be made about the mode of entry into the markets that are considered profitable. As mentioned in the chapter, there are four possible modes of entry to international markets—exports, licensing/franchising, joint ventures, and partly or wholly owned

---

[32] Cavusgil S. Tamer, "Guidelines for Export Market Research," *Business Horizons*, 1985, 28(6), 27–33.

subsidiaries. The fast-food industry has historically worked on setting up franchises; however, Tasty Burgers should look into legal, political, and cultural issues in each of the countries that have been selected for entry. They must identify partners who are willing to adhere to the moral and ethical standards set by Tasty Burgers in the US.

Tasty Burgers has to conduct research that answers several strategic questions so as to determine the price and positioning of the product. The first step will be to test if the product will be accepted in its present form or if any modifications have to be made in each of the foreign markets. Local eating habits and religious sentiments have to be taken into account. Researchers will then have to determine the price that consumers are willing to pay for the product. The existing fast-food chains can be used as a point of reference in this matter. The advertising media has to be researched, and the most cost-effective way of introducing and promoting Tasty Burgers will have to be worked out.

Based on the research results, Tasty Burgers should decide if they want to use the sprinkler strategy or the waterfall strategy in these countries. Both the strategies have their benefits and drawbacks. If Tasty Burgers adopts the waterfall strategy, they will be rolling out their investments in a phased manner. They can learn from their mistakes in one city and avoid making the same costly blunders in all other cities; however, with this kind of approach, competitors may beat them at opening outlets in new cities that could turn out to be very profitable. With the sprinkler strategy, Tasty Burgers preserve their first mover advantage, but could end up making the same costly mistakes in all the cities, multiplying their losses many times.

The next stage will be the problem orientation of Tasty Burgers. The corporate attitude dictates this to a great extent. They could set up all their outlets in these foreign markets exactly the same way as their US outlets—the ethnocentric approach. They could decide to customize their product and management strategies in these countries—the polycentric approach. They could also decide to take it on a case-by-case basis and make changes that are absolutely necessary—the geocentric approach. However, the success of Tasty Burgers depends on their ability to adapt their products to meet consumer preferences in each of these countries, as shown by marketing research.

One factor that could be a detriment to the success of Tasty Burgers is the SRC. Management cannot work under the assumption that the factors that led to the success of Tasty Burgers in the US will help them achieve their goals in international markets.

SUMMARY

This chapter deals with the first stages of the global marketing research process, namely, identifying the needs of the firm, defining the problem, and deciding the unit of analysis. The firm will have to decide on the information requirements for it to set up business in international markets. Once this has been decided, the research objective will have to be drawn and the problem will have to be defined in precise terms, making allowance for biases like the SRC. The firm will then have to decide on the unit of analysis—whether it wishes to target one country, one region, or go global. The mode of entry for each of these markets will have to be decided. There are four choices available to companies to set up business in international markets—exporting, licensing, joint ventures, and wholly owned subsidiaries. Another aspect with regard to going international is whether to target many markets simultaneously or follow a more cautious approach and enter one market at a time. Marketing research is used to determine the best alternative. Once a decision to enter has been made, the firm will have to decide on the extent of customization that it needs to make to penetrate local markets in these countries. When making strategic decisions in foreign countries, researchers must bear in mind the problem of SRC——defining problems in a foreign culture in terms of one's native culture. The chapter discusses ways in which SRC can be avoided.

QUESTIONS AND PROBLEMS

1. Nuturama, a US-based health-focused fast-food chain, thinks there exists a market for their products in European countries. Explain the steps involved in the process of market selection.
2. Assume that research on market selection stated that Switzerland was the best market to start out with. What is the best mode of entry that can be adopted by Nuturama? List any assumptions that have been made to arrive at the mode of entry.
3. What are the information requirements for Nuturama in Switerland during the following phases of the product life cycle:
   a. Entry phase
   b. Growth phase
   c. Maturity phase
4. What are the various challenges researchers face when obtaining information for global marketing research?

5

Secondary Data Research

Companies usually understand that they need to conduct research to get a deeper insight into the problem at hand. But, where should you start? You possibly cannot test all hypotheses, answer all your questions with survey research. Researchers use secondary data as a starting point to get a deeper look into the problem itself. Secondary data refers to readily available data that was collected for a purpose other than solving the present problem. Other than being the most economical and easiest means of access to information, secondary data provides great direction to researchers, which is why it is recommended to conduct some secondary research prior to commissioning a primary research study. It provides a clear guidance to the researcher by pointing out the gaps in the information that is available, so that the discrepancies can be addressed with the help of primary data. It is tempting for managers to test everything with consumers; however, a lot of information is already collected by someone else that can be used efficiently, thereby reducing considerable amount of cost and time. The amount of data that is available can be overwhelming; therefore, it is a researcher's job to conduct a thorough search for secondary data sources in areas of interest and utilize data that is relevant to their research.

SOURCES OF SECONDARY DATA

Secondary data can be sourced either from the internal company records or from external information providers. The internal records of the company are the cheapest and the most relevant source for secondary data. External sources of information include government publications, trade journals, periodicals, newspapers, books, annual reports, store audits, consumer purchase panels, and many more. The usual procedure is to start with the most available, least expensive source. Figure 5.1 provides the classification of the sources of secondary data.

Internal Sources of Data

As the name suggests, this refers to the information that can be obtained within the organization. The advantages of using internal sources of information are: (a) easy availability, (b) continuous accessibility, and (c) pertinence. The internal sources data can be broadly classified into: operational database, customer feedback, and customer database.

FIGURE 5.1
CLASSIFICATION OF SECONDARY SOURCES OF DATA[1]

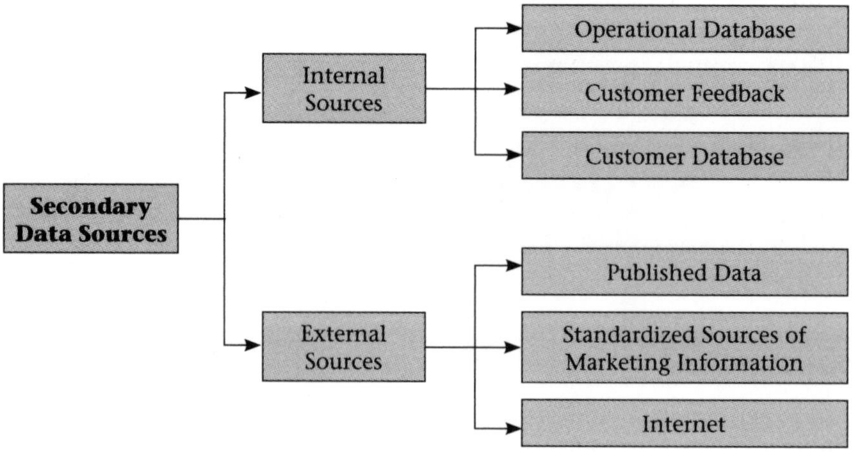

Operational Database

This database typically collates information from the accounting, marketing, and operations departments, and houses data at the company and customer levels. With advances in IT and supply chain management, customers are now more tightly tied to suppliers, thereby improving the timeliness and depth of the sales information available to managers. For instance, the integration of supply chain systems of Wal-Mart and P&G have enabled both companies to track, measure, and analyze their category performance and identify new ways to drive sales. This helps them with instant access to data regarding operations, sales, and customers.

Customer Feedback

This valuable source of information enables a company to listen to the customer and design product offerings that match their exact needs. This can be achieved by tracking information regarding product returns, service records, customer correspondence, customer suggestions, and complaint letters. This type of data offers a wealth of information as to the customer satisfaction levels and the awareness level of the products.

Customer Database

This database contains customer-level information that can be sorted and analyzed to produce useful information. Records of frequent customers and their transactions are maintained, and the companies use this data to find out what is common among its customers. A direct usage for such databases is in developing and implementing rewards programs. For instance, Stew Leonard's, the Connecticut-based grocery retailer, estimated that an average customer at their

---

[1] Adapted from Aaker et al., *Marketing Research*, 11th edition.

store spends around $100 a week, shops around 50 weeks a year, and remains in the area for around 10 years. So, in terms of customer value, Stew Leonard's is looking at around $50,000 annually from each of its customers.[2] This data can also be used to find out about customers' product preferences, form of payment, and so on. These customer databases are now being used extensively by marketing managers for formulating relationship marketing strategies.

External Sources of Data

External sources of data pertain to information sources located outside the organization. They can be broadly categorized as published data, standardized sources of marketing information, and the Internet.

Published Data

Published data are by far the most popular source of secondary information. Not only are the data readily available, often they are sufficient to answer the research question. However, the researcher is confronted with the problem of matching a specific need for information with a bewildering array of secondary data sources of variable and often indeterminate quality. It is, therefore, imperative for the researcher to undertake a flexible search procedure that will ensure that no pertinent source is overlooked, and then adhere to some general criteria for evaluating quality of data. The major published sources are the various government publications (federal, state, provincial, and local), periodicals and journals, and publicly available reports from such private groups as foundations, publishers, trade associations, unions, and companies. Of all these sources, the most valuable data for the marketing researcher come from government census information and various registration requirements. The census report typically includes births, deaths, marriages, income tax returns, unemployment records, export declarations, automobile registrations, and property tax records, among others.

Typically, governments of developed countries offer a wealth of useful data free of cost or for a very nominal charge. One of the most comprehensive sources of information is the National Trade Data Bank maintained by the US Department of Commerce. The best way to go about this is to start with the Annual Statistical Abstract of the US. This abstract contains a host of information, including population totals and trends, population projections, GDP, GNP, and much other useful information. The abstract's source notes provide more detailed information to a marketer. The Trade Information Center is a one-stop shop for providing information collected from 19 federal agencies. International trade specialists are available at the toll free number 1-800-USA-TRADE and provide assistance and advice to marketers on how to use government information.

Many other countries also provide trade data. If the information is published in the local language, embassies and consulates provide translations. Foreign embassies in Washington, DC will be able to provide a lot of useful information. There are international magazines targeting people who want to go international with their businesses. *The Statistical Yearbook* published by the United Nations contains trade data on products and information on exports and imports by country. The United Nations' Statistical Yearbook also provides information

---

[2] N. Hill and J. Alexander, *Handbook of Customer Satisfaction and Loyalty Measurement* (Hampshire: Gower Publishing Company, 2000), 2nd edition.

on worldwide demographics. The World Bank's World Atlas gives information on population, growth trends, and GDP. The World Bank also publishes a World Development Report that summarizes information on indicators such as life expectancy at birth and school enrollment in various countries. The Organization for Economic Cooperation and Development publishes quarterly and annual trade data on its member nations. The International Monetary Fund and the World Bank publish occasional staff papers discussing regional or country-specific issues in depth.

Standardized Sources of Marketing Information

These sources refer to the information commonly used for marketing research studies. The popular sources of information include store audits reports, consumer purchase panels, compilations, directories, Nielsen's television index, country guides, consulting research reports, and marketing databases. Retrieving information from these sources has also become easier over time. Recent advances in computer technology have resulted in more efficient methods of cataloging, storing, and retrieving published data. The growth in the number of databases available electronically through computers has been dramatic. It is estimated that over 5,000 online databases are available to researchers and analysts working in almost every area of business, science, law, education, and the social sciences. Some of the popular databases are ESOMAR, *The Economist*, Dun and Bradstreet Identifier, World Bank data, International Monetary Fund data, Standard and Poor's database, Data-Star, among others. Apart from the online versions of databases, the information is also now available for download and on CD-ROM. This provides the additional feature of data portability.

Internet

The Internet is an important tool that has added a new dimension to traditional marketing research intelligence. With volumes of relevant information available at the click of a mouse, decision making has assumed new dimensions. Also, the number of Internet users around the world is constantly growing. This has created a vast and expanding network of online resources such as online consumer reports and forums that provide valuable product information. Chapter 6 provides an in-depth coverage regarding Internet and its role in marketing research.

Increasingly, the ability to surf the Internet and its equivalents is essential to amassing pertinent data to support international trade decisions. Electronic databases accessible via the Internet carry marketing information ranging from latest news on product development to new writings in the academic and trade press, and updates in international trade statistics. There are also several profile analysis studies conducted that could help researchers analyze and target the potential customers in a better manner. For instance, the popular belief is that Japan is a homogeneous market and that there will either be mass response or no response. Psychographic analysis and segmentation of the Japanese market indicates otherwise. Ten segments have been identified and each of these segments can be targeted with custom programs.[3]

With such a wide variety of information sources available, the usual procedure to obtain secondary information is to start out with the most available and least expensive source. With

---

[3] Lewis C. Winters, "International Psychographics," *Marketing Research* (1992), vol. 4, pp. 48–49.

this as a reference point, the researcher can go from one source to another. However, the overall concentration should be on the relevancy of the information required.

SYNDICATED DATA SOURCES

Syndicated data is an important source of external data for global marketing research. Typically collected and compiled by commercial research firms using standardized procedures, such data sources provide rich information on a wide variety of topics regarding the industry, products, and firms. Since most of data compiled here is collected from the point of sale, it also reflects consumer preferences and sentiments. Further, such data sources also provide the benefit obtaining customized and tailored reports based on the client firm's requirements. Companies providing such data usually compile the data using one of the three ways—consumer panels, store audits, and scanner data. Many research organizations such as AC Nielsen and Information Resources, Inc. provide syndicated data in the US. For the purpose of marketing research, it becomes necessary for the researcher to identify syndicated data sources for the country of interest. There are many websites that provide information on sources of syndicated data in various countries.

Consumer panels are essentially samples of households that have agreed to share specific information over a long period of time, typically, information on product purchase information, buying habits, and media habits. The research firms *recruit* such households to share information regarding their purchase behavior through structured and standardized questionnaires. This collection of information typically occurs over a period of time whereby consumers report back on a weekly or monthly basis. After collecting substantial amount of data, the research firms sell it to their clients after sufficiently personalizing and tailoring it to meet the clients' research needs.

There are various companies that supply panel data, such as AC Nielsen, Information Resources Inc., TNS, and Synovate Consumer Opinion Panel.[4] Online panels are available from companies like Survey Sampling International (SSI), SSI's European subsidiary, Bloomerce Access Panels, Europe, Harris Interactive, E-Rewards.com, and Opinion Outpost. These sources are extremely helpful for any researcher as they are well-established resources. For instance, SSI has been in the business of creating and managing global online panels for 15 years. Measuring and tracking attitudes and behaviors has become extremely easy with these tools.[5] Moreover, SSI offers a lot of specialty panels like SSI Auto Pane, SSI Mother of Babies Panel, SSI Health and Patient Panel, SSI Mobile Panel, and the like, which enables businesses to reach their target segments efficiently. Exhibit 5.1 describes consumer profiles in Europe and Exhibit 5.2 talks about specific consumer categories in the UK.

---

[4] "Marketing Power AMA Resource," http://www.marketingpower.com/Community/ARC/Pages/Research/SecondaryData/PanelData.aspx (Retrieved on June 2, 2013).

[5] SSI Global Panel Book, http://www.surveysampling.com/ssi-media/Corporate/Fact-Sheets-2013/Global-Panel-Book-2013.image (Retrieved on June 2, 2013).

Exhibit 5.1

Geodemographic Profiling: MOSAIC and EuroMOSAIC[6]

Consumers can be classified in several ways: on the basis of personal demographics such as age and income, according to values and attitudes (psychographics), and on the basis of their behavior (behavior graphics). Geodemographic classifications group consumers together on the basis of the neighborhood they live in. The logic behind this is that neighborhoods that are similar across a wide range of demographic measures will offer similar potential across most products, brands, services, and media.

This type of classification has a number of advantages. Marketing researchers can obtain better representativeness and greater coverage for surveys by using preclassified profiles. These lists also provide flexibility as they can be used for a number of products and various activities. Speed is another big advantage offered by these lists. Availability of readymade segments will make it easier for marketing researchers to conduct surveys and other research studies. They also make it easy for researchers to extrapolate market potential across similar segments without having to repeat the studies.

Geodemographic classification exists for most countries in Western Europe, North America, and Australia. The size of a typical neighborhood cluster can vary from as little as 15 households in Great Britain to as many as 800 households in Sweden. A given segmentation could include statistics from the census, credit rating agencies, electoral registers, mail-order purchases, car registrations, and many other sources. For instance, in Great Britain, 80 separate measures were used to define 52 distinct MOSAIC types that were organized into 12 cluster groups. On the basis of the zip code, each household is allocated a MOSAIC code between 1 and 52. The MOSAIC distribution of population in Great Britain is given in Exhibit 5.2. Profiles are a very powerful tool and can be built in a number of ways as demonstrated below.

- Profiling the whole customer file against the Great Britain average to establish which MOSAIC types the majority of the consumers are likely to fall in.
- Profiling a customer file against a catchment base to establish which MOSAIC types are under- and over-represented compared to the areas in which customers live.
- Profiling one segment of a customer file against all customers to establish which MOSAIC types buy each of a range of different products sold.
- Profiling the average level of spending and sales to establish which MOSAIC types prove to be the most profitable customers.

The emergence of a single European market has meant that a number of companies are adopting marketing strategies for Europe as a whole. Hence, the profiling system has to be expanded to encompass all of Europe. EuroMOSAIC is a system that classifies 310 million individuals on the basis of the neighborhoods they live in. Global marketing researchers use this profiling to define their population and target segments. EuroMOSAIC identifies 10 different lifestyle categories that are consistent across all countries and are derived from 300 or more separate MOSAIC segments describing consumers in different European countries.

---

[6] Margaret Crimp and Len Tiu Wright, *The Marketing Research Process* (Harlow: Prentice Hall, 1995), 4th edition. Reprinted by permission of Pearson Education Ltd.

Exhibit 5.2

MOSAIC UK Groups[7]

Group	Description	% Population	% HHlds	Type	Description	% Population	% HHlds
A	Alpha territory	4.28	3.54	A01	Global power brokers	0.32	0.3
				A02	Voices of authority	1.45	1.18
				A03	Business class	1.83	1.5
				A04	Serious money	0.68	0.56
B	Professional rewards	9.54	8.23	B05	Mid-career climbers	2.9	2.3
				B06	Yesterday's captains	1.8	1.84
				B07	Distinctive success	0.48	0.48
				B08	Dormitory villagers	1.81	1.29
				B09	Escape to the country	1.41	1.31
				B10	Parish guardians	1.14	1.0
C	Rural solitude	4.84	4.4	C11	Squires among locals	1.01	0.85
				C12	Country-loving elders	1.32	1.31
				C13	Modern agribusiness	1.61	1.36
				C14	Farming today	0.53	0.53
				C15	Upland struggle	0.36	0.34
D	Small town diversity	9.21	8.75	D16	Side street singles	1.21	1.17
				D17	Jacks of all trades	2.6	1.99
				D18	Hardworking families	2.87	2.63
				D19	Innate conservatives	2.53	2.96
E	Active retirement	–	–	E20	Golden retirement	0.52	0.67
				E21	Bungalow quietude	1.42	1.79
				E22	Beachcombers	0.57	0.6
				E23	Balcony downsizers	0.9	1.29
F	Suburban mindsets	13.16	11.18	F24	Garden suburbia	2.82	2.14
				F25	Production managers	2.31	2.63
				F26	Mid-market families	3.75	2.7
				F27	Shop floor affluence	2.82	2.73
				F28	Asian attainment	1.45	0.98

---

[7] "Mosaic United Kingdom—A Report by Experian," 2009, http://www.experian.co.uk/assets/business-strategies/brochures/Mosaic_UK_2009_brochure.pdf (Retrieved on June 2, 2013).

Group	Description	% Population	% HHlds	Type	Description	% Population	% HHlds
G	Career and kids	5.34	5.78	G29	Footloose managers	1.11	1.67
				G30	Soccer dads and mums	1.34	1.34
				G31	Domestic comfort	1.24	1.09
				G32	Childcare years	1.46	1.52
				G33	Military dependents	0.19	0.17
H	New home-makers	3.99	5.91	H34	Buy-to-let territory	1.08	1.79
				H35	Brownfield pioneers	1.13	1.38
				H36	Foot on the ladder	1.48	2.37
				H37	First to move in	0.3	0.37
I	Ex-council community	10.6	8.67	I38	Settled ex-tenants	2.08	2.06
				I39	Choice right to buy	1.9	1.72
				I40	Legacy of labor	3.46	2.68
				I41	Stressed borrowers	3.15	2.2
J	Claimant cultures	4.52	5.16	J42	Worn-out workers	1.82	2.3
				J43	Streetwise kids	0.9	1.05
				J44	New parents in need	1.8	1.8
K	Upper floor living	4.3	5.18	K45	Small block singles	1.26	1.77
				K46	Tenement living	0.62	0.8
				K47	Deprived view	0.36	0.5
				K48	Multi-cultural towers	1.09	1.11
				K49	Re-housed migrants	0.97	0.99
L	Elderly needs	4.04	5.96	L50	Pensioners in blocks	0.89	1.31
				L51	Sheltered seniors	0.67	1.12
				L52	Meals on wheels	0.51	0.86
				L53	Low spending elders	1.98	2.68
M	Industrial heritage	7.39	7.4	M54	Clocking off	2.18	2.25
				M55	Backyard regeneration	2.4	2.06
				M56	Small wage owners	2.81	3.09
N	Terraced melting pot	6.54	7.02	N57	Back-to-back basics	2.5	1.97
				N58	Asian identities	1.06	0.88
				N59	Low-key starters	1.6	2.72
				N60	Global fusion	1.38	1.44

Group	Description	% Population	% HHlds	Type	Description	% Population	% HHlds
0	Liberal opinions	8.84	8.48	061	Convivial homeowners	1.74	1.68
				062	Crash pad professionals	1.41	1.09
				063	Urban cool	1.25	1.1
				064	Bright young things	1.36	1.52
				065	Anti-materialists	1.12	1.03
				066	University fringe	1.1	0.93
				067	Study buddies	0.87	1.14

Store audits are audit data collected by research firms wherein auditors from the research firm visit a sample of stores at fixed intervals for the purpose of counting stocks and recording deliveries to estimate retail sales. These store audit results then are projected—to arrive at nationwide and regional estimates of total sales, inventories, and so forth—and reported to the client at specified time periods (usually every six to eight weeks). During each store visit, the auditor also may collect such observable information as shelf prices, display space, the presence of special displays, and in-store promotion activities.

Scanner data include data on retail purchases covering information on the product, the price, and any other in-store promotion data. The scanner data are used mainly to study the behavior of the consumer when different elements of the marketing mix are varied. They are also used to study and forecast the sales of a new product. Even retailers are using scanner data to conduct experiments that would advise them on the various pricing options and optimum price at which they can maximize their total contribution. Retailers such as Wal-Mart and Safeway are pioneers in implementing insights from scanner data into their retail strategy. For instance, Safeway used scanner data to test alternative placement of products within a store. Results showed, for example, that foil-packaged sauce mixes should not be displayed together, but should be spread around the store according to their contents (e.g., spaghetti sauce mix near bottled spaghetti sauce, gravy mix near canned gravy, and so on).

Marketers experience a lot of confusion when trying to learn to decide where to enter the global arena, what to sell, and how to sell it.[8] The organization must collect and analyze pertinent information to support the basic go/no-go decision before getting into the issues addressed by conventional marketing research. The key to accomplishing this is to make effective use of secondary research. Secondary research will not answer all the specific questions that a marketer may have, but when it is done right, it is a low-cost way to shed light on macro-decisions that should be made before moving on to the next steps in the research process.

---

[8] Michael R. Czinkota, "Take a Short-Cut to Global Research," *Marketing News*, March 13, 1995, p. 3.

ELECTRONIC POINT OF SALE (EPOS) SCANNING

Bar-coding, computerized information, radio frequency identification (RFID) tags, QR codes, and more recently mobile checkouts are all part of the changing trend in the retail auditing. Apart from helping retailers manage their sales and inventory management processes, such technologies are good sources of secondary data that companies can use. In countries like the US and Canada, EPoS data is widely used to research purposes also. Consumer panels are recruited to track purchase patterns. Consumers are asked to present an electronic card at the checkout counter and the sale is recorded. This data helps researchers study buying habits of people across different demographic sections, as well as discerning brand loyalty, switching patterns, and impact of promotions on sales.

The RFID tags are a step above the point of sale scanners. To check out, customers just have to roll their loaded shopping cart past an RFID scanner. In less than a second, the scanner would scan the information on every item in the cart. In fact, shoppers can also walk past the RFID scanner even after bagging their items and still have their items scanned, thereby reducing the checkout time. Although instant checkout sounds like a technological benefit every shopper would appreciate right away, RFID tags on groceries have not caught on. The reason for this is the high cost of the tiny tag components and the slender margins of grocery product manufacturers. So while the supermarket industry led the way in the adoption of bar codes, other industries will lead the way to the adoption of RFID tags. Supermarket shoppers can be certain that the cost of the RFID tags will steadily decrease and will eventually be financially viable to be included in the product.

Another technological evolution in the point of sale gadgets is the shopping buddy. Developed by IBM, the shopping buddy is equipped with a scanner that lets shoppers save time by scanning items as they add them to the cart, bag the groceries themselves, and head to the checkout counters. Stop & Shop was one of the first grocery retailers to try out this technology in 2003. The retailer activated the shopping buddy with a Stop & Shop card that was equipped to retrieve customers' past shopping history, help shoppers find specific products, and allow customers to order deli items without waiting in line.

The introduction of QR codes was another major development in the point of sale technology. Originally created for the Japanese automobile industry, the QR code system quickly spread to other industries as they enabled fast readability and greater storage capacity compared to standard barcodes. Now QR codes are being used in wide range of industries and their various applications such as logistics, manufacturing bases, inventory management, consumer advertising, and marketing, among others.

In the field of marketing, QR codes have been designed to contain useful information such as URL for a website, or some basic product information, thereby securing easy and effortless access to the product information. QR codes storing such information may appear in magazines, on signs, on buses, on business cards, or on almost any object about which users might need information. Users with a camera phone equipped with the correct reader application can scan the image of the QR code to display text, contact information, connect to a wireless network, or open a web page in the phone's browser. A recent study by comScore found that 14 million mobile users in the US (or 6.2% of the total mobile audience) scanned a QR code on their mobile device in June 2011. The study also found that a mobile user that scanned a QR code during the month was more likely to be male (60.5% of code-scanning audience), aged between 18 and 34 years (53.4%), and have a household income of $100k or above (36.1%).

Further, the study found that users are most likely to scan codes found in newspapers/ magazines and on product packaging, and do so while at home or in a store.[9]

Capitalizing on the mobile revolution, an increasing number of mobile applications for point of sale purposes are being developed. Recently, Stop & Shop launched an in-store handheld scanner named *Scan It! Mobile* that allows customers to use their mobile device to scan and bag their groceries while they shop. The scanner operates via an app on the iPhone® 3GS or 4G, and allows customers to complete an entire shopping trip on their mobile devices. This mobile application by Stop & Shop is based on their original *Scan It!* application that was launched in 2007. The *Scan It!* was an upgrade over the shopping buddy and provided shoppers with a smaller handheld device to scan items and receive personalized offers.[10] As the mobile technology expands, we can expect more such applications to enter the marketplace.

USES OF SECONDARY DATA

Secondary data can be used by researchers in many ways. This type of data is most suited for the following applications:[11]

Estimation of Demand

Companies typically earmark valuable marketing resources based on the region, segment, or territory. When companies assess the potential of each customer segment they cater to, allocation of resources is done in relation with each of the customer segments. For instance, Ford is spending more than $1 billion in an effort to bolster its Lincoln brand. Toward this end, they have realized that producing better cars alone would not suffice. They have identified that a luxury car-buying experience that will attract younger, better-educated, and wealthier buyers holds the key. For a brand that has customers primarily in the seventies and eighties age bracket, Ford is going after a much younger customer segment in addition to satisfying their preferred attributes of customers—having a median income of $143,000 and college-educated.[12]

The estimation of demand can be done in two ways. The first method is from the desegregated sales data about the industry. This method is known as the *direct data method*. The sales information required for this method may come from government sources, industry surveys, or trade associations. However, such data are useful for establishing relative market potentials only if the sales can be broken down by the organization's sales or operating territories, as this permits a direct comparison of the share of company sales and industry sales in each territory. For instance, Gartner research firm reports that worldwide PC shipments amounted to 79.2 million units in the first quarter of 2013. Of this, HP accounts for 11.7 million units, Lenovo 11.7 million units, Dell 8.3 million units, and Acer Group 6.8 million units. Further, this first

---

[9] "14 Million Americans Scanned QR Codes on their Mobile Phones in June 2011," *comScore. Inc.*, August 12, 2011.

[10] "Ready, Set, Scan: Stop & Shop Launches Scan It! Mobile App," Stop & Shop Press Release, July 7, 2011.

[11] Aaker et al., *Marketing Research*, 11th edition.

[12] Craig Trudell, "Lincoln Tries Cheese to Lure Mercedes Buyers to Showrooms," *Bloomberg*, June 13, 2013.

quarter performance represents an 11.2% decline in the number of shipments compared to the first quarter of 2012.[13]

In the second method known as the *corollary data method*, the absence of industry sales data for each territory is compensated by using another variable, that is (a) available for each sales territory or region, and (b) correlated highly with the sales of the product. For example, the territory demand for child-care services or baby food is correlated highly with the number of births in the area during the previous three years. Thus, the share of births in all geographic areas within the territory of interest would be a good proxy for the relative market potential within that territory.

Scanning the Competitive Environment

Secondary data helps companies keep track of the important market developments and trends in the marketplace. Given the ever-changing market dynamics, companies will benefit immensely by keeping themselves abreast of the changes in attitudes, fashions, fads, and changes in legislation, among others. This calls for closely following newspapers, general magazines, industry magazines, and periodicals. For instance, the Indian government recently announced that global retailers entering India will not be able to use the franchise route to set up shop, and that the front-end stores set up by the multi-brand retailers (such as Tesco, Carrefour, Wal-Mart) will have to be company-owned and -operated. Further, the foreign retailers will be required to compulsorily place 50% of their investments in back-end infrastructure specifically for their retail chain.[14] For companies like Tesco, Carrefour, and Wal-Mart that have operations in India, keeping track of information such as this will help them plan their investment routes and local logistics.

Segmentation and Targeting

The strategy of market segmentation permits companies to better deal with competition in the marketplace by differentiating their offerings. The product offerings are typically differentiated upon price, packaging, promotion, distribution, and service, among others. Segmenting the market can be done on the basis of geography (e.g., region, city, and climate), demography (e.g., age, gender, income, education, and occupation), psychography (e.g., needs, attitudes, perception, and lifestyle), sociocultural factors (e.g., religion, race, and culture), usage situation (e.g., personal, fun, and gift), time of usage (e.g., work, leisure, day, and night), and benefit (e.g., convenience, economy, and social acceptance).

Effective segmentation demands that firms group their customers into relatively homogeneous groups. In the US setting, the *North American Industry Classification System* and *Dun's Market Identifiers* are used by companies selling industrial goods to segment their markets. In India, the *RK SWAMY BBDO Guide to Urban Markets* uses around 18 variables to develop market indices for over 750 towns with a population over 50,000 that accounts for around 77% of the urban population. Similarly, *MICA Rural Market Ratings* uses six variables to develop market

---

[13] Venkatesh Ganesh, "How HP is Trying to Stay Relevant in Devices Space," *Business Line*, July 9, 2013.

[14] "Govt Nixes Franchise Route for Multi-Brand Retail Stores; Clarifies Sourcing Norms," *Business Line*, June 6, 2013.

ratings for 459 districts in India. With the help of such compilations, companies can appropriately segment the market.

Developing a Business Intelligence (BI) System

A BI system contains data on the environment and the competitors. It forms an integral part of the marketing decision support system. Both primary and secondary data form a part of the BI system. Gartner research has reported that global BI, corporate performance management, and analytics applications/performance management software revenue amounted to $13.1 billion in 2012, representing only a slight growth of 6.8% from 2011. The findings also identified the following five key market dynamics that affected BI software spends and growth in 2012: (a) tough macroeconomic situation and confusion regarding the definition of analytics, (b) involvement of big data and BI, (c) BI spending moving outside of IT, (d) data discovery becoming a mainstream architecture, and (e) software as a service.[15] With such a dynamic marketplace, it is important to have an advanced BI system that tracks all the relevant information about the marketplace to place the companies ahead of the competition.

ADVANTAGES OF SECONDARY DATA

In today's times, the most significant advantage of secondary data is its accessibility and availability. It is very easily accessible and widely available to every marketer/researcher, some at a fee and others free of cost. Moreover, it is extremely quick when using online retrieving techniques. Other major benefits that secondary data offer a researcher are savings in cost and time. The process involved in collecting secondary data is fairly straightforward. The researcher needs to spend some time in a library or on the Internet looking for related sources of data. Even if the data had to be bought from another agency, it would still work out cheaper than collecting primary data in a foreign country. Secondary data can warn the researcher that the project is not feasible or financially viable even before more time and money is spent in primary data collection.

In some cases, secondary data may be the only recourse available for conducting research. For instance, ascertaining the market demand for hybrid cars in the emerging economies by gathering primary data may be a tough proposition. Instead, secondary data available on this will be of valuable assistance to the researcher. Similarly, data on historical trends and occurrences can be obtained only through secondary data. Further, when competitive information regarding sales and profit figures is needed, secondary sources such as trade publications and industry reports would be better suited to get this data than the competitors themselves.

DISADVANTAGES OF SECONDARY DATA

Secondary data does have some disadvantages.[16] A critical shortcoming is the data not being collected to answer the specific question the researcher has. Also, at a global stage, availabil-

---

[15] "Global Biz Intelligence, CPM Software Revenue at $13 bn in 2012: Gartner," *Business Line*, June 6, 2013.

[16] This section is adapted from Cateora, *International Marketing*, 9th edition.

ity of secondary data is still an issue. The US and most developed nations have an extensive array of secondary data that are collected through various government and private sources; however, developing countries do not have agencies that collect data on a regular basis. Hence, accessing even basic information like income, wholesale and retail prices for goods and services, and telephone numbers may prove to be a challenge.

Even if secondary data is available, it may not have the level of accuracy that is needed for confident decision making. Some of the statistics may be too optimistic, reflecting national pride rather than practical reality. In many countries, businesses falsely report relevant figures like income and sales to avoid taxation. In some cases, errors are intentional; in some others, they are a result of sloppy recording.[17] It is necessary for researchers to harbor healthy skepticism about secondary data collected from foreign countries regardless of the source of the data.

In a lot of countries, especially the developing countries, data may be outdated and may have been collected on an infrequent and unpredictable schedule. Rapid changes in the global economy make it necessary that the data be current. Even if some countries were collecting reliable data on a regular basis in the recent past, there is no historical data available to compare and study the trends.

Another related problem with secondary data is the method in which data is collected and reported. There is a lot of variation in these aspects between countries. It becomes impossible to compare data between countries when conducting a multi-country study.

Secondary data must be checked and interpreted carefully for it to be of any use to the research study. It is extremely difficult to validate data that has been collected from some countries. The researcher has to find out who collected the data and how it was collected. Further, the research also has to investigate if there was any reason for the data to be misrepresented and check if it is internally consistent and logical in light of known sources and market factors. This can be a very challenging task in global marketing research. Exhibit 5.3 presents the lack of reliability in China's economic data.

PROBLEMS IN COLLECTING SECONDARY DATA

All the problems that researchers face in domestic marketing research tend to be exacerbated in global marketing research. There is a general dearth of statistical summary data, especially in less-developed countries with primitive statistics and research services. Even in countries that do provide data sources, there is the problem of comparability of data. For example, in Germany, the expense incurred in buying a television would be classified as entertainment expense, whereas in the US, it would be classified as furniture expense. Even when referring to certain terms, different countries have different meanings. For instance, the term *supermarket* in a Japanese context typically refers to two- or three-storey buildings that sell food products, products for daily needs, and clothing on each floor. Some of these stores even sell furniture, electric home appliances, stationery, and have a restaurant. The supermarket in the American context is, however, very different from the Japanese context.

More comparability problems arise in the way different foreign countries process statistical data. Table 5.1 provides the standard age categories for classifying statistical data covering consumer purchase in four different countries.

---

[17] Tom Lester, "Common Markets," *Marketing*, November 9, 1989, p. 41.

Exhibit 5.3

China's Economic Data Raises More Questions[18]

A recently published report by the US–China Economic and Security Review Commission on the reliability of China's economic data reveals that China's official statistics are not as reliable as those produced in the US and Europe.

Specifically, the statistics suffer from three deficiencies—gathering, measurement, and presentation of data. First, the way the Chinese government gathers the data is not complete, that is, the sample surveys gathered to measure the economy do not cover the services and private sector. Second, the measurement of data is found wanting in many areas as the methods of statistical work that are adopted vary across reporting units in China's economy. Further, there is a lack of transparency about the weights used to calculate inflation, and the consumer price index does not adequately factor in the role of the Chinese service sector and private industry. Finally, the presentation of data is also questionable as China's statistics frequently undergo substantial revisions even after they are made public.

In addition to this, manipulation of data remains an important cause of unreliable statistics. In the enterprise sector, for instance, both private and state-owned enterprises have incentives to misreport income and output—in some cases to avoid taxes and regulation, in other cases to appease officials. Further, when the data is cross-checked with other economic indicators the inconsistency in the data shows up. For example, nominal GDP published at the provincial and national levels does not always add up, and the different measures of national output—the production and expenditure methods—are contradictory as well.

This problem of unreliable data is especially relevant in the international research context when viewed from the words of Li Keqiang, then a regional Communist Party head, in 2007. The current Premier's comments, revealed in a diplomatic cable published by WikiLeaks in late 2010, reveal that the figures that go into China's gross domestic product are *man-made* and *for reference only*. Comments such as these only highlight the lack of transparency and reliability of data that continues to bog China's progress toward a more open, transparent, and market-oriented economy.

These differences and difficulties among countries often mean that multiple markets must be researched, including poorer countries where a profit potential is questionable, rather than a single large market, like the US.

EVALUATING THE VALUE OF RESEARCH

Before proceeding with the research, it is necessary to have an estimate for the value of information, that is, the value of obtaining answers to research questions. This will help the company decide how much, if anything at all, should be spent on the research. The value of

---

[18] Iacob N. Koch-Weser, "The Reliability of China's Economic Data: An Analysis of National Output," US–China Economic and Security Review Commission Staff Research Project, January 28, 2013; "China Economic Data Questioned as Electricity Use Slows," *Bloomberg News*, July 13, 2012.

TABLE 5.1
AGE CLASSIFICATION ACROSS COUNTRIES[19]

Australia	India	Turkey	USA
Under 15 years	Under 6 years	Under 14 years	Under 5 years
15–44 years	7–14 years	15–64 years	5–17 years
45–64 years	15–59 years	65 years and over	18–24 years
65 years and over	60 years and over		25–44 years
			45–64 years
			65 years and over

research will depend on the importance of the decision that is to be based on the information, the uncertainty surrounding the situation, and the influence of the research information on the decision. It stands to reason that if the decision is likely to have significant impact on the long-term plans of the organization, it would be deemed very valuable. By the same logic, if the outcomes already known with certainty and the research information will not have any impact on the decision, the information will have no value.

These concepts are better illustrated by a simple example. Consider the decision to introduce a new product. The uncertainty in this case is whether or not the product is going to succeed. The probability of success is given as 0.6 and the probability of failure is given as 0.4. Country A and Country B represent two scenarios faced by the company.

	Success	Failure
Country A		
Introduce	$4 million	$1 million
Do not introduce	$0	$0
Country B		
Introduce	$4 million	–$2.5 million
Do not introduce	$0	$0

If the product is introduced in Country A, irrespective of the uncertainty involved with the success or failure of the product, the firm makes money. If the product succeeds in the market, the firm makes $4 million, and if it fails, the company makes $1 million. This is a straightforward decision—the company should introduce the product. Any research conducted to get the exact success and failure probabilities will not add value to the decision. This is a case where research does not have any value.

However, in Country B, the firm cannot make an unequivocal decision to introduce the product. If the product fails in the market, the firm could sustain a loss of $2.5 million. In this scenario, if research information can give perfect information about the success or failure of the product, it can save the company $2.5 million in the event that the product fails. Given

[19] Australian Census Bureau; Office of the Registrar General and Census Commissioner, India; Turkish Statistical Institute; United States Census Bureau.

the existing information with the probability of failure being 0.4, the value of perfect information will be 0.4 times $2.5 million, that is, $1 million. Since market information is unlikely to be perfect, the actual value of the information will be less than $1 million. The value of information will be dependent on the company's opinions on the probability of success and failure of its products.

GUIDELINES FOR EFFECTIVE ONLINE SECONDARY DATA RESEARCH

Secondary research can be daunting for a lot of companies at first. But, there is merit in exploring this area before investing huge time and capital in primary research. There is a likely chance that someone else has conducted a similar research that can provide great insights to you. As discussed earlier, there are huge advantages to using secondary research. With the advancements in technology, conducting secondary research has become a lot simpler due to the easy access to online information. However, it is definitely challenging to mine the right kind of information due to the variety and variability of the available content.

Internet is the most trusted companion of most researchers today. Internet provides a great platform to search for all the relevant research conducted by others at the click of a button. As we know, Google dominates the Internet search market today. Google's simple yet effective offering has made it the leader of the market. At the onset of any project, a researcher can search for information, content, or reports that can guide them to results or data that they can use to conduct further analysis.

While search is an easy and effective tool, it is quite a challenge to search for relevant content online. It is important to understand the logic behind how the search engines search the web pages to be able to use the resources effectively. For instance, Google provides information to enhance your searching experience and improve your search in their support section;[20] use of quotes returns the search results for the exact word/phrase and use of (–) dash before a word excludes the word from your search (especially useful to find words that have totally different meaning, for instance, Apple computers versus Apple fruit).

Although most people depend on the Internet to throw results instantly, to get richer information, one needs to know where to look. It is good to insert those news sources or websites or journals that you think might carry the kind of information you are looking for. Moreover, the use of words *statistics, research, reports, survey, study,* etc. can enrich your search results while looking for secondary data. There are various resources available that can be of great help to marketers while starting the secondary research. Some of these are:[21]

- Whitepapers, articles, research reports, or survey results found on trade publication and trade associations' websites
- Trade publication and trade association-sponsored webinars
- Federal and State Census reports segmented by industry and business type
- Reports available online from providers like IbisWorld, Mintel, Business Source Complete, etc. Some of these reports could be at a fee while others are free. Institutions

---

[20] Google Help, https://support.google.com/websearch/answer/136861 (Retrieved on June 2, 2013).

[21] J. Castanzo, "Tips for Conducting Secondary Research Online," August 2, 2011, http://www.godfrey.com/How-We-Think/B2B-Insights-Blog/Research/Tips-for-Conducting-Secondary-Research-Online.aspx (Retrieved on June 2, 2013).

like ESOMAR also have reports published frequently that can provide a broad under-standing of the industry, country, or a particular region that may be of interest to the marketer. Also, companies like "Pew Internet and American Life" explore the impact of the Internet on citizens in general. These are just a few examples of the resources avail-able to a researcher to explore and exploit while conducting secondary research online

- Practitioners and seasoned researchers write blogs that can provide great insights to a marketer or a researcher. It is possible to subscribe (RSS) to news sources like, say, CNN, BBC, New York Times, etc., as well as blogs that might be of relevance to your industry or business. The RSS feature channels the content that you are interested in to you in an efficient manner
- Social media and mobile play a significant role in the amount of data generated today. These can be a great source for companies to gain insights on the qualitative aspects of the product/service or an issue

Although search is a powerful and a useful tool, the research should guard himself against some of the disadvantages of Internet. Authenticity and validity of the reports, articles, or whitepapers should be looked at by the researcher. Moreover, copyright issues could arise if care is not taken while using the reports for your use. Citing the source provides more cred-ibility to the user.

GLOBAL MARKETING RESEARCH IN PRACTICE

Continuing with the example of Tasty Burgers wanting to enter UK, Brazil, India, and Saudi Arabia, this chapter takes a look at conducting secondary research. The first step in secondary research is to obtain general data on all these countries. This would include economic data such as GNP/GDP and per capita income; political data, such as stability of the government and the legal system in each of these countries; infrastructure availability, such as transporta-tion, communication, and advertising media, the social structure; and the attitude of people toward foreign products. This will give researchers a feel for the viability of each of these coun-tries as potential expansion markets. There are many sources from which this information can be obtained. The embassies of these countries in the US would be a good place to start. Many magazines and trade journals will also carry information on business climates in foreign countries. Another potentially good source is the Internet. Conducting secondary research on the Internet is explained in great detail in Chapter 6. There are many websites that contain country statistics and demographics. The onus of verifying the authenticity of the source and the information is on the researcher. It is always best to collect the same information from multiple sources and crosscheck them. This way the possibility of error is minimized. It must be borne in mind that secondary data will not always be in a format that the researcher wants, and hence, they may not always be comparable. Some of the sources that can be used have been mentioned earlier in this chapter.

It is also important to obtain information on competing products and other local and foreign fast-food chains that have set up business in these countries. This will help Tasty Burgers decide if the products they offer need to be modified for any of these countries. If other American fast-food chains have already set up business in any of these countries, it is necessary that Tasty Burgers find out their market share and profit margins. This will be required to decide if that particular market can support another fast-food chain. Information about suppliers and distribution networks and potential franchise costs will also have to be obtained. It is possible to sign up for a multi-client study with one of the information providers in the US. It may also be beneficial to contact information brokers in each of these countries and contract them to gather data.

The key in secondary research is to consider the costs of gathering data and compare that against the future potential benefits. Secondary data is a useful place to start but, as mentioned earlier, is neither completely accurate nor is it available in the exact format that researchers want. A cost–benefit analysis has to be performed before deciding the time and resources to be spent in gathering secondary data.

SUMMARY

This chapter deals with secondary data—its sources, advantages, and drawbacks. It is important to note that the sources of secondary data are numerous and this book mentions only a selected few. This chapter should have convinced the reader of the importance of looking into various secondary data sources before launching the research study. Many research studies can be undertaken with the wealth of information available from the company's internal records or other secondary data sources. With the growing power of computers and the Internet, accessing data is becoming very easy. It is possible for researchers to obtain a list of marketing research companies in the country of interest to them.

Secondary data have many advantages and disadvantages. They are relatively cheap in that they can be obtained in a short span of time. In many cases, they help decision making without having to resort to primary research. Past history and consumer behavior data can be obtained only through secondary research. On the other hand, there is lack of adequate secondary data that is authentic. Many developing countries have data that is outdated or inaccurate. There is also the problem of comparison of data that has been collected from different countries. It is important that a cost–benefit study be performed to ensure that the benefits of collecting secondary data outweigh the costs.

QUESTIONS AND PROBLEMS

1. Obtain sales information for a particular industry as well as all the sales for all major firms in that industry in 2013 through the use of secondary data sources. After computing the market shares of these major firms, obtain information on the market shares of these same firms using another source. What are the differences? Why do they exist?
2. Suppose you are opening a new retail store that will sell sporting equipment and clothing. What secondary data are available in your area to help you decide where to locate the store? Would the same data be relevant to someone opening a Sport and Fitness Center?
3. After obtaining the data for coffee consumption in the US, calculate the country's per capita consumption of coffee and compare it to that of France. Is there are notable difference? If so, what accounts for it?

4. Of the products listed below, for which industry associations would it beneficial to contact in order to obtain secondary data?
   a. Smartphones
   b. Imported liquors
   c. Hybrid vehicles
   d. Foreign rugs
   e. Frozen dinner packages.
5. If Tasty Burgers moves forward with its expansion plan towards the UK, Brazil, India, and Saudi Arabia, what are certain elements of competitors that they must evaluate? How will secondary data sources be useful in this case?

6

Marketing Research on the Internet

INTRODUCTION

The unprecedented expansion of Internet and its users has taken a lot of people by surprise. In 2013, 41% of world's households are connected to the Internet according to the latest ITU report "The World in 2013."[1] Half of these users come from developing countries. This is exciting for companies planning to expand their business in international shores. The world is now open for trade with huge number of prospective consumers waiting to benefit from the best of products and services that companies have to offer. Although the staggering growth of Internet is visible in developed countries, the scenario in developing countries is slightly different. Of the households without Internet connections, 90% come from developing countries. However, the trend is encouraging enough for marketers to indulge in online trade. Table 6.1 highlights some interesting facts and statistics that illustrate the progress of the Internet in the past 10 years.[2]

While Internet is reshaping the business world by enabling e-commerce and communication across national borders, the mobile revolution has taken it to the next level. With constant innovations in mobile technology like the location-based services, companies now have newer ways to conduct business. Interaction with their customers has changed from a one-way communication to a two-way channel. Customers are constantly communicating their preferences and opinions via different media online. Moreover, they are getting increasingly demanding about the products and services that are being offered in market today. Internet and mobile technology have enabled consumers to look for the information they need themselves instead of accepting the information provided by marketers/store representatives. Word of mouth has always been a strong influence for consumers. However, with Internet and the boom in social media, there is a way to measure this today. It allows marketers to collect huge amount of information about their customers and their reactions to the products and services offered by them. Increasingly, consumers are seeking for suggestions and giving

---

[1] "The World in 2013—ICT Facts And Figures," http://www.itu.int/en/ITU-D/Statistics/Documents/facts/ICTFactsFigures2013.pdf (Retrieved on June 3, 2013).

[2] C. Erickson, "Internet a Decade Later—Infographic," August 22, 2012, http://mashable.com/2012/08/22/the-internet-a-decade-later/(Retrieved on June 2, 2013).

TABLE 6.1
INTERNET—THEN AND NOW![3]

	2002	2013
Internet users	569 million (i.e., 9.1% of the world population)	2.80 billion[4] (i.e., 39% of the world population)
Total websites	3 million	672 million[5]
Web browser	Internet Explorer: 95% Other: 5%	Chrome: 41% Firefox: 27% Internet Explorer: 23% Opera: 2% Others: 7%[6]
Speeds	It took 12.5 minutes to download a 5 MB song on a 56k modem	It now takes less than 1 minute to download a 5 MB song on a DSL line
Page loading time	16 seconds	7.25 seconds[7]
Social networking	Friendster that was launched then had 3 million users	Facebook, the number 1 social networking site has 1.2 billion users

suggestions online.[8] While a marketer is aware of these emerging trends, it is difficult to accurately measure and analyze these small nuances of customer interaction with a firm. Hence, marketing research has gained special importance in this Internet age.

Even for a firm, the Internet is becoming a powerful tool. The continuous innovations aid in the development of sophisticated software to analyze the enormous data that is getting collected every day. Although the emerging trends in the online world are impressive, it is extremely challenging for marketers to analyze every detail of consumer interaction and presence online, thereby making the job of a researcher much more complex. More and more consumers are looking to shop online in the comfort of their homes or offices. This adds a new dimension to the already existing competition in the marketplace for most firms. The costs outweigh the benefits of the Internet by a huge margin. Conducting online surveys are cheaper using the Internet, researching for information on latest trends is a lot easier, conducting secondary research too is way cheaper and easier as already seen in Chapter 5. This chapter will explain how the Internet can be used in global marketing research environment.

---

[3] Adapted and updated from C. Erickson, "Internet a Decade Later—Infographic," August 22, 2012, http://mashable.com/2012/08/22/the-internet-a-decade-later/(Retrieved on June 2, 2013).

[4] "Internet World Stats—Usage and Population Statistics," http://www.internetworldstats.com/stats.htm (Retrieved on September 26, 2014).

[5] "Internet Live Stats," http://www.internetlivestats.com/total-number-of-websites/(Retrieved on September 29, 2014).

[6] "World-Wide Internet Usage Facts and Statistics—2013," http://www.factshunt.com/2014/01/world-wide-internet-usage-facts-and.html (Retrieved on September 29, 2014).

[7] "Top Retail Websites Not Getting Faster: Average Web Page Load Time Is 7.25 Seconds [Report]," http://marketingland.com/retail-website-load-times-continue-to-decline-with-a-22-decrease-during-the-last-year-37604 (Retrieved on September 26, 2014).

[8] H. Leggatt, "High Percentage of Consumers Seeking and Giving Product Advice Online," February 1, 2007, http://www.bizreport.com/2007/02/high_percentage_of_consumers_seeking_and_giving_product_advice_online.html (Retrieved on June 3, 2013).

CURRENT TRENDS IN INTERNET

The world today is increasingly becoming digital. It is exciting to see the amount of information available at the click of a button. On a typical day, Internet users (a) consume enough information to fill 169 million DVDs, (b) send 294 million e-mails, and (c) post 2 million blog entries.[9]

Internet has changed many things—from the way companies conduct business to the way in which people interact with each other and the companies. Every person using the Internet leaves some form of digital footprint. It enables companies to track a customer's data so as to serve them with customized product/service offerings. Keeping the privacy issues separate, this definitely benefits both parties. Firms get rich data to devise strategies that can attract, retain, or win back customers. A customer, on the other hand, gets a tailor-made product that is customized specifically to their needs. Today in 2013, 2.7 billion people, comprising of almost 40% of the world's population, are online.[10] It is extremely interesting to observe the fast-paced evolution of technology.

In the last decade or so, the adoption of broadband has been sensational. In developed countries like the US, 65% of American adults have a high-speed broadband connection at home. Figure 6.1 illustrates the remarkable trend in adoption of broadband versus dial-up by the Internet users who are aged 18 or higher. As fixed-broadband services become more affordable, penetration has been increasing.[11]

FIGURE 6.1
BROADBAND AND DIAL-UP ADOPTION, 2000–2013[12]

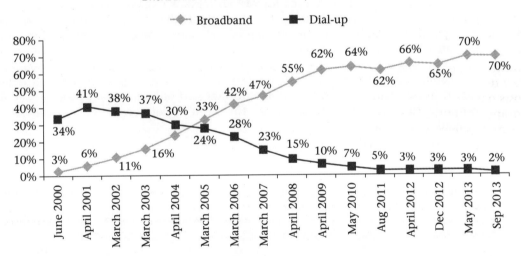

[9] F. Berkman, "How the World Consumes Social Media," January 17, 2013, http://mashable.com/2013/01/17/social-media-global/(Retrieved on June 3, 2013).

[10] "The World in 2013—ICT Facts And Figures," http://www.itu.int/en/ITU-D/Statistics/Documents/facts/ICTFactsFigures2013.pdf (Retrieved on June 3, 2013).

[11] Ibid.

[12] Adapted from Pew Research Center's Internet and American Life Project surveys, http://www.pewinternet.org/data-trend/internet-use/connection-type/(Retrieved on September 30, 2014).

Among people who use the Internet, the figures have been startling. Research findings show that an average American user spends around 23 hours every week (i.e., nearly 14% of the total time in a week) in activities including e-mailing, texting, using social media, and other types of communication.13 According to this survey, respondents spent nearly eight hours a week checking e-mail, nearly seven hours a week checking their Facebook account, and five hours per week on YouTube. The niche social network users are more attached, and among the tech-connected respondent pool, more than 80% of users of each site logged in at least once a week.[14]

Research also suggests that more men than women use Internet globally.[15] While women have increasingly started to use online and social media platforms in both developed and developing countries, a gender gap still exists. The gap is much more profound in developing nations where 16% fewer women use the Internet than men as compared to 2% in developed nations. However, once women are online, they are more connected than men.[16] Communication and social networking have been key drivers for men and women, but women seem to be increasingly spending more time on these activities as compared to men.

The presence of the baby boomer generation is increasing online, thereby engaging in various social activities on the Web. For a marketer, it is important to pay special attention to this target group as majority of the household spending decisions are made by women. In countries with a large market for e-commerce, women are driving purchase in the online world. In terms of transactions and spending, women contribute more than men. Table 6.2 points to some interesting marketing statistics about the baby boomer women.

China ranks number 1 in terms of the number of Internet users, followed by US, India, Japan, Brazil, Russia, Germany, Indonesia, UK, and France, in that order.[17] Across the world, consumers interact with each other online for various reasons like browsing for information about new product/service, sharing information about themselves with their friends and relatives, interacting with firms, browsing to educate oneself about some topic, etc. The amount of data generated by users is enormous. Every minute, YouTube users upload 48 hours of new video, Facebook users share 684,478 pieces of content, Instagram users share 3,600 new photos, and Tumblr sees 27,778 new posts published.[18] The latest report on Internet usage indicates the increase in the amount of information created online over a period of time is going to continue to increase. Figure 6.2 shows the trend of data or content generation of digital information over time.

---

[13] "American Spend 23 hours per Week Online/Texting," *Business News Daily*, July 3, 2013, http://mashable.com/2013/07/03/americans-time-online-texting/(Retrieved on August 15, 2013).

[14] "Social Usage Involves More Platforms, More Often," *E-Marketer*, July 2, 2013, http://www.emarketer.com/Article/Social-Usage-Involves-More-Platforms-More-Often/1010019 (Retrieved on August 15, 2013).

[15] "The World in 2013—ICT Facts And Figures," http://www.itu.int/en/ITU-D/Statistics/Documents/facts/ICTFactsFigures2013.pdf (Retrieved on June 3, 2013).

[16] Comcast Report: "Women on the Web—How Women Are Shaping the Internet," June 2010, http://www.comscore.com/Insights/Presentations-and-Whitepapers/2010/Women-on-the-Web-How-Women-are-Shaping-the-Internet (Retrieved in June 2013).

[17] "Top 20 Countries with Highest Number of Internet Users," June 30, 2012, http://www.internetworldstats.com/top20.htm (Retrieved in June 2013).

[18] N. Spencer, "How Much Data Is Created Every Minute," June 19, 2012, http://www.visualnews.com/2012/06/19/how-much-data-created-every-minute/(Retrieved in June 2013).

TABLE 6.2
INTERESTING MARKETING STATISTICS ON THE BABY BOOMER WOMEN[19]

Net worth of women age 50 and older	$19 Trillion
Consumer purchases made by women	85%
Home purchases	91%
Vacations	92%
Shop online at least once a day	22%
Feel advertisers don't understand them	91%
Would get rid of their TV if they had to lose one digital device	58%
Pass along information about deals or finds to others	92%
Women who influence household consumer electronic purchases	61%
New businesses started by women	70%
Average number of contacts in their e-mail lists	171
New cars	65%
Bank accounts	89%

FIGURE 6.2
GLOBAL DIGITAL INFORMATION SHARED AND CREATED[20]

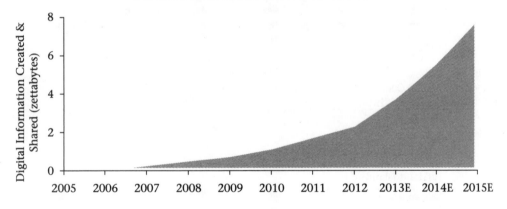

However, most of these data are mostly unstructured. While it is important for marketers to know what types of customers are online to be able to provide appropriate products and services, it is also critical to understand what language they are interacting in to be able to accordingly communicate and engage them with their brands. Figure 6.3 throws some light in

---

[19] Adapted from Statistics Brain, October 6, 2012, http://www.statisticbrain.com/financial-facts-on-baby-boomer-women/(Retrieved on June 2, 2013). Stats are for women born between 1946 and 1964.

[20] Adapted from K. Knibbs, "Five Surprising Things We Learned from the 2013 Internet Trends Report," June 3, 2013, http://www.digitaltrends.com/social-media/top-x-things-we-learned-from-the-2013-internet-trends-report/(Retrieved in August 2013).

this regard. By far, English is the most dominant language on the Web, followed by Chinese. If one had to translate these figures for marketers, it means that if one had a website in English, they could potentially reach approximately 536 million users online. While Google dominates the search market in English, Baidu is the go-to search for the Chinese consumer.

Although China leads the world in the number of users due to its sheer population figures, it does not feature in the Top 10 list of countries with the highest Internet penetration levels, as seen from Table 6.3.

FIGURE 6.3
TOP 10 LANGUAGES IN THE INTERNET 2010—IN MILLIONS OF USERS[21]

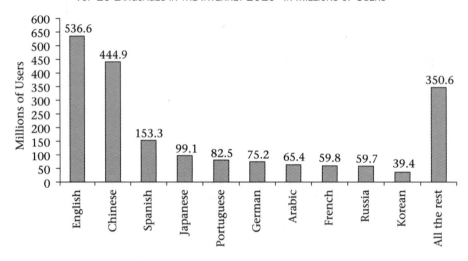

TABLE 6.3
TOP 10 COUNTRIES WORLDWIDE WITH THE HIGHEST INTERNET PENETRATION RATE[22]

Iceland	97.8%
Norway	97.2%
Sweden	92.9%
Falkland Islands	92.4%
Luxembourg	91.4%
Greenland	90.2%
Australia	89.8%
Netherlands	89.5%
Denmark	89.0%
Finland	88.6%

---

[21] Adapted from Internet World Stats, http://www.internetworldstats.com/stats7.htm (Retrieved on June 2, 2013).

[22] Ibid.

SECONDARY RESEARCH ON THE INTERNET

As seen in Chapter 5, Internet has enhanced secondary data research for researchers. Information for research can be obtained at a company level, industry level (such as databases and directories) or at the macro level (government, organizations, etc.). Moreover, finding information about competitors is an important activity for any marketing unit. Companies can find the product and financial information of competitors through their websites, if displayed. Pricing information can be sought online for companies engaged in online trade. While it is possible to gather such information on the company websites, information on competitive promotion and distribution is hard to find. Search engines are better suited for this purpose. As discussed in Chapter 5, search criteria play an important role in display of accurate results. Also, there are customer search providers available to help obtain the information for a certain fee, which is discussed in detail in later paragraphs.

While performing secondary research over the Internet, one should bear in mind the statistics mentioned above in terms of the penetration of Internet, the language and profile of users interacting online. Even today, a large part of the population in the developing countries does not have access to the Web. Moreover, it is a good practice for researchers to check for the validity of data and authenticity of the source before investing resources on the strategies derived from the data.

Custom Search Services

With the growing interest in the use of Internet for business, a number of companies are offering specialized search services for a fee. This could be either a one-time custom search or regular news deliveries. These custom-search services specialize in one or two areas like telecommunications or food processing and offer their services in the form of a regular newsletter to subscribers. Service charges depend on the frequency with which information is delivered to the client, the usage (one-time or for the whole project), the periodicity (weekly, monthly, yearly), the object (document fee, fee per researched publication), the amount of text (number of characters), or any combination of these. For example, Dow Jones News/Retrieval Service provides customized business and financial news and information. Its service scans more than 6,000 business publications from around the world, and the user can search 55 million business articles. The user retrieves the headlines of the articles for free and pays $2.95 for each article viewed. Also, the customer can select *topic folders* from a list of 1,200 preconfigured folders tracking information relevant to a user's particular needs.[23]

Agents[24]

Agents work differently from custom-search services. With intense competition, intelligent agents are increasingly being used for monitoring information. So an agent can be used to provide constant important information relevant to the product—for example, pricing of

---

[23] Aaker et al., *Marketing Research*, 11th edition.
[24] Ibid.

competitors' products. An intelligent agent would monitor websites of all manufacturers and retailers, collect price and availability information, and deliver easy-to-skim summaries.

There are many ways in which agents function. Some are available on the Internet and preprogrammed for particular search tasks, such as Bargain Finders. This commercial application will most likely gain tremendous significance in the near future. Other types of agents include software purchased by the user, who then has to specify downloading criteria. Most often, searches are scheduled at night so they do not have to wait to download documents. Agent technology is on the verge of entering the mainstream of Web search, and the future is likely to bring many innovations in this area.

Search Engines

There are several search engines that can be used—Google, Bing, Yahoo, Ask, AOL. Google by far leads the way with 66.7% market share, followed by Bing at 17.4% and Yahoo at 12%.[25] It is easy to see how secondary research is greatly simplified by the Internet and the search engines. Global marketing researchers can conduct a thorough search on the Internet and form initial hypotheses even before stepping out of the borders of their home country. This has a significant impact on keeping the costs down. There are websites that provide detailed information such as the geographic, economic, political, and demographic data about countries of interest. Many countries have also established government agencies that provide free information to businesses wanting to enter those countries. Search strategies shared in Chapter 5 can come in handy while trying to search for specific items. Conducting a search in the Internet can be done at three different levels—company level, industry level, or the macro level. Following are examples of how this information can be collected only using the Internet.

Competitive Intelligence Analysis

In this type of study, the researcher studies a particular company in a specific country. For example, a researcher may be contracted by Ford to gather information about their competitor marketing actions in Indonesia. In such a study, the researcher typically looks out for information on: (a) the overall auto industry in Indonesia and its future outlook; (b) country-specific auto industry information such as the population of Indonesia, the number of cars sold in Indonesia, the manufacturers having a significant presence in Indonesia, trade fair information, industry information, and best market opportunities; (c) important trade-related information such as information like trade barriers, tariffs, business organizations, commercial policies, foreign investment, incentives, taxation, and regulatory agencies; (d) information on the marketing practices of car manufacturers and the promotional plans offered by them to car buyers obtained from the official websites of the car companies; (e) product-related information such as price and features of different car models of competitors, the number and location of car dealerships, financing schemes, and special promotions, among others; and

---

[25] J. Slegg, "Google, Bing Both Win More Market Share," June 18, 2013, http://searchenginewatch.com/article/2275863/Google-Bing-Both-Win-More-Search-Market-Share (Retrieved on July 3, 2013).

(f) specific information requested by Ford to be included in the study. A compilation of all this information would be a good way to learn about competitor actions.

Industry Analysis

In this type of study, the researcher studies a particular industry in a specific country. An example of this would be that of a US breakfast cereal manufacturer wanting to enter the Indian market. Such a study calls for a thorough understanding of the Indian cereals market in terms of the market size, market share of other cereal manufacturers (if any), the Indian perception of cereals, and the popular breakfast items that could pose a threat to the market share of cereals in India. Specifically, the researcher must look out for information on: (a) cultural factors that are likely to determine the acceptance of the cereal in India (e.g., country history, geographical settings, education levels, political system, legal system, religion, living conditions, healthcare facilities, and languages); (b) economic factors that inform about the overall market characteristics (e.g., population demographics, macro-economic indicators, natural resources, science and technology, infrastructure, international trade, trade restrictions, work conditions, and media); (c) industry factors that are specific to the cereals industry (e.g., market size, growth, seasonality, new product prospects, product rivalry, and power of buyers and suppliers); (d) product factors that deal with specific product characteristics (e.g., pricing pattern, distribution channels, selling practices, advertising and promotion, product usage patterns, and service levels); (e) customer characteristics (e.g., customer demographics, customer profile, buying habits, purchase decision, and timing and frequency of purchase); and (f) competitor information (e.g., current marketing strategy, performance metrics, key success factors, SWOT analysis, and future growth plans). The information on all these factors should be sufficient in conducting the research study and formulate a few hypotheses about launching the breakfast cereals in India.

Buyer Behavior

This type of study calls for an understanding into the buying characteristics in a specific market. An example of this study would be that of a national distribution chain in Germany having to decide whether it should include consumer-ready food products in its portfolio. This study would, therefore, involve studying the retail food market in Germany and the existing distribution setup to get a better understanding of buyer behavior. Specifically, this would require gathering information regarding: (a) the product (e.g., information on the innovativeness of the product, product usage patterns, product feature preferences, how it scores over the competition, and the problems and resistances to customers accepting the proposed product); (b) the market (e.g., geographical region(s) considered, forms of transportation available for distribution, communications methods to be adopted, estimated industry sales, estimated sales for the company, industry regulations, and required licenses and certifications to produce the product); (c) the customer purchases (e.g., buying and shopping habits, frequency of purchase, price sensitivity, and usage conditions); (d) the distribution setup (e.g., type of outlets that would carry this product, involvement of middlemen, billing and delivery conditions to the stores, and credit policies to the stores); (e) advertising and promotion (e.g., advertising media used to reach the target audience, and sales promotion tools to be used); (f) pricing (e.g., markups, retailer margins and discounts, types of discounts, and pricing compared to the competitor offerings); and (g) competitive positioning (e.g., competitor brands and products in the market, product features and packaging aspects of the competing products, competitor pricing structure, advertising and promotion methods adopted by the competitor, and distribution setup of the competition). All this information would be a good place to begin to understand the market potential for consumer-ready foods in Germany.

New Business-to-Business (B2B) Market

This type of study involves understanding a B2B market for a specialized product in a specific country. For instance, a researcher may be required to prepare a report on iron foundries in China that can produce cast-iron products like sewer covers, drain pipes, and pipe fittings that are used in the construction industry. In such a project, the researcher typically looks for information on: (a) the list of products that are typically made using the iron casting method; (b) the industries that use such products (e.g., construction, engineering, drilling and well service, exploration, engineering and technical services, oil producing and processing companies, hospitals, educational institutions, mining industry, and government agencies like the health department, road and highways department, public works department, and railway department); (c) the available production methods of iron casting; (d) number of factories producing such cast-iron products; (e) the availability pattern of raw materials for production facilities; (f) the market size and estimated sales of such products; and (g) government regulations, licenses, and approvals involved in the production and usage of such products. All this information will provide the researcher with basic information required to get started on the project. With this data in hand, the researcher can decide on the next step of designing an instrument to collect primary data, if the client wants to proceed with this project.

PRIMARY RESEARCH ON THE INTERNET

Internet has emerged as a popular medium for collecting data in recent times. As seen earlier in the previous section, Internet is being used increasingly in the area of secondary research. In terms of primary research, the Internet has made a lot of things simpler, faster, and more efficient. At the heart of the matter lies the flexibility to develop more sophisticated questionnaires, complex skipping patterns, use of different stimuli like audio/video or text, etc. The Internet has also widened the scope of conducting research online. A researcher can now reach a wider sample while conducting primary research at almost no cost; larger sample means more robustness and more accuracy. It also enabled the collection of data from much diverse audience. In addition, the physical barrier of place is removed, which enables one to collect responses from respondents in any part of the world. The interviewer bias is eliminated as well. The respondents now self-administer the questionnaire and respond at a time suitable to them. A very popular advantage of conducting primary research over the Internet is the time and cost savings in terms of coding of data. It also is more accurate as it eliminates the problem of manual data entry.

Sampling bias has been an issue for online survey research. Moreover, although time is saved due to the elimination of coding of data at the back end, the front-end setup time has increased. So even though Internet survey research is useful, there is merit in understanding the drawbacks of the methodology before we apply it. There are a number of ways to collect primary information from a respondent. These are discussed as follows.

E-mail Surveys

Questionnaires are usually sent out to respondents and the responses are collected via electronic mail. E-mail is used as a medium to send and receive the information from respondents. Provision is also made in the questionnaires to complete the form online and return it to the researcher. Table 6.4 provides the list of advantages and disadvantages of e-mail surveys.

TABLE 6.4
ADVANTAGES AND DISADVANTAGES OF E-MAIL SURVEYS

Advantages	Disadvantages
• It provides greater speed of delivering electronic mail over the regular postal mail. In case the respondent fails to receive the questionnaire, it can be resent instantly, unlike the postal mail which can take anywhere from one to three days. • Speed of receiving responses and feedback is much higher in this form versus the traditional methods. • The cost savings in e-mail surveys is enormous when compared to regular mail. • There is an absence of interviewer bias (in case of face-to-face) and a moderator bias (in case of direct interviews or focus groups). The survey is usually read only by the recipient. • It involves asynchronous communication. That is, it is up to the user to receive, read and respond to the firm collecting the response at a time that is suitable.	• A large number of e-mails turn out to be spam/junk/unsolicited e-mails. In 2010, 107 trillion e-mails were sent on the Internet, out of which 89.1% were spam.[26] • Research for certain product categories may have to be done among audiences that cannot be reached via e-mail/Internet. In such cases, this method cannot be useful. • Security related to electronic e-mail is lower than traditional media. Respondents may fear that providing information online may reveal their identity. • Response rate has been an issue. While you can resend questionnaires very easily at no extra cost, it is easier for respondents to simply ignore, thereby affecting the response rate for surveys. • The same respondent can fill in survey responses using different e-mail addresses, especially when the completion of a survey is attached to a reward.

Interactive Forms

Electronic interactive media forms allow marketers to tailor the message for each respondent. Today's consumers do not receive information from the manufacturer alone; they interact and engage with their friends and relatives or browse the Web to seek more detailed information and reviews prior to purchase. Interactive media has enhanced the online sharing experience for customers. Electronic dating services are a good example of electronic interactive media. The interaction occurs with the help of digital technology. Survey respondents today are no more passive and they involve themselves in a two-way communication using electronic interactive media.[27]

---

[26] Pingdom, "Internet 2010 in Numbers," January 12, 2011, http://royal.pingdom.com/2011/01/12/internet-2010-in-numbers/(Retrieved in June 2013).

[27] W. G. Zikmund; J. C. Carr, and M. Griffin, "Business Research Methods," 2012, CengageBrain.com, pp. 205–234.

Online Panels

Online panels are like a ready-to-survey sample of people who have already shared their willingness to participate in marketing research studies for some incentive/reward as decided by the recruiting company. Online panels are great for researchers as respondents agree to participate in the survey and share their views online. Since respondents are participating willingly, the response is a lot richer. Harris Interactive and Synovate are some of the many companies offering online panels across the world. Since recruitment of respondents is already done, researchers and marketers can save considerable amount of time when they use services offered by these companies. Also, sometimes the marketer or the researcher may not have the resources to go and recruit respondents. In such occasions too, online panels serve to be extremely useful.

The recruitment plays a vital role in the whole process. In the process of covering a wide audience, the recruiter should not lose focus on the sampling technique. The sample has to be representative and it is a researcher's job to ensure that the online panel company providing the respondents has fair practices in place. Respondents are given incentives to participate in surveys. Also, respondents provide their demographic and psychographic details to the recruiting firm based on which they are profiled for corresponding studies in the future. Maintenance of the online panel is another responsibility of the recruiting agency. It is important for the recruiter to update the information and ensure practices are in place to get information from the respondent from time to time. Failure to do so may result in incorrect profiling and the marketers would be seeking responses from respondents they do not wish to interview.

Online Focus Groups

The Internet has facilitated qualitative research by making online focus groups possible. Now, researchers can recruit respondents from any part of the world and seek information on *why* they do or do not do certain things, buy or do not buy certain products or services, like or do not like a particular communication, etc. Further, it is also possible to screen and moderate respondents for focus groups completely online.

Respondents are comfortably placed in their homes in front of their computer screens engaging with other respondents in similar situation. While some critics argue about the lack of face-to-face interaction, online focus groups still is a great alternative to the traditional approach in a lot of situations.

User-generated Reviews

Consumer reviews have become a part of everything that is present online. More and more consumers are seeking reviews online before any purchase, including high involvement items like cars or homes. While e-commerce is picking up, consumers are increasingly spending more time in online product research. [28] According to a study, 50% of consumers spend

---

[28] G. Charlton, "E-Commerce Consumer Reviews: Why You Need Them and How to Use Them," March 21, 2012, http://econsultancy.com/us/blog/9366-e-commerce-consumer-reviews-why-you-need-them-and-how-to-use-them (Retrieved in June 2013).

around 75% or more of their total shopping time conducting online product research, and a further 15% of consumers spending more than 90% or more of their shopping time in this manner.[29] For instance, a 2011 study found that visitors who read consumer packaged goods reviews have a 6% higher average order value than visitors who do not read reviews.[30] In the British setting, recommendations from friends are the most influential driver for UK shopping habits followed closely by consumer reviews. Therefore, it is important for companies to have a platform where consumers can provide reviews of their experience with the product/service. User-generated reviews also have a sense of authenticity and a connection that consumers feel which allows them to trust the reviews and base their product decisions on that.

While consumer reviews does provide helpful information to aid purchase decisions, caution has to be exercised in selecting the source of reviews. Notably, researchers have to be wary about paid or fake reviews. Such comments, whether intended to promote or damage the product, can heavily bias the overall sentiment and thus wrongly influence the market research process. Generally, comments with zero caveats, empty adjectives, purely extreme emotions, or comments made by the same author in a lot of other places specify signals of opinion spams.[31] In some cases, researchers may refer wiki posts for product information. This source is not always reliable (as against peer-reviewed scientific evidence) for product research, owing to the open editing policy of Wikipedia.

The exchange of views and ideas has increased manifold due to the emergence of social media, and has provided people a platform to discuss products and social issues in an online setting. The next section on social media will illustrate the significance and the importance of it in global marketing research.

SOCIAL MEDIA

In 2012, 50% of all Internet users signed into a social network.[32] The increase in the use of the Internet by consumers in their daily lives can be partially attributed to the growth of social media in recent years. Earlier, consumers used e-mails and chat as a way to interact and exchange views and ideas with each other. But social media has changed that from a one-on-one interaction to a shared view and communication. The term *socializing* has a new meaning with the gaining popularity of social media channels. So what constitutes as social media? As Lisa Buyer puts it, "Social media is today's most transparent, engaging and interactive form of public relations. It combines the true grit of real time content with the beauty of authentic peer-to-peer communication."[33] As an extension of interactive Web, social media allows its users to not only contribute by sharing articles, pictures or videos but also create their own content. According to Harish Manwani, Unilever's Chief Operating Officer and Hindustan

---

[29] Marketing Charts, "Customer Reviews Affect 6 in 10 Online Shoppers," September 1, 2011, http://www.marketingcharts.com/direct/customer-reviews-affect-6-in-10-online-shoppers-19019/(Retrieved in June 2013).

[30] "The Conversation Index Vol. 1," October 2011, Bazaarvoice.com.

[31] Arjun Mukherjee, Bing Liu, and Natalie Glance, "Spotting Fake Reviewer Groups in Consumer Reviews", ACM Digital Library, April 2012.

[32] F. Berkman, "How the World Consumes Social Media," January 17, 2013, http://mashable.com/2013/01/17/social-media-global/(Retrieved on June 3, 2013).

[33] Heidi Cohen, "30 Social Media Definitions," May 9, 2011, http://heidicohen.com/social-media-definition/(Retrieved in June 2013).

Unilever Limited Chairman, "The consumer is taking ownership of the content and the social media is creating the content about products."[34] Globally too, the adoption of social media has been phenomenal. According to a Forrester study, "Global Social Media Adoption in 2012," more than 86% of online US adults and 79% of European online adults engage with social media. In BRIC countries, some 93% of online users use social tools.[35] The adoption of social networking among females is outstanding. Table 6.5 illustrates percent women and men using different popular social networking websites. This information is extremely useful for marketers to accordingly engage their consumers in the social platform.

TABLE 6.5

MALE VERSUS FEMALE USERS OF SOCIAL MEDIA SITES[36]

	Male (%)	Female (%)
Facebook	40	60
Twitter	40	60
Pinterest	21	79
Google+	71	29
LinkedIn	45	55

The expansion of the numbers of online social networks and blogs is outstanding. It attracts consumers from a wide range of demographic segments. Internet users are turning to one another as trusted sources for everything from pie recipes to product reviews. Marketers have considered this ongoing/growing trend rather seriously and have increased their online ad spending budgets. In 2012, the online ad spending reached $37 billion.[37] Below are some of the popular social media channels[38]:

- *Blogs:* Online journals used to store information. Two popular types of blog are corporate blogs (e.g., Google Blog, Coca-Cola Conversation, and Delta Airlines—Under the Wing) and micro blogs (e.g., Twitter, Tumblr, and Plurk). While corporate blogs are used to create consumer involvement with a company's marketing activities, micro blogs allow users to exchange small elements of content such as short sentences, individual images, or video links.
- *Social networks:* Platforms that allow users to create and connect personal networks, such as Facebook, Twitter, MySpace, and LinkedIn.
- *Content communities:* Websites that store and share particular types of content such as YouTube, Google Video (video sharing), or Flickr (photo sharing).

---

[34] "Social Media Forcing Change in Corporate Strategy: HUL Chief," *Hindu*, March 20, 2013.

[35] P. Crowe, "8 in 10 Internet Users Engage in Social Media Globally," July 5, 2012, http://www.globalresponse.com/2012/07/8-in-10-internet-users-engage-in-social-media-globally/(Retrieved in June 2013).

[36] "100 Social Network Facts and Statistics for 2012 Infographic," http://www.mediabistro.com/alltwitter/files/2013/01/100-social-media-stats.png (Retrieved on June 3, 2013).

[37] M. Walsh, "Online Ad Spending Up 15% to $37 Billion in 2012," April 16, 2013, http://www.mediapost.com/publications/article/198161/#axzz2Ykex7cPo (Retrieved in June 2013).

[38] Aaker et al., *Marketing Research*, 11th edition.

- *Social coupons:* Websites that offer online daily deals and discounts, such as Groupon and Living Social.

Word of mouth has always been a strong influencer in marketing. Social media has made this aspect of word of mouth communication trackable and quantifiable. Also, the reach is tremendous. One can communicate with thousands of people at the same time sitting in their living room. In words of CEO of Amazon Jeff Bezos, "If you make customers unhappy in a physical world, they might each tell 6 people. If you make customers unhappy on the Internet, they can each tell 6,000 friends."[39] Some facts and figures about major social networks have been listed in Exhibit 6.1.

LEVERAGING BIG DATA

Big Data refers to the ever-increasing volume, velocity, variety, variability, and complexity of information. From marketing and sales data to online browsing history to social media activity, data today only keeps getting more voluminous. With technologies readily available to handle such huge and varied data, Big Data analytics can help organizations draw more accurate marketing insights that can in turn be translated into informed business decisions.

Big Data technologies, with their powerful parallel computing techniques, enable us to mine the huge data volume with ease. When diligently used, it can help businesses identify new markets, focus on opportunities, review current performance, maximize sales effectiveness, understand customer engagement, customer retention, and loyalty.[40] The concept of data analytics may not be new, but the fact that the data for analysis, even though very large, can still be easily available and minable is probably a reason why Big Data is regarded very high in the field of business analytics.

Facebook, the social networking giant, has proved itself to be an extensive Big Data specialist, through its various real-time analytical operations. Facebook takes note of every log in, log out, every *like*, *comment* or *share*, fan page visit or ad click and uses it diligently for analysis. The data collected is literally stored forever, and deleted only for security, privacy, or regulatory reasons. For this purpose, Facebook maintains several Hadoop clusters each consisting of several thousand servers. The largest cluster stores more than 100 petabytes.[41] To answer a specific query, data is often pulled out of the warehouse to be studied. Facebook uses personal data of its customers to publish ads real time on the user timeline. It also uses this information to suggest new friends and pages that may be of user interest. Amazon, too, has a well-setup Big Data infrastructure that is used to iteratively build its product recommender engine. The Amazon recommender system uses the clickstream data and historical purchase of around 152 million customers to suggest similar or newer the customers could buy.[42]

---

[39] Collins Olua, "Dave Carroll Versus United Airlines (When Customer Service Fails)," January 25, 2011, from http://www.ebusinessjournals.com/2011/01/25/dave-carroll-versus-united-airlines-when-customer-service-fails/(Retrieved in June 2013).

[40] SAS Institute Inc., "Big Data, Bigger Marketing", http://www.sas.com/en_us/insights/big-data/big-data-marketing.html (Retrieved on September 26, 2014).

[41] Wade Roush, "Facebook Doesn't Have Big Data. It Has Ginormous Data," February 14, 2013, http://www.xconomy.com/san-francisco/2013/02/14/how-facebook-uses-ginormous-data-to-grow-its-business/ (Retrieved as on September 30, 2013).

[42] "How Amazon Is Leveraging Big Data," http://www.bigdata-startups.com/BigData-startup/amazon-leveraging-big-data/(Retrieved on May 5, 2014).

Exhibit 6.1

Key Social Media Facts, Figures, and Statistics for 2013[43]

Facebook

Daily active users: 665 million

Monthly active users: 1.1 billion

Millions of mobile users that access Facebook monthly: 751 million

Mobile only active users: 189 million

Percentage revenue that mobile generates by its ads: 30%

Google+

Position in social network: Second largest social network

Monthly active users (according to a GlobalWebIndex study): 359 million

Growth in active users from June 2012 through to March 2013: 33%

Twitter

Position: Fastest growing social network in the world

Monthly active users: 288 million

Percent of the world's Internet population using Twitter every month: 21%

Registered accounts: Over 500 million

Twitter's fastest growing age demographic is 55–64-year-olds, registering an increase in active users of 79%

YouTube

Unique monthly visitors: 1 billion

Duration of videos watched every month: 6 billion hours

YouTube reaches more US adults aged 18–34 than any cable network

LinkedIn

Position: Largest professional business networks on the planet

Users: Over 200 million

Activity: 2 new users join it every second

Penetration: 64% of users are outside the US

As it can be seen from the examples, Web data is one big contributor to Big Data. With aggregation of tons of weblogs, the metrics used to drive decisions become extremely important. Some direct metrics that are tracked include the number of page visits, page views, newsletter subscribers, active members, social media followers, and the time spent on any web page. The more important metrics, however, are the derived metrics that can be used to provide actionable insights. Some examples include understanding who is visiting the website, from where do they visit, which web pages are most frequently visited, what channels are

---

[43] Adapted from J. Bullas, "21 Awesome Social Media Facts, Figures and Statistics for 2013," 2013, http://www.jeffbullas.com/2013/05/06/21-awesome-social-media-facts-figures-and-statistics-for-2013/(Retrieved on June 3, 2013).

driving customers, which conversions are deepening relationships or generating revenue, and how different are the regular visitors from the infrequent visitors, among others.[44]

With respect to the analytics tools, most of the Big Data analytics tools are built on Hadoop, which is the most widely used open-source software framework for storage and large-scale processing of data sets on clusters of commodity hardware. Hadoop has its own data warehouse called Hive to provide data summarization, query, and analysis, while simultaneously hosting another high-level language called Pig that serves as a platform for analyzing large data sets through user programs. Some competitive Big Data tools include SpliceMachine, mongoDB, and Pentaho.[45]

With enormous data available at one's disposal, businesses may sometimes run into problems with choosing the right data, knowing which analytical tools to use and figuring the way to go from data to insight to impact.[46] Big Data can be overwhelming at times, but these challenges can be overcome if one is clear with the business objective at hand.

The advent and growth of Big Data has not only eased business analysis, but has opened up numerous avenues for job offerings in this space. As of January 2014 alone, around 140,000–190,000 Big Data scientists were in demand world-wide. This can partly be understood by the fact that even though Big Data technologies have revolutionized the way data can be gathered and analyzed, its applications in marketing and elsewhere still remain human decisions.[47]

GLOBAL MARKETING RESEARCH IN PRACTICE

The Internet is one of the most important sources of secondary data. Tasty Burgers could make good use of the Internet to obtain preliminary information on the countries of to them. In the previous chapter, we outlined the different kinds of secondary data that are required to make a preliminary judgment on the four countries. Economic data include variables such as GDP, GNP, per capita income, and purchasing power parity. Social data include legal systems, social structures, and infrastructure such as transportation, communication, and media services. Demographic data would cover population, population density in a given region, income ranges, and standard of living. There are many websites that provide these data. A search engine could be used to identify these sites. One such site is the CIA World Factbook, which is available at http://www.odci.gov/cia/publications/factbook. This site provides basic data for all countries of interest and is also well updated. There are several websites maintained by the Indian and Brazilian statistical institutes that can be identified by using "Indian statistics" or "Brazilian statistics" as the search criterion. It is also possible to obtain information about the fast-food industry and suppliers of breads, vegetables, and meats in each of these markets. It is important to interject a word of caution for those who use the Internet as a source of information. There is no control in terms of the information that is posted on the Web. Hence, the authenticity of the source and the information must always be verified.

---

[44] Jayson DeMers, "2014 Is the Year of Digital Marketing Analytics: What It Means for Your Company," February 10, 2014, http://www.forbes.com/sites/jaysondemers/2014/02/10/2014-is-the-year-of-digital-marketing-analytics-what-it-means-for-your-company/(Retrieved in September 2014).

[45] William Toll, "Top 45 Big Data Tools for Developers," March 20, 2014, http://blog.profitbricks.com/top-45-big-data-tools-for-developers/(Retrieved in September 2014).

[46] SAS Institute Inc., "Big Data, Bigger Marketing".

[47] Rob Salkowitz, "From Big Data to Smart Data: Using Data to Drive Personalized Brand Experience," January 22, 2014 http://www.mediaplant.net/report/details/bigdata (Retrieved on September 26, 2014).

SUMMARY

Internet has changed the way we interact with each other. Therefore, it also has changed the way firms and companies conduct businesses. Marketing and marketing research, both domestic and international, have gone through major reforms in terms of methodology of conducting research. Since the world is more connected than ever before, international researchers have been able to leverage the advances in digital technology and use it to their advantage. The Internet has contributed to increasing the speed of communication while decreasing the cost for both primary and secondary research.

This chapter provides a brief overview of the impact of Internet on primary and secondary research, relevant statistics pertaining to the Internet and social media. Conducting primary research on the Internet is beginning to become popular and this chapter takes a look at some of the methods.

QUESTIONS AND PROBLEMS

1. YoungForever, a popular American chain of fashion retailers, wants to enter the Indian market. Briefly outline how you would leverage the Internet to carry out the market research for this operation.
2. What are the various online ways of receiving customer inputs about a product? How do you think social media has changed the market research process?
3. Do you think the current marketing world's buzz about Big Data is justified? What capabilities do Big Data technologies bring that earlier-generation infrastructure do not?
4. John Smith has to make a holiday trip from Seoul to Los Angeles. He searched on the Internet for the lowest price offering and bought his ticket. Demonstrate the search process that John used to get his ticket.
5. Pick any company of your choice, and
   a. Identify its website
   b. Browse through the website
   c. List the type of information that is available
   d. Identify any country-specific or international operators of the firm

7
CHAPTER

Primary Data Research

INTRODUCTION

This chapter focuses on the collection of primary data for global marketing research. We address the different types of primary research, the various issues involved in collecting primary data, the biases that can occur, and the benefits and costs of collecting primary data.

Primary data may be required for various reasons. When a specific research objective is to be addressed, primary data are collected. Primary data are usually collected to aid in a specific project, such as a product launch. A company may choose to collect primary data on a continuous basis also. This may be used to plan its corporate strategy and for future research activities. A variety of methods, ranging from qualitative research to surveys to experiments, comprise primary data. Exhibit 7.1 illustrates how Kellogg's used primary research for the development and launch of Crunchy Nut Bites in the UK.

Exhibit 7.1

Kellogg's Crunchy Nut Bites[1]

Many companies are product-oriented, i.e., they focus on developing brands. However, Kellogg's is more market-oriented and focuses on the customer needs that they can meet with the help of their products. In order to develop a brand extension of their successful Crunchy Nut Cereal, one of the most important brands for Kellogg's in UK since its launch in 1980, Kellogg's used a combination of primary and secondary research to finally develop a brand extension in order to provide consumers with different flavor and texture, thereby gaining more market share in the breakfast cereal category. A combination of qualitative and quantitative techniques was used throughout

---

[1] Adapted from "New Products from Market Research—A Kellogg's Case Study," 2014, http://businesscasestudies.co.uk/kelloggs/new-products-from-market-research/introduction.html#axzz2ZQJFooTr (Retrieved on May 10, 2014).

the research phase. Following were the steps taken by Kellogg's during the development process of their new product.

Step 1: Product Opportunity Identification: They used secondary research to gain in-depth knowledge about the innovation trends in the cereal market, including information about new products, flavors, etc. Using the results from secondary research, Kellogg's carried out primary research with consumers in a focus-group setting. This focus group was carried out with the objective to get more product suggestions that could be a part of the parent brand "Crunchy Nut" cereals. As a result of this exercise, they got a range of potential flavors and textures that consumers were interested in.

Step 2: Ideation: Still, it wasn't just one idea that stood out. With a few shortlisted options, they set out to refine it further with the help of a quantitative concept-testing study. They developed the ideas into concepts and tested them with a different set of consumers. The ideas were now developed into full-blown concept boards with images, pictures and product description and insight statement. The results indicated that a new Crunchy Nut Bites idea was perceived as the most appealing amongst all the ideas tested providing the proportion of people who were prospects to buy the product when launched.

Step 3: Idea Implementation: Having finalized on the concept, the team of Kellogg's developed the prototype recipe. These were again refined using another quantitative and qualitative survey. They used qualitative research to understand the eating experience and specific aspects of the new flavor and texture with the consumers. Quantitative survey helped them select the finalists among the prototype recipes that were developed. This stage also included testing of the packaging design with consumers, which is how they closed on a final packaging design for Crunchy Nut Bites.

Step 4: Generating Sales Forecasts: Prior to launch, Kellogg's has to put their new product through one final test, that is, in home use test. This included placing the new product with the consumers who had liked the idea or were prospective buyers to actually rate the product itself. This was a quantitative survey that they carried out to measure the appeal of the new product, their propensity to buy the product when actually launched in market, their evaluation of the product, and aspects they liked or disliked about product. This extensive research helped them arrive at a sales estimate/forecast for Crunchy Nut Bites. This forecast was then used by the finance department to set the budgets, organize the supply chain, and schedule food production.

It is clear how Kellogg's used market research throughout the whole development process from the initial idea to the planning of production and delivery. Kellogg's launched Crunchy Nut Bites in September 2008 extending the Crunchy Nut family of products, bringing new consumers to the brand with increased consumption. As per the sales data, this was one of the best performing brands to launch in the breakfast cereal category with a sales value of £6.9 million in its first full year of sales (IRI sales data). Kellogg's maximized their chances with this product launch with the help of market research at every stage of their developmental cycle ensuring that the product extension fit right in with the consumers.

Despite the wide variety of primary research methods, some methods are better suited to one category of research than another. It is also essential for the researchers to note that not all data collection methods work in all countries. This is due to differences in availability of infrastructure, cultural differences, geographic limitations, and language barriers. Since the process of primary data collection is a costly affair, researchers should obtain preliminary information on the country of interest before starting the actual data collection process.

As mentioned in Chapter 5, secondary research helps in easing the pressure off primary data collection. Various organizations publish information that could be used to decide the data collection methods beforehand. Exhibit 7.2 presents a global picture of market research presented by ESOMAR.

Exhibit 7.2

2012 ESOMAR Global Market Research[2]

In the 2012 Global Market Research report prepared by ESOMAR, the findings show that the total world turnover in 2011 rose to $33.5 billion, representing an increase of 3.8% from 2010. After adjusting for inflation, the increase amounts to just 0.4%. The report also identified gains and losses across global country markets that show stark variations. The global market research turnover is provided below:

Region	2011		2010	
	Research Turnover ($ billion)	Net Growth Rate (%)	Research Turnover ($ billion)	Net Growth Rate (%)
Europe	14,140	−1.3	13,143	1.0
North America	11,188	1.7	10,614	3.1
Asia Pacific	5,754	1.7	5,082	3.5
Latin America	1,858	1.3	1,828	13.9
Middle East and Africa	601	−1.3	573	4.3
World	33,540	0.4	31,239	2.8

In terms of areas of spending, the report found that in 2011 the top three areas of market research spending were market measurement studies (18%), qualitative studies (16%), and audience research studies (15%). The other research studies that companies around the world also spent for are as follows:

Type of Research Study	Percentage of Spending
Market Measurement	18
Other Qualitative Studies	16
Media Audience/Research	15
Stakeholder Measurement, including CRM	9
Other Studies	8
Advertising/Brand Tracking	7

---

[2] Adapted from ESOMAR, "Global Market Research 2012," ESOMAR Industry Report, in cooperation with KPMG Advisory.

Type of Research Study	Percentage of Spending
New Product/Service Development	7
Usage and Attitude	6
Market Modeling	4
Advertising Pre-testing (Copy)	3
Opinion Research/Polling	3
Other B2B Studies	2
Other Omnibus/Shared Cost Surveys	2

The report also examined the role of online research among the options available for a researcher. The findings showed that the online research is gaining more prominence and accounted for 22% of total market research investment. It has surpassed research investments into other traditional methods such as face-to-face studies (11%), telephone surveys (13%), and group discussions (13%). The report also highlighted the variations in investments toward online research. For instance, Japan was found to be the highest user of the online medium (nearly 40% of all research), followed closely by New Zealand (38%). The other top users of the online medium are as follows:

Country	Online Research Spend as a Percentage of Total Spend in 2011
Japan	40
New Zealand	38
Netherlands	36
Finland	35
Canada	35
Bulgaria	35
Sweden	34
Australia	29
UK	28
Germany	22

The report also highlighted the changing dynamics in terms of the role of online media and the nature of studies undertaken. While online research was not part of a researcher's toolkit, it is now widely accepted by the industry as it covers a wide range of people and services. Further, with the constant demand for faster turnaround of research projects and quick actionable insights from clients, online research has enabled research companies to achieve similar results for the same or lesser money. Additionally, the report also tracked these changing dynamics and calls for re-evaluating the existing definitions of research, and places focus on guidelines and standards designed for a new digital age.

TYPES OF PRIMARY RESEARCH

Primary research can be of three types: exploratory research, descriptive research, and causal research. The difference is in the requirements in terms of time and expense. The purpose of each of these types of research is also different and their utility to companies can vary from purely tactical to strategic and long-term. A vast majority of the global marketing research studies are descriptive in nature. Often, exploratory research is insufficient to make important corporate decisions and causal research is too time-consuming. Most companies are satisfied with obtaining a thorough understanding of the market, which enables them to make reasonably accurate decisions. This section deals with the three types of primary data collection in detail.

Exploratory Research

Exploratory research is most appropriate when the primary objective is to identify problems, to define problems more precisely, or to investigate the possibility of new alternative courses of action. Exploratory research can also aid in formulating hypotheses regarding potential problems or opportunities present in the decision situation. In some cases, this could be the only step in further research activity. Exploratory research is characterized by the need for great flexibility and versatility. The researcher has very little knowledge about the situation being researched and needs to be able to adapt quickly to newly emerging situations in order to make research worthwhile. Exploratory research focuses on qualitative rather than quantitative data collection and the researcher is looking for quick answers to the research problem on hand. As a result, this type of research is less rigorous and, therefore, less reliable than descriptive and causal research. Exploratory research is used when the objective is to define the problem or provide an overview of the situation. It is more economical in terms of time and money. Exploratory research is used extensively in global marketing research. When researchers are asked to solve a problem or identify an opportunity in a foreign country they are not familiar with, they have to resort to exploratory research to learn and understand that culture.

Descriptive Research

Descriptive Research aims at providing a description of the existing market phenomena. Such research is often used to determine the frequency of occurrence of market events, such as frequency of customers visiting a store, machines needing to be replaced, or lawyers being consulted. Descriptive research can also be used, in a non-causal fashion, to the degree to which marketing variables are related to one another. Based on this determination, predictions can be made about future occurrences in the market. In an international setting, the researcher typically uses descriptive research to look for similarities and differences between markets and consumer groups. Similarities can then be exploited through standardization, whereas differences can help in formulating adaptive business strategy.

Descriptive studies require large quantities of data, as the need for accurate portrayal of the population studied is more stringent. Hypotheses are pre-formulated and subsequently tested with the collected data. The research design needs to be carefully planned and structured. The intent of descriptive research is to maximize accuracy and minimize systematic error. The researcher aims to increase the reliability by keeping the measurement process as free from random error as possible.

Causal Research

Casual research aims at identifying the precise cause-and-effect relationships present in the market. The level of precision is higher than that for other types of research because reasonable unambiguous conclusions regarding causality must be presented. Hence, causal research is often the most demanding in terms of time and financial resources. To extract causality from a variety of unrelated factors, researchers often need to resort to longitudinal and experimental measures. Longitudinal measures are required because after-the-fact measurement alone cannot fully explain the effect of causality. Experimentation is necessary to introduce systematic variation of factors and then measure the effect of these variations. Causal research is useful only if the research objective is to identify these inter-relationships and if this knowledge makes a contribution to the corporate decision-making process.

Experimental Design[3]

Experimental design is a set of procedures that guide an experimental study by specifying: (a) what independent variables are to be manipulated, (b) what dependent variables are to be measured, (c) what levels of the experimental treatment are to be used, (d) how to select test units and assign them to different groups, (e) how to control for selection bias, and (f) how to minimize the influence of extraneous variables on the results of the experiment. This technique is based on the principle of manipulating a treatment variable and observing changes in a response variable. This enables the researcher to draw conclusions about causality, especially if the experiment has been controlled for all other factors that can cause changes in the response variable.

In establishing a causal relationship between variables, it is necessary to determine which variable is the cause and which is the result. While looking for causal relationships, the researcher should look for evidences of strong associations between the action taken and the observed outcome and that the action preceded the outcome. The researcher should also be capable of eliminating every other possible or probable cause for the observed outcome. The other important factor to be considered is the time lag between the cause and the effect.

In many international marketing situations, the results are not apparent immediately. Even though experimental designs are applicable to all social and cultural backgrounds, it is very difficult to design an experiment that is comparable or equivalent in all countries and cultures. Experiments, by their very nature, incorporate differences of culture in terms of marketing practices, distribution channels, and purchase patterns. Hence, transferring the same design across countries could result in erroneous results. The data must be adjusted to account for built-in national and cultural biases.[4] The following six notations are commonly used while conducting experiments:

---

[3] Aaker et al., *Marketing Research*, 11th edition.
[4] Charles S. Mayer, "Multinational Marketing Research: The Magnifying Glass of Methodological Problems," *European Research* (1978), vol. 6, pp. 77–83.

1. *O:* This denotes a formal observation or measurement of the dependent variable that is made as part of the experimental study. When more than one measurement of the dependent variable is being used, symbols such as O_1, O_2, and so on will be used. The ordering of *O*s from left to right will represent the time sequence in which they occur.
2. *X:* This denotes the test units' exposure to the experimental manipulation or treatment. When more test units are exposed to more than one experimental treatment, symbols such as X_1, X_2, and so forth will be used. The ordering of *X*s from left to right will represent the time sequence in which they occur.
3. *EG:* This denotes an experimental group of test units that are exposed to the experimental treatment. In case of more than one experimental group, symbols such as EG_1, EG_2, and so on will be used.
4. *CG:* This denotes a control group of test units that are not exposed to the experimental treatment. In case of more than one control group, symbols such as CG_1, CG_2, and so on will be used.
5. *R:* This denotes random assignment of test units and experimental treatments to groups. Randomization ensures control over extraneous variables and increases the reliability of the experiment.
6. *M:* This denotes that both the experimental group and the control group are matched on the basis of some relevant characteristics. Matching helps reduce the experimental error that arises out of selection bias.

Experimental designs are generally divided into three categories: pre-experimental, true experimental, and quasi-experimental designs.

Pre-experimental Designs

Pre-experimental designs are similar to exploratory types of studies that have almost no control over the influence of extraneous factors on the results of the experiment. This category of design has little or no value in establishing causal inferences, but can lead to hypotheses about causal relationships. The common pre-experimental designs used in global marketing research are as follows.

One Group, After-Only Design

The design involves applying the experimental treatment to a subject or group, and measuring the results. For instance, a home improvement store might run a two-week advertising campaign in Duluth, Georgia, during April, highlighting the beauty of well-maintained lawns. Upon subsequent analysis, an uptick in cleaning equipment sales and number of customer visits to the gardening department at the store may serve to justify the advertising expenditure. This experimental design can be described with the following notation:

$$EG \quad X \quad O$$

One problem with this design is that it leaves open the possibility that the results could be explained by events external to the design. For instance, increase in sales of cleaning supplies and more customer visits to the cleaning supplies department might be linked to the spring-cleaning initiatives by the customers, and not necessarily triggered by the advertising campaign. These confounding effects that are external to the design are termed as history effects. In marketing studies, the history effects can be seen in the actions of competitors, retaliatory or otherwise. In some situations, competitors deliberately run special promotions in markets in which others are experimenting, to foul them up. The longer the time period involved, the greater is the likelihood that history will account for the observed results.

Another problem with this design is known as maturation. This refers to changes within respondents that are a consequence of time, including aging, growing tired, or becoming hungrier. For instance, suppose the experimental treatment is a one-year delinquency-prevention program. At the year's end, the program is evaluated by measuring the number of subjects who have jobs and the incidence of crime. If 18-year-olds are more likely than 17-year-olds to hold jobs and avoid crime, then the findings may be the result of the young people maturing during the year, and not because of the delinquency program.

Non-matched Control Group Design

One approach to control for history and maturation effects is to introduce a control group. Data on garden equipment sales and store visits might be readily available for Savannah, Georgia. Thus, the data obtained in Savannah could be compared with that of Duluth. This design would be:

$$\begin{array}{ccc} EG & X & O_1 \\ \hline CG & & O_2 \end{array}$$

The top line refers to the city of Duluth and the bottom line to the city of Savannah, which, of course, receives no experimental treatment. The results of interest would then be O_1–O_2. A dotted horizontal line means that the groups are separate, and that the experimental treatment does not reach the control group. If people in Duluth read the advertisement in the Savannah newspaper, such would not be the case.

However, this design suffers from selection bias. It may be that the response to the experiment is strictly a function of the city selected, Duluth. The type of homes, income, lifestyle, and climate in Duluth could influence the experiment. If two, three, or more test cities and a like number of control cities were used, the selection bias very likely would be reduced, but it still would be there.

Matched Control Group Design

One approach to reducing selection bias is to match the experimental and control groups. Thus, if climate is expected to affect a community's reaction to lawn maintenance advertising, cities can be matched based on their average temperature. A control city, similar to that of Duluth in terms of temperature, can be selected. Of course, another city may be found that matches Duluth in other dimensions besides temperature, such as the type of homes, or income levels. This design can be denoted as:

$$EG \quad M \quad X \quad O_1$$
$$CG \quad M \qquad O_2$$

where M indicates that the two groups are matched with respect to some variable of interest.

The use of matched control groups is very beneficial when the sample design and cost considerations limit the size of the sample. It is very costly to run a test marketing program with subsequent measurement in a city or a small group of cities, and the researchers are often constrained to a single test city, or at most two or three. In such cases, attempting to match the control city or cities with the test city or cities might be appropriate.

One Group, Before–After Design

The designs considered thus far have been *after-only* designs. Another approach to improving the control is to add a before measure, noted as follows:

$$EG \quad O_1 \quad X \quad O_2$$

The before measure that acts as a control group implies that if the city is large, the O_1 measure also will be large. The interest is then in the change from O_1 to O_2, correcting for seasonal patterns. The before measure can be added to any design already presented. It will enhance sensitivity by adding another method to control for confounding variables.

True Experimental Designs

True experiments use random assignment of subjects to groups. The main objective in this type of designs is to control and minimize threats to internal validity, which include effects of mortality, testing, history, selection, and maturation. This helps researchers rule out competing hypotheses. As true experimental designs use random assignment of subjects, they control for internal validity to a great extent. The common true experimental designs used in global marketing research are as follows.

Two-Group, After-Only Design

This design uses a test group, which is subjected to the experimental treatment and a control group, which is used for comparison purposes. Members are assigned to the experimental group and the test group in a random fashion. The researcher can measure the differences in the test group and control group and get an understanding of the impact of the treatment. Because the subjects are randomly assigned to the test and control group, when the sample size is large enough, the two groups will be matched in all dimensions. Since no measurements are taken before the treatment is applied, there can be no bias because of testing effect.

For instance, we had 30 retail stores to use in our test. We randomly assign 15 to the test condition, and use the remaining 15 as a control. Because of the randomization, it would be unlikely that the test retail stores differ from the control retail stores on conditions like revenue, number of customers, number of products, and so on. All of these factors should tend to average out. Of course, as the sample size increases, the degree of matching achieved by randomization also increases. A randomized two-group, after-only design can be represented as:

$$EG \quad R \quad X \quad O_1$$
$$CG \quad R \qquad\quad O_2$$

where R indicates that subjects are randomly assigned to the test and control groups. Randomization works very well in cases where the sample size is large enough such that the test and control groups are similar; however, this method does not eliminate biases created due to history and maturation effects. Hence, the two-group, before–after design is used to control for this.

Two-Group, Before–After Design

As was done in the previous design, there are two groups—an experimental group and a control group. In this design, measurements are taken from both the groups before and after the treatment have been applied. This method reveals the effect of the experimental treatment on the test group.

For instance, the Campbell Soup Company conducted a series of 19 before–after, randomized control group experiments in the 1970s to evaluate alternative advertising strategies for many of its products, including Campbell's condensed soups, Soup for One soups, Chunky soups, Franco-American pasta, Swanson frozen dinners, and V-8 cocktail vegetable juice.[5] The studies tested increased advertising, shifts to different media, shifts to different markets, and new creative approaches. Five key conclusions emerged from the experiments. First, in five tests of increased advertising expenditures, consumers did not respond to being told the same thing more often. Second, three of five experiments, including the Chunky soup experiment, in which the test advertising reached more people, did result in increased sales. Third, improved creative efforts did result in increased sales in three of five experiments that tested new advertising. Fourth, in the experiments where significant sales increases occurred, they usually occurred within a relatively short time period, three or four periods. A two-group, before–after design is denoted as:

$$EG \quad R \quad O_1 \quad X \quad O_2$$
$$CG \quad R \quad O_3 \qquad\quad O_4$$

where the control group helps control for history and maturation effects and also controls for the reactive effect of O_1 on O_2. The disadvantage with this method is that it may sensitize the members of the experimental group to the procedure and hence cause them behave in an unnatural manner.

---

[5] J. O. Eastlack, Jr, and Ambar G. Rao, "Conducting Advertising Experiments in the Real World: The Campbell Soup Company Experience," *Marketing Science* 5, no. 3 (Winter 1989): 245–259.

Solomon Four-Group Design

The Solomon Four-Group design offers a possible solution to the problems faced in the two previous designs. This procedure uses four groups—two experimental groups and two control groups. Observations are made for one experimental group and one control group before the treatment. The treatment is then applied to both the experimental groups. Observations are then made for all four groups. This method is very expensive, as the sample size required is twice that for the other designs. However, this design controls for all the biases in the experimental procedure and gives a clear picture of the effect of the experiment. This experiment can be denoted as:

$$EG \quad R \quad O_1 \quad X \quad O_2$$
$$CG \quad R \quad O_3 \quad \quad O_4$$
$$EG \quad R \quad \quad X \quad O_5$$
$$CG \quad R \quad \quad \quad O_6$$

Quasi-Experimental Designs

Quasi-experimental designs are used in situations where random assignment of subjects is not feasible or practical. In these cases, the researcher should be aware of the factors that can be potential threats to internal validity and should control for them. Field experiments allow the researcher to make causal inferences in a real-world situation. The natural setting provides greater generalizability to the results.

Quasi-experimental designs include procedures such as trend analysis and time-series measures. In these methods, there is no random assigning of subjects. An example of an experimental design was the study conducted to evaluate the impact shelf facings on the sales of a given product, which in this case was fruit juice. In the US, most grocery stores display these products in four columns. Hence, the shelf facings were changed to three and five columns and the change in sales was observed. The researchers made sure that there were no other variables such as change in price and competitors' promotions going on in the stores that could have a confounding effect on the experiment. The same procedure was to be conducted in the UK and Japan; however, the key to conducting experiments in the international scenario is adopting the procedure to suit the country characteristics. In the UK, the average number of columns for display of fruit juice is three. Hence, the experiment changed this to two and four and made a note of the difference in sales. The average number of columns for display in Japan is two and this was changed to one and three. Suitable changes have to be made in the experimental procedure to make it meaningful in that specific country context.

Problems in Experimental Designs[6]

International field experiments are unusual because the organizational settings in which such research is feasible are hard to find, and the complexities are also high. When combined with

---

[6] Betty Jane Punnet, "Designing Field Experiments for Management Research Outside North America," *International Studies of Management and Organization* XVIII, no. 3 (1988): 44–54.

the influence of cultural differences, this can lead to various problems, some of which are mentioned below.

- A lack of familiarity with the research process on the part of the subject group or the organization can mean that experimental research is seen as an attempt to impose the researcher's values on the subjects. It can be particularly difficult to gain access to the organization under these circumstances.
- The administrative aspects of conducting research, such as gathering information and being present at the site, may, in themselves, be unusual and constitute a form of treatment that confounds the effect of the intended treatment. This is even more likely in international settings than in domestic settings because research projects are unusual in the former.
- The researcher is often different from the subject population in terms of education, status, prestige, etc. In some cases, the researcher is seen as an authority figure, and subjects may then respond by trying to please the researcher by giving the *right* response or alternatively try to thwart the researcher by giving the *wrong* response.
- The researcher may be considered of a lower status in some cases because of race, sex, or age. In such cases, subjects may refuse to cooperate or may deliberately try to distort the results.
- It may be desirable for the experiment to be carried out by the organization members in order to implement treatment as naturally as possible. If they are unfamiliar with the research process, it may be difficult for such people to understand the need to follow procedures rigorously.
- Differing customs and conditions may have unexpected results. It is relatively easy in a familiar environment to isolate possible confounds to an experiment. In an unfamiliar environment, the researcher may be unaware of variables that are important, and may overlook them.
- Obtaining subjects' consent for research and debriefing them regarding the purpose of the research may be difficult if they are not familiar with the research process or the theory that is being tested.

Biases in Experimental Design

Researches encounter biases in experimental designs, which contribute to distorting the results. Some of the more common biases are the following:[7]

- *History effect:* Events external to the experiment that affects the responses of the people involved in the experiment.
- *Mortality:* Members of a group leave the group in large numbers; hence, groups that start out as matched groups may not remain that way as the experiment progresses.
- *Selection:* There could be a conscious or unconscious bias in selecting the subjects so that the groups are not matched or there is a predisposition toward subjects with certain traits.
- *Testing effect:* If the subjects are aware that they are being tested in some manner, they may exhibit behavior that is not natural to them.

---

[7] Richard L. Sandhusen, *Global Marketing* (Hauppauge, NY: Barron's Educational Series, 1994), pp. 67–69.

- *Measurement or instrument error:* There could be differences in measuring the before and after findings or there could be a change of instrument during the course of the experiment. This could lead to changes in measurements.

ISSUES IN PRIMARY DATA COLLECTION

Collecting primary data does not always mean that researchers have to set foot in the country that is being studied. The data could be collected from within the US by talking to students from the nation of interest, the local embassy personnel, tourists, or even experts in the US who have in-depth knowledge about that country. One word of caution—even though the information collected may be technically correct, it should not be considered representative of the general population. This can be used in exploratory research to get a feel for the problem and to formulate hypotheses.

Once the decision has been made to visit the country of interest, the researcher must be very clear on the information that needs to be collected. The target segment should be very specific. For instance, if the research is meant for working women, parts of the country with maximum concentration of working women must be concentrated upon. The idea is to collect the maximum amount of useful information with minimum expense of time and effort. At this juncture, it is prudent to mention that the researcher should also be very clear on the decision-making process. If the study is on selling financial services, the researcher should have a clear idea of whether the decision is made jointly by a married couple or if the male partner decides for the family.

The researcher should have an idea of the client's capabilities and limitations before deciding on the data sources. Many clients tend to place a lot of faith in their own employees and sometimes this could backfire on the researcher. An employee of the client's firm claiming to know all about another nation may not be the best source for information. The same goes with friends who offer to help. As there is no financial obligation on the part of this person, the information could be substandard or even erroneous. The researcher will have to carry this cross at a later stage in the research process.

EMIC Versus ETIC Dilemma

One of the major problems faced by a global marketing researcher is that of comparability of data. It is common fact that each country is unique and people of different nationalities exhibit different values, attitudes, and behaviors. Hence, the researcher is required to design the study in a manner that suits the specific country of interest. This may be useful in gathering accurate data about one country. However, in a multi-country study, this will make data across countries incomparable. For the sake of comparability of data, researchers may design standard techniques to be used across countries. This could, however, result in loss of precision.

Given the preceding dilemma, two schools of global marketing research have emerged. The *EMIC* school believes in the uniqueness of each country and culture and emphasizes studying the peculiarities of each country, identifying and understanding the uniqueness. The study is typically culture-specific and inferences have to be made about cross-cultural similarities and differences in a subjective manner.

At the other end of the spectrum is the *ETIC* school, which is primarily concerned with identifying the universal values, attitudes, and behavior. The research techniques in this case are culture-free, making comparisons across cultures easy and objective. Applying the same techniques across cultures can, however, lead to methodological problems. These schools of thought represent the two polar extremes on the continuum of cross-cultural research methodology. The researcher tends toward one or the other depending on the purpose of the research and the number of countries or cultures studied.

Both these ideologies are correct in their own way. For a multi-country study to be useful, information should be comparable. At the same time, if a research study has to be useful to users in the country where it is conducted, the uniqueness that come with the data has to be retained. The ideal survey instrument would encompass both the EMIC and ETIC schools of thought. This can be accomplished by getting the local users involved in the research study right from the beginning. The research design should not be totally standardized. It has to make allowances for peculiarities of each country. This becomes very important when *soft* data like lifestyle and attitudes are researched.

TYPES OF PRIMARY SOURCES

Selection of a specific research technique depends on a lot of factors, such as the following:

- The purpose for which the data is collected. Standardized techniques can be used for collecting objective data, but may not be very useful in collecting subjective data.
- Researchers need to use open-ended questions to get unstructured data.
- The environment in which the data is to be collected affects the technique to be used. Researchers can control the environment in which the data is to be collected or they can collect it from the real world.
- The type of data sought—historical data or future intentions to purchase a product.
- National and cultural differences and individual preferences also affect the research technique adopted. For instance, researchers in the US prefer the survey method. Japanese researchers prefer to collect data from the dealers and other channel members.[8]

Interviews

Interviews are a popular form of collecting primary data. These interviews help researchers to obtain in-depth information about the topic under study. Since interviews are unstructured or semi-structured, there is maximum freedom to respond, within the boundaries of the topic. Such interviews are normally taped (with the permission of the respondent) for future analysis. A one-on-one or telephone interview can always yield good results, provided the right person is being interviewed. While telephone interview offers the advantage of being cost-effective and requiring minimal field staff, a personal interview technique can reduce the error due to non-response. A caveat here is the interviewer bias that researchers should watch out for.

---

[8] Czinkota and Ronkainen, *International Marketing*, 5th edition, p. 256.

Focus Groups

Focus groups are another popular method of collecting primary data. A group of knowledgeable people is gathered for a limited time period and they discuss a specific topic. As it involves a lot of individuals, many hidden issues surface, something that would not have happened in an individual interview. Discussions are recorded on tape and subsequently analyzed in detail. Focus groups provide more qualitative data and information on subjective matters like attitudes, perceptions and other covert factors. In the international setting, the researcher must understand the cultural traits and adapt the process accordingly to stimulate a frank and open exchange of ideas. Focus groups are a popular form of primary research where researchers try and tap into the customer sentiments in a collective environment to understand their attitudes toward events or products or services. Clients are involved in this process from a hidden room and can immediately signal the moderator if they need clarification on a particular thought/idea. In an international setting, technology has broadened the scope of conducting focus groups. As seen in Chapter 6, focus groups are increasingly being conducted over the Internet. Internet has melted boundaries and shrunk the world into a smaller place giving the researcher conducting global marketing research the ability to reach consumers who are not nearly in the same location as the researcher himself/herself.

Observational Techniques

Observational techniques require the researcher to play the role of a non-participating observer of activity and behavior. Observation can be personal or conducted through some mechanical devices. It can be obtrusive or non-obtrusive. In global marketing research, observational techniques are mainly used to develop an understanding of practices that have not been previously encountered. These techniques can also help understand phenomena that would be difficult to assess with other techniques.

Also, observational techniques aid in acquiring a more accurate picture of the behavior. Instead of asking consumers how long they took to shop or what was the path they followed while doing their grocery shopping, researchers can observe these activities firsthand and draw conclusions. It is more accurate as some consumers may not know this kind of information about themselves or they would not be comfortable sharing the information with the researcher, which creates biases in data analysis. For instance, P&G conducted observational studies to redesign its Swiffer mop by visiting homes across the US. This led to the launch on the Swiffer CarpetFlick in August 2005 that had inputs from the end users.[9] In the international context, this technique is used to observe previously unobserved traits and practices.

Observational techniques have their pitfalls. Once the subject is aware of being observed, the reactions may not be normal. In an international setting, use of multiple languages can cause some issues. For example, in Belgium, four different languages are spoken and the language can vary from one store to another. Different countries have different rules regarding observational research. Europe, for instance, requires the researcher conducting in-store research to conduct photo audits of the shelves, store checks, and in-store interviews way in advance.[10] Moreover, country-wise shopping patterns differ. For instance, some of the developing nations have not adopted the mall format of shopping completely. This brings in additional variables for a researcher to consider in terms of style and format of shopping for goods.

---

[9] Sarah Ellison, "Studying Messy Habits to Sweep Up a Market," *Wall Street Journal*, July 14, 2005.

[10] Czinkota and Ronkainen, *International Marketing*, 8th edition.

Surveys

Surveys are the most popular form of gathering primary data. Surveys are usually conducted with the help of questionnaires that are administered personally, through mail or by telephone. In global marketing research, survey techniques face a lot of stumbling blocks. Surveys are conducted with the assumption that the target population is able to understand and respond to the questionnaire. This may not always be the case. Most third world countries do not have widespread availability of telephones, which make telephone surveys impossible. A lot of these countries do not have an organized postal system and mailing addresses to majority of the sample population may not be available. In Venezuela, for example, houses do not have numbers but have individual names. Reaching a respondent at the right address could be a cumbersome task. Mail surveys have also been subjected to a lot of scams. In some countries, the postal employees pocket the incentive that has been mailed with the questionnaire. In Italy, for instance, a lot of mail got delivered to paper mills for recycling. Despite all these problems, survey remains the most popular method of collecting data for global marketing research. A lot of the issues of interviews have been offset by technology. It is much cheaper to conduct interviews online. Chapter 6 discussed this topic in detail on how Internet changed marketing research with the online surveying techniques.

Online International Omnibus Surveys

Omnibus surveys have been very popular for a long time. In these surveys, respondents are asked about a wide range of topics in the same interview. Several companies pay for these surveys and the clients paying for this get to ask relevant questions to the consumers. These multiclient marketing surveys are extremely popular because of two primary reasons: (a) cost savings—the respondent screening and recruitment costs are shared by all clients involved, and (b) time savings—since these are ongoing, it saves time as opposed to commissioning a separate primary research study. The time and cost savings are magnified when such studies are conducted at a global stage. Multi-country studies are expensive and require a lot of coordinated resources to successfully carry out research projects as intended. With the help of two powerful forces, Omnibus and Internet, companies have a quicker and easier way to find information from their customers.

Companies can use Omnibus surveys for a lot of purposes. Identifying the winning concept, to checking for awareness of a new product or a particular incident, checking for effectiveness of the promotional campaign to understanding detailed consumer experience. Ipsos MORI conducted one such study for a client who wanted to learn if *spamming* was a cost-effective way of approaching future customers for a variety of online services and product categories.[11] They used the Online Omnibus in GB, France, Germany, the US, Canada, and Brazil to measure: (a) the proportion of spam mail being deleted without even being read, (b) the demographic groups most susceptible to spam marketing, (c) the service/product categories yielding the greatest success as a result of spamming, and (d) satisfaction levels with the post-spam purchase process.

---

[11] "Ipsos MORI—Online Omnibus," http://www.ipsos-mori.com/researchareas/omnibusservices/onlineomnibus.aspx (Retrieved in June 2013).

PROBLEMS WITH COLLECTION OF PRIMARY DATA

The problems with collection of primary data can be broadly classified under three main categories: methodological problems, practical problems, and operational problems.[12] We will now discuss each category in detail.

Methodological Problems

Cultural Bias

Each researcher brings into his or her study a set of values, beliefs, and assumptions that are molded by his or her culture. Even when they are aware of this bias, it is very difficult for them to guard against it. The SRC, as noted in earlier chapters, allows the values, beliefs, and attitudes of the researcher to affect the way in which he/she interprets the verbal and non-verbal cues of respondents in a foreign culture. This effect is even more pronounced when the researcher is conducting a study in a culture that is vastly different from his/her own. For instance, Kraft has recognized the differing tastes in coffee across countries and has launched various versions for the British (who drink coffee with milk), the French (who drink it black), and the Latin Americans (who prefer chicory in their coffee). However, General Foods had a failed launch when they positioned Tang as a substitute for orange juice at breakfast, only to realize later that the French drank little orange juice and almost never ate at breakfast.[13] Therefore, researchers analyzing products and international markets must be wary of their own biases affecting the study results.

Language Problems

Most North American research is conducted in English, but in international research, use of the English language alone may create problems such as no response or short, uninformative answers, misunderstanding, and difficulty in gaining access to local government officials or local partners. Also, people who speak a second language fluently think differently in another language. The researcher may get subtly different answers to the same question, depending on the language it was posed on. For instance, India has no national language. As per the 2001 census, the Indian government has recognized 29 *official* languages that are used by more than a million native speakers. In addition to this, there are 60 languages that have more than 100,000 native speakers, and 122 languages have more than 10,000 native speakers. In such a market, researchers must be careful in understanding and interpreting market phenomena, as meanings are likely to differ across languages.

Translation can overcome these problems, but the terms often do not translate directly. If a translator or interpreter is used, that person must be fluent in both languages and be familiar with the particular research area. The researcher and translator must meet before beginning the research. Translation is also important for the interview protocol, which is the outline of

---

[12] Ugar Yavas and Erdner Kaynak, "Current Status of Marketing Research in Developing Countries: Problems and Opportunities," *Journal of International Marketing and Market Research* 5, no. 2 (1980): 79–89.

[13] Kotler et al., *Marketing Management*.

questions to be used. When *back* translations are used, it is found that there are as many mistakes if not more, as in the original translations.

Incomplete Research Design

Certain companies may not fit into the research design developed by the researcher. The first challenge is to locate enough good and bad performers with other characteristics necessary to satisfy the research design. Choice of research sites is very important. They should be chosen to keep as many variables as possible constant. A 2×2 matrix is often a good format.

The problem of identification is often the problem of sample size. Methodological debate over research with large samples versus research with small samples and lack of potential research sites within a country to satisfy a project design are common problems encountered. In the absence of adequate sites or lack of access to them, the researcher must consider other solutions. For example, if eight sites are desired, but only four can be accessed, alternative solutions must be sought. One strategy is to proceed with the companies that have given access and simultaneously begin the search for additional sites, but this entails thinking through which are the most important variables to control and establishing a hierarchy. This should be used to guide the search for new sites and to make decisions about accepting them. Flexibility must be built in, with fallback options clearly outlined.

The Problem of Access

In order to learn how organizations cope with restrictive investment policies, localization pressures, and initiating and managing joint ventures in the developing world, they must get into the field and talk with the principal actors in these situations. Assuming that an appropriate sample of companies has been identified, the next problem is to gain access to them as research sites. Depending on how sensitive the research question is, the access problem can be heightened.

To access people in organizations, the first step is to locate the appropriate person in corporate headquarters. Cooperation and probability of success are enhanced if the researcher can enter the company at the top. The initial letter should be directed to the president or vice-president of the international organization. It is possible that such people may not be available, the issue may be too sensitive to expose to an outsider, or the organization may not fit the research design at all. Many companies may be unwilling to contribute to academic research. The research proposal must be expressed in terms acceptable to executives and must try to confer a practical benefit on respondents. Business rather than academic terms must be used. For example, company executives are not interested in whether the researcher is using multiple regression, factor analysis, or content analysis. It has been found useful to offer the interviewee a summary of the results when the study is complete.

The viewpoints of the host country government, the local partners, the local general manager, local employees, and so on must be kept in mind. Each party will have a different logic guiding its actions, but local government officials and joint venture partners may be less accessible and probably less interested in academic research than even North American organizations. Accessing individuals may also prove to be problematic in some countries.

In Mexico, the upper socioeconomic classes are difficult to reach because of barriers like the housing structure of walls, gates, and the intervening servants.[14]

Confidentiality and Trust

Confidential data of sensitive nature, relating to, say, the functioning of a sovereign nation or pertaining to local operating problems or intercompany conflicts, may need to be researched. The researcher must convince concerned parties that he/she will not violate their trust. The promise of confidentiality and the keeping of the promise are very important. Confidentiality usually involves keeping actual names of companies or people secret. This prevents the researcher from evaluating the work completely, but this weakness is insignificant because otherwise, one would never be able to gain access for research purposes. Further, companies should believe that the researcher is actually preserving confidentiality.

Researchers must also be sensitive to the time required for interviews and answering questionnaires. The interviewee should be apprised of the purpose of the research at the beginning of the interview. Permission to take notes or use a tape recorder should be asked, though a negative answer may often be forthcoming. Notes must be updated as soon as possible after the interview. A thank you letter and other materials promised should be sent immediately after the interview. Apart from common courtesy, the letter reminds the interviewee of a potential situation that should have been discussed during the interview such as follow-up telephone calls or an additional visit for clarification.

The Problem of Analysis and Communication of Results

After recording the narrative history, a preliminary analysis should be made to ensure that all questions regarding completeness of data are answered. This may uncover areas for further probing or even force the researcher to modify the framework appropriately.

During the final analysis, the researcher will search the data for performance- related patterns. Because most of the information is qualitative data from questionnaires, there is an enormous amount of responsibility for the researcher to write well. Good writing is essential in narrative histories and observed patterns. Qualitative techniques, such as content analysis, may also be used.

Practical Problems

Time

Quick, competent studies of adaptation are rare. For a researcher, time spent is an invaluable resource in conducting studies. Hence, careful and meticulous planning would help the researcher to keep to timelines by avoiding delays. Since time eventually translates to expense, careful scheduling of field research has to be efficient. This also encompasses identifying

---

[14] Kalim, "Quality Standards," pp. 11–26.

alternate sources of data collection and a well-thought-out research design. A rough checklist to outline the progression of an international field research project will be handy in adhering to timelines. A rule of thumb in international studies is to calculate the anticipated time and then double it. There will be periods of downtime when interviewing, for example, because the researcher has to work around executive's busy schedules.

Expense

Time eventually translates into expense. Field research is the most expensive kind of international research; therefore, it has to be as efficient as possible. A well-thought-out research design is necessary before launching on actual data collection. If traditional academic sources are not sufficient, non-traditional sources must be considered. In Canada, the Canadian International Development Agency and External Affairs and in the US, the US Agency for International Development could be considered.

Technological Requirements

This refers to ensuring that the support features, with respect to resources such as telephones, fax machines, e-mail and mail facilities, and transportation facilities, are available and are maintained in proper functioning order. In the international setting, a researcher might face problems in transportation facilities when working in less-developed countries by way of poor roads and improper connectivity. Such logistical and resource needs must be properly ensured and alternatives for them identified. Another problem could be the compatibility issues when using multiple software packages. This has to carefully done so as to avoid any delay in translation process.

Operational Difficulties

1. An initial problem could be securing research permission, especially in developing countries. Some countries take three to six months to grant permission, particularly if the research topic is a sensitive one for the nation or if it requires travel outside the capital city. A sister organization in the country—a university or a management institution—could help with the process.
2. Telephones may not be dependable. A personal visit to the office to request an appointment may work better. If funding permits, hiring someone to do the telephoning and training them well may be the keys to success. The trade-offs must be considered, such as the fact that a foreign voice can often get an appointment that a local person would have difficulty getting, or a local person may be better able to secure appointments than a foreign researcher.
3. Mail systems are unreliable in some countries. Letters may be lost or delayed. Even courier service is not foolproof. The letter may reach the wrong person in the organization. A project carried out by a certain team of researchers showed that the actual addressee did not receive almost 25% of letters sent by courier though they had been signed for at the organization.

4. Travel to research sites can be difficult. Poor road conditions, bad traffic, infrequent or expensive air travel, and hazards of traveling by bus may be other problems.

5. Actual and perceived physical risk to researchers is also present. It is important to not look too prosperous—merge with the locals in terms of dress. It would serve well to inquire about the safety of areas where one travels by foot, etc.

6. Keeping a close eye on possessions and placing one's address prominently on one's briefcase are important.

7. The researcher also has to work around problems like people having died, moved elsewhere, or not wanting to talk about certain things the researcher is interested in.

8. The computer used by the researcher at home may be incompatible with the one he uses on the field. Even if made by the same company, there may be incompatibility among software packages. For example, variations and incompatibilities between software available in different countries can lead to a series of problems with respect to translation and analysis for the researcher.

In the ultimate analysis, clinical field research involves issues of access, trust, schedules, confidentiality, and feedback of transcribed interviews. Clinical research may not suit everyone, but there may be a fit between a method and a researcher's personality. The implementation phase may be fraught with ambiguity, anxiety, and frustration.

ADVANTAGES AND DISADVANTAGES OF PRIMARY DATA COLLECTION

As compared to secondary data, primary data have a lot of advantages and disadvantages. This section of the chapter deals with them in detail.

Primary data are accurate and precise as they are collected with the specific project in mind. In case of secondary data, they have been collected for purposes other than the research study and, hence, will be useful in giving only a general idea. Secondary data cannot be used to make strategic decisions. Inferences and conclusions can be drawn only with the help of primary data. Also, secondary data are collected in different formats in different countries and are in some cases not comparable. This makes it difficult for researchers to use secondary data in multi-country research. Primary data can be collected in a manner that is preferred for the specific research study.

The one major disadvantage with primary data is the resources involved in collecting it. Companies have to invest significant amount of time, manpower, and capital into gathering primary data of acceptable quality. This is more pronounced in global marketing research as the national and cultural differences mentioned earlier have a significant impact on the data collection methods.

ESTABLISHING EQUIVALENCE IN INTERNATIONAL MARKETING RESEARCH[15]

The results of a study are based on the assumption that the groups are a representative sample of the defined population and the results are a true measure of the sample. In reality, however, a number of biases can complicate the analysis and interpretation of data. Bias, thus, may be

---

[15] Douglas and Craig, *International Marketing Research*, pp. 78–82.

defined as any factor that tends to produce results or conclusions that differ systematically from the truth. The cause of bias in a research may be from many sources including errors in statistical analysis, failure to distinguish between independent and dependent observations, or failure to adjust for confusing variables. Therefore, it becomes necessary to examine the various aspects of the data collection process and establish their equivalence, and more so in a multi-country research. The types of equivalence are briefly explained in Figure 7.1.

FIGURE 7.1
EQUIVALENCES IN INTERNATIONAL MARKETING RESEARCH

Construct Equivalence

Construct equivalence deals with the function of the product or service that is being researched and not the method used in collecting the information. Different countries that are being studied must have the same perception or use for the product that is being researched. If this is not the case, comparison of data becomes meaningless. If, for example, we are studying the bicycle market, we need to understand that they come under the category of recreational sports in the US; however, in India and China, they are considered as a basic means of transportation. In Japan, people substitute noncarbonated drinks for fruit juices, whereas in the US these two categories are considered distinct products.[16] Researchers need to be concerned with the information that is needed for the study and not with the means used to collect the same. For instance, telephone interviews may be used in the US. In a third world country, researchers may have to resort to mail interviews or personal interviews to obtain the same information. This is explained in detail in the chapter on designing questionnaires.

Measurement Equivalence

Measurement equivalence is concerned with the scales used for measuring various aspects of the research study. In a multi-country study, researchers need to modify the units of measurement. In Great Britain and most Commonwealth nations, the standard for measurement is the metric scale. This change of units will have to be taken care of when designing the research instrument. It has generally been observed that it is easier to establish measurement equivalence between demographic variables than between psychographic variables. While in

---

[16] Charles S. Mayer, "The Lessons of Multi National Marketing Research," *Business Horizons*, December 1978, p. 10.

the US, researchers use a five- or a seven-point scale, it is very common to use a 20-point scale in France. This type of equivalence further includes equivalence pertaining to calibration, translation, and metric. The chapter on development of scales considers this in detail.

Sampling Equivalence

Sampling equivalence concerns the decision-making process. If, for instance, the study in on purchasing habits regarding toys, researchers need to understand that in the US, children decide the toys they want to buy. In another country, the parents could make this decision. Hence, to obtain useful information, children should be interviewed in the US and parents should be interviewed in the other country. This will be explained in detail in the chapter on Sampling.

Analysis Equivalence

Analysis equivalence is the fourth and last aspect of equivalence that a global marketing researcher should be concerned about. When doing data analysis, the researcher should take into account the different biases that might exist in different cultures. Different cultures differ widely in their assessment of situations and problems. Accordingly, they tend to choose different ratings on a given scale. For instance, the Japanese have a tendency to choose the neutral point, so it is prudent to avoid a scale with a neutral point to obtain useful information. Americans do not typically go into details with open-ended questions. Latin Americans and Italians tend to exaggerate their response. These factors must be kept in mind when designing the scales for measurement. The chapter on data analysis deals with this aspect.

To establish equivalence with respect to all the four aspects mentioned above, researchers normally conduct comparisons of results across countries, while simultaneously analyzing and checking for reliability.

The main difference between a domestic and a global marketing research study is the need to establish equivalence as far as construct, measurement, and sampling are concerned. This is easier said than done in case of global marketing research. For starters, it is very difficult to compare across cultures. People from different nations have different values, beliefs, and lifestyles and in general view the world very differently. It would be impractical to hope that a Frenchman and a Korean would agree to all of the same ideas. In many cases, homogeneity in ideas and values is not even possible within a single country, so it may be necessary for the researcher to adapt the research design to collect comparable data from various countries.

In many cases, researchers try to follow one methodology in all the countries that are being studied. If, for instance, telephone surveys were used as the primary means of collecting primary data, this would be very effective in the developed nations where most households have a telephone and the list of telephone numbers is easily accessible. Unfortunately, this may prove to be a very costly method in the developing countries where the cost of making a telephone call is very high. Moreover, not all households have a telephone connection and reaching the target sample may not be possible. In such countries, the methodology will have to be adapted. The goal is to ensure that the data are comparable. Comparability of the research instrument comes a distant second.

The same principles could be applied to measurement and sampling equivalence. The scales used to measure various aspects should be modified according to the country where they are to be used. The sampling frame should also be modified. For instance, if a company were interested in researching the office supplies market, in the US all information regarding buying behavior could be collected by talking to the office secretary; however, in some cultures that are still highly bureaucratic, it may be necessary to interview someone higher up in the corporate ladder. To obtain information that is comparable, researchers should understand the decision-making process and target the right sample.

Establishing equivalence for a global marketing research study is a mammoth task that calls for a lot of judgmental decisions on the part of the researcher. The researcher will have to call upon past experience to decide the methodology that will work in the country of interest. A survey was conducted to study the stress levels at workplace in different cities and it was stated that Hong Kong was the most stressful city. The importance of establishing equivalence in terms of construct, measurement, sample, and analysis could be illustrated by the results of this survey. The survey compared cities like New York and London to Hong Kong and opinions of working men and women were obtained. Due to a great deal of diversity among the people surveyed, definition of stress is bound to vary widely. A New Yorker could consider the commute stressful, whereas a person in Hong Kong could consider peer pressure to be the most stressful aspect of the job. It is also important that the samples in all these cities be equivalent. This could prove very tricky because a physician in London may not have the same work pressure that a physician in New York has. Hence, it is important that the researcher consider all these aspects before coming to a conclusion.

GLOBAL MARKETING RESEARCH IN PRACTICE

Tasty Burgers will have a reasonably clear picture of the market size in each of the four countries—UK, Brazil, India, and Saudi Arabia—with the secondary data available to them. This will help them eliminate some markets where secondary data clearly indicates there is no potential for growth; however, it is very important to conduct primary research for those markets where they plan to expand. Primary data, as defined in this chapter, is data that has been collected specifically for this project and should be able to provide answers to all the research questions.

The first step is to analyze the extent of information available about a given market. Usually, there is a plethora of information available for developed countries; hence, researchers should have in-depth information about the UK. However, in case of developing countries, such as Brazil and India, reliable demographic and economic data are not available easily. Even if they were available, they would not have been updated in the recent past. Saudi Arabia is another country where there is dearth of information. In these cases, it becomes necessary to perform exploratory research to test the viability of the project in these countries. A detailed study involves time and resources, which should be allocated only if exploratory research proves that there is market potential.

Exploratory research will involve studying the major cities in each of these countries and determining which one of these cities would be a good place to set up the first outlet. Researchers could study the existing fast-food market in each of these countries and determine the products for which there is a great demand. An informal survey of clientele in other fast-food chains could be conducted to find out if they are satisfied with the products being offered by competitors. The survey could be used to find out if the theme used by Tasty Burgers would sell in each of these markets.

Descriptive research involves thorough investigation into all the aspects that are required to set up business in each of these countries. The most efficient and reliable forms of data collection methods will have to be decided for each of the countries. It may not be possible to use the same method of data collection, as there are significant national and cultural differences among these countries. Care should be taken to ensure that construct, measurement, and sampling equivalence are maintained. The subsequent chapters on measurement scales, sampling, and designing the questionnaire will discuss how this can be achieved.

SUMMARY

This chapter deals with collecting primary data for global marketing research. Depending on the research purpose, a choice is made among exploratory, descriptive, and causal research. Exploratory research is most appropriate when the primary objective is to identify problems, define problems more precisely, or to investigate the possibility of new alternative courses of action. Descriptive research aims at providing a description of the existing market phenomena. Causal research aims at identifying the precise cause-and-effect relationships present in the market. The different methods of collecting primary data, like qualitative methods, surveys, and observational methods, are described in detail. The chapter also deals with the problems that are specific to primary data collection in international research and are categorized under three major headings: methodological problems, practical problems, and operational problems. The chapter also outlines the advantages and disadvantages of primary data. The most important aspect of primary data collection is establishing equivalence. There are various aspects to establishing equivalence and each aspect is explained in great detail in the following chapters.

QUESTIONS AND PROBLEMS

1. A group of customers at a well-known retail store in a particular city are sent mail on upcoming offers and sales discounts. The results are used to establish the effectiveness of this campaign to other cities in order to increase overall sales.
   a. What kind of experimental design is this an example of?
   b. What are the potential hazards in drawing the above conclusion from this type of experiment?
2. List some of the threats to internal validity you learned in this chapter. What type of experimental design offers the most effective control and minimization of such threats?
3. List the different types of primary research and describe them briefly.
4. Coca-Cola wants to conduct a blind taste test in the Philippines to test the preference of Coke over Pepsi. In the blind taste test, the respondents are asked to taste unlabeled colas and report their preference. Evaluate the validity of this experiment.
5. What are the factors that affect experimental designs in global marketing research?
6. Compare and contrast EMIC and ETIC schools of thought.
7. Define and describe the components of establishing equivalence in global marketing research.

8

CHAPTER _____

Qualitative and Observational Research

INTRODUCTION[1]

In most global marketing research studies, it is not possible to find secondary data that will help solve all the research problems. Collecting primary data becomes a necessity. In most cases, the researcher does not have enough information to formulate the research question. It becomes imperative that the researcher conduct exploratory research to get a better understanding of the problem. Qualitative and observational data help the researcher get a better feel for the problem before launching into the actual research process.

NEED FOR QUALITATIVE RESEARCH

Qualitative research enables researchers to understand consumer needs, expectations, and perceptions. Information regarding the consumer perspective helps the researcher to become oriented to the range and complexity of consumer activity and concerns. For instance, Del Monte closely interacted with their customers through their online community called "I Love my Dog" when they were developing a new breakfast treat for dogs. Based on the interaction, the company identified a need for something that had a bacon-and-egg taste along with vitamins and minerals. With continuous involvement of the online community throughout the product development process, the company launched fortified "Sausage Breakfast Bites." The constant interaction and inputs enabled them to develop and launch this product in nearly half the time usually taken to launch a new product.[2] In the international context, qualitative research takes on an added meaning as the regional and cultural differences accentuate the attitudinal variations among people. For instance, the prevailing mindset in Asia that pale or white skin is beautiful has been identified through research.[3] This has led cosmetic companies like P&G, Unilever, and L'Oreal to launch products that appeal to this expectation. Examples of such products include P&G's skin-whitening products from Olay and SK-II, the green tea flavored toothpaste from Crest, and Tide Naturals detergent for countries like India where a significant portion of the population washes clothes by hand. Therefore, qualitative studies

_____

[1] Adapted from Kumar et al., *Essentials of Marketing Research*.

[2] Emily Steel, "The New Focus Groups: Online Networks Proprietary Panels Help Consumer Companies Shape Products, Ads," *Wall Street Journal*, January 14, 2008.

[3] Anita Chang Beattie, "Early Foothold in China Pays Off," *Advertising Age*, October 29, 2012.

bring to light the feelings, thoughts, intentions, and behaviors of customers that significantly influence the success of products in the global marketplace.

Qualitative data are collected to know more about things that cannot be directly measured and observed. The basic assumption behind qualitative methods is that an individual's organization of a relatively unstructured stimulus indicates the person's basic perception of the phenomenon and his or her reaction to it. The more unstructured and ambiguous a stimulus is, the more the subjects can and will project their emotions, needs, motive, attitudes, and values. The structure of a stimulus is the degree of choice available to the subject. A highly structured stimulus gives the subject very clear alternatives and leaves very little choice to the subject, whereas a stimulus of low structure has a wide range of alternatives.

Qualitative methods are less structured and more intense than questionnaire-based interviews. There is a longer and more flexible relationship with the respondent, so that the resulting data give the researcher greater insight and newer perspectives. Qualitative research relies on a small sample which may not be representative of the target population. Qualitative research can be used for various purposes. In exploratory research, it can be used to define a problem in greater detail. It is used to generate hypotheses that can be researched in detail. It is used by researchers to test new product concepts and for pretesting questionnaires. In international research, qualitative research is used to learn the consumers' vantage point and vocabulary and to get a better understanding of the way decisions are made and products are used in a foreign culture.

All too often, researchers tend to view qualitative research as an alternative to and in competition with, quantitative research. It has to be understood that each merely represents different tools available to the researcher. Quantitative research addresses the *who, what, when,* and *where* of consumer behavior. Qualitative research tends to focus on the why—the reasons behind the overt behavior. There is also a popular fallacy in the research community that qualitative research can be used only for the purpose of exploratory research. Qualitative research aims to understand consumer behavior instead of measuring it, so it is typically used to increase researchers' knowledge, clarify issues, define problems, formulate hypotheses, and generate ideas. It helps researchers understand cultural and personal meanings attached to objects and experiences.[4]

TYPES OF QUALITATIVE RESEARCH[5]

There are different methods of conducting qualitative methods, and this section explains each of them in detail. The methods differ from one another in terms of the structure imposed on data collection, the environment in which the data is collected (real shopping world or simulated), the extent to which the respondent is aware of the study, and the sample size.

Individual Interviews

Individual interviews are conducted face-to-face with the respondent so the subject matter can be explored in detail. In-depth interviews are of two basic types:

---

[4] David Aaker, V. Kumar, Robert P. Leone, and George S. Day, *Marketing Research* (Hoboken: Wiley Publications), 11th edition.

[5] This section adapted from Aaker et al., *Marketing Research*, 6th edition.

1. *Nondirective interviews:* The respondent is given the freedom to respond within the bounds of the topics of interest to the interviewer. Success in such interviews depends on establishing a relaxed atmosphere and the ability of the interviewer to probe the respondent and guide the discussion back to the topic in case of any digression. These sessions may last one to two hours and may be recorded for interpreting at a later time.
2. *Semi-structured or focused individual interviews:* The interviewer attempts to cover a specific list of topics or subareas. The timing, exact wording, and the time allotted to each question is left to the interviewer's discretion. These types of interviews are useful with busy executives to obtain basic information on the subject of interest. The open nature of the interviews allows the interviewer to pursue a discussion in detail if required.

Three techniques have been widely used in conducting in-depth interviews. The first technique is called *laddering*. In this technique, the questions progress from product characteristics to user characteristics. The technique attempts to use tangible product aspects to elicit response from the customers with regard to the intangible aspects, like feelings and attitudes. If the topic being researched is about a clothing store, respondents will be quizzed on each attribute they list, and then probed to see why it is important to the respondent. This probe continues until the researcher connects the attribute listed to value derived from it. An example of such a process might resemble the following line of questioning:

Interviewer:	Why do you like the Clothing Store A?	
Respondent:	They carry a wide range.	(*Store Attribute*)
Interviewer:	Why is that important?	
Respondent:	I can get the clothes for my size.	(*Store Attribute*)
Interviewer:	Why is that important?	
Respondent:	The clothes will fit me well.	(*Consequence of shopping there*)
Interviewer:	Why is that important?	
Respondent:	I will look and feel good.	(*Value derived from the store*)

In the above dialogue, the focus has moved from a very tangible aspect of a clothing store (i.e., a wide range of clothes) to an intangible aspect (i.e., contribution to self-esteem by looking and feeling good).

The second technique is called *hidden-issue questioning*. The focus in these interviews is not on the socially shared values but rather on personal *sore spots*—not on general lifestyles, but on deeply felt personal concerns. It should be noted that this line of questioning is different from focusing on socially shared values. Instead, the researcher focuses on deeply held personal concerns that are not often expressed through a direct line of questioning. For instance, the interviewer could ask the participant about their ideal image of a social life. Following their answer, the follow-up question can be focused around determining the traits that would be excluded from their perfect life. For example, if the question reveals that the respondent would not like to feel *left out* from the social community, then this is an area that the company should address. One way of addressing this concern may lie in developing user communities that interact and discuss the product. Communities such as Harley Owners Group, the SAP Community Network, and Intuit's Live Community are a few examples of user communities that bring in close interaction among *like-minded* customers and create a close social bond.

The third technique, *symbolic analysis*, attempts to analyze the symbolic meaning of objects by comparing them with their opposites. This technique helps the researcher to find out what certain things really mean to the respondent. For instance, after ascertaining that the respondent uses mobile phones, an interviewer might ask what they would do if mobile phones did not exist. The respondent might respond that they would not be able to instantly communicate with their friends, family, and coworkers, and will have to depend on writing letters, or make long trips to meet them. From this, the interviewer can gather that, to the participant, mobile phones represent an immediate and instantaneous way to keep in touch with their contacts. Mobile phone companies may use this information to develop ads that highlight fewer dropped calls and better call reception to appeal to their subscribers.

Conducting personal interviews over the telephone is beginning to gain greater acceptance in countries that have an extensive telephone network. Respondents are becoming more receptive to the idea of saving time by giving the interview over the telephone. It is also far more economical for the firm conducting the study. Increasingly, the computer is also being used for interviews. The interviewer conducts the interview with a headset and keys the responses directly into the computer. The responses can be printed out at a later time. Some computer programs provide for frequency counts and averages for responses to the closed-ended questions.

Focus Groups

A focus group discussion is the process of obtaining possible ideas or solutions to a marketing problem from a group of respondents by discussing it. The participants are representative of the target markets and emphasis is placed on the group interaction. Each participant is encouraged to express views on the topic of discussion and elaborate on or react to the views of other participants. The discussion is moderated by an interviewer who stimulates the discussion and guides the group back to the topic at hand whenever there is a digression.

Focus group discussions offer more stimulation than interviews and are known to elicit more spontaneity and candor. Focus groups are used to:

- Generate and test ideas for new products, product concepts, and product positioning
- Generate hypotheses that can be studied in later research
- Collect information that can be used for designing questionnaires
- Check if marketing strategies are transferable across countries

Focus groups can be of different types. Exploratory focus groups are used to generate hypotheses for testing or concepts for future research. Experiencing focus groups allow the researcher to experience the emotional framework in which the product is being used. Clinical focus groups are used to gain insight into the true motivations and feelings in the consumers' minds that are subconscious in nature. Clinical focus groups require a moderator with expertise in psychology and sociology.

As a rule, three to four group sessions are usually sufficient to get most of the information on the topic of interest. The first discussion reveals a lot of information to the analyst. The second and subsequent discussions produce a lot of information, but not much of it is new. Exceptions to this occur if there are distinct segments to cover and these segments have widely varying opinions on the topic being discussed.

In the international setting, it is important for moderators to be conversant with the language and also the patterns of social interaction and the nonverbal clues used by people in that part of the world. The moderator should also bear in mind other practices peculiar to that region. For instance, in the Middle East, women do not have as much freedom as women in the Western world. In some Asian countries, the moderator must take special interest in introductions if the discussion is to be truly open and candid. In global marketing research, the role of the moderator becomes crucial, as he or she tends to reflect the norms, attitudes, and response patterns typical of a specific cultural context and these attitudes and responses may be projected into the findings.[6]

The moderator first looks at the research purpose and the research questions. A checklist is then prepared on the specific issues to be covered in the discussion. The moderator uses this checklist as a general guide to prevent digression by the group. The usual method of introducing topics is to start with a general topic and gradually proceed to specific topics. The group selected for the discussion should provide for both the similarity and contrast within a group. It is necessary to combine participants from different social classes and age groups because of differences in their perceptions, experiences, and verbal skills. Recruiting a focus group requires a great deal of understanding of the topic and of the potential members of the group. For instance, in the UK, conducting focus group sessions for ethnically sensitive topics poses quite a challenge.[7] While it is necessary to ensure that the group is representative of the population that is being targeted, it is impossible to recruit a perfectly *Asian* focus group. Creating a group of three Hindus, two Sikhs, two Moslems and a Christian is asking for problems. Young West Indians in groups can also be very difficult to research as they strive very hard to keep their street identity intact. Though the usual group size is about 8–12 members, smaller group sizes may also be used. Exhibit 8.1 presents the required skills of the moderator and the assistant moderator.

For a focus group to deliver useful results, the analyst must be culturally sensitive, more so in global marketing research. The analyst should keep in mind the dynamics that are peculiar to the specific nation or culture. Certain cultures may be excessively conservative in their approach to a new idea or a concept. For instance, the French have been proven to resist innovations of any kind. In some cases, the participants may be excessively critical of one thing and uncritical of something else. The Japanese hesitate to criticize new product ideas. There is also a very strong group mentality among the Asian culture while most Americans tend to be individualistic. In Asia, this translates to the group rejecting somebody that does not *belong*. Care should be taken to address this issue while selecting the panel members. Even though each country is unique in its cultural characteristics, there are some common differences that should be addressed:[8]

- *Time frame:* Many companies in the US and Canada are used to completing the research project in a relatively short period of time. This is not possible with international research. Lead times tend to be much longer, more so in the Far East. A good estimate would be to calculate the time required for the research in the US and double it for Europe. It would be even longer for Asia.
- *Structure:* Most focus groups panels consist of four to six people, versus eight to ten in the US. The focus group interviews themselves last for almost 4 hours. Specific instructions have to be given to research organizations that are coordinating the project in the foreign country.

---

[6] Naresh K. Malhotra, James Agarwal, and Mark Peterson, "Methodological Issues in Cross-Cultural Marketing, A State-of-the-Art Review," *International Marketing Review* 13, no. 5 (1996): 7–43.

[7] Peter Chisnall, *Marketing Research* (Berkshire: McGraw Hill Publications, 1997), 5th edition, p. 185.

[8] Adapted from Thomas L. Greenbaum, "Understanding Focus Group Research Aboard," *Marketing News* 30, no. 12 (3 June 1996): H14.

Exhibit 8.1

Required Skills of the Moderator and the Assistant Moderator[9]

The moderator in a focus group should possess critical skills such as:

- Able to start the discussion quickly and smoothly. This involves making a crisp welcome message that gives the purpose of the meeting, the overview of the topic, ground rules to be adhered to, and the first question to start the discussion.
- Able to establish a quick rapport so that the group gets to the topic of interest in as little time as possible. That is, make the participants feel comfortable and willing to contribute.
- Demonstrable knowledge about the topic, and display genuine interest in the views of the participants. Also should be adept with the idiomatic expressions, the casual lingo, cultural references, and nonverbal cues attached to the topic of discussion.
- Encourage discussions within the group yet maintain focus on the main topic at hand.
- Ensure that there is a balance in conversation so that one person does not dominate the meeting.
- Avoid use of technical jargon and sophisticated terminology.
- Be mentally well-prepared by being free of any distractions, and being attentive to the comments made.
- Be able to diffuse any conflicts that may take place from the various interactions.
- Use probing phrases (e.g., "Would you explain further?", "Can you provide an example?") and pause intelligently in order to elicit more information and invite participants to contribute more.
- Be flexible in implementing the interview agenda so that the group does not lose its spontaneity.
- Make sure that the group stays focus on the main topic, yet does not exercise control to the extent that members are hesitant to voice perspective.
- Use an appropriate conclusion that summarizes the discussion, reviews the comments made and looks out for any points that were left out; and thank the group for contributing to the discussion.

The assistant moderator in a focus group should possess critical skills such as:

- Ensure that participants feel welcome at the discussion and are comfortable.
- Help the smooth flow of the discussion by arranging the room, equipping the room with any electronic audiovisual equipment, help in operating the equipment, and providing refreshments to keep the participants in good spirits.
- Take thorough notes of the various interactions and topics that are discussed throughout the meeting.
- Abstain from participation throughout the discussions unless specifically asked to by the moderator.
- Meet with the moderator at the end of the discussion to give a summary of the entire meeting, and provide them with input on the pros and cons of the meeting.

---

[9] Adapted from Richard A. Krueger and Mary Anne Casey, "Designing and Conducting Focus Group Interviews," in *Social Analysis, Selected Tools and Techniques*, eds, Richard A. Krueger et al. (October 2002), pp. 4–23, (Retrieved in June 2013); "Guidelines for Conducting a Focus Group," 2005, http://assessment. aas.duke.edu/documents/How_to_Conduct_a_Focus_Group.pdf (Retrieved on May 6, 2014).

- *Recruiting and rescreening:* Panelists for focus groups in the US are screened and recruited in a rigid manner. These processes must be monitored very carefully.
- *Approach:* Foreign moderators are not as structured and as authoritative as US moderators. This can result in long periods of silence and digression. This is because foreign moderators feel it is necessary to allow the group to settle down and establish trust to build up the necessary comfort. Foreign focus groups tend to use fewer external stimuli, such as photos and visual aids.

Focus groups have become very popular in the recent past. The technology used to conduct focus group interviews has also improved tremendously. Conference rooms with one-way mirrors are used to allow researchers to observe the group dynamics so nonverbal cues may be observed and recorded. Telephone focus groups are conducted for participants who are extremely busy. These are conducted through conference calling facility. Two-way focus groups are also becoming common. In this case, one group listens and learns from a related group.

Projective Techniques

The central feature of all projective techniques is the presentation of an ambiguous, unstructured object, activity, or person that a respondent is asked to interpret and explain.[10] The more ambiguous the stimulus, the more the respondents have to project themselves into the task, thereby revealing hidden feelings and opinions. These techniques are used when the researchers believe that the respondents cannot or will not respond to direct questions about certain behaviors and attitudes. Some people strive to give the socially correct answer all the time to avoid a bad self-image. Sometimes the respondent may be too polite to correct the interviewer. In all the proceeding cases, researchers make use of projective techniques to get down to the real reason behind consumer behavior.

There are different categories of projective techniques. The *word-association technique* asks the respondents to give the first word or phrase that comes to mind after the researcher presents a word or phrase. The researcher reads out a list of words quickly to avoid respondents' defense mechanism from setting in. Responses are analyzed by calculating the frequency with which any word is given as a response, the amount of time that elapses before a response is given, and the number of respondents who do not respond at all to a test within a reasonable amount of time. Word association tests produce hundreds of words and ideas. They can be used to conduct associative research on competitive brands. They can also be used to obtain reactions to potential brand names and advertising slogans. *Completion tests* involve giving the respondent an incomplete and ambiguous sentence, which is to be completed with a phrase. The sentences are usually in third person and the respondent is encouraged to respond with the first thought that comes to mind. In the *picture interpretation technique* the respondent is shown an ambiguous picture and asked to describe it. This technique is very flexible, as the picture can be readily adapted to many kinds of marketing problems. *Third-person techniques* involve asking respondents how friends, neighbors, or the average person would think or react to a situation. The respondents will, to some extent, project their own attitudes on to this third person and reveal more of their true feelings. In *role-playing*, the respondent assumes

---

[10] Harold S. Kassarjian, "Projective Methods," in *Handbook of Marketing Research*, ed., Robert Ferber (New York: McGraw Hill, 1974), pp. 3–87.

the role or behavior of another person and in the process may project their own attitudes into the role that they are playing.

Protocol

In the protocol method, the respondent is asked to think aloud while a decision is being made or a problem is being solved. Hence, this serves as a record of the respondent's thought process. These methods are designed to specifically prevent the researcher from imposing his views on the respondent. The respondent is free to make the decision based on factors that are important to him or her. The common method used is to record the respondent's opinions as he or she is in the process of making the decision. If the researcher is looking for information on buying behavior in a grocery store, he accompanies the respondent as the latter goes through the shopping process. The respondent is asked to talk aloud as the purchase decision is made. In some cases, respondents are given a recorder so that they can talk into it as they shop. This may not be effective as most people feel embarrassed to talk into a microphone while they shop.

TYPES OF OBSERVATIONAL METHODS

Observation can produce insights into customer behavior that other methods cannot. It can be used to study a wide variety of topics ranging from shopping behavior to patterns in pedestrian traffic. Observational methods can be very useful in producing new ideas for product development, product complements, and substitutes. For instance, it was observed that clients at a community mental health center engaged in odd behavior, parking far from the facility, even though ample parking was available nearby. When they were asked about this, clients admitted that they did not want to be seen entering the facility. The center then redesigned the entrance and changed the signs.[11]

These methods are limited to providing information on current behavior. Observational methods are less expensive than other methods and very accurate. In some cases, observation may the only alternative available to the researcher. There are different types of observation and they are discussed briefly in the following paragraphs.

Direct Observation

Direct observation is when an observer disguised as a shopper watches shoppers approach a product category. The observer gathers information on aspects like the time spent in the display area, the ease of finding the product, and whether the customer read the package. In some cases, the observer is asked to mingle with the customers to find out if they have any problems with service. Better results are obtained if the customers are not aware that they are being watched so that they perform the shopping activities without being conscious.

---

[11] Sydney J. Levy, "Dreams, Fairy Tales, Animals, and Cars," *Psychology and Marketing* 2 (Summer 1985): 67–82.

Contrived Observation

Contrived observation involves studying the behavior of people placed in a contrived observation situation. This will reveal some of their beliefs, attitudes, and motives. A variation of the same method uses teams of observers disguised as customers observing the interaction between the customer and the personnel handling the service desk. Though this method has been useful in providing insights into aspects like discriminatory treatment of minorities, there have been some questions about the ethics involved in this method.

Content Analysis

Content analysis is used to analyze written material into meaningful units using carefully applied rules. It is defined as the objective, systematic, and quantitative description of the manifest of the content of communication and includes observation as well as analysis. The material may be analyzed in terms of words, characters, themes, space and time measures, or topics. The categories for classifying and analyzing the material are developed and the written matter is broken down according to prescribed rules. For instance, this method can be used to analyze advertisements.

Physical Trace Measures

Physical trace measures involve recording the natural *residue* of behavior. For instance, if the researcher was interested in finding out the alcohol consumption in a town without checking the retail store sales, the number of empty bottles from the garbage will give a rough estimate of the alcohol consumption. This method may not work in all the countries of interest to the researcher because the developing countries do not have an organized garbage disposal system. Hence, it is necessary for the researcher to first determine if tracing physical evidence will be helpful in the study.

Humanistic Inquiry

Humanistic inquiry involves immersing the researcher in the system that is being studied rather than the traditional method where the researcher is a dispassionate observer. The researcher maintains one log for recording the hypotheses formed during the process. The second set of notes is a methodological log where investigative techniques used during the process are recorded. An external auditor is employed to determine if the interpretation of the data gathered has been impartial.

Behavior Recording Devices

Behavior recording devices have been developed to overcome deficiencies of human observers. Some of these devices do not require the direct participation of the respondents. The people meter developed by AC Nielsen is attached to a television set to record continually to which channel the set is tuned to. If the variables to be observed are beyond human capacity, special devices have to be used. Eye movement recorders are popular and have been used to record the experience of viewing pictures of advertisements, packages, signs, or shelf displays. These devices help in observing the time spent by the respondent with the various elements of the visual stimulus. Voice-pitch analysis examines variations in the pitch of the respondent's voice, and the greater the variation, the greater is the emotional involvement of the respondent.

ADVANTAGES AND DISADVANTAGES OF QUALITATIVE AND OBSERVATIONAL RESEARCH

Each of the qualitative and observational methods described above has both benefits and shortcomings. It is the researcher's decision to choose one method over another. Most researchers prefer to use the same methodology for obtaining data in all the countries that are being studied. While choosing a method, the researcher will have to keep in mind traits and habits that are peculiar to each country and choose the one method that will get the best results. In some cases, researchers may even have to settle for using different instruments in different countries to obtain comparable data.

Interviews

Interviews are a very good source of obtaining information. In face-to-face interviews, the interviewer has the flexibility to probe the respondent and direct the interview in a manner that will help the study best. This method is very effective with busy executives who are the decision-makers and will be able to give authentic information for the study. Advances in technology have made possible telephone interviews that are very cost-effective and provide the researcher with a wealth of information. The drawback in this method is that it is dependent on the interviewing skills and the personal biases of the researcher. The interviewer must be sufficiently skilled to establish a good rapport with the respondent and pursue a line of questioning which will provide the best results. Another problem in this method is recording the responses. Some respondents do not like to be tape-recorded, and the interviewer has to be fast enough to record all the important details of the response. In the international context, interviews must be used with discretion. For instance, the Japanese do not like being interviewed over the telephone. In Hong Kong, the researcher will not be allowed inside the home. Interviews will have to be conducted through an aperture in the front door. In the Middle East, women will not give any interviews, especially to male interviewers. The researcher will have to take care not to flout any traditions.

Focus Group

Focus group sessions are very successful if the number of participants is restricted between five and nine and all the participants are allowed to express their opinions. Since most people are comfortable in a group, they are a lot more candid in focus groups than in interviews; however, the moderator should watch out for a few stumbling blocks. Sometimes, one or two members of the panel get very aggressive and force their views on the remaining panel members. This should be stopped before any real damage is done. Focus groups can also yield misleading results if conducted poorly. As is usually the case, in the international setting, researchers will have to be aware of the importance of culture in the discussion process. In the Eastern countries, researchers will have to spend some time in detailed introductions. Only after the panel members know one another will they get comfortable enough to be candid with their views. In many cultures, members are conscious of their social status and disagreement is considered impolite. Exhibit 8.2 illustrates the use of focus groups for gathering information.

Projective Techniques

In global marketing research, projective techniques are very useful, as they do not impose a specific cultural referent on the respondent; however, interpretation of the results is highly subjective. It is very difficult to establish rules regarding coding and analyzing for these methods. Comparing across nations may also prove to be a challenge.

Protocols

Protocols are very useful in providing information regarding effectiveness of advertising and promotional campaigns. They let the researchers know exactly what the customers think of a marketing strategy. They also give an insight into the different uses that customers have for a single product and the substitutes that are used frequently. Protocols help examine the importance that customers attach to factors like store layout, shelf displays, interaction with store personnel, crowding at the checkout counters, and so on. They also help researchers understand the terminology used by consumers in relation to a product. Protocols have their disadvantages. They are very unstructured. The onus of interpreting them and attributing national and cultural differences is on the researcher. On many occasions, the customer may not verbalize the entire thought process and so the researcher ends up with partial information.

Observational Methods

These methods are costly and time-consuming. People tend to react differently if they discover that they are being observed. They also have the added restriction that researchers cannot measure motives, attitudes, or intentions. Hence, they cannot be very useful in diagnostic studies. The interpretation of the results is highly subjective and is entirely dependent on the observer. There is the added complexity of the usage of multiple languages. It may also be very difficult to execute some of the methods mentioned earlier in some countries. If the

---

[12] Adapted from Joanna L. Krotz, "Dos and Don'ts for Using Marketing Focus Groups," Microsoft Business, 2011, http://www.microsoft.com/business/en-us/resources/marketing/market-research/dos-and-donts-for-using-marketing-focus-groups.aspx?fbid=f6-znzgl1Jk (Retrieved on May 12, 2014).

researcher were planning on using physical evidence in a developing country, the research would yield incorrect results, as garbage disposal is not an organized activity in many of these countries. It may be very difficult to convince a retailer in Japan to consent to a covert observation of customers.

FREQUENCY AND EASE OF USE

The choice of the research method depends largely on the research purpose, environment, and researcher. If the researcher wishes to gain insight into the problem or understand the differences with respect to domestic research, qualitative methods would be preferred. Protocols are used if the research study focuses on the decision-making process rather than the actual behavior itself. Protocols can also be conducted in a laboratory or any other controlled atmosphere and are used in situations where it is not practical to conduct the study in the real world. Interviews are very frequently used in international marketing studies, primarily because of the complexity introduced due to national and cultural differences. Interviews are very structured and help the researcher in retaining control over the data to be collected.

Observation techniques are used frequently when the researcher is conducting exploratory research to become familiar with the shopping habits in a foreign country; however, in some cultures, people are averse to being observed. It has also been the experience of researchers that customers tend to behave differently when they are aware of being observed; therefore, many researchers prefer to observe discretely. Observation methods are in general useful in studying how people purchase in different environments, especially when the process differs considerably between the different countries that are being studied. If the researcher is not familiar with the usage patterns in a certain country, observational methods serve to educate the researcher and help decide the best method of collecting data.

CULTURAL INFLUENCES

Designing the research instrument for a global marketing research project is tricky. Researchers should make sure that they understand the product usage and other acceptable substitutes to the product before they launch the data collection process. The research instrument should be able to provide the researchers with useful data about the specific country, while at the same time, it should be comparable to the data collected from other countries. Questions can be structured or unstructured—this is dependent on the culture. It has been observed that Eastern cultures provide good information on open-ended questions, whereas Americans prefer to avoid such questions; however, open-ended questions are subject to interpretation by the researcher and this could lead to biases.

Researchers have to be very careful with the manner in which the questions are worded. Some societies resent being asked direct questions on sensitive issues like income and lifestyle. In most Latin American cultures, tax evasion is very common and so questions regarding income are viewed with a great deal of suspicion. In such cases, researchers should phrase the question in a subtle manner. Demographic and psychographic data may vary considerably. What is considered a lower working class in one country may be the middle class in another country. The researcher should determine the class structure in the country before looking for information in the appropriate segments in that culture. Language plays a very important role in qualitative research. A lot of vital information and subtle nuances can be lost in translation. In some countries with multiple cultures, differences in usage in a single language can add to the complexity of the task.

Chivas Regal carried out an international qualitative study in 1990 to help its managers evaluate a number of global advertising concepts for Chivas Regal whiskey. One of the aspects of this study was the treatment of Japan as a special case. There were 14 in-depth interviews and two group discussions that used one local moderator and three other researchers as unobtrusive observers. The interviews and groups progressed through a stage of building rapport to the actual research topics. The moderator and two observers were Japanese while one observer was an American bilingual. This was done to ensure that the researchers were in tune with the cultural significance of responses.[13]

BIASES IN QUALITATIVE AND OBSERVATIONAL RESEARCH

Global marketing research involves researchers belonging to one culture or country studying the lifestyles, attitudes, values, and beliefs of consumers in another culture. There are vast differences between countries and between cultures even within one country. There is a very high possibility of the researcher misinterpreting the words and actions of consumers in another country. In any research study, the interpretation of the data collected ultimately rests with the researchers and any misinterpretation on their part could lead to erroneous results; hence, it is very important to know what the different sources of biases are and how to avoid them.

One of the major sources of biases in global marketing research is the research design and approach taken by the researcher. The researcher allows their own values, beliefs, and attitudes to affect the way in which they interprets the verbal and nonverbal cues of respondents in a foreign culture (SRC). This effect is even more pronounced when the researcher is conducting a study in a culture that is vastly different from their own. For instance, an American researcher conducting a study in Canada might have a mistaken notion that geographic proximity implies similarity in habits and attitudes. This would be a blunder, especially if the researcher were to approach respondents with a business-like attitude that most Americans approve and practice. Canadians like to take their time in getting to know the person and establishing a rapport before getting down to business. If researchers keep an open mind and try to spend some time familiarizing themselves with the foreign culture, the study will be more effective.

Another major source of bias is communication. A lot of vital information is lost in translations and global marketing research is heavily dependent on translations and back translations. First, the survey instrument has to be translated to the native language so that the respondent may understand it. Then the response has to be translated to the language used by researchers in the study. It is very important that the right message be conveyed in each of the translations. This could prove to be tricky because some languages have many dialects and are used differently in different regions. An example would be Hindi, the language spoken by many in northern parts of India. There are many versions of this language depending on the region that it is spoken in. Most studies use professional translators. Even so, a lot of miscommunication occurs at every stage of the translation process. This contributes significantly to the bias.

The third source of bias is interpreting the results. This is a major aspect of qualitative and observational techniques. Interpretation is entirely dependent on the researcher and this is where SRC comes into play once again. The researcher may have problems attributing the

---

[13] Clive Nancarrow, Len Tiu Wright, and Chris Woolsten, "Pre-Testing International Press Advertising," *Qualitative Market Research: An International Journal* 1, no. 1 (1998): 25–38.

right reasons for a purchase behavior. If for instance, in a developing country, a consumer were to choose a product that has been packaged in aluminum container instead of a plastic carton, the reason could simply be that the consumer plans to use this container for storage purposes after the contents have been used. An American researcher could not be faulted for attributing reasons of efficient recycling as the motive for this purchase. This error in interpretation could mean a big blunder when it comes to positioning the product.

Avoiding biases in global marketing research requires a lot of effort from the researcher. The first step would be to try and understand the research problem from the perspective of the foreign country. This is easier said than done because the root of the problem may the researcher's lack of sensitivity to and understanding of such cultural nuances. A feasible alternative is to include researchers from different cultural backgrounds in the research team so that the team as a whole can consider all the different facets of the research problem. At every stage of the research process, the researcher who is familiar with that specific culture takes the lead in conducting the study and the results are then compared across countries. In some cases, researchers find it easier to develop research instruments specific to one country and then coordinate and compare across countries. Here again, both researchers who are familiar with the country and those who are not examine the instruments and the data and draw conclusions. This second method of considering one country at a time and then comparing is preferable even though it is time-consuming. This method also poses a number of interaction problems, as researchers from different cultural backgrounds have to be in constant touch with one another. Another means used to avoid biases is to use many different instruments to measure the same variables. Convergent results for any given variable would indicate absence of biases.

LANDMARK DEVELOPMENTS

Global marketing research has come a long way in the area of qualitative and observational research. This section examines some of the landmark developments that have occurred over the past few decades.

Measuring Minds

Lifestyle segmentation schemes emerged on the marketing research scene in the early 1990s. Starting from demographics, the research methods gradually moved onto psychographics, the Values, Attitudes, and Lifestyles (VALS), and the refurbished VALS 2 program, all in an effort to understand the consumer psyche to increase revenues. Techniques like benefits probes, role-playing, and photo collages competed with large-scale psychographic segmentations at advertising agencies. Learning about consumers and emotions regarding specific brands provided the key to good advertising.

With an increasingly complex marketplace, one can no longer explain markets using a few customer segments. Multiple segments must be used, but it is impossible to keep all of them straight. In the beginning, the ability to generalize while fragmenting the mass market was the salient feature of psychographics. It grew from sociology, psychology, economics, and anthropology to facilitate understanding of large consumer groups. Sociological inquiries began when Harvard-educated psychologist Daniel Yankelovich and market researcher Florence Skelly noticed that societal changes influenced markets greatly. In the early 1960s, Playtex asked Yankelovich, Skelly, and White to ascertain the reason for the downturn of the girdle market. It was found that women, wanting a more natural look, had changing perceptions of their bodies and did not want girdles anymore. Another study for Chrysler confirmed that people were buying cars less for status than as a means of personal self-expression. These researchers co-founded Yankelovich Lifestyle Monitor. The Monitor was developed in 1970 as a way to chart changing societal attitudes and their impact on businesses, and continues to do so by identifying the changing trends on the basis of annual interviews.

Computers have made possible the cross-tabulation of large numbers of survey questions. Combining statistical theories, psychographics provide a quantitative way of studying customer qualities. It gives researchers a market segmentation method that went beyond demographics. In an attempt to better understand the marketplace, researchers have placed more emphasis on brand- or product-specific attitudes and behavior. When the original VALS program was developed by Arnold Mitchell in 1978, many top advertisers and agencies embraced the typology as the newest microscope with which to understand the complexities of the US marketplace. By the late 1980s, critics charged that it was too theoretical and not predictive enough of consumer behavior. There was also alleged to be too much variation in the size and homogeneity of the groups for them to be useful. Therefore, SRI International recognized that its VALS program needed updating and introduced a new version in 1989 that focuses on product use.

The VALS 2 program, with its eight consumer types, answered these criticisms posed at the original VALS program. Each consumer type now accounted for between 8% and 17% of the population, compared with between 2% and 38% in the original VALS. The new types were based on consumption of 170 different categories of products. While the original VALS was intended as a model of social behavior, VALS 2 focused on predicting consumer behavior by defining segments on the basis of product use. In other words, VALS 2 evaluated consumption tendencies of people, rather than their style of relating to other people, their spiritual goals, or their ethnic values.

How They Feel

Agencies are reusing old projective techniques to get at the emotions that influence brand choice. For this, BBDO Worldwide uses a trademarked technique called Photosort. Consumers express their feelings about brands through a specially developed photo deck showing pictures of different types of people from executives to college students. Respondents connect people with the brands they think they use. A photosort for General Electric revealed that consumers associated the brand with conservative, older, business types. To change that image GE adopted the "Bring Good Things to Life" campaign. Another photosort for Visa found the card had a wholesome, female, middle-of-the road image in customer's minds. The "Everywhere You Want To Be" campaign strove to interest more high-income men.

The Thematic Apperception Test was another successful technique that brought in another layer of understanding the hidden feelings and opinions of people. In this test, the respondent is shown an ambiguous picture in the form of a line drawing, illustration, or photograph, and asked to describe it. This test was applied to discern whether the advertising of Coors and Lowenbrau had established associations with their use-contexts—Coors with hiking, wholesomeness, and health, and Lowenbrau with a barbecue-type setting, friends, and warmth.[14]

---

[14] David A. Aaker and Douglas M. Stayman, "Implementing the Concept of Transformational Advertising," *Psychology and Marketing*, May–June 1992, pp. 237–253.

One of the images depicted a break after a daytime hike on a mountain; the other showed a small evening barbecue with close friends. During the scene, the beer served was either Coors or Lowenbrau. Respondents were asked to project themselves into the scene and indicate, on a five-point scale, the extent to which they would feel *warm, friendly, healthy,* and *wholesome.* The results showed that Coors was evaluated higher in the mountain setting and Lowenbrau in the barbecue setting, as expected, but that the other (word) associations were not sensitive (related) to the setting. For example, in the hiking context, Coors was higher on the *warm* and *friendly* dimensions, as well as on *healthy* and *wholesome.* Other projective techniques that have evolved over the decades include Rorschach's inkblot tests, sentence completion, picture aspiration tests, and case studies.

Brand Clutter

With increase in product categories and explosion in the number of similar brands, advertisers identified the need to study how customers relate to their brands. As spending choices increase, agencies look for nuances in selling. Techniques such as one-on-one interviews, asking people to attach personalities to brands, and probes were often used to better understand customers' feelings toward the brand. For instance, Grey Advertising developed the Benefit Chain to better understand the consumers' feelings. A self-administered probing technique, the Benefit Chain used layers of carbon paper to record the observations of consumers about the products. On the first layer, consumers use their own words to describe a product's two most important benefits. On the next, they write down the secondary benefits and so on. This process allows consumers to express in their own words the benefits that they value and the level of consciousness at which these appear. A benefit chain done for Minute Rice, for example, revealed that the product's emphasis on perfect rice every time had outlived its effectiveness.

Understanding the Psychographics

The longest running agency psychographic study is DDB Needham's Lifestyle Study, which has been conducted annually since 1975. Each year, 4,000 adults nationwide respond to a 1,000-question mailed survey that includes attitudes and opinions, activities, personal and family product use, product ownership, media habits, and demographics. Lifestyle analysis is used to profile target audiences and identify trends.

Large-scale custom research provides extra selling points with clients and exclusive market insights for agencies that can afford it. Grey has fielded major studies on the *ultra* consumer, the 50-plus market, and other household segments. Backer Spielvogel Bates Worldwide has a program called Global Scan that currently segments markets in 18 countries by psychographics. NW Ayer has segmented the baby-boom generation based on psychographics and purchase behavior. Ogilvy and Mather has a consumer trend scanning program called New Wave that tracks major trends affecting consumption. Exhibit 8.3 provides a different flavor of consumer segmentation by analyzing their social responsibilities.

Agencies like Leo Burnett in Chicago and NW Ayer in New York pioneered evolutions in psychographic research that quantifies personalities, lifestyles, and emotions. Leo Burnett's Emotional Lexicon is an interactive computerized system that studies emotions derived from product categories. It leads the subject through an interview and contains words or phrases that represent 143 emotional dimensions that can be reduced to 15 key emotional points.

Exhibit 8.3

Global Segmentation of Social Responsibility Roles[15]

The segmentation schemes being generated have now extended beyond the realm of traditional marketing activities such as advertising, promotions, and buyer behavior to include activities like corporate social responsibility. Cone Communications recently published a study titled *Global Consumer Responsibility Segmentation* that categorizes global consumers based on their views and roles in addressing social and environmental issues, as identified through their purchases. The segmentation identified the following four distinct personalities:

- *Old guard:* This segment of consumers is likely to be male and aged above 55 years. These consumers do not believe they play a role in addressing social or environmental issues through their purchasing decisions. Their purchase decisions are primarily based on values such as price, quality and convenience. In fact, among those that do buy a socially responsible product, 32% say it is merely by chance.
- *Happy go-lucky:* Equally likely to be male or female, this segment consists of consumers in the 18–34 age group. These consumers believe that their role is to buy products that they consider to be socially and environmentally responsible. However, they will buy those products only if they are convenient. Even though nearly 72% of these consumers believe that they can positively influence social issues through their purchasing habits, they are not contented with just *good deeds*. They also need to *feel good* about the purchases. In fact, nearly 31% of these consumers indicate *making me feel good* as the primary benefit from socially responsible purchases.
- *Bleeding heart:* Typically aged around 18–34 years and most likely to be female, these consumers feel that their role is to proactively seek socially responsible product options every time they shop, or as often as possible. They also feel that the foremost benefit they derive from such purchases is the awareness that they can positively impact society. However, their purchase behavior comes with a caveat. Nearly 92% of these consumers are likely to boycott products or services they find negligent, and nearly 57% have already done so.
- *Ringleader:* Typically aged above 35 years, and equally likely to be male or female, these consumers believe that their role is not only to purchase socially responsible products every time they shop, but also encourage others to do the same. In fact, nearly 45% of these consumers have advocated for such products because they strongly feel that individuals can have a significant impact on social issues. Further, almost 92% value and consider the corporate social responsibility efforts of companies when deciding which products to recommend to their friends.

---

[15] Adapted from Cone Communications, "Global Consumer Responsibility Segmentation: Cookie Cutter Communications Won't Cut It," May 24, 2013, http://www.conecomm.com/global-csr-segmentation (Retrieved in July 2013).

For example, it is possible to study people who like low-calorie beer as opposed to regular beer and determine whether the difference is based on the rational level of calories. NW Ayer's Version of the emotional lexicon consists of a questionnaire with phrases that rate according to 50 emotion brands, reactions to advertising, and feelings after using a product. The responses are cross-tabulated and can be graphically represented in perceptual maps.

In the international context, psychographic segmentations vary depending on the local culture and lifestyle. For instance, Japan VALS™, the Japanese version of VALS, has categorized the Japanese consumers into ten segments along two important parameters—*life orientation* and *attitudes toward social change*. While the life orientation parameter also includes aspects such as traditional approaches, occupations, innovation, and self-expression, the attitudes toward social change parameter also includes aspects pertaining to being sustaining, pragmatic, adapting, and innovating.[16] Likewise, in the Indian market, the RK Swamy/BBDO advertising agency operating in India has developed the *RK SWAMY BBDO Guide to Urban Markets* for understanding the complex Indian market. The index developed by the agency uses around 18 variables to develop market indices for over 750 towns with a population over 50,000 that accounts for around 77% of the urban population. Further, the *MICA Rural Market Ratings* uses six variables to develop market ratings for 459 districts in India. Similarly, syndicated reports from agencies such as the AC Nielsen–ORG-Marg Retail Index and the National Readership Survey provide consumer and industry information that are grouped under relevant categories.

In the British context, McCann-Erickson London identified a set of lifestyles that applied to the British consumers. They lifestyle segments were: (a) the *Avant-Gardians* who were always interested in change, (b) the Pontificators who were traditional people following the British customs and values, (c) the Chameleons who changed with the society and times, and (d) the Sleepwalkers who were contented with their existing levels of achievements.[17] Similarly, D'Arcy, Masius, Benton, & Bowles (DMB&B) published *The Russian Consumer: A New Perspective and a Marketing Approach* that categorized the Russian population into five groups. They were: (a) the *Kuptsi* or the merchant segment, (b) the *Cossacks* comprising of ambitious, independent and status-seeking individuals, (c) the students, (d) the business executives, and (e) the *Russian Souls* comprising of individuals who were passive, fearful of choices, and hopeful.[18]

It's All Semantics

The criticism of psychographics arises largely due to semantics. Psychographics, once thought to mean segmentation by lifestyle, has now come to include product-specific attitudes, emotions, and behavior. The word was first published in the November 1965 issue of *Grey Matter*, an internal publication of Grey advertising. Even before the actual term was coined, the concept was used in its broadest sense. In 1964, Daniel Yankelovich published a paper in the *Harvard Business Review* in which he outlined what he called non-demographic segmentation. He recommended segmentation of markets should be done according to consumer, product-specific values, and attitudes. He warned that personality typologies were useless in predicting

---

[16] Kotler et al., *Marketing Management*.

[17] Kotler, *Marketing Management*, 10th edition.

[18] Stuart Elliott, "Sampling Tastes of a Changing Russia," *New York Times*, April 1, 1992, pp. D1, D19.

brand choice. He felt that personality differences are too deep to have much bearing on product choices that are rather superficial.

Zaltman Metaphor Elicitation Technique

The Zaltman Metaphor Elicitation Technique (ZMET) was developed by Gerald Zaltman, a marketing professor at the Harvard Business School, to draw upon the conscious and unconscious thoughts of consumers by exploring their metaphoric expressions. This in-depth methodology is built on the assumption that most thoughts and feelings are shaped by a set of *deep metaphors*. These deep metaphors are basic understanding that consumers have about their surroundings and its constituents. Largely unconscious and universal, these metaphors reflect everything people hear, see, or do.[19] The metaphors are classified into the following seven categories as provided in Table 8.1.

TABLE 8.1

METAPHORS DESCRIBING FEELINGS AND THOUGHTS

Metaphor Category	Feelings and Thoughts that Are Indicated
Balance	Equilibrium and the interplay of natural elements
Transformation	Changes in substance and circumstances
Journey	Meeting of the past, present, and the future
Container	Inclusion, exclusion, and other boundaries
Connection	Need to relate to oneself and others
Resource	Acquisitions and their consequences
Control	Sense of mastery, vulnerability, and well-being

According to this technique, the participants are first asked to select a minimum of 12 images that reflect their thoughts and feelings about the research topic. Participants are given instructions in advance to collect these using their own sources like magazines, photos, family journals, etc. After they have collected the images, the researcher conducts a one-to-one interview with the participants wherein the images are explored and advanced interview techniques are used to elicit the hidden feelings. Finally, the participants are asked to use a computer program to create a collage with the selected images that communicates their subconscious thoughts and feelings about the topic.

This technique has been used to good measure for designing and implementing marketing actions.[20] For instance, using this technique, Nestlé Crunch found that the candy bar reminded participants of their pleasant childhood memories. Similarly, DuPont realized that their pantyhose had a strong *love–hate* relationship among the users, as evidenced by images such as steel bands strangling trees and tall flowers in a vase. In the case of Motorola, the consistent appearance of images of dogs when reviewing their new security system suggested the feeling of being secure as being important to the participants. Apart from marketing

---

[19] Gerald Zaltman and Lindsay Zaltman, *Marketing Metaphoria: What Deep Metaphors Reveal About the Minds of Consumers* (Boston: Harvard Business School, 2008).

[20] Daniel Pink, "Metaphor Marketing," *Fast Company*, March/April 1998, pp. 214–229.

studies, ZMET has also been used in academic and not-for-profit environments to study a range of topics including the experience of mountain biking,[21] and how Americans are dealing with the economic crisis.[22]

Neuromarketing

Among the latest developments in the field of marketing research is the concept of neuromarketing. This branch of research focuses on monitoring brain activity to understand the consumer responses to marketing actions. Several technologies within this field are being used by researchers to uncover various facets of neurological behavior. The popular technologies include:

- Electroencephalography (EEG) that records electrical activity in the brain in combination with other physiological cues such as skin temperature and eye movement in response to ads.
- Magnetic resonance imaging (MRI) that focuses on the frequency, location, and timing of neuronal activity as a response to external stimuli such as scents, colors, images, and sounds.
- Functional magnetic resonance imaging (fMRI) that measures the brain activity by detecting associated changes in blood flow in response to marketing actions.
- Electromyography (EMG) that evaluates and records the electrical activity produced by skeletal muscles when they are electrically or neurologically activated as a result of exposure to marketing messages.
- Facial Electromyography (fEMG) that measures facial muscle activity by detecting the tiny electrical impulses that are generated when exposed to positive and negative stimuli.

The science of neuromarketing is being used increasingly and with impressive results. One area of marketing that has benefited immensely by the use of this technique is advertising. Research for various companies has consistently revealed that subjects display the varying levels of brain activity for the ads they are exposed to. In some cases, customers' liking of an ad (as identified by studying the brain activity) has been found to be different from their originally stated preference to the brands.[23] This shows that while consumers may *claim* to prefer certain brands, their preference may not extend to the marketing messages of the brand. Findings such as this are important for marketers, as it could potentially make or mar the popularity of the brand in the marketplace.

Similarly, Volkswagen gleaned some interesting insights about their "The Force" ad aired during the 2011 Super Bowl. The ad shows a small kid dressed up as Darth Vader who unsuccessfully attempts to show "The Force" on his parents' exercise bike, the washing machine, on the kitchen counter, and even the family dog is almost ready to accept defeat. When his

---

[21] Alison Balmat, "The Meaning of a Bike," January 1, 2000, http://news.psu.edu/story/141419/2000/01/01/research/meaning-bike (Retrieved on May 25, 2014).

[22] Rob Walker, "S.U.V. and Sympathy," *New York Times*, March 22, 2009, p. MM21 (New York edition).

[23] Carolyn Yoon, Angela H. Gutchess, Fred Feinberg, and Thad A. Polk, "A Functional Magnetic Resonance Imaging Study of Neural Dissociations between Brand and Person Judgments," *Journal of Consumer Research* 33 (2006): 31–40.

father arrives home in his Passat, the boy decides to try his *power* for one final time on the car. Seeing this from inside the house, his dad decides to humor him by starting the car's ignition with the remote control. The boy turns around, truly astonished that The Force worked. The fMRI research performed on this ad by Sands Research, Texas, recorded the highest *neuro-engagement score* ever. This is also reflected in the winning of the "2011 Best Commercial" award by Adweek, and two Gold Lions at Cannes.[24] The popularity of this ad can also be seen in the 12 million YouTube views it garnered even before the game started, and as of this writing, the ad has been viewed nearly 58 million times.

Neuromarketing is also being used for comparative brand studies to see how brands are being perceived and used vis-à-vis their competitors. A recent study delved into the classic comparison of Pepsi and Coca-Cola using the fMRI technique and produced some interesting results.[25] The study selected 67 participants and scanned their brains while being given a blind taste test of Coca-Cola and Pepsi. After the tasting, around half the participants chose Pepsi, since Pepsi tended to produce a stronger response than Coke in their brain. But when the subjects were told they were drinking Coke, three-quarters said that Coke tasted better. Their brain activity had also changed. The area of the brain that is responsible for high-level cognitive powers (the lateral prefrontal cortex), and the area responsible for memory (the hippocampus) were now being used, indicating that the consumers were thinking about Coke and relating it to memories and other impressions. Therefore, it was clear that Pepsi was losing out to Coke, not because Coke tasted better, but because of Coke's superior brand experience.

Another study using the same technique conducted by Daimler-Chrysler found that images of sports cars brought forward responses from the reward center of the brain (the medial prefrontal cortex). This is also the same area that shows increased activity when drugs or alcohol are consumed. Therefore, these studies clearly highlight the importance of precise branding and promotion campaigns to create a favorable and long-lasting brand experience among the users. All these insightful results have made several companies such as Coca-Cola, The Home Depot, and P&G repose belief in this form of research and use it for their product and marketing studies.

While the traction gained by this field of marketing has largely been due to the inclusion of sophisticated technology that enables marketers to listen to the consumers' minds, it has also benefited by the ambiguous and sometimes inaccurate information uncovered when using other traditional observational techniques such as focus groups. An estimated $154 billion is expected to be spent on advertising in the US this year, according to TNS Media Intelligence.[26] Despite this high amount of spending, companies do not often get reliable results from focus groups. As said by Zaltman, creator of ZMET, "The correlation between stated intent and actual behavior is usually low and negative."[27] He cites several products and even TV shows (e.g., *Seinfeld* and the British comedy, *Coupling*, for the US market) that have uncovered misleading information while using focus groups. When viewed from this light, results

---

[24] Alex Hannaford, "'Neuromarketing': Can Science Predict What We'll Buy?" *Telegraph*, April 13, 2013.

[25] Samuel M. McClure, Jian Li, Damon Tomlin, Kim S. Cypert, Latané M. Montague, and P. Read Montague, "Neural Correlates of Behavioral Preference for Culturally Familiar Drinks," *Neuron* 44, no. 2 (2004): 379–387.

[26] Donna Mitchell-Magaldi, "Turning Heads—Neuromarketing Must Overcome Some Obstacles to Gain Acceptance," *Industry* and *Innovation Marketplace Review*, Nerac Inc., April 26, 2007.

[27] Gerald Zaltman, *How Customers Think: Essential Insights into the Mind of the Market* (Boston: Harvard Business Review Press, 2003).

from neuromarketing research have yielded more dependable insights that have been found to be more effective in designing advertising and marketing campaigns. As a result, this new method of research offers much promise in companies' quest toward designing and developing products that are more suited to address consumer needs and wants, while enhancing their bottom line.

Despite the higher accuracy in study results, this field of research is still in the nascent stages of development. This is largely due to the cost involved. Though comparative estimates of this research with other traditional forms of research are unavailable, the cost of MRI scanners alone runs into a few millions of dollars. Add to this the other components of research such as participant selection, administering the study, the number of scans to be performed, and the subsequent data analysis; the entire cost of research will be pegged well above the affordability of several companies, especially the small businesses.

In addition to the challenge of high costs, this field of research also faces stiff opposition from rights and ethics groups. Experts and consumer advocacy groups fear that this type of research may be used to infringe on personal privacy. Further, psychologists also worry about the adverse effects such neuromarketing applications will have on people with buying disorders, other compulsive disorders, and vulnerable groups such as children and young adults.[28] When this research is used to understand consumer thoughts and feelings, the concern is that marketing of unhealthy and undesirable products will be made easy. In addition, medical complexities involved with administering the MRI scans also concern the medical community. Consumers with surgical implants and pacemakers should never be placed in an MRI. In some cases, the MRI scanner may also cause dizziness, nausea, and burns associated with magnetic field friction.

As it stands now, although studying the human brain has thrown some interesting insights about the interworking of the human anatomy, transforming such insights into actionable marketing campaigns continue to be a challenge as seen from a financial and ethical standpoint. While neuroscientists will continue to benefit from the funding it would bring them and academicians from cutting-edge research studies, marketers and companies will still need more evidence to justify the costs and return on investment for this field of research to become mainstream.

Mobile Phone Tracking

As technology pervades into everyday life, retailers are finding newer ways to collect data about how consumers shop. This has led to the recent practice of tracking movement of customers by following the wi-fi signals from their smartphones.[29] With the growth of big data, companies are looking to add more data points about customers that can help marketers accurately analyze customers' in-store behavior.

Nordstrom was the first major retailer to try out this new technology in October 2012. Using the system and service provided by Euclid, Nordstrom stores were fitted with sensors that collected information from customer smartphones as they attempted to connect to Wi-Fi service. Through these sensors, information such as the departments visited, time spent in

---

[28] Donna Mitchell-Magaldi, "Head Games—Neuromarketing Applies the Power of MRI to Study Our Reaction to Ads," *Industry* and *Innovation Marketplace Review*, Nerac Inc., March 26, 2007.

[29] Stephanie Clifford and Quentin Hardy, "Attention, Shoppers: Store Is Tracking Your Cell," *New York Times*, July 15, 2013, pp. A1.

each department, and overall store traffic patterns were collected. Essentially, the system was designed to track phone signals and thereby determine the departments visited by the consumers. While the store management said that only the signals were being tracked and that no personally identifiable information regarding the mobile users were collected, the experiment was not taken too kindly by the shoppers. Consumers were irked by the physical surveillance and deemed it to be an invasion of privacy. Following the spate of consumer complaints, Nordstrom called off the program in May 2013.

Among the various companies selling such software, the services offered by them cover a wide range. Some of the prominent features of such systems include: (a) identifying shoppers' store navigation patterns to design appropriate store layouts; (b) determining time spent in each department to assist stores in planning their manpower resources; (c) differentiating shoppers based on gender (male versus female) and age (children versus adults) to identify shopper preferences of different customer segments; (d) recognizing returning shoppers (via the unique identification codes used while tracking) to collect information on repeat visits and average time between visits; (e) drawing maps of customer visits within the store to decide on the type and placing of store displays; (f) analyzing facial cues to determine customers' *happiness levels* within the store; and (g) tailoring marketing messages to a customer's gender, age, and mood, as measured by facial recognition.

Despite Nordstrom's experience, a surprising number of retailers are experimenting with such technologies. Retailers like Family Dollar, Cabela's, Benetton, Warby Parker, and UK-based Mothercare are testing these technologies to gather information that would advise them on planning their storefronts and promotional campaigns. Coupled with the wide variety of tracking services on the offer and the strides made by online retailers, brick-and-mortar retailers are increasingly looking at such options that will put them back on the reckoning to woo consumers to their stores.

Facial Recognition

The recent development in the field of observational studies is the use of facial recognition technology. Using a computer application, researchers can now identify or verify a person from a digital image or a video image by comparing selected facial features with a facial database. This technology is being extensively used by private and government security agencies and the state and federal justice departments. For instance, the US Department of State operates one of the largest face recognition systems in the world with over 75 million photographs that is actively used for visa processing. Other popular uses of this technology include routine surveillance at public events (Florida police used this technology at 2001 Super Bowl and identified people with minor criminal records), and for identification purposes (the Mexican government used this technology in the 2000 presidential election to prevent voter fraud).

This technology has now found a use in marketing as well. Recently, NEC IT Solutions created a facial recognition software program that can be used by retailers to identify VIPs or celebrities who walk into their stores.[30] The British software company already supplies similar software to security services to help identify terrorists and criminals. This software tracks people that walk into the stores while registering and analyzing people's faces. It then compares the facial measurements against a database containing images of VIPs and celebrities. When a positive match is identified, the software alerts the staff through computer, iPad, or

---

[30] Brenda Salinas, ""High-End Stores Use Facial Recognition Tools To Spot VIPs," *NPR*, July 21, 2013.

smartphone of the VIP's entry into the store. Along with the alert, the program sends information specific to the VIP such as dress size, favorite buys, or shopping history. The company claims that the software works well not only when the VIP is wearing other fashion accessories like sunglasses or hats, but also when they have undergone other physical changes such as changes in weight, hair color, facial hair, and age. As of this writing, this technology is being tested in various premium stores and hotels in the US, the UK, and Asia.

GLOBAL MARKETING RESEARCH IN PRACTICE

Qualitative and observational methods are some of the most important means of data collection for Tasty Burgers. Qualitative methods involve informal or semi-structured interviews, focus groups, and projective techniques. Not all these methods are equally effective in all the four countries. Focus groups work well in cultures where people are generally used to being frank and holding an independent opinion. It will be a very good method of data collection in the UK; however, in India, where most people succumb to peer pressure and do not want to appear very different from the rest of the society, focus groups may not be the ideal method. Individual semi-structured interviews may be more effective in drawing honest responses. Japanese consumers tend to be more hesitant to criticize a new product than their Western counterparts.[31] In Saudi Arabia, women are not allowed to talk to strange men, and, hence, it may be necessary to have women moderators or interviewers to gather data from that segment of the society. It is important to ensure that the interviewers and focus group moderators are culturally sensitive and respect the religious beliefs, particularly those of respondents in India and Saudi Arabia, because the line dividing the social or political life and religion is very narrow.

Observational methods help researchers gather information that has not been voiced by the respondents. These methods will prove very helpful to Tasty Burgers in societies where people mask their true feelings in public in order to adhere to socially accepted roles. For instance, in India many people claim to be vegetarians because the religious beliefs of Hindus forbid them from eating beef; however, many of these people also consume meat unknown to their family and friends. These people will publicly deny trying any of the products that include meat. Observation unknown to the subjects will provide researchers better estimates of product sales. It may not be possible to engage in observational methods in all countries. For instance, in Saudi Arabia, it may not be possible for researchers to observe the snacking habits of women, as restaurants have separate sections for women and families.

SUMMARY

This chapter discusses the use of qualitative and observational methods in global marketing research. Qualitative methods include individual interviews, focus groups, projective techniques, and protocol. Direct observation, contrived observation, content analysis, physical trace measures, humanistic inquiry, and behavior recording devices come under observational methods. The chapter also discusses the advantages, disadvantages, and frequency and ease of use of these methods in global marketing research. Cultural influences make a big difference

---

[31] David B. Montgomery, "Understanding the Japanese Customers, Competitors, and Collaborators," *Japan and the World Economy* (1991), vol. 3, pp. 61–91.

in recording and interpreting behavior, and researchers should be sensitive to the local culture in foreign countries.

The purpose of marketing research is to ensure that the company has not overlooked any major element of the problem or all alternative options available have been considered. Research is an iterative process wherein every stage is an improvement over the previous one. Qualitative and observational methods help researchers in exploratory research and in getting familiar with the international markets. The advantages and disadvantages of each method are also discussed here.

QUESTIONS AND PROBLEMS

1. Compare and contrast the focus group and individual in-depth interview methods of qualitative research. [Hint: Attempt to discuss in terms of the level of group interactions, peer pressure, respondent competition, ease of conducting, and amount of information gathered in each of these methods.]
2. In 2004, P&G was researching to build a better air freshener and decided to seek customer inputs to get the desired *scent experience*. What are your suggestions on the qualitative or observational research techniques that could be used in such an initiative?
3. YourFriendlyStore, the neighborhood all-purpose store, has of late been receiving complaints and concerns about gender biases with respect to prices, sales assistance, and credit. Which technique described in this chapter would you use to study this case?
4. A study at a market research center hypothesizes that because of the growing number of teenagers, advertisers would use more teenaged models in their promotions. Which method do you think could test this hypothesis the best?
5. What are the significant differences between nondirective and semi-structured individual interviews? In what circumstances would a nondirective interview be more useful than a semi-structured interview?
6. A local consumer organization is interested in the differences in food prices among major international markets. How should it proceed in order to obtain meaningful comparisons?
7. What difficulties might be encountered when conducting a qualitative interview in an international context?
8. When would you recommend observational methods in different countries? Why?

9

CHAPTER

Survey Research

INTRODUCTION

Survey research is one of the popular means of collecting primary data. As seen in Chapter 6, with the emergence of Internet, it has become a popular channel to collect primary data, and cheaper to conduct surveys. This chapter discusses in detail the most popular forms of survey research, and reviews the usefulness of each of these methods in international research settings. There are a number of different ways in which surveys can be conducted. As technology for communication progresses, the number of survey methods also increases. E-mail and mobile technology have added to the many different ways in which the survey instrument can be communicated to the respondent.

In global marketing research, the choice of a specific survey method is a difficult one because of the difference in technological developments in different countries. To provide a flavor of survey research, Table 9.1 provides the percentage of research turnover (quantitative studies only) across European countries.

TYPES OF SURVEYS

The four most prevalent methods of conducting surveys are personal interviews, telephone interviews, mail surveys, and online surveys. This section discusses each of these methods.

Personal Interviews

Personal interviews can be classified into different types depending on the method by which the interviews are conducted. There are four entities involved in a personal interview—the researcher, the interviewer, the respondent, and the interview environment. The human factor affects the outcome of the interview since the researcher, the interviewer, and the respondent have certain characteristics, some acquired and some inherent. During a personal interview, the interviewer and the interviewee influence one another in the interview environment. The researcher decides on the interview environment depending on the type of data to be collected. The different methods of conducting a personal interview are discussed below.

TABLE 9.1

PERCENTAGE OF RESEARCH TURNOVER ACROSS EUROPEAN NATIONS (QUANTITATIVE STUDIES ONLY)[1]

Country	Mail	Telephone	Face-to-Face	Online	Other
Austria	3	20	22	8	2
Belgium	1	32	32	9	3
Croatia	1	23	33	1	31
Czech Republic	1	18	44	5	14
Denmark	9	18	9	24	28
Finland	5	40	5	33	3
France	2	12	15	12	46
Greece	1	18	41	1	28
Hungary	4	16	45	14	5
Latvia	0	17	41	5	22
Netherlands	5	18	11	25	15
Norway	8	39	10	23	3
Poland	0	11	35	10	26
Portugal	0	19	21	3	38
Russia	1	21	35	5	13
Slovak Republic	1	14	42	2	24
Slovenia	8	27	23	4	14
Spain	2	26	27	11	15
Sweden	12	36	7	22	12
Switzerland	5	49	21	10	1
UK	8	17	21	18	23

Door-to-door Interviewing

In door-to-door interviewing, consumers are interviewed in their homes. This has been considered the best method due to a number of factors. First, it is a personal, face-to-face interview with advantages like feedback from the respondent, and possibility of instant clarifications regarding the survey questions. Second, it offers the ability to explain complicated tasks, use special questionnaire techniques, and show the respondent product concepts and other stimuli for evaluation. Finally, the consumer is seen as being at ease in a familiar, comfortable, and secure environment; and, therefore, able to answer more freely. This type of interviewing also allows the interviewer to look out for body language and other nonverbal cues. This will add to the quality of the information collected. This is the only viable method of conducting in-depth interviews and some in-home product tests. However, personal interviews tend to be more preferred outside the US and Canada, owing to lower costs involved in administering the survey.[2]

---

[1] Adapted from ESOMAR, "Global Market Research," ESOMAR Industry Report, Amsterdam, 2008, http://www.roymorgan.com/~/media/Files/Papers/2008/20080903.pdf (Retrieved on May 6, 2014).

[2] D. Monk, "Marketing Research in Canada," *European Research* (1984), vol. 15, pp. 271–274.

Executive Interviewing

The industrial version of door-to-door interviewing is called executive interviewing. Business people are interviewed in their offices concerning industrial products or services. This type of interviewing is typically very expensive. First, identifying the survey participants who meet the survey criteria is a laborious task. Having located the qualifying participant, getting them to meet for an interview takes a lot of time. Finally, spending valuable time in traveling to the meeting place, only to undergo long waits and even cancellations, is a common feature. The interviewer must be very experienced, as the interview topic could be very complicated.

Mall Intercept Surveys

When funds are limited, researchers resort to mall intercept surveys. Interviewers are stationed at the entrances to malls and they approach shoppers in a random manner. The interviews are conducted either at that location or the respondents are invited to a special facility in the mall. The survey costs in this method are low, as the interviewers do not incur traveling expenses, and a high number of respondents can be contacted in a given time frame. However, the sample obtained from shopping malls is not representative of the general population. This method is very popular in the US and Canada; however, it is not commonly used in either European countries or developing countries.[3]

Despite the low cost outlay, mall intercept surveys do face cost/quality issues. While this method has ensured better, faster, and cheaper service, it has not been without any costs attached to it. Specifically, issues such as the quality of the study, the efficiency of using resources, and the subsequent satisfaction of the client have come into question. In situations where significantly low incidence levels are expected or when the data collected must meet special parameters for analysis or modeling, small bases (number of interviews in a given location) are appropriate. However, key players are mistakenly choosing smaller bases (and, therefore, more locations on a single project), assuming that it will lead to faster completion of the interviewing process and save money.

Self-administered Questionnaires

In self-administered questionnaires, there is no interviewer involved. This contributes to reduction in costs. The other benefit with self-administered questionnaires is that interviewer bias is eliminated. The flip side is that there is no one available to clarify any doubts that the respondent may have. This method is used in malls, airlines, and other places where the researcher is assured of a captive audience. Businesses in the service sector, like hotels and restaurants, use this frequently to assess the quality of their service.

Purchase Intercept Technique

Another technique related to mall interception is called purchase intercept technique. This technique involves intercepting the customers while they are shopping and interviewing them about their purchase behavior. This is a combination of in-store observation and in-store interviewing to assess the shopping behavior of the respondents and the reasons for that behavior. The researcher usually observes the customers in a store unobtrusively while they are shopping and then interviews them as soon as the purchase has been made. This technique is superior

---

[3] B. P. Kaiser, "Marketing Research in Sweden," *European Research* (1988), 16 (1): 64–70.

because of better buyer recall. As very little time has elapsed between the purchase and the interview, the respondent is able to remember the details clearly. However, the interviewer can contact only people who make purchases, and so the sample may not be representative. Researchers could also have problems gaining access to the stores.

Omnibus Surveys

Omnibus surveys are regularly scheduled personal interview surveys conducted on a weekly, monthly, or quarterly basis. These surveys are conducted for different clients on different topics. The questionnaire contains many question sequences, each provided by a different client. This method is very useful when the respondent needs to answer only a limited number of questions. The total cost is reduced because many clients share it. This method is particularly useful in continuous tracking studies because the procedure is standardized and the results can be tabulated very easily. Sometimes researchers use the split-run method to get better results. In a split-run method, some members of the sample surveyed receive one questionnaire and some receive another version. This method of survey has proved to be very useful in studying low-incidence activities such as ownership of exotic pets.

Telephone Interviews

With improvements in technology in most parts of the world, telephone interviewing is gaining popularity among researchers, especially when the sample size required for the study is large. This is also effective in keeping costs low. Many respondents who may not be available for a face-to-face interview will be willing to do a telephone interview. Further, the popularity of mobile phones is changing the face of telephone interviews around the world.

The process of conducting a telephone interview is very similar to that of a face-to-face interview. The process differs in selecting the sample. Researchers could use random dialing procedure or select numbers from a pre-specified list, such as a directory or a customer list. In developed countries where most individuals or businesses are listed in a directory, picking numbers from a telephone directory has been the traditionally used method. For instance, as of 2011, France had 63 telephone lines per hundred people, and Hong Kong had 215 mobile cellular telephone subscriptions per hundred people—among the highest in the world.[4] In such countries as the Netherlands, the number of telephone interviews far exceeds personal interviews.[5]

However, the case of Finland shows a dramatic picture with respect to telephones. In 2010, more than 99% of households had one or more mobile phones, while only 20.7% had a landline telephone, and less than 20% of households had both types of telephones. Further, 79.1% of households had only mobile telephones, and less than 1% only a landline telephone. This trend of declining number of landline telephones has been happening over the past decade, and it is possible that landline telephones will disappear completely in the future. At present, nearly all of the landline telephones in Finland are owned by the elderly people. In 2010, 38% of pensioners' households had a landline telephone, and 2.6% of them had only a landline telephone. Other user segments that had a similar ownership profile of landline telephones included farmers (28% owing a landline, and 2.3% only a landline), and entrepreneurs (32%

---

[4] World Bank, 2011 World Development Indicators.

[5] J. C. J. Ososteveen, "The State of Marketing Research in Europe," *European Research* (1986), 14 (3): 100–135.

owning a landline, but they all owned mobile phones as well). In view of all this, more than 90% of all telephone interviews in Finland are conducted on a mobile telephone.[6]

Telephone interviews may not work very well in countries like Germany, where there is lot of resistance to telephone interviews.[7] This may not be possible in countries or states where the number of unlisted telephone numbers is very high. There is also the possibility that such a selection may not be representative of the general population, as people who have unlisted numbers tend to be significantly different from the rest of the population.

Random Digit Dialing (RDD)

To overcome this bias created by telephone directories, researchers resort to RDD. In a complete RDD method, all the digits of the telephone number (the area code, prefix, and the exchange suffix) are selected randomly. This implies that in a given country, all telephone numbers stand an equal chance of being called. The drawback in this method is that not all numbers may be in service and so many calls could be made to nonexistent numbers, which in turn leads to waste of time and money. Moreover, a completely RDD leads to telephone numbers which are of no interest to the researcher—outside the geographic scope of the study, government numbers, a business number when the research is on households, etc. Exhibit 9.1 gives a list of countries for which samples are available.

Exhibit 9.1

Coverage Expands for Global Telephone Samples[8]

SSI is a global provider of sampling solutions for survey research. Ordering landline or wireless telephone sample with SSI-SNAP is as easy as clicking the mouse. All the user has to do is download an SSI-SNAP application to their desktop. The simple menu options enable the user to build the right sample for their project through SSI-SNAP™ which communicates directly with SSI, delivering the custom sample to the user quickly. Being in the industry for over 36 years, it provides users with a trusted sample. Help is available at every step from live expert consultants to a comprehensive help function. With the coverage of wireless and mobile sample in 12 countries, the sample has the most updated demographics with detailed choice of geographic breakdowns. Users can calculate the numbers they need using their simple calculator on the website. The software installation is completely free of cost. SSI's RDD telephone samples along with directory listed and special targets are the available sampling methods for a user. Global representation, efficiency, and cost-effective sampling are built into SSI-SNAP. Geography file updates, mandatory for ensuring proper geographic representation, are immediately available for downloading. These samples are extensively used in many industries. Recently, an RDD telephone sample of 1,500 US adults was used by Kaiser Foundation Tracking Poll study.[9]

---

[6] Vesa Kuusela and Matti Simpanen, "Finland," in *Telephone Surveys in Europe*, eds Sabine Häder, Michael Häder, and Mike Kühne (Heidelberg: Springer, 2012), pp. 37–45.

[7] D. N. Aldridge, "Multi-Country Research," *Applied Marketing and Social Research 2*, 1987, pp. 359–377.

[8] Adapted from http://www.surveysampling.com (Retrieved on July 23, 2013).

[9] "SSI Sample Is Source for Kaiser Foundation Tracking Poll," http://www.surveysampling.com/KnowledgeLink/news/SSI-News/SSI-Source-for-Tracking-Poll (Retrieved in July 2013).

Nearly 98% of US households can be reached via telephone today.[10] Therefore, for any kind of survey which requires a wide audience like syndicated research, political polling studies, and other such marketing research projects, telephone sampling is a choice of most researchers. The explosion of mobile technology, however, has declined the landline ownership, calling for a change in the traditional way of conducting telephone surveys. Also, the number portability and other such issues that arise have to be taken care of before using a sample for a study. Researchers have to be cognizant of the recent changes in the telecommunications industry to be able to ensure that their samples are robust and representative enough to ensure accuracy of their research project. Table 9.2 points to some statistics about the coverage data for telephone frames as of 2013.

TABLE 9.2
COVERAGE DATA FOR TELEPHONE FRAMES

Total US households (in millions)*	123.1
Telephone households (in millions)*	118.3
Percentage of telephone households*	96.1
Non-telephone households (in millions)*	4.8
Percentage of non-telephone households*	3.9
Mobile cellular subscriptions (in millions)**	305.7
Mobile cellular subscriptions (per 100 people)**	95.5

*US Census Bureau, Current Population Survey, and **World Development Indicators.*

Systematic Random Digit Dialing (SRDD)

A variation of the RDD called SRDD is used in most cases. Here, the researcher specifies the area code and the prefix for the telephone numbers to be called, thus, avoiding sections of the population that are not useful for the study. The researcher determines a starting number (seed point) and a constant which is added to systematically to the number generated. This produces the list of telephone numbers to be called. Not all the numbers called will result in successful interviews; therefore, researchers have to generate at least four times as many telephone numbers as the sample size. The advantage in this method is that each telephone number has an equal chance of being called. At the same time, because the researcher controls the exchange prefix, it is possible to focus the study in a specific geographic area. If the study requires sampling with geographic dispersion, the researcher only needs to add more seed numbers and generate more lists. The list can be generated with the help of computers. A simpler version of the SRDD method is called plus-one dialing. This involves selecting random numbers from telephone directories and adding "1" to the last four digits in the number. These methods ensure that unlisted numbers are also included in the sample. Exhibit 9.2 provides a brief illustration of SRDD process.

---

[10] Linda Piekarski, "The Pros and Cons of Sampling Mode", *Quirks Marketing Research Review*, December 2008 http://www.quirks.com/pdf/200812_quirks.pdf (Retrieved in July 2013).

Exhibit 9.2

An Illustration of the SRDD Process[11]

Suppose an interviewer wants to poll 1,000 ($n = 1,000$) respondents on the eve of the presidential election in a particular area (with the area code prefix as 743). There are a total of 10,000 ($k = 10,000$) numbers with the prefix 743, that is, 743-0000 to 743-9999. The first step in the SRDD process is to compute the sampling interval (I) given by kn, which in this case is equal to 10. The interviewer then randomly chooses a telephone number in the interval 743-0000 to 743-0010. Once a number is chosen (say, 743-0005), then, to generate additional numbers, the value of I is added to each of the previously selected numbers. In other words, the telephone numbers to call would be 743-0005, 743-(0005 + I), 743-(0005 + $2I$),..., 743-[0005 + (n –1)I].

Telephone Prenotification Method

Telephone interviews are also being increasingly used in global marketing research as a method of screening and notifying the respondents. Surveys are very expensive in international markets and the costs can be justified only with very high response rates. Telephones are used in conjunction with other modes of survey to ensure excellent response rates. This was used in a survey conducted by the author for a software company to measure market potential in global markets for their products. Germany was one of the countries included in the study. The method adopted was to call up potential respondents and inform them of the purpose of the study and enlist their cooperation. The respondents were then sent a questionnaire either by fax or by e-mail. The respondents were once again contacted by telephone if they did not send in their responses within a specified time. This resulted in a very high response rate, and as a consequence, only a small sample size was required. This method of enlisting cooperation beforehand is found to work well among busy executives. Exhibit 9.3 gives some pointers on timing telephone calls.

The outcome of a telephone interview may be very different in international research. In the US, interviewers are used to getting through the number more often than not. Most telephones are also hooked up to an answering machine or voice mail. The typical procedure is to leave a message and call back at a later time. In most other countries, the phone lines may not be functional for considerable periods of time. Even when they are in working order, the researcher could get a busy signal, as there is no concept of call waiting. It is very rare that the call is picked up by an answering machine. In case of industrial surveys, getting through to the decision maker could be very cumbersome because of bureaucratic management styles. The interviewer could at best wean an appointment from a secretary. The cost is also very high. There is a charge for most local calls, and state-to-state calls are considerably more expensive than they are in the US. There is the added complication of some cultures refusing to part with any information over the telephone. All this has to be borne in mind when considering the telephone as the medium of data collection.

---

[11] Aaker et al., *Marketing Research*, 11th edition.

Exhibit 9.3

Timing the Telephone Call[12]

When conducting research, it has been noticed that the exact timing of an interview can go a long way in generating a high-quality level of response. After analyzing telephone calls made at different times of the day/week, researchers were able to notice certain trends:

1. Consumers displayed a high preference for conducting interview between 6 p.m. and 9 p.m.
2. The best time to reach homemakers or contact individuals at work is between 9 a.m. and 4:30 p.m.
3. Interviewers' patterns of working were more related to their preferences than the working practices of any marketing research agency.
4. Higher chance of successful response if interviewer focused more on what *time* of the day interview should be held rather than what *day* of the week.
5. Encouraging interviewers to make evening calls may lead to better response rates and minimize costs.

It has been generally found that the reliability of the Mexican telephone network is questionable (only 17 telephone lines per 100 people as of 2011).[13] As a result, some companies chose to bypass it by using private satellite networks to provide their own telecommunication lines. In Argentina, one has to hold the phone for hours waiting for a dial tone. In Russia too, it has been reported that nearly 40–60% of telephone survey calls result in direct refusals and interrupted interviews, which is higher than the direct refusal rates for face-to-face interviews.[14] In China, there are no residential telephone directories. Many Chinese are not used to taking phone calls, and, hence, there is no standard procedure for hanging up. Sometimes, they give a warning before hanging up abruptly, and some other times they hold the receiver farther and farther away from the mouth before finally fading away. These are some of the problems encountered in telephone surveys in global marketing research.

There are a few tips that come in handy when conducting a telephone interview. The introduction is a very important part because this helps establish a rapport with the client. It is absolutely necessary that the interviewer have a pleasant voice and sound friendly over the telephone. The introduction to the topic of the study should be brief and precise. It is also important that the telephone call be made at a time when the respondent is most likely to be available. For instance, if the study requires that professional be interviewed, they should be contacted at home after working hours or over the weekends. However, the call should not be made very late into the evening as it will intrude into their sleep time and the respondents

---

[12] Aaker et al., *Marketing Research*, 11th edition; Chisnall, *Marketing Research*, 5th edition (Reprinted by permission of Professor P. M. Chisnall).

[13] "Dialling for Dollars, Far from Home," *Business Week*, January 13, 1992; Ray Converse and Shelley Galbraith, "Eastern Europe," *Business America*, June 18, 1990; "China's Budding Phone Market, Industry Still Has Its Wires Crossed," *San Jose Mercury News*, March 6, 1994.

[14] Anna Andreenkova, "Russia," in *Telephone Surveys in Europe*, eds Sabine Häder, Michael Häder, and Mike Kühne (Heidelberg: Springer, 2012), pp. 3–16.

may not cooperate. The interviewer should also make a detailed report of each call—the day and the time the call was made, the outcome, the length of the call, if the respondent should be contacted again, and so forth. This step is very important for collating the data.

Mail Surveys

This is a method of survey where the questionnaire is mailed to potential respondents who complete the survey and mail it back. In a mail interview, the individuals to be sampled should be identified and their mailing addresses should be obtained. This is commonly used in countries where the literacy level is high.[15] Mailing lists can be obtained from various sources such as telephone directories, organization membership rosters, publication subscription lists or other commercial sources. The only precondition is that the mailing list must be current and must closely relate to the group being studied. As can be expected, obtaining a valid mailing list that is current and representative of the general population is a cumbersome task. Also, mail surveys are also subjected to mailing costs. Among the European nations, postal rates in Bulgaria are the highest at €2.26 after adjusting for labor costs and purchasing power. In comparison to most European operators, the US Postal Service (USPS) letter rates are amongst the cheapest at €0.46. Additionally, USPS is covering a much vaster geographical area than the European postal operators. In an international context, the USPS is offering a very fair deal on their products. Table 9.3 provides the postal rates in the 27 member states in the EU.

In the day and age of digital marketing, traditional channels of direct mail still perform better on the response rate of customers. The response rate for a direct mail to an existing customer average 3.40% while it is 0.12% for e-mail.[16] While mailing lists are readily available today, small businesses may not be able to afford them. Postal service—USPS—is trying to address this issue faced by several small businesses. Exhibit 9.4 explains the key feature of USPS's Every Door Direct Mail service in the US.

There are other decisions that would have to be made before mailing a survey. Although they may seem relatively mechanical, these could affect the efficiency and quality of the mailing survey. Some of the aspects that need to be considered are the length of the questionnaire, the content, layout, color and format, the method of addressing the respondent, the contents of a cover letter, the incentive that would be given to the respondents, the type of return envelope and postage. The choice of incentives is very critical to the success of mail surveys in cross-national research.[17] Researchers should also decide on the time and effort to be spent in follow up in the form of post cards, letters, or telephone calls. These decisions will have a significant impact on the response rates, the quality of information collected, and cost of executing the mailing survey. Respondents could be screened using a preliminary notification.

---

[15] T. Vahvelainen, "Marketing Research in the Nordic Countries," *European Research* (1985), vol. 13, pp. 76–79; T. Vahvelainen "Marketing Research in Finland," *European Research* (1987), 15 (1): 62–66; E. H. Demby, "ESOMAR Urges Changes in Reporting Demographics, Issues Worldwide Report," *Marketing News* 24, no.1 (January 8, 1990): 24–25.

[16] "DMA Response Rate Report," 2012, http://www.targetmarketingmag.com/article/direct-mail-response-rates-dipping-says-dma-report/1 (Retrieved in July 2013).

[17] David Jobber, Hafiz Mirza, and Kee H. Wee, "Incentives and Response-Rates to Cross National Business Surveys: A Logit Model Analysis," *Journal of International Business Studies* 4 (1991): 711–721.

TABLE 9.3
STANDARD LETTER MAILING COSTS AMONG EUROPEAN NATIONS[18]

Country	Postal Rate (€)	Country	Postal Rate (€)
Bulgaria	2.26	UK	0.64
Latvia	1.54	Greece	0.62
Lithuania	1.38	Switzerland	0.61
Slovakia	1.28	Sweden	0.60
Romania	1.21	Austria	0.59
Poland	1.02	Luxembourg	0.58
Norway	0.94	Germany	0.55
Denmark	0.90	France	0.54
Hungary	0.89	Ireland	0.51
Estonia	0.83	Cyprus	0.47
Portugal	0.80	Netherlands	0.44
Finland	0.73	Spain	0.44
Czech Republic	0.68	Slovenia	0.38
Italy	0.65	Malta	0.35
Belgium	0.64		

Exhibit 9.4

Every Door Direct Mail[19]

Every Door Direct Mail is a service available to companies who would like to send their mail to all residents in a particular area. A lot of businesses actually send out materials such as mail surveys, catalogues, information about their product or services, etc. to all residents in a specific locality. Every Door Direct Mail does not require the company to have a mailing list in place. Using this service from USPS, companies can simply map out the area they wish to target, select a delivery route, and the drop off dates from the convenience of their laptops or computers. It is great for local businesses as they can send out coupons, menus, event calendars, satisfaction survey, store maps, etc.

While mail surveys form one type of self-administered surveys, other types are where the questionnaires are faxed across to the respondents or simply e-mailed or handed over to them in person. The rapid Internet penetration has resulted in an increase in the use of

---

[18] Adapted from Deutsche Post, "Letter Prices in Europe," March 2011.
[19] Adapted from https://www.usps.com/business/every-door-direct-mail.htm (Retrieved in July 2013).

online surveys by businesses. These are efficient, fast, and inexpensive. In the international context especially, online surveys are becoming more popular due to the nature and scope of its execution. It is fairly easy for a researcher sitting in US to conduct primary research among consumers in Asia via online surveys. It is not only inexpensive and quick, but also extremely convenient and efficient. By enabling the researcher to have more access and control of the data collection process, it makes way for the creation of in-depth questionnaires, thereby achieving a lot more out of a single survey. The gaining popularity of online surveys has urged more and more people to join online panels as well.

Online Surveys

The Internet has become known for the generation and dissemination of information, connectivity among the users, and the social networking possibilities. Given these attractive features, the Internet has emerged as a reliable source for researchers to seek opinions and test new concepts. As of June 2012, there were an estimated 2.4 billion Internet users around the world. While Asia is home to more than 1 billion Internet users, the growth of number of Internet users as compared to 2000 estimates is the highest in Africa (36 times), followed by the Middle East (26 times), and Latin America/Caribbean (13 times).[20] Among the BRIC countries, India posted the sharpest growth in unique website visitors between 2011 and 2012 at 41% (62.6 million users), followed by Russia at 20% (59 million users), Brazil at 6% (52 million users), and China at 5% (336 million users).[21]

In terms of the gender composition, an estimated 1.3 billion women (37% of all women) are online, compared with 1.5 billion men (41% of all men). There are an estimated 826 million women Internet users and 980 million male Internet users in the developing countries. In contrast, 475 million female Internet users and 483 million male Internet users are from the developed countries. The gender divide is stark in the developing countries than the developed countries. In the developing world, 16% fewer women than men use the Internet, compared to only 2% fewer women than men in the developed world.[22] In terms of popular languages used on the Internet, English tops the list with nearly 565 million users around the world in 2011, followed by Chinese with 509 million users, and Spanish with 165 million users. However, in terms of growth rates between 2000 and 2011, the number of Arabic language users grew the most by 25 times, followed by Russian users by 18 times, and Chinese users by 14 times.[23]

With such a dynamic growth pattern around the world, researchers are turning to this medium more often for their survey needs. A variety of international marketing studies are now possible with such a wide Internet audience base. Some of the popular uses for online surveys are: (a) e-mail surveys and consumer panels, (b) online focus groups, (c) website

---

[20] "Internet Users in the World Statistics," June 30, 2012, http://www.internetworldstats.com/stats. htm (Retrieved in July 2013).

[21] "No Sign of Slowing Web Uptake in India," September 18, 2012, http://www.emarketer.com/Article/ No-Sign-of-Slowing-Web-Uptake-India/1009356 (Retrieved on April 10, 2014).

[22] "The World in 2013—ICT Facts And Figures," http://www.itu.int/en/ITU-D/Statistics/Documents/ facts/ICTFactsFigures2013.pdf (Retrieved on June 3, 2013).

[23] "Top Ten Languages Used in the Web," May 31, 2011, http://www.internetworldstats.com/stats7. htm (Retrieved in July 2013).

effectiveness, (d) advertising measurement, (e) opt-in e-mail marketing lists, (f) opinion research, (g) new product development, and (h) customer satisfaction surveys.

While online surveys are often hosted in domains that are controlled by the organization conducting the research, private websites offering paid and free online survey options are also popular among researchers. Some of these websites include QuestionPro, Zoomerang, PollDaddy, Survey Monkey, and Kwik Surveys. These websites make online research easy for researchers by providing a range of services that include survey question types and templates, survey themes based on the type of surveys, statistics regarding survey completion, mobile/tablet compatible surveys, reminder e-mail functionality, social network integration, multilingual surveys, downloadable data and reports in multiple file formats, data analysis and report generation, secure and password protected administrator section, and helpdesk support for the administrators, among others. While the paid versions from these websites provide the whole gamut of services targeted to the research topic and the organization, the free versions also provide significant cost savings despite the limited services available.

Online surveys have been used in several studies outside of the marketing domain as well, such as health awareness, social development, and opinion polls on governmental policies. Typically, the online surveys are made available to the respondent either as part of user forums or as privately addressed e-mails, with the requirement of having the respondent complete the survey and submit it. An online questionnaire should ensure a mix of multiple choice questions, fields for comments, the inclusion of multimedia tools (image and/or video), and provide integration with social networks. The appeal of online surveys to researchers stems primarily for the benefit of cost savings (printing questionnaires and travel costs for the researcher), and instant delivery of the survey instrument. However, online surveys have to be carefully analyzed for any sampling issues that they might raise and the validity of responses collected online.

ADVANTAGES AND DISADVANTAGES OF SURVEY METHODS

This section considers the benefits and drawbacks of each of the four methods in the international context.[24]

The Personal Interview

Most researchers consider this to be the most flexible method of obtaining data. The interview is a face-to-face encounter and can put the respondent at ease. The interviewer will clarify any doubts that the respondent may have during the course of the survey. The rate of non-response error will be marginal. The interviewer has a high degree of flexibility to rephrase the questions on more comfortable grounds or probe the respondent on any aspect of the survey. This is the ideal method for studies that focus on complex topics or those that require lot of information. The interviewer can also exercise the option of interviewing other members of the household if they can contribute significantly to the study. In West African countries where the literacy rate is very low (e.g., adult literacy rate in Mali was 31%, Guinea was 41%, and Sierra Leone was 42% in 2010), this may be the only way of gathering information

---

[24] Monk, "Marketing Research in Canada"; Jack J. Honomichl, "Survey Results Positive," *Advertising Age* 55 (November 1984): 23.

from respondents.[25] Even though the cost of personal interviews is very high, this is the most effective method of data collection in less-developed countries.[26]

As contradictory as it sounds, the presence of the interviewer is also the biggest disadvantage of personal interviews. Respondents may provide wrong answers to some questions with a desire to appear prestigious and sophisticated. In some cases, the presence of the interviewer could make some respondents uncomfortable and reticent. In many cultures, like Latin America, interviewers are treated with a lot suspicion. Similarly, in Belarus and Middle Asian countries, conversation on topics relating to consumer goods, media preferences, evaluation of government policies, and views on governmental actions and policies are considered threatening and undesirable.[27] For the interview to be fruitful, the interviewer has to put a lot of effort in winning the trust of the respondent.

Studies have also shown that there is a significant impact of the interaction effects of gender and ethnicity on the quality of response.[28] There is the possibility of interviewer bias, which is very pronounced in global marketing research. For instance, interviewing housewives in Middle Eastern countries will be difficult if the interviewer is male. The interviewer could misinterpret the response due to a lack of understanding of the foreign culture or language problems. Some countries have different dialects and differences in usage of the same language in different parts of the country. This makes the task of the interviewer more difficult. There could also be problems in interpreting nonverbal cues in a foreign country. An example would be shaking of one's head. While it means a negative reply in most parts of the world, the Japanese use it to indicate a positive answer. Last, but not the least of all, the cost of personal interviews is very high. Exhibit 9.5 provides a few tips for effective interpretations in international surveys.

The Telephone Interview

Telephone interviews cost less than personal interviews and can be done in a very short period of time. The non-response rate is generally very low. If the respondent cannot be contacted on the first attempt, it is very easy to call back again at a later time. In countries that have a very good telephone network, such as Switzerland, it is possible to contact people who meet all the specifications of the target population. In Switzerland, there is no legal restriction upon calling published telephone numbers even for marketing purposes. This has made the RDD option of telephone survey reasonably feasible.[29] Further, declining costs of telephone calls have made it possible for interviewers to a cover a broadly distributed sample. It has also been observed that international calls produce better results consistently. The fact that they require no field staff serves to lower costs further. With advances in technology, interviewers can key in the responses directly into a computer, simplifying the task of data preparation.

[25] Friedrich Huebler and Weixin Lu, "Adult and Youth Literacy, 1990-2015 Analysis of Data for 41 Selected Countries," *UNESCO Institute for Statistics*, (UNESCO Publishing, 2012) http://www.uis.unesco.org/Education/Documents/UIS-literacy-statistics-1990-2015-en.pdf (Retrieved on April 10, 2014).

[26] Naresh K. Malhotra, "A Methodology for Measuring Consumer Preferences in Developing Countries," *International Marketing Review* (Autumn 1988), vol. 5, pp. 52–65.

[27] Andreenkova, "Russia."

[28] Cynthia Webster, "Hispanic and Anglo Interviewer and Respondent Ethnicity and Gender: The Impact of Survey Response Quality," *Journal of Marketing Research* (February 1996), vol. 33, pp. 62–72.

[29] Michèle Ernst Stähli, "Switzerland," in *Telephone Surveys in Europe*, eds Sabine Häder, Michael Häder, and Mike Kühne (Springer, 2012), pp. 3–16.

Exhibit 9.5

Tips for Effective Interpretations[30]

Language is perhaps the most important barrier when researching international markets. Therefore, irrespective of the research instrument being used, ensuring exact interpretations is vital in deriving insightful results. The following tips would be of help to researchers using interpreters.

1. *An interpreter is different from a translator!* While it may seem obvious, people generally use one for the other. Therefore, it is critical to understand their terminologies. A translator is someone who works with the written word and translates a written text in one language into a written text in another language. In contrast, an interpreter works with the spoken word or oral communication, and is used for real-time communication in a foreign country.
2. *It's all about the meaning.* Interpreters do not translate. Rather, they communicate what researchers mean in the listener's language. There are plenty of examples of marketing gaffes that have relied heavily on literal translations and have produced erroneous and often embarrassing results. Therefore, it is not about the literal translation—it is the appropriate rendering of your meaning in the other language.
3. *A pause goes a long way.* If you speak for too long without a pause, the interpreter will find it more difficult to render your meaning, and your listeners will get bored or lose focus. Therefore, a pause helps the interpreter to collect, assimilate, and effectively interpret the message into the foreign language.
4. *Go easy on the slangs.* The focus should be on the message that has to be communicated. This calls for easy and straight talk that does not involve slangs, humor, pun, or play with words. This helps the interpreter to concentrate on interpreting the message correctly.
5. *Look at your counterpart, not the interpreter!* In the most ideal setting, the interpreter should be invisible, with only the interpreted messages going back and forth. This is possible only if the researcher focuses his attention on the counterpart, and using the ears only with the interpreter. Such an approach also helps the researcher to pick up the nonverbal cues from the counterpart.

Telephone interviews must be kept as short as possible as respondents fail to cooperate for very long interviews. The problem of interviewer bias is present as in the case of personal interviews. Telephone interviews do not permit the use of visual aids to aid the survey process. In developing countries, the percentage of population that owns telephone is very low. Telephone interviews will be able to contact only the upper echelons of the society. The sample interviewed over the telephone will not be representative of the majority. Even if a telephone network exists, there may not be a reliable directory that lists the telephone numbers. RDD will not be very effective because many telephones may not be in working order. In some countries like Japan, people tend to think of telephone interviews as disrespectful.

---

[30] Adapted from Anne Orban, "Qualitatively Speaking: Ten Tips for Using Interpreters in International Research," *Quirk's Marketing Research Review*, November 2005, p. 20.

Respondents will cooperate only in personal interviews. Telephone interviews will not be cost-effective in Europe because the charges are very high, especially in Germany.

The Mail Survey

Mail surveys can cover a broader respondent base and do not require any field staff. They are free from interviewer bias. The cost of mailing questionnaires to respondents selected from a sample tends to be low when compared to personal interviews or telephone interviews. This method can be used effectively for industrial surveys where the respondents are highly knowledgeable and the topic of the survey is very specific. Further, since the questionnaire is answered at the respondent's discretion, the replies are likely to be more thoughtful and others can be consulted for necessary information. Mail surveys generally are superior when sensitive or potentially embarrassing topics, such as sexual behavior and finances, are covered (so long as the respondent is convinced that the answers will be kept in confidence).

The non-response rate in a mail survey is very high and this causes some problems. Even though the cost of mailing questionnaires is relatively low, because of poor response, the cost-per-survey may be very high. The other problem is that there could be a significant bias because of low response rate. There is no control over the questionnaire once it has been mailed out. Respondents may answer questions selectively, ignoring personal issues. They could misinterpret some questions. Additionally, mail surveys cannot control for the identity of the respondent (i.e., is the addressee responding or someone else), whom the respondent consults for the answers, and how the questions are being interpreted by the respondent. Further, great care and effort are required to compile mailing lists that do not have flaws such as obsolescence, omissions, and duplications.

In global marketing research, mail surveys are made difficult by the fact that current mailing lists may not be available. In many places, such as Hong Kong, people live on boats and have no formal addresses. There are no house or site numbers in Venezuela and addresses are identified by house names such as Casa Rosa or Casa Rio. Even if researchers were to look into magazine subscription lists, they tend to include citizens who are better educated and wealthier than the average folks. This introduces sampling biases in the survey. There could also be a significant loss of questionnaires and responses once they are mailed out. In Brazil, 30% of the mail does not get delivered. The postal system in many less-developed countries does not provide the service of forwarding mail. Low levels of literacy could also mean that even if it were possible to get the addresses, not all people would be able to respond. Including incentives in the mail to ensure cooperation is also not possible because of mail thefts. Conducting a multi-country mail survey also poses some practical problems for researchers—it is not possible to get return envelopes for such a survey. Researchers need to be aware of all these problems before deciding on a mail survey for global marketing research.

A lot of the problems faced by mail surveys are overcome by online surveys. While the non-response rates are higher in online than mail surveys, researcher can send out surveys to many more respondents as the cost of e-mailing to a larger group is almost nothing. The return envelope problem does not exist in online survey. All the respondent needs to do is click on a link provided to them in their e-mail and fill in the form. Online surveys reduce the time involved with the data coding process. In an international setting, it is extremely beneficial as the survey responses are recorded online and the physical location of the country where the research is being conducted does not play any role in data coding process. Online surveys are quick to conduct and provide more control to the researchers in terms of selection of panel members.

The Online Survey[31]

Online surveys are changing the role marketing research and how surveys are being administered. Their prominence as an attractive option is due its advantages over the traditional survey methods, in terms of high quality, faster turnaround in administering the surveys, and being relatively inexpensive.

As no interviewers are involved in administering these surveys, the possibility of interviewer error and bias is eliminated. Further, Web-based surveys give researchers much more control over data quality. Logic checks can be built into the survey so that contradictory or nonsensical answers are not allowed, eliminating the need for data cleaning and editing. With an online survey, the questionnaire is posted on a secure website where clients can instantaneously view results as soon as any respondent has completed the interview. In some cases, invitations to surveys are also posted on banners in certain websites that attract high traffic. These website visitors would click on the banner and would be redirected to a secure website to conduct a brief interview. Upon completion of the survey, respondents are automatically returned to the website where they were redirected from.

Despite the benefits provided by online surveys, their validity depends on the sample selection, survey design, response tendencies, and technology challenges. In e-research, the choice of sampling units is in the form of e-mail addresses, electronic subscription groups, and heavily visited websites. Unfortunately, people change their e-mail addresses very often, thus, creating problems in obtaining well-defined samples. Another problem is the poor translation of well-designed surveys into electronic versions. This results in lower response rates for the surveys, which in turn lowers their statistical value and validity. Adding to this complexity is the presence of multilingual online surveys where translation is a major concern area, and the respondents will not have any guidance in understanding and answering questions.

Therefore, online surveys need continuous monitoring to determine their direction, appropriate use, and long-term effectiveness. However, online surveys do continue to attract more number of researchers as more people get on to the Internet for longer periods of time.

FREQUENCY AND EASE OF USE

In global marketing research, mail surveys are usually used for industrial products. The response rate is good and the cost per survey is low. The adoption of online surveys for this purpose is increasing. Obtaining the mailing list for such products is easy. For consumer research, this method will be effective only in industrialized nations where the literacy levels are high and mailing lists are available. In most developing countries, obtaining a mailing list will be expensive. Even if one were available, most potential respondents will not be able

---

[31] Dick McCullough, "Web-Based Market Research Ushers in New Age," *Marketing News*, September 14, 1998.

to respond because they are not literate. Other methods of survey research will have to be adopted in these countries.

Telephone interviews are dependent on the quality of the lines, which can vary substantially between countries. There are many countries where telephone connections are not widely available. Any survey conducted by telephone will be biased toward the upper classes in that country; therefore, this method is used if the population to be surveyed consists of lawyers, doctors, and other professionals who are in the upper income level. The second factor that decides the use of telephone surveys is the availability of telephone directories or lists that are valid and current. Cost per call is an aspect that researchers cannot ignore. In many countries, a hefty charge is levied on domestic or state-to-state calls. It may not be practical for the researcher to conduct lengthy surveys over the telephone.

Personal interviewing is considered the most flexible method of survey research. It is the most frequently used method of conducting surveys in global marketing research. Even though the cost of conducting personal interviews is very high, it can be cost-effective in a foreign country because of the very high response rate. The preference for personal interviews arises because of the problems posed by mail surveys and telephone interviews. Telephone interviews are generally ruled out because of the high cost. Mail surveys are not very effective because most people do not mail the questionnaire back. Incentives do not help as most people in developing countries barely make ends meet and consider the incentive as a means of sustenance rather than as an obligation on their part to respond to the survey. There have been instances of mail thefts in cases where the postal employees become aware of the incentive included in the envelope. Besides, the cultural differences are so great that they can be captured only in personal interviews. In countries like India and China, the language, culture, and habits vary widely from region to region. Researchers will be able to gather all this data only by face-to-face interviews. In general, surveys for developing countries should be backed with observational studies because it may not be possible to obtain information from all classes of respondents.[32]

REQUIREMENTS

The researcher conducting the survey has to have four basic requirements: (a) understanding of the research project, (b) knowledge of the industry, (c) familiarity with the national and cultural traits in the countries where the research is being conducted, and (d) fluency with the language.

Conducting a survey is a complex task of gaining the trust and building rapport so that the respondent is comfortable with divulging information to a virtual stranger. This is a lot easier if the researcher is able to converse with the respondent in his/her own language. It is also better for the researcher to blend in with the culture rather than stand out. This can be achieved if the researcher is familiar with important customs and traditions in the part of the world where the survey is being conducted.

Industry knowledge and an understanding of the project are required because it will help the researcher design the survey better. It also becomes vital when the survey respondents are professionals and experts in the area that is being researched. They are likely to respect and respond better to someone who has a good knowledge of the technical aspects.

---

[32] Naresh K. Malhotra, "Administration of Questionnaires for Collecting Quantitative Data in International Marketing Research," *Journal of Global Marketing* 2 (1991): 63–92.

Audits and Surveys conducts surveys on a regular basis for Coca-Cola Company to measure the awareness of Coke in all the countries where it is being sold. The master plan for the research is designed by the headquarters in New York. The project is executed by researchers for Audits and Surveys in all these different countries. The questionnaire is originally designed in English and in each of these countries researchers translate it to the local language for the purpose of conducting the survey with the locals. The results are then translated back to English and sent to the New York office where the final analysis is completed. It is evident that researchers in all these different countries should be fluent in English as well as the local language.

As many research companies point out, no one person can be an expert in all the industries and all the regions. People tend to specialize in a particular area, and with experience, gain insights into one or two cultures different from their own. A research company, however, will have the benefit of the combined knowledge and experience of all these researches and is in a position to conduct surveys in any industry and in any part of the world.

APPLICABILITY

The chapter on primary research stresses the importance of establishing equivalence with respect to construct, measurement, sampling, and analysis. This is the stage in the research process where the researcher has to be concerned about establishing construct and measurement equivalence. The survey instrument used in surveys is a questionnaire, which has to be designed in a manner such that the data collected is comparable. This is better explained with the help of an example.

Consider a research study on car ownership among high-income homes in various countries. The researcher could formulate a hypothesis stating that the number of garages in a residence is an indicator of the number of the cars owned. This would be a reasonably accurate estimation in the US because every house comes with built-in garages. The problem arises when this questionnaire is used for surveys outside of the US. In many countries, most houses do not have garages. People use unconventional parking spots like the sidewalks and the front yard. Therefore, if the researcher wants the same hypothesis to hold good in other countries also, he should find all the acceptable substitutes to a garage in these countries and incorporate all these choices in the questionnaire. Only then will the results of the research be considered valid.

As can be understood from this example, it is very important for the survey instrument to be applicable in a given country, in a given situation, if the research is to be fruitful. Once again, it brings us back to importance of cultural and national differences and the necessity for the researcher to be culturally sensitive.

CULTURAL INFLUENCES

Chapter 1 illustrated a lot of examples of the cultural differences among countries, and thereby the impact of the same on marketing. This chapter focuses on the vast differences in the reactions of different cultures toward surveys. Personal interviews last longer in France, Germany, and Italy, as the interviewers provide elaborate descriptions for all the terms that have no direct translation into that language. Therefore, care should be taken to ensure that the survey does not last more than 20 or 25 minutes in the US because this would mean a 35–40-minute survey in any of the above-mentioned countries. There is also a high rate of refusal in these countries because a lot of people are subject to too many surveys. The other factor that should be considered is that Germans are very conscientious about time. If they are told that the survey will last half an hour, at the end of the half hour, they ask you to stop. The French and the Italians are a lot more flexible with their time. The English are too polite to cut off the interviewer. People in the Scandinavian countries have lower refusal rates and are generally very cooperative. People in most Mediterranean countries, with the possible exception of Spain, like to converse a lot. Among the Asian countries, the Japanese consider it impolite if they are surveyed over the telephone. They have to be interviewed personally. In Hong Kong, researchers are not allowed inside the residence. They will have to question the respondents through a small aperture in the front door of the house. In the Middle Eastern countries, women cannot be interviewed in their houses without the presence of men. Researchers will have to bear all this in mind while launching a survey. In most Middle Eastern countries, lunch lasts for two to four hours and people have a relaxed attitude toward punctuality.[33]

PROBLEMS SPECIFIC TO DEVELOPING COUNTRIES[34]

Language is likely to present a very big problem in conducting surveys, especially in countries where multiple dialects are spoken. Most of these countries are also characterized by low levels of literacy. Under these circumstances, written questionnaires are useless. Getting good research staff is also likely to be a problem in many of these countries. For instance, interviewers in India tend to be generalists, and are not regarded very highly since the status of the marketing research is poor. Interviewers should be of the same racial group as the respondents. There could be a lot of respondent bias in developing countries. Thai and Indonesian women are not likely to talk to strangers, while Indian women require some known acquaintance to accompany the interviewer. Businessmen in some cultures view interviewers as industrial spies and refuse to divulge facts and figures. In many countries like Hong Kong, China, and India, the best way to obtain an interview might be to just go knocking on the doors rather than trying to fix up an appointment over the telephone.

SOURCES OF BIAS IN SURVEYS

Bias in survey[35] research can be attributed to three major sources—the respondent, the interviewer, and the topic of survey.

Respondents in many countries, particularly in Asia, provide responses which they think would please the interviewer. As known as socially desirable responding, this refers to "the tendency for people to present themselves favorably according to current cultural norms."[36] Research has identified that socially desirable responding consists of two factors, namely, impression management (people's deliberate tendency to present themselves in a

---

[33] Sak Onkvisit and John J. Shaw, *International Marketing—Analysis and Strategy* (Upper Saddle River, NJ: Prentice Hall, 1997), 3rd edition, p. 224.

[34] Joanna Kinsey, *Marketing in Developing Countries* (London: Macmillan Education, 1994).

[35] Ibid.

[36] D. G. Mick, "Are Studies of Dark Side Variables Confounded by Socially Desirable Responding? The Case of Materialism," *Journal of Consumer Research*, 1996, vol. 23, pp. 106–119.

positive manner) and self-deceptive enhancement (people's tendency to provide self-reports that are honest but positively biased). Impression management is closely related to faking, dissimulation, lying, and deceiving others. Self-deceptive enhancement is a predisposition to see oneself in a positive light, and is a form of rigid overconfidence.[37]

The moral and cultural obligations of people in these societies imply that they will go to any extent to prevent the interviewer from getting upset. The norms of many societies demand that respondents be courteous to strangers. Therefore, more often than not their responses are not indicators of their true feelings and opinions. To avoid this, it may be preferable to conceal the sponsors of the study. Interviewers should be trained adequately to overcome these obstacles. The questions should be worded in manner that will reduce courtesy bias. This could be achieved by phrasing the question as applicable to a third party: "People think that..." rather than "What do you think ...."

Another source of bias is the respondents' behavior exhibited through agreement tendency, yea-saying, and positivity. This behavior is referred to as the response style of acquiescence is defined as the tendency to agree with items regardless of content.[38] This often occurs with topics that are controversial. Research has explained that acquiescence is negatively related to verbal ability, logical consistency of attitudes, and social taste.[39] Further, research in the survey research and sociological literatures shows that acquiescence may reflect either deference shown by lower-status respondents to higher-status interviewers, or uncritical acceptance of sweeping generalizations and suggestive statements by respondents low in cognitive abilities.[40] Researchers have to try and understand values and topics that are likely to induce this behavior and make allowances for these. Cultural traits like modesty make a lot of difference in the survey. The Japanese are a modest society and tend to understate things while the Latin Americans tend to exaggerate their income and lifestyle. Even within a given country, factors like age, sex, and education play an important role in contributing to the bias. Respondents who are not well-educated try harder to please the interviewer.

Specific cultural traits too can cause bias. It has been found that the Chinese in Malaysia tend to be more reticent than Malaysians or Indians and consequently give more "No" and "Don't know" answers to open-ended questions. The Middle Eastern respondents tend to exaggerate, especially in aspects like class, income, position, and achievement. This can be overcome by using correlation techniques.

The presence of the interviewer adds to the bias in surveys. If the interviewer is not familiar with the country and its traditions, they could misinterpret the verbal and nonverbal responses given by the respondent. If the survey has open-ended questions, the interviewer may miss certain vital points. The research analyst could attribute wrong intentions to some of the responses or actions recorded during the course of the survey.

---

[37] D. L. Paulhus, "Measurement and Control of Response Bias," in *Measures of Personality and Social Psychological Attitudes*, eds, J. P. Robinson, P. R. Shaver, and L. S. Wright (San Diego, CA: Academic Press, 1991), pp. 17–59. ·

[38] Paulhus, "Measurement and Control of Response Bias"; J. D. Winkler, D. E. Kanouse, and J.E. Ware, Jr, "Controlling for Acquiescence Response Set in Scale Development," *Journal of Applied Psychology* 67 (1982): 555–561.

[39] S. Messick, "Psychology and Methodology of Response Styles," in *Improving Inquiry in Social Science: A Volume in Honor of Lee J. Cronbach*, eds, R. E. Snow and D. E. Wiley (Hillsdale, NJ: Erlbaum, 1991), pp. 161–200.

[40] H. Schuman and S. Presser, *Questions and Answers in Attitude Surveys* (New York: Academic Press, 1981).

The topic that is being researched also can cause bias. Some topics are socially sensitive in some countries. For instance, Latin Americans are touchy about alcoholism and Indians consider sex a taboo topic. In some surveys, respondents refuse to answer all the questions, leading to non-response bias.

NEW APPROACHES TO SURVEY RESEARCH

The constant change in technology creates innovative opportunities for researchers to use the technology in surveying consumers. While Internet is bringing its own set of innovation to the table, mobile technology is revolutionizing the way people communicate with each other. The use of Internet in marketing research surveys has been discussed in detail in Chapter 6. The further addition to this innovation chain is the proliferation of social media and the mobile technology. The quick adoption of mobile devices has made the researchers to pay attention to this medium for their research. Researchers are constantly worried about increasing the response rate and there is an increasing interest among them to use mobile for survey due to its adoption among all age groups. While the adoption of this technology among adults is high, among teens it is baffling. The survey results from the survey conducted by Pew Research Center indicate that 23% of teens have a tablet computer, a level comparable to general adult population. Also, one in four teens is a *cell-mostly* Internet user. These customers mostly go online using their phone and do not use some other device such as a desktop or laptop computer.[41] 95% of teens use the Internet. 93% of teens have a computer or have access to one at home. Seven in ten (71%) teens with home computer access say the laptop or desktop they use most often is one they share with other family members. This kind of information plays a key role for any marketer marketing to this particular group of customers.

It is interesting to note that mobile surveys are also a great addition to the face-to-face personal interview. Researchers are battling between three mobile survey tools: (a) software that is connected to the Internet, (b) customized software, and (c) dedicated applications (or apps).[42] The multi-platform portability is the issue that is concerning most researchers today. The future of mobile surveys will have to provide answers to such concerns that arise with the increased adoption and use. Exhibit 9.6 illustrates an example of survey conducted using the mobile platform.

GLOBAL MARKETING RESEARCH IN PRACTICE

Data gathered from secondary research, observation, and qualitative methods would help Tasty Burgers identify the questions that need to be asked to potential clients. The design of the questionnaire will be discussed in Chapter 11. This chapter deals with modes of conducting surveys. As discussed in this chapter, there are four methods of conducting a survey—personal interviews, telephone interviews, mail surveys, and online surveys.

---

[41] M. Madden et al., "Teens and Technology 2013," March 13, 2013, http://www.pewinternet.org/Reports/2013/Teens-and-Tech.aspx (Retrieved in July 2013).

[42] E. Perreault, "Mobile Surveys: Advantages, Tools & Perspectives," April 2, 2013, http://blog.voxco.com/2013/04/02/mobile-surveys-advantages-tools-and-perspectives/(Retrieved in July 2013).

Exhibit 9.6

Survey on Mobile[43]

Sage North America conducted a mobile survey among 476 small and midsized businesses in Canada. The Sage SMB Survey on Mobile Devices indicated that Canadian business owners find the use of mobile technology to have a positive effect on their company's productivity.

Nancy Harris, the senior vice president and General Manager of Sage 50 Accounting-Canadian Edition says, "Mobile devices have become so pervasive that many of us feel like these devices are an extension of ourselves, so it makes sense that the majority of business owners Sage surveyed in Canada are incorporating mobile devices to increase productivity."

Key Findings

1. Nearly 83% of respondents feel mobile technology has a positive effect on the productivity of their business.
2. Almost 78% of respondents use devices such as laptops, tablets, or smartphones for work-related information.
3. Remote access has increased over the past year with laptops increasing by 48%, tablets by 64%, and smartphones by 78%.
4. Around 45% of respondents have a bring-your-own-device policy in place.
5. E-mail is the most popular work-related item that is accessed on a mobile device.

It has already been mentioned that the mail survey provides the lowest response rate. Generally, this method is not employed in global marketing research as the cost per returned response tends to be very high. The telephone is usually a very good means of conducting surveys. It provides better response rates and the interviewer can clarify any doubts that the respondent might have. It is the method that will be used by Tasty Burgers in the UK. In Brazil, Saudi Arabia, and India, the penetration of telephones is very low and only a very small segment of the population can be reached. More often than not, the lines will not be functional and even if they were, telephone calls work out to be very expensive. People are also reluctant to impart personal information over the telephone. The best survey method in these countries will be personal interviews.

SUMMARY

This chapter deals with personal interviews, telephone interviews, and mail surveys. The advantages and disadvantages of each method and the applicability in global marketing research are discussed in detail. In global marketing research, one encounters a lot of

---

[43] Adapted from Sage North America, "Sage SMB Survey on Mobile Devices Finds Canadian Businesses Using Mobile Technology to Positively Affect Their Business," March 18, 2013, http://www.marketwire.com/press-release/sage-smb-survey-on-mobile-devices-finds-canadian-businesses-using-mobile-technology-1768986.htm (Retrieved in July 2013).

constraints in terms of nature and complexity of problem, lack of adequate knowledge and information, and available budget. The researcher has a few basic data collection methods at his disposal and global marketing research calls for a great deal of adaptation of these methods. These methods could be used in combination in a given country. In a multi-country study, different methods could be used in different countries. The stress is on the comparability and usefulness of data rather than on the use of identical instruments. This is a judgment call that has to be made by the researcher. It has been generally found that survey methods are the most popular means of collecting primary data in global marketing research—the personal interview, in particular. Improvements in technology, like the e-mail, have made surveys a lot easier and faster. The mobile technology has brought technology in the pockets of consumers. The impact of this technology on research is discussed in this chapter.

 QUESTIONS AND PROBLEMS

1. A retail store in the US that had habitually been conducting door-to-door surveys suddenly has a reduced budget to carry out its market research activities. Which survey technique could the store resort to in such a situation? What benefits from a personal interview may the new survey lose out on?

2. Biased opinions are a common problem in handling survey responses. Which survey method, according to you, generates the highest biasing effect?

3. As a market research manager, what, according to you, are some ethical guidelines that you should follow in all of the survey methods mentioned in this chapter?

4. What kind of data collection procedure would you recommend to research the question of why female shoppers choose a particular retail store, in the Middle East, to buy clothing?

5. You are a senior analyst in the marketing research department of a major chemical company.
   a. Your company has a patent on a chemical that, when combined with plastic, gives it near metallic properties. You have been asked to find out international users for this chemical and also forecast its total market potential.
   b. What information, if any, that could be obtained from respondents, would be useful for this research?
   c. What techniques are applicable for obtaining each item of information?
   d. Design a survey to obtain the information desired. Prepare all instructions, collection forms, and other materials required to obtain such information.
   e. Estimate the cost of conducting the survey you have designed.

10

Scale Development

INTRODUCTION

Globalization has led to increased competition among domestic and multinational firms in both domestic and foreign markets. Researchers have the challenging task of developing measures that will be useful in assessing customer attitudes and preferences for both domestic and foreign products.

The attitudes of customers shape their behavior, and attitudes are based on the information they have about the product. What companies are really trying to do in the marketplace is to understand and ultimately influence customer behavior. It is, however, very difficult to follow the target segments and try to observe their behavior and come to reasonable conclusions. Hence, marketers try to work on understanding attitudes, as attitudes are thought to be windows to behavior. It is easier to talk to potential consumers and gain an insight into the attitudes they have toward a product or concept. Favorable attitudes can translate into purchases and unfavorable attitudes will mean that the product or concept needs to be modified to suit their tastes better. It is possible to measure customer attitude with respect to specific features of a product. This chapter deals with measurement of attitudes and the tools used for this process. In international marketing, the main method used is the survey, which has already been discussed in the earlier chapter. This chapter deals with development of scales that are used to measure attitudes.

ATTITUDES

Attitude is defined as "an overall evaluation that enables one to respond in a consistently favorable or unfavorable manner with respect to a given object or alternative."[1] Attitudes are mental states used by consumers to perceive their surroundings and are composed of three parts:

- The *cognitive* or *knowledge* part represents the information that a person has about an object. This represents awareness of the object's existence, beliefs about the object's characteristics, and judgments about the relative importance of each characteristic.

---

[1] de Mooij, *Global Marketing and Advertising*.

- The second component is the *affective* or *liking* component that is an overall feeling of liking or disliking that a person has toward the object. This component causes consumers to prefer one object or concept to others, and hence, measure of preferences is a good indicator of the attitude.
- The last component is the *intention* component that represents the person's expectations of future behavior toward the object. Intentions are restricted by time periods that depend on the buying habits and planning horizons.

Consumer perception varies substantially among cultures. In the country of origin (COO) studies, it was observed that most consumers perceived Mexican products to be inferior to those made in Japan and the US. Over time, Japanese products have developed a significant advantage over US products in terms of perceptions of better quality.[2]

MEASUREMENT AND SCALING

Measurement is defined as the process of assigning numbers or other symbols to certain characteristics of the object of interest, according to some pre-specified rules. Usually, numbers are assigned because of the ease of handling them in mathematical and statistical analyses. Certain rules should be followed while assigning numbers for measurement. There should be a one-to-one correspondence between the number and the characteristic, and this assignment should be constant over time. Scaling is the process of creating a continuum on which objects are located according to the amount of the measured characteristic they possess.

Level of measurement defines the relationship among values that are assigned to the attributes of a variable. Interpretation of data is simplified if the level of measurement is known. Based on the level of measurement, four categories of scales can be defined as follows.

- *Nominal scale:* If a number has been assigned to establish the identity of an object, it is called a nominal scale. In a nominal scale, objects are assigned to mutually exclusive, labeled categories. That is, if one entity is assigned the same number as another, then the two entities are identical with respect to a nominal variable. Otherwise, they are just different. Sex, geographic location, and marital status are examples of nominally scaled variables. The only arithmetic operation that can be performed on such a scale is a count of each category. The section numbers of different courses offered in a university course catalog is an example of this scale. These numbers help distinguish one section from all others and any comparison between these numbers would be meaningless. The objects are mutually exclusive and there are no necessary relationships among categories. The numbers do not imply any order among the variables. An example would be labeling all respondents who are single as 1, all respondents who are married as 2, and all who are married but divorced as 3.
- *Ordinal scale:* In an ordinal scale, objects are ranked and arranged in a particular order with regard to some common variable. This scale provides information as to which object has more of a characteristic and which has less of it. Since, the differences between the ranks are not known, a mean cannot be drawn based on this scale.

---

[2] John R. Darling and Van R. Wood, "A Longitudinal Study Comparing Perceptions of US and Japanese Products in a Third/Neutral Country: Finland 1975 to 1985," *Journal of International Business Studies* 3 (1990): 427–450.

However, median and mode can be computed on such a scale. This scale merely tells us which object has more of the characteristic we are interested in and which object has less of it. There is no information on how much difference there is between the objects. For example, graduate students from a university could be asked to rank courses offered by the marketing department. A rating that one course gets would be on an ordinal scale. Some students would rate this course the best, some others would rate it the second best, and so on. It is not possible to compute a mean ranking for the course because the difference between the best, second best, etc. are not known. Hence, statistical computation is limited to median and mode calculation.

- *Interval scale:* The problem of computing the difference between two categories is taken care of in the next scale called the interval scale. In this scale, the numbers that are used to rank the objects also represent equal increments of the attribute being measured. This implies that ordinal scales give room for comparing differences. For example, Fahrenheit and Celsius temperatures are measured with different interval scales and have different zero points. Further, the entire range of statistical operations can be employed to analyze the resulting number, including addition and subtraction. Consequently, it is possible to compute the mean, standard deviation, correlation, etc. and conduct regression analysis, t-tests, and ANOVA tests.

- *Ratio scale:* This scale is a modified version of the interval scale, with a meaningful zero point. With this scale, it is possible to say how much greater or lesser one object is than another. This scale also gives the opportunity to compare absolute comparisons of magnitude. For instance, it is possible to say that a product costing $10 is twice as expensive as one costing $5.

Table 10.1 gives a summary of the above types of scales and their applications.

TABLE 10.1

TYPES OF SCALES AND THEIR PROPERTIES

Type of Measurement Scale	Types of Attitude Scale	Rules for Assigning Number	Typical Applications	Statistics/Statistical Tests
Nominal	Dichotomous (*yes* or *no* scales)	Objects are either identical or different	Classification (by sex, geography, social status)	Percentages, mode/chi-square
Ordinal	Comparative, rank-ordered, itemized category, and paired comparison	Objects are greater or smaller	Rankings (preference, class standing)	Percentile, median, rank-order correlation/ Friedman ANOVA
Interval	Likert, Thurstone, Stapel, associative, semantic differential	Intervals between adjacent ranks are equal	Index numbers, temperature scales, attitude measures	Mean, standard deviation, product moment correlation tests/t-tests, ANOVA, regression, factor analysis
Ratio	Certain scales with special instructions	A meaningful zero to help compare absolute magnitudes	Sales, income, units produced, costs, age	Geometric and harmonic mean, coefficient of variation

TYPES OF SCALES

A scale can have many dimensions depending on the attribute it is trying to measure and how the construct is defined. This could be illustrated with an example. If we think that the choice of a specific brand of car is dependent only on price, the scale has to have only one dimension. Price is completely capable of explaining the purchase decision. In reality, however, this is not true. Customers look for various aspects like performance, style, name of the manufacturer, and price. Hence, the purchase decision has many dimensions, each of which has to be tested to determine the impact it has on the final decision.

Attitudinal scales can be broadly classified as single-item and multiple-item scales. Single-item scales are those that have only one item to measure a construct. However, attitudes toward most products are complex and cannot be measured completely with one scale question. There are many different facets that must be measured to get a complete picture of the true attitude of customers. Multiple-item scales are used in such situations. There are different types of single-item and multiple-item scales and some of them have been considered in detail in this section. Figure 10.1 illustrates the different types of attitudinal scales.

FIGURE 10.1

TYPES OF ATTITUDINAL SCALES

Attitude Measurement Scales		
Single-Item Scales	**Multiple-Item Scales**	**Continuous Scales**
• Itemized Category Scales • Comparative Scales • Rank Order Scales • Q-Sort Scales • Constant Sum Scales • Pictorial Scales	• Likert Scales • Semantic Differential Scales • Thurstone Scales • Stapel Scales • Associative Scales	Contains infinite categories, and respondents rate items by placing a mark on the line. The line is labeled at each end, with scale points (e.g., 1 to 10) marked under the line. Constructing the scale is easy, but scoring is difficult.

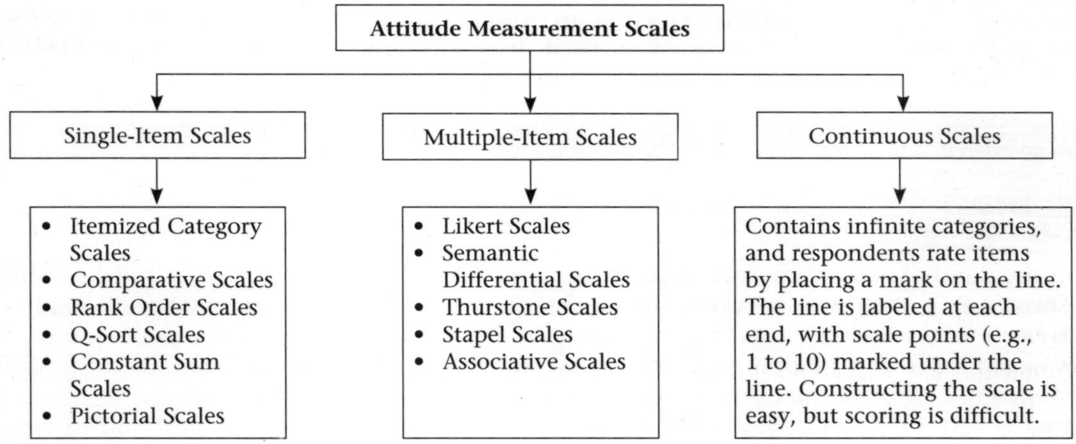

Single-Item Scales

The most widely used single-item scale is the *itemized-category scale*. This scale gives the respondent options to indicate his/her opinions about the object being measured. There can be several different variations of this scale. The researcher can choose to label all the categories as shown below.

Give us your opinion about the local hospital:

___ *Very satisfied*   ___ *Moderately satisfied*   ___ *Somewhat satisfied*   ___ *Not satisfied*

It is also possible to label only the extreme categories.

Give us your opinion about the local hospital:				
Highly satisfied				Highly dissatisfied
+2	+1	0	−1	−2

As can be seen from the examples above, there may or may not be a neutral point. The scale can be balanced as in the second exhibit or it can be unbalanced, tending toward more favorable or more unfavorable, as shown below.

Give us your opinion about the following national news channels:				
	Excellent	Very good	Average	Below average
HNN News	____	____	____	____
News Now	____	____	____	____
News Hub	____	____	____	____

The same scale can be modified to include an explicit comparison in the statement. It is then called a *comparative scale*. The question used in the example above would be modified as shown below.

As compared to HNN News, how would you rate your local news station?
___ Excellent   ___ Very good   ___ Average   ___ Below average

Another kind of single-item scale requires the respondents to arrange the objects in ascending or descending order with regard to some criterion. This is called the *rank-order scale*. Ranking has been used widely in international surveys as it corresponds to the choices that consumers would make in a shopping scenario. However, these require a lot of mental effort on the respondents' part and hence may not be very accurate if the number of objects to be compared is very high. Usually, consumers have a very good idea about the best and worst in the list. However, if there are too many objects, the differentiation for items in the middle becomes very obscure. The optimum number that can be used is five or six. If there are more than six objects, two-stage ranking can be followed. In the first stage, the respondents are asked to rank the objects into two or three classes. In the second stage, the respondents are asked to rank the objects in each class individually.

When the number of objects to be ranked is very high, say 100, ranking becomes very difficult even in two stages. In such cases, *Q-sort scaling* is followed. Consider the example of a car manufacturer wanting to study the most preferred features for a specific model. The product design team comes up with 100 different product concepts, each with minor variations. Respondents are handed out 100 cards, each containing one version of the product. They are then asked to sort these cards into 12 piles such that one pile contains five of the most preferred versions and another pile contains five of the least preferred versions. The other 10 piles contain versions of the product in the decreasing order of preferences. After this has been completed, researchers pick out the most preferred pile or some of the better-preferred piles and ask respondents to rank these versions. As the number of piles increases, the reliability of the results also increases. Figure 10.2 illustrates the plot of the number of cards in each pile.

FIGURE 10.2

PLOT OF NUMBER OF CARDS ON EACH FILE

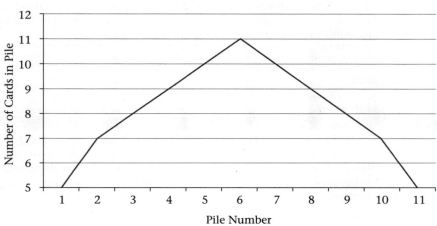

Constant-sum scales ask respondents to allocate a fixed number of points among different categories such that the division of points reflects their relative preferences. This is illustrated in the example below.

Allocate 100 points among these factors so that the points indicate how important each of these factors is in your choice of a news channel.	
Authenticity of information	_____
Quick coverage of news	_____
In-depth analysis of news stories	_____
Coverage of wide range of topics	_____
Coverage of local, national, and international news	_____
Total	**100**

In global marketing research, researchers should be prepared for the event that the target population may be illiterate. There are also times when the study involves children who have not yet learned to read or write. Communicating ideas and concepts through written matter becomes a challenge. In such situations, they resort to *pictorial scales* where the various categories are depicted pictorially. Respondents indicate their agreement or disagreement by indicating the corresponding position on the pictorial scale. The funny face scale is a very commonly used pictorial scale.

The type of scale to be used is dependent on the experience, preference, and judgment of the researcher. However, certain aspects have to be borne in mind when using single-item scales. There cannot be too many scale categories in the questionnaire even though theoretically the number can vary from 2 to infinity. In mail surveys and personal interviews, respondents can handle five to seven categories with reasonable accuracy. This number is further reduced in telephone interviews. The adjectives used to describe the categories are dependent on the country where the research is conducted. Some cultures require strong adjectives, whereas in some others, the adjectives should be suitably toned down. Depending on the country, researchers should also decide whether to use a unipolar or a bipolar scale and whether to provide a neutral point or not. It has been pointed out that certain cultures like the Japanese tend to stick with the neutral when they have the choice. In such cases, researchers should avoid providing a neutral choice to force a decision from the respondent.

Multiple-Item Scales

When it is not possible for the researcher to capture the entire range of attitudes that the respondent might have toward an object using a single scale question, multiple-item scales are used. Figure 10.3 is a flow chart of the steps involved in multi-item scale development. These scales obtain information about the respondent's attitude along different aspects of the object and then combine all these to form an average score indicative of the overall attitude of the respondent toward the object. Some of the frequently employed multiple-item scales are explained in this section.

FIGURE 10.3
STEPS IN MULTIPLE-ITEM SCALE DEVELOPMENT

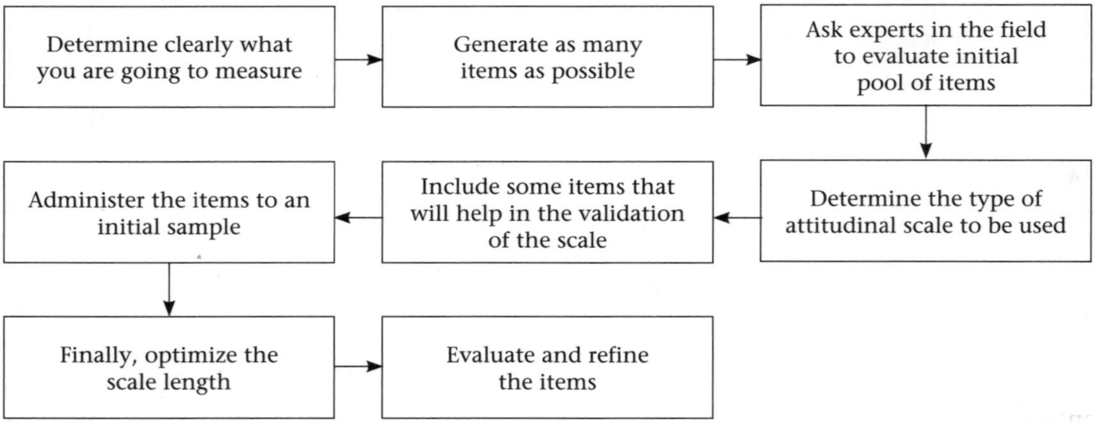

Likert scales require a respondent to indicate the degree of agreement or disagreement with a number of statements related to the characteristics of the object. They are also called summated scales, because the scores on the individual items are summed to produce a total score for the respondent. A Likert scale usually consists of two parts, the item part and the evaluative part. The item part is essentially a statement about a certain product, event, or attitude. The evaluative part is a list of response categories ranging from "strongly agree" to "strongly disagree." An example is provided below that contains statements representing a common construct (i.e., performance). This enables the researcher to sum the scores to produce an average score.

	Strongly Agree	Somewhat Agree	Neither Agree nor Disagree	Somewhat Disagree	Strongly Disagree
News channel covers local news very well					
News channel covers national and world news very well					
News channel covers wide variety of topics very well					
News channel provides authentic information					
News channel covers the information quickly					

Thurstone scales help researchers obtain a one-dimensional scale with interval properties, and for this reason they are called the method of equal-appearing intervals. The procedure for administering a Thurstone scale is a two-step process. At first, researchers generate a number of adjectives, usually 100, reflecting all degrees of favorableness toward the object. A group of judges then classify these according to their degree of favorableness or unfavorableness. Intervals between categories are treated as equal. The scale value for each category is the median value assigned by the judges. Adjectives for which there has been no consensus among the judges are discarded. This results in a scale consisting of 10–20 categories representing different degrees of favorableness. The second step is to ask respondents to rate different aspects of the object on different categories in this scale. This procedure is time-consuming and very expensive to construct. It is also possible that the scale categories could depend on the judges selected for the process.

Semantic differential scales are used widely in global marketing research to reflect the set of beliefs or attitudes the respondent has about an object. Different aspects of the object are presented to the respondent in the format described below and the respondent chooses the one that matches closely with his/her opinions. There may or may not be a neutral point depending on the country where the questionnaire is being administered. Care should be taken to see that the adjectives used to describe the categories are relevant in the country where the survey is being conducted and respondents understand the implications of the categories. It is sometimes necessary to reverse the positive and negative poles of the scale to avoid a halo effect where the respondent allows previous judgments to affect subsequent judgments. It is possible to assign scores to the categories and provide an average score for different objects. A profile analysis is an application wherein the mean ratings for each category are plotted to get a visual comparison of the ratings. This aids researchers in getting a quick look at how different objects have been rated along different categories. Figure 10.4 gives a sample profile analysis.

Give us your opinion about two news channels—News Now and News Hub.

Good local coverage	___	___	___	___	___	*Bad local coverage*
Reliable	___	___	___	___	___	*Unreliable*
Good global coverage	___	___	___	___	___	*Bad global coverage*
Fast news coverage	___	___	___	___	___	*Slow news coverage*

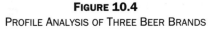

FIGURE 10.4
PROFILE ANALYSIS OF THREE BEER BRANDS

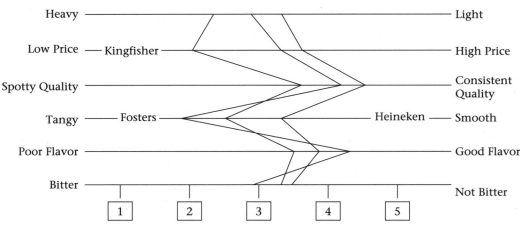

Stapel scales are a simpler version of semantic differential scales where the categories have only one pole. Respondents give a score to the category depending on their preference, and a higher positive score implies higher preference.

A simple technique of multiple-item scaling called *associative scaling* is used frequently in global marketing research. This method overcomes the limitations of semantic differential scaling where the respondent should be familiar with all the objects to respond usefully. In associative scaling, the respondent is asked to associate one alternative with each question.

SCALES IN CROSS-NATIONAL RESEARCH

The previous sections of this chapter discussed the various types of scales that are typically used in domestic marketing research. The question remains whether the same scales can be administered to respondents all over the world.[3] Low educational or literacy levels in some countries will have to be taken into account when the decision is taken to administer the same scale. Literacy and educational levels have a certain impact on the response formats of the scales employed. Moreover, culture in a country can also affect the responses and may induce some cultural biases. Likert and semantic differential scales are culture-bound and should be treated as culture-specific instruments.[4]

Researchers can develop scales that use a self-defined cultural norm as a base referent. For instance, respondents can be asked to indicate their own anchor point and position relative to culture-specific practices. This approach can be used to measure attitudes toward cultural

---

[3] Most international research studies conducted use different kinds of scales in their research. A few examples are: Daniel C. Fieldman and David C. Thomas, "Career Management Issues Facing Expatriates," *Journal of Business Studies* (Second Quarter 1992); vol. 23, pp. 271–293. Earl Newmann, "Organization Predictors of Expatriate job Satisfaction," *Journal of Business Studies* (First Quarter 1993), vol. 24, pp. 61–81.

[4] Julie H. Yu, Charles Keown, and Laurence Jacobs, "Attitude Scale Methodology: Cross-Cultural Implications," *Journal of International Consumer Marketing* 6, no. 2 (1993): 45–64.

norms (e.g., attitude toward marital roles). In this regard, researchers must also test the significance and appropriateness of anchors when using Likert scale or a semantic differential scale in international studies.[5] For instance, when a preliminary questionnaire was administered in a study of US–Japanese channel relationships, it was found that the Japanese managers did not adequately understand the scale anchors *agree/disagree*. Consequently, the anchors had to be changed to *definitely true*, *somewhat true*, and *not at all true* to convey the intended meaning.[6]

Another issue that is important in international research is whether response formats, particularly their calibration, need to be adapted for specific countries and cultures. For example, in France, a 20-point scale is commonly used to rate performance in primary and secondary schools. Consequently, it has been suggested that 20-point scales should also be used in marketing research. In general, verbal scales are more effective among less-educated respondents, but a more appropriate procedure for illiterate respondents would be scales with pictorial stimuli. For example, in the case of lifestyle, pictures of different lifestyle segments may be shown to the respondents, and they may be asked to indicate how similar they perceive themselves to be to the one in the picture. Some other devices such as the *funny faces* and the *thermometer* scale are also used among the less-educated respondents.

GLOBAL OR PAN-CULTURAL SCALES[7]

Research has been conducted to find out whether there is a pan-cultural scale. The semantic differential scale seems to come closest to being a truly pan-cultural scale. It consistently gives similar results in terms of concepts or dimensions that are used to evaluate stimuli, and also accounts for a major portion of the variation in response when it is administered in different countries. However, studies have shown that Likert and semantic differential scales are also culture-specific (with EMIC properties) even in culturally similar countries such as Japan, South Korea, and China.[8] An alternative approach that has been attempted is to apply techniques that use a base referent, a self-defined cultural norm. This type of approach is likely to be particularly useful in evaluating attitudinal positions where evidence exists to suggest that these are defined relative to the dominant cultural norm.

Designing scales for global marketing research calls for a great deal of adaptation on the researchers' part. It has to be decided whether a single scale can be used in all the countries or whether it should be customized to suit each country. Americans use a five- or seven-point scale. However, people in many other countries, like France, are familiar with a 20-point scale. Semantics play a very important role in the accuracy with which a scale measures any given attribute. Many cultures tend to overstate their feelings while many others are more modest. Hence, *excellent* may connote very different levels of perfection to Japanese and Italians. Adjustments for these linguistic differences have to be made. It has been observed that verbal rating scales work the best in the international context. All respondents are used to verbally expressing their feelings, irrespective of the country or culture they belong to. There could,

---

[5] Naresh K. Malhotra, James Agarwal, and Mark Peterson, "Methodological Issues in Cross-Cultural Marketing Research: A State-of-the-Art Review," *International Marketing Review* 13, no. 5 (1996): 7–43.

[6] J. L. Johnson, T. Sakano, J. A. Cote, and N. Onzo, "The Exercise of Interfirm Power and Its Repercussions in US–Japanese Channel Relationships," *Journal of Marketing* 57 (1993): 1–10.

[7] Douglas and Craig, *International Marketing Research*.

[8] J.H. Yu, C.F. Keown, and L.W. Jacobs, *Journal of International Consumer Marketing*, 1993.

however, be a problem with these scales. In some countries, 1 would be rated as the best while in some others it would be the least favored choice. The researcher should clarify this before asking respondents to rate attributes. The concept of the midpoint of the scale will have to be explained to respondents in many countries. Even if respondents understand the concept of midpoint or the neutral category, scales have to be modified to take into account the predisposition of many cultures to stick with the middle response category.

Bearing in mind the drawbacks of administering scales to respondents in other countries, the one scale that has consistently provided accurate results is the semantic differential scale. Since the adjectives on the polar ends of the scale are opposite in meaning, it is easy for the respondent to understand and answer the questions in a manner that is useful to the researcher.

MEASUREMENT OF EQUIVALENCE[9]

In global marketing research, the very meaning of a scale may change because of cultural influences. Consequently, global marketing research calls for appropriate equivalence and comparability checks. It is important for the researcher to be able to compare data across countries, and hence, it is essential to examine the various aspects of data collection process and establish their equivalence. It is difficult to state with conviction whether the similarities and differences are real or if they are due to measurement problems. The issue of measurement equivalence must be addressed to reduce threats of measurement reliability and validity.[10] There is always the trade-off between capturing more variance more accurately by adding more categories and reducing the number of categories to make the scale less susceptible to response bias.[11]

It is important that data collected from various regions is comparable, otherwise it could lead to the researcher drawing erroneous conclusions. This is illustrated by the following example of a survey conducted in Europe to study the bathing habits of women.[12] Initial data suggested that percentage of Belgian women taking baths was far higher than any other nationality. However, a closer look at the data revealed that the time period was not comparable. In Belgium, the women were asked if they had taken a bath in the last seven days. In all other countries, the question had been, "Have you had a bath in the last three days?"

Measurement equivalence relates to establishing equivalence in terms of procedure used to measure concepts or attitudes.[13] Three aspects will have to be considered to establish measurement equivalence:

Calibration equivalence: Calibration equivalence refers to the calibration system used in the measurement. This would include monetary units, measures of weight, distance and

---

[9] Douglas and Craig, *International Marketing Research*.

[10] Alma T. Mintu, Rojer Calantone, and Jule B. Gassenheimer, "Towards Improving Cross-Cultural Research: Extending Churchill's Research Paradigm," *Journal of International Consumer Marketin,* 1995, 7 (2): 5–23.

[11] Michael Mullen, "Diagnostic Measurement Equivalence in Cross-National Research," *Journal of International Business Studies* 3 (1995): 25–41.

[12] C. Min-Han, Byoung-Woo Lee, and Kong Kyun Ro, "The Choice Survey Mode in Country Image Studies," *Journal of Business Research* 29 (1994): 151–162.

[13] Margaret Crimp and Len Tiu Wright, *The Marketing Research Process* (Herfordshire: Prentice Hall, 1995) , 4th edition.

volume, and perceptual cues such as color, shape, or form. In global marketing research, this issue has to be taken care of since various countries around the world follow different units of weights and measures. For instance, Americans are used to weighing things by the pound or ton while the British and most of the Commonwealth countries use the gram and kilogram. If the wrong terminology is used, responses will not be accurate. The same holds true for currency measures also. One billion in the US may not mean the same amount in some other country (e.g., the UK). Researchers should also take care to establish equivalence in terms of interpretation of perceptual cues. Colors mean different things to different cultures.[14] White, for example, is considered as a symbol of purity and peace in the Western world. The Japanese consider it a color of mourning.[15]

Translation equivalence: The research instrument has to be translated such that respondents in all countries involved in the study understand it. The instrument should also contain equivalent meaning in each research context. This becomes more complicated when the researcher has to interpret and translate nonverbal clues. As has been pointed out earlier, the stress in this book is not on the equivalence of the instrument translated into another language. The stress is on the equivalence of the information collected. It may not be possible to translate a questionnaire verbatim into another language because of lack of equivalent words in the foreign language. For instance, there is no equivalent term for *husband* in Japanese. The researcher should focus on conveying the intent of the question to the respondent and obtain an answer that can be comparable across countries.

Metric equivalence: This is the scoring or scalar equivalence of the measure used. The researcher has to ensure equivalence of the scaling or scoring procedure used to establish the measure. Care should also be taken to establish equivalence in terms of the responses to a given measure in different countries. The scales used in different countries may vary depending on the culture and education level of the respondents. In the US, typically researchers use a five- or a seven-point scale. However, there are countries where scales can have as many as 20 categories. When the sample consists predominantly of people incapable of reading, pictorial scales are used. The specific country also determines whether the scale should be unipolar or bipolar and whether there should be a neutral point in the scale. Researchers studying the Japanese market design scales with no neutral point as the Japanese have a tendency to remain neutral if given a choice. The researcher should also ensure equivalence of the response to a given measure in different countries. For instance, researchers need to tone down income data from Latin American countries, as most managers in Latin American countries tend to exaggerate their income.[16]

Profile analysis can be used as a means of examining metric equivalence. This involves calculating the mean for each measure and plotting it on a graph. The points are connected by lines. If these lines are not parallel, it can be taken as an indication that difference between two data sets is not caused by systematic response bias. It must be noted that even if the lines

---

[14] Laurence Jacobs, Charles Keown, Reginald Worthley, and Kyung-II Ghymn, "Cross-Cultural Color Comparisons: Global Marketers Beware," *International Marketing Review* 8, no. 3 (1991): 21–30.

[15] Ibid.

[16] Ki-Taek Chun, John B. Campbell, and Jong Hae Yoo, "Extreme Response Style Cross-Cultural Research," *Journal of Cross Cultural Psychology* 5 no. 5 (1974): 465–480.

are parallel, the differences between means could be caused by real differences and not necessarily by response set bias.[17]

ACCURACY OF ATTITUDE MEASUREMENT

Attitude measures, in common with all measures used in marketing, must be both accurate and useful. In this section, the focus is on those aspects of attitude measures that contribute to accuracy: validity, reliability, sensitivity, generalizability, and relevancy.

Validity

An attitude measure has validity if it measures what it is supposed to measure. If this is the case, then differences in attitude scores will reflect differences among the objects or individuals on the characteristic being measured. This is a very troublesome question. For example, how is a researcher to know whether measured differences in the attitudes of managers, consumer activists, and consumers toward marketing practices, regulation, and the contribution of the consumer movement are true differences? There have been three basic approaches to this question of validity assessment.

Face, or *consensus*, *validity* is used when the measurement so self-evidently reflects or represents the various aspects of the phenomenon that there can be little quarrel with it. For instance, buyers' recognition of advertisements is usually accepted at face value as an indication of past ad exposure. This faith typically is supported by little more than common sense, despite evidence that recognition scores are influenced by reader interest.

Criterion validity is more defensible, for it is based on empirical evidence that the attitude measure correlates with other *criterion* variables. If the two variables are measured at the same time, *concurrent validity* is established. Better yet, if the attitude measure can predict some future event, then *predictive validity* has been established. A measure of brand preference or buying intentions is valid if it can be shown through sales records to predict future sales. This is the most important type of validity for decision-making purposes, for the very nature of decisions requires predictions of uncertain future events.

Although face, concurrent, and predictive validity provide necessary evidence of overall validity, often they are not sufficient. The characteristic of these three approaches is that they provide evidence on *convergent validity*. That is, an attitude measure can adequately represent a characteristic or variable if it correlates or *converges* with other supposed measures of that variable. Unfortunately, an attitude measure may converge with measures of other variables in addition to the one of interest. Thus, it is also necessary to establish *discriminant validity* through "low correlations between the measure of interest and other measures that are supposedly not measuring the same variable or concept." Advertising recognition measures often fail this second test. While they correlate or converge with past ad exposure, which is what we want, they also are correlated with number of magazines read and product interest.

Construct validity can be considered only after discriminant and convergent validity have been established.[18] It is achieved when a logical argument can be advanced to defend

---

[17] Mullen, "Diagnostic Measurement Equivalence in Cross-National Research."

[18] F. M. Andrews, "Construct Validity and Error Components of Survey Measures," *Public Opinion Quarterly*, Summer 1984, pp. 432.

a particular measure. The argument aims first to define the concept or construct explicitly and then to show that the measurement, or operational definition, logically connects the empirical phenomenon to the concept. The extreme difficulty of this kind of validation lies in the unobservable nature of many of the constructs (such as social class, personality, or attitudes) used to explain marketing behavior. For example, is occupation a good operational definition of social class, or does it measure some other characteristic? One way to assess construct validity is to test whether or not the measure confirms hypotheses generated from the theory based on the concepts. Since theory development is at a youthful stage in marketing, the theory itself may be incorrect, making this approach hazardous. This is one reason why little construct validation is attempted in marketing. A more significant reason is the lack of well-established measures that can be used in a variety of circumstances. Instead, marketing researchers tend to develop measures for each specific problem or survey and rely on face validity.

Reliability

So far we have been talking about systematic errors between an observed score (X_o) and a true score (X_t), which will determine whether a measure is valid. However, the total error of a measurement consists of this systematic error component (X_s) and a random error component (X_r). Random error is manifested by lack of consistency (unreliability) in repeated or equivalent measures of the same object or person. As a result, any measurement can be expressed as a function of several components:

$$X_o = X_t + X_s + X_r$$
Observed score = true score + systematic error + random error

To interpret this equation, remember that a valid measure is one that reflects the true score. In this situation, $X_o = X_t$ and both X_s and X_r are zero. Thus, if we know the measure is valid, it has to be reliable. The converse is not necessarily true. A measure may be highly reliable, $X_r = 0$, and still have a substantial systematic error that distorts the validity. But, if the measure is not reliable, it cannot be valid since at a minimum we are left with $X_o = X_t + X_r$. In brief, reliability is a necessary but not a sufficient condition for validity.

Although *reliability* is less important, it is easier to measure, and so receives relatively more emphasis. Studies have shown that the same scales may have different reliabilities in different cultures and can adversely affect the comparability of cross-cultural findings.[19] Therefore, the substantive relationships among constructs must be adjusted for unequal reliabilities before valid inferences can be drawn. The basic methods for establishing reliability can be classified according to whether they measure stability of results over time or internal consistency of items in an attitude scale.[20]

Stability over time is assessed by repeating the measurement with the same instrument and the same respondents at two points in time and correlating the results. To the extent

[19] H. L. Davis, S. P. Douglas, and A. J. Silk, "Measure Unreliability: A Hidden Threat to Cross-National Marketing Research," *Journal of Marketing* 45, no. 2 (1981): 98–109.

[20] J. Paul Peter, "Reliability: A Review of Psychometric Basis and Recent Marketing Practices," *Journal of Marketing Research* 16 (1979): 6–17.

that random fluctuations result in different scores for the two administrations, this correlation and hence the reliability will be lowered. The problems of this test–retest method are similar to those encountered during any pretest–post-test measurement of attitudes. The first administration may sensitize the respondent to the subject and lead to attitude change. The likelihood of a true change in attitude (versus a random fluctuation) is increased further if the interval between the test and the retest is too long. For most topics, this would be more than two weeks. If the interval is too short, however, there may be a carryover from the test to the retest: attempts to remember the responses in the first test, boredom or annoyance at the imposition, and so forth. Because of these problems, a very short interval will bias the reliability estimate upward, whereas longer periods have the opposite effect.[21]

The equivalence approach to assessing reliability is appropriate for attitude scales composed of multiple items that presumably measure the same underlying unidimensional attitude. The split-half method assumes that these items can be divided into two equivalent subsets that then can be compared. A number of methods have been devised to divide the items randomly into two halves and compute a measure of similarity of the total scores of the two halves across the sample. An average split-half measure of similarity—coefficient alpha—can be obtained from a procedure that has the effect of comparing every item to every other item.

Sensitivity

The third characteristic of a good attitude measure is *sensitivity,* or the ability to discriminate among meaningful differences in attitudes. Such sensitivity is achieved by increasing the number of scale categories; however, the more categories there are, the lower the reliability. This is because very coarse response categories, such as "yes" or "no," in response to an attitude question can absorb a great deal of response variability before a change would be noted using the test–retest method. Conversely, the use of a large number of response categories when there are only a few distinct attitude positions would be subject to a considerable, but unwarranted, amount of random fluctuation.

Generalizability

This refers to the ease of scale administration and interpretation in different research settings and situations.[22] Thus, the generalizability of a multi-item scale is determined by whether it can be applied in a wide variety of data collection modes, whether it can be used to obtain data from a wide variety of individuals, and under what conditions it can be interpreted. As in the case of reliability and validity, generalizability is not an absolute, but rather is a matter of degree.

---

[21] Ravi Parameswaran and Attila Yaprak, "A Cross-National Comparison of Consumer Research Measures," *Journal of International Business Studies* (Spring 1987), vol. 18, pp. 35–49

[22] For a discussion of generalizability theory and its applications in marketing research, see Joseph O. Rentz, "Generalizability Theory: A Comprehensive Method for Assessing and Improving the Dependability of Marketing Measures," *Journal of Marketing Research* 24 (1987): 19–28.

Relevancy

Relevancy of a scale refers to how meaningful it is to apply the scale to measure a construct. Mathematically, it is represented as the product of reliability and validity.

$$\text{Relevance} = \text{Reliability} \times \text{Validity}$$

If reliability and validity are evaluated by means of correlation coefficients, the implications are:

- The relevance of a scale can vary from 0 (no relevance) to 1 (complete relevance).
- If either reliability or validity is low, the scale will possess little relevance.
- Both reliability and validity are necessary for scale relevance.

PSYCHOPHYSIOLOGICAL APPROACHES TO SCALE DEVELOPMENT[23]

As scientific advancements continue to emerge from various domains of research, the interdisciplinary nature of the field of marketing naturally lends itself to incorporating such applications from other fields of knowledge. In this regard, the fields of study that have significantly impacted marketing research include IT, biology, neurology, physiology, and psychology, among others. The above-mentioned fields have developed techniques that have been applied in several marketing research studies. Popular among these techniques include eye movement analysis, electrodermal analysis, pupillary response, and facial muscle activity. This section tracks the progress and use of these techniques in marketing research.

Eye Movement Analysis

In this technique, the eye movement is measured by recording either the number of fixations or dwell time of the eyes during a participant's exposure to some visual messages. Measurements on eye patterns regarding how much information is received and how much is retained help researchers distinguish between the automatic and voluntary responses received by external messages.[24] Marketing research studies have found that eye movement is related to attention,[25] memory,[26] and information

---

[23] Yong Jian Wang and Michael S. Minor, "Validity, Reliability, and Applicability of Psychophysiological Techniques in Marketing Research," *Psychology* and *Marketing* 25, no. 2 (2008): 197–232.

[24] D. W. Stewart, and D. H. Furse, "Applying Psychophysiological Measures to Marketing and Advertising Research Problems," *Current Issues* and *Research in Advertising* 5 (1982): 1–38.

[25] L. Bogart and B. S. Tolley, "The Search for Information in Newspaper Advertising," *Journal of Advertising Research* 28 (1988): 9–19; R. Pieters, E. Rosbergen, and M. Wedel, "Visual Attention to Repeated Print Advertising: A Test of Scanpath Theory," *Journal of Marketing Research* 36 (1999): 424–438; R. Pieters and M. Wedel, "Attention Capture and Transfer in Advertising: Brand, Pictorial, and Text-Size Effects," *Journal of Marketing* 68 (2004): 36–50.

[26] H. E. Krugman, "Brain Wave Measures of Media Involvement," *Journal of Advertising Research* 1 (1971): 3–9; D. M. Krugman, R. J. Fox, J. E. Fletcher, P. M. Fischer, and T. H. Rojas, "Do Adolescents Attend to Warnings in Cigarette Advertising? An Eye Tracking Approach," *Journal of Advertising Research*

processing.[27] While there are studies that have established this technique's high predictive capacity on recall and memory based on either dwell time[28] or the number of fixations,[29] other studies have posited that this technique has only a mediating role of cognitive learning.[30] The reliability of eye movement measures has also been questioned in certain research studies based on the observation that eye movement patterns can be influenced by participants' excessive blinking or tear fluid.[31] Such a scenario would restrict the opportunity of recruiting certain individuals with various eye problems for eye movement experiments in marketing research.

Electrodermal Analysis

This technique tracks the level of resistance or conductivity of human skin by passing electric current.[32] By tracking the changing in the sweat glands, researchers can deduce the psychological activity to be the result of interest, arousal, or pleasure.[33] Electrodermal activities can be monitored through either galvanic skin response or skin conductance response. Galvanic skin response is recorded by a galvanometer to assess the ability of the skin to conduct electricity. Skin conductance response can also be employed to monitor skin conductance (the reciprocal of skin resistance) by polygraphic recording. In marketing research, electrodermal activity has been intensively used to measure attention,[34] arousal,[35] anxiety, and warmth as

34 (1994): 39–52; M. Wedel and R. Pieters, "Eye Fixations on Advertisements and Memory for Brands: A Model and Findings," *Marketing Science* 19 (2000): 297–312.

[27] A. S. King, "Pupil Size, Eye Direction, and Message Appeal: Some Preliminary Findings," *Journal of Marketing* 36 (1972): 55–58; W. Kroeber-Riel and B. Barton, "Scanning Ads: Effects of Position and Arousal Potential of Ad Elements," *Current Issues* and *Research in Advertising* 3 (1980): 147–163; W. Kroeber-Riel, "Effects of Emotional Pictorial Elements in Ads Analyzed by Means of Eye Movement Monitoring," *Advances in Consumer Research* 11 (1984): 591–596.

[28] Krugman et al., "Do Adolescents Attend to Warnings in Cigarette Advertising?" *Journal of Advertising Research*, 1994, 34, 39–52

[29] Wedel and Pieters, "Eye Fixations on Advertisements and Memory for Brands." *Marketing Science*, 2000, 19, 297–312

[30] W. Kroeber-Riel, and B. Barton, "Scanning Ads: Effects of Position and Arousal Potential of Ad Elements," *Current Issues & Research in Advertising*, 1980, 3, 147–163.

[31] R. Pieters, E. Rosbergen, and M. Wedel, "Visual Attention to Repeated Print Advertising: A Test of Scanpath Theory," *Journal of Marketing Research*, 1999, 36, 424–438

[32] P. J. Watson and R. J. Gatchel, "Autonomic Measures of Advertising," *Journal of Advertising Research* 19 (1979): 15–26.

[33] J. M. Klebba, "Physiological Measures of Research: A Review of Brain Activity, Electrodermal Response, Pupil Dilation, and Voice Analysis Methods and Studies," *Current Issues* and *Research in Advertising* 8 (1985): 53–76.

[34] P. D. Bolls, D. D. Muehling, and K. Yoon, "The Effects of Television Commercial Pacing on Viewers' Attention and Memory," *Journal of Marketing Communications* 9 (2003): 17–28.

[35] A. Groeppel-Klein and D. Baun, "The Role of Customers' Arousal for Retail Stores: Results from an Experimental Pilot Study Using Electrodermal Activity as Indicator," *Advances in Consumer Research* 28 (2001): 412–419; P. D. Bolls, A. Lang, and R. F. Potter, "The Effects of Message Valence and Listener Arousal on Attention, Memory, and Facial Muscular Responses to Radio Advertisements," *Communication Research* 28 (2001): 627–651.

affective processes,[36] and enables researchers to identify the magnitude of a response with considerable accuracy.

While the technique's usefulness in uncovering psychological activity has been shown, contrary study findings do exist. For instance, it was found that electrodermal response was not valid in measuring attention, and as an indicator of warmth to external messages.[37] Further, studies have also provided few cautionary notes while using this technique for research. It has been observed that the placement of electrode is critical to the accuracy of results, as the results tend to be biased when the placement sites are not carefully chosen, cleaned, and controlled. Also, the impact and sensitivity to stimuli needs to be better understood in order to make this technique applicable in experimental conditions. Additionally, it has also been suggested that this technique should be administered at various time intervals to ensure reliability of results.[38]

Pupillary Response

This technique measures the physiological changes in an individual's pupil size in response to visual messages, and is found to be an indicator to responses such as pleasure and arousal.[39] In marketing, it has been used to ascertain the effectiveness of advertisements, with the technique's significant discriminatory power on the effectiveness of advertising messages.[40] Despite this technique's applicability in marketing research, researchers have identified challenges regarding its validity. Some of these challenges include identifying the relevant psychological changes that were conveyed through the pupil dilation;[41] and the lack of continued usage of this technique in marketing studies since the 1970s that raises issues on its reliability. Further, researchers have identified the need to specify the causal relationship between psychological processes such as attention, pleasure, or information processing, and physiological indicators (pupil size), so that this technique can be used for future research.[42]

---

[36] D. A. Aaker, D. M. Stayman, and M. R. Hagerty, "Warmth in Advertising: Measurement, Impact, and Sequence Effects," *Journal of Consumer Research* 12 (1986): 365–381; A. E. Stem and C. S. Bozman, "Respondent Anxiety Reduction with the Randomized Response Technique," *Advances in Consumer Research* 15, no. 1 (1988): 595–599.

[37] P. Vanden Abeele and D. L. MacLachlan, "Process Tracing of Physiological Responses to Dynamic Commercial Stimuli," *Advances in Consumer Research* 21 (1994): 226–232; P. Vanden Abeele and D. L. MacLachlan, "Process Tracing of Emotional Responses to TV Ads: Revisiting the Warmth Monitor," *Journal of Consumer Research* 20 (1994): 586–600.

[38] Stewart and Furse, "Applying Psychophysiological Measures to Marketing and Advertising Research Problems."; J. T. Cacioppo and R. E. Petty, *Social Psychophysiology* (New York: Guilford Press, 1983).

[39] E. H. Hess, "Attitude and Pupil Size," *Scientific American* 212 (1965): 46–54.

[40] F. J. Van Bortel, "Commercial Applications of Pupillometrics," in *Application of the Sciences in Marketing Management*, eds. F. M. Bass, C. E. King, and E. A. Pessemier (New York: Wiley, 1968); J. E. Stafford, A. E. Birdwell, and C. E. Van Tassel, "Integrated Advertising: White Backlash," *Journal of Advertising Research* 10 (1970): 15–20.

[41] Watson and Gatchel, "Autonomic Measures of Advertising."

[42] R. D. Blackwell, J. S. Hensel, and B. Sternthal, "Pupil Dilation: What Does It Measure?" *Journal of Advertising Research* 10 (1970): 15–18.

Facial Muscle Activity

Unlike the other techniques covered above, facial muscle activity is a voluntary physiological indicator and is measured by electrical signals caused by the contraction of facial muscle fibers, usually when electrodes placed on the face. Using this technique, EMG has been the most frequently used measurement device in marketing research. The applications of technique in marketing studies include the identification of the directions of affective responses (i.e., pleasure versus displeasure) to messages such as radio advertisements.[43] Studies have found that the physiological reaction using this technique along with the positive affective response was robust across different stimuli. However, a caveat when using this technique is that the electric signal produced by an EMG device can be influenced by participants' physical movements or bodily sensitivity. Therefore, future research using this technique should set the experiment process in a way wherein the participant is distracted during electrode placement.[44]

The techniques listed above are but only a sample that is being used in marketing research. While these techniques are significant developments in the field of marketing research, there is scope for further development of similar techniques that can help researchers. Further, using a combination of techniques to understand a phenomenon would be a good future progress for this branch of research. Even though the physiological techniques pose certain research challenges, its advantages over behavioral and verbal measures are manifold. Given these positive aspects, this area of research can be expected to undergo a major boost and will realize its potential for researchers.

CULTURAL ISSUES

Communication depends, to a great extent, on the cultural background of the respondent, and so designing scales also becomes culture-dependent. In certain cultures, communication is based entirely on explicit messages. The Swiss, for instance, talk very literally. The Japanese on the other hand are not as precise in their communication. Personal pronouns are not explicitly expressed and the number of tenses is largely reduced. In Japanese, both the spoken and written words have multiple meanings so that the listener needs to have some contextual clarification.[45] This becomes very important when deciding on the type of scale to be used. In certain countries, comparison between objects has to be made explicit. The scale ideas will also be conveyed with clarity.

The educational system of a country reflects the culture and heritage of the country to a great extent. Education, to a great extent, shapes the way people in a certain country think or act. It has also been proved that one of the most efficient ways of studying the national character is to observe the education systems and the child-rearing practices followed in the country. Education can also have a great impact on how receptive the people are to foreign products and concepts. This affects not just the researchers but also the companies who plan

---

[43] J. A. Wiles and T. B. Cornwell, "A Review of Methods Utilized in Measuring Affect, Feelings, and Emotion in Advertising," *Current Issues* and *Research in Advertising* 13 (1990): 241–275.

[44] P. D. Bolls, A. Lang, and R. F. Potter, "The Effects of Message Valence and Listener Arousal on Attention, Memory, and Facial Muscular Responses to Radio Advertisements," *Communication Research* 28 (2001): 627–651.

[45] Jean-Claude Usunier, *Marketing Across Cultures* (Hertfordshire: Prentice Hall, 1996), 2nd edition.

to market their products in the foreign country. For the purpose of designing scales, it is very important that the researchers have an idea of the education levels of the target population. The knowledge and awareness of the respondent will decide the type of scale that can be used. A simple example would be conducting research in interior parts of the developing world where the population is mainly illiterate. Pictorial scales will have to be used so as to convey the intention to the respondents. It has been seen that people from China, Japan, and Hong Kong tend to use the middle category in the scale as opposed to people from the US, Germany, and the UK. Hence, scales must have even-numbered categories when they are being administered in China, Japan, and Hong Kong. This decreases the central tendencies and increases the variance in the questionnaire.[46]

GLOBAL MARKETING RESEARCH IN PRACTICE

Tasty Burgers will have to design a questionnaire to collect information through the use of surveys. As discussed in the previous chapter, researchers can use telephone surveys in the UK and personal interviews in Brazil, India, and Saudi Arabia. The surveys are aimed at collecting demographic data of people who visit fast-food restaurants on a regular basis. Tasty Burgers would also like to know customer preferences in terms of food and beverages and average amount spent in a given visit to fast-food restaurants. This will help them decide the ideal product mix for maximizing profits.

One of the concerns that researchers have will be the type of scales that can be used in the questionnaire. This is dependent on the country and type of survey mechanism that is used. Typically in the UK five or seven point scales are used. Since telephones are used there, it would be better to use a five-point scale. This makes it easier for the interviewer to read out the scales to the respondent. The respondent will also be more comfortable remembering just five degrees of any attribute rather than seven. In Brazil, India, and Saudi Arabia, personal interviews are used. Here, the interviewer has more flexibility with the questionnaire script. For ease of comparison, it may be better to retain a five-point scale. However, the interviewer could use examples to explain or clarify a certain point. For instance, if the question asks respondents to rate the burgers sold by a leading competitor on five levels—excellent, good, average, below average and bad.

It is good practice in global marketing research to collect data on an absolute level and on a comparative basis. This can be done by setting one product as a basis for comparison and asking respondents to compare all other products to the base product. The basis for comparison should be a product that is positioned similarly in all countries. For instance, McDonald's is positioned as a fast-food chain affordable even by the lower-income class in the US. However, in India, their target market is the middle and upper income groups. Hence, Tasty Burgers should look for a product that is aimed at all the segments, including the lower income groups, and use that as a basis of comparison. This way the interviewer will be able to gain more insights into the fast-food market. This may not be possible with a telephone interview unless the question has been specifically worked into the script.

Care should be taken to use the currency of the country where the scale is being used. If required, the values could be translated back to dollars for easy comparison. An expert on the

---

[46] Steven X. Si and John B. Cullen, "Response Categories and Potential Cultural Bias: Effects of an Explicit Middle Point in Cross-Cultural Scales," *International Journal of Organizational Analysis*, 1998, 6 (3): 218–230.

local culture should be involved while setting categories for the scales. As has been mentioned in this chapter, cultural differences play an important role in scale design.

SUMMARY

This chapter deals with measurement of attitudes and development of scales that are used in this process. Attitude is defined as an overall evaluation that enables one to respond in a consistently favorable or unfavorable manner with respect to a given object or alternative. The three components of attitude are the cognitive part, the affective part, and the intention part. Measurement is defined as the process of assigning numbers or other symbols to certain characteristics of the object of interest, according to some pre-specified rules. This chapter discusses four types of scales that are used in measurement—the nominal scale, the ordinal scale, the interval scale, and the ratio scale. Scales can be classified as single-item and multi-item scales.

The focus of this chapter is on the modifications required to administer scales in different countries. It is important for researchers to bear in mind that the objective should be to collect data that is comparable across countries. The scales that are being used should reflect this equivalence. In particular, researchers should ensure that scales meet the criteria for calibration equivalence, translation equivalence, and metric equivalence. Researchers should also take care to see that validity, reliability, and sensitivity of scales are maintained across different countries.

QUESTIONS AND PROBLEMS

1. What is measurement? What are the scales of measurement and what information is provided by each?
2. Identify the type of scale and justify your answer.
   a. During which season of the year were you born?
      _____Winter _____Spring _____Summer _____Fall
   b. How satisfied are you with the Ford Taurus that you have bought?
      _____Very satisfied _____Satisfied _____Neither satisfied nor dissatisfied
      _____Dissatisfied _____Very dissatisfied
   c. On an average, how many cigarettes do you smoke in a day?
      _____Over 1 pack _____1/2 pack to 1 pack _____Less than 1/2 pack
   d. Rank the following according to your preference.
      _____Tide _____Surf _____Cheer _____Wisk _____Bold
3. How would you select a set of phrases or adjectives for use in a semantic-differential scale to evaluate the image of banks and other consumer financial institutions in Australia, Japan, India, and Germany? Would the procedure differ if you were going to use a Likert scale?
4. Under what circumstances can attitude measures be expected to be good predictors of subsequent behavior? Is there any value to measuring attitudes in situations where attitudes are likely to be poor predictors?

5. Explain the concepts of reliability and validity in your own words. What is the relationship between them?
6. Carter Toys, the US-based manufacturer of the popular PollyDolly, feels that a strong sales potential exists for the doll in foreign markets. The management has identified the selection of suitable foreign country markets as being its first priority. Worldwide Research Corp. has been employed to conduct a survey of the three countries that are currently under consideration: UK, Japan, and Kenya.
   a. Can the same questionnaire be used to survey all three countries? Give reasons for your answer.
   b. What factors must be considered in selecting a suitable scale to be used in each country?
   c. Recommend the most suitable scale for use in each country?

11

Questionnaire Design

INTRODUCTION

Questionnaire is a form containing a set of questions, especially one addressed to a statistically significant number of subjects as a way of gathering information for a survey.[1] This chapter will discuss the designing of questionnaires in detail, various types of questioning, and the issues involved in developing questionnaire in an international marketing setup. Questionnaire brings in a sophisticated and systematic way of analyzing the results post the survey. It brings in a level of standardization that allows the researcher to compare results across multiple respondents and geographic locations. There are many things at play in terms of the actual designing of the questionnaire: the wording, to the length to the style and methodology. All of these will be discussed in greater detail in respective sections of this chapter.

One of the most important problems faced by researchers in global marketing research is the difference in perceptions due to cultural and regional differences; Exhibit 11.1 is a humorous demonstration of the same. Designing a questionnaire and translating it to several languages without compromising on the intended objective of the question is a challenge.

Exhibit 11.1

Opinions[2]

Four men, a Saudi, a Russian, a North Korean, and a New Yorker, are walking down the street. A marketing researcher asks them, "Excuse me, what is your opinion on the meat shortage?" The Saudi says, "What's a shortage?," the Russian says, "What's meat?," the Korean says, "What's an opinion?," and the New Yorker says, "Excuse me? What's excuse me?"

---

[1] *The Free Dictionary*, http://www.thefreedictionary.com/questionnaire (Retrieved in June 2013).

[2] John Tierney, " The BIG CITY; You could Look It Up", *The New York Times*, September 24, 1985, http://www.nytimes.com/1995/09/24/magazine/the-big-city-you-could-look-it-up.html (Retrieved on April 14, 2012).

Survey research plays a very important role in today's dynamic, need-to-know-right-away business environment. Survey results are often the primary, if not the sole, vehicle for making important decisions. Hence, it is very critical that surveys be conducted in an accurate, unbiased manner. An important component of survey research is the development of the survey instrument—the questionnaire, which is a set of questions designed to evoke useful answers. The questionnaire is the vehicle of communication between those seeking insight (the survey sponsor) and those from whom insight is sought (the respondents). It is the role of the researcher to ensure that the sponsor's inquiries are accurately translated into appropriate questions for respondents, and that the respondents correctly interpret the questions. The researcher must then correctly interpret the survey results and translate the findings into meaningful marketing terms.[3]

Questionnaires make it possible for the researcher to quantify various aspects of the research that are being studied. Designing a good questionnaire is considered an art. Questionnaires are not merely a collection of questions with the intention of eliciting some information from the respondent. The researcher must be very clear on the type of information that is needed for the research and questionnaire should be tailor-made to collect this information.

Researchers follow a specific sequence of steps to design a questionnaire. Figure 11.1 gives a flowchart of the steps involved in questionnaire design. The first step is to decide what variables need to be measured; this is nothing but revisiting the objective of conducting research in the first place. This involves going back to the research problem and the research questions. Researchers will also have to check back on the data collected during the course of secondary research and the hypotheses formulated when exploratory research was conducted. Using this, the researcher is required to decide on the questions to be asked in order to address the research issue that is being faced. The first step also includes a clear thought process on the researcher's part regarding how he/she would like to analyze the data that is being collected. This step is very crucial as it sets clear expectations and provides accurate scope of what the researcher can and cannot achieve with the current research.

The next step is to decide on the content and format of each question. Content refers to the general idea that the question is trying to address. Format refers to the way of asking this question including the scale type to be used. Next comes the actual wording of the questions. Each question should be unbiased. The researcher should make sure the level of understanding or knowledge needed at the respondent's end is realistic. Also, the questionnaire wording should not be loaded toward either extreme, leading the respondents to answer based on the desired outcome of the research objectives. An important step in the questionnaire designing process from a global marketing research standpoint is the translation of questionnaires. Typically, research is conducted in the local language being used in the particular region. It is critical for researchers to administer the questionnaire in the local language. For this purpose, once the questionnaire is designed in English, it is translated into the desired foreign language. To ensure equivalency, the questionnaire is translated back into English; however, the research is conducted using the foreign language questionnaire. The sequence of questions should be checked for logical continuity. The last step is to pretest the questionnaire and rectify any problems that may show up. Pretesting questionnaires is an extremely critical step in any study. It is during pretest that the researcher can evaluate the questionnaire accurately as it mirrors the actual interview process with the respondent.

---

[3] Kris Hodges, "Ask a Silly Question...," in *Marketing 98/99*, ed., John E. Richardson (Guilford, CT: Dushkin/McGraw-Hill, 1998), pp. 98–100.

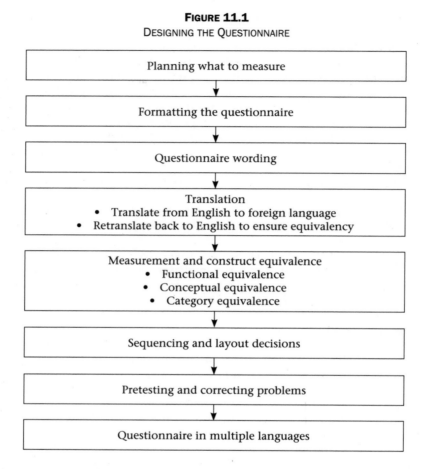

FIGURE 11.1
DESIGNING THE QUESTIONNAIRE

Planning what to measure

Formatting the questionnaire

Questionnaire wording

Translation
- Translate from English to foreign language
- Retranslate back to English to ensure equivalency

Measurement and construct equivalence
- Functional equivalence
- Conceptual equivalence
- Category equivalence

Sequencing and layout decisions

Pretesting and correcting problems

Questionnaire in multiple languages

While designing the questionnaire, the researcher has to bear in mind three factors that could have a great impact on the effectiveness of the questionnaire. First, the potential respondent should be able to understand the question. This implies that the language, the context, and the topic that is being investigated should be familiar to the respondent. Second, the respondent must have adequate knowledge to answer the question. The assumption behind survey research is that all the responses are indicative of the true nature of the respondents' attitudes and feelings. This basic assumption fails if the respondent does not possess the knowledge required to give an intelligent answer. Finally, the respondent should be willing to participate in the survey without any external pressure. This is necessary to ensure unbiased responses that reflect the true feelings of the respondents.

QUESTIONNAIRE DEVELOPMENT

Table 11.1 gives data organization of a typical questionnaire. The focus of global marketing research, as stressed in earlier chapters, will be on equivalence of information collected and not on equivalence of the instrument used to collect the data; hence, questionnaires do not

TABLE 11.1

ORGANIZATION OF A TYPICAL QUESTIONNAIRE[4]

Location	Type	Function	Example
Starting questions	Broad, general questions	To break the ice and establish a rapport with the respondent	Do you own a mobile phone?
Next few questions	Simple and direct questions	To reassure the respondent that the survey is simple and easy to answer	What brands of mobile phones did you consider when you bought it?
Questions up to a third of a questionnaire	Focused questions	Relate more to the research objectives and convey the area of research	What attributes did you consider when you purchased your mobile phone?
Major portion of the questionnaire	Focused questions; some may be difficult and complicated	To obtain most of the information required for the research	Rank the following attributes of a mobile phone based on their importance to you
Last few questions	Personal questions that may be perceived by the respondent as sensitive	To get classification and demographic information about the respondent	What is the highest level of education you have attained?

have to be identical across all countries in a multi-country study. The objective is to ensure that the questionnaires convey the purpose of the study to the respondent and elicit responses that will be useful for the research. Information that can be collected by a questionnaire falls under three main categories: demographic data, psychographic data, and behavioral data.

Demographic data reveal information about the respondent, such as age, sex, marital status, income, education, occupation, size of the family, and so on. This may not be a simple task in global marketing research. Some cultures support polygamy and so a person may have several spouses. There are societies where divorce and cohabitation of unmarried couples is common. This kind of data could be very difficult to capture in a questionnaire unless the researcher is aware of them and asks the respondent very specific questions. Income varies from country to country and the definition of classes—high income, middle income, and low income—also varies widely. Adequate data on this should be collected before designing the questionnaire. For instance, in some developing nations where the average annual income could be an equivalent of $500, it makes no sense for the questionnaire to include salary ranges from $25,000 upwards.

Education is another factor that varies widely between countries. There is a large disparity in the number of years spent in formative schooling and college education. The method and content of education also varies substantially. Definitions and product usage varies widely from country to country. Each country has a different definition for *urban* and *rural*. Before conducting the research, this must be clarified for each country. The definition of *family* is dependent on the specific country. In the Western cultures, nuclear families are the order of the day, while in many Eastern cultures, people continue to live in joint families. There could be differences in the place of residence. It could be a *house* in some parts of the world,

[4] Adapted from Aaker et al., *Marketing Research*, 6th edition.

apartments in some others, and *flats* in certain countries. The questionnaire will have to be designed in a manner such that respondents from all the countries surveyed should be able to interpret it in a similar manner.

Psychographic, attitudinal, and lifestyle data prove to be the most difficult in terms of questionnaire design for a multi-country study. Many concepts that researchers may be used to in their home countries may not exist in other countries where the survey is being conducted. Even if the concepts exist, designing questions to convey the same meaning in a foreign language is a mammoth task that requires a lot of effort in terms of translations and back-translations.

A simple example would be the attitude of people toward credit. In the US, credit cards, car loans, and mortgages are a part of the daily life for most people. However, some cultures in Asia frown upon credit of any form and consider it an insult to be indebted to another person or organization. Purchase of durable goods and luxury items will be made only if the individual is capable of paying for the item in full. Even within the US, the immigrants are found to have slightly lower poverty rates than US-born New Yorkers.[5] For instance, immigrants accounted for $215 billion in economic activity in New York City in 2008, which represented about 32% of the gross city product. Further, the 10 neighborhoods with the highest concentration of foreign-born residents had stronger economic growth than the rest of New York City between 2000 and 2007. Therefore, even within the US setting, it has been observed that many immigrants do not trust credit, tend to be better savers, and are more prudent with their finances than Americans in general.[6]

Another difference is in the role of women in different cultures. In the Western world, most women have careers and play an important role as equal partners to men. In many Middle Eastern countries, women are predominantly considered as homemakers and are not included in making decisions. Hence, if the study pertained to attitudes of women, the questionnaire and survey method will be different for women in the US and women in the Middle East.

Behavioral data tracks the actual action taken by the consumer in terms of buying the product, and the ways in which the product is used. The researcher should be able to collect information on whether the behavior is dependent on a sociocultural or economic environment.

There should also be adequate data on the various substitutes that could be used in a given country or culture. For instance, in the US, most products are sold as specific brands. The questionnaire can ask the respondents to name the brand of pasta or rice that they use most frequently. The tradition of shopping at a grocery or department chain is also very common. This may not be the case in other countries. In India, for instance, it is very common to buy vegetables and greens on the sidewalks, where vendors sell them from mobile carts. Therefore, asking the respondents the brand names for these items does not make practical sense. This scenario was observed in a survey conducted by Reader's Digest in the 1970s that suggested that the consumption of spaghetti and macaroni was significantly higher in France and Western Germany than in Italy.[7] On close examination, it was found that the questions asked in all countries were concerned with packaged and branded spaghetti, whereas many Italians

---

[5] New York State Comptroller, "The Role of Immigrants in the New York City Economy," Report 17, January 2010.

[6] Natalia V. Osipova, "Immigrants Baffled by US Debt Culture," October 24, 2012, http://www.voicesofny.org/2012/10/immigrants-baffled-by-us-debt-culture/(Retrieved in July 2013).

[7] Charles S. Mayer, "Multinational Marketing Research: The Magnifying Glass of Methodological Problems."

buy their spaghetti loose. This is the classic case of designing the survey instrument without getting a thorough understanding of buyer behavior.

The research study determines the questions that should be included in the questionnaire and the order in which they should be asked. The researcher has to decide on the degree of freedom that can be given to the respondent in terms of answering the question. The question could be close-ended—the respondent has to choose among the alternatives put forth by the researcher. With close-ended questions, the researcher may also decide to code the response—1 for "yes" and 0 for "no" and so on. The other option is the open-ended question where the respondent has the freedom of expressing independent opinions on the subject. With open-ended questions, the researcher has to record the response verbatim. The questions could be direct or indirect. The researcher may also use visual cues to get an opinion from the respondent. The next section discusses the type of questions that can be used to design a questionnaire.

Question Format

The questionnaire design has to ensure data equivalence in global marketing research. The format, content, and wording of the questions should be such that the respondent is able to comprehend and respond in a manner that is useful for the study. For example, in a developed country, a white-collar worker may be part of the middle class, whereas in a less developed country, the same person would be a part of the upper class.[8] Hence, the questionnaire must be designed accordingly in different countries. The format, content, and wording of the questions must be decided after the respondent profile in understood. Also, there has to be a decision in terms of the freedom provided to the respondent to answer a particular question. For example, a researcher should decide if a question can yield a better response by being an open-ended question versus a close-ended question. In terms of format, content, and wording, questions can be categorized under the following types: open- versus close-ended, direct versus indirect, and verbal versus nonverbal.

Open- Versus Close-Ended Questions

Close-ended questions offer a set of choices, and the respondent has to choose one among the several alternatives available. Open-ended questions give the respondent the freedom to provide his/her response. There are compelling arguments in favor of both open- and close-ended questions. Close-ended questions have the advantage of easy analysis. All the possible responses can be pre-coded and keyed into a computer prior to the survey. However, they also have a drawback in the sense that a thorough research has to be conducted and all possible options must be included in the response set. This poses quite a challenge in international research because the researcher has to first conduct an extensive study of buyer behavior and gather data on all acceptable uses and substitutes for the product in that country. Certain cultures tend to remain neutral when they are offered the option among different choices. This tends to cause significant bias in the survey. The other problem with close-ended questions is that respondents from different cultures may interpret the choices very differently. Exhibit 11.2 gives an example of the impact of close-ended versus open-ended questions.

---

[8] Czinkota and Ronkainen, *International Marketing*, 5th edition.

Exhibit 11.2

Open-Ended or Close-Ended?[9]

Open-ended or close-ended is a very tricky choice. The impact of the same can be seen from the following example.

In a poll conducted after the presidential election in 2008, people's responses to the same questions asked in different formats provided a very different set of results. Consider the question: "What one issue mattered most to you in deciding how you voted for president?" One was asked as a close-ended question while the other was asked as an open-ended one. The close-ended version entailed five options for respondents to choose from, along with allowance to choose an option that was not on the list and specify the same. It was observed that on explicitly offering *economy* as a response, more than half of respondents (58%) chose this answer. However, only 35% volunteered the *economy* as a response in the open-ended format.

Moreover, among respondents who were asked the close-ended version, only 8% of them provided a response other than the five options explicitly mentioned on the questionnaire, as opposed to 43% of those asked the open-ended version, who delivered responses that were not listed in the close-ended version of the question. All of the other issues were chosen at least slightly more often when explicitly offered in the close-ended version than in the open-ended version. The following table shows the results of this question in both formats.

Question	What one issue mattered most to you in deciding how you voted for president?	
Answer	Open-Ended* (in %)	Close-Ended# (in %)
The Economy	35	58
The War in Iraq	5	10
Healthcare	4	8
Terrorism	6	8
Energy Policy	–	6
Others	43	8
Candidate Mentions	9	–
Moral Values/Social Issues	7	–
Taxes/Dist. of Income	7	–
Other Issues	5	–
Other Political Mentions	3	–
Change	3	–
Other	9	–
Don't Know	7	2
	100	100

* Unprompted first response to open-ended question
# First choice from five options read to respondents

---

[9] Adapted from Pew Research Center for the People and the Press, "Open and Closed-Ended Questions," 2013, http://www.people-press.org/methodology/questionnaire-design/open-and-closed-ended-questions/(Retrieved as in July 2013).

In a global marketing research setup, it is tough for researchers to create a robust list of options for close-ended questions. One common practice among researchers is to conduct a pilot study with open-ended questions to discover most common answers and then use the same for developing the close-ended question response list including the most common responses as answer choices. This is one way to avoid making mistakes in creation of scale in a country that the researcher is not very familiar with.

In cases where the researcher is not sure about the purchasing behavior, it may be better to use open-ended questions. They do not impose any restrictions on the respondents and hence eliminate cultural bias because of a lack of understanding on the part of the researcher. The researcher does not have to be familiar with the entire range of responses that can be obtained for that specific question. The limitation is obvious—these questions cannot be precoded. The process of coding and tabulating them once the data has been collected is very tedious. The length of the response and consideration given to the question before filling out the response are dependent on the time given to the respondent. If the respondent is pressed for time, the response may be hurried and half-hearted.

Some of the factors that affect the decision to design the question as open-ended or close-ended in global marketing research are level of literacy, education, and communication skills of the respondent. If the respondents are highly literate and very familiar with the survey topic, open-ended questions will enable the researcher to collect a lot of information. Similarly, open-ended questions will serve their purpose only if the respondent is very articulate and is able to communicate clearly to the researcher. These questions have to be used with caution in international research to avoid bias due to differences in levels of education. The usefulness of these questions is also dependent on the interviewer's ability to record the responses thoroughly. Open-ended questions are used mostly in exploratory research where the primary objective is to gain insight into the research subject. Respondents are asked to list all possible options that come to their minds at the time of the survey. Responses that repeat very often are examined in greater depth.

Direct Versus Indirect Questions

Direct questions avoid ambiguity regarding the question content and meaning. Indirect questions probe the respondent by asking them to list choices of their friends or peers rather than their own. Direct questions can be used when the topic is not controversial or when it is about a topic that would make the respondent uncomfortable. However, for sensitive topics, it is more beneficial to use the indirect approach. In global marketing research, the researcher may have to spend some time finding out what is sensitive to people of a certain culture. For instance, while it is very common to discuss sexual preferences in the US, this is a taboo topic in many Asian cultures. Any information required on this topic should be asked in an indirect manner. Similarly, tax evasion is a very common occurrence in many Latin American countries and respondents are extremely suspicious of anybody asking questions regarding income and taxes.

Verbal Versus Nonverbal Questions

Most questionnaires are designed in a manner such that the questions can be read out to the respondents (interviews) or the respondent can read the questions (mail survey). However, in some cases, it may be necessary for researchers to use nonverbal cues, if the target sample consists mainly of children or if the research is undertaken in countries where the literacy levels are very low. In order to assist the respondent in understanding the questions better, picture cards or other visual aids are used. In some cases, product samples may also be shown to the respondents. This may be necessary to ensure that the respondent is familiar with the product and its uses. This method is sometimes used even when the literacy levels are high. In some cases, the researcher may want to subject one portion of the sample to nonverbal cues to ensure that the translation of the questionnaire is done correctly. Here, the associations and uses that people have will have to be accounted for. For example, a side-to-side facial movement in Asian cultures indicates an agreement, whereas in many Western cultures it is considered a disagreement. Therefore, nonverbal cues cannot be considered free of cultural bias.

Wording and Translation

Wording of the questions is a very important aspect of questionnaire design. There are instances where different words could mean the same thing. In such cases, the researcher should make sure that the words used in the questionnaire are the ones that are commonly used in the country where the questionnaire is being administered. For instance, the baby carriage or the stroller in the US is known as a pram in the UK.[10] Similarly, the *Scotch tape* commonly used in the US, Canada, Italy, Russia, and Ukraine is known as *Sellotape* in Australia, Ireland, New Zealand, and the UK.

Further, a question that is not understood by the respondent may be left unanswered or erroneously answered. Either way, this causes a lot of bias in the survey. It is very important to remember the profile of the sample population. The respondent base should dictate the wording, tone, and structure of the questions. For instance, asking homemakers technical details about the air-conditioning in their residences will not make any sense.

It is also necessary to keep in mind that respondents have limited attention spans, and asking long-winded questions will only result in them losing track of the question midway. A better option would be to break up the questions into smaller chunks that can be understood and responded to easily. If there are a lot of options which the respondent needs to consider before coming to a decision, these options must be presented in written form rather than the respondent having to listen to the interviewer read them. In a telephone interview, it is very important for the interviewer to make an oral transition from one type of question or subject area to another. This will help respondents anticipate change and shift them into a new mindset.

Questions have to be phrased in a manner such that they are free from bias and ambiguity. This becomes very important in global marketing research because of the different ways in which the same phrase can be interpreted. Consider the question "Don't you think this

---

[10] Sak Onkvisit and John J. Shaw, *International Marketing—Analysis and Strategy* (Upper Saddle River, NJ: Prentice Hall, 1997), third edition, p. 214.

advertising is appealing?" When an American answers "Yes," this usually means, "Yes, I agree with what you say." However, in Asian countries, this can mean a number of things. It could mean the other person is just acknowledging the fact that somebody is addressing them. It could also mean that the person understood what was being said but did not necessarily mean agreement with what was being said. It could also mean complete agreement or complete disagreement. Also, not only is the wording of question important; the scales have an impact too. Exhibit 11.3 illustrates this with an example. Some of the biggest blunders in marketing have been caused by using the wrong words or the right words in the wrong context.

Exhibit 11.3

Multilingual Marketing Research[11]

Weijters, Gueuens, and Baumgarter point to how consumers are influenced by the specific labels used to mark the endpoints of a survey response scale. In an international marketing context and especially in multi-country studies, this plays a vital role as we deal with the translation of questions and scales in multiple languages. The response category labels that are used in different languages have to be equivalent. If not, this could bias the survey results heavily.

Consider the *agree–disagree* scale. Often, participants are required to indicate their agreement or disagreement with certain set of statements using the *agree–disagree* scale with category labels that say *strongly (dis)agree* or *completely (dis)agree*.

A new study indicates that the survey results of a multilingual study could be skewed if the respondents do not know the meaning of the translated terms. In the study, English- and French-speaking consumers from the US, the UK, Canada, and France were used as test subjects. It appeared that the respondents endorsed the endpoints of the agreement scales depending on their familiarity of the labels. For instance, if the associated labels were often used in every-day language (such as *completely agree* or *tout à fait d'accord*), response categories got more responses. However, when the scales were less commonly used labels (such as *extremely agree* or *extrêmement d'accord*), the endorsements dropped. This trend was true for both the English and the French language.

Another research showed that the self-reported awareness of the cholesterol level of different types of food was a lot stronger when the Dutch equivalent of *completely disagree* to *completely agree* was used as against the *strongly disagree* and *strongly agree*.

So, it is clear from the two examples mentioned above that the importance of using the right labels when creating survey lists for research cannot be stressed upon more. Not only is the question wording important, the labels too have to be carefully evaluated so as to conduct an unbiased research and make sure that the response category labels used in different languages are equivalent in terms of familiarity.

---

[11] Adapted from Bert Weijters, Maggie Geuens, and Hans Baumgartner. "The Effect of Familiarity with the Response Category Labels on Item Response to Likert Scales," *Journal of Consumer Research* (2013), volume 40, pp. 368–381.

The issue of question format is an important one when constructing a questionnaire for cross-national research.[12] The researcher may lack experience with consumer purchase behavior or relevant determinants of response in another country or cultural context. Use of open-ended questions may, thus, be desirable in a number of situations. Since they do not impose any structure or response categories, open-ended questions avoid the imposition of cultural bias by the researcher. However, open-ended questions will have to be used with care in cross-national research, in order to ensure that bias does not occur as a result of differences in levels of education. Another consideration is whether direct or indirect questions should be utilized. Direct questions avoid any ambiguity concerning question content and meaning. On the other hand, respondents may be reluctant to answer certain types of questions. An additional consideration in instrument design is the extent to which nonverbal, as opposed to verbal, stimuli are utilized in order to facilitate respondent comprehension. Particularly where research is conducted in countries or cultures with high levels of illiteracy, as, for example, Africa and the Far East, it is often desirable to use nonverbal stimuli such as show cards. In short, whatever be the format of questioning, the main focus must be on their use in surveys in order to ensure that respondents understand verbal questions, relevant products, and product concepts.

Language Considerations

A key aspect of designing the questionnaire in global marketing research is to get familiar with the local language, keep the language as simple as possible, and avoid lengthy explanations and instructions. This way the researcher can ensure that all the respondents will be able to understand the questions and respond meaningfully. Care should be taken to ensure that there is no ambiguity for the respondent. As far as possible, the choices will have to be clearly specified. If, for instance, the researcher wants to find out how frequently the respondent indulges in a certain activity, specific options like *once a week* should be provided. Phrases like *often* and *usually* should be avoided as respondents attach different meanings to these words. Exhibit 11.4 gives some tips on questionnaire design.

Questions should not be combined together as this will cause a lot of confusion for the respondent and will make it difficult for the researcher to analyze the response. Consider a survey of recent car buyers to check for the satisfaction levels. The question asked of respondents was "Are you satisfied with the design and performance of the car?" The customer could be satisfied with one aspect but not with the other, and there is no provision for the respondent to explicitly state that he/she is satisfied with the design but not the performance (or vice versa). Even if the respondent answers the question with "Yes" or "No," the researcher is not in a position to decide whether the response refers to the design aspect or the performance aspect.

The questionnaire should not in any way reflect the opinions of the researcher on the subject matter. This could be in the form of including choices as a part of the question, such as "What do you spend the most money on—clothes or dining out?" Here the choice is limited to one of the two choices offered by the researcher, whereas the respondent could be spending the maximum amount on some other activity. Any words that convey strong emotions or affect the self-esteem of the respondents should also be avoided. One way to avoid these

---

[12] Shelby Hunt, Richard D. Sparkman, and James B. Wilcox, "The Pretest in Survey Research: Issues and Preliminary Findings," *Journal of Marketing Research* (1982), vol. 19, pp. 269–273.

Exhibit 11.4

Tips on Questionnaire Design[13]

Designing a questionnaire for global marketing research involves lot of preparation by the researcher. Following are some of the pitfalls to avoid when designing questionnaires.

- Have a clear understanding of the issue and main purpose behind the questionnaire.
- Understand how the questions are to be worded.
- Make sure the questions are laid out in a sequential manner, thus, showing a connection between them and a sense of thoroughness.
- Group questions in appropriate subtopics, and have a firm understanding of what is to be asked.
- Make sure there are no errors in the questionnaire.
- Make the respondent comfortable with the questioning process by opening up with a more generic question regarding the topic.
- Do not use questions that can generate vague and broad responses that do not further enhance the purpose of the questionnaire.
- Instructions should not confuse the respondents. Keep the instructions short and precise.

pitfalls is to test the questionnaire on a small number of respondents from the target segment and rectify any mistakes at a very early stage.

Another important facet of global marketing research is translation of questionnaires and responses. Examples of blunders in the research study arising from errors in translation abound. For instance, the Spanish-language version of Microsoft launched in Spain and Mexico offered *savage* and *man-eater* as synonyms for the word *Indian*.[14] It is important to note that accurate translation is important for both verbal and nonverbal stimuli and responses. The procedure normally followed in translating a questionnaire is very elaborate and involved. A professional translator translates the original English version of the questionnaire into the foreign language. This foreign version is then translated back into English by another person who is not familiar with the original version. This is done to ensure that the questionnaire is consistent in terms of content in both the languages. Though this process is very time-consuming and expensive, many researchers use it because of its effectiveness. It should be noted that back translation assumes that equivalent terms and concepts exist in all languages that are of relevance to the researcher. This does not always have to be true.

There are several drawbacks with this method. The foremost problem is that the mental representation of verbal information is different in different cultures.[15] Professional translators may not be familiar with commonly used idioms. Translators are usually not very conversant

[13] Adapted from Aaker et al., *Marketing Research*, 11th edition.

[14] "Microsoft Says Sorry, i.e., Oops," *Deseret News*, July 6, 1996.

[15] Bernd Schmitt, Yingang Pan, and Nader T. Tavossili, "Language and Consumer Memory: The Impact of Linguistic Differences between Chinese and English," *Journal of Consumer Research* 21 (1994): 419–431.

with the art of marketing and persuasion, and the translated version of the questionnaire often does not have a ring of authenticity to it.[16]

Besides, in countries like India and China, where thousands of dialects are spoken, it is impossible for translators to be fluent in all of them. The original questionnaire is designed in a certain language and will carry the tone and style of that language and will be dominant in that language structure. The basic assumption in the method of back-translation is that equivalent terms and phrases exist in all the languages that the questionnaire is to be translated. This may not always be the case. For instance, Japanese does not have an exact equivalent for the word *husband*. Term selection is particularly problematic in the information systems industry where Americans have invented many words for which there are no equivalents in any other language. In circumstances like this, researchers have to settle for a colloquial equivalent. This is a strong argument in favor of focusing on the comparability of data collected rather than on the questionnaire itself. Researchers should concentrate on conveying the purpose of the survey and recording the responses in the best and most efficient manner possible. The instrument used to achieve this objective is secondary.

Pretesting questionnaires is of utmost important in international marketing studies. Pretesting is done to ensure that all versions of the questionnaire are interpreted in a similar manner by respondents from various countries. It is also important to check for clarity and fluency before the questionnaires can be used in the survey. In global marketing research, equal importance should be given to translating nonverbal cues and responses. Adequate time and effort should be invested in pretesting perceptual and visual cues to avoid miscommunication arising as a result of difference in interpretations. It is also useful to have redundancy in the questionnaires to help researchers in cross-checking the validity of responses.[17]

CULTURAL ISSUES

Even though the questionnaire has been designed and translated carefully to meet the needs of several countries or cultures, this situation of response bias due to cultural differences does arise. Some of the factors that may lead to these biases are discussed in this section.

In drafting a questionnaire, knowledge of the social, psychological, and ethnic aspects of the society is essential.[18] This is a good indication of how people are likely to respond to certain topics, how they will react toward questions that are private, and the amount of time they will be willing to spend for an interview. The wording, length, and form of the questionnaire should depend on the verbosity, sophistication, credibility, conformity, and extremism of response of the sample population. The type of scales used, the language of the questionnaire, and the concept being tested should be comprehended by the respondents. As an example, if a questionnaire was to be designed for a national study of Philippines, the questionnaire would have to be translated into nine different languages. In India, this would be several hundred. In regions where literacy levels are very low, pictorial scales have to be used and visual aids have to be provided to ensure that the respondents are clear on the concepts that are

---

[16] Simon Anholt, "The Problem of International Work: Why Copy Can't Be Translated," *DM News*, January 23, 1995, p. 13.

[17] Naghi Namakforoosh, "Data Collection Methods Hold Key to Research in Mexico," *Marketing News*, 28 (1994): 28.

[18] Joanna Kinsey, *Marketing in Developing Countries* (England: Macmillan Education, 1994).

being tested. It has generally been found that open-ended questions provide better results and reduce cultural biases to a great extent. However, the trade-off is the difficulty in coding an open-ended question, which can generate thousands of responses in a multi-country study.

Translation is another major problem that researchers face in global marketing research. A study conducted to investigate trust and commitment and the importance of these attributes in relationship with management found that there are no direct translations of concepts related to trust in Japanese. *Amae* translates literally as *indulgent dependency* and *giri-ninjo* as an *obligation to show compassion to those who show it to you*. However, these ideas are not fully consistent with Western ideas of trust, and they apply only to Japanese–Japanese interaction.[19] This study focused on US–Japanese interaction, and the lack of adequate terminology made it difficult for researchers to convey their questions accurately.

The desire to be socially correct or provide answers that may be felt to be desired by the interviewer is present in almost everyone. This is, however, stronger in some cultures than in others. The Japanese almost always try to respond in a manner that they feel the interviewer wants them to so that they do not upset or cause any distress to the interviewer. Respondents in several poorer countries consider the survey as an honor bestowed upon them and will go to any lengths to please the interviewer. The other factor that causes bias is the desire to give socially acceptable answers. This is common in many cultures where the respondents feel the need to live up to a certain lifestyle or appear sophisticated. Therefore, the responses will be what they think they should answer rather than what they actually feel about the subject.

CONSTRUCT EQUIVALENCE

This concept has already been introduced in the earlier chapters. Construct equivalence deals with the function of the product or service that is being researched and not the method used in collecting information. The researcher has to establish that the constructs being studied in different countries are equivalent. There could be substantial differences in the way the same product is perceived in different regions. Countries that are being researched must have the same perception or use for the product being studied. If not, the comparison of data becomes meaningless. For instance, in the UK, Germany, and Scandinavia, beer is regarded as an alcoholic beverage, whereas in Greece, Spain, and Italy, it is treated more as a soft drink and compared to Coca-Cola. This understanding is vital in drawing conclusions and results based on the research. Construct equivalence consists of three parts—functional equivalence, conceptual equivalence, and category equivalence.

Functional Equivalence

Functional equivalence involves establishing that given concept or behavior serves the same purpose or function from country to country. We can consider the example of bicycles. While in the US, they are primarily used as a means of recreation, in many developing countries they serve as a mode of transportation. Hence, in the US, the relevant competing products

---

[19] Jean L. Johnson, Tomoaki Sakano, Kevin Voss, and Hideyuku Takenouchi, "Marketing Performance in US–Japanese Cooperative Alliances: Effects of Multiple Dimensions of Trust and Commitment in Cultural Interface," Working Paper, 1998, Washington State University.

would be other recreational sports items like roller blades and skiing equipment. In those other countries, we would have to have a different set of competing products, like alternate modes of transportation. As far as activities go, people from different cultures do things differently. Shopping for groceries is a chore in the US to be completed as efficiently as possible, and most food retailers make it easier with self-service aisles and shopping carts. In many countries, this is considered a social activity and there is a lot of interaction between the grocer and the customer. Similarly, there could be differences in the way people perceive objects in various countries around the world. Cars are considered a necessity in the US, while they are a luxury and a status symbol in many developing countries. All these factors will play an important role in the design of the questionnaire. Researchers have to make sure that they ask the questions in the right context.

Conceptual Equivalence

Conceptual equivalence deals with individual interpretation of objects and stimuli. The focus in this aspect of construct equivalence is on individual variations in attitudes and behavior rather than societal norms and behavior (as was the case in functional equivalence). Researchers try to understand the extent to which people from different cultures exhibit personality traits, such as aggression, authoritarianism, or need for affiliation. Social interaction, rituals, and practices vary widely between countries. In the UK, engagement implies a commitment to marry, whereas in Italy or Spain, it merely means having a boyfriend or girlfriend.

Category Equivalence

The last aspect of construct equivalence is called category equivalence. This relates to the categories in which relevant objects or other stimuli are placed. In many countries, beer is considered a soft drink. Many countries differ in the way they classify soft drinks, carbonated sodas, powdered or liquid concentrates, etc. The same holds true for the dessert market. Many cultures consider sweets as a part of the dessert. However, in China, sweets are not included as a part of the meal. In many Middle Eastern and African countries, marital status could include several wives. Even occupations are placed in different categories in different countries. Less-developed countries give much importance to professions like teacher or a religious minister.

Differences in culture, economic status, social structure, and product usage can cause wide variation in responses to the same given question. For instance, the American Customer Satisfaction Index represents overall satisfaction as a function of customer expectations, perceived quality, and perceived value.[20] The model is designed to take into account multiple indicators to measure customer satisfaction. This is done because the constructs used in the model represent different types of customer evaluations that cannot be measure directly. Using multiple indicators results in an index that is general enough to be comparable across firms, industries, sectors, and nations. While this index is applicable to the international context also, special care needs to be taken when designing the questionnaire. Customer

---

[20] Claes Fornell, Michael D. Johnson, Eugene W. Anderson, Jaesung Cha, and Barbara Everitt Bryant, "The American Customer Satisfaction Index: Nature, Purpose, and Findings," *Journal of Marketing* 60 (1996): 7–20.

expectations and perceived quality and value are culturally and nationally sensitive constructs. They would depend on the product, its price in a given country, the substitutes available, and the usage methods.

Consider, for instance, the product category of passenger cars and measure customer satisfaction in the US and India. The average customer in the US considers cars a necessity. There is ample choice and the cost of a car as a percentage of annual income is not very high. However, in many developing countries, cars are considered a luxury that is within the reach of only a small percentage of the population. As a percentage of the annual income, the cost of cars is very high and there is only limited choice. Hence, the customer perception of value, quality, and their expectations of a car are bound to be different.

A questionnaire that does not take into account all these differences will not capture the real picture. To start with the basics, translating the questionnaire will prove to be a problem. It is not possible to get a precise translation for the word *perceive* in many languages worldwide. Even if the meaning were conveyed adequately, differences could arise due to variances in the perception of the product—the car in this case itself in this case.

Assume that Ford is conducting a customer satisfaction study for its Fiesta line of cars. Even though the sixth-generation Fiesta (Mark VI) was launched worldwide in 2010, using the same questionnaire to test the satisfaction across country markets would not work. This is because of the differences in the car make in the various countries. For instance, Fiesta is available in four body styles, including 3- and 5-door hatchbacks, 4-door saloon, and 2-door van, across various countries. Whereas the 5-door hatchback is sold globally except India, the 4-door saloon is sold in China, North and South America, and parts of Australasia, the 3-door hatchback is sold in Europe, Australasia, and parts of Asia such as Singapore, and the 3-door van is sold only in Europe. Similarly, there are other differences in exterior and interior accessories, fuel type (petrol versus diesel), and the type of standard features that vary from the base model to the top model. Given the variations in the attributes, asking the questions in an absolute sense does not provide accurate results. Therefore, there is no one *single* questionnaire that can be used across all the countries.

Even when developing different questionnaires for different countries, questions have to be asked in comparative terms and researchers have to provide anchors that are comparable in order to obtain comparable results. One way to go about this would be to pick a model that is being used by a certain segment of the society and ask for satisfaction relative to this model. In this regard, the competing cars will have to be identified in each of the markets are used in generating the questions. For instance, in the US, the question could be phrased as "Compared to the Nissan Versa, how does Fiesta rate on all the following factors?" (Provide a list of attributes that need comparison). In India, the same question could be worded as "Compared to the Volkswagen Vento, how does Fiesta rate on all the following factors?"

There are certain aspects that are culture-sensitive. For instance, Americans are used to speaking up their minds, and hence any dissatisfaction that they feel toward the car will be reflected in the response. However, Asians are not so candid and may hide any negative opinions for fear of hurting the feelings of the interviewer. In such situations, adjustments will have to be made to the scales and the interviewer will have to go to great lengths to convince the respondent of the importance of an honest response. This requires that the researcher have in-depth understanding of the foreign culture.

Designing the questionnaire in the correct manner is only solving half the problem. Analyzing the results is the other major component, and it is always preferable to include researchers who are familiar with the foreign country or culture in the analysis.

GUIDELINES FOR ONLINE QUESTIONNAIRE DESIGN

As seen earlier, Internet has changed the way marketing research is carried out in many countries. Many developed nations use online surveys instead of the traditional pen and paper methods. Is the questionnaire design for online surveys same as pen and paper surveys? In fact, the online surveys are better than the traditional ones in many ways. Some of these are outlined below:

- Online format allows researcher to build in complex skipping patters and make the questions more relevant and precise for respondents to answer.
- Researchers can design the survey in such a manner that the respondent's answer can be plugged in and the follow-up questions can be generated accordingly. For example, consider the case where the question reads, "Which of the following is your favorite restaurant?" to which the respondent answers "Olive Garden." In an online survey, the researcher has the flexibility to use this response to design the follow-up question on the following lines, "Would you recommend 'Olive Garden' to your friends and relatives?"
- As an extension to the previous point, the researcher has the flexibility to reduce the response list based on prior selection. For instance, while asking to rate the most often used brand, researcher can filter out the non-aware brands as recorded earlier by the respondent. This makes the response list more relevant.
- Researchers can use different media to test various aspects of their study. Unlike the pen and paper format, audio or video clips can be inserted very easily in online surveys.
- Statements can be randomized. While administering a questionnaire in pen and paper format, apart from the starting point, there is a way to randomize statements. In the online questionnaires, all statements can be truly randomized to remove the order bias of the statements.
- Online surveys can be designed to look good. As opposed to the pen and paper surveys, online surveys can be made exciting to engage the respondents while answering the survey.

Websites like Survey Monkey, Zoomerang and the like are making survey designing extremely easy. While such software products make the actual designing of questionnaire easy, the knowledge of important concepts spoken earlier in the chapter is still very essential. Chapter 9 provides a good snapshot of online survey options that researchers can use.

Following are some of the design aspects that a researcher should be cognizant of while creating an online questionnaire.[21]

1. *Welcome screen:* Welcome screen is the first screen that a respondent sees. It provides the research with an opportunity to explain the purpose of the survey to the respondents, establish confidentiality terms, and provide information about the collection of incentives.
2. *First question:* It is observed that respondents abandon the survey if it tends to get boring. So the first question sets the tone for the rest of the questionnaire.

---

[21] Valerie M. Sue and Lois A. Ritter, *Conducting Online Surveys* (London: SAGE Publications, 2012), second edition.

3. *Color:* Pen and paper surveys tend to be black and white only as color questionnaires would increase the cost of printing and mailing tremendously. Researchers can engage the respondent with effective use of colors on screen and make it fun for respondents to answer the survey. However, careful use of color is advised, without overdoing it and distracting the respondents from the main purpose. Colors signify certain emotions, feelings, and have meanings associated with them. Table 11.2 lists some examples of common color associations for adults in the US.

4. *Technological changes:* While technology enables researchers to show their creativity in terms of the questionnaire design, they should be aware of the technical issues that multiple platforms can run into. There is a difference in the visual appearance depending on the operating system, the browsers, screen configurations, wrap-around text, etc. Incompatibility with one of the operating systems can result in non-response. Today, researchers should be aware that mobile technology is being widely adopted by consumers, and as a result, surveys should be mobile-compatible as well so that respondents get an option of answering questions while they are on the go.

5. *Include instructions:* Since online surveys are self-administered, it is very important to include specific instructions for respondents. An example of online survey instruction is shown in Exhibit 11.5. While these initial instructions are included in most surveys, specific instructions for answering each question are very important. For example, Single response questions should say, "Choose only one answer," multiple response questions should say, "Choose all that apply," and open-ended questions should include "Please be as specific as possible."

TABLE 11.2
COLOR ASSOCIATIONS FOR ADULTS IN THE US[22]

Color	Negative Associations	Positive Associations
Blue	Sadness, depression	Male, sky, water, peace, truth, calm
Purple	–	Royalty, luxury
Pink	–	Female, cute, soft, gentle
Orange	Caution	Autumn, Halloween, creativity
White	Cold, sterility, clinical	Winter, virginity, clean, innocent, truth, peace, snow
Black	Death, evil, mourning, night, mystery, fear	Formality, style, power, depth
Yellow	Illness, hazard	Happiness, sunshine, optimism, summer
Gray	Gloomy, conservative, boring	Maturity, dignity
Red	Danger, aggression, blood, hot, stop	Power, love, fire, passion, intimacy, courage
Brown	Bland	Earth, nature
Green	Inexperience, misfortune	Money, freshness, envy, nature, growth

[22] Adapted from Sue and Ritter, *Conducting Online Surveys*, second edition.

Exhibit 11.5

Instructions for Online Survey Respondents[23]

- The survey is very simple to complete and should only take about 10 minutes or less of your time.
- If you are unsure about a specific service provided by your organization, you may choose to skip that question and complete it after you have obtained the information needed (re-clicking the link at a later time will return you automatically to uncompleted items, or you may also click the *Back* key anytime while taking the survey).
- Only one response per individual please.
- You may move back to a previous page and revise your responses at any time. When all answers are completed, simply click the *Submit* tab and you will be asked to select your gift of appreciation. The first 50 respondents are eligible to receive NIKE running/walking shoes!
- All surveys should be completed by July 14, 2006!
- Should you wish to complete the survey by hand, we will be happy to mail a hard copy to you.
- Please contact us at 555-555-5555 if you need assistance. Remember: all surveys should be completed by July 14, 2006!
- Thank you for your participation.

Click here to begin the survey!

6. *Formats of response options:* There are many ways in which researchers can gather responses. The response list can be in the form of radio buttons, check boxes, drop-down menus, rank-order metrics, constant sum, and open-ended text boxes. Researcher has scope to choose any of these depending on the best fit for the type of question and the level of understanding of the audience, that is, respondents. One can also include logic checks and accordingly display error messages to the respondent to resolve the issue. Logic checks and error messages are extremely important; without these, many questionnaires filled will not be used in research analysis due to non-response bias.

7. *Forced response:* An extension of logic checks and display of error messages is forcing response from respondents for certain questions. If the forced response option is not implemented, the actual response to questions might be very low. While the researcher can avoid forcing respondents on questions that he/she may find difficult to answer, it is crucial to get a response to important questions that the respondent may avoid simply to move ahead in the questionnaire and complete the survey.

8. *Navigation guides:* Some researchers include a navigation guide that serves as a roadmap for respondents to understand where exactly they are in the survey reducing the frustration levels of completing the survey soon.

9. *Font:* Font size and type has an impact on the ease of reading for respondents. Figure 11.2 illustrates top three fonts by category for ease of choosing.

---

[23] *Source*: Adapted from Sue and Ritter, *Conducting Online Surveys*, second edition.

FIGURE 11.2
TOP THREE FONTS IN EACH CATEGORY[24]

Rank	Reading Time (in seconds)	Perceived Legibility	Perceived as Being Businesslike	Perceived as Youthful and Fun	Font Preference
1	Tahoma (270)	Courier	Times New Roman	Comic Sans MS	Arial
2	Times New Roman (273)	Comic and Verdana	Courier	Bradley	Verdana and Georgia
3	Verdana (280)	Times New Roman	Schoolbook	Verdana	Comic

10. *Additional Cues:* In addition to the discussed items, researcher can choose to include images, audio and visual stimuli. At the end, a "Thank you for participation" screen is displayed to conclude the online survey.

GLOBAL MARKETING RESEARCH IN PRACTICE

This section discusses the practical aspects of designing and administering a survey questionnaire for global marketing research. The first aspect that a researcher needs to look into is the population characteristics. It may be possible for the researcher to obtain a complete list of the people who make up the population. However, this would depend on the population and the location. For instance, whereas a comprehensive list of all pulmonologists in New York is a reasonable goal, the same may not be available in a developing country. Even within developed countries, if the population was defined as all women who use shampoos and conditioners in Atlanta, it may be difficult to get a complete list. Even if the list were available, it would be difficult to get a complete list. This task would be more tedious in a developing nation such as Brazil or India where shampoo purchases are not usually tracked. Hence, defining the population and deciding whether to go for the complete list or just choosing a representative sample is the first step in a survey.

Once the population has been defined, designing the questionnaire will depend on the population characteristics. It is safe to assume that any randomly selected women in Atlanta will be aware of the concept of shampoo. However, in Kenya, as in many parts of the less-developed world where cheaper and more traditional ingredients are prevalent, many women do not use bottled shampoos. Hence, the questionnaire must have a screening question at the start to ensure that respondents use shampoos.

Language issues have to be addressed in all global marketing research surveys. For the Miami area, the researcher may be better off having designing questionnaires in both English and Spanish. For the survey in Kenya, questionnaires must be designed in English and the local language. Further, when administering surveys in Asian and Middle-Eastern countries, many cultures do not take kindly to strangers striking up conversation with women. There could

---

[24] Adapted from M. L. Bernard, M. M. Mills, M. Peterson, and K. Storrer, "A Comparison of Popular Online Fonts: Which Is Best and When?" *Usability News 3.2*, 2001, http://usabilitynews.org/a-comparison-of-popular-online-fonts-which-is-best-and-when/(Retrieved as in July 2013).

also be substantial differences in the method of administering the questionnaire. Depending on the availability of time, telephone interviews, mail surveys, or mall intercept surveys could also be used. However, mail surveys will produce poor response rates in many less developed countries, as the postal system is not efficient. Incentives may have to be offered in many countries to improve response rates.[25] It may also not be possible to obtain the mailing list. Hence, personal intercept or store intercept surveys seem to be best way to collect information. The researcher needs to identify locations in various parts of the city that could give the best *hit* rates.

The type of questions that can be asked also varies widely from country to country. If an open-ended question were asked in US, most respondents would be verbose, telling the researcher exactly what they feel. However, many oriental cultures do not encourage verbosity, and an open-ended question in China and other Asian countries will not get very good results. For this reason, it may be better to opt for close-ended questions in these countries and ask respondents to choose from a pre-specified list of choices. The researcher will also have to watch out for various kinds of biases that are prevalent in less developed countries. Many women in Asian countries may claim to use shampoos just so they can appear trendy and sophisticated. Respondents could also answer the questionnaire because they are too polite to refuse the interviewer.

Ultimately, all surveys are dependent on the resources available to the researcher. Hence, cost becomes a major factor in deciding the type of survey, length of the questionnaire, number of people to be surveyed, and the geographic coverage.

SUMMARY

Surveys are an important source of primary information for researchers, and questionnaires are used to collect information through surveys. Questionnaires make it possible for the researcher to quantify various aspects of the research that are being studied. There are three factors that are considered very important in a questionnaire: the respondent should understand the question, should possess adequate knowledge to answer the question, and should be willing to participate in the survey without any external pressure. Questionnaires gather data that fall under three categories: demographic data, psychographic data, and behavioral data. Questions in a survey can be open- or close-ended, direct or indirect, and verbal or nonverbal. The type of question used will be determined by the topic that is being researched and the country or culture where the rese-arch is being conducted. Questionnaires should always be pretested to make sure they achieve the objective planned by the researcher. A questionnaire has to meet the requirements of construct equivalence for it to be a valid data collection tool in global marketing research. Construct equivalence can be broken into three components: functional equivalence, conceptual equivalence, and category equivalence. The researcher should be cognizant of the technological aspects discussed in the chapter while designing online survey questionnaires.

[25] Charles Keown, "Foreign Mail Surveys: Response Rates Using Monetary Incentives," *Journal of International Business Studies* (Fall 1985), volume 16, pp. 151–153.

QUESTIONS AND PROBLEMS

1. Little Kids, a US-based manufacturer of the popular board game *Fun with Science*, feels that a strong sales potential exists for educational toys in the emerging markets. The management has identified the selection of suitable emerging country markets as being its first priority. Worldwide Research Corp. has been employed to conduct a survey of the three countries that are currently under consideration: Brazil, Turkey, and South Africa.

   a. Can the same questionnaire be used to survey all three countries? Give reasons for your answer.

   b. What factors must be considered in selecting a suitable scale to be used in each country?

   c. Recommend the most suitable scale for use in each country.

2. The finance committee of St. John's Residents' Association has reported a fall in the level of donations to the association despite the fact that residents' participation in community activities has not declined. This decline in financial contribution is creating a strain on the continuity of community services such as security, recreational amenities, and regular maintenance and up-keep of the neighborhood. In an effort to boost donations, the committee has decided to conduct personal interviews of all residents to determine each member's habits regarding donations to the association.

   a. How might this survey method bias the results of the study? Each member of the committee has been given a questionnaire from which to conduct the personal interviews. The first four questions are as follows:
      (i)   How often do you attend the association meetings during a year?
      (ii) Are you aware that the association's only form of income is the donations from its residents?
      (iii) Do you donate to the association every year?
      (iv) How much, on average, do you donate?

   b. How would the following factors affect the results of this study?
      (i)   Question order
      (ii) Question wording
      (iii) Subject matter
      (iv) Interviewer's affiliation to the association

3. Discuss about the translation problems encountered in designing global marketing research questionnaires.

4. "Questionnaire design for descriptive research is more difficult than for an exploratory research." Discuss this statement.

12

CHAPTER _____

Sampling

INTRODUCTION

The purpose of global marketing research is to study the characteristics and preferences of a population. *Population* is defined as the set of all objects that possess some common set of characteristics with respect to some marketing research problems. A survey that contacts all members of a population is called a *census*. In most research studies, it is not very practical to conduct a census because of limitations in terms of resources and time. Researchers choose a subset of elements from the population and this subset is called the *sample*. From this subset, they then make an inference about the population based on the relevant information obtained from the sample. The critical assumption in this case is that the sample is representative of the population and any data collected from the sample can be applied to all members of the population.

It is important to bear in mind that using samples can introduce a bias in the research project. Even if the researcher is able to specify the population of interest, it may not be possible to access the entire population. The sample that has been selected may include some members who do not belong to the population. There is also the possibility that some segments of the population are left out of the sample. Also, the members of the sample may not always give the correct response.

STATISTICAL BASIS FOR SAMPLING

It is important to familiarize the reader with some terms that are used frequently in conjunction with sampling.[1] A sampling unit that has been contacted by the researcher provides a *response*, which will be used as a basis for analysis. Any function of this response is called a *statistic*. A statistic can be described as the value obtained across all responses for a certain measure, like the sample mean or the sample variance. A *sampling distribution* is the probability distribution of the statistic. The total error in a survey can be split into two major components. If the difference between the population parameter and sample statistic is only because of sampling, this is called *sampling error*. This could be mainly because of choosing a sample of size that is smaller than the population. In most cases, the sampling error can be reduced to a great extent by using a relatively larger sample. Determination of the appropriate sample

---

[1] William Trochim, "Statistical Terms in Sampling," October 2006, http://www.socialresearchmethods.net/kb/sampstat.php (Retrieved in October 2014).

size is discussed later in this chapter. It must be remembered that the statistically determined sample size is the number of complete responses that must be received by the researcher. The response rate in a given country for a given method must be identified and an adequate number of people must be contacted.

If there is a difference between the population parameter and the sampling statistic that is not due to sampling error, it is called *non-sampling error*. Non-sampling errors can be due to errors in measurement, errors in recording the responses, errors in analyzing the data, and non-response error.

THE SAMPLING PROCESS

When a decision is made to use a sample, a number of factors must be taken into consideration. Figure 12.1 represents the flowchart for the sampling process.

FIGURE 12.1
THE SAMPLING PROCESS

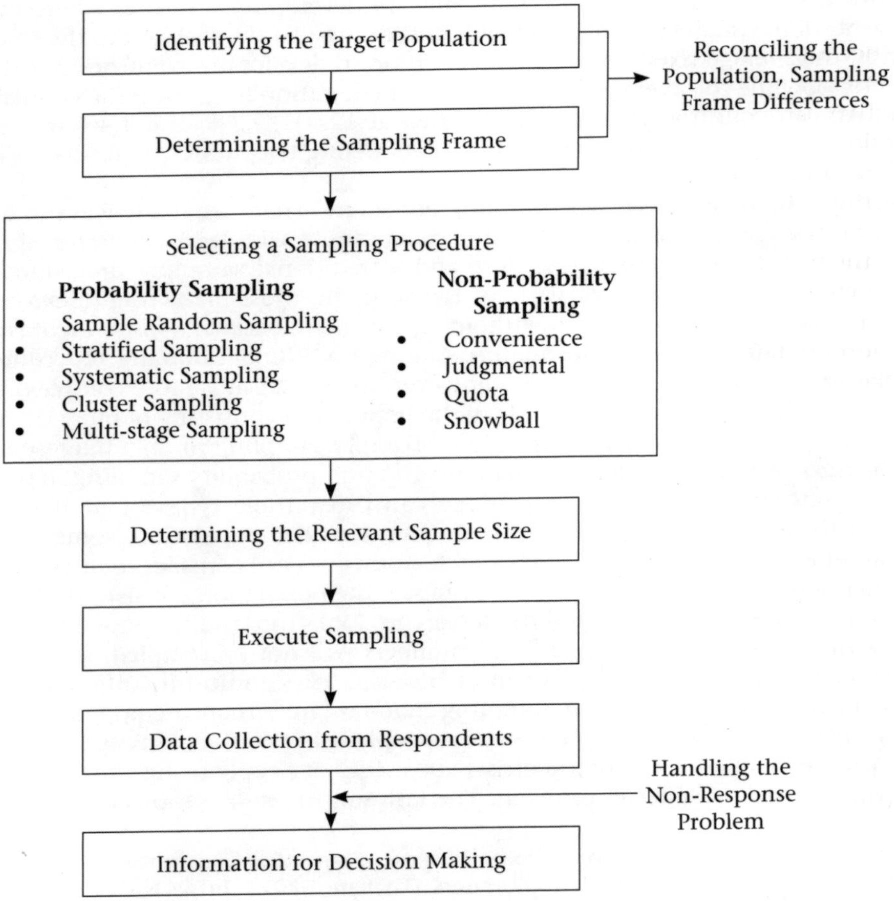

The first step in the sampling process is to determine the target population. This has to be defined clearly and precisely, as the narrower the definition is, the better the results from the sample obtained will be. In global marketing research, this attains more importance due to differences in decision-making processes among various countries. A good knowledge about the market will aid the researcher in deciding the target population and sample size. Before proceeding to the second stage, the differences pertaining to population and sampling frame have to be addressed. This will also help researchers establish the sampling unit. A sampling unit may consist of individuals, households, or organizations. The assumption behind the sampling unit is that all responding members of the unit provide information for the whole unit. Here again, the researcher needs to know the market well enough to decide this. For instance, if the family is considered as a sampling unit, the researcher needs to clarify the definition of a family in that country.

The next step is to decide the sampling frame. The sampling frame is a list of population members used to obtain a sample. In global marketing research, this can create problems as documented information sources are found wanting. Also, the decision-making process may vary among countries. For instance, in Japan decisions are still made by consensus of every family member.[2] A list of members belonging to the sampling frame should then be obtained. While in developed countries this information can be easily obtained from professional organizations and database marketing companies, in developing countries where marketing research is still in its infancy, finding a reliable source may pose a problem to the researchers. For instance, the average fixed telephone penetration in developing countries is 2013 is estimated at 11.1%, while the average fixed telephone penetration in Asia-Pacific countries, Arab states, and African countries in 2013 is estimated at 12.9%, 9.3%, and 1.4%, respectively.[3] With such low levels of telephone penetration, conducting telephone-based surveys is bound to yield unreliable results.

The third step involves selecting a sampling procedure. There are many ways of obtaining a sample and many decisions associated with generating a sample. A researcher should first choose between using a Bayesian procedure and a traditional sampling procedure. Next, a decision is made to sample with or without replacement. Most marketing research projects employ a traditional sampling method without replacement, because a respondent is not contacted twice to obtain the same information. Among traditional sampling procedures, some are informal or even casual. In most cases, however, the situation is more complex. It is then necessary to obtain a representative sample of the population consisting of more than a handful of units. The preferred approach is to use probability sampling to obtain a representative sample. The next section will discuss probability and non-probability sampling in detail.

Improper definition of the sampling frame can cause three types of problems for the researcher. If the sampling frame chosen is smaller than the population, some members of the population are not sampled and the research study does not consider their tastes and attitudes. This is called a *subset problem*. If, for instance, the population consists of all telephone owners in a given geographic area and the researcher looks into the telephone directory, this would be a subset problem, as the unlisted numbers will not be sampled. It has also been found that the people with unlisted telephone numbers are significantly different from those with listed telephone numbers. If the sampling frame is larger than the population, we have a *superset problem*. If the population consists of people using contact lens and the researcher obtains a sample database form optometrists consisting of people using eyeglasses and contact lens, this becomes a superset problem. The last and the most serious error is the *subset/*

---

[2] Edward Leslie, "Some Observations on Doing Business in Japan," *Business America*, 1992, pp. 2–4.

[3] ITU World Telecommunication, "ICT Indicators Database," 2013, http://www.itu.int/ict/statistics (Retrieved on April 25, 2013).

superset problem. This occurs when the researcher leaves out some members of the sampling frame while including others that do not belong to the sampling frame. Assume a researcher is interested in contacting small business owner with at least 44 million in sales. If the researcher uses a business list which contains all businesses (not strictly small businesses) with over $5 million in sales, a subset/superset problem results.

In the fourth step, the sample size is determined. The size of a sample can be determined by using statistical techniques or through some ad hoc methods. Ad hoc methods are used when a person knows from experience what sample size to adopt or when there are some constraints that determine the sample size. The rule of thumb and comparable studies are some ways in which sample size can be determined through ad hoc methods. Determination of sample size depends on four factors: (a) the number of groups and sub-groups that will be analyzed, (b) the value of information in the study, (c) the cost of the sample, and (d) the variability of the population.

In the fifth and sixth steps, the sampling is executed and using the sampling design, data is collected from the respondents. The object of sampling is to obtain a body of data that are representative of the population. Unfortunately, some sample members become non-respondents because they (a) refuse to respond, (b) lack the ability to respond, or (c) are inaccessible.

Non-response can be a serious problem. It means that the sample size has to be large enough to allow for non-response. Further, it also indicates the possibility that those who respond differ from non-respondents in a meaningful way, thereby creating biases. The seriousness of non-response bias depends on the extent of the non-response. If the percentage involved is small, the bias is small. A way to correct the response bias is to replace each non-respondent with a *matched* member of the sample. Three more approaches are: (a) to improve the research design to reduce the number of non-responses, (b) to repeat the contact in order to reduce non-responses, and (c) to attempt to estimate the non-response bias. Therefore, the non-response problem has to be handled before proceeding to the decision-making stage.

Owing to uncertainties regarding the definition of population and sampling frame, selecting a sampling procedure is very crucial in global marketing research. The roadmap provided in this section would help the researcher to understand the sampling process and use appropriate sampling techniques. The types of sampling are provided in the following section.

TYPES OF SAMPLING

Selecting a sampling procedure is very crucial in global marketing research owing to uncertainties regarding the definition of the population and sampling frame. Theoretically, however, sampling methods can be classified under two broad headings: probability sampling and non-probability sampling. In probability sampling, each member of the population has a known probability of being selected. However, the researcher needs to have a definite sampling frame and also have prior information on the objects or sampling units before getting started on the sampling process.

Probability sampling has several advantages. It permits the researcher to demonstrate the representativeness of the sample. It helps researchers state the variation introduced by using a sample instead of a census. It also helps researchers identify possible biases introduced due to sampling.

In global marketing research, it is not always possible to obtain a sampling frame. In such circumstances, non-probability methods work best. There are no significant costs involved in developing a sampling frame; however, it is also not possible to guarantee the representativeness of the sample. The responses can contain hidden biases and uncertainties that cannot be explained. Increasing the sample size does not help overcome these biases. Hence, researchers prefer to avoid non-probability sampling methods whenever possible.

Probability Sampling

A sample can be obtained by using the principle of probability theory. In this procedure, researchers first specify the population to be sampled and the sample size. Generally speaking, the sample size depends on the accuracy required by the study, the resources available to the researcher, and the reliability of the sampling list collected by the researcher. Probability sampling involves four specific considerations. First, the target population must be specified. Second, the method for selecting the sample needs to be developed. Third, the sample size must be determined. The sample size will depend on the accuracy needs, the variation within the population, and the cost. Finally, the non-response problem must be addressed. The various types of probability sampling are discussed below.

Simple Random Sampling

Simple random sampling is the method of sampling where a group of subjects is selected from the population entirely by chance and the probability of choosing any given member from the population is the same. This method is used when the population from which the sample is to be chosen is homogeneous. Small sheets of paper with names written out on them are mixed together in a bowl and the desired number of names is drawn out. This method works very well for small sample sizes; however, if a large number of people have to be chosen from a population, it becomes very tedious. Another way of picking out a random sample is by generating a random-number table. Exhibit 12.1 gives a list of computer-generated random-number tables that can be used to pick out a sample. The researcher can start anywhere in the list and proceed horizontally or vertically. These numbers can then be used to generate a sample. Increasingly, computers are being used to generate random numbers. An example of random sampling could be choosing a set of teenagers from all countries across the world. Since teenagers worldwide are assumed to have similar opinions and exhibit similar behavior, this will be a random sample from a homogeneous group.

Exhibit 12.1

Computer-Generated Random Numbers

99	55	62	70	92	44	32
95	17	81	83	83	04	49
39	58	81	09	62	08	66
50	45	60	33	01	07	98
33	12	36	23	47	11	85
63	99	89	85	29	53	93
78	37	87	06	43	97	48
59	73	56	45	65	99	24
52	06	03	04	79	88	44

Stratified Random Sampling

Stratified random sampling, also called proportional sampling, is a two-step process in which accuracy and efficiency is improved relative to simple random sampling. There are factors that divide the population into clear-cut groups or strata and the first step in stratified sampling is to identify these strata. Each of these groups will contain members of the population who are homogeneous to a great extent. The second step is to sample members from each of these relatively homogeneous groups; however, there are marked differences between the groups themselves (e.g., males and females). These differences have to be accounted for when a sample is selected from a population. This can be achieved by stratified sampling. An example would be a car manufacturer trying to find out the factors that are considered most important to new car buyers. Assume that the manufacturer has conducted exploratory studies that revealed that males and females have different criteria for evaluating cars. The population for this study will be all adults of ages 18 and above who are interested in buying a new car in the next calendar year. The population could then be divided into males and females and simple random sampling could be employed for each of these groups.

Stratified Sampling

Stratified sampling can be proportional, that is, the number of members chosen from each group is directly or inversely proportional to the size of the group. However, when the groups are very small, proportional sampling will not provide an adequate sample. In such instances, disproportional samples are used. Stratified sampling ensures that the sample will be representative of the population. It also goes one step further and guarantees that each subgroup in a given population is represented as well, no matter how small the subgroup may be. Stratified sampling is used very frequently in global marketing research. If the study involves understanding the breakfast cereal market in North America, the population would include Canada, the US, and Mexico. The sample will have to include a proportional number of Canadians, Americans, and Mexicans. It is possible to go one step further and stratify the Canadian population based on the eating habits of the various ethnic groups.

Systematic Random Sampling

Systematic random sampling is used in cases where the researcher knows that the list of population members to be sampled is in some order: random, cyclical, or monotonic. Thus, if the population contains 1,000 (= N) people and a sample size of 100 (= n) is desired, every 10th (= I, sampling interval) person is selected for the sample. A starting point could be randomly chosen between the first name and the I-th name initially, and then every I-th name is chosen.

Systematic random sampling is used most frequently in telephone interviews. If the population consists of all people belonging to a given geographic territory and has telephone numbers starting with the same prefix, systematic RDD could be used to obtain a representative sample. If the researcher is interested in conducting telephone surveys in an area where the first three digits of the telephone number (the area code) are 408 and the next three numbers are 560, the possible list of 10,000 telephone numbers that can be surveyed are (408) 560-0000 through (408) 560-9999. Assume that the required sample size is 1,000. Every tenth number in the list could be used starting with a randomly selected phone number between (408) 560-0000 and (408) 560-0010. It has been proved that households with unlisted numbers possess different characteristics from those with phone numbers that are listed in directories. This method eliminates any bias that could be created by ignoring the unlisted numbers in that population.

The one drawback with all the random sampling methods discussed above is geographic coverage. If the population is spread over a wider area, it becomes difficult to obtain a representative sample. This problem can be overcome by using cluster sampling.

Cluster Sampling

Cluster sampling is a technique where the entire population is divided into similar groups, or clusters that are very similar, and each cluster represents a mini-population. A random sample of these clusters is then selected. Once clusters have been selected for sampling, all members in these clusters are surveyed. This is different from stratified sampling in that all members of the cluster that has been selected in the sampling process are interviewed.

Multi-stage Sampling

Multi-stage sampling is performed in several stages. In global marketing research, owing to lack of information and high cost of research, most researchers opt for this sampling technique. Consider a soft drink manufacturer conducting a study to find out the brand awareness of the beverage they manufacture. All the countries where the brand awareness study is to be conducted are first divided into regions that are similar on a predetermined set of attributes, such as per capita income or annual sales of the beverage. These regions are then broken down into countries and the countries are further broken down into cities. Clusters of residential areas are identified in each of these cities. Researchers then draw a random sample of a certain number of clusters depending on the sample size they need. All members in these clusters are surveyed. The results obtained for the selected clusters can be extrapolated to get the awareness figures for the whole region. Depending on the complexity of the information required and the geographic territory that needs to be covered, multi-stage sampling can involve as many as three or four stages. Exhibit 12.2 gives the sample characteristics adopted in census measurement across four countries.

Non-probability Sampling

In non-probability sampling, researchers typically do not develop a sampling frame. As a result, sampling efficiency and precision are absent in these methods; however, they are used in exploratory research, pretesting questionnaires, and surveying homogeneous population. In many global marketing research studies, non-probability sampling methods are used frequently because of the novelty of the research process in these countries. For instance, the research project undertaken to study cellular telephone usage targeted countries like Egypt, Jordan, Saudi Arabia, and the UAE. Even though all these countries may have a very good penetration of cellular telephones, it is not possible to do a random sampling of the target population. It is socially unacceptable for strangers to go knocking on doors asking for information. Non-probability methods are used in these cases. Some of the popular non-probability methods are as follows.

Judgmental sampling

Judgmental sampling is done when the researcher knows the market well enough to choose a sample using expert judgment. For instance, when conducting a survey in a mall to obtain the opinions of working women on a certain cosmetic, interviewers may decide to talk to women who appear to be employed. When conducting surveys in malls, interviewers usually talk to people who appear to be willing to respond. This is based on the assumption that all people coming to that mall have similar attitudes and opinions. This may not always be the case, and the survey may induce a bias. Judgmental sampling is used in cases where the researcher needs quick results. This method can be used with reasonable accuracy when the sample size is very small, like in an exploratory research or a questionnaire pretest.

Exhibit 12.2

Sample Characteristics Used in Census Across Four Countries[4]

Sample Characteristics	Brazil	France	India	USA
Sample design	Systematic sampling of every 2.13 households	Adopts a "Rolling Census." Enumerated each year: 20% of communes under 10,000 population (taken in their entirety); 8% of housing units sampled from communes of 10,000 or more population.	Two-staged, stratified systematic sampling Stage 1: In rural sector, regions are stratified based on population and crop pattern. Census villages are selected from region strata systematically with probability proportional to population. In urban sector, districts are stratified by population. Urban blocks are selected from district strata circular systematically with equal probability. Stage 2: Selected large villages/blocks are split into rural or urban, some of which are randomly selected to form the strata for Stage 2, along with small villages/blocks selected in Stage 1. Households are selected from Stage 2 strata by circular systematically with a random start. Affluent households are over-sampled. The ratio of affluent to other households is 2:8 in rural/urban sector.	–
Sample unit	Households	Private dwellings and individuals in group quarters	Households	Households
Sample fraction (in %)	5	33 (approx.)	0.06	1
Sample Size	9,693,058	19,973,287	602,833	3,061,692

---

[4] *Source*: Compiled from 4 webpages within IPUMS International, Minnesota Population Center, University of Minnesota (https://international.ipums.org/international/). The 4 individual webpages are: Brazil (https://international.ipums.org/international/sample_designs/sample_designs_br.shtml); France (https://international.ipums.org/international/sample_designs/sample_designs_fr.shtml); India (https://international.ipums.org/international/sample_designs/sample_designs_in.shtml); and USA (https://international.ipums.org/international/sample_designs/sample_designs_us.shtml).

Snowball Sampling

Snowball sampling is used when the population consists of individuals in specialized areas. This method starts out with the researcher identifying one individual or unit that has all the population characteristics. This individual is then asked to give a list of names of all others who meet the population characteristics. This method is effective in sampling highly specialized population segments. This is an easy way of sampling segments like astronauts, deep-sea divers, and families with triplets. The drawback in this method is that people who are socially visible tend to get selected. The cellular telephone study that was mentioned at the beginning of this chapter used snowball sampling. This way, the interviewer would start with interviewing one respondent who fits the profile. This respondent would then be asked to provide names and addresses of acquaintances who also meet the requirements for the population. This is the one of the more effective ways to interview women in the Middle East and many Asian countries.

Convenience Sampling

Convenience sampling is used to obtain information quickly and inexpensively. Selection criteria could be as simple as the first few commuters getting of a local subway, students enrolled for a class in a certain university. This method is not very accurate and can be used only in exploratory research.

Quota Sampling

Quota sampling is judgmental sampling with the condition that a certain minimum number be included from each specified subgroup. The subgroups are typically formed on the basis of some demographic variable such as age, sex, location, and income. Consider a research that involves studying the television preferences of teenagers. The researcher wants to sample teenage boys and girls from local schools who visit a mall that is located in the same area. The researcher can work under the assumption that all teenagers who visit the mall attend local schools and are not visiting from another city. If it is known that the percentage of teenage boys in the area is 60% and the required sample size is 300, the researcher should interview 180 teenage boys visiting the mall.

In their haste to meet quotas, researchers sometimes ignore problems that are related to statistical principles. Consider the following example of a study conducted in the US and Canada to evaluate the impact of the free trade agreement on employment. The study will be sampling male and female workers. The distribution of this population in two cities is given in Table 12.1.

TABLE 12.1
POPULATION DISTRIBUTION

	Male	Female	Total	Percent
USA	300	200	500	50
Canada	200	300	500	50
Total	500	500	1,000	100
Percent	50	50	100	

The study requires a sample of 100 people, so researchers decide to go in for 50 Americans and 50 Canadians. Further, they decide to have a sample with 50% males. The quotas could then be as given in Table 12.2. It can be observed in the table that the marginal frequencies—50% and 50%—match; however, the joint frequencies in each cell—30%, 20%, and 30%—do not match. This type of error should be avoided when selecting quotas.

TABLE 12.2
POPULATION QUOTAS

	Male	Female	Total	Percent
USA	50	0	50	50
Canada	0	50	50	50
Total	50	50	100	100
Percent	50	50	100	

Online Sampling

From the start of this book, the plethora of changes that Internet has brought to marketing research has been discussed in context of international marketing. Chapter 6 discussed the benefits of online surveys while conducting international research. Online sampling techniques are an extension to the same discussion. For a researcher, it is critical to understand the source where the sample is being pulled. To obtain a representative sample while conducting an online survey, researchers' understanding of the source of the sample, how it is pulled, and how it is managed during the interviewing process is very important.[5] Some of the types of online samples are discussed below.[6]

- *Web-screened samples:* These are also known as Web intercepts or River samples. These participants are screened and directed to surveys for which they qualify. These are not panelists as the information is limited to what is collected during the screening process. The control is lower and so is the response rate for this sample.
- *List sample:* Like Web-screened sample, the information captured about the respondent is limited. List sample includes participants who agree to receive e-mail messages pertaining to the topic of their interest; however, they still have not agreed to participate in research survey. Similar to Web-screened samples, the control as well as the response rates tend to be low.
- *Database sample:* More and more people are subscribing to database samples. In a database sample, the recruiting company has richer information about the respondents as compared to the above mentioned types. In addition to that, the controls too tend to be better for database sample. The application is not just for research purpose; many companies use database sample for marketing to send out direct marketing communication and attract potential customers to their firms. Again, these are still not the same as panel sample although some databases are positioned as panels. Response rate for database samples tends to be lower than panels.

---

[5] C. Maginnis, "Online Sample—Can You Trust It?" July 2003, http://www.quirks.com/articles/a2003/20030708.aspx (Retrieved in July 2013).

[6] Ibid.

- *Online panels:* The primary purpose of developing an online panel is to conduct online survey research. With the available technology, development, implementation, and maintenance of online panels have increased in recent years. The recruiting company knows detailed information about the panelist, and has control over the project. Further, the response rate tends to be higher as these panelists have volunteered to be a part of the panel. Panelists are incentivized for their participation by the recruiting company.

The availability of online samples makes it lucrative for the companies to conduct online research. Is it always useful? A company should identify the nature of their research before launching an online study. Following questions should be considered:[7]

1. Can the survey be self-administered?
2. Can the information about the product or service be effectively communicated on a computer monitor?
3. Can the target respondent be reached via e-mail?
4. Can members of the cyber-population reflect the client's target market?

If the answers to all of these are positive, then online samples should be sought. A general comparison of survey models is illustrated in Table 12.3.

TABLE 12.3

GENERAL COMPARISON OF SURVEY MODES[8]

Item	Mail	Telephone	Web
Overall Response Rate	Good, with proper incentives	Good, but increasingly more difficult	Good with e-mail invite; poor otherwise
Item Response Rate	Good	Good	Excellent for screen layout, poor to good for scroll layout
Self-Selection Bias	Minor	Minor, but increasingly a problem	Minor using targeted e-mail invite; considerable if simply posted on a web page
Cost	Expensive for large samples; better for smaller samples	Less expensive for larger samples	Normally the least expensive, particularly for large samples
Turnaround Time	Poor	Good	Excellent
Data Entry Accuracy	Requires keypunch verification	Good with CATI system	Excellent with proper layout, plus, can use pop-up verification
Length of Time for Respondent to Complete Surveys	Slow	Reasonable	Can be fast
Open-Ended Responses	Good	Good	Uncertain: Research has found contradictory results

---

[7] C. Maginnis, "Online Sample—Can You Trust It?".

[8] Scott Dimetrosky, Sami Khawaja, and Phil Degens, "Best Practices for Online Survey Research," *Quirks Marketing Research Review*, January 2001.

Advantages and Disadvantages of Sampling Techniques

Simple random sampling is easy to conduct when the required sampling frame and the target population list are available. This is not always the case in global marketing research. Locating people, addresses, and streets can be a complicated task. For instance, in many Asian countries, residences are identified by names rather than numbers. Even when numbers are used, they are not in a sequential order. Many parts of these countries do not have street maps; therefore, simple random sampling may prove very costly and time consuming in global marketing research.

Stratified sampling can be very effective in making the sample representative of the population by giving greater importance to segments of the population who have a more significant impact on the study. However, in the international context, identifying this segment of the population could present problems.

Systematic random sampling works very well with telephone interviews, even in countries that do not have most of the telephone numbers listed. However, it is very difficult to use for mail or personal interviews because obtaining the list of respondents and their mailing addresses could prove very cumbersome in some countries.

Cluster sampling involves surveying only certain subgroups of the selected sample. If the researcher is conducting a study of Germany and decides to sample only major cities like Frankfurt and Berlin, there would significant savings in terms of time and cost. A critical assumption in this method is that the population characteristics of people living in Frankfurt and Berlin are similar. Otherwise, significant bias may be introduced in the study.

Judgment sampling provides an efficient way of obtaining the sample if done by an expert in the area of interest. This is particularly true of industrial marketing research, which calls for in-depth knowledge on the part of the respondent. In countries with low levels of literacy, the researcher is free to sample educated people who are better informed than the general population. The flip side to this method being, in the international context, that the researcher may not always know the market very well. It is also possible that ignoring the vast majority of the population and selecting only certain specific category of respondents may introduce bias in the research study.

Snowball sampling relies primarily on the initial respondents to obtain a list of more respondents. The problem with this technique is that the initial respondents tend to give names of people who are similar to them in terms of demographics. This could lead to the selection of a sample that is not representative of the population.

Convenience sampling is a very simple method where respondents who are willing or are easy to contact are surveyed. The advantage is the low cost of conducting the surveys and availability of information in a very short span of time. However, this method could introduce substantial bias as it may not be representative of the population.

Quota sampling is an appropriate method for surveying people from a specific industry. This method ensures that a representative sample is obtained quickly and with relatively low expense. Since the judgment of the researcher is involved, it is necessary that researchers be knowledgeable of the markets where the study is being conducted. Exhibit 12.3 summarizes a method developed to eliminate the disadvantages of quota sampling.

Online surveys have a huge advantage over offline surveys in terms of cost, speed of completion of survey, and even response rates. However, sample biases and representativeness concerns have been raised by many for online survey samples. Table 12.4 provides a snapshot view of the advantages and disadvantages of some of the earlier discussed techniques.

Exhibit 12.3

Usage of Quota Sampling[9]

A recent study used quota sampling to quantify the use of sunbeds (tanning beds) in young people between the ages 11 and 17 across England, identify geographical variation, and explore patterns of use, including supervision. This study was conducted across six cities—Liverpool, Stoke/Stafford, Sunderland, Bath/Gloucester, Oxford/Cambridge, and Southampton.

The number of interviews carried out in each zip/postcode was decided by the proportion of domestic households in that region relative to the total in the city. Within each zip/postcode, a list of streets was compiled for conducting the interviews. Since the goal of the study was to study the sunbed usage among young adults, obtaining an equal number of boys and girls was essential. To achieve this, interviews were conducted by using an interlocking age within gender quota. The face-to-face interviews were conducted at home or a convenient location, and written parental permission was obtained for children under the age of 14.

Of the 3,101 respondents, the study found that 6% of children had used sunbeds, and 15% of children had not used one but might do so in the future. The usage of sunbeds was significantly higher in the 15–17 years category (11.2%) compared to the 11–14 years category (1.8%). However, the inclination to use a sunbed in the future was higher in younger children (15.6%), compared to the older children (14.1%).

The reasons for not using sunbeds were also identified. The reasons and the responses from the two age categories are: (a) lack of interest (53.4% for 11–14-year-olds versus 55.8% for 15–17-year-olds), (b) health risks (38.7% for 11–14-year-olds versus 46% for 15–17-year-olds), (c) practical reasons such as access to sunbed centers and the expenses associated with it (13.4% for 11–14-year-olds versus 13.5% for 15–17-year-olds), (d) not allowed/advised to do so (6.3% for 11–14-year-olds versus 1.6% for 15–17-year-olds), and (e) other reasons (7.6% for 11–14-year-olds versus 4.1% for 15–17-year-olds).

The study also found that the usage of sunbeds was consistently higher in girls than in boys and in those from lower rather than higher social grades. There was also geographical variation. While the sunbed usage by 11–17-year-olds was higher in Scotland and Wales than in England, across England, the usage was more common in children from the north than the rest of the country.

The study also found the supervision to be inadequate. Across the six cities, around 23% said they had used a sunbed at home and 19% of children used sunbeds in a tanning/beauty salon or gym/leisure center that had not been supervised. Where *supervision* was provided, it was unsatisfactory, with only 37% reporting that they were informed of the risks.

From a sampling techniques standpoint, this study clearly shows the importance of quota sampling that was used to bring out the differences in the usage of sunbeds across age and gender for a specific set of respondents.

[9] Catherine S. Thomson, Sarah Woolnough, Matthew Wickenden, Sara Hiom, and Chris J. Twelves (2010), The BMJ, 340: c877. Retrieved from http://www.bmj.com/content/340/bmj.c877 (accessed on 21 October 2014)

TABLE **12.4**
SAMPLING TECHNIQUES: ADVANTAGES AND DISADVANTAGES[10]

Technique	Descriptions	Advantages	Disadvantages
Volunteer, Accidental, Convenience	Either asking for volunteers, or the consequence of not all those selected finally participating, or a set of subjects who just happen to be available	Inexpensive way of ensuring sufficient numbers of a study	Can be highly unrepresentative
Quota	Select individuals as they come to fill a quota by characteristics proportional to populations	Ensures selection of adequate numbers of subjects with appropriate characteristics	Not possible to prove that the sample is representative of designated population
Snowball	Subjects with desired traits or characteristics give names of further appropriate subjects	Possible to include members of groups where no lists or identifiable clusters even exist (e.g., drug abusers, criminals)	No way of knowing whether the sample is representative of the population
Purposive	Hand-pick subjects on the basis of specific characteristics	Ensures balance of group sizes when multiple groups are to be selected	Samples are not easily defensible as being representative of populations due to potential subjectivity of researcher
Stage	Combination of clusters (randomly selecting clusters) and random or stratified random sampling of individuals	Can make up probability sample by random at stages and within groups; possible to select random sample when population lists are very localized	Complex, combines limitations of cluster and stratified random sampling
Simple Random	Random sample from whole population	Highly representative if all subjects participate; the ideal	Not possible without complete list of population members; potentially uneconomical to achieve; can be disruptive to isolate members from a group; time-scale may be too long, data/sample could change
Stratified Random	Random sample from identifiable groups (strata), subgroups, etc.	Can ensure that specific groups are represented, even proportionally, in the sample(s) (e.g., by gender), by selecting individuals from strata list	More complex, requires greater effort than simple random; strata must be carefully defined

(Table 12.4 Contd)

---

[10] Adapted from T. R. Black, *Doing Quantitative Research in the Social Sciences: An Integrated Approach to Research Design, Measurement, and Statistics* (Thousand Oaks, CA: SAGE Publications, 1999), p. 118.

(Table 12.4 Contd)

Technique	Descriptions	Advantages	Disadvantages
Cluster	Random samples of successive clusters of subjects (e.g., by institution) until small groups are chosen as units	Possible to select randomly when no single list of population members exists, but local lists do; data collected on groups may avoid introduction of confounding by isolating members	Clusters in a level must be equivalent and some natural ones are not for essential characteristics (e.g., geographic: numbers equal, but unemployment rates differ)

DETERMINING THE SAMPLE SIZE

The size of a sample can be determined either by using statistical techniques or through some ad hoc methods. Ad hoc methods are used when a person knows from experience what sample size to adopt or when there are some constraints, such as budgetary constraints, that dictate the sample size. This section discusses a few common ad hoc methods for determining sample size.

Rules of Thumb

One approach to determining sample size is to use some rules of thumb. Researchers suggest that the sample should be large enough so that when it is divided into groups, each group will have a minimum sample size of 100 or more.[11] Suppose that the opinion of people from various countries regarding a computer software package is desired. In particular, estimation is to be made of the percentage who felt that some of the advanced features (which means that the package will be priced substantially higher) are required. Suppose, further, that a comparison is desired among those who: (a) use these features frequently, (b) use the features occasionally, and (c) never use these features. Thus, the sample size should be such that each of these groups has at least 100 people. If the frequent users, the smallest group, are thought to be about 10% of the population, then under simple random sampling a sample size of 1,000 would be needed to generate a group of 100 subjects.

In almost every study, a comparison between groups provides useful information and is often the motivating reason for the study. It is, therefore, necessary to consider the smallest group and to make sure that it is of sufficient size to provide the needed reliability.

In addition to considering comparisons between major groups, the analysis might consider subgroups. For example, there might be an interest in breaking down the group of frequent users by age and comparing the usage by teenagers, young adults, middle-aged persons, and senior citizens. Research also suggests that for such minor breakdowns the minimum sample size in each subgroup should be 20–50.[12] The assumption is that less accuracy is needed for the subgroups. Suppose that the smallest subgroup of frequent users, the experienced pro-

---

[11] Seymour Sudman, *Applied Sampling* (New York: Academic Press, 1976), p. 50.
[12] Ibid.

grammers, is about 1% of the population and it is desired to have 20 in each subgroup. Under simple random sampling, a sample size of about 2,000 might be recommended in this case.

If one of the groups or subgroups of the population is a relatively small percentage of the population, then it is sensible to use disproportionate sampling. Suppose that only 10% of the population watches educational television, and the opinions of this group are to be compared with those of others in the population. If telephone interviewing is involved, people might be contacted randomly until 100 people who do not watch educational television are identified. The interviewing would then continue, but all respondents would be screened, and only those who watch educational television would be interviewed. The result would be a sample of 200, half of who watch educational television.

Budget Constraints

Often, there is a strict budget constraint. A museum director might be able to spare only $500 for a study, and no more. If data analysis will require $100 and a respondent interview is $5, then the maximum affordable sample size is 80. The question then becomes whether a sample size of 80 is worthwhile, or if the study should be changed or simply not conducted.

Comparable Studies

Another approach is to find similar studies and use their sample sizes as a guide. The studies should be comparable in terms of the number of groups into which the sample is divided for comparison purposes. They also should have achieved a satisfactory level of reliability.

Table 12.5, which is based on a summary of several hundred studies, provides a very rough idea of a typical sample size. Note that the typical sample size tends to be larger for national studies than for regional studies. A possible reason is that national studies generally address issues with more financial impact and, therefore, require a bit more accuracy. Note, also, that samples involving institutions tend to be smaller than those involving people or households. The reason is probably that institutions are more costly to sample than people.

TABLE 12.5
TYPICAL SAMPLE SIZES FOR STUDIES OF HUMAN AND INSTITUTIONAL POPULATIONS[13]

No. of Subgroup Analyses	People or Households		Institutions	
	National	Regional or Special	National	Regional or Special
None or few	1,000–1,500	200–500	200–500	50–200
Average	1,500–2,500	500–1,000	500–1,000	200–500
Many	2,500+	1,000+	1,000+	500+

[13] Seymour Sudman, *Applied Sampling*, p. 87. Reprinted by permission.

Factors Determining Sample Size

Sample size really depends on four factors. The first is the number of groups and subgroups within the sample that will be analyzed. The second is the value of the information in the study in general, and the accuracy required of the results in particular. At one extreme, the research need not be conducted if the study is of little importance. The third factor is the cost of the sample. A cost–benefit analysis must be considered. A larger sample size can be justified if sampling costs are low than if sampling costs are high. The final factor is the variability of the population. If all members of the population have identical opinions on an issue, a sample of one is satisfactory. As the variability within the population increases, the sample size also will need to be larger.

Let us assume that we are interested in the attitudes of symphony season-ticket holders toward changing the starting time of weekday performances from 8:00 p.m. to 7:30 p.m. The population comprises the 10,000 symphony season-ticket holders. Of these ticket holders, 3,000 respond "Definitely yes" (which is coded as +2). Another 2,000 would respond "Prefer yes" (coded as +1), and so on. The needed information is the average, or mean, response of the population (the 10,000 season-ticket holders), which is termed as μ:

$$\mu = \text{population mean} = 0.3$$

This population mean is one population characteristic of interest. Normally, it is unknown, and our goal is to determine its value as closely as possible, by taking a sample from the population.

Another population characteristic of interest is the population variance, σ^2, and its square root, the population standard deviation (σ). The population variance is a measure of the population dispersion, the degree to which the different season-ticket holders differ from one another in terms of their attitude. It is based on the degree to which a response differs from the population average response (μ). This difference is squared (making all values positive) and averaged across all responses. In our example, the population variance is

$$\sigma^2 = \text{population variance} = 2.22$$

and

$$\sigma = \text{population standard deviation} = 1.49$$

The problem is that the population mean is not known but must be estimated from a sample. Assume that a simple random sample of size 10 is taken from the population. The 10 people selected and their respective attitudes are shown in Table 12.6.

Just as the population has a set of characteristics, each sample also has a set of characteristics. One sample characteristic is the sample average, or mean:

$$\overline{X} = \frac{1}{10} \sum_{j=1}^{10} X_j = 0.5$$

Two means have now been introduced, and it is important to keep them separate. One is the population mean (μ), a population characteristic. The second is the sample mean, $\overline{X}$, a sample

TABLE 12.6
ATTITUDE OF BROADWAY TICKET HOLDERS

Nakamichi	$X_1 = +1$
John S.	$X_2 = +2$
Paula R.	$X_3 = +2$
Francois T.	$X_4 = 0$
Werner R.	$X_5 = +1$
Vinod K.	$X_6 = +1$
Amir K.	$X_7 = -1$
Jose F.	$X_8 = +1$
Spiros M.	$X_9 = -2$
Zhang T.	$X_{10} = 0$

characteristic. Because $\overline{X}$ is a sample characteristic, it will change if a new sample is obtained. The sample mean $\overline{X}$ is used to estimate the unknown population mean (μ).

Another sample characteristic or statistic is the sample variance (s^2), which can be used to estimate the population variance (s^2). Under simple random sampling, the sample variance is

$$s^2 = \frac{1}{n-1} \sum_{j=1}^{n} (X_j - \overline{X})^2 = 1.61$$

Note that s^2 will be small if the sample responses are similar, and large if they are spread out. The corresponding sample standard deviation is simply

$$S = \text{sample standard deviation} = \sqrt{s^2} \rightarrow = 1.27$$

Again, it is important to make a distinction between the population variance (σ^2) and the sample variance (s^2).

Of course, all samples will not generate the same value of $\overline{X}$ (or s). If another simple random sample of size 10 were taken from the population, $\overline{X}$ might be 0.3 or 1.2 or 0.4, or whatever. The point is that $\overline{X}$ will vary from sample to sample.

Intuitively, it is reasonable to believe that the variation in $\overline{X}$ will be larger as the variance in the population σ^2 is larger. At one extreme, if there is no variation in the population, there will be no variation in $\overline{X}$. It also is reasonable to believe that as the size of the sample increases, the variation in $\overline{X}$ will decrease. When the sample is small, it takes only one or two extreme scores to substantially affect the sample mean, thus generating a relatively large or small $\overline{X}$. As the sample size increases, these extreme values will have less impact when they do appear, because they will be averaged with more values. The variation in $\overline{X}$ is measured by its standard error, which is

$$\sigma_{\overline{X}} = \text{standard error of } X = \sigma_x/\sqrt{n} = 1.49/\sqrt{10} = 0.47$$

($\sigma_{\overline{X}}$ can be written simply as σ). Note that the standard error of $\overline{X}$ depends on n, the sample size. If n is altered, the standard error will change accordingly, as Table 12.7 shows.

TABLE 12.7

INCREASING SAMPLE SIZE

Sample Size	$\sigma_{\overline{X}}$	$\sigma_{\overline{X}} = \sigma_x \Big/ \sqrt{n}$
10	1.49	0.470
40	1.49	0.235
100	1.49	0.149
500	1.49	0.067

Now we are finally ready to use these concepts to help determine sample size. To proceed, the analyst must specify size of the sampling error that is desired and the confidence level; for example, the 95% confidence level.

This specification will depend on a trade-off between the value of more accurate information and the cost of an increased sample size. For a given confidence level, a smaller sampling error will *cost* in terms of a larger sample size. Similarly, for a given sampling error, a higher confidence level will *cost* in terms of a larger sample size. These statements will become more tangible in the context of some examples.

Using the general formula for the interval estimate (recall that s and s_x are the same),

$$\overline{X} \pm \text{sampling error, or } \overline{X} \pm z\sigma_x/\sqrt{n}$$

we know that

$$\text{Sampling error} = z\sigma/\sqrt{n}$$

Dividing through by the sampling error and multiplying by $\sqrt{n}$

$$\sqrt{n} = z\sigma/(\text{sampling error})$$

and squaring both sides, we get an expression for sample size

$$n = z^2\sigma^2/(\text{sampling error})^2$$

Thus, if we know the required confidence level, and, therefore, z, and also know the allowed sampling error, then the needed sample size is specified by the formula.

Let us assume that we need to have a 95% confidence level and that our sampling error in estimating the population mean does not exceed 0.3. In this case, the sampling error = 0.3, and, because the confidence level is 95%, $z = 2$. The population standard deviation is 1.49, so the sample size should be

$$n = 2^2(1.49)^2/(0.3)^2 = 98.7 \approx 99$$

If the confidence level is changed from 95% to 90%, the sample size can be reduced, because we do not have to be as certain of the resulting estimate. The z term is then 5/3 and the sample size is

$$n = (z\sigma)^2/(\text{sampling error})^2 = (5/3)^2(1.49)^2/(0.3)^2 = 68.5 \approx 69$$

If the allowed error is increased, the sample size will also decrease, even if a 95% confidence level is retained. In our example, if the allowed error is increased to 0.5, then the sample size is

$$n = (z\sigma)^2/(\text{sampling error})^2 = 4(1.49)^2/(0.5)^2 = 35.5 \approx 36$$

It should be noted that the sample size calculation is independent of the size of the population. A common misconception is that a *good* sample should include a relatively high percentage of the sampling frame. Actually, the size of the sample will be determined in the same manner, whether the population is 1,000 or 1,000,000. There should be no concern that the sample contains a reasonable percentage of the population. Of course, if the population is small, the sample size can be reduced. Obviously, the sample size should not exceed the population.

Determining the Population Standard Deviation

The procedure just displayed assumes that the population standard deviation is known. In most practical situations, it is not known, and it must be estimated by using one of several available approaches.

One method is to use a sample standard deviation obtained from a previous comparable survey or from a pilot survey. Another approach is to estimate *s* subjectively. Suppose the task is to estimate the income of a community. It might be possible to say that 95% of the people will have a monthly income of between $4,000 and $20,000. Assuming a normal distribution, there will be four population standard deviations between the two figures, so that one population standard deviation will be equal to $4,000.

Another approach is to take a *worst-case* situation. In our example, the largest population variance would occur if half the population would respond with a +2 and the other half with a −2. The population variance would then be 4. The recommended sample size, at a 95% confidence level and a 0.3 allowable error, would be 178. Note that the sample size would be larger than desired, and, thus, the desired accuracy would be exceeded. The logic is that it is acceptable to err on the side of being too accurate.

Proportions

When proportions are to be estimated (the proportion of people with negative feelings about a change in the symphony's starting time, for example), the procedure is to use the sample proportion to estimate the unknown population proportion, π. Because this estimate is based on a sample, it has a population variance, namely,

$$\sigma^2_p = \pi(1-\pi)/n$$

where
π = population proportion
p = sample proportion (corresponding to X), used to estimate the unknown

$\sigma^2{}_p$ = population variance of p.
The formula for sample size is then

$$n = z^2 \, \pi(1-\pi)/(\text{sampling error})^2$$

As Figure 12.2 shows, the worst case (where the population variance is at its maximum) occurs when the population proportion is equal to 0.50:

$$\pi(1-\pi) = 0.25$$
$$\pi = 0.50$$

FIGURE 12.2

A GRAPH OF π $(1-\pi)$

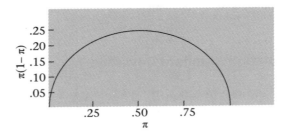

Because the population proportion is unknown, a common procedure is to assume the worst case. The formula for sample size then simplifies to

$$n = z^2 \, (0.25)/(\text{sampling error})^2$$

Thus, if the population proportion is to be estimated within an error of 0.05 (or 5 percentage points) at a 95% confidence level, the needed sample size is

$$n = 2^2(0.25)/(0.05)^2 = 400$$

since z equals 2, corresponding to a 95% confidence level, and the allowed sampling error equals 0.05. Figure 12.3 summarizes the two sample size formulas.

FIGURE 12.3

SOME USEFUL SAMPLE SIZE FORMULAS

In general,
sample size = $n = z^2 \sigma^2 \div (\text{sampling error})^2$
where,
$z = 2$ for a 95% confidence interval
$z = 5/3$ for a 90% confidence interval
σ = population standard deviation
and
sampling error = allowed sampling error
For proportions,
sample size $= n = z^2 (0.25) \div (\text{sampling error})^2$

Sampling error (also known as *accuracy* or *precision error*) can be defined in relative rather than absolute terms. In other words, a researcher might require that the sample estimate be within plus or minus G percentage points of the population value. Therefore,

$$D = G\mu$$

The sample size formula may be written as

$$n = \sigma^2 z^2 / (\text{sampling error})^2$$

where

$$c = (\sigma/\mu)$$

which is known as the *coefficient of variation*.

Several Questions

A survey instrument or an experiment will usually not be based on just one question— sometimes hundreds can be involved. It will usually not be worthwhile to go through such a process for all questions. A reasonable approach is to pick a few representative questions and determine the sample size from them. The most crucial ones with the highest expected variance should be included.

Cost–Benefit Analysis

Selection of the sampling procedure is an issue that needs great deal of attention in global marketing research. Owing to the national differences, sampling procedures have different degrees of reliability in different countries. Therefore, it is important for the researcher to use the procedure that is most effective in the country of interest. In a multi-country study, it is not necessary to use one method across all countries. It may be preferable to use different methods or procedures that provide equivalent sampling reliability. It is important for the researcher to focus on comparability in terms of response rates and quality of responses. The specific method that is used is secondary. There will also be considerable difference in costs when different sampling methods are used. It is possible that standardizing the sampling methods results in centralized coding and analysis; however, the benefits of standardization may be far outweighed by the costs incurred in administering a specific sampling plan or due to loss of accuracy in sampling. For instance, if the research study called for random sampling in all countries, the cost of obtaining lists of potential respondents may be exorbitant in some countries. In such cases, the researcher should compromise on the sampling technique and opt for the method that is most cost-efficient while maintaining the accuracy and reliability of the study.

SAMPLING EQUIVALENCE

In global marketing research, it is important to make sure that the samples drawn from different countries are comparable. The stress is not on equivalence of the method used or the profile from which the sample has been drawn, but rather on the equivalence of the information collected from the sample. Two different aspects need to be taken care of to ensure this.

The first step is to decide who should be contacted for the survey and whether the study needs to have a single respondent or multiple respondents within a household. This is typically dependent on the decision-making process involved and could vary widely among countries. A decision that is made by an individual in one country could be made jointly by two or more people in some other country. In the corporate world, decisions are made at different levels in the corporate ladder. The target segment could vary among countries. All these differences have to be accounted for if the population sampled is to yield results that can be compared across borders. Examples for this aspect of sampling are numerous. For instance, the decision to make a large investment would be a joint decision with most married couples in the US. In the Middle East, however, women are not consulted in such matters. If the study involves asking respondents about their investment habits, to get complete information, we need to talk to both the partners in the US, while it is sufficient to survey the male partner in the Middle East. Children have a major say in a lot of purchase decisions in the US, while this is not likely so in many other countries. This goes to show that different categories of people will have to be surveyed to obtain similar information.

The second issue deals with the extent to which the sample is representative of the population. In most developed countries, information regarding potential markets and sampling frames is easily available. However, in Japan, the residential list that was most popularly used in sampling studies has been made inaccessible to researchers.[14] Developing countries do not have such extensive databases and so obtaining the sampling frame to suit the needs of the research could be difficult. Researchers will have to employ different methods in different countries to obtain representative samples. In remote parts of certain developing countries where literacy levels are low, researchers have to survey folks who are reasonably well educated. This automatically induces a bias, as the portion of the population not surveyed will be substantially different. In situations like this, judgment sampling or snowball sampling is more effective. The other part of this issue is whether the data from one segment or country can be extrapolated to other countries or segments. It is possible to group countries into clusters based on demographic and psychographic similarities. Sampling results can be extrapolated for such clusters. Many researchers use the Nielson Regions for this purpose; however, extrapolation at national level may produce significant bias in global marketing research.

CULTURAL ISSUES

Identifying the right kind of sampling and using the appropriate sampling method for a global marketing research project depends on a number of factors, the foremost of which would be the cultural differences in these countries. There are several practical problems faced by the researcher. A research study conducted for a software development company based in the US

---

[14] Kazuaki Katori, "Recent Developments and Future Trends in Marketing Research in Japan Using New Electronic Media," *Journal of Advertising Research* (1990), vol. 12, pp. 53–57.

highlights all these issues. The study involved finding the market potential for software applications in Great Britain, Germany, Japan, France, and Belgium. The target sample was the chief information officers, system managers, and system development professionals of major companies in all these countries. The main issue was to find the equivalent sample in all these countries. There was the option of sampling people with identical or similar titles; however, this would not have provided information that can be compared across all five countries. The first step in this study was to understand the responsibilities and job descriptions of each of the categories that need to be sampled. The next step was to identify professionals who perform similar functions and carry similar job responsibilities in all these countries, irrespective of the job titles. The responses from this sample could be compared across countries. In the end, it helps to pay attention to sampling design issues without getting too obsessed with them.[15]

MODIFICATIONS REQUIRED FOR DEVELOPING COUNTRIES[16]

It is a lot more difficult for researchers to obtain samples in developing countries because of nonexistent or poor sampling frames. Most of these countries do not have registers, age and sex breakdowns, telephone directories, maps, or numbering on dwelling units. It is very difficult to get details of universal characteristics from which a meaningful sample can be drawn. Even if any of the above resources are available, they are very outdated and inaccurate. Due to lack of sampling resources, it is possible that large segments of the population are excluded from the sampling process. An example would be Brazil, where Rio de Janeiro and São Paulo have different sampling frames because sampling resources tend to be distributed differentially throughout the country. A *national urban sample* combining these different sampling frames in different cities is likely to yield less than perfectly accurate results. An additional problem in rapidly growing cites is maintaining adequate sampling frames. The expense involved in keeping them up-to-date is prohibitively high. In many cases, it becomes very important to specify terms, such as the exact meaning of a dwelling unit in the given research context. Consequently, coverage and comparability of existing sampling frames in developing countries often leave much to be desired and modifications in the sampling procedure are necessary.

Important fallout of this is that convenience, judgment, quota, and snowball sampling are used more frequently in developing countries than probability sampling methods. They are more cost effective and yield better results than probability sampling methods. Convenience sampling, though the cheapest method, is not likely to be very effective. Judgment sampling in these countries is based on the assumption that some members are better informed than others. An example would be asking the opinions of the village head, the priest, or any other local authority and assuming these opinions reflect that of the territory. Quota sampling requires that the researcher have some idea about the region to set aside quotas in a logical manner. Snowball sampling obtains a list of people to be interviewed from one interviewee. The best way to work out a sampling plan for developing countries is for the researcher to observe and devise their own sampling frames.

Another important factor that needs to be considered for developing countries is that the markets are likely to be more fragmented, different markets within developing countries.

---

[15] Uma Sekharan, "Methodological and Theoretical Issues and Advancements in Cross-Cultural Research," *Journal of International Business Studies* 4 (1991): 711–721.

[16] Kinsey, *Marketing in Developing Countries.*

Each sample should be representative of the population that represents a potential market. An example could be widely varying income levels in a given geographic territory. It becomes necessary to choose an appropriate clustering procedure.

GLOBAL MARKETING RESEARCH IN PRACTICE

Sampling is a very important aspect of the marketing research process and has a big impact on the validity of results. In the international scenario, this tends to be crucial because of the lack of information available to the researcher. This section attempts to help researchers avoid some common pitfalls of sampling with the help of examples from practical research problems conducted in the past.

A refrigerator manufacturer is interested in understanding the decision-making process involved in purchasing one in several countries around the world. Some of the countries identified for the research process are the US, Great Britain, and Indonesia. An appropriate sampling method has to be decided for each of these countries. In the US and Great Britain, researchers decide to opt for random sampling of households in a geographically dispersed manner such that the sample is representative of these countries as a whole. The logic behind this decision is fairly clear—almost every household in these two countries has a refrigerator and so the probability of reaching a household that does not own one is negligible. It is also very easy to obtain a list of names and phone numbers in both these countries. Consider the case of Indonesia, where random sampling would be impossible due to low percentage of refrigerator ownership. A more appropriate method will be snowball sampling or convenience sampling. There is also the problem of obtaining the names and addresses of all the people to be contacted.

Selecting a sampling frame could also be a complicated decision in many countries. Consider the case of a financial services company wanting to evaluate customer satisfaction in various countries. For a researcher in the US, this would be a simple task—design a questionnaire that would allow customers to rate the company on different aspects of customer service. This questionnaire could then be administered to customers; however, in some countries, this simple procedure could prove very difficult to implement. In Brazil, the survey will be completely unsuccessful because any survey pertaining to personal finances is perceived as an audit by the tax department. In some Middle Eastern countries, the male members of the household make all the investment decisions, so even if the records indicate a female client, it would be useful to contact the spouse or the guardian. The sampling frame has to be redefined depending on the decision-making process. In most third world countries, the concept of service is alien to customers and companies. Anything beyond basic service is considered a favor bestowed upon the customer. In such situations, questioning customers on service aspects does not make any sense.

Anticipating changes in economic, political, and social setup in different countries is very important to research studies, especially to sampling. A survey conducted to study public opinion in the former Soviet Union is an example.[17] Researchers anticipated the break-up of the Soviet Union and that the Baltic States would leave the Union. As these states were too small make a major impact on the results, researchers decided to exclude them from the study.

---

[17] James L. Gibson, "Mass Opposition to the Soviet Putsch of August 1991: Collective Action, Rational Choice, and Democratic Values in the Former Soviet Union," *American Political Review* 91, no. 3 (1993), pp. 671–684.

A thorough understanding of the country is required even before the decision to choose a sampling method is considered.

In this section, we present a practical research problem with emphasis on the sampling method adopted for an international market.[18] Psychographics is an approach used to define and measure the lifestyles of consumers. It is a popular method employed by advertisers and marketers because it can provide more detailed information about consumers then basic demographic variables. Psychographic research involves two phases: the first phase includes determining the appropriate psychographic statements; the second phase focuses on developing a typology of consumers. A key factor is to capitalize consumer differences by identifying segments of consumers who differ significantly within the population, while also identifying consumers who display similar behavior.

This study had two objectives. The first was to generate the psychographic dimensions of various customers in India and Taiwan, and the second was to develop a typology of female consumers based on their psychographic patterns. The chosen sample was restricted to working females between the ages of 18 and 35. The reason for selecting this age group is that it constitutes a relatively large percentage of the female population in the three regions, as well as appearing to be a very lucrative market segment.

Previous studies conducted in India identified five distinct segments on the basis of respondents' income and professional levels. These are listed in Exhibit 12.4. Similar studies conducted in Taiwan provided eight different segments, listed in Exhibit 12.5.

Exhibit 12.4

Segmentation in India[19]

Segment	Characteristics
Deprived	Comprised of individuals who are primarily living under the poverty line. Typically consists of unskilled laborers, and individuals who work on a part-time or seasonal basis.
Aspirers	Consists of low-wage earners and small-time vendors. Much of the money spent by these individuals is on basic necessities.
Seekers	Most diverse group of individuals, ranging from government employees to self-employed individuals. The diversity also pertains to other characteristics such as age, education, and attitudes.
Strivers	Comprised of many successful professionals, bureaucrats, government officials, and farmers. Most individuals in the group have a significant amount of savings, and are generally labeled as the beginning benchmark for successful people in India.
Global Indians	Generally includes owners of large businesses, politicians, and executives of major corporations. Beginning to include graduates from some of India's top educational institutions.

[18] Jackie L. M. Tam and Susan H. C. Tai, "The Psychographic Segmentation of the Female Market in Greater China," *International Marketing Review* 15, no. 1 (1998): 61–77.

[19] Adapted from Jonathan Ablett et al., "The 'Bird of Gold': The Rise of India's Consumer Market," McKinsey Global Institute, May 2007 (Retrieved on October 20, 2014).

Exhibit 12.5

Segmentation in Taiwan[20]

Segment	Characteristics
Traditional Homebodies	Less affluent, had little interest in buying or trying new products; about 16% of the population
Confident Traditionalists	Middle-aged, predominantly male group; had a high self-image and a keen sense of social norms and expectations (12%)
Discontented Moderns	Relatively affluent and younger; tended to follow Japanese and Western trends but maintained a number of traditional attitudes (17%)
Rebellious Youths	Generally aged between 15 and 24 with a strong sense of individualism; impulsive buyers when it came to things that aroused their interest (7%)
Young Strivers	Average age of 29; competitive and materialistic natures; appeared to be the most likely group to succeed in future (13%)
Middle-Class Hopefuls	Average 31 years; moderate spenders and willing to take a few risks with their finances (8%)
Family-Centered Fatalists	Primarily females aged 42 years. Not particularly affluent; tended to live slower-paced lives (13%)
Lethargics	Average age of 32; did not stand out in any way but were buyers of mass consumer products (14%)

While consumers in Taiwan were primarily categorized by geographical factors, the segmentation of customers is India was done primarily on an income-level basis. Despite having decreased in size over the past two decades, a significant portion of the customers in India were comprised of individuals living under the poverty line. In addition, the percentage of Indians that were categorized as *elite*, despite having increase in size by over tenfold, continued to make up less than 2%.

The questionnaire design was completed after reviewing a lot of literature. The final version of the questionnaire consisted of three parts. The first part comprised interest and opinion statements, the second part contained frequency of participation activity statements, and the third part consisted of items relating to demographic information. The selection of lifestyle statements was based on three criteria: they had to be relevant to females, valuable to marketers, and measurable.

The target population were working individuals with a majority of those targeted in Taiwan, being women between the ages of 18 and 35. The objective was to obtain three groups of females who were matched in terms of age characteristics rather than in the representativeness

[20] From "Research note: Psychographic segmentation of the female market in greater China", by Jackie L.M.Tam and Ms. Susan Tai in International Marketing Review, Vol. 15, Iss. 1, 1998. Reprinted by permission of MCB University Press.

of the working female population in each region. The majority of the respondents from Taiwan were found to be single with more than 60% having attained university education. This could be accounted for by the fact that job markets in India and Taiwan are very competitive. The researchers performed factor analysis and cluster analysis on the data. Each of these methods is explained in detail in Chapter 15.

SUMMARY

This chapter deals in depth with the sampling procedures that can be made use of in global marketing research. Researchers choose a subset of elements from the population and from this subset called the sample. A sampling distribution is the probability distribution of the statistic. If the difference between the population parameter and sample statistic is only because of sampling, this is called sampling error. If there is a difference between the population parameter and the sampling statistic that is not due to sampling error, it is called non-sampling error. If the sampling frame chosen is smaller than the population, some members of the population are not sampled, and, hence, the research study does not consider their tastes and attitudes. This is called a subset problem. If the sampling frame is larger than the population, we have a superset problem. Sampling methods can be classified as probability sampling and non-probability sampling. In probability sampling, each member of the population has a known probability of being selected. The chapter discusses in detail many different probability and non-probability sampling methods and the advantages and disadvantages of each of these methods. The chapter also explains the statistical basis for the selection of a sample size and the means of achieving sampling equivalence in global marketing research. It is important to note that defining the population, choosing a sampling frame, and selecting a sampling procedure are very country-specific and are constrained by the resources available.

QUESTIONS AND PROBLEMS

1. A city council is concerned about the low usage of its city transit system by its residents. To determine how the transit system can increase its patronage, the council plans to sample all people who have the regular-rider monthly pass for the transit system. Comment.
2. A soft drink manufacturer is planning to introduce a new flavor in their Asian markets. They are confident that 25% of the population will buy it. A critical question is how frequently buyers will use it. A judgment has been made that 95% of them will use it between 1 and 17 times per month. On that basis, the population standard deviation is estimated to be 4.
   a. Explain how the standard deviation estimate was obtained.
   b. What sample size is required if an accuracy of ±1 is needed at the 90% level, and at the 95% level? (The sampling error should not exceed 1.)
   c. Repeat (b) for an accuracy of ±0.4
   d. What considerations should be introduced in selecting the confidence level and desired accuracy?

3. Develop a population list or sampling frame for an attitude study when the target population is:
   a. All those who rode on a public transit system during the last month in New York
   b. Retail sporting goods stores in London
   c. Stores that sell tennis rackets in India
   d. Watchers of evening television in Brazil.
4. When operating in a developing country such as India that is characterized by polarized income levels and buying habits, how would you establish sampling equivalence?
5. For research studies across countries,
   a. How does the sampling procedure employed in an international environment differ from that used domestically?
   b. What are the relevant issues to be considered before a researcher can decide to use the same sampling procedure across countries?
6. A pet food manufacturer wanted to get opinions from 4,000 pet store managers on a new type of dog food. An associate provided a list of such stores, divided into 400 large and 3,600 small stores. He drew a random sample of 200 stores and was disappointed to find only 19 large stores in the sample, since they represented more than 30% of the potential volume. A friend suggested that he draw a second sample. What do you recommend? What other pieces of information would you like to have?
7. Good Foods Inc., an organic grocery store operating in a fast growing city with a population of 100,000 in a developing country, is planning on offering door-delivery of grocery purchases. Currently, the store serves customers within a 10-mile radius of the store. In the proposed service, the store guarantees same-day delivery. The store believes that this move will enable them to increase their customer base.
   a. What sampling frame would the owner use to establish how many households lie within this delivery area?
   b. It was found that 1,000 households are within the current delivery area, which is 5% of the total number of households in the city. The store management wants to conduct this study throughout the city, and has decided to collect a random sample of 2,000 households.
   c. What percentage of the total population will be represented in the sample?
   d. Recommend a sampling method that is most suitable for this study, and support your answer.
8. Discuss the differences between proportionate and disproportionate stratified sampling.

Section III

Data Analysis and
Reporting the Results

13 | **Simple Data Analysis   303**

14 | **Advanced Data Analysis   322**

15 | **Multivariate Data Analysis   346**

16 | **Presenting the Results   366**

13

CHAPTER _____

Simple Data Analysis

INTRODUCTION

Data analysis is the researcher's means of converting the information collected into defensible actionable sets of conclusions and reports. Once the data has been collected, appropriate data analysis methods have to be chosen. The choice of the method depends on the type of data collected—some data analysis methods require certain specific types of data.

It is pertinent to remember that data analysis tools help researchers quantify findings. The accuracy of the study, however, rests on the research design. Data analysis cannot be called upon to rescue a badly designed study.

Data analysis has several advantages. It can help researchers develop insights into a seemingly unrelated set of variables and numbers. These insights can help prevent managers from making erroneous decisions that could lead to financial disasters. It also helps maintain continuity in the research process to the extent that it helps researchers analyze and understand work done by others.

DATA PREPARATION[1]

The basic steps to be followed for data analysis in global marketing research are the same as those for domestic research. The first step is data preparation. This involves logging the data, checking data for accuracy, editing if required, entering the data into the computer, transforming the data, and developing and documenting a database structure.

Data Logging

In any research project, responses from various sources come in at different times. It is very important that all this data be stored in a single location until the researcher is ready to analyze the data. The most preferred way of doing this is to set up some kind of database and append information as responses keep trickling in. It is also necessary to retain the original response sheet and give each one an ID (an identification symbol, such as a number) so that verification becomes easier if the response sheet needs to be cross-checked at the data editing stage.

_____

[1] William Trochim, "Data Preparation," October 2006, http://www.socialresearchmethods.net/kb/statprep.php (Retrieved in October 2014).

Data Editing

Data editing is performed to identify omissions, ambiguities, and errors in responses. These errors can result from a number of sources. The interviewer could have missed out on some instructions, thereby inducing error in the responses. Responses sometimes fail to answer certain sections or specific questions, inadvertently or deliberately. The response might not be legible. There could be logical inconsistencies in the responses filled out by respondents. There may be cases where the respondents are not eligible to participate in the study.

The preferred method of solving these problems is by contacting the respondents again.[2] In global marketing research projects, where the costs of primary data collection are prohibitively high, this could prove to be an impractical solution. The next best alternative is to throw out the questionnaires that are flawed in some manner, and it is apparent that the respondent has not understood the purpose of the study. A less extreme measure is to discard only those questions that are unacceptable and retain the responses to the remainder of the questionnaire. It is also possible to extrapolate the results for certain questions by using the mean profile values.

Data Coding

Coding the questionnaire involves identifying the respondents and the variables used in the survey. It is mandatory that every research project have a coding sheet that describes the data and where it is located. Description of data should contain information such as:

- Name of the variable
- What the variable represents in the research project
- The format of the variable—data, currency, text, etc.
- The units used to describe the variable—dollars, kilograms, etc.
- The location of the variable in the database
- The ID of the response sheet from where the value is obtained
- Any other notes if necessary

Coding close-ended questions is a lot easier than coding open-ended questions.[3] In case of open-ended questions, the researcher has to generate a list of all possible responses that can be expected for that question. If the responses do not match properly, the researcher has to exercise judgment and place the responses in one of the previously listed categories. In an international market research study, this tends to be more complicated because it may be very difficult to generate the initial list of all possible responses owing to differences in purchasing and product usage habits. Even if such a list were generated, because of differences in language and use of idioms, it may be difficult for the researcher to classify responses into one of the categories in the list.

---

[2] Naresh K. Malhotra, "Analyzing Marketing Research Data with Incomplete Information on the Dependent Variable," *Journal of International Marketing Research* 24.1 (1987): 74–84.

[3] For additional details, please refer Philip S. Siedel, "Coding," in *Handbook of Marketing Research*, ed., Robert Ferber (New York: McGraw-Hill, 1974); Pamela L. Alreck and Robert B. Settle, *The Survey Research Handbook* (Homewood, IL: Richard D. Irwin, 1985), pp. 254–286.

Another aspect that needs to be paid attention to in global marketing research is coordination of coding patterns across countries so that the different categories are harmonized. This is achieved by deciding the guidelines for coding in a centralized location and having local agencies implement equivalent versions of the same in their individual countries. The central office has to verify the coding sheet before using it for analysis. Once the response sheet has been coded, the data can be entered into the computer. It is preferable to proofread the data to make sure there are no errors.

Data Adjustment

Raw data is rarely used in marketing research. Data transformation is a mandatory step in every research project. Some of the more common data transformation methods are discussed below.

In many cases, respondents do not provide answers to all the questions in the questionnaire. There could be several reasons for this ranging from oversight to reluctance in divulging information to sensitive topics. The method of treating this missing data depends on the research project. In many cases, it is simply ignored and analysis is carried on with other available data. Some statistical packages require that a certain value, such as 0, be entered to indicate a missing value. This has to be checked prior to using the package.

When designing scales for a questionnaire, researchers tend to reverse the scale categories for some questions to prevent bias in responses. For instance, there could be one question that asks the respondent to give a score of 5 for the most preferred category and 1 for the least preferred category. In another question, the researcher may reverse this and ask the respondent to give 1 for the most preferred and 5 for the least preferred. When conducting data analysis, all this data needs to be coded uniformly so that all the least preferred values are represented in the same manner, as are the most preferred values. Data needs to be adjusted for this.

Another aspect that will have to be taken care of is combining categories. In certain data analysis techniques that are discussed later, it will be observed that each category needs to have a certain minimum number of observations for the statistical test to yield significant results. Hence, if the sample size is not large enough, to meet these requirements, two or more categories have to be combined. In a questionnaire containing the following question:

What is your annual income?

- Less than $20,000
- $20,000–$39,999
- $40,000–$59,999
- $60,000–$79,999
- $80,000–$99,999
- $100,000 or above

if the responses in any or all of these categories are found to be less than the statistically required number, the categories can be combined so that the requirements are met. The new list of categories could be

- Less than $20,000
- $20,000–$59,999

- $60,000–$99,999
- $100,000 or above

Data should also be checked for reliability, implying that the researcher should verify from experts if the data is acceptable given the specific country or culture. This becomes a necessity in countries or contexts where little or no prior research has been done. In case of multi-country research, where the instrument has been adopted to suit different cultures, because of linguistic and conceptual differences, data collected may not be reliable across all countries. Checking for reliability becomes critical in global marketing research, even though it is usually expensive and time-consuming. Data should also be checked for equivalency of currency measures, metric equivalence, and numerical equivalence.

Statistical adjustment is done so that the quality of the data is enhanced. There are many procedures available to the researcher to statistically adjust data and some of them are mentioned below.

Weighting is a procedure by which each response in the database is assigned a number so that the response can be more representative of the population.[4] If the researcher is aware of the population characteristics that are of interest to the study, it is possible to give weights according to some predetermined rules. For instance, the researcher can decide to attach higher weights to responses from heavy users of a product so that their opinions are given more importance.

Variable re-specification is a procedure in which existing variables are modified to create new variables or a given set of variables is collapsed to create fewer variables. Creating new variables can be achieved by taking a ratio of two existing variables, using the square root or log of an existing variable or using dummy variables. Dummy variables are used mainly to classify qualitative variables.

Scale transformation is another common data adjustment procedure used and it involves manipulation of scale values to ensure comparability with other scales. Standardization is a popular scale transformation technique. This method enables researchers to compare widely varying data.[5] If it were hypothesized that sales of a product are dependent on two variables—advertising dollars and price. If the researcher were to run a regression using data on both these variables, the statistical package would give the regression equation. However, it would be difficult to state the impact of each of these individual variables on the product sales, as they would be in different units. The regression equation could be altered by changing the units on one or both these variables. Hence, researchers use standardizing to eliminate the effect of the units used. Mathematically, this is achieved by subtracting the values from the mean and dividing the difference by the standard deviations. This can be applied only to interval or ratio scaled data.

DATA ANALYSIS

The first step in data analysis is to identify each variable independent of other variables. This is done by tabulating the data. Tabulation helps the researcher understand the distribution of variables and calculates some key descriptive statistics.

---

[4] For additional details on weighting, please refer Trevor Sharot, "Weighting Survey Results," *Journal of the Marketing Research Society* 28 (July 1986): 269–284.

[5] Ronald E. Frank, "Use of Transformations," *Journal of Marketing Research* 3.3 (1996): 247–253.

Descriptive statistics generated during the tabulation phase fall under three categories. The first category represents the central tendency of the variable. This could be represented by the mean, the mode, or the median. The second category represents dispersion. This is estimated using the range, variation (or standard deviation), and the coefficient of variation. The third category represents the shape of the distribution and is measured using skewness or kurtosis.

Descriptive statistics are useful in summarizing large sets of data. However, there is loss of information as one single number is used to communicate all the information related to an entire data set. These statistics are used extensively for nominally scaled variables. When relations among and between nominally scaled variables are of interest, cross-tabulations are used. Cross-tabulation is considered an integral part of data analysis and is used even if complicated data analysis procedures are to be performed on the data set. In some cases, interval- and ratio-scaled data are treated as nominal variables and cross-tabulation is performed on the data.

STATISTICAL TECHNIQUES

Statistical techniques are broadly classified as univariate and multivariate techniques depending on the number of variables that have to be analyzed. *Univariate techniques* are used when the variables in the data set are to be analyzed in isolation. When there are multiple measures of each observation and two or more variables are to be analyzed simultaneously, *multivariate techniques* are used. A classification of univariate and multivariate techniques is given in Figure 13.1. This chapter focuses on univariate methods. Chapter 14 will deal with ANOVA, correlation analysis, and regression analysis. Chapter 15 will deal with multivariate techniques.

Hypothesis Testing

A research project starts out by formulating some hypotheses about the population. This has to be tested in the data analysis stage. Researchers usually base the hypothesis on some prior knowledge of the population. The data that has been collected has to be tested to see if there is a significant difference between the population statistic and the sample statistic. Empirical results should pass the test before any further tests are conducted. Hypothesis testing is used to make a judgment about the difference between a population parameter and a sample parameter or two sample parameters.

Hypothesis testing starts out with a *null* and an *alternate hypothesis*. The null hypothesis is the value or the difference between population and sample parameters that is being tested. It must be emphasized that the purpose of hypothesis testing is to make a judgment about the difference between the sample statistic and the hypothesized population parameter.

For hypothesis testing, the researcher needs to know the probability distribution of the sample. This would be dependent on the purpose of the test. Table 13.2 gives a list of different hypothesis tests, the probability distributions, and the conditions under which they can be used in each case. When dealing with a sampling distribution, the number of degrees of freedom is an important aspect that has to be considered. Degrees of freedom (df) refer to the number of unconstrained data used in calculating a test statistic. If the sample size is n, the degrees of freedom associated with the mean are n. However, the sample variance has only $(n-1)$ degrees of freedom. One degree of freedom is lost in calculating the sample mean, which is a requirement to calculate the sample variance.

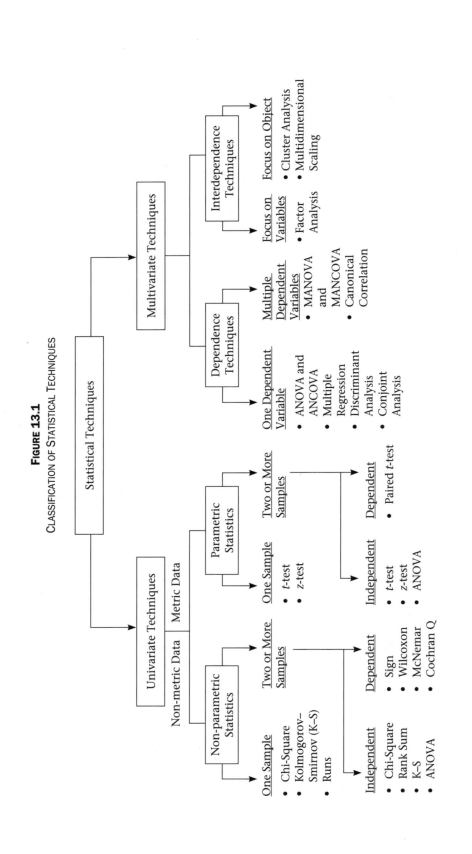

FIGURE 13.1
CLASSIFICATION OF STATISTICAL TECHNIQUES

TABLE 13.1

DATA ANALYSIS OUTCOME

In Population	Accept Null Hypothesis	Reject Null Hypothesis
Null Hypothesis True	Correct decision	Type I error
Null Hypothesis False	Type II error	Correct decision

Testing is done at a given level of significance, which is the percentage of sample means that lies outside the cutoff limits. This is also called the critical value.[6] Let us consider a given sample mean, a sample size of n, and a significance level of 5%. This implies that if a sample of size n is picked from the population repeatedly, the probability of finding the sample mean outside the cutoff value is 5%. The cutoff value is decided by the sampling distribution of the mean. It is advisable to use large sample sizes (greater than 30) to get a fairly accurate measure.

The significance level is represented by α and is also called Type I error. Type I error is defined as the probability of rejecting the null hypothesis when it is true. The probability of accepting the null hypothesis when it is false is called Type II error and is represented by β. Table 13.1 gives a clear idea of Type I and Type II errors. Ideally, any hypothesis should reduce the value of α and β. Since $(1 - \beta)$ provides a good measure of how small the value of β is, it is called the power of the test. It is observed that in trying to reduce the possibility of Type I error, Type II error necessarily increases.

Researchers make their decision on a certain significance level based on the penalties associated with accepting a wrong null hypothesis and rejecting a correct null hypothesis. The other aspect of a hypothesis test is to decide whether it is a one-sided or a two-sided test. This depends on the objective of the test. If we were interested in finding out whether one parameter is larger than or smaller than another parameter, we would conduct a one-tailed test. There would be one critical value and the null hypothesis would be rejected if the calculated value of the statistic were to fall in the critical region. However, if we were interested in finding out whether a population parameter lies between certain bounds or outside of it, we would use a two-tailed test. Depending on the sampling distribution, there would be one or two critical values and the null hypothesis would be rejected if the calculated value of the parameter fell in the critical region. Table 13.2 provides the conditions under which various statistical tests can be used for different purposes.

The remainder of the chapter will deal with various hypothesis testing procedures, illustrated mainly with the use of examples.

I—Hypothesis Testing of Single Mean with a Known Population Variance

An exporter has an optimum target of 5,000 units to be shipped each day. If there is a change in the production process, the machines have to be tuned. An inspection is done once a month to ensure that all 100 units are on target. Historically, the standard deviation for the process is known to be 250. The sample for the month of April showed that an average of

---

[6] Alan G. Sawyer and Paul J. Peter, " The Significance of Statistical Significance Tests in Marketing Research," *Journal of Marketing Research* (May 1982), 122-131

TABLE 13.2

HYPOTHESIS TESTING AND ASSOCIATED STATISTICAL TESTS[7]

Hypothesis Testing	No. of Groups/ Samples	Purpose	Statistical Test	Assumptions/ Comments
Frequency	One	Goodness of fit	X^2	
Distributions	Two	Tests of independence	X^2	
Proportions	One	Comparing sample and populations proportions	Z	If σ is known, and for large samples
		Comparing sample and populations proportions	T	If σ is unknown, and for small samples
	Two	Comparing two sample proportions	Z	If σ is known
		Comparing two sample proportions	T	If σ is unknown
Means	One	Comparing sample and population mean	Z	If σ is known
		Comparing sample and population mean	T	If σ is unknown
	Two	Comparing two sample means	Z	If σ is known
		Comparing two sample means (from independent samples)	T	If σ is unknown
		Comparing two sample means (from related samples)	T	If σ is unknown
	Two or more	Comparing multiple sample means	F	Using ANOVA framework (discussed in next chapter)
Variance	One	Comparing sample and population variances	X^2	
	Two	Comparing sample variances	F	

Legend: σ = population standard deviation.

4,960 units had been shipped every day. The company would like to test at a significance level of 0.05 whether this difference is significant enough to stop the process and tune the machines. The hypothesis testing is done as follows.

Null hypothesis:	H_0: $\mu = 5{,}000$ (Hypothesized value of the population mean)
Alternative hypothesis:	H_a: $\mu \neq 5{,}000$ (The true mean value is not 5,000)
Sample size:	$n = 100$

---

[7] Aaker et al., *Marketing Research*, 11th edition.

Sample mean: $x = 4,960$
Population std. deviation: $s = 250$
Significance level: $\alpha = 0.05$

Since the population standard deviation is known, and the size of the sample is large enough to be treated as infinite, the normal distribution can be used. The first step, then, is to calculate the standard error of the mean. This is done using the formula:

$$\text{Standard error of mean } \sigma_x = \sigma/\sqrt{n}$$

Because this is a two-tailed test with a significance level α of 0.05, using the normal distribution table, the Z-value for 0.975 $[1 - (0.05/2)]$ of the area under the curve is found to be 1.96. The calculated Z-score is

$$Z = \frac{\bar{x} - \mu}{\sigma x} = \frac{(4,960 - 5,000)}{25} = -1.6$$

Figure 13.2 provides a graphical description of the hypothesis test. The rejection rule is to reject the null hypothesis in favor of the alternative hypothesis if $|Z_{calc}| > Z_{\alpha/2}$. Because $1.6 < 1.96$, the management is convinced that its production process meet the competitive standards of a quality rating of 5,000 points.

The example explained above is called a two-tailed test because we test for values lying in two critical regions. The one-tailed test has only one critical region and we would be testing whether the sample mean is greater or less than the critical value.

For the same example, if the manufacturer is interested in knowing if the process is manufacturing at least 5,000 units on average per day and would like to test this at a significance level of 0.01. The hypothesis testing would be set up as follows.

Null hypothesis: H_0: $\mu \geq 5,000$ (Hypothesized value of the population mean)
Alternative hypothesis: H_a: $\mu < 5,000$ (The true mean value is less than 5,000)
Sample size: $n = 50$

FIGURE 13.2
THE NORMAL DISTRIBUTION: TWO-TAILED TEST

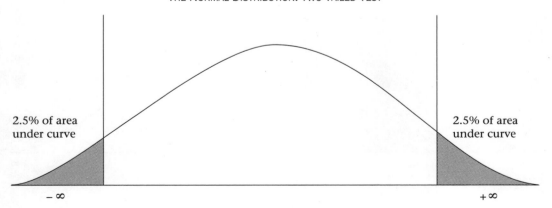

2.5% of area under curve

2.5% of area under curve

$-\infty$

$+\infty$

Sample mean: $\bar{x} = 4{,}970$
Population std. deviation: $s = 250$
Significance level: $\alpha = .01$
Standard error of mean: $\sigma_x = \sigma/\sqrt{n} = 250/7.07 = 35.36$

$$Z = \frac{\bar{x} - \mu}{\sigma_x} = \frac{(4{,}970 - 5{,}000)}{35.36} = -0.85$$

Since this is now a one-tailed test (left-tailed test) with a significance level of 0.01, using the normal distribution table, the Z-value for 0.99 ($1 - 0.01$) of the area under the left tail of the curve can be found to be –2.33. The calculated Z-score is –0.85. The rejection rule for a left-tailed test is to reject the null hypothesis in favor of the alternative hypothesis if $Z_{calc} < -Z_\alpha$. Since –0.85 > –2.33, we fail to reject the null hypothesis. This test is illustrated in Figure 13.3.

II—Hypothesis Testing of Single Mean with an Unknown Population Variance

In most cases, the population variation, and hence the population standard deviation, are not known. We have to use an estimate for the standard deviation when calculating the standard error. This will change the probability distribution of the sample means. We now use a T-distribution instead of a standard normal distribution. However, for large sample sizes ($n>30$) the T-distribution approaches the standard normal distribution and the two can be used interchangeably. To illustrate the use of a T-distribution, consider the previous example with a sample size of 25. It is observed that the average production is 4,962 units and the

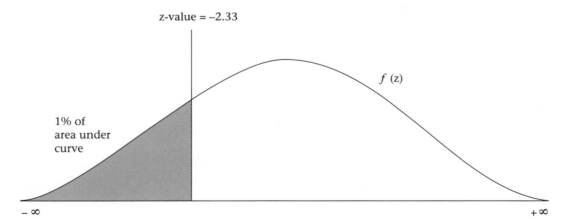

FIGURE 13.3
THE NORMAL DISTRIBUTION: ONE-TAILED TEST

z-value = –2.33

$f\,(z)$

1% of
area under
curve

$-\infty$

$+\infty$

sample standard deviation (represented by s) is 245. To test whether the difference in the mean is statistically significant, we conduct the following hypothesis test.

Null hypothesis:	H_0: $\mu \geq 5,000$ (Hypothesized value of the population mean)
Alternative hypothesis:	H_a: $\mu < 5,000$ (The true mean value is less than 5,000)
Sample size:	$n = 25$
Sample mean:	$x = 4,962$
Population std. deviation:	$s = 245$
Significance level:	$\alpha = .01$
Standard error of mean:	$\sigma_x = \sigma/\sqrt{n} = 250/7.07 = 35.36$

Because the population standard deviation is not known, the sample standard deviation can be used as an estimate of the population standard deviation. Also, since an estimate for the population standard deviation is being used, the standard error of the mean will also be an estimate, given by

$$S_{\bar{x}} = \frac{s}{\sqrt{n}} = \frac{245}{\sqrt{25}} = 49$$

As discussed earlier, if σ is not known, the appropriate probability distribution will be the T-distribution. The appropriate T-distribution will have $n - 1$ (in our case 24) degrees of freedom. The *t*-value from the tables is 2.492. The calculated *t*-value is given by

$$t_{calc} = \frac{(X - \mu)}{S_x} = (4,962 - 5,000)/49 = -0.78d$$

The rejection rule for a left-tailed t-test is to reject the null hypothesis in favor of the alternative hypothesis if $t_{calc} < -t^{\alpha}_{n-1}$. Here, –0.78 is greater than –2.492; hence, we fail to reject the null hypothesis.

There are a number of situations where the researcher should be able to state the difference between two sample means. For instance, if a business manager is planning on setting up a manufacturing plant in a foreign country and is interested in knowing the production costs in the two nations, since wages form an important part of the cost structure, the researcher is asked to determine if there is a significant difference in the average wages in both these countries.

The researcher samples 400 employees in a similar industry in country A and determines that the average wage is $105.70 and the standard deviation is $5.00. The corresponding numbers for country B are $112.80 and $4.80. The results are to be reported with a confidence level of 99%.

If the employees in two countries are different people, then the sample is considered to be independent. On the contrary, if the researcher wants to compare the wages for a given set of employees in two different time periods within a country, then the samples are not independent. This will have to be treated as a matched pair and the hypothesis testing for the difference is done in a slightly different manner.

III—Hypothesis Testing of Differences in Means for Independent Samples with a Known Population Variance

The null and alternate hypothesis can be set up in the following manner.

Null hypothesis:	H_0: $\mu_1 - \mu_2 = 0$
Alternate hypothesis:	H_a: $\mu_1 - \mu_2 \neq 0$

Reject H_0 if $|Z_{calc}| > Z_{\alpha/2}$
Since we use large sample sizes, we can adopt the approximation of using the sample standard deviation instead of the population standard deviation. The standard error of difference in means

$$S_{\bar{x}_1 - \bar{x}_2} = \sqrt{\frac{s_1^2}{n_1} + \frac{s_2^2}{n_2}} = \sqrt{\frac{(5.00)^2}{400} + \frac{(4.80)^2}{576}} = \$0.32$$

where

s_1 = standard deviation of sample 1
s_2 = standard deviation of sample 2
n_1 = size of sample 1
n_2 = size of sample 2
and the calculated value of Z is

$$Z_{calc} = \frac{(\bar{x}_1 - \bar{x}_2) - (\mu_1 - \mu_2)}{S_{\bar{x}_1 - \bar{x}_2}} = \frac{(105.70 - 112.80) - 0}{0.32} = -22.19$$

where

$(\bar{x}_1 - \bar{x}_2)$ = difference between sample means
$(\mu_1 - \mu_2)$ = difference between the population means.

For $\alpha = 0.01$ and a two-tailed test, the Z-table value is 2.58. Since $|Z_{calc}|$ is greater than $Z_{\alpha/2}$, the null hypothesis is rejected. This means that the mean daily wages of males and females are not equal.

For unknown σ, whether or not it is assumed to be equal across the two samples, the T-distribution is used. Table 13.3 gives information on the computation of the test statistic, degrees of freedom (df), and standard error.

IV—Hypothesis Testing of Differences in Means for Related Samples

A manufacturer wants to test if his product is cheaper by at least $20 in country A than in country B. This can be done by using hypothesis testing. The prices quoted are as follows:

Country A	237	135	183	225	147	146	214	157	157	144
Country B	153	114	181	186	134	166	189	113	188	111
Difference	84	21	2	39	13	−20	25	44	31	33

TABLE 13.3
PROCEDURE FOR TESTING TWO MEANS

Unknown or Assumed to Be Equal	Unknown or Not Assumed to Be Equal
Compute	Compute

$$t = \frac{(\overline{x}_1 - \overline{x}_2) - (\mu_1 - \mu_2)}{s_{\overline{x}_1 - \overline{x}_2}}$$ $$t = \frac{(\overline{x}_1 - \overline{x}_2) - (\mu_1) - (\mu_2)}{s_{\overline{x}_1 - \overline{x}_2}}$$

where   where

$$s_{\overline{x}_1 - \overline{x}_2} = s_p \sqrt{\frac{1}{n_1} + \frac{1}{n_2}}$$ $$s_{\overline{x}_1 - \overline{x}_2} = \sqrt{\frac{s_1^2}{n_1} + \frac{s_2^2}{n_2}}$$

where   where

$$s_p^2 = \frac{(n_1 - 1)s_1^2 + (n_2 - 1)s_2^2}{n_1 + n_2 - 2}$$ $$g = \frac{\dfrac{s_1^2}{n_1}}{\left(\dfrac{s_1^2}{n_1}\right) + \left(\dfrac{s_2^2}{n_2}\right)}$$

and

df = n1 + n2–2 (degrees of freedom)

and

$$df = \frac{(n_1 - 1) - (n_2 - 1)}{(n_2 - 1)g^2 + (1 - g)^2(n_1 - 1)}$$

The rejection rule is the same as before.

The difference is denoted as D.

Null hypothesis $H_0: D \geq 20$
Alternative hypothesis $H_a: D < 20$

The appropriate test statistic is

$$t = \frac{\overline{D} - d}{s_{\overline{D}} \Big/ \sqrt{n}}$$

where

d = hypothesized valued difference; in our case $d = 20$

n = sample size (10).
Then

$$\overline{D} = \frac{1}{n}\sum_{i=1}^{n}D_i = \frac{210}{10} = 21$$

Thus,

$$s_D^2 = \frac{1}{n-1} = \left(\sum_{i=1}^{n}D_i^2 - n\overline{D}^2\right) = \frac{1}{9}[14,202 - 10(21)^2] = 1,088$$

$$s_{\overline{D}} = 32.98$$

$$t = \frac{21-20}{32.98\Big/\sqrt{20}} = 0.96$$

The rejection rule is the same as before. If $\alpha = 0.05$, for 9 (i.e., $n-1$) degrees of freedom and a one-tail test, the critical t-value is -1.833. Because the calculated t-value of 0.096 2–1.833, the null hypothesis is not rejected. Therefore, the manufacturer's claim is valid.

V—Testing of Sample and Population Proportions

There are many instances where the researcher is interested in sample proportions. Testing the statistical significance of sample proportions or difference in proportions is shown below.

An author claims that 95% of the students in a certain school use his book for reference. The publisher wants to test this statement and surveys 225 students from the school. The survey reveals that 87% of the students use this book. The publisher would like to determine if this difference is statistically significant. The hypothesis testing is done in the following manner.

$p_o = 0.95$: hypothesized value of the proportion of students using book
$q_o = 0.05$: hypothesized value of the proportion of students not using the book
$p = 0.87$: sample proportion of students using the book
$q = 0.13$: sample proportion of students not using the book
Null hypothesis: $\qquad\qquad$ H_0: $p = 0.95$
Alternative hypothesis: $\qquad$ H_a: $p \neq 0.95$
Sample size: $\qquad\qquad\qquad$ $n = 225$
Significance level: $\qquad\qquad$ $\alpha = 0.05$

The first step in the hypothesis test of proportions is to calculate the standard error of the proportion using the hypothesized, that is,

$$\sigma_p = \sqrt{\frac{p_o q_o}{n}} = \sqrt{\frac{0.95 \times 0.05}{225}} = 0.0145$$

Since np and nq are each larger than 5, the normal approximation of the binomial distribution can be used. Hence, the appropriate Z-value for .975 of the area under the curve can be obtained from the Z-tables as 1.96. Thus, the limits of the acceptance region are

$$p_0 \pm 1.96\sigma_p = 0.95 \pm (1.96 \times 0.0145) = (0.922, 0.978)$$

As 0.87 does not fall within the acceptance region, the publisher should reject the author's claims (the null hypothesis).

VI—Testing of Two Sample Proportions

A cosmetic manufacturer is planning on entering a foreign market as a first step toward going global. Preliminary research has narrowed the choices down to two potential markets. A survey of 100 women was conducted as a part of the survey in both these countries. Eighty-four percent of the women surveyed in country A said they would definitely buy the product as against 82% in country B. The manufacturer is interested in finding out if the difference is significant enough to help make a decision. Hypothesis testing could be used to check if the difference is statistically significant.

$p_a = 0.84$ = proportion of potential users in country A
$n_1 = 100$ = sample size from country A
$p_b = .82$ = proportion of potential users in country B
$n_2 = 100$ = sample size from country B
Null hypothesis: $H_0: p_a = p_b$
Alternative hypothesis: $H_a: p_a \neq p_b$
Significance level: $\alpha = 0.05$

As in the case of the pooled variance estimate of difference in means, the best estimate of p (the proportion of success), if the two proportions are hypothesized to be equal, is

$$p = \{(n_1 p_a) + (n_2 p_b)\}/(n_1 + n_2) = \{(100 \times 0.84) + (100 \times 0.82)\}/200 = 0.83$$

$$q = 0.17$$

Now an estimate of σ_{pj-pl} can be obtained using

$$\sigma_{p_j - p_l} = \sqrt{\frac{pq}{n_1} + \frac{pq}{n_2}}$$

$$= \sqrt{\frac{(0.83)(0.17)}{100} + \frac{(0.83)(0.17)}{100}}$$

$$= 0.053$$

The Z-value can be calculated using

$$Z_{calc} = \{(p_a - p_b) - (0)\}/(\sigma_{pa-pb}) = 0.02/0.053 = 0.38$$

The Z-value obtained from the table is 1.96 (for $\alpha = 0.05$). Hence, we fail to reject the null hypothesis.

With all the hypothesis testing problems, decisions can be made based on *p*-values, which are an alternative to significance levels. The *p*-value is defined as the largest significance level at which the null hypothesis is accepted. In general, it can be stated that the smaller the *p*-value, the greater is the confidence in the sample findings.

One factor that could have significant impact on the results of hypothesis testing is the sample size. The basic purpose of hypothesis testing is to test whether the information obtained from the sample is a chance occurrence or a representation of population characteristics. If the sample size is large, the probability of a chance occurrence is greatly reduced. This can be inferred mathematically from the formula used to test the statistic. The standard error, which is a measure of variability, reduces if the sample size increases.

Chi-Square Test

With the use of descriptive statistics, it is possible to obtain cross-tabulation for two variables. Chi-square test is used to test the statistical independence of these two variables. Alternatively, it may also be used as a test of goodness of fit. In both these cases, we would apply the chi-square distribution. If the variables were independent, they would have a continuous probability distribution approximately represented by the chi-square distribution. The area under the curve for a chi-square distribution is 1.0. There are many chi-square distributions depending on the degrees of freedom.

Test of Independence

Statistical independence implies that knowledge of value of one variable would not offer any information about the value of the other variable. The following example illustrates the procedure for testing statistical independence. We wish to find out if pet ownership is a trait related to the geographical location. The distribution of pet ownership is given in Table 13.4.

The next step is to calculate the expected values for each cell. For this, we look at the probability of the observation falling in the given cell. Since we start the procedure by assuming independence of the two variables, the probability of an observation falling in a given cell will be the joint probability of that cell. For any given cell, the joint probability is given by

TABLE 13.4

DISTRIBUTION OF PET OWNERSHIP

	Own Pets	Do Not Own Pets	Row Total	Probability
Europe	22	18	40	0.20
Americas	48	52	100	0.50
Asia Pacific	10	50	60	0.30
Column total	80	120	200	1.0
Probability	0.40	0.60	1.0	–

TABLE 13.5
EXPECTED DISTRIBUTION FOR PET OWNERSHIP

	Own Pets	Do Not Own Pets	Row Total	Probability
Europe	16	24	40	0.20
Americas	40	60	100	0.50
Asia Pacific	24	36	60	0.30
Column total	80	120	200	1.0
Probability	0.40	0.60	1.0	–

$$P(\text{given row}) \times P(\text{given column})$$

Based on this we obtain the table of expected values for this set of observations, as indicated in the Table 13.5.

Null hypothesis: H_0 = Pet ownership independent of region
Alternate hypothesis: H_a = Pet ownership not independent of region

The chi-square (χ^2) test statistic is given by

$$x^2 = \sum_{i=1}^{k} \frac{(O_i - E_i)^2}{E_i}$$

O represents the observed value, E represents the expected value. The degrees of freedom are given by $(r - 1) \times (c - 1)$, where r stands for the number of rows and c stands for the number of columns. The above example has $(2 - 1) \times (3 - 1) = 2$ degrees of freedom.

The calculated value of the χ^2 expression is 20.03. From the table, we observe that for a χ^2 with 2 degrees of freedom, the value is 5.99. Since 20.03 falls in the critical region, we reject the null hypothesis and conclude that pet ownership is not independent of region.

The strength of association for a χ^2 is given by

$$C = \sqrt{\frac{X^2}{X^2 + n}}$$

Substituting the values, we obtain

$$C = \sqrt{\frac{20.03}{20.03 + 200}} = 0.30$$

It must be noted that the results of a χ^2 test are valid only if the expected frequency in each contingency table is more than 5. The results are dependent on the sample size. It is difficult to extrapolate the results to a sample of any size and compare results across two samples of different sizes.

Test of Goodness of Fit

This test is used to check whether a given set of observations corresponds to a certain *expected* pattern or a specific probability distribution. Consider the example of a computer manufacturer who is interested in knowing the sales of their mainframe computers in the US, Great Britain, Singapore, and Japan. Past data indicate that the percentage of sales has been 30, 25, 25, and 20%, respectively. For the current year, the manufacturer sold 2,500 units. The individual breakup is given in Table 13.6.

The hypothesis testing is done in the following manner.

Null hypothesis: H_0 = sales follow the expected pattern
Alternate hypothesis: H_a = sales do not follow the expected pattern

As in the previous case, we calculate the expected sales in each of these countries. They are given in Table 13.7.

The chi-square (χ^2) test statistic is given by

$$\chi^2 = \sum_{i=1}^{k} \frac{(O_i - E_i)^2}{E_i}$$

Substituting the numbers, we obtain $\chi^2 = 59.42$. The degrees of freedom in this case are 3. From the tables, we obtain a value of 7.81. Since the calculated value falls in the critical region, we can reject the null hypothesis and conclude that sales do not follow the expected pattern.

TABLE 13.6

MAINFRAME COMPUTER SALES

Country	Number Sold
USA	680
UK	520
Singapore	675
Japan	625

TABLE 13.7

EXPECTED MAINFRAME COMPUTER SALES

Country	Probability	Expected Frequency
USA	0.3	0.3 × 2,500 = 750
UK	0.25	0.25 × 2,500 = 625
Singapore	0.25	0.25 × 2,500 = 625
Japan	0.2	0.2 × 2,500 = 500

SUMMARY

Data analysis tools help researchers quantify findings. However, the accuracy of the study rests on the research design and data analysis cannot be called upon to rescue a badly designed study. Data preparation involves logging the data, checking for accuracy, editing, entering the data into the computer, transforming the data, and developing and documenting the database. Data analysis starts with tabulating the data and obtaining descriptive statistics. Statistical methods for analyzing data are classified as univariate and multivariate methods, based on the number of variables that have to be analyzed. The data analysis techniques that have been explained in this chapter are hypothesis testing, testing of proportions and chi-square test for test of independence, and test of goodness of fit.

 QUESTIONS AND PROBLEMS

1. When 200 people who were traveling to Europe for the winter holidays were sampled, 86 respondents said they visited Spain. Test the null hypothesis that half of all the travelers visited Spain.
2. An automobile parts and service retailer sampled at random 100 of their customers to know which brand of audio system appealed to them the most. Of these sample customers, 35 opted for Bose audio system. Test the null hypothesis that 45% of customers of the retailer prefer this brand, as against the alternative that the true percentage is lower.
3. It is known that among the people that shopped for *Better Living* brand of wall paints at a major home improvement store, 62% of the population bought the matte finish paints, 23% bought the glossy finish paints, and 15% bought the satin finish paints. A sample of 80 purchases of *Better Living* wall paints shows that 74% opted for matte finish paints, 17% opted for glossy finish paints, and 9% opted for satin finish paints. Test the null hypothesis that the distribution of purchasers surveyed was the same as distribution of shoppers at the store.
4. Explain the steps involved in preparing data for analysis.
5. A snack food manufacturer claims that putting up stalls in the venues of all the major sporting events in the upcoming year will increase product sales in supermarkets by an average of 40 cases a week. For a random sample of 25 supermarkets, the average sales increase was 31.3 cases and the sample standard deviation was 12.2 cases. Test, at the 5% level, the null hypothesis that the population mean sales increase is at least 40 cases, stating any assumption you make.
6. A coffee shop randomly sampled their customers and found that their newly launched lemon mint chai had a mean preference of 5.1 (on a 1 to 7 scale, where 7 denotes most preferred). In the previous surveys, the mean preference has always been 5.0. Has the mean preference changed now? (Use $\alpha = 0.10$ and $\sigma = 0.10$)
7. What are some of the data transformation methods used by researchers to analyze data?

14

CHAPTER _____

Advanced Data Analysis

INTRODUCTION

This chapter reviews six advanced techniques for conducting analysis. First, the ANOVA technique is discussed. This is an important statistical technique used in experimental studies. It allows the researcher to test for statistically significant differences between treatment means and to estimate the differences between the means. Second, the chapter reviews the correlation technique. The correlation analysis involves measuring the strength of linear relationship between two variables. Third, the regression technique that is used to relate two or more variables is covered. The objective in regression analysis is to build a prediction equation, called the regression model, relating the dependent variable to one or more predictor variables. Fourth, the pooled time-series cross-sectional (TSCS) analysis technique is presented. This technique is often used in global marketing research where data is available across a set of units (such as people, countries, regions, brands, etc.) over time. Fifth, the genetic algorithms (GAs) are discussed. A GA is a search approach that closely imitates the process of natural evolution. This technique is often used to generate solutions to problems related to optimization and search queries, and finds applications in various domains of knowledge. Finally, the Hierarchical Bayes (HB) models are discussed. The HB models represent a group of sub-models, and the Bayes theorem is used to integrate them together and account for the uncertainty contained in the data.

ANALYSIS OF VARIANCE

This technique is mainly used to analyze experimental data. Researchers use this method to determine if differences observed across treatments in an experiment are caused by the change in treatment condition from one level to another, or they are merely due to chance. The following example illustrates the use of ANOVA in statistics.

Products manufactured from three countries—Venezuela, Japan, and Australia—are selected for comparing the sales performance in Canada. To determine the influence of the COO effect on sales, five cities are chosen in Canada. The sales for these products from three different COO levels are noted and tabulated in Table 14.1.

TABLE 14.1

SALES FOR DIFFERENT COO LEVELS

| Country of Origin (COO) Levels | Cities | | | | | |
	1	2	3	4	5	Mean
Venezuela	8	12	10	9	11	10
Japan	7	10	6	8	9	8
Australia	4	8	7	9	7	7

One-Factor Analysis of Variance

Suppose that we wish to study one qualitative factor with levels 1, 2, . . . , r. (In the case of the COO experiment, the number of levels is 3.) That is, we wish to study the effects of these r treatments on a response variable (in this case, sales). The ANOVA of a one-factor model is sometimes called a one-way ANOVA. As a preliminary step in one-way ANOVA, we wish to determine whether or not there are any statistically significant differences between the treatment means $\mu_1, \mu_2, \mu_3, . . . , \mu_r$ (μ_r being the mean value of the population of all possible values of the response variable that could potentially be observed using treatment r). To do this we test the null hypothesis,

$$H_0: \mu_1 = \mu_2 = \mu_3 = . . . = \mu_r$$

(This hypothesis says that all treatments have the same effect on the mean response.) against the alternative hypothesis,

$$H_1: \text{at least 2 of } \mu_1, \mu_2, . . . , \mu_r \text{ are different}$$

(This hypothesis says that at least two treatments have different effects on the mean response.)

Essentially, in the case of the COO experiment, the null hypothesis will be that differences in COO have no effect on sales. The differences between sample means in each COO could be caused by the fact that a sample of only 5 was employed for each COO. The alternative hypothesis is that the COO effect on sales would not be the same for each COO.

To test these hypotheses, we need to compute the ratio between the *between-treatment* variance and *within-treatment* variance. Here, we define *between-treatment variance* as the variance in the response variable for different treatments. On the other hand, *within-treatment variance* is defined as the variance in the response variable for a given treatment. If we can show that the *between* variance is significantly larger than the *within* variance, then we can reject the null hypothesis.

Variation Among Country of Origin

Consider the COO experiment illustrated in Figure 16.5. To test the null hypothesis, first focus on the variation among mean COO levels ($X_1 = 10$, $X_2 = 8$, and $X_3 = 7$). Then consider the variation within COO e.g., the cities in Venezuela as COO level had sales of 8, 12, 10, 9, and 11). Under the null hypothesis that COO effect has no effect on sales, each of these estimates should be similar. If the estimate based on variation among cities of different COO effect is inflated, doubt will be cast on the null hypothesis.

The *between* variance estimate is based on the variation between the sample mean values of each row (COO effect), which is calculated using the formula

$$SS_r = \sum_{p=1}^{r} n_p \left(\overline{X}_p - \overline{\overline{X}} \right)^2$$

where,

SS_r = sum of squares between COO levels (rows), also called the treatment sum of squares or the variation explained by the COO level
X_p = mean sales at price level p (e.g., X1 = 10)
X = overall mean (in this case = $8^1/_3$)
n = number of observations at each price level ($n = 5$)
p = treatment or COO ($p = 1, 2, 3$)
r = number of treatments or countries ($r = 3$)

Hence, in this example, the treatment sum of squares can be calculated to be

$$SS_r = 5[(10 - 25/3)^2 + (8 - 25/3)^2 + (7 - 25/3)^2] = 23.3$$

Clearly, as the difference between means gets larger, so will the treatment sum of squares. The *between* variance estimate is termed MSS_r (the mean sum of squares between COO and is an estimate of the variance among cities), and is obtained by dividing the SS_r by its associated degree of freedom (df), which here is the number of treatments (rows) less 1. Thus,

$$MSS_r = \frac{SS_r}{r-1} = \frac{23.3}{3-1} = 11.65$$

Variation within Country of Origin

The *within* variance estimate is based on the variation within each COO (row), which is calculated using the formula

$$SS_u = \sum_{i=1}^{n_p} \sum_{p=1}^{r} \left(X_{ip} - \overline{X} \right)^2$$

where

SS_u = sum of squares unexplained by the COO (row), also called the error sum of squares or the variation within the COO
X_{ip} = sales of observations (cities) i at COO p

n_p = number of observations at each COO (n_p = 5 for all p-s)
p = treatment or COO level (p = 1, 2, 3)
r = number of treatments or COO levels (r = 3)

Hence, in this example, the error sum of squares (or unexplained variations) can be calculated to be

$$SS_u = (8 - 10)^2 + (12 - 10)^2 + \cdots + (7 - 7)^2$$

$$= 34$$

The *within* variance estimate is termed MSS_u (the mean sum of squares unexplained by the COO level, an estimate of the variance within cities) and is generated by dividing SS_u by its associated degrees of freedom, which is equal to $r(n - 1)$ when the group sizes are unequal or 12 also equal to total sample size (N) minus the total number of treatment levels (r) for equal group sizes. Thus,

$$MSS_u = \frac{SS_u}{n - r} = \frac{34}{12} = 2.8$$

Having calculated the variation explained by the treatment (COO level) and the variation unexplained by it, an addition of these two factors would give the total variation or the sum of squares total (SS_t). Thus,

$$SS_t = SS_r + SS_u$$

which is,

$$57.3 = 23.3 + 34$$

Table 14.2 provides the source table for ANOVA.

TABLE 14.2
SOURCE TABLE FOR ANOVA

Source of Variation	Variation, Sum of Squares (SS)	Degrees of Freedom (df)	Variance Estimate, Mean Sum of Squares (MSS)	F-ratio
Between COO Levels Variation	$SS_r = \sum_{p=1}^{r} n_p (\bar{X}_p - \bar{\bar{X}})^2$	r–1 = 2	$MSS_r = \frac{SS_r}{2} = 11.65$	$\frac{MSS_r}{MSS_u} = 4.16$
Within COO Levels Variation	$SS_u = \sum_{i=1}^{5}\sum_{p=1}^{3}(X_{ip} - \bar{X}_p)^2 = 34$	n–r = 12	$MSS_u = \frac{SS_u}{12} = 2.8$	
Total	$SS_t = \sum_{i=1}^{5}\sum_{p=1}^{3}(X_{ip} - \bar{\bar{X}})^2 = 57.3$	n–1 = 14		

F-Statistic and *p*-Value

We now consider the ratio of the two estimates of the variance (the *between* and *within*) of the store sales. This ratio is termed an *F-ratio* or *F-statistic*:

$$F = MSS_r \, / \, MSS_u$$

$$= 11.65/2.8 = 4.16$$

If the null hypothesis that COO levels have no effect on sales is true, then our variance estimates using the difference between the sample means, MSS_r, should be the same as those based on the within-row (COO-level) variations. The *F*-ratio should then be close to 1. If, however, the hypothesis is not true and the different COO levels generate different sales levels, the MSS_r term will be large reflecting the different COO levels. As a result, the *F*-ratio will tend to become large.

The *p*-value is the probability that the *F*-ratio would be larger than 4.16, given the null hypothesis. To generate the *p*-value, the *F*-probability distribution is used. Associated with each *F*-ratio are the numerator (MSS_r) degrees of freedom (2) and the denominator (MSS_u) degrees of freedom (12). Knowing this pair of degrees of freedom, a table of the *F*-distribution can be used to determine, at least approximately, the *p*-value. The *F*-distribution table provides the following *p*-values for our case, in which the degrees of freedom are 2 and 12.

F-Statistic	p-Value
1.56	0.25
2.81	0.10
3.89	0.05
6.93	0.01

Thus, the *p*-value associated with 4.16 is not in the table, but would be about 0.04. If the null hypothesis were true, there would be a 0.04 probability of getting an *F*-statistic of 4.16 or larger. Therefore, the evidence that the null hypothesis is not true is fairly substantial. The observed difference between sample means could have occurred by accident even if the null hypothesis was true, but the probability is low (1 chance in 25). Since the *p*-value is less than 0.05, we can say that the *F*-statistic is significant at the 0.05 level. Note: The ANOVA *approach and the regression approach to one-factor* ANOVA *give the same value for the F-statistic.*

Strength of Association

A good descriptive statistic for measuring the strength of association is to compute ρ (rho), the ratio of the sums of squares for the treatment (SS_r) to the total sums of squares (SS_t). Rho is a measure of the proportion of variance accounted for in the sample data. In our example, $r = 23.3/57.3 = 0.407$. In other words, 40.7% of the total variation in the data is explained by the treatment (price levels). However, since the sample value (r) tends to be upward-biased, it is useful to have an estimate of the population strength of association (ω^2—omega squared) between the treatment and the dependent variable. A sample estimate of this population value can be computed as

$$\varpi^2 = \frac{SS_r - (r-1)MSS_u}{SS_r + MSS_u} = \frac{23.3 - 2(2.8)}{57.3 + 2.8} = 0.295$$

In other words, 29.5% of the total variation in the sales data is accounted for by the treatment (or the COO).

CORRELATION ANALYSIS

The *Pearson correlation coefficient* measures the degree to which there is a linear association between two interval-scaled variables. A positive correlation reflects a tendency for a high value in one variable to be associated with a high value in the second. A negative correlation reflects an association between a high value in one variable and a low value in the second variable. If it is based on an entire population, the measure is termed the population correlation (ρ). If it is based on a sample, it is termed sample correlation (r). If two variables are plotted on a two-dimensional graph, called a scatter diagram, the sample correlation reflects the tendency for the points to cluster systematically about a straight line rising or falling from left to right. The sample correlation r always lies between -1 and 1. An r of 1 indicates a perfect positive linear association between the two variables, whereas if r is -1, there is perfect negative linear association. A zero correlation coefficient reflects the absence of any linear association.

Simple Correlation Coefficient

A reasonable measure of association between the two variables is the covariance between the two variables:[1]

$$\overline{\text{Cov}(x, y)} = \Sigma \overline{(X_i - X)} \times (Y_i - Y)$$

The second step of the method for calculating the sample correlation is to divide the association expression by the sample size:

$$\frac{1}{(n-1)} \times \sum \left(X_i - \overline{X}\right) \times \left(Y_i - \overline{Y}\right)$$

This expression is called the sample covariance. Thus, the covariance between X and Y (denoted Cov_{XY}), measures the extent to which X and Y are related. The size of the covariance measure could be changed simply by changing the units of one of the variables. However, if we divide the measure by the sample standard deviations for X and Y. The result is the sample

---

[1] Dawn Iacobucci and Gilbert A. Churchill, Jr, *Marketing Research: Methodological Foundations* (Ohio: Cengage Learning, 2009), 10th edition.

correlation coefficient, which will not be affected by a change in the measurement units of one or both of the variables:

$$r_{xy} = \frac{1}{(n-1)} \times \sum \frac{X_i - \overline{X}}{S_x} \times \frac{\left(Y_i - \overline{Y}\right)}{S_y}$$

This expression for the sample correlation coefficient (*r*) is called the *Pearson product-moment correlation coefficient*. This is expressed in simpler terms as

$$r_{xy} = \frac{Cov_{XY}}{S_x \times S_y}$$

The product-moment correlation coefficient has several important properties. It is independent of sample size and units of measurement. It lies between −1 and +1, and hence, the interpretation is intuitively reasonable. It is used in regression analysis, which is explained in the next section of this chapter.

It should be understood that even though the correlation coefficient (*r*) provides a measure of association between two variables, *it does not imply any causal relationship* between the variables. Correlation can measure only the nature and degree of association between variables. It cannot imply causation. It should also be noted that the sample correlation coefficient could be seriously affected by outliers or extreme observations. The correlation coefficient provides a measure of the relationship between two questions or variables. The underlying assumption is that *the variables are intervally scaled*, such as age or income. Table 14.3 gives the computation of the correlation coefficient.

Partial Correlation Coefficient

The Pearson correlation coefficient provides a measure of linear association between two variables. When there are more than two variables involved in the relationship, partial correlation analysis is used. The *partial correlation coefficient* provides a measure of association between two variables after controlling for the effects of one or more additional variables. For example, the relationship between the advertising expenditures and sales of a brand is influenced by several other variables. For the sake of simplicity, let us assume that the relationship is affected by a third variable, the use of coupons. If the brand manager is interested in measuring the relationship between the dollar amount spent on advertisements (*X*) and the associated sales of the brand (*Y*), he or she has to control for the effect of coupons (*Z*). The partial correlation coefficient can, thus, be expressed as

$$r_{XY,Z} = \frac{r_{XY} - r_{XZ} \times r_{YZ}}{\sqrt{\left(1 - r_{XZ}^2\right)} \times \sqrt{\left(1 - r_{YZ}^2\right)}}$$

Although the correlation analysis provides a measure of the strength of the association between two variables, it tells us little or nothing about the nature of the relationship. Hence,

TABLE 14.3
COMPUTATION OF CORRELATION COEFFICIENT

	Japan Sales		**China Sales**		
	Y_i	$Y_i - \bar{Y}$	X_i	$X_i - \bar{X}$	$(X_i - \bar{X})(Y_i - \bar{Y})$
Store A	3	−6	7	−4	24
Store B	8	−1	13	2	−2
Store C	17	8	13	2	16
Store D	4	−5	11	0	0
Store E	15	6	16	5	30
Store F	7	−2	6	−5	10
Total	54	0	66	0	$78 = \sum_i (X_i - \bar{X})(Y_i - \bar{Y})$
Average	$\bar{Y} = 9$		$\bar{X} = 11$		$15.6 = \dfrac{1}{n-1}\sum_i (X_i - \bar{X})(Y_i - \bar{Y})$

$$r_{YX} = \frac{1}{n-1} \frac{\sum_i (X_i - \bar{X})(Y_i - \bar{Y})}{S_X S_Y} = \frac{78}{5(3.85)(5.76)} = 0.70$$

$$S_X = 3.85 = \sqrt{\frac{1}{n-1}\sum_i (X_i - \bar{X})^2}$$

$$S_Y = 5.76 = \sqrt{\frac{1}{n-1}\sum_i (Y_i - \bar{Y})^2}$$

regression analysis is used to understand the nature of the relationship between two or more variables.

Spearman Rank Correlation Coefficient

The *Spearman rank correlation coefficient* is an index of the correlation between two rank-order variables. The correlation between the ranks tells us very little about the degree of the linear relationship between the underlying variables. Furthermore, the square of the rank correlation coefficient is not to be interpreted as similar to the population coefficient of determination. Thus, we cannot say it is the proportion of the total variation in Y explained by its association with the variation in X.

Consider the following example. Assume two respondents A and B rank-ordered 10 brands of cereals in terms of their preferences. The ranking data for the two respondents are provided in Table 14.4. The question of interest is whether the two respondents have similar preferences. It is possible to answer this question by computing the rank-order correlation between the two sets of ranks.

TABLE 14.4
RANKING FOR CEREAL IN TWO COUNTRIES

Brand	1	2	3	4	5	6	7	8	9	10
Respondent A (Singapore)	6	9	1	3	4	5	8	7	2	10
Respondent B (Russia)	5	10	4	7	2	6	8	3	1	9

TABLE 14.5
COMPUTATION OF CORRELATION COEFFICIENT

Brand I	Respondent A (Singapore)	Respondent B (Russia)	Difference D_I	Squares of Difference, D_I^2
1	6	5	1	1
2	9	10	−1	1
3	1	4	−3	9
4	3	7	−4	16
5	4	2	2	4
6	5	6	−1	1
7	8	8	0	0
8	7	3	4	16
9	2	1	1	1
10	10	9	1	1
				$\Sigma D_I^2 = 50$

For the rank correlation, ranks enter into the calculation of the coefficient. Thus, we have a very simple computational form when no ties exist, as shown here.

$$r_s = 1 - \frac{6\left(\sum_i D_I^2\right)}{n(n^2 - 1)}$$

where D_I is defined as the difference between the ranks associated with the particular brand I, and n is the number of brands evaluated.

The Spearman rank correlation is a very simple value to compute. All we need to know are the number n of objects (i.e., brands ranked) and the difference in the rankings of each individual, D_I. The term r_s is a correlation coefficient computed for the ranks. We now illustrate the computation of this coefficient. The data are listed in Table 14.5.

Now, we can substitute values into the equation for r_s. We have $n = 10$ and $\Sigma D_I^2 = 50$. So

$$r_s = 1 - \frac{6 \times 50}{10(10^2 - 1)} = 1 - \frac{300}{990} = 1 - 0.303 = 0.697$$

The Spearman correlation is 0.697, which can be considered to be on the higher side. The results imply that respondents from Singapore and Russia have similar rankings of the cereal brands.

If a tie occurs in the rankings, we can still use the Spearman correlation equation. However, the means and variances of the ranks no longer have the simple relationship to n as in the case where no ties exist. If ties occur, the simplest procedure is to assign mean ranks to sets of tied measurements. When two or more items are tied in order, each item is assigned the mean of the ranks they would otherwise occupy.

REGRESSION ANALYSIS[2]

Regression analysis is a statistical technique that relates two or more variables. There is an independent variable called the predictor, which determines the value of the variable of interest to the research. The variable of interest is called the dependent or response variable. Regression analysis helps the researcher build a model that can predict the value of the dependent variable on the basis of the independent variable. If the study involves determining the relationship between the dependent variable and one independent variable, it is called simple regression. Regression analysis that involves more than one independent variable is called multiple regression analysis.

Simple linear regression starts with the specification of one dependent and one predictor variable. For instance, consider the sales of a given product in several countries. Our goal is to determine the impact of per capita income on sales of the product in these countries. The following regression model may be hypothesized.

$$Y_i = \beta_0 + \beta_1 X_i + \varepsilon_i$$

where,

Y_i—the sales of the product in a given country i.
X_i—per capita income in a given country i.
β_0—model parameter that represents the mean value of the dependent variable (Y) when the value of the independent variable X is zero. This is also called the Y intercept.
β_1—a model parameter that represents the slope that measures the change in the value of the independent variable associated with a one-unit increase in the value of the X variable.
ε_i—an error term that describes the effects on Y_i of all factors other than the value of X_i.

Table 14.6 explains the computation of the regression coefficients.

There are several assumptions to be made while conducting regression analysis, the most important being that the selected variables do, in fact, explain or predict the dependent variable, and that no other important variable has been omitted. A second assumption is that the relationship between the independent and dependent variable is linear and additive. A third assumption is that there is a random error term that absorbs the effects of measurement error and the influences of the variables that are not included in the regression equation.

---

[2] For a more detailed discussion of regression analysis, please refer Aaker et al., *Marketing Research*, 11th edition.

TABLE 14.6

COMPUTATION OF REGRESSION COEFFICIENTS

If

$$y = \alpha + \beta x + \varepsilon$$

where

α is the intercept term,
β is the slope coefficient, and
ε is the error term,

the estimated equation is given by,

$$\hat{y} = a + bx$$

The estimate of the slope coefficient is given by

$$b = \frac{\sum xy - \sum x \sum y}{n\sum x^2 - \left(\sum x\right)^2}$$

r = correlation between x and y
S_x, S_y = standard deviations of x and y

$$a = \bar{y} - b\bar{x}$$

The model requires that the researcher input values for the dependent and independent variables. The statistical package will output regression coefficients along with their associated beta coefficient and t-values. This is used to evaluate the strength of the relationship between the respective independent variables and the dependent variables. All statistical packages also give the value of R^2, which gives an indication of the goodness of fit of the model.

A study conducted to examine the reaction of customers to new products in different countries uses regression analysis as a data analysis tool. The study tries to predict how consumers in a given country react to a new product and the time it would take for the product to achieve a certain level of market penetration in that country. The study focused on diffusion patterns of new products and technologies in different ways in which a new product gets adopted in a culture and the reasons for differences in adoption process between countries.

The data used in the studies are the sales data for five product categories across multiple countries.[3] The product categories include consumer durables such as VCRs, microwave ovens, cellular phones, home computers, and CD players. The countries used are Australia, Belgium, Denmark, Finland, France, Germany, Italy, the Netherlands, Norway, Portugal, Spain, Sweden, Switzerland, and the UK. Data was collected from the first year the product

---

[3] V. Kumar, Ganesh Jaishankar, and Raj Echambadi, "A Cross-National Diffusion Research: What We Know and How Certain Are We," *Journal of Product Innovation Management* (1998), 15 (3).

was introduced in the country to the most recent available. The time-effect of the diffusion pattern was tested in concept using regression analysis. The regression analysis revealed that imitation coefficient for country i is dependent on cosmopolitanism, mobility of the population and the proportion of women in workforce. This is represented by the regression equation,

$$(\text{Imitation coefficient})_i = \beta_0 + \beta_1 (\text{cosmopolitanism})_i + \beta_2 (\text{mobility})_i +$$

$$\beta_3 (\text{women on labor force})_i$$

The findings are summarized in Table 14.7.

Interpretation of Regression Model Parameters

The parameter values in Table 14.7 offer many insights. First, the hypothesized effects for each of the independent variables were supported. For example, in case of a CD player, the larger the cosmopolitanism in the country and lower the proportion of women in not required labor force, the larger is the propensity to innovate. Similar interpretations can be made for propensity to imitate. If one is interested in evaluating the relative importance of the independent variables, then standardized regression coefficients have to be computed as shown here.

$$\beta_{\text{cosmo}} = b_{\text{cosmo}} \times \frac{S_{\text{cosmo}}}{S_{\text{innovate}}}$$

where S_{cosmo} and S_{innovate} are standard deviations of the cosmopolitanism and propensity to innovate, and b_{cosmo} is the un-standardized regression coefficient. In general, the most important variable has the largest standardized regression coefficient provided all the assumptions of the regression model are met.

Testing the Significance of the Independent Variable

If β_1 is zero, there will be no effect of cosmopolitanism on imitation coefficient, and hence, the model specified does not serve any purpose. Hence, it makes sense to conduct a hypothesis test to verify if β_1 is zero. If there is sufficient evidence that β_1 is zero, the model should be discarded. The estimate of β_1, b_1 has a variance associated with it and is denoted by S_{b_1}. One way of evaluating the magnitude of b_1 is to conduct the following statistical hypothesis test.

Null Hypothesis: H_0: $\beta_1 = 0$
Alternate Hypothesis: H_a: $\beta_1 \neq 0$

The test statistic is given by

$$t = \frac{b_1 - \beta_1}{S_{b_1}}$$

TABLE 14.7

SIMULTANEOUS ESTIMATION OF CROSS-SECTIONAL AND TIME-SERIES FACTORS INFLUENCING THE CROSS-NATIONAL DIFFUSION PARAMETERS

Variables	Past Research Hypothesis	CD Player	Microwave Oven	VCR	Cellular Phone	Home Computer	Support for Hypothesis
Propensity to Innovate							
Cosmopolitanism	Positive	0.0202 (12.56)	0.0069 (42.02)	0.0174 (34.13)	-0.0091 (-2.06)	0.0357 (11.64)	Yes
Women In Labor Force	Negative	-0.0047 (-6.63)	-0.0018 (-29.45)	-0.0034 (-18.57)	0.0364 (21.11)	-0.0164 (-14.11)	Yes
Propensity to Imitate							
Cosmopolitanism	Negative	-0.1409 (-10.93)	0.1205 (6.35)	-0.1044 (-24.60)	-0.2823 (-2.26)	-0.2658 (-12.34)	Yes
Mobility	Positive	0.0779 (6.53)	1.1660 (18.00)	-0.1923 (-25.65)	-0.9200 (-5.90)	0.2585 (5.13)	Yes
Women in labor force	Positive	0.0500 (6.43)	-0.1410 (-10.89)	0.0135 (3.99)	-0.2901 (-8.41)	0.0319 (2.11)	Yes
Time lag	Positive	0.3678 (46.91)	0.0534 (15.20)	0.0226 (38.57)	0.0499 (6.11)	0.0366 (4.77)	Yes

Note: *t*-statistics represented in parentheses. All coefficients are significant at the 0.05 level.
Source: Kumar et al. (1998).[4]

---

[4] V. Kumar, Ganesh Jaishankar, and Raj Echambadi. (1998), *Journal of Product Innovation Management* (1998), pp. 255–268.

The calculated test statistic has a T-distribution. By fixing α at a certain level, say 0.05, and applying the rule for a two-tailed test, we can or cannot reject the null hypothesis.

POOLED TIME-SERIES CROSS-SECTIONAL ANALYSIS[5]

This technique is often used in global marketing research where data is available across a set of units (such as people, countries, regions, brands, etc.) over time. In other words, we can represent this type of data as: $i = 1, 2,..., N$, where i indicates information available across time t, represented as $t = 1, 2,..., T$. The final look of such a data will have multiple observations ($N \times T$) on each unit over time.

Typically, TSCS data has more time periods in comparison to the units themselves. The focus of researchers with this type of data lies in the differences in the units, and the characteristics displayed by them. For instance, consider a data set that tracks the penetration of mobile phone technology in ASEAN countries. Such a data set could track the 10 member countries across, say, 15–20 years or more. By studying such a data set, researchers can identify and track each country's mobile phone growth patterns over time.

Based on this, it would be easy to visualize a TSCS data as a collection of stacks of data. That is, it can be viewed as stacks of data, placed on top of each other, wherein, each stack of data contains variables across time periods for a specified unit or cross-section (e.g., mobile phone penetration in one member country of ASEAN, across 20 years). The placing of one stack over another is analogous to combining different units of data (e.g., mobile phone penetration in each member country of ASEAN).

Examples of such data sets frequently used in international population studies include: (a) the Household, Income and Labor Dynamics in Australia, a household-based panel that helps in researching issues such as poverty trends, financial planning during retirement, physical and mental health trends, and an international comparison of wealth and happiness; (b) the Survey of Income and Program Participation data that provides information about the income of American individuals and households and their participation in income transfer programs; and (c) the Chinese Family Panel Studies that contains data pertaining to social, economic, education, health, and other family parameters that will help researchers understand social and economic changes in individual, family, and community.

In general, a pooled linear regression model can be estimated using the Ordinary Least Squares (OLS) procedure represented as follows:

$$y_{it} = \beta_1 + \sum_{m=2}^{m} \beta_m x_{mit} + e_{it}$$

where,

$i = 1, 2,..., N$, and indicates a cross-sectional unit
$t = 1, 2,..., T$, and indicates a time period, and
$m = 1, 2,..., M$, and indicates a specific explanatory variable.

---

[5] Federico Podestà, "Recent Developments in Quantitative Comparative Methodology: The Case of Pooled Time Series Cross-Section Analysis," DSS Papers Society SOC 3-02, 2002, www.unibs.it/sites/default/files/ricerca/allegati/1233pode202.pdf (Retrieved on March 14, 2014).

Therefore, y_{it} refers to a dependent variable (e.g., a continuous variable such as sales), and x_{it} refers to the independent variables for a specific unit i at time t. Further, β_1 and β_m refer to the intercept and the variable coefficients, respectively, along with e_{it}, a random error term.

As with any technique, the pooled TSCS analysis too has advantages and disadvantages attached to its usage. They are listed in this section.

Advantages of Pooled TSCS Analysis

- **Better explanatory power:** Most often, analyses based on time-series data or cross-sectional data are characterized by limited data. That is, in the case of time-series data, information is limited to one specific unit over a time period. On the other hand, the cross-sectional data contains information on a specific number of units at a specific time period. Consequently, the limited nature of data contained in these types of data sets leads to a relatively smaller sample size. Therefore, the total number of the potential explanatory variables exceeds the degree of freedom required to model the relationship between the dependent and independent variables, thereby adversely impacting the explanatory power of the model.

  On the contrary, a pooled TSCS data set has ($N{\times}T$) observations wherein, data on a set of variables is available over a period of time. This not only increases the sample size, but also the number of variables. As a result, this enables researchers to test the impact of a large number of predictors of the level and change in the dependent variable, thereby improving the explanatory power of the model.[6]

- **Focus on the variables of interest:** In cross-sectional or time-series analysis, it is possible that certain variables do not get sufficient attention owing to minor variations in them across time and units. However, pooled data that has a sufficiently larger data set (by combining units and time) will likely reveal higher variability of data as compared to a simple time-series or cross-section analysis.[7]

- **Capturing simultaneous variations:** In addition to tracing the changes across only time or only units, the pooled TSCS analysis also enables researchers to capture variation between the two dimensions simultaneously. This is possible because of the structure of the database that contains data across time and units. Therefore, instead of building a cross-section model (that explains variation for all countries at one point in time) or a time-series model (that explains variation for one country across various time periods), a pooled model is tested for all countries through time and the inherent variations contained between them.[8]

[6] M. G. Schmidt, "Determinants of Social Expenditure in Liberal Democracies," *Acta Politica* 32, no. 2 (1997): 153–173.

[7] A. Hicks, "Introduction to Pooling," in *The Comparative Political Economy of the Welfare State*, eds, T. Janoski and A. Hicks (Cambridge: Cambridge University Press, 1994).

[8] P. Pennings, H. Keman, and J. Kleinnijenhuis, *Doing Research in Political Science: An Introduction to Comparative Methods and Statistics* (California: SAGE Publications, 2006), 2nd edition.

Disadvantages of Pooled TSCS Analysis

Despite the popularity of this technique and the benefits it provides to researchers, studies have identified methodological issues with this technique that researchers must be aware of. Specifically, studies have shown that this technique often violates the standard OLS assumptions about the error process that requires that all the errors exhibit homoscedasticity and that all of the errors are independent of each other.[9] Further, it has been found that when the OLS procedure is applied to pooled data, it is likely to generate biased, inefficient, and/or inconsistent estimates. This is because the errors for regression equations estimated from pooled data using OLS procedure tend to generate the following five complications.[10]

- Errors tend to be serially correlated, such that errors in country i at time t are correlated with errors in country i at time $t + 1$. This is because observations and traits that characterize them tend to be interdependent across time. For instance, country-specific information such as GDP growth and population tend not to be independent over time, and are largely dependent on the previous time period.
- Errors tend to be contemporaneously correlated across countries, such that errors in country i at time t are correlated with errors in country j at time t. Further, it is possible for errors in the statistical model for one nation (e.g., the US) to resemble the errors of its neighboring nation(s) (e.g., Mexico and Canada). Additionally, it is also possible that errors in countries of a certain geographic region (e.g., Southeast Asian countries) may be linked together, but be independent of errors with countries of another geographic region (e.g., the Middle East countries).
- Errors tend to be heteroscedastic, such that countries with higher values on variables tend to have less restricted and, hence, higher variances on them. For instance, the US tends to have more volatile as well as higher unemployment rates than the Switzerland. This means that the variance in employment rates will tend to be greater for bigger nations with large heterogeneous labor forces than for small, homogeneous nations. Further, errors could also be heteroscedastic because of differences in the scales of the dependent variable among countries (e.g., level of government spending on education may differ between India and China).
- Errors could reflect/conceal unit and period effects in certain cases. That is, it is possible to have regression estimates that have observed heteroscedasticity and auto-correlated errors based on a model misspecification. The model misspecification typically occurs when the level of dependent variable across units and time periods are not homogeneous (as required by OLS estimation). In such case, the least squares estimator will not be a good predictor of the time periods and the cross-sectional units, and the level of heteroscedasticity and auto-correlation will also be substantially inflated.
- Errors might be non-random across time and/or units because parameters are heterogeneous across subsets of units. In other words, since processes linking dependent and independent variables tend to vary across subsets of nations or/and period, errors tend to reflect some causal heterogeneity across space, time, or both. This issue could also be due to model misspecification.

---

[9] N. Beck and J. N. Katz, "What to Do (and Not to Do) with Time-Series Cross-Section Data," *American Political Journal Review* 89 (1995): 634–647; J. A. Stimson, "Regression in Space and Time: A Statistical Essay," *American Journal of Political Sciences* 29, no. 4 (1985): 914–947.

[10] A. Hicks, "Introduction to Pooling."

GENETIC ALGORITHMS[11]

A genetic algorithm (GA) is a search approach that closely imitates the process of natural evolution. This technique is often used to generate solutions to problems related to optimization and search queries, and finds applications in various domains such as bioinformatics, computational science, engineering, economics, marketing, and manufacturing, among others.

In the field of marketing, GA is used in studies involving macro-level diffusion models. A simple GA is composed of three operators: reproduction, crossover, and mutation. Using these three operations, the GA iterates through the following three steps.

In the first step, individual strings of a generation (parent generation) are copied to the next generation (child) according to their objective function values, f. This step is referred to as the *reproduction* stage. For a diffusion model to identify the sales of a product, the objective function f can be thought of as the sum of squared errors between the predicted values of sales and the actual value of sales. Selecting strings according to their fitness values means that strings with a higher fitness value have a higher probability of contributing one or more offspring(s) in the next generation. The probabilities could depend on the proportion of solutions present in a parent generation, based on linear ranking system of the solutions or based on a tournament selection. This operator is an artificial version of natural selection, a Darwinian survival of the fittest among string creatures.

In the second step, a simple *crossover* happens. There are two ways this can happen. First, members of the newly reproduced strings (or new generation) are paired at random. Second, each pair of strings undergoes crossing over as follows: an integer position K along the string is selected uniformly at random between 1 and the string length less 1 [1, 1 – 1]. Two new strings are created by swapping all characters between positions $K + 1$ and l. The mechanics of reproduction and crossover are simple, involving random number generation, string copies, and some partial string exchanges. Nonetheless, the combined emphasis of reproduction and the structured, though randomized, information exchange of crossover give GA much of their power.

In the final step, a cell is randomly changed in the string or the solution vector. This is known as the *mutation* process. Through this process, the algorithm attempts to ensure a globally optimal solution. If the algorithm is trapped in a local minimum, the mutation operator randomly shifts the solution to another point in the search space, thus, removing itself out of the trap.

The above steps are repeated until the algorithm is halted. The decision to halt the program can depend either on a pre-fixed number of generations, the time elapsed in the evolutionary process, or the change in the optimal solution in the previous n generations. The composition of the final generation of strings—the best strings—is the GA's solution to the problem. It should be noted that when new strings are created, the old ones (those belonging to the previous generation) are discarded. Because the reproduction process tends to choose the *fittest* members of a generation, the generations tend to evolve. Thus, an initial population of relatively undistinguished solutions evolves to yield a set of solutions that cover the optimal region in the final generation. To obtain the optimal solution, one can either use a gradient search algorithm such as hill climbing from the mean value in the final generation or use the

---

[11] Rajkumar Venkatesan, Trichy V. Krishnan, and V. Kumar, "Evolutionary Estimation of Macro-Level Diffusion Models Using Genetic Algorithms: An Alternative to Nonlinear Least Squares," *Marketing Science* 23, no. 3 (2004): 451–464.

solution with the best fitness in the last generation as the optimal solution. which method to choose to find the optimal solution vector depends on the terminate the iterations.

Alongside this technique, other algorithms such as the sequential-search-based least-squares (SSB-NLS) have also been used. Despite the fact that the two techniq. identical objective function, the SSB-NLS and GA have several important and substan. ferences due to which SSB-NLS and GA need not always provide the same solutions, as i. fied by several studies.[12] They are:

- SSB-NLS technique uses single-point gradient search algorithms to locate the parameters that optimize the objective function (minimum sum of squared errors).
- GA uses parallel, evolutionary search algorithms to locate parameters that optimize the objective function (minimum sum of squared errors in this case).
- Theoretically, GA is expected to have a higher probability of convergence to global optimum solutions when data points are less, number of parameters is large, the parameter space is multi-modal, and the model is inherently nonlinear.[13] However, SSB-NLS is dependent on smooth, and mostly quadratic, surfaces to ensure convergence to local optimal—with the expectation that if appropriate starting values are chosen the local optimum will represent the global optimal solution.[14]
- The estimates from GA provide better fit and forecasting performance as compared to SSB-NLS for highly nonlinear functions,[15] and they represent inherently two different classes of optimization techniques that have different properties.[16]

Although the GA has several benefits from an estimation standpoint, the technique does have two limitations. First, the search can entail many evaluations of the objective function and, consequently, a longer execution time when compared to SSB-NLS. However, with present day computational power, this limitation can be easily overcome. Second, one has to carefully select the convergence criteria to obtain an optimal solution. Although the complexity of coding involved in implementing GA is a major impediment to its widespread applicability, many software packages (e.g., MatLab, S-Plus, C++, and Excel) are being released with wide-ranging functions and applications built into them, and these software packages can be run even on commonly available spreadsheets.

[12] P. Del Moral and L. Miclo, "Asymptotic Results for Genetic Algorithms with Applications to Nonlinear Estimation," in *Theoretical Aspects of Evolutionary Computation*, eds, L. Kallel, B. Naudts, and A. Rogers (Berlin: Springer-Verlag, 2001), pp. 439–494; Robert E. Dorsey and Walter J. Mayer, "Genetic Algorithms for Estimation Problems with Multiple Optima, Nondifferentiability, and Other Irregular Features," *Journal of Business Economics and Statistics* 13, no. 1 (1995): 53–66; Ralf Salomon, "Evolutionary Algorithms and Gradient Search: Similarities and Differences," *IEEE Trans. on Evolutionary Computations* (1998), 2(2): 45–55.

[13] Moral and Miclo, "Asymptotic Results for Genetic Algorithms with Applications to Nonlinear Estimation."

[14] G. A. F. Seber and C. J. Wild, *Nonlinear Regression* (New York: John Wiley and Sons, 1989), p. 92.

[15] Robert E. Dorsey and Walter J. Mayer, "Genetic Algorithms for Estimation Problems with Multiple Optima, Nondifferentiability, and Other Irregular Features," *Journal of Business Economics and Statistics* 13, no. 1 (1995): 53–66.

[16] Salomon, "Evolutionary Algorithms and Gradient Search."

HIERARCHICAL BAYES MODELS[17]

Hierarchical Bayes (HB) models are models in a hierarchical form that are estimated using Bayesian methods. The hierarchical model is a group of sub-models, and the Bayes theorem is used to integrate them together and account for the uncertainty contained in the data. A typical design and structure of this model in marketing research studies would be one model for within-unit analysis (that could describe the behavior of individual respondents over time), and another model for across-unit analysis (that could be used to describe the diversity, or heterogeneity, of the units). Computational methods have been developed to implement the Bayes theorem through the use of simple, repetitive calculations performed by computers. These computational methods are referred to as Markov chain Monte Carlo (MCMC) methods and are used in tandem with hierarchical models. The Bayes theorem is designed to keep track of uncertainty, through conditional probability. It brings together concepts such as the probability about the outcome of events based on prior knowledge about things, and statements about prior knowledge about things based on observed data.

To illustrate the Bayes theorem at work, consider an American snack food company that is in the testing phase of a Chinese version of their best-selling product by adding a new ingredient. The two conditions here are—new ingredient (I+) and no new ingredient (I–). Similarly, when they test the product in China, they are faced with two outcomes—liked by the Chinese (L+) and not liked by the Chinese (L–). A market researcher commissioned to study this would be likely to look at two aspects—the sensitivity [denoted as $P(L+ \mid I+)$], and the specificity [denoted as $P(L- \mid I-)$]. Here, large values of $P(L+ \mid I+)$ indicate that Chinese consumers are sensitive toward liking the new product given that the new ingredient has been added; large values of $P(L- \mid I-)$ indicate that Chinese consumers are right in indicating the non-likeability of the product due to the absence of the ingredient. The researcher is also likely to measure the sensitivity and specificity by testing the product with and without the new ingredient in other Asian countries that are known to have liked and not liked the product, and in the process gather important statistics regarding the new product.

However, the approach of the company management could be different. The company's prior experience and knowledge in product development would dictate them to know $P(I+ \mid L+)$ if Chinese consumers liked the product, and not $P(L+ \mid I+)$. In other words, they would want to know the impact of adding/not adding the ingredient, given the reaction of Chinese consumers. Further, the company has just one test result for China, not many. Since the sample involved is small (one, in this example), the company would want to be careful by not basing their decisions on hypothetical outcomes across multiple studies.

In such a scenario, the Bayes theorem will help the company move from $P(L \mid I)$ to $P(I \mid L)$. The conditional probability is as follows:

$$P(I+ \mid L+) = \frac{P(L+ \mid I+) \times P(I+)}{P(L+)} \text{ and}$$

---

[17] Greg M. Allenby, Peter E. Rossi, and Robert E. McCulloch, "Hierarchical Bayes Models: A Practitioner's Guide," January 2005, http://ssrn.com/abstract=655541; Greg M. Allenby, Peter E. Rossi, and Robert E. McCulloch, *Bayesian Statistics and Marketing* (New York: John Wiley and Sons, 2005).

$$P(I- \,|\, L+) = \frac{P(L+ \,|\, I-) \times P(I-)}{P(L+)}$$

In terms of odds ratio, this can be presented as:

$$\frac{P(I+ \,|\, L+)}{P(I- \,|\, L+)} = \frac{P(L+ \,|\, I+)}{P(L+ \,|\, I-)} \times \frac{P(I+)}{P(I-)} \quad \text{or,}$$

Posterior odds = (Likelihood ratio) × (Prior odds)

Therefore, the Bayes theorem is used to move from the likelihood, which conditions on the addition of the new ingredient, to a statistics that is directly relevant to the company management and allows them to update their prior knowledge and understanding about developing new products for various countries. In other words, the Bayes theorem takes a large-sample concept like sensitivity and specificity and transforms it into a statistic so that inference can be made about a single country. In addition, it combines these measures with prior beliefs expressed in the form of probabilities.

Although simple and intuitive in form, the Bayesian methods have not become popular because of the complexities involved in the analytical calculations. However, the MCMC methods have eliminated this difficulty. The MCMC methods substitute a set of repetitive calculations that simulate draws from this distribution rather than deriving the analytic form of the posterior distribution. These draws are then used to calculate the parameter estimates and the confidence intervals. The HB model is brought into form by setting up a Markov chain that generates draws from posterior distribution of the model parameters.

To illustrate the development of the HB model, consider a simple regression model:

$$y_t = \beta x_t + \varepsilon_t \qquad \text{where } \varepsilon_t \sim \text{Normal}(0, \sigma^2)$$

where prior distributions for the regression coefficients are typically assumed to be distributed according to a normal distribution:

$$\pi(\beta) = \frac{1}{\sqrt{2\pi\sigma^2}} \exp\left[\frac{-1}{2\sigma^2}(\beta - \bar{\beta})^2\right]$$

and, similarly, a prior distribution is assumed for the variance term, $\varpi(\sigma^2)$. The above is the formula for a bell-shaped curve centered at $\bar{\beta}_1$ and standard deviation equal to σ. This prior distribution was combined with the likelihood, which reflected the information contained in the data about the parameter as follows:

$$\pi(y_t \,|\, \beta, \sigma^2, x_t) = \prod_{t=1}^{T} \frac{1}{\sqrt{2\pi\sigma^2}} \exp\left[\frac{-1}{2\sigma^2}(y_t - \beta x_t)^2\right]$$

The Markov chain for the model can be described as follows:

1. Draw β given the data $\{y_t, x_t\}$ and the most recent draw of σ^2
2. Draw σ^2 given the data $\{y_t, x_t\}$ and the most recent draw of β
3. Repeat.

While the idea behind MCMC methods is simple, its implementation requires the derivations of the appropriate (conditional) distributions for generating the draws. Modern computing methods and software provide assistance to the researcher in generating the draws, thereby securing a wider reach for this technique in the field of marketing.

As a technique that is expanding in usage, it does have some immediate challenges that researchers have to contend with. First, off-the-shelf software programs for estimating HB models are limited in number and applicability. Further, customizable programs that can help researchers estimate these models are still in the early stages of development, and will take some more time to provide researchers with a comprehensive program to work with. Second, researchers must be comfortable with the fact that HB models do not *converge* in the fashion many estimation models do. Therefore, even after several thousand iterations, there will be some variation in the average parameter estimates. Finally, instead of a point estimate of values for each respondent, the HB model provides a distribution of estimates for each respondent. While this is powerful in terms of understanding uncertainty, it adds to the complexity of the analysis, particularly in the case of market simulation.

In summary, the Bayesian models provide researchers the freedom to study the complexities and uncertainties of human behavior in a more realistic manner. With its simple and intuitive form, this technique can help researchers understand several complex phenomena and yield better insights for the marketplace. With advances in computing power, this technique will be made more accessible to researchers for a wide range of marketing issues.

SUMMARY

The goal of one-factor ANOVA is to estimate and compare the effects of different treatments on the response variable. Statistical experiments are mostly used to determine if the effects of various treatments on the response variable are different, and to estimate how different they are. The ANOVA table can be expanded to accommodate n factors. Correlation analysis involves measuring the strength of a linear relationship between two variables. The objective in regression analysis is to build a prediction equation, called the regression model, relating the dependent variable to one or more predictor variables.

A pooled TSCS analysis is a collection of data across a set of units (such as people, countries, regions, brands, etc.) over time. While they do offer benefits such as better explanatory power, ability to focus on the variables of interest, and capture simultaneous variations, they suffer from drawbacks such as correlation among the errors, heteroscedasticity, and contemporaneous correlation, among others. GAs provide a search-based approach that closely imitates the process of natural evolution. This technique is often used to generate solutions to problems related to optimization and search queries. This technique has been found to be better than other search-based algorithms in terms of better fit and performance. However, it still suffers from a longer execution time and complexities in coding. The HB models are models in a hierarchical form that are estimated using Bayesian methods. The hierarchical model is a group of sub-models, and the Bayes theorem is used to integrate them together and account for the uncertainty contained in the data. Even though this technique provides the much-needed assistance to researchers in modeling uncertainties, they do pose challenges in the form of limited availability of software programs for estimating these models, variations in the average parameter estimates, and presence of a distribution of estimates for each respondent instead of point estimate.

 QUESTIONS AND PROBLEMS

1. The Ob–Gyn department of St. Patrick's Presbyterian Hospital maintains the age and weight chart of the newborn babies. Given below are a random sample of the age (in months) and weights (in pounds) of babies that currently visit the hospital.

Age	4.5	5.5	3.0	2.0	1.5	6.5	7.5	9.0
Weight	13.0	16.5	11.5	11.0	10.0	17.0	18.5	20.0

   a. Determine the sample correlation between age and weight.
   b. Test at 5% level that the population correlation coefficient is zero.
2. A major grocery retailer was interested in knowing the impact of advertising expenditure on store traffic. You are called in as a consultant to help them out. You are provided with a random sample of 20 stores. For each store in the sample, the number of people entering the store (Y_i) on a given Saturday is provided, along with the amount spent on advertising for each store in the previous day (X_i). The information is provided in the table below.

No. of Stores	Store Traffic, Y_i	Advertising Dollars, X_i	$X_i \times Y_i$	X_i^2
1	90	40	3,600	1,600
2	125	75	9,375	5,625
3	320	100	32,000	10,000
4	200	110	22,000	12,100
5	600	190	114,000	36,100
6	450	200	90,000	40,000
7	400	300	120,000	90,000
8	700	310	217,000	96,100
9	800	380	304,000	144,400
10	810	410	332,100	168,100
11	1,000	480	480,000	230,400
12	1,170	500	585,000	250,000

(Table Contd)

(Table Contd)

No. of Stores	Store Traffic, Y_i	Advertising Dollars, X_i	$X_i \times Y_i$	X_i^2
13	1,200	520	624,000	270,400
14	1,500	550	825,000	302,500
15	1,000	560	560,000	313,600
16	900	580	522,000	336,400
17	700	690	483,000	476,100
18	1,000	700	700,000	490,000
19	1,300	710	923,000	504,100
20	1,350	800	1,080,000	640,000
Sum	15,615.00	8,205.00	8,026,075	4,417,525
Mean	780.75	410.25		

    a. Estimate the linear regression of advertising expenditure on store traffic.

    b. If advertising expenses of 750 are planned, what effect on store traffic would you expect?

3. An analyst for an oil company has developed a formal linear regression model to predict the sales of 50 of their filling stations. The estimated model is

$$\hat{Y} = b_0 + b_1 X_1$$

where

$\hat{Y}$ = average monthly sales in gallons
X = square foot area of station property
$X_1 = X - \bar{X}$(difference from the mean).

Some empirical results were

Variable	Mean	Range of Data	Reg. Coefficient	t-Value	r^2
Y		5,000–80,000 gal.	$b_0 = 10,000$		
X	10,000	3,000–20,000 sq. ft	$b_1 = 3.1$	2	0.3

    a. What does r^2 mean?

    b. Interpret the parameter estimates b_0 and b_1.

4. An experiment was conducted to determine which of three advertisements to use in introducing a new personal computer. A total of 120 people who were thinking of buying a personal computer were split randomly into three groups of 40 each. Each group was shown a different advertisement and each person was asked his or her likelihood of buying the advertised brand. A scale of 1 (very unlikely) to 7 (very likely) was used. The results showed that the average likelihood of purchase was:

Advertisement A: 5.5
Advertisement B: 5.8
Advertisement C: 5.2

The ANOVA table was as follows:

Source of Variation	SS	df	MSS	F-Ratio	p-Value
Due to Advertisements	12	2	6.0		
Unexplained	234	117	2.0		
Total	246	119			

a. What is the appropriate null hypothesis? The alternative hypothesis?
b. What are the *F*-ratio and the *p*-value?
c. Is the result significant at the 0.10 level, the 0.05 level, and the 0.01 level?
d. Are there any differences among the impacts of the three advertisements?

15

Multivariate Data Analysis

INTRODUCTION

This chapter discusses multivariate data techniques. The techniques discussed here are called multivariate data analysis techniques because they involve the simultaneous analysis of two or more variables. Multivariate techniques can be classified as interdependence or dependence techniques based on whether two or more variables have been designated as dependent on one or more independent variable. In dependence techniques, the value taken by the dependent variable could be predicted once the researcher knows the values of independent variables. In interdependence techniques, researchers concentrate on the interaction between variables. Here variables are not classified as dependent or independent.

INTERDEPENDENCE TECHNIQUES

The three interdependence techniques that are used most frequently in global marketing research are factor analysis, cluster analysis, and multidimensional scaling.

Factor Analysis

Factor analysis is a technique in which researchers look for a small number of factors that could explain the correlation between a large number of variables. It allows the researcher to study the variance of a number of variables in relation to a set of underlying factors. In marketing research, factor analysis is used primarily as a means of data reduction and transformation. Data may be available for a large number of attributes in a global marketing research project. This could be reduced to a manageable level by identifying the basic factors that underlie these attributes. This procedure can also be used to identify factors that are not correlated. Factor analysis can also be used to give appropriate weights to the variables when combining them into a scale. Some areas of marketing research that use factor analysis are development of personality scales, identification of key product attributes, and so on.

In general, factor analysis can be summarized as a method of transforming the original variables into new, non-correlated variables, called *factors*. One measure of the amount of information conveyed by the factors is their variance and for this purpose, factors are typically arranged in order of decreasing variances. The first factor will have the maximum variance. Once the first factor and its loading are fixed, the principal components will locate a second factor that maximizes the variance it explains. This is continued until the analyst determines that the useful numbers of factors has been obtained. Once the factors have been generated, it is useful to rotate the factors using one of the many rotation schemes. This helps in better interpretation of factors.[1]

Factor

A factor is a variable or a construct that is not directly observable but needs to be inferred from the input variables. A factor model has a small set of independent variables termed factors, which are hypothesized to cause or explain the dependent variable. The coefficients of factors, called factor loadings, link the factors to the variables, and are used to help interpret the factors. Since the primary goal of factor analysis is to reduce the number of variables in the model, an obvious question is how many factors can be used. Theoretically, there can be as many factors as variables, but this would serve no purpose. Hence, the thumb rule used is that the factors must explain at least as much variation as an average variable. The logic behind this is that if the factor has to replace one or more variables in the model, it must absorb at least as much variance as an original input variable.

Eigenvalue Criteria

An *eigenvalue* represents the amount of variance in the original variables that is associated with the factor. Only factors with eigenvalues greater than 1.0 are retained in the model; other factors are not included in the model. Put in another manner, the sum of the square of the factor loadings of each variable on a factor represents the eigenvalue of the total variance explained by the factor. A factor with eigenvalue less than 1.0 is not better than a single variable, since, due to standardization, each variable has a variance of 1.0. A factor should be able to explain at least the variance in one variable. If this is not possible, it is better to have the original variable.

Scree Plot Criteria

A *scree plot* is a plot of eigenvalues against the number of factors. The shape of the plot is used to determine the number of factors. Typically, the plot has a distinct break between the steep slope of factors with large eigenvalues and a gradual trailing off associated with the rest of the factors. This gradual trailing off is referred to as the *scree*. Experimental evidence indicates that the point at which the scree begins denotes the true number of factors.

Percentage of Variance Criteria

The number of factors extracted is determined so that the cumulative percentage of variance extracted by the variance reaches a satisfactory level. The level of variance that is satisfactory depends on the research problem. Typically, a criterion of factors explaining at least 70% of the variance is sought.

Factor Interpretation

The input to a factor analysis program is a set of variables for each individual or object in the sample. A matrix of correlations can also be used as input. The most important part of the output is the factor loadings—correlation between factors and variables. Factor analysis works

---

[1] For a detailed description of Factor Analysis, refer Aaker et al., *Marketing Research*, 11th edition.

on the assumption that there are factors underlying the variables and that the variables completely and adequately represent these factors.

Factor Scores

A factor is a variable, and the output of most factor analysis programs is the values for each factor for all respondents. These values are termed *factor scores*. Factor scores will be used in subsequent analyses instead of the original variables because they have fewer factors than variables and the factors are conceptually meaningful. The factor is a derived variable in the sense that the factor score is calculated from knowledge of the variables associated with it. Factors can be represented as linear contributions of original variables.

Communality

Communality is the percentage of a variable's variance that contributes to the correlation with other variables or is *common* to other variables.

Variance Explained

The percentage of variance explained is a summary measure indicating how much of the total original variance of all five variables the factor represents.[2] The percentage-of-variance-explained statistic can be useful in evaluating and interpreting a factor.

Factor Rotation

Factor analysis can generate several solutions (loadings and factor scores) for any data set. Each solution is termed a particular factor rotation and is generated by a factor rotation scheme. Each time the factors are rotated, the pattern of loadings changes, as does the interpretation of the factors. Geometrically, rotation means simply that the dimensions are rotated. There are many such rotation programs, such as varimax rotation (for orthogonal rotation) and promax rotation (for oblique rotation).

Factor analysis has several disadvantages. It is a highly subjective method and rests completely on the judgment of the analyst. It does not make use of any regularly used statistical tests, and hence, it is difficult to know if the results are significant or merely an accident. The determination of the number of factors, their interpretation, and the rotation to select (if one set of factors displeases the analyst, rotation may be continued indefinitely) involves subjective judgment.

A related limitation is that no statistical tests are regularly employed in factor analysis.[3] As a result, it is often difficult to know if the results are merely accidental or really reflect something meaningful. Consequently, a standard procedure of factor analysis should be to divide the sample randomly into two or more groups and independently run a factor analysis of each group. If the same factors emerge in each analysis, then one may be more confident that the results do not represent a statistical accident.

---

[2] The percentage of variance explained is proportional to the sum of squared loadings associated with that factor. Thus, a factor's percent of explained variance depends in part on the number of variables on which the factor has high loadings. A variable's communality actually is equal to the sum of the squared factor loadings of that variable.

[3] David W. Stewart, "The Application and Misapplication of Factor Analysis in Marketing Research," *Journal of Marketing Research* 18 (1981): 51–62.

An example of practical usage of factor analysis in global marketing research is the study conducted to measure consumer innovativeness in the US, Germany, and France.[4] International markets frequently present managers with many challenges. The local consumers will perceive their products as new products or innovations. To market their products successfully, managers should know the pattern of acceptance of new products around the world. The study focused on a concept called domain-specific innovativeness scale (DSI) which had been developed earlier and was used to measure innovativeness or tendency of consumers to be among the first to try new products in a specific product field after they appear in the marketplace. The DSI has been validated for both goods and services in English-speaking countries. However, this study considered the French and German versions to measure innovativeness among French- and German-speaking people. The study also provides an opportunity to evaluate cross-culturally some aspects of the diffusion theory of marketing.

Innovativeness has been described as a normally distributed characteristic in the consumer population. In addition, innovativeness is domain-specific. Consumers who are likely to adopt the latest new product in one field may be laggards in another. The DSI index is a six-item Likert scale intended to reliably and validly measure consumer innovativeness in a specific product field. The DSI was developed as a balanced scale—three items positively worded and three items negatively worded. The scale demonstrates high internal consistency and has shown to be free from social desirability and acquiescence response artifacts. Criterion validity has been established because the scale is positively correlated with measures of behaviors that it should be positively related to. It exhibits positive correlation with measures of product involvement, positive correlation with product knowledge and zero correlation with a measure of opinion seeking. For the purpose of this study, DSI was hypothesized to be unidimensional, internally consistent, free from social desirability and acquiescence. It was also hypothesized to be positively correlated with measures of product usage, product involvement, and product knowledge and uncorrelated with a measure of opinion seeking, replicating previous studies, and thereby demonstrating nomological validity.

A study that aimed to develop an individual-level measure of consumer-based brand equity used factor analysis as one of the tools for analyzing data.[5] Drawing upon earlier studies,[6] this study used data from American, Korean American, and Korean consumers. The study surveyed 12 brands: six athletic shoes (Adidas, Asics, LA Gear, Nike, Puma, and Reebok), four films (Agfa, Fuji, Kodak, and Konica), and two color television sets (Samsung and Sony). The brands were selected on three criteria. First, it was ensured that the brands were available in both Korea and the US. Second, the brands had to be markedly different in terms of market share. Finally, the selected brands had different countries of origin. The US is the COO for LA Gear, Nike, Reebok, and Kodak, Germany for Adidas, Puma, and Agfa, Japan for Asics, Fuji, Konica, and Sony, and South Korea for Samsung.

After pilot testing the questionnaire, the study decided upon six items for perceived quality, three for brand loyalty, three for brand awareness, and five for brand associations that were to be included in the main study. At this stage, three levels of analyses were conducted to develop a brand equity measure. First, an individual analysis was performed to determine

[4] Ronald E. Goldsmith, Francois d'Hauteville, and Leisa R. Flynn, "Theory and Measurement of Consumer Innovativeness," *European Journal of Marketing* 32, no. 3 (1998): 340–353.

[5] B. Yoo, and N. Donthu, "Developing and Validating a Multi-Dimensional Consumer-Based Brand Equity Scale," *Journal of Business Research* 52, no. 1 (2001): 1–14.

[6] D. A. Aaker, *Managing Brand Equity* (New York: Free Press, 1991); K. L. Keller, "Conceptualizing, Measuring and Managing Customer-Based Brand Equity," *Journal of Marketing* 57, no. 1 (1993): 1–22.

whether common items and dimensions were found in each sample. Second, a multigroup analysis was conducted to examine factorial invariance of the items selected in the individual analysis to enable cross-cultural comparisons of the constructs. Finally, a pooled analysis was conducted to identify culture-free universal dimensions of brand equity in the pooled sample.

These analyses resulted in the 10-item measure of multidimensional brand equity (MBE) as a scale of consumer-based brand equity. Because of the cross-cultural invariance, the scores of the MBE and its dimensions can be compared cross-culturally, and the different scores may be considered indicative of true cross-cultural differences in the constructs. The 10 items reflected the three dimensions of brand loyalty, perceived quality, and brand awareness/associations. Across cultures, Nike and Kodak were the highest in the MBE index and in every brand equity dimension. Sony received higher evaluations than Samsung in the American market, but Koreans preferred Samsung to Sony. Exhibits 15.1(a–d) illustrate the application of the MBE formula on the 12 brands.

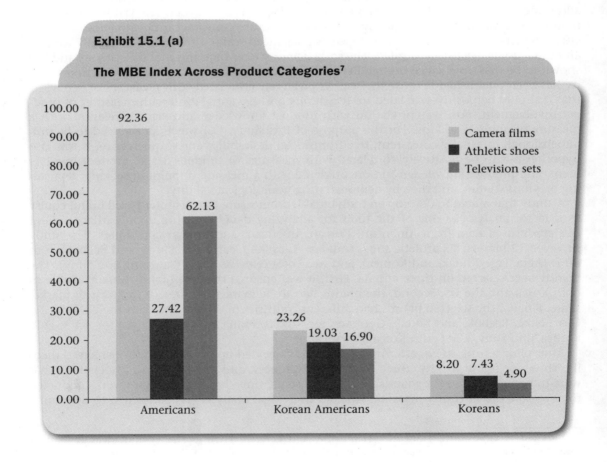

Exhibit 15.1 (a)

The MBE Index Across Product Categories[7]

- Camera films
- Athletic shoes
- Television sets

Americans: 92.36, 27.42, 62.13
Korean Americans: 23.26, 19.03, 16.90
Koreans: 8.20, 7.43, 4.90

[7] Yoo and Donthu, "Developing and Validating a Multi-Dimensional Consumer-Based Brand Equity Scale."

Exhibit 15.1 (b)

The MBE Index of Camera Film Brands Across Cultures[8]

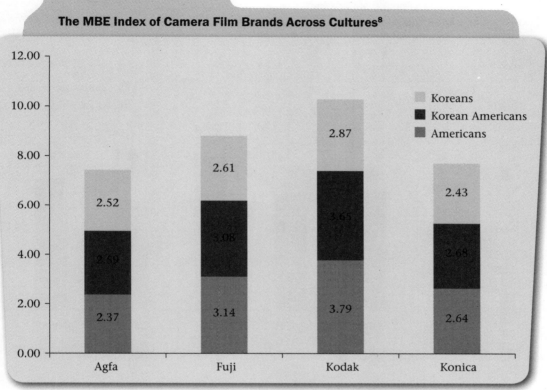

To assess MBE's convergent validity, the study further developed a four-item unidimensional (direct) measure of brand equity, which they labeled as *overall brand equity*. A strong and significant correlation was found between the two measures. The correlation between the MBE index and the mean score composite was 1.00 for Americans, 0.98 for Korean Americans, and 0.99 for Koreans. The other composite score, made from a sum of the raw scores of the 10 items, was also highly correlated to the MBE index. The correlation between the MBE index and the raw score composite was 0.97 for Americans, 0.91 for Korean Americans, and 0.94 for Koreans. These results suggested that the composite score based on the mean or raw scores can be used as an excellent proxy for the MBE index, in particular in non-Korean or non-American countries.

---

[8] Yoo and Donthu, "Developing and Validating a Multi-Dimensional Consumer-Based Brand Equity Scale."

Exhibit 15.1 (c)

The MBE Index of Athletic Shoes Across Cultures[9]

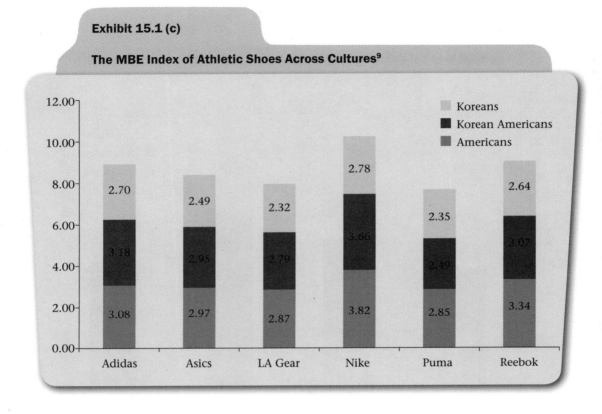

Cluster Analysis

In cluster analysis, variables are placed in subgroups or clusters. These clusters are formed by the cluster analysis procedure itself by using a group of ad hoc computational procedures. Cluster analysis is mainly used to place objects in groups or clusters based on the attributes they possess. Objects that are placed in a certain cluster have a higher association with other objects in the same cluster and lesser association with objects in any other cluster. Groups formed by cluster analysis have minimum within-group variability and maximum between-group variability. It is possible to have a number of alternative sets of clusters. The researcher then chooses the one set that is most appropriate for the situation.

---

[9] Yoo and Donthu, "Developing and Validating a Multi-Dimensional Consumer-Based Brand Equity Scale."

Exhibit 15.1 (d)

The MBE Index of Television Sets Across Cultures[10]

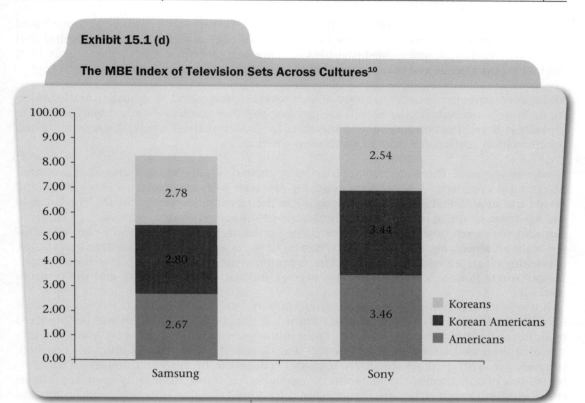

The cluster analysis typically involves six stages.[11] In the first step, the problem to be investigated is defined. Second, an appropriate similarity measure is selected to group objects together. Third, decisions on how to group the objects are made. Fourth, the desired number of clusters is decided. Fifth, the clusters are evaluated and profiles are created to describe them for managerial relevance. Finally, the clusters are validated against some information to make sure they produce meaningful results. The following sections provide a brief description of the stages involved.

Problem definition: In this stage, individuals or objects that form natural groupings or clusters are defined and identified. Often in marketing studies, one goal of marketing managers is to identify similar consumer segments so that marketing programs can be developed and tailored to each segment. Therefore, the aim of such a clustering might be to cluster customers

---

[10] Yoo and Donthu, "Developing and Validating a Multi-Dimensional Consumer-Based Brand Equity Scale."

[11] For a detailed description of Cluster Analysis, refer Aaker et al., *Marketing Research*, 11th edition.

based on the product benefits they seek. Alternatively, customers can also be grouped based on their lifestyles. The result could be one group that likes outdoor activities, another that enjoys entertainment, and a third that likes cooking and gardening. Each segment may have distinct product needs and may respond differently to advertising approaches.

Measures of similarity: In order to group objects together, some kind of similarity or dissimilarity measure is needed. Similar objects are grouped together and those farther apart are put in separate clusters. The commonly used measures for cluster analysis are: (a) distance measures, (b) correlation coefficients, and (c) association coefficients.

Clustering approach: There are two approaches to clustering—hierarchical approach and non-hierarchical approach. A *hierarchical clustering* can start with all objects in one cluster, and divide and subdivide them until all objects are in their own single-object cluster. This is called the *top-down*, or decision, approach. The *bottom-up*, or agglomerative, approach, in contrast, can start with each object in its own (single-object) cluster and systematically combine clusters until all objects are in one cluster. When an object is associated with another in a cluster, it remains clustered with that object. The commonly used methods of hierarchical clustering are single linkage, complete linkage, average linkage, Ward's method, and the centroid method.

A *non-hierarchical clustering* program differs only in that it permits objects to leave one cluster and join another as clusters are being formed, if the clustering criterion will be improved by doing so. In this approach, a cluster center initially is selected, and all objects within a pre-specified threshold distance are included in that cluster. If a three-cluster solution is desired, three-cluster centers are specified. These cluster centers can be random numbers or the cluster centers obtained from the hierarchical approach. The most commonly used non-hierarchical clustering approaches are the sequential threshold, parallel threshold, and optimizing procedures.

Number of clusters: Several approaches are used to determine the number of clusters. In the first approach, the number of clusters is specified in advance. This could be done for logical or managerial reasons. In the second approach, the level of clustering can be specified with respect to the clustering criterion. For instance, if the clustering criterion is easily interpretable, such as the average within-cluster similarity, it might be reasonable to establish a certain level that would dictate the number of clusters. In the third approach, the number of clusters is determined from the pattern of clusters the program generates. The distances between clusters at successive steps may serve as a useful guideline, and the analyst may choose to stop when the distance exceeds a specified value or when the successive distances between steps make a sudden jump. Finally, the ratio of total within-group variance to between-group variance can be plotted against the number of clusters. The point at which an elbow or a sharp bend occurs indicates an appropriate number of clusters. Increasing the number of clusters beyond this point probably is not useful, and decreasing the number can result in combining unrelated categories into one cluster.

Evaluating and profiling the clusters: Once clusters are developed, they will have to be profiled to draw up a meaningful description of the clusters. One frequently used measure is the centroid—the average value of the objects in the cluster on each of the variables making up each object's profile. If the data are interval-scaled and clustering is performed in the original variables space, this measure appears quite natural as a summary description.

Statistical inference: There are no established procedures of testing the statistical reliability of clusters. This is largely due to the difficulty in specifying realistic null hypothesis. However, some ad hoc methods are available that researchers can use. For instance, two or more different clustering routines can be applied to the same data and the resultant clusters and distance measures can be compared. Another approach is to split the data randomly into halves, perform separate clustering, and then examine the average profile values of each cluster across subsamples. Alternatively, simulation procedures that employ random-number generators can be used to create a data set with the properties matching the overall properties of the original data but containing no clusters. The same clustering methods can be used on both the real and the artificial data, and the resultant solutions can be compared.

Exhibit 15.2 shows the results of a cluster analysis that was performed to understand how social media behavior could be used by higher education institutions in the Netherlands for communication and recruitment purposes. The study explores the main characteristics of the future university students and analyses the way they use the social media in their everyday life, and the effect it has on their decision-making process, particularly in the selection of higher education studies. Segmenting future university students like this can help develop or refine social-media-based communication strategies, effectively reaching future students and providing them with better information in order to help them make the right study choices.

Exhibit 15.2

Clusters for Future Students in The Netherlands (on the Basis of Social Media Usage)[12]

Segment: Social Media Users	Profile
Social users (40.7%)	The largest of the three clusters; the users of this group use their social media accounts predominantly for the purposes of entertainment and socialization.
Informational users (29.7%)	This class of users leverages the social media to not only perform activities of entertainment and socialization, but also carry out information-seeking activities. They also engage in information-adding activities like sharing of pictures and videos.
Beginner users (29.5%)	This group is characterized by very low levels of profile usage for entertainment and socialization.

[12] Efthymios Constantinides and Marc C. Zinck Stagno, "Potential of the Social Media as Instruments of Higher Education Marketing: A Segmentation Study," *Journal of Marketing for Higher Education* 21, no. 1 (2011): 7–24.

Multidimensional Scaling

Multidimensional scaling encompasses a set of computational procedures that can summarize an input matrix of associations between variables or objects.[13] It has been mainly used by marketing researchers to study relationships among objects, like different brands of a certain product category. Multidimensional scaling technique can be used to analyze consumer perceptions and preferences for various brands. It is also applied to identify the product attributes that are important to consumers, the most preferred attributes, combinations of attributes that give the product a competitive edge, and substitutes that are available for consumers.

An example of multidimensional scaling technique used in global marketing research is the study conducted to determine patterns of convergence and divergence among industrialized nations.[14] The objective was to analyze if increased trade and travel between countries helps bring countries together. This study examined similarities in macro-environmental characteristics of 18 industrialized nations over a 28-year period. The study started out with three propositions:

1. Industrialized countries are becoming more similar in terms of macro-environmental characteristics
2. Physical distance is declining in importance as a determinant of difference between nations
3. Individualism and power distance are important determinants of patterns of macro-environmental evolution

The original data set consisted of 42 variables representing economic, demographic, market infrastructure, and quality of life variables. Four criteria were used to reduce the variables to 15.

1. Availability of data for all time periods
2. Redundancy of variables, giving rise to problems of multi-collinearity
3. Elimination of variables with no variance over the time period studied
4. Selection of variables with a high coefficient of variation across countries

Multidimensional scaling was used to test the first proposition. Patterns of convergence and/or divergence of the macro-environmental factors over the 28-year period were observed. A dissimilarities matrix for the 15 macro-environmental variables was calculated using Euclidean distance measure. The resulting 72 × 72 (18 countries × 4 time periods) matrix was served as input to a multidimensional scaling routine.

Examination of the three-dimensional mapping solution for the 18 countries and the four time periods in Figures 15.1 and 15.2 suggests that, rather than converging in terms of macro-environmental characteristics, countries are becoming more divergent. In the 1960s, countries form a tight cluster predominantly in the upper right quadrant. The US is the only exception being in the upper left quadrant. By 1970, the clustering had begun to shift toward the left. However, major shifts occurred between 1980 and 1988. All countries moved dramatically

---

[13] Efthymios Constantinides and Marc C. Zinck Stagno (2011), *Journal of Marketing for Higher Education*, pp. 7–24.

[14] Samuel Craig, Susan Douglas, and Andreas Grein, "Patterns of Convergence and Divergence Among Industrialized Nations: 1960–1988," *Journal of International Business Studies* (1992).

FIGURE 15.1

MULTIDIMENSIONAL MAP OF EUROPEAN COUNTRIES, THE US, AND JAPAN (DIMENSION 2: COST OF LIVING)

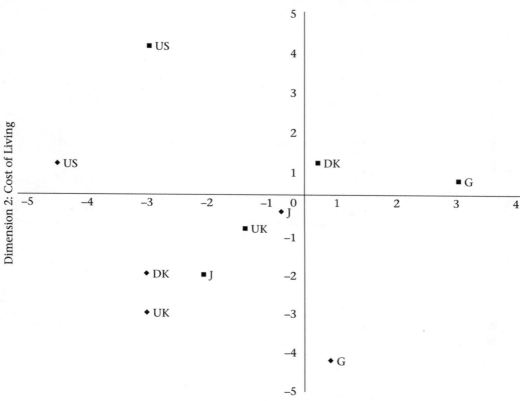

Dimension 1: Standard of Living

◆ 1988   ■ 1960

toward the left and became increasingly dispersed. The increasing divergence is further con-firmed by the examination of the mean dissimilarity of countries for the 15 macro-environ-mental variables for the four time periods.

Closer observation of the figures show that not only does the distance between countries increase over the period studied, but in addition, there is a marked shift from left to right on Dimension 1. Examination of the variable that accounts for most of the variation on this dimension suggests that it reflects overall standard of living.

Dimension 1 accounts for the largest portion of the variation in country dissimilarity. Consequently, most of the original variables used to establish the three dimensions correlate with Dimension 1. This dimension seems to capture the standard of living, as reflected by per capita income and increase in number of passenger cars. It also incorporates aspects of communications network (number of telephones and radios) and real wealth. Countries that exhibit the greatest movement in this direction were the Mediterranean countries marked by social power structures and social inequality.

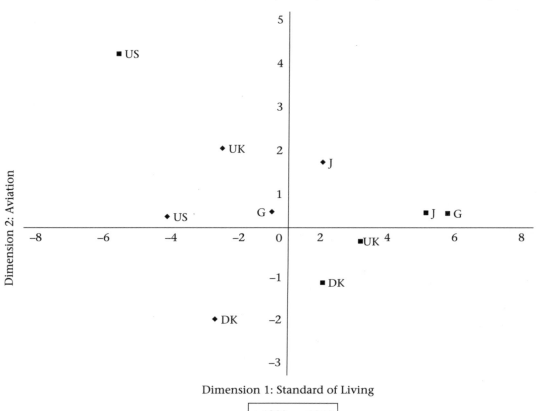

FIGURE 15.2
MULTIDIMENSIONAL MAP OF EUROPEAN COUNTRIES, THE US, AND JAPAN (DIMENSION 2: AVIATION)

Dimension 1: Standard of Living

◆ 1988   ■ 1960

DEPENDENCE TECHNIQUES

Dependence methods that are discussed in this chapter are discriminant analysis, and conjoint analysis.

Discriminant Analysis

The basic idea of discriminant analysis is to find a linear combination of independent variables that makes the mean scores across categories of the dependent variable on this linear combination maximally different.[15] As in case of regression analysis, discriminant analysis is

---

[15] Thomas Kinnear, James Taylor, Lester Johnson, and Robert Armstrong, *Australian Marketing Research*, (Sydney: McGraw-Hill Book Company, 1993).

used for prediction and description. This technique is used to classify objects into two or more alternative groups on the basis of a set of measurements. The groups are distinct and each individual object belongs to one of the groups. Discriminant analysis aims to:

1. Determine linear combinations of predictor variables that would form groups, so as to have maximum between-group variation relative to within-group variation
2. Develop procedures that help in placing new objects in one of the previously formed groups
3. Test if there are significant differences between groups
4. Determine variables that contribute the most to the group variations

Discriminant analysis is used primarily to identify variables that contribute to differences in the defined groups with the use of discriminant functions. The model requires variable values for the independent variables and the dependent variable. Discriminant analysis will provide the characteristics of the discriminant function and the significance of the function. F-tests are used for determining the significance of the discriminant function. The program also gives the raw and standard discriminant weights to assist in the classification of objects.

Discriminant analysis works on the assumptions that all the independent variables (say p independent variables) must have a multivariate normal distribution. The $p \times p$ variance–covariance matrix of the independent variables in each of the two groups must be the same.

The following example illustrates the use of discriminant analysis. The researchers surveyed CEOs of small businesses to explore their interest in foreign markets. 200 small businesses were sent questionnaires and 98 were returned. The researchers created a variable called *export interest* (EI) from the original variable, *willingness to export*. *Willingness to export* was rated a 4 or 5 if the company had an interest to enter foreign markets. Otherwise, it was rated 1, 2, or 3. The EI variable would assume the value 2 if *willingness to export* had 4 or 5, and 1 if the *willingness to export* had 1, 2, or 3. This leads to two groups—one exhibiting high interest to export (EI = 2) and one with low interest (EI = 1). The independent variables for the discriminant analysis used in this case were workforce size (Size), the firm's revenues (Rev), years of operation in the domestic market (Years) and the number of products currently produced by the firm (Prod). This will set up a discriminant function with four independent variables. The results are summarized in Tables 15.1 and 15.2.

TABLE 15.1

RESULTS OF DISCRIMINANT ANALYSIS[16]

Variables	Pooled-Within Discriminant Loadings	Total-Sample Standardized Discriminant Coefficients	Raw Canonical Coefficients
Size	0.585	0.825	0.077
Rev	0.249	0.196	0.300
Years	0.541	0.824	0.895
Prod	0.358	0.156	0.061

---

[16] Aaker et al., *Marketing Research*, 11th edition.

TABLE 15.2

CLASSIFICATION MATRIX[17]

Post Interest	High	Low	Total
Actual High	16 (72.73%)	6 (27.27%)	22 (100%)
Actual Low	9 (23.68%)	29 (76.32%)	38 (100%)
Total	25 (41.67%)	35 (58.33%)	60 (100%)
Hit Ratio = (16 + 29) / 60 = 75%			

Based on the examination of the standardized discriminant function coefficient for the predictor variables, we can conclude that workforce size (0.83) and years of operation in domestic market (0.82) are the two most discriminating variables of the level of EI. The classification matrix yields a hit ratio, or the percentage of cases correctly classified, of 75%, which is better than a chance classification of sorting every firm to the largest group (38 / 60 = 0.63 or 63%).

Conjoint Analysis

Conjoint analysis is an extremely powerful data analysis tool that is being used increasingly in global marketing research. This procedure deals with the joint effects of two or more independent variables on the ordering of a dependent variable. It provides a quantitative measure of the relative importance of one attribute as opposed to another. Data are obtained by giving respondents descriptions of concepts that represent the possible combinations of levels of attributes. It is also possible to obtain paired comparison judgments to get an understanding of the degree of preference of one profile over another. The computer program assigns values (known as part-worth utilities) for each level of the attribute. When these values are summed for each of the concepts being considered, the rank-order of these total value scores should match the respondents' rank-ordering of preference as closely as possible. The combination with the highest utility should be the one that was originally most preferred and the combination with the least utility should be the least preferred. The greater the difference between the highest- and the lowest-valued levels of the attribute, the more important is the attribute.

Respondent preferences can be obtained by asking them to consider two attributes at a time or making an overall judgment of a full profile of attributes. The full-profile approach is preferred in many cases because of the following advantages:

- All concepts are considered at the same time, and hence it is a more realistic approach
- Researcher has the option of using a ranking or a rating scale
- Respondents rate all attributes at the same time, and hence have to spend less time and energy

Unfortunately, as the number of attributes gets larger, judging becomes complex and puts a lot of strain on the respondents. This could result in loss of accuracy. Under these circumstances,

---

[17] Aaker et al., *Marketing Research*, 11th edition.

it is better to opt for the pair-wise trade-off method. There are certain disadvantages associated with the pair-wise trade-off method that researchers should be aware of.

- This method is tedious and time-consuming. Consequently, respondents may not be very accurate all the time
- There could be interactions among attributes, and when asked to rate the attributes separately, the respondents may not know how to deal with them. For instance, when asked to rate price and quality as separate attributes, those who associate price with quality could be unsure of how to rank the two
- There is loss of realism as respondents consider only two attributes at a time

Conjoint analysis was used to analyze data collected for direct mail response optimization for a charity institution in the Netherlands.[18] The objective of this study was to improve the effectiveness of direct mail by determining the optimal mailing design. The researchers first established the theoretical framework for response optimization. Past research in the area of direct mailing shows that the response depends on the following factors, in the order of importance:

1. The quality of the list
2. The characteristics of the (commercial) offer
3. The creative elements or the design of the mailing
4. The timing of the mailing

Studying the respondents' process of responding to the direct mail, they identified three critical behavioral components:

1. The prospective respondent opening the envelope
2. The prospective respondent taking notice of the elements of the mailing package and the offer
3. Responding to the offer

When the four factors were linked to the process of responding to the direct mail, the following conclusions emerged. The design characteristics of the direct mail influence its attractiveness, which in turn influences the probability of opening the envelope—a prerequisite for taking notice of the contents. The attractiveness of the contents of the mail influences the probability of taking notice of the offer that is made to the potential customer. Finally, the attractiveness of the offer itself influences the probability of responding.

Using conjoint analysis provides the researchers with a lot of flexibility. The respondents can be asked to judge a set of experimentally constructed envelopes with respect to their attractiveness. Using relative importances and part-worth utilities, it is possible to draw conclusions about the optimal design. However, this would be questioning the respondents in a setting that is not realistic. Hence, the researchers opted to use conjoint field-experiments. Each household in the sample receives one of the experimentally varied mailings.

---

[18] Marco Vriens, Hiek R. van der Scheer, Janny C. Hoekstra, and Jan Roelf Bult, "Conjoint Experiments for Direct Mail Response Optimization," *European Journal of Marketing* 32, no. 3 (1998): 323–339.

The design and implementation of a conjoint experiment consists of a number of steps in data collection and data analysis. These include:

1. Selection and definition of attributes
2. Determination of relevant levels within the characteristics
3. Thinking about the preference model
4. The choice of data collection method
5. Construction of stimuli
6. The definition of the dependent variable
7. The choice of data collection procedure

The characteristics included in the envelope experiment are listed in Exhibit 15.3.

Exhibit 15.3

Envelope Experiment[19]

Characteristics	Levels (Number of Levels)
Format	A5, Cabinet, or Ola (3)
Extra Imprint	Hologram, extra window in envelope, or none (3)
Type of Paper	Paper without chlorine or recycling paper (2)
Streamer	Typed, handwritten, or none (3)
Sender	Full name or abbreviated form (2)
Addition	Lottery or none (2)

The population of interest from which the sample was drawn was provided by the charity institution—people in the database who had donated at least once in the last three years. From the original sample of 1,692 people, 360 indicated willingness to cooperate in the study. Only 200 appeared at the time of the interview and 170 valid questionnaires were received. The relative importances of various characteristics (in percentages) as indicated by three major respondent segments are listed in Table 15.3.

Segment 1 consisted of respondents in the age group 35–50, having children, and residing outside the main city. Segment 2 was characterized by respondents over the age of 65. Segment 3 was made up of respondents below 35 years of age, having no children, and living inside the main city.

For situations in which it is not possible to link segmentation results to background characteristics, the weighted average relative importances are computed using segment sizes for weights.

---

[19] "Envelope Experiment," from Marco Vriens, Hiek R. van der Scheer, Janny C. Hoekstra and Jan Roelf Bult, "Conjoint Experiments for Direct Mail Response Optimization," *European Journal of Marketing*, Vol.32 (3/4), 1998 pp. 323-339. Reprinted with permission from MCB University Press.

TABLE 15.3

RELATIVE IMPORTANCE OF ATTRIBUTES BY SEGMENTS[20]

Attribute	Segment 1	Segment 2	Segment 3	Weighted
Format	17.1	14.3	33.5	20.6
Extra Imprint	41.1	22.4	45.5	34.2
Type of Paper	4.2	41.4	9.5	21.9
Streamer	19.2	8.4	2.7	9.7
Sender	6.5	2.5	8.1	5.2
Addition	11.8	11.2	0.7	8.3

Whether the institution decides to send three distinct envelopes instead of one to the three segments depends on whether the gains of such a strategy outweigh the extra costs.

There were differences in terms of the letter sent to respondents. The characteristics are listed in Exhibit 15.4. Test-letters were mailed to 48,000 households, and 54.4% response was obtained. Exhibit 15.5 summarizes the response figures. It was observed that by using customized letters for different segments, there was an average increase in donations of 5%. Because the direct mailing involves millions of households, this could prove substantial in absolute terms.

Exhibit 15.4

Letter Experiment Characteristics[21]

Characteristics	Levels
Payment Advice	Attached or not attached
Brochure	Present or absent
Illustration	Top left, top right, or none
Amplifier	Many, few, or none
Post Scriptum	Summary or new information
Signature	Professor or director
Address	Letter or payment advice

---

[20] "Relative Importance of Attributes by Segments," from Marco Vriens, Hiek R. van der Scheer, Janny C. Hoekstra and Jan Roelf Bult, "Conjoint Experiments for Direct Mail Response Optimization," *European Journal of Marketing*, Vol.32 (3/4), 1998 pp. 323-339. Reprinted with permission from MCB University Press.

[21] "Characteristics included in the letter experiment," from Marco Vriens, Hiek R. van der Scheer, Janny C. Hoekstra and Jan Roelf Bult, "Conjoint Experiments for Direct Mail Response Optimization," *European Journal of Marketing*, 1998, 32 (3/4): 323-339. Reprinted with permission from MCB University Press.

Exhibit 15.5

Exhibit 15.5. Letter Experiment Responses[22]

Characteristics	Levels	Response (%)	Donations*
Payment Advice	Attached	52.94	9.57
	Not attached	55.83	9.69
Brochure	Present	54.43	9.63
	Absent	54.35	9.63
Illustration	Top left	55.91	9.77
	Top right	49.51	9.02
	None	56.25	9.97
Amplifier	Many	55.54	9.73
	Few	53.52	9.51
	None	55.46	9.86
Post Scriptum	Summary	56.11	9.79
	New information	52.17	9.42
Signature	Professor	55.61	9.84
	Director	53.18	9.42
Address	Letter	54.50	9.63
	Payment advice	54.28	9.63
Overall		54.39	9.63

*Note: *Average donation (in NLG) of all households.*

The study concluded that between segments there were large differences with respect to mean relative importances of the characteristics as well as with respect to the optimal level. The availability of household characteristics is a prerequisite for applying the segmentation results. If this is not available, optimal mailing for the whole population should be determined and used.

SUMMARY

Multivariate techniques can be classified as interdependence or dependence techniques based on whether two or more variables have been designated as dependent on one or more

[22] "Characteristics included in the letter experiment," from Marco Vriens, Hiek R. van der Scheer, Janny C. Hoekstra and Jan Roelf Bult, "Conjoint Experiments for Direct Mail Response Optimization," *European Journal of Marketing*, Vol.32 (3/4), 1998 pp. 323-339. Reprinted with permission from MCB University Press.

independent variables. Factor analysis is used to identify underlying dimensions or constructs in data and to reduce the number of variables by eliminating redundancy. Cluster analysis is used to group variables, objects, or people. Multidimensional scaling is used to identify dimensions by which objects are perceived or evaluated, to position objects with respect to those dimensions, and to make positioning decisions for new and old products. Conjoint analysis is used to predict the buying or usage of a new product that is still in concept form. It is also used to determine the relative importance of various attributes to respondents, based on their making trade-off decisions. Discriminant analysis is used primarily to identify variables that contribute to differences in a priori defined groups with the use of discriminant functions. It can also be used to classify into one or more groups that have already been defined.

 QUESTIONS AND PROBLEMS

1. What is factor analysis and how does it help researchers in analyzing data?
2. How is the number of clusters in a solution determined?
3. How does multidimensional scaling differ from factor and cluster analysis?
4. What is discriminant analysis used for?
5. What are the steps involved in the design and implementation of a conjoint experiment?

16

Presenting the Results

INTRODUCTION

Research does not stop with finding the solutions to the proposed problems. Communicating the proposed solution to the stakeholders plays a very important role. Often, researchers get too involved in the technical aspects of analyzing data, forgetting the fact that the application of mathematical and statistical outputs is most important. Presentation of results plays a very significant role in marketing and has a special place in the context of global marketing research. A typical marketing research process will involve two presentations—the proposal and the findings. Presenting the proposal is very important to the researcher as the client makes a decision to proceed with the study based on this presentation. Presenting the results is also important as it addresses the decisions associated with the research purpose. Some managers evaluate the entire research process solely on the basis of the presentation, so researchers have a lot riding on the presentation. Results are presented in both written and oral formats, and guidelines for both of these formats are discussed in this chapter.

WRITTEN REPORT

A written report should be addressed to a specific audience, who in this case would be the decision makers. Clarity of thought and language is sine qua non. Visual aids, figures, and tables should be used wherever appropriate. Care should be taken to ensure that the report does not sound condescending. This becomes a crucial issue in many cultures where one is expected to act in deference to age, title, and gender. The report should address all the information needs of the research study. Researchers should perfect the art of conveying all the findings in a clear and concise manner. It should be remembered that managers who commission the study are extremely busy people and will not waste time and effort wading through reams of data to find the relevant data. It is entirely possible that the results do not fit into the preconceived ideas that one or more decision makers have and may not be accepted as valid results. It is important for the researcher to remain objective, even though the easy way out would be to make the report look more acceptable. The researcher should also be capable of defending the results if required.

There is no pre-specified format in which a written report may be prepared for a global marketing research study; however, it is a generally accepted practice in the marketing research industry for all written reports to contain the following:[1]

1. A *title page* that captures the essence of the study. It should include the name of the marketing research company and the name of the organization sponsoring the study. A confidential report should also include the names of the individuals who should receive it.
2. The *table of contents* with page references. This should include all the topics covered in the report, along with any tables or graphs or other visual aids used for the presentation.
3. The *executive summary*, which provides a snapshot of the entire research process. Because most decision makers read only the executive summary, it should contain information on those aspects of the research process that have the most impact on decision making. It should contain the research purpose, the main results, and all the recommendations put forth by the researcher.
4. The *body* of the report should be detailed and should document the research process from the beginning to the end.

    *   It is normal practice to start with an *introduction*, which depends on the audience. If the decision makers are not familiar with the research project and the marketing research process in general, it is vital that the introduction be extensive. It should include the nature of the decision problem and the circumstances under which the research was undertaken.
    *   The *methodology* followed will have to be detailed. This section of the report must contain research design—research question, hypotheses that have been tested, population definition, sampling plan, data collection procedures, and data analysis techniques.
    *   The *results* of the research have to be presented, keeping in mind the nature of the problem and the decisions that have to be made. This section should contain very few, if any at all, technical terms that cannot be understood by laymen.
    *   Care should be taken to explain the *limitations* of the research process. These could arise from discrepancies in sampling, data collection, and analysis stages.

5. *Recommendations* are a logical extension of the research findings and call for considerable experience and judgment on the part of the researcher. Recommendations should be practical and management must be in a position to take action.

Most researchers are not trained for report writing, and hence, they overlook the need for a good writing style. The pointers given below should be considered important for a good report.

*   Main headings and subheadings should be used to communicate the content or the main idea of the material discussed
*   As far as possible, the report should be in present tense
*   Active voice makes reports more lively and interesting

---

[1] Adapted from H. L. Gordon, "Eight Ways to Dress a Research Report," *Advertising Age*, October 20, 1980, p. S-37.

- Tables and graphs should be used whenever communicating data, as they are easier to follow and visually pleasing
- Use quotations to communicate the respondents' comments. This could help brand managers a lot

ORAL PRESENTATION

Most clients prefer to have an oral presentation in addition to a written report. Here is a checklist that will help researchers in making an effective presentation:

- Practice the presentation and have somebody listen to it. This will take care of holes in the presentation and make it more effective
- Before the presentation, check all equipment. Make sure the lights, microphones, projectors, and all other visual aids are in working order. Make contingency plans in case of failure of any equipment
- Get a feel for the audience. Begin the presentation by giving an overview of the research process
- Introduce research topics that are controversial toward the end of the presentation. The audience will be more open to radical changes once they are confident of the validity of the research process
- A golden rule for oral presentations: Do not read. Keep your notes handy and refer to them to make sure you are not leaving out any important points, but face the audience during the presentation
- Use visual aids to emphasize important points like facts and figures. These aids make the presentation more organized and easier to understand
- Avoid mannerisms and movements that distract the audience from the presentation. Do not add fillers such as "you know" and "okay" to sentences
- Listen to the audience when they ask a question. Allow the audience member to complete the question before answering. This is very important in some cultures where anticipating a question and answering it in advance is considered a sign of rudeness
- If you do not understand the question, repeat it and ask for a clarification. In a similar manner, if you do not know the answer to the question, do not fake a reply
- Keep the answers brief and support them with evidence whenever possible

It is helpful to use charts and graphs in both oral and written presentations. These figures help researchers summarize and convey a lot of information in a manner that is easy for the audience to follow. There are a number of software packages that allow researchers to generate these figures with little effort.

VALIDITY, RELIABILITY, AND GENERALIZABILITY IN PRESENTATIONS

Whether a presentation is oral or written, researchers have to address issues of validity, reliability, and generalizability. Even though it is important to keep the presentation brief, there are certain facts about the research project that must be conveyed to the audience. For instance, it is vital that the sample size chosen for the sampling process and the logic behind it be mentioned as a part of the presentation. Special translation or wording methods used in questionnaire design must be conveyed to the audience. Another aspect that must be remembered is to avoid generalizations. It is possible that the research study makes some important conclusions about a specific nationality or culture, say, the French; however, these results cannot be generalized to include the Germans or any other European nationalities.

INTEGRATING ADVANCES IN COMMUNICATION TECHNOLOGY

Data Visualization

Big data phenomenon has revolutionized the marketing research industry. Big data not only means more data to analyze, it has made presentation of this wealth of information challenging. Presenting of results has come a long way. It plays a special role in the international marketing context as the information is being shared across multiple countries. Today, there are a lot of softwares and tools available to visualize and present the data to the audience. The main goal of data visualization is to communicate information clearly and effectively.[2] Businesses now have online visualization tools such as Google Chart API, Visual.ly, and the like. Desktop applications like Processing are allowing firms to go beyond the simple online Web-based widgets to a more powerful desktop-based application.[3] Professional tools like SPSS, SAS, and R are being used by businesses and academicians alike.

Integrating New Technology and Presentation

In a global marketing research context, presentation of findings is probably the most important step in the whole process. It is at this stage that all the objectives of the study are realized. Microsoft Office products have become ubiquitous, with Microsoft PowerPoint being the solution for presentations on most computers. However, as the world is moving toward cloud storage, there is a huge demand for free Web-based technology solutions, even for presentations.

Prezi is one example of a Web-based alternative to Microsoft PowerPoint. It creates some good-quality, animated presentations. Moreover, since it is all stored in cloud, one does not have to worry about carrying a jump drive with the final version. The themes and templates make it easier even for non-designers to make aesthetically better looking presentations. Other animated presentation software tools include GoAnimate, Google Docs, SlideRocket, and the like. The focus is more now to develop applications that can allow users to make fancy presentations even through their mobile devices like smartphones and tablets. Haiku Deck is one such application that allows users to create presentations on their iPad tablets.

Open-source platforms are on the rise too. For example, there are free software tools like Open Office that support all operating systems to benefit the public. *Impress* is a part of Open Office suite of business software to build presentations. With features very similar to PowerPoint, users can get used to it pretty quickly.

---

[2] V. Friedman, "Data Visualization and Infographics," January 14, 2008 http://www.smashingmagazine.com/2008/01/14/monday-inspiration-data-visualization-and-infographics/ (Retrieved in July 2013).

[3] B. Suda, "Top 20 Data Visualization Tools," September 17, 2012, http://www.netmagazine.com/features/top-20-data-visualisation-tools (Retrieved in July 2013).

Using Tablets at Work

In the rapidly evolving technology world, gadgets are increasingly being developed to aid in work productivity. Tablets and mobile devices are no more restricted to entertainment and communication devices. They can be armed with productivity software that can help users work on the go without losing the benefit of working with feature-rich, workhorse applications that come standard in laptops and desktop computers. Consider the following numbers and trends from Forrester Research that indicate the growing popularity of tablets in the workforce:[4]

- The number of anytime, anywhere information workers—those who use three or more devices, work from multiple locations, and use many apps—has risen from 23% of the global workforce in 2011 to 29% in 2012.
- Nearly 25% of information workers using tablets and 22% of all information workers use a file sync/share solution like Box, Dropbox, SugarSync, or YouSendIt—and 70% of employees using Dropbox use it for work or work and personal files.
- Nearly 36% of information workers use tablets for presentations, compared to 27% who use PCs.
- By 2017,
  - The global installed base of tablets will reach 905 million.
  - Nearly 60% of online consumers in North America (US/Canada) and 42% of online consumers in Europe will own a tablet. Further, tablets will reach majority status in leading Asian markets like Singapore and South Korea.
  - The total worldwide sales will reach 381 million units.
- Trends emerging over the next few years include
  - In addition to company-issued and bring-your-own tablets, an ownership model wherein workers bear part of the cost of a tablet to get the specific device of their choice will emerge.
  - The hyper-portability of tablets in industries such as the healthcare, wherein doctors and nurses will use them for patient-facing scenarios (e.g., displaying test results) as well as for treatment-related scenarios (e.g., keying-in information into patient records and monitoring health conditions).
  - Tablets transcending hierarchy within an organization, wherein company-issued tablets will move beyond executives and traveling salespeople to other roles.

In terms of shipments, International Data Corporation (IDC) reports that in the first three months of 2013, a total of 49.2 million tablets were shipped to retailers for sale. This amounted to more than all the tablet devices shipped in the entire first half of 2012. Further, it is expected that tablets sales will surpass portable PCs in 2013 and all PCs in 2015.[5]

---

[4] Ted Schadler, "2013 Mobile Workforce Adoption Trends," February 4, 2013, http://www.vmware.com/files/pdf/Forrester_2013_Mobile_Workforce_Adoption_Trends_Feb2013.pdf (Retrieved on March 24, 2014); J. P. Gownder, "Global Business and Consumer Tablet Forecast Update, 2013 To 2017," *Forest Research*, August 5, 2013, http://blogs.forrester.com/jp_gownder/13-08-02-global_business_and_consumer_tablet_forecast_update_2013_to_2017_0# (Retrieved on March 26, 2014).

[5] "IDC Forecasts Worldwide Tablet Shipments to Surpass Portable PC Shipments in 2013, Total PC Shipments in 2015," *Press Release*, 28 May 2013.

In terms of ownership, the Pew Internet and American Life Project reports that tablet adoption rose from 18% in 2012 to 34% in 2013. The report also claimed that 35–44 year olds were the most likely to own a tablet and said that tablet ownership was also most likely if users were colleague graduates (49%), parents, and in a household earning at least $75,000 per year.[6]

This feverish pace of tablet usage is significantly impacted by the development of apps that run the tablets. Juniper Research predicts that nearly $8.8 billion worth of tablet apps were sold in 2013, and revenue for tablet apps is expected to outsell those of smartphones by 2017. While non-work-related apps continued to drive the growth of apps, the business and productivity apps are beginning to show growth prospects.[7] These trends clearly indicate the growing presence of tablets and their importance in carrying out work-related tasks with much ease and creativity through productivity apps. Exhibit 16.1 showcases one such productivity app designed for tablets.

Exhibit 16.1

Let's *Quip*[8]

Quip is a cross-platform word processor and collaborative tool for tablets that enables creating and sharing documents with ease. The features include real-time collaborative editing, a cross-platform instant messaging tool, offline editing, folders, checklists, live tracking of document edits via a news feed, tagging users using @mentions, push notifications for alerts, and read-receipts.

Quip's *basic* version can be freely downloaded on iPhone or iPad by creating an account. However, the *full* version—Quip *Business*—is priced at $12 a month per user, and allows collaboration for up to 250 different users through the website. Using the power of cloud computing, the tablet and PC versions of this app also allow for seamless transition between the two, as users can access their documents by logging in to their account on their PCs. The PC version also enables users to download documents in PDF format or print them directly, apart from basic formatting options and inserting artwork into documents.

Sharing of documents can be done with members from the contact list (on phone and tablet) through e-mails or text messages. Alerts will be sent to collaborators whenever someone sends a message, shares a document with them, or makes an edit. News feeds (known as *Diffs*) are similar to the track changes option in MS Word that highlights additions in green and deletions in red. Further, folders can also be shared and archived (with easy retrieval) for effective and clutter-free management of work-in-progress documents.

---

[6] Kathryn Zickuhr, "Tablet Ownership 2013," Pew Research Center, June 10, 2013, http://pewinternet. org/Reports/2013/Tablet- Ownership-2013.aspx (Retrieved on March 26, 2014).

[7] "The State of the Tablet Market," *TabTimes*, August 13, 2013, http://tabtimes.com/resources/the-state-of-the-tablet-market (Retrieved on March 18, 2014).

[8] Adapted from Videep Vijay Kumar, "Productivity in the Mobile Era," *Hindu*, August 14, 2013, http://www.thehindu.com/sci-tech/technology/productivity-in-the-mobile-era/article5022189.ece (Retrieved on March 20, 2014).

SUMMARY

Communication skills are important in marketing research in terms of having to present the research proposal and the research results to the client. The type of presentation and its nature should be based on the audience so that the presentation has maximum impact. A typical presentation includes an overview of the project followed by a body and a summary. This chapter presents guidelines that can help make a presentation effective, and the increasing role of technology that can help in collaboration and presentation of results.

Section IV

Marketing Research Approaches across the Global Markets

17 | Asia-Pacific   375

18 | Europe   400

19 | Latin America   419

20 | Middle East and Africa   441

21 | North America   463

17

Asia-Pacific

The countries that comprise the Asia-Pacific region tend to be extremely diverse in terms of culture as well as market characteristics. Several countries in Asia can be categorized as high-context cultures where there is significant emphasis placed on authority figures to endorse or suggest product usage. While advertising and marketing serve as effective means to determine consumer interest and purchase, the role of word of mouth and of role models is to be noted as well. Most Asian countries can be classified as collectivistic, where familial decision-making patterns as well as group interaction tend to be high as compared to the US.

The differences in purchasing power as well as infrastructure are to be noted when trying to reach the entire Asia-Pacific market. The newly industrialized economies of Hong Kong, Singapore, and South Korea are markedly different from the South Asian economies, India, Pakistan, and Bangladesh, as are some of the ASEAN countries comprised of Malaysia, the Philippines, Indonesia, Thailand, Burma, Brunei, Vietnam, Cambodia, and Laos. The economic volatility of these countries implies that companies should consider not only the demographic and psychographic characteristics prior to marketing but also look into the chief aspect of affordability. There are also significant differences in tastes that should be taken into account. In the Philippines, while McDonald's used their standard menu, a rival company adapted its menu to suit the local tastes. McDonald's soon found that they had only 10% of the market share in the metro Manila, and the rival's business was booming.[1]

REGIONAL CHARACTERISTICS

The World Bank estimates that over 1.98 billion people live in East Asia and Pacific today, representing almost one-third of the world's population. Regional trade agreements help to bring these consumers together into cohesive trade blocs, further encouraging and facilitating international trade. US companies are able to reach these consumers in a manageable fashion by targeting surveys to the appropriate respondents. The economic transformation occurring throughout most Pacific Rim countries has been called an *economic explosion*. Of the

---

[1] *ABS-CBN News*, "How Jollibee Beat McDonald's in Philippines," November 2, 2013, http://www.abs-cbnnews.com/business/02/11/13/how-jollibee-beat-mcdonalds-philippines (Retrieved on August 2, 2013).

$18.8 trillion in world exports in 2013, Asia accounted for nearly 33%.[2] With the exploding economic growth, consumers' standards of living and their ability to purchase US goods and services through the mail will grow as well. As large multinational companies invest and begin operating in the Pacific Rim, more and more Americans are moving there. In Japan alone, there are over 49,815 US citizens on business assignments (and 60,000 in Hong Kong). Many of these potential consumers live on comfortable expatriate compensation packages, enjoy receiving mail from home, and like buying American products.

Education and overall industrialization is increasing throughout most Pacific Rim countries. This trend results in more sophisticated consumers who have a greater proficiency in the marketplace, and are more likely to buy through non-traditional marketing channels. In many countries, people are moving away from agricultural employment to manufacturing and service-oriented jobs. This means consumers have a higher disposable income per household, and also have less time to shop in retail shops. Figures 17.1 and 17.2 illustrate the growth of Internet commerce and Internet penetration in the Asia-Pacific region.

Table 17.1 gives the reader a brief glimpse of some of the country characteristics for marketing in Asia and the Pacific Rim. Credit cards make it easier for companies to establish direct marketing channels. Increasing use of mobile and Web-based technologies to set up payment mechanisms require high credit card proliferation in the market of interest. Domestic list availability is of particular significance to marketing researchers. The ease with which mailing lists can be obtained to a large extent will decide the method used for data collection. This will also help in direct marketing. Import restrictions will determine the mode of doing business in any of these markets. China, for instance, has very high import requirements; however, the size of the market is favorable for companies to go in for direct investment and establish manufacturing bases in China. It is apparent from the table that the countries are vastly different in these characteristics. This makes it necessary for marketing researchers to adopt different methods in each of these countries to gather data that is comparable.

FIGURE 17.1

ASIA'S E-COMMERCE POTENTIAL[3]

Global e-commerce has taken off in the last two decades. While China is ahead of other Asian countries in terms of their readiness for e-commerce, Korea ranks third-highest in terms of the number of debit/credit cards per capita as per Forrester Readiness Index: eCommerce report, 2013. Some of the interesting statistics relating to Asia's e-commerce potential are highlighted below:

- Will generate B2C e-commerce sales of over $1 trillion by 2017
- Will have 4.8 billion mobile subscribers by 2020
- Will contribute around 6.9% of Asia-Pacific's GDP by 2020
- Will support 6.1 million jobs by 2020.

---

[2] World Trade Organization Statistics Database, http://stat.wto.org/Home/WSDBHome.aspx? Language=E (Retrieved on August 12, 2013).

[3] GSMA, "Asia Pacific Is Home to Half the World's Mobile Subscribers Says New GSMA Study," press release. Groupe Speciale Mobile Association (GSMA), June 9, 2014. Retrieved from http://www.gsma.com/newsroom/asia-pacific-home-half-worlds-mobile-subscribers/ on May 6, 2014; "Global B2C Ecommerce Sales to Hit $1.5 Trillion This Year Driven by Growth in Emerging Markets," February 3, 2013. Retrieved from http://www.emarketer.com/Article/Global-B2C-Ecommerce-Sales-Hit-15-Trillion-This-Year-Driven-by-Growth-Emerging-Markets/1010575 (accessed on May 6, 2014).

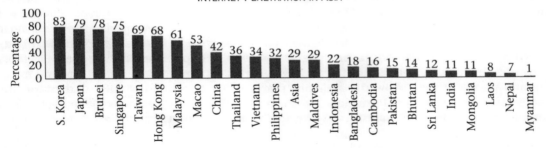

FIGURE 17.2
INTERNET PENETRATION IN ASIA[4]

TABLE 17.1
COUNTRY CHARACTERISTICS FOR MARKETING[5]

Country	Fixed Broadband Subscribers in 2013 (per 100 People)	Time to Import in 2014 (Days)
Australia	25.01	8
Brunei	5.71	15
China	13.63	24
Hong Kong	30.75	5
Indonesia	1.30	26
Japan	28.84	11
Malaysia	8.22	8
New Zealand	29.21	9
Philippines	2.61	15
Singapore	25.70	4
Thailand	7.35	13

CULTURE

It has been repeatedly emphasized in the previous chapters that cultural sensitivity is important, especially when conducting a survey research. Each Asian country has a unique culture and history, and if US companies neglect these issues, the results can be disastrous. This can lead to decision makers getting erroneous information and making wrong decisions that

---

[4] Adapted from The next web (Retrieved from http://wearesocial.sg/blog/2013/01/social-digital-mobilechina-jan-2013/we-are-social-internet-penetration-in-asia-2/ on June 2013).

[5] "Fixed Broadband Internet Subscribers (per 100 People)", http://data.worldbank.org/indicator/IT.NET.BBND.P2 (Retrieved on May 6, 2014); "Trading Across Borders," http://doingbusiness.org/data/exploretopics/trading-across-borders (Retrieved on May 6, 2014).

could cost the company millions of dollars. There is a greater fear that the company could have its reputation compromised and lose all the goodwill that has built up over the years. (It must be noted that Australia and New Zealand are in the Pacific Rim; however, they are not considered Asian countries.) Sometimes, little things that are overlooked can make a huge difference. For example, if an advertisement campaign were to show an automobile driving down the road in Thailand or Hong Kong, it would do well to remember that people in these countries drive on the left side of the road. While this certainly would not violate any major cultural norms, it may show the audience that a researcher does not fully understand the marketplace or has not paid sufficient attention to details. While each specific marketplace is unique, the following general issues can be applied to the region as a whole:

- In most Asian cultures, trying to solicit an immediate response from a potential consumer is contrary to traditional buying habits. For example, running a television advertisement which ends "operators are standing by now" will fall on deaf ears. The advertiser should carefully word the *offer* in a mailing and generally steer away from hard-sell approaches
- A majority of Asians generally put their family names before their given names. Thus, Soung Chi Lan should be referred to as Mr Soung. Be aware of these issues when developing a database and/or while mailing a survey questionnaire
- Name/brand recognition is paramount throughout the region and helps create a comfort zone to facilitate the buying process. Consider using testimonials and providing a list of local or regional clients
- Asians are generally more conservative than their Western counterparts and place a great deal of importance on loyalty, respect, age, and gender. Relationships are important throughout the region and must be developed accordingly
- Regionally speaking, using a teaser on the envelope is not as popular as in the US

When designing the survey, researchers should consider that numbers, shapes, and colors may have very different (sometimes negative) connotations in some Pacific Rim countries. Some examples are listed here. In Japan, the numbers 4 and 9 signify death, and odd numbers are considered unlucky. Black and white colors are the funeral colors and bright red and other bold colors are inappropriate for a mailing campaign. People in Hong Kong believe that the number 8 signifies prosperity or good fortune, the number 4 signifies death, and the number 3 signifies life. Red and yellow are considered lucky colors, and blue and white are the Chinese funeral colors. In South Korea, the number 10 and red ink are said to bring bad luck. Exhibit 17.1 summarizes the results of a survey conducted by *The Economist*, which highlights the optimism of many Asian economies.

SEASONALITY AND HOLIDAYS

The timing of a marketing campaign can have a significant impact on its success or failure. This fundamental truth holds as much water in the Pacific Rim as it does in the US. The holidays followed in each of these countries can help companies design and administer marketing mailers, and determine when (and when not) to schedule the campaigns. In general, Exhibit 17.2 lists some of the major holidays and seasons that are observed in the Pacific Rim.

Exhibit 17.1

Optimism Makes Asia Stand Out[6]

A recent Nielsen survey (Q1-2013) found that consumers in Indonesia were the happiest. Further, Indonesia was also found to be the world's most optimistic country with 122 points. The reasons for Indonesia's optimism included a 6% economic growth in the past three years, resilience to the weakening global economy, increase in minimum wage up to 40% in some regions, and a 15% stock market rally so far this year. Out of the 10 most confident countries globally, 7 were from the Asia-Pacific region that included Asian countries such as India, Philippines, and Thailand.

According to Nielsen, saving money was the main priority for consumers in the Asia-Pacific region, with 62% of those surveyed indicating that they save spare cash once essential living costs have been covered. According to Nielsen, Asia-Pacific consumers are at least two times more likely to have spare cash after taking care of their necessities than any other part of the world.

Asian optimism is a potent contributor to economic growth, but even more potent is the fact that Asians are not satisfied with their existing circumstances and are making changes for a better future. The picture that emerges of Asia is that of peoples who both believe that the present circumstances are unsatisfactory and that the future will be better.

Exhibit 17.2

Prominent Seasons/Holidays in the Pacific Rim[7]

Season/Holiday	Months	Countries
Ramadan Feast	Varies from year to year	Muslim countries such as Indonesia and Malaysia
Chinese New Year	Late January	Most Eastern Asian countries
Summer months in Southern Hemisphere	December–February	New Zealand/Australia
Golden Week	Late April to early May	Japan
Obon Festival	Late July to late August	Japan

---

[6] Adapted from Dhara Ranasinghe, "Where Do the World's Happiest Customer Live," *CNBC*, May 1, 2013, http://www.cnbc.com/id/100692893 (Retrieved on May 6, 2014).

[7] United States Postal Service, *Marketing Resource Guide to the Pacific Rim*, ed., William A. Delphos (Washington, DC: United States Postal Service, 1993), p. 150.

LANGUAGE AND TRANSLATION ISSUES

There are over 1,000 different languages spoken in the Pacific Rim today, including English. Therefore, it is important to consider the following points:

- The long history of the British influence in the region has resulted in a number of Asians who speak English.
- Many Asian business executives (and consumers) have studied in English-speaking countries and, therefore, know and/or speak this language.
- In some Asian countries, the English language carries with it an intrinsic value that can be used as a marketing tool.

Mobile Internet Marketing

With the improvements in mobile technology, it has been easier for marketers to reach out to consumers. E-mail and online messaging are some of the most popular ways to reach out to consumers. People now access e-mails and online messages not only through their laptops and desktops but also through smartphones like iPhones, Android phones, and so on. This trend is dominant in Asia as shown in the graph.

For instance, in Hong Kong, India, China, Singapore, and Malaysia, about 1 in 4 people use smartphone to access e-mail and online messages, while in Japan, 1 in 10 use smartphone to access e-mail and online messages. Marketers are adapting this new technology to reach out to their customers.[8] Direct mail has been long substituted by e-mails, and now mobile Internet marketing is making waves in the Asia-Pacific regions.

SECONDARY SOURCES OF INFORMATION

There is significant amount of published information that can help companies compete in these markets. Many of these resources go unused because executives cannot locate the pertinent information. Listed in the following paragraphs are some of the possible avenues that can be looked into for obtaining secondary data.

US Department of Commerce

The US Department of Commerce provides a PacRim Hotline called FlashFacts. This service is available free-of-charge, seven days a week, 24 hours a day. By calling (in Washington, DC) (202) 482-2954 (from a touch-tone telephone), companies can receive reports of one to seven pages directly on their fax machines. A complete directory of all available reports can also be ordered by calling the hotline and following the directions or by visiting their website.

---

[8] International Post Corporation, "IPC Strategic Perspectives: On Direct Mail Growing the Business in Asia," October 2009, http://www.ipc.be/~/media/Documents/PUBLIC/strategic-perspectives/2009%20 Strategic%20Perspectives/IPC%20SP%20DM%20growing%20the%20business%20in%20Asia.pdf (Retrieved on May 6, 2014).

National Technical Information Service

Many useful US government publications are available by contacting the National Technical Information Service (NTIS). During the earliest stages of a market research process, companies can contact the NTIS and have them send a directory of available publications covering the Pacific Rim. The e-mail address, website, physical address, and phone numbers of the publisher corresponding to a country can be found at http://www.ntis.gov/help/cooperate.aspx.

Computerized Information

A number of market research resources are now available through electronic media. This greatly facilitates keeping information up-to-date, as well as disseminating the information to the business community. The following services can provide valuable, timely information on Pacific Rim markets:

- The US government provides valuable information and guidance regarding exporting to other countries and the prevailing regulations for US exporters and this can be obtained from http://export.gov/index.asp
- The US Department of State publishes background of all countries in the world. They also publish a fact sheet which has details about the relationship between the country and US. This information can be accessed from http://www.state.gov/aboutstate/
- The US Commercial Service publishes international market research information on all the countries in the world, and this can be accessed from http://www.buyusainfo.net/adsearch.cfm?search_type=int&loadnav=no
- The US Census Bureau publishes information regarding US trade details with other countries, and this can be obtained from http://www.census.gov/foreign-trade/data/
- The World Trade Organization also publishes reports regarding US trade with other countries. The 2013 report on world trade published by the WTO can be retrieved from http://wto.org/english/res_e/publications_e/wtr13_e.htm

AUSTRALIA

Country Characteristics[9]

Population: 22,507,617 (July 2014 est.)
Land Area: 7,682,300 sq km
Language: English 76.8%, Mandarin 1.6%, Italian 1.4%, Greek 1.2%, Cantonese 1.2%, Vietnamese 1.1%, other 10.4%, unspecified 5.0% (2011 est.)
Literacy Rate: 99% (2003 est.)

---

[9] CIA, "Australia," in *The World Factbook*, https://www.cia.gov/library/publications/the-world-factbook/geos/as.html (Retrieved on August 5, 2013).

Religion: Protestant 28.8%, Catholic 25.3%, Eastern Orthodox 2.6%, other Christian 4.5%, Buddhist 2.5%, Muslim 2.2%, Hindu 1.3%, other 8.4%, unspecified 2.2%, none 22.3% (2006 est.)

GDP—Purchasing Power Parity: $998.3 billion (2013 est.)

GDP per Capita—Purchasing Power Parity: $43,000 (2013 est.)

GDP—Real Growth Rate: 2.5% (2013 est.)

Inflation Rate—Consumer Price Index: 2.4% (2013 est.)

Business Characteristics

While Australians tend to be friendly and easy-going, this behavior does not carry over to business relations. Most expect a code of etiquette with emphasis on the verbal as well as nonverbal aspects. For instance, it is considered appropriate to offer your business card, but you might not receive one in return because most Australians do not carry name cards. It is customary to shake hands when greeting, as it is at the conclusion of a meeting. It is also acceptable for people to introduce themselves without waiting to be introduced and most Australians would perceive this as informal and outgoing.

Market Research in Australia

The Australian market is extremely urbanized—82% of the people live in cities. Targeting such markets involves the foreign companies to evaluate the ease of access to the markets. The majority of Australia lives in the country's southern region in the major cities such as Sydney, Melbourne, and Canberra. Table 17.2 gives readers an idea of the communication infrastructure used in marketing that is available in Australia and New Zealand.

More than 80% of the Australian population has access to the Internet. Since such a wide reach of the Internet enables coverage of diverse segment of the population, online surveys are very popular in Australia. Typically online surveys are sent through e-mail either to a client-specific database or research panels to which people sign up in exchange of gifts. The other widely used survey technique in Australia is the Computer Assisted Telephone Interview (CATI). CATI is very efficient as it increases the speed and accuracy of carrying out telephone interviews. CATI and online survey mechanisms have replaced the traditional methods of surveys—face-to-face and mail—in Australia. One of the main aspects to be considered would be

TABLE 17.2

MARKET RESEARCH—INFRASTRUCTURAL ANALYSIS

Country	Australia	New Zealand
Internet Users in 2013 (in million)*	19.55	3.81
Internet Penetration in 2013 (% population)*	86.90	86.60
Facebook Users in 2012 (in million)*	11.81	2.29
Landlines in Use in 2012 (in million)**	10.47	1.88
Mobile Lines in Use 2012 (in million)**	24.40	4.92

*Internet World Stats; **CIA World Factbook.*

the size of the major cities in Australia. Though this is a significant problem, the accuracy and reliability of the secondary data available substantiates efficient marketing research ventures by foreign firms.

The Australian market is similar to that of the US in terms of technological progress. Media research is available for all media sources and this includes meter measurement of TV audiences. Both Australia and New Zealand can be rated highly in terms of news awareness. Though readership of the print media has reduced, online newspapers are becoming more and more popular. Penetration of televisions is also very high. On the whole, the entire region is highly literate and media-conscious and on average has advanced methods of communication. This would translate to conducting effective market research in Australia.

Random sampling has been recommended as the most suitable since there is immense cultural diversity in the Australian market that needs to be captured. The influx of immigrants to Australia from several Asian countries implies that consumption patterns, as well as consumer characteristics, differ drastically between such groups.

CHINA

Country Characteristics[10]

Population: 1,355,692,576 (July 2014 est.)
Land Area: 9,326,410 sq. km
Language: Standard Chinese or Mandarin, Yue (Cantonese), Wu (Shanghainese), Minbei (Fuzhou), Minnan (Hokkien-Taiwanese), Xiang, Gan, Hakka dialects, minority languages
Literacy Rate: 95.1% (2010 est.)
Religion: Buddhist 18.2%, Christian 5.1%, Muslim 1.8%, folk religion 21.9%, Hindu < 0.1%, Jewish < 0.1%, other 0.7%, unaffiliated 52.2%, officially atheist (2010 est.)
GDP—Purchasing Power Parity: $13.39 trillion (2013 est.)
GDP per Capita—Purchasing Power Parity: $9,800 (2013 est.)
GDP—Real Growth Rate: 7.7% (2013 est.)
Inflation Rate—Consumer Price Index: 2.6% (2013 est.)

Marketing and Consumer Behavior in China

Over the past few years, there has been a notable change in consumer behavior in China. Increasingly, Chinese consumers are exhibiting similar behavioral tendencies as other affluent nations. A fast-growing segment of customers is becoming more self-indulgent, more individualistic in wants, and more loyal to favorite brands. Traditionally, Chinese consumers were value seekers; they were inclined to follow general trends.[11] Though a majority of the Chinese

---

[10] CIA, "China," in *The World Factbook*, https://www.cia.gov/library/publications/the-world-factbook/geos/ch.html (Retrieved on August 5, 2013).

[11] Yuval Atsmon, Max Magni, and Lihua Li, "From Mass to Mainstream: Keeping Pace with China's Rapidly Changing Consumers," September 2012, https://solutions.mckinsey.com/insightschina/_SiteNote/WWW/GetFile.aspx?uri=%2Finsightschina%2Fdefault%2Fen-us%2Fabout%2Four_publicatio ns%2FFiles%2Fwp2055036759%2FMcKinsey%20Insights%20China%20-%20From%20mass%20to%20

consumers still fall under this category of traditional consumers, with higher income level and more disposable cash, it is expected that more consumers would shift toward becoming self-indulgent consumers in the coming years. These types of self-indulgent, brand-conscious, and savvy customers are more prevalent in bigger cities and in urban clusters along China's coast.

Chinese consumers are spending more on recreational activities, and the trend of *eating-out* is on the rise. Yet, consumers are also cautious and still believe saving money as an essential like ever before. Consumers display clear favoritism for foreign brands in some segments like electronics; however, when it comes to personal care, household care, and food and beverages, consumers like to stick to domestic brands. Additionally, consumers with more disposable income display a tendency to prefer foreign products in the personal care, household care, and food and beverages category also. Big trustworthy brands that offer plenty of functional benefits with little frill will attract more consumers.

Business Characteristics

The Chinese give a lot of importance to value of time and most meetings commence on time. They place a lot of emphasis on precision and detail when designing contracts. They pay close attention to long-standing relationships because it is believed that the culture of each company is better understood by building long-term relationships. It does take a significant amount of time for a company entering China to understand the legal aspects as well as the culture in negotiating deals. In establishing business deals, the company that invests in understanding and appreciating the Chinese culture succeeds. On the other side, Chinese understand the cultural differences and would not expect foreigners to get fully acclimatized to their tradition. They would go with their assessment of their partners rather than the custom alignment.[12] In order to prevent *loss of face*, most Chinese would prefer to work on a one-on-one basis with the party and not through an intermediary.

In terms of nonverbal communication, it would help to assess the status of the officials who have convened to discuss the contract. Most Chinese meetings are devoted to pleasantries in order to wait for the most opportune moment to discuss formal aspects of the contract or the business. Also, most Chinese tend to become rigid in posture when their position is in jeopardy. It is important to understand the difficulty in establishing a nationwide strategy given the regional differences, which are similar to the vast differences that exist in India.

Product Positioning

A common concern for Western firms selling in China is the product pricing and positioning strategies that they should adopt. Chinese consumers are quickly becoming sophisticated, and they are now interested in both quality and value. However, Chinese consumers value western brands more and are willing to pay more for these products, as they think these western

---

mainstream%20%E2%80%93%20Keeping%20pace%20with%20China%E2%80%99s%20rapidly%20changing%20consumers_fd6a761f-2b88-4e8f-a7cc-8afac03a88f1.pdf (Retrieved on August 5, 2013).

[12] CNN, "Doing Business in China: Five Tips for Success," October 21, 2011, http://edition.cnn.com/2011/10/21/business/china-business-investors-culture (Retrieved on August 5, 2013).

brands would elevate their status.[13] The distribution system in China is surely an aspect that most marketers would have to consider. It is extremely difficult to find a national system of distribution or a national system of transportation that can get goods from one part of China to another.[14] The demographics of Chinese consumers according to a recent Gallup survey are explained in Exhibit 17.3.

Exhibit 17.3

Collecting Information on Chinese Consumers[15]

Until recently, consumer research in China had been ad hoc in nature and was largely confined to tier-1 cities like Beijing. This meant that only the wealthiest 5% of the Chinese population was researched. With the rapid growth and urbanization, it is impossible to ignore the growing middle class. This means that companies need to understand the behavior of consumers across a wider set of geographic and demographic barriers. To understand this wider set of consumers is not easy and this comes with its own set of problems. Market researchers are often faced with the question of how best to collect and analyze data from such a diverse mix of consumers.

Researchers face another important issue. With the mobile explosion and rapid Internet penetration in China, researches find themselves with lot many tools like online survey, social media, and such to collect data from consumers. The key challenge for the researcher lies in managing these different streams of information, and deciding the best-suited methods to target the various consumer demographics.

Further, there is an increase in ownership of cars among Chinese consumers. As of 2011, 11 cities had more than 1 million cars. The trend of owning a new car is increasing as it is seen as a status symbol. Not only the desire to own a car or the new economic status of the consumer is attributed to the increased number of cars on the road, but also the abundance of automobiles developed and produced by China's automobile industry for the common people.

The recognition of the multinational brands is an indication of the effectiveness of the strategies that are implemented by these multinational brands. Chinese consumers prefer to buy multinational brands for two reasons. First, for the status-conscious consumer, owning multinational brands is a form of endorsement of their status. Second, Chinese consumers are fascinated by the innovative technology/ideas behind the multinational brands, which they feel is lacking in the domestic market.

---

[13] Derrick Daye, "Brand Positioning for Chinese Market," *Brand Strategy Insider*, August 28, 2012, http://www.brandingstrategyinsider.com/2012/08/brand-positioning-for-chinese-markets.html#.UgAOl4FKb4c (Retrieved on August 5, 2013).

[14] Matthew Rouse, "Chinese Distribution Is Complex," *The Manzella Report*, May 1, 2009, http://www.manzellareport.com/index.php/manufacturing/210-chinese-distribution-is-complex-companies-may-be-forced-to-build-their-own-networks (Retrieved on August 5, 2013).

[15] Adapted from Asia Research Online, "Understanding the Chinese Consumer," May 2012, http://asia-research.net/2012/05/understanding-the-chinese-consumer/ (Retrieved on August 6, 2013); People's Daily Online, "Number of Private Cars in China Exceed 70 Million," July 20, 2011, http://english.peopledaily.com.cn/90001/90776/90882/7446361.html (Retrieved on August 6, 2013); and China.org.cn, "Chinese Prefer Foreign Brands," August 6, 2012, http://www.china.org.cn/business/2012-08/06/content_26140532.htm (Retrieved on August 6, 2013).

There are several guidelines for identifying the factors that should be looked into by the company entering China. First, specific regions that are of interest and the kind of infrastructure that is available in those regions must be considered. Second, it would be beneficial to consider the customers' expectations in this respect, that is, the nature and type of organizations that they consider to be satisfactory. Perhaps one of the main prerequisites to functioning in China is to understand the business culture. This would be facilitated if consultants were approached for suggestions. Exhibit 17.4 explains the attitude of workers in China. It would also be appropriate to obtain a list of government and financial institutions in order to understand the dealings that need to be done, as well as groundwork which would have to be accomplished prior to functioning in China. The concept of *guanxi* is prevalent in China and refers to the favors given and owed, as well as the equivalent of bribing. However, the Chinese government is tightening its anti-corruption laws in the country.

Exhibit 17.4

Attitudes of Workers in China[16]

The Chinese find it extremely difficult to say "no" as they think it would cause embarrassment and loss of face; hence, they tend to agree with things even if they are uncomfortable. They do this as a courtesy, rarely with malicious intent, although it can be a real problem in the workplace. If bad news needs to be told, Chinese will be reluctant to break it. Sometimes, they will use an intermediary for communication, or perhaps they will imply bad news without being blunt. To cut through such murkiness, it is best to explain to your Chinese coworkers that you appreciate direct communications and that you will not be upset at bearers of bad news.

Market Research in China

One of the biggest problems in conducting primary research in China is the language. Most often, it is not adequate to have a literal translation of the questionnaire, which would not capture the full essence of the research. It would be valuable for the company to invest in translators who can interpret the jargon specific to the industry and appropriately relate to the audience. The issues concerning the various jargons in China are explained in Exhibit 17.5.

Commercial market research industry in China is a very young and growing industry. The first Chinese market research provider, Guangzhou Marketing Research, was established only in 1988. As in any developing industry, practices have been undergoing significant changes.

---

[16] Adapted from "China Communication Styles: World Business Culture," http://www.worldbusinessculture.com/Chinese-Business-Communication-Style.html (Retrieved on August 6, 2013).

Exhibit 17.5

Dialects and Idioms[17]

Mandarin, or *pu tong hua* in Chinese, is the official national language in China; however, the problem is compounded by the existence of several dialects that are somewhat similar but exist as separate entities. In terms of the script, the individual dialects are exactly the same, though the phonetic usage, as well as the accent, could affect the usage. If a person who speaks Cantonese meets a person fluent in Hokkien or Hakka, it is most likely that they would converse in Mandarin.

Data Collection

Different methods of data collection such as door-knock surveys, central-location test, mail surveys, phone surveys, and Web surveys are prevalent in China today. With mobile and Internet technology becoming popular, online and telephone surveys are gaining popularity in China. However, face-to-face interview is still preferred in some cases. When interviewing executives in a large company, a quasi-government official, or a medical officer, it is ideal to conduct a face-to-face interview. Chinese expect human interaction during interviews and consider face-to-face interview as a mark of respect. This is in big contrast to western cultures, where senior executives prefer to be interviewed by phone in order to save time.

Also, when interviewing consumers in second- and third-tier cities, face-to-face interviewing is preferred. This is due to the fact that prices vary widely from city to city, and there is no significant cost difference in conducting face-to-face interviews versus Web/telephone interviews in second- and third-tier cities. Also, field providers in small cities have their practice more firmly built upon traditional methodologies.

The most prevalent method of data collection is phone interviews, particularly in the B2B scenario. Most Chinese research centers are equipped with a CATI center. However, since many dialects are spoken in China, telephone interviews are not as efficient as they would be in countries where people speak a single language. Telephone interviews are generally conducted in Mandarin. If the respondent and the interviewer are from different dialects, there is a high probability that they might not understand each other and interview might take longer time than usual. To combat this issue, well-trained interviewers and experienced field providers are important in China, unlike in linguistically more homogeneous countries. Though mobile phone usage is becoming very popular in China, surveys through text messages or cold calls, which target the mobile platform, are mostly unwelcome.

Web surveys are not very popular among researchers in China. Since researchers are skeptical about the sample representativeness and authenticity of respondents, when using Web surveys, Web surveys are not a widely accepted practice in the industry. As the Chinese market matures, online surveys will become popular. While in the meantime, stringent

---

[17] Adapted from China Business: World Trade Press Country Business Guide (1994) 174.

quality control and data cleaning procedures are the only remedy to the quality concerns raised by online surveys.

Sampling

Sample for a market research is generally drawn from three sources: client list, public sources, and field provider proprietary database.

Client list: In studies that involve research on a client's existing customers, the sample is sourced from a client-provided list extracted from client's database. In several cases, the client's database is not up to date, and hence, researchers need to add buffers when sampling using these databases.

Public sources: Residential phone directories do not exist as Chinese government prohibits publishing of a comprehensive list of telephone numbers. Even in the business side, only yellow-pages-style directories exist. Basically, industries who do not advertise themselves will not be listed in the business directories. Also, it has to be noted that preparation of sample frame and the configuration of the dialer software is not carefully considered in some call centers.

Commercial databases are published and sold by providers such as Dun and Bradstreet. These databases are very usual when it comes to developed countries. Given that socialistic legacy of complicated organization of state-owned, quasi-state-owned, and other businesses, these databases do not always reflect the reality, and databases from government-related agencies are biased toward government-related companies.

Field provider proprietary database: Like other markets, there are field providers in China who aggregate contacts of people to form a proprietary database. It is often unclear to researchers how these databases are built as field providers are unwilling to provide specific details about the database. Network sampling seems to be the usual mechanism by which field providers build their databases. At times, an ad hoc search is conducted based on the research requirements. But otherwise, most of the respondents on the field provider database are highly interconnected (A refers B, B refers C, C refers D, and so on). Hence, probability sampling cannot be obtained from these databases and the respondents in the pool essentially comprise of a convenience sample.

INDIA

A country of more than a billion people, India offers a fascinating insight into the manner in which marketing research is to be performed. This is especially true because India is such a diverse society, with vast differences in economic levels, caste, and religion-based composition, as well as a multiplicity of languages.

Country Characteristics[18]

Population: 1,236,344,631 (July 2014 est.)
Land Area: 2,973,193 sq. km
Language: Hindi 41%, Bengali 8.1%, Telugu 7.2%, Marathi 7%, Tamil 5.9%, Urdu 5%, Gujarati 4.5%, Kannada 3.7%, Malayalam 3.2%, Oriya 3.2%, Punjabi 2.8%, Assamese 1.3%, Maithili 1.2%, other 5.9% (Note: English enjoys the status of subsidiary official language, but is the most important language for national, political, and commercial communication.)
Literacy Rate: 61%
Religion: Hindu 80.5%, Muslim 13.4%, Christian 2.3%, Sikh 1.9%, other 1.8%, unspecified 0.1% (2001 census)
GDP—Purchasing Power Parity: $4.99 trillion (2013 est.)
GDP per Capita—Purchasing Power Parity: $4,000 (2013 est.)
GDP—Real Growth Rate: 3.2% (2013 est.)
Inflation Rate—Consumer Price Index: 9.6% (2013 est.)

Business Characteristics

Conducting business in India requires considering certain cultural aspects and nuances. Hinduism dominates every aspect of Indian life, and often seeps into relationships and culture. Although not strictly adhered to in the big cities and amongst the westernized circles, the role of religion should be considered. The use of the first name for address should be avoided. The usual method used will be press one's palms together in front of the chest and say "*Namaste*," meaning "Greetings to you." The attitude toward women is one of respect and the distance between men and women is one that should be maintained when addressing them. For instance, a young woman generally does not take the hand of a man who is not her husband. Women who have been educated generally do not perceive this to be objectionable, though it is preferable to extend a verbal greeting. Attitude toward time is lax in India, with most people being complacent about the provision of service.

In conducting business, it would be appropriate to chart the dimensions of the contractual agreement in order to have a document to refer to over an extended period of time. Bargaining for goods and services is considered to be part and parcel of Indian business environment. Though a significant number of retail outlets have sprung up in the past few years, most of the business dealings with small business owners tend to be dominated by bargain transactions. Indians usually consider business to be separate from personal life, though when inviting people to their homes, their hospitality extends to trying to make the guest more at home, either through cultural exchange or divulging personal information. Exhibit 17.6 gives some pointers on the cultural aspects of conducting marketing research in India.

---

[18] CIA, "India," in *The World Factbook*, https://www.cia.gov/library/publications/the-world-factbook/geos/in.html (Retrieved on August 5, 2012).

Exhibit 17.6

Cultural *Dos* and *Don'ts* in India[19]

- Hindi is the national language; however, when doing business, English is mainly spoken.
- While it is acceptable for men to shake hands with men, men shaking hands with women may be frowned upon.
- Common to greet someone with the Indian greeting "Namaste."
- The caste system is complicated and difficult to understand. This is also a sensitive area to many Indians and, hence, it is best to stay away from this topic.
- Use last names upon meeting someone for the first time and mention any higher academic or other titles.
- Hospitality is an outstanding feature of the Indian society. All guests, whether they are expected or not, are welcomed into the home and given some refreshments. Indians expect this to be reciprocated.
- Clothing is casual, as temperatures are usually hot.
- While dining with Indians, it is important to remember that only right hands are used for eating.
- Putting your hands on your hips is rude.
- Touching someone with your foot is rude, as is pointing with your feet.

Market Research in India

As India is transforming into an industrialized country, market research is gaining importance as the need for accurate information of demand becomes essential. It has taken a significant amount of time for companies to realize the importance of market research in the allocation of funds and human resources in carrying out the activities of the corporation effectively. The two main challenges that are faced in market research are ensuring market coverage that represents all parts of India, and recruiting interviewers to conduct market research. Technology is helping the market research industry to answer these two challenges.

India being a diverse nation with different regions speaking different languages and practicing various customs and habits, it becomes essential to cover different regions of India for a successful survey. Market research is yet to gain popularity as a profession among young adults in India. Therefore, the presence of market research companies in India is few, and characterized by independent market researchers who consult with companies on a contract basis. Exhibit 17.7 explains the manner in which McDonald's has adapted its business style to suit the Indian culture.

---

[19] Adapted from Kwintessential, "Doing Business in India," http://www.kwintessential.co.uk/etiquette/doing-business-india.html (Retrieved on May 8, 2014); and Aimee Groth, "12 Essential Tips for Doing Business in India," ," Business Insider, January 6, 2012. Retrieved from http://www.businessinsider.com/12-things-you-need-to-know-about-doing-business-in-india-2012-1?op=1 (accessed on May 18, 2014).

Exhibit 17.7

McDonald's in India[20]

McDonald's success across the globe has been their ability to adapt to local taste without losing their brand image. Keeping up to their brand image, they have adapted well to the Indian market. Adhering to the religious beliefs of Indians, McDonald dropped beef and pork from their menus for a long time. Recently, they have decided to open outlets by mid-2013 that would serve only vegetarian menu options in the pilgrimage cities of India. This move shows the adaptability of McDonald's in accommodating the local preferences of the market. Even though McDonald's has only 270 outlets in India (from a world tally of 33,000 outlets), the fast-food chain is willing to customize its offering as they see a huge market potential in India. With changing economic conditions and a rising trend in eating out, India promises several development opportunities for US restaurant chains, similar to China.

Data Collection

As a part of recent developments, mobile market research tools help manage field work over large distances and ensure high quality of data. Smartphones and tablets help in gathering data and immediately transfer it back to the agency.

Telephone

The problem with telephone data collection is that the infrastructure is often inadequate and expensive to construct or develop. Furthermore, the problem with *reach* also exists because the research to be conducted tends to focus only on metropolitan cities. India is a large country with an immense consumer base that is relatively untapped. Given the rural and urban differences, it would be ideal to get information regarding purchase behavior. However, the infrastructure does not support a consistent national research to be conducted. India has an estimated 28.5 million landlines, 904.5 million mobile lines, and a telephone density (number of land and mobile phones per 100 persons) of 75.2% as of 2014.[21] With the advent of mobile technology, the reach to rural consumers has expanded, but even now, the rural population is not as widely connected as the urban population.

Focus Groups

Focus groups are a very effective way to understand the Indian market, especially for the new entrants. Indians like to participate in the focus group discussions, and hence, finding respondents will not be an issue. Since the cost of arranging for pick up and drop for respondents for focus group discussions is not expensive, picking up the respondents would ensure

---

[20] Adapted from "In India, McDonald's Plans Vegetarian Outlets," *Wall Street Journal*, September 5, 2012.

[21] Department of Telecommunications, Ministry of Communications and Information Technology, Government of India, "Annual Report 2013–2014," http://www.dot.gov.in/sites/default/files/AR%20 2013-14%20English%20%282%29_1.pdf (Retrieved on May 6, 2014).

high show rate. Focus groups should be formed keeping in mind the socioeconomic divide in India and the regional differences in attitudes. Incentives should be given only after interviews, as incentives would make Indians feel obliged and they would not be able to share their feelings correctly.[22]

Mail Surveys

Two major problems with conducting mail surveys involve the size of the population, and the lack of a good database of consumers for targeting purposes. The size of the market is large and diverse enough to warrant such a method of data collection; however, the reliability of the postal system further complicates the issue with irregular delivery of mail, as well as postal strikes.

Fax

Similar to telephones, this mode of collecting consumer responses has not extended beyond business dealings. The problems with power outages, telephone lines, and inconsistent connections prove to be major hurdles to this otherwise effective mode of data collection. With the growth of Internet, e-mail, and mobile technologies, the use of faxes for data collection is on the wane.

E-mail and the Internet

The development of the Internet as a tool in market research has improved significantly over the years; however, infrastructural issues still remain. This is partly due to the state of telecommunications, and the cost of setting up such a system on a home-to-home basis. The average computer in India costs anywhere from ₹30,000 to ₹40,000 ($1 = approx. ₹62 in 2015) and the cost of establishing the network connection could range from ₹1,000 to ₹5,000. Furthermore, Web surfing in itself is charged by the hour, which means that individuals do not have the privilege to stay online for extended periods of time. Though Internet penetration is estimated to be around 19% in 2014, online survey through mobile phones is more promising as mobile presence is increasing.[23] However, a major concern regarding mobile surveys is the low literacy rate (61%).[24] Exhibit 17.8 gives a brief overview of conducting marketing research in India.

An Insight into the Indian Consumer Market

The middle class population in India is estimated to be around 300 million people.[25] The peril in marketing to Indian consumers as a whole is that this middle-income class varies significantly in terms of level of education, purchasing power, and consumption (based upon the geographical location). Considering just income as a determinant is often misleading, given that the scale ranges from low-middle to upper-middle income levels. Marketing in India would require the company to tailor its product design and pricing strategies in order

---

[22] Quirk's Marketing Research Media, "Qualitatively Speaking: Use Focus Groups to Understand India's Massive Markets," http://www.quirks.com/articles/a2004/20041109.aspx (Retrieved on August 12, 2013).

[23] Retrieved from http://www.internetlivestats.com/internet-users/india/ on May 6, 2014.

[24] CIA, "India."

[25] Sambuddha Mitra Mustafi, "India's Middle Class: Growth Engine or Loose Wheel?" *New York Times*, May 13, 2013, http://india.blogs.nytimes.com/2013/05/13/indias-middle-class-growth-engine-or-loose-wheel/?_r=0 (Accessed on August 12, 2013).

to address the differences between India and the Western world. It would help the company to understand the shifts that are currently taking place in India, the mobility between classes, the rural-urban migration, and the impact of new media.

Exhibit 17.8

Marketing Research in India[26]

With more than a billion people spread across 28 states and 7 union territories, India has 21 different languages and more than 1,700 minor languages and dialects and many different religions. With such a large population and vast regional differences, selecting an appropriate sample of the population is a mammoth task. This raises several problems regarding translation between the various languages and dialects.

Postal system in India is not very efficient, so mail surveys are not effective. Telephone interviews are expensive and rural areas are not well covered, even with the advent of the mobile technology. Thus, telephone interviews cannot be used to cover all regions of India. The best method of data collection would be personal interviews in areas which are not covered by telephone. Labor is cheap and people are usually receptive to the idea of being interviewed in public or in their homes.

Online survey is definitely a lucrative option when compared to telephone surveys, as it is economical and relatively easier method to collect data. India's development is diverse—certain sectors like banking and IT are well developed while manufacturing is not. Hence, not all sectors can be reached through online surveys. Also, given that India is a multilingual country, conducting an online survey in several languages would be a researcher's nightmare. Given these drawbacks of online surveys in India, face-to-face and telephone surveys still are the effective ways to reach diverse Indian consumers.

In the fast-moving consumer goods (FMCG) market, food products are the leading segment with 43% of the overall market.[27] Despite the high level of inflation over the past few years, which makes affordability an important issue, there has been a consistent rise in the spending levels. Increase in credit facilities offered, as well as price competition, has resulted in a boost to consumer spending in India. This is a specific aspect that market researchers should address in trying to collect information by attempting to obtain data on the various segments of the diverse population.

Challenges Facing Market Research in India

India's GDP growth has been predicted to be around 6–9% till 2025. This optimistic prediction is based on the fact that there is substantial growth opportunity in Indian businesses and the growing middle class with more disposable income.[28] A booming economy like India

[26] Adapted from Value Notes, "Online Survey in India: When Does It Work?," May 31, 2013. Retrieved from http://www.valuenotes.biz/online-survey-india-work/ (accessed on June 3, 2014).

[27] IBEF, "Indian Consumer Market," http://www.ibef.org/industry/fmcg-presentation (Retrieved on August 12, 2013).

[28] McKinsey, "The 'Bird of Gold': The Rise of Indian Consumer Market," http://www.mckinsey.com/insights/asia-pacific/the_bird_of_gold (Retrieved on August 13, 2013).

is not only a lucrative market for the local companies, but also an attractive proposition for global companies.[29] With a growing middle class, it is obvious that there is an increasing need for companies to capture and understand real-time consumer behavior and transactions. The diverse nature of consumers across all regions in India calls for a detailed market research. Companies have started to invest in market research activities in India to understand their customers from different regions in India so that they would be able to cater to all kinds of customers in India. However, there are many challenges that impede the growth of the industry.

The two main problems that inhibited data collection in the past have been lack of infrastructure and the attitude of the retailer/consumer. Advancements in mobile technology have helped in solving one of the issues. With the growth of mobile subscriptions and advancements in technology, setting up hardware (tablets or smartphones can be used as a replacement for computers) in rural parts of the country has become easy. This has paved way for easier data collection even from rural parts of the country. Having said this, it has to be noted that basic infrastructure like power is not guaranteed in all parts of the country. One might be able to provide the retailer with necessary hardware and software needed for data collection, but without power, data collection will not be effective.

The other problem of retailers being hesitant to share their transactional data has been changing, but the attitude has not changed completely. Retailers are now more open to the idea of sharing data and have started to appreciate the technology that enables data collection. Nonetheless, this still is a concern in collecting data. The only way to get all the retailers to share their data is by educating them about the benefits that market research would bring in to their business.[30]

JAPAN

The Japanese market has been considered insurmountable for most market researchers. However, the success stories of consumer products like McDonald's and Coca-Cola and high-technology categories like IBM and Apple indicate that there is an immense openness which can be utilized.

Country Characteristics[31]

Population: 127,103,388 (July 2014 est.)
Land Area: 364,485 sq. km
Language: Japanese
Literacy Rate: 99%

---

[29] Business Line, "Govt Nixes Franchise Route for Multi-Brand Retail Stores," http://www.thehindubusinessline.com/industry-and-economy/govt-nixes-franchise-route-for-multibrand-retail-stores-clarifies-sourcing-norms/article4788426.ece (Retrieved on August 13, 2013).

[30] V. Rajesh. "Dig through the data goldmine." *The Hindu Business Line*, July 25, 2013. Retrieved from http://www.thehindubusinessline.com/features/weekend-life/dig-through-the-data-goldmine/article4949282.ece (accessed on August 13, 2013).

[31] CIA, "Japan," in *The World Factbook*, https://www.cia.gov/library/publications/the-world-factbook/geos/ja.html (Retrieved on August 5, 2012).

Religion: Shintoism 83.9%, Buddhism 71.4%, Christianity 2%, other 7.8%. (Note: Total exceeds 100% because many people belong to both Shintoism and Buddhism.)
GDP—Purchasing Power Parity: $4.729 trillion (2013 est.)
GDP per Capita—Purchasing Power Parity: $37,100 (2013 est.)
GDP—Real Growth Rate: 2% (2013 est.)
Inflation Rate—Consumer Price Index: 0.2% (2013 est.)

Cultural Characteristics[32]

Japanese people tend to operate as a group in general and this tendency reflects in their purchase behavior as well. Their purchase of a product is guided by not the utility or worth of the product but rather by how well the product is accepted in their community/friends/relatives. While shopping, Japanese people tend to consider the opinion of the salesman/friends and others more than consumers. Hence, it becomes crucial for the salespeople to be seen as friendly, knowledgeable advisors. Since product purchase is largely influenced by the acceptance of the community in Japan, it becomes essential to target all the communities in Japan as part of the marketing plan. The overall appearance of a product is more important to the average consumer than the performance of the product. Therefore, due diligence needs to be done with respect to product design/appearance. Japanese consumers either buy a product for their utility or for the status. There is a clear divide in the prices that they pay for these two categories of goods. Any intermediately priced item does not sell well in Japan.

Business Characteristics

The Japanese get familiar with the culture of the people whom they deal with. Japanese are very polite people and try to accommodate everybody's needs and wishes. When approaching the Japanese, one should take caution in not being too direct, because this would mean that if they are not able to answer or accommodate the query, that would result in them losing face in front of the foreign party. Given the level of collectivism in the Japanese society, it translates to such a system in the workplace. Most executives convene as a group, and often it is difficult to determine who is at the top of the hierarchy.

Politeness, sensitivity, and good manners form the foundation of businesses in Japan. Being loyal to a company is considered a virtue and many executives spend a number of years with the company. This translates to a long-term relationship with partners in business scenarios. Significant emphasis is placed on the actual interaction with the clients. The Japanese tend to be very formal in their meetings. Time is sacrosanct in Japan and they would like to be aware of any delays in advance.[33] They prefer formal dressing in client meetings and give a lot of importance to business cards. The meeting is generally more formal and rigid when compared to the US culture. Exhibit 17.9 provides a few useful tips in navigating the Japanese market.

---

[32] Intelligence Bridges, "Where Your Intelligence Cross to Japan," http://www.intelbridges.com/japanesedisposition.html (Retrieved on August 12, 2013).

[33] Venture Japan, "Japanese Business Culture," http://www.venturejapan.com/japanese-business-etiquette.htm (Retrieved on August 12, 2013).

Exhibit 17.9

Useful Tips for the Japanese Market[34]

Business cards are a must while meeting Japanese clients. Business cards need to be exchanged during meetings. Accept business cards with respect and keep them safe, as forgetting to pick up their business card is considered impolite, and is considered as a proxy for the lack of interest in a long-term relationship.

It is important to maintain a long-term relationship with the Japanese, since this is the *sole* criterion that is favored. Rather than using lower prices or better deals as means to determine their business ventures, the Japanese prefer to have a consistent management style to work with.

Myths About Dealing with Japanese Business Organizations[35]

Over the years, some fallacies have emerged about the way Japanese conduct business. Some of the more common ones follow:

- The last market one should enter is Japan
- The on-the-job training of American managers abroad can be combined with their simultaneous roles as trainers of our Japanese staff
- No Japanese company makes profit in the first year
- Japanese executives expect a huge salary and heavy summer and winter bonuses each year
- Millions of dollars need to be spent for the first five years of business in Japan
- Selling in Japan is more expensive than any other market; hence, Japanese distributors are justified in demanding 50–70% of the revenues
- Bilingual employees expect two times the salary that they would get from a local company
- Japanese employees are expected to be hired for life and it is difficult to dismiss an employee even if there is a reason

Exhibit 17.10 showcases typical characteristics of the Japanese culture and the impact it has on companies' ability to grow their business.

---

[34] Adapted from Venture Japan, "Japanese Business Culture," http://www.venturejapan.com/japanese-business-etiquette.htm (Retrieved on August 12, 2013).

[35] Venture Japan, "Japanese Business Myths," http://www.venturejapan.com/japan-business-myths.htm (Retrieved on August 12, 2013).

Exhibit 17.10

Japan's Corporate Culture[36]

The importance given to reverence and respect of elders in society has long been a staple of Japanese culture. The Japanese are known to be some of the most polite, humble, noble, and well-mannered people in the world. However, the impact that this mentality has had on their ability to grow their corporate culture and expand businesses has been questioned on many occasions. The respect that is given to figures of authority has been viewed as a hindrance to the professional growth of Japanese corporations. The idea of being proactive within an organization, or delivering input and suggestions to superiors, can come across as disrespectful and out of line. It is viewed by some that opportunities are left on the table and that by discouraging a culture that promotes new ideas and suggestions, the company's potential to grow is severely restricted. Recent studies have shown that nearly two-thirds of Japanese companies are not experiencing profits, and moving forward, it remains to be seen which will be able to last.

Market Research in Japan

The differences in survey research in Japan further complicate the cultural issues that can impede conducting market research. While these represent significant areas that have to be addressed by the company, they also reflect on the problem in trying to conduct research in a similar manner as in the US. Some of the common practices to be followed and some others that ought to be avoided are listed in Exhibit 17.11.

Data Collection

Door-to door interview is a major data collection method in Japan, although there has been an increase in use of telephone and the Internet for surveys. The cultural aspect is intrinsically tied with this method. A growing number of women are now working or spending a significant amount of time away from home, reducing their accessibility for phone surveys or door-to-door interviews. The use of interphones in several apartment complexes also has affected the degree to which the potential respondents can filter and block out the researcher.

Recently, in Japan, many businesses have adopted telephone surveys and telemarketing. Hence, there has been a surge of cold telephone calls to consumers in Japan. This has not been taken well by the Japanese consumers. Consumers are annoyed and not interested in cold calls. It becomes increasingly necessary for the interviewer to clearly state the purpose of the call at the very beginning of the survey. It is also essential to have interviewers

---

[36] Adapted from Nick Thomson, "Japanese culture: Help or hindrance for business growth? The Guardian 17 October 2014.

Exhibit 17.11

Cultural *Dos* and *Don'ts* in Japan[37]

- The Japanese are an extremely group-oriented and community-based people
- Avoid making too much direct eye contact as it can be interpreted as challenging and can make most Japanese uncomfortable
- Many Japanese are not comfortable with shaking hands, so it is best to take cue from them before offering your own hand
- It is best to be polite to everybody in the company as employees are loyal to their companies, stay around, and rise through the ranks. Today's employees could become tomorrow's executives
- "Yes" from Japanese does not always mean acceptance. When asked the question, "Don't you think so?" they often respond, "Yes, I don't think so."

who are aware of the cultural sensitivities to conduct these interviews. Many a time, respondents expect incentives to answer surveys.[38]

Several Japanese companies are looking at cost efficiency as a main prerogative in determining the kind of survey research method to employ. The emphasis is more on the ease of access to the sample as well as the speed with which the results are obtained and tabulated. The growing reliance on qualitative means of measurement versus the quantitative aspect would mean that companies rely on the provision of value-added services by marketing research firms. Exhibit 17.12 provides the sources for obtaining data in Japan.

Exhibit 17.12

Sources of Data for Japan

The Japanese Ministry of Internal Affairs and Communication publish statistics related to economic/financial conditions of Japan, business activities, family income and expenditure, housing, etc. These data can be accessed from http://www.stat.go.jp/english/data/.

Another good source of marketing-related information is http://www.allon.info/index.html. This website gives a plethora of information about market segmentation in Japan, and market share ranking in Japan, apart from information regarding the general demographics of Japan.

---

[37] Adapted from Venture Japan, "Japanese Business Culture," http://www.venturejapan.com/japanese-business-etiquette.htm (Retrieved in August 2013); "Where Your Intelligence Cross to Japan," *Intelligence Bridges*, March 16, 2014. Retrieved from http://www.intelbridges.com/japanesedisposition.html (accessed on August 2013).

[38] Quirk's Marketing Research Media, "Simplifying Research in Japan," http://www.quirks.com/articles/a2001/20011104.aspx?searchID=633178253&sort=9 (Retrieved on August 12, 2013).

Facsimile (Fax): The use of the fax machines in reaching the Japanese customers is facilitated by having a home reporter who has access to several respondents who fit the criteria for personal interviews. Benefits of this method include large reach, speed, low cost (though this would depend upon the installation charges and equipment), volume of the questionnaire (two-pronged benefit in which it has the reach of a telephone survey and the feasible length of a mail survey), and visual aids (words and figures). The disadvantages of conducting surveys through fax machines include low penetration amongst residents, and are used mainly as a tool to reach business respondents. The cost in installing machines in selected respondents' houses is very high. The user ability may also restrict the full usage of the fax machine.

Online/mobile surveys: The Internet has been gaining popularity as an effective survey tool. With 78.2% Internet penetration and 90.4% mobile phone penetration in Japan as of 2010,[39] market researchers are able to reach a wide set of consumers with the online surveys. However, in conducting global surveys, care should be taken to customize the survey for the Japanese consumers.

SUMMARY

This chapter presents an overall outlook of Asia-Pacific and provides data about personal and business habits that will be useful to the marketing researcher. Specifically, the countries of Australia, China, India, and Japan are discussed. Some of the topics that have been covered include the infrastructure available in these countries, the penetration of media, cultural habits, and sources of data.

---

[39] Industry Report. Telecoms and technology—Japan.

18

CHAPTER _____

Europe

INTRODUCTION

Ever since the creation of the *single market* in 1993, the EU has come a long way in terms of creating a unified community. This has been possible only through the establishment of *four freedoms* of movement of goods, services, people, and money. This has led to the creation of more than 200 laws covering tax policy, business regulations, professional qualifications, and other barriers to open frontiers. Exhibit 18.1 provides a comparison of the transformation over the past two decades in the market structure within EU.

The basic fact when targeting Europe is to consider it as an amalgamation of several nations rather than a geographically homogeneous group. People in such countries are used to local markets and specify the research based upon the kind of companies that exist within the confines of the continent. This has changed dramatically with the influx of US investment. Market research in the US starts with referring to demographic data,[1] while a significant portion of European research is initiated with information from governmental or public-based data. The problem becomes acute when the researcher assumes that the national institute handling such output is consistent across Europe. For example, Institut National dela Statistique et des Études Économiques (National Institute of Statistics and Economic Studies) (INSEE) in France is markedly accurate in its estimations of consumer profiles while Italian sources tend to be raw in their presentation.

REGIONAL CHARACTERISTICS

Analyzing data on consumer behavior in terms of purchase habits will be easy in Europe because this is similar to the kind of research that is being conducted in the US. The use of consumer panels and people meters, for example, helps translate the usage rates as well as perspectives, which will make sense due to the relative comparison made. Table 18.1 lists the television viewing culture of certain European countries.

---

[1] Blayne Cutler, "Reaching the Real Europe," *American Demographics*, October 1990, pp. 38–43.

Exhibit 18.1

EU—The Journey Thus Far[2]

	1992	2012
EU countries	12	27
EU consumers (in millions)	345	500
Countries in the euro area	NA	17
Possibility of basic Internet access	NA	95%
Regular Internet use	NA	68%
EU citizens banking online	0%	37%
Population buying online	NA	43%
Mobile phone use	Less than 1%	Over 100%
Internet access at home	NA	73%
Online research for goods and services as of 2010	NA	56%
Car ownership (per 1,000 inhabitants)	345	477
Number of companies (in millions)	12	21
Value of goods traded between EU countries (in billions) as of 2010	€800	€2,538
Value of goods traded between the EU and the rest of the world (in billions) as of 2010	€500	€2,850

TABLE 18.1
AVERAGE DAILY TELEVISION VIEWING TIME IN 2012[3]

Country	Minutes per Day per Person
Italy	255
Poland	243
UK	241
Spain	246
France	230
Germany	222
Brazil	216

[2] Adapted from "The European Union Explained—Consumers," February 2013, http://europa.eu/pol/cons/flipbook/en/files/consumers.pdf (Retrieved on August 18, 2013).
[3] Adapted from "Average Daily TV Viewing Time per Person in Selected Countries in 2012," *Statistica*, 2013, http://www.statista.com/statistics/214353/average-daily-tv-viewing-time-per-person-in-selected-countries/ (Retrieved on August15, 2013).

Perhaps one of the biggest concerns for an American marketer working in Europe would be the kind of emphasis being placed on obtaining quantitative information as substantiation for the inferences being made on the local markets. Unlike the Japanese and Korean marketers, numbers and raw data are placed higher on the list of priorities compared to analyzing the business culture. Europe leads the market research industry with a turnover of $14,140 million.

Mobile density in Europe has risen tremendously since the 1990s, when the US and Japan recorded far greater mobile subscribers. The introduction of the GSM standard, along with a wide variety of value-added services and mobile devices at various price points, spurred the growth of mobile subscribers in Europe. According to Eurobarometer, Europe has recorded a mobile density rate of 128%, as against 100% in Japan and 104% in the US. The high mobile density rate is a result of over 650 million active SIM cards available with 450 million people, translating to more than one subscription per person on average.[4] As a result of this rapid growth in mobile subscription, the growth in mobile messaging traffic (SMS and MMS) also has been robust. Table 18.2 presents the number of mobile subscriptions and the use of SMS in 2009 within the European nations.

TABLE 18.2
MOBILE SUBSCRIPTIONS AND THE USE OF SMS IN EUROPE[5]

Country	Mobile Subscriptions (per 100 Inhabitants)	Average Number of SMS Messages Sent (per Inhabitant)
Greece	180	677
Italy	151	NA
Portugal	151	2,397
Lithuania	148	2,757
Luxembourg	146	889
Finland	145	713
Bulgaria	139	87
Czech Republic	136	730
Cyprus	133	1,984
Germany	132	420
UK	130	NA
Sweden	126	1,758
Denmark	124	2,413
Netherlands	122	495
Ireland	119	2,677
Hungary	118	188
Poland	118	1,224

(Table 18.2 Contd.)

[4] Eurobarometer, "Wireless Intelligence; E-Communications Household Survey," 2010.
[5] Adapted from Eurostat, http://epp.eurostat.ec.europa.eu/statistics_explained/index.php/Telecommunication_statistics (Accessed on August 18, 2013).

(Table 18.2 Contd.)

Country	Mobile Subscriptions (per 100 Inhabitants)	Average Number of SMS Messages Sent (per Inhabitant)
Romania	118	346
Estonia	117	163
Spain	111	180
Belgium	108	1,374
Slovenia	103	491
Malta	102	1,201
Slovakia	102	252
Latvia	99	NA
France	95	978
Austria	83	687
Switzerland	121	736
Norway	111	1,328
Iceland	106	459
Liechtenstein	97	NA
FYR of Macedonia	95	229
Croatia	91	787
Turkey	88	1,793

Given these developments, mobile devices have become ubiquitous to the European citizen's personal and business life, owing to the presence of other applications such as watch, calculator, alarm clock, personal information management device, GPS navigator, music player, and camera, among others. Even among business users, mobile communication services have become essential, especially for the estimated 50% of employees who spend at least two to three days away from their workplace.[6]

EUROPEAN STATISTICAL SOURCES

There are some very good secondary data sources available for Europe, some of which are the following:

1. *European Central Bank.* The European Central Bank collects necessary and relevant data and disseminates impartial, accurate statistics, which complies with European and internationally accepted standards
2. *European Official Statistics: A Guide to Databases.* Almost 120 publicly accessible databases within the field of official statistics are listed. Information contained here covers virtually all social and economic sectors

---

[6] IDC, "Worldwide Mobile Worker Platform, 2009–2013 Forecast."

3. *European Official Statistics: Sources of Information.* Provides a list of over 250 government bodies, organizations, ministries, and banks that publish information
4. *Eurostat—Your Partner for European Statistics: A Guide to the Statistical Office of the European Communities.* Contains information on where relevant statistical data can be obtained about the EU
5. *Europe in Figures.* Provides information on the present state of the Union. It is an excellent source of information for understanding current and future developments in Europe
6. *Eurostat Yearbook.* Contains information on the people, the land and environment, national economy, and trade and industry and in the Union

EUROPE—ONE ECONOMY?

When trying to perceive the EU or the European Economic Community (EEC) as a large bloc, a market researcher has to exercise restraint in standardizing across the continent. Operating a chain of retail outlets from Great Britain to the Czech Republic requires careful attention to the piquancy in the individual markets. With widely different infrastructures, varying economic growth rates, and diverse cultures, this continent holds several conditions and constraints for the marketer, and is far from being straightforward. For example, it is very common to find that retail outlets may not extend the service that is similar to that of the West. The shopping experience would be entirely different in some places of East Europe. One cannot pick up the items they need and take it to the cashier for billing. Shoppers might have to ask the person at the counter for the item they are looking for and then pay at the cashier.[7]

Despite the fact that members of the EEC portray themselves to be connected by a currency as well as heightened trade relations, the two biggest problems are that the national identities are maintained as separate and distinct and there is a huge difference in the per capita wealth of the old Europe and the emerging markets of Eastern Europe.[8] Depending on the markets (countries), the market preferences and tastes vary, and it is best to cater to the taste and preferences of the local market.

There are many ways that one can approach marketing research in Europe. One approach would be to address the consumers geographically. When a foreign company prepares to enter any country in Europe, it would need to evaluate the kind of consumer behavior in terms of the differences to the company's COO. Exhibit 18.2 shows how Russia is unique in terms of the beverage industry.

The EU is committed to eliminating all internal economic barriers to trade and creating a single market. According to 2012 estimates from Eurostat, these 28 countries have a combined population of 507 million and constitute one of the wealthiest markets in the world.

---

[7] About.com, "Top 7 Tips for Shopping in Eastern Europe," http://goeasteurope.about.com/od/easterneuropeanhistory/tp/shopping.htm (Retrieved on August 13, 2013).

[8] Forbes, "Is Eastern Europe Economically Converging with the West?" August 12, 2012, http://www.forbes.com/sites/markadomanis/2012/07/14/is-eastern-europe-economically-converging-with-the-west/ (Retrieved on August 13, 2013).

Exhibit 18.2

Beverage Industry in Russia[9]

In a world that is reigned supreme by the two soft-drink giants, Coca-Cola and Pepsi Co, Russia is perhaps the only country which has still not been *conquered*. In the soft-drink market, carbonated drinks account for only 39% of the total soft drink sales as of 2011. The rest of the business comes from bottled water and vegetable and fruit juices. Russia as a nation has become more health-conscious, and citizens of Russia prefer healthier drinks to carbonated drinks. With an increase in disposable income due to stable economy and health-conscious citizens, there is a huge potential for growth in the non-carbonated soft drinks sector in Russia. Not only do Russian consumers look for healthier alternatives, they also look for cheaper options. Local brands which are cheaper are more popular among masses.

In fact, Europe is home to seven of the world's 15 richest countries. Collectively, the GDP is nearly €13 trillion ($17.5 trillion), with per capita GDP of €25,500 ($34,000).[10] By comparison, the US GDP is $15.7 trillion, with per capita GDP of US$ 49,965.[11]

The European marketplace consists of more than just EU-member countries. The European Free Trade Association (EFTA) countries, Iceland, Liechtenstein, Norway, and Switzerland, also represent excellent opportunities to US direct marketers. The market structure of the EFTA members is closely aligned to the EU; this is evident from the fact that many member countries applied for EU membership in the past and are now part of EU. To support this, EFTA countries have agreed to work with the EU in the creation of a European Economic Area. This agreement is widely viewed as a preliminary stage for the incorporation of the seven EFTA countries into the EU.

CULTURE

Despite the vast size and wealth of this New Europe, it is important to realize that Europe should not, and cannot, be considered a single marketplace. For example, the 28 nations of the EU have 24 official languages, 13 currencies (including the euro), numerous payment options, and different national cultures. To communicate effectively with European customers, researchers must understand their culture. This requires a significant amount of cultural sensitivity and is especially important when developing an advertising campaign and when writing the copy. Europeans have unique cultures and histories, and if these issues are neglected, a researcher's reputation can be tarnished.

---

[9] Adapted from "Just the Facts: The Russian Soft Drinks Market," December 6, 2010. Accessed on August 18, 2013 from http://www.just-drinks.com/news/just-the-facts-the-russian-soft-drinks-market_id102578.aspx

[10] Eurostat, http://epp.eurostat.ec.europa.eu/portal/page/portal/eurostat/home/ (Retrieved on August 14, 2013).

[11] World Bank National Accounts Data.

Even the finer details should be accounted for and incorporated into a campaign. For example, when writing dates in Europe, the day (numeric) is placed first, followed by the month, and then the year. Thus, 7/2/13 is February 7, 2013 in the UK, but is July 2, 2013 in the US. A mistake in this area would not violate any major cultural norms but may show the target audience that a US company does not fully understand the marketplace. Some of the cultural aspects that need to be remembered are listed in Exhibit 18.3.

Exhibit 18.3

Cultural *Dos* and *Don'ts* in Europe[12]

- Most countries can speak English as their main professional business language.
- The French are proud of their language and they prefer to speak it.
- The city-based Germans speak good business English, but they are not comfortable conversing in English.
- Handshakes are a common form of greeting upon initial meeting.
- First names are commonly used to address one another. However, titles, such as Dr or Prof., are commonly used as well.
- Meetings with the French tend to be formal and lengthy. They also consider it impolite to start a business conversation in French and revert to English.
- The Germans are very keen on punctuality and to be on time is essential. Business atmosphere is formal and a working knowledge is greatly appreciated.
- When doing business with the British, they expect printed cards to be exchanged.
- Dining is a common form of generosity and hospitality in Europe.
- Most European countries do not see a need to establish personal relationships prior to business interactions.

SEASONALITY AND HOLIDAYS

As a general rule, Europe is *Closed for Business* during the month of August when many people take their vacations and companies tend to run on a skeleton staff. US companies should also realize that Christmas holidays are sometimes celebrated differently in Europe. For example, in the Netherlands, gifts are exchanged on St. Nicholas Day, almost two weeks before December 25, and in Spain, gifts are exchanged on Epiphany—two weeks after Christmas.

LANGUAGE ISSUES

One of the most important decisions that a researcher will make is whether to translate the questionnaire or not. This decision depends on several factors, including the target audience,

---

[12] Adapted from "Passport to Trade: A Bridge to Success," http://businessculture.org/western-europe/ (Retrieved on May 8, 2014); "Don't Be the Ugly American," http://away.com/stores/travel-guides/europe/ european-customs-guide-1.html (Retrieved on May 15, 2014).

the type of product, and the nature of the survey. In general, translation is recommended unless it is certain that the target audience reads English. In the end, however, the language issue should be addressed on a case-by-case basis. Many companies find it acceptable to translate only certain parts of the questionnaire (i.e., the incentives, the return instructions, and so on). Additionally, English can be written alongside the local language to ensure that the widest possible audience is being reached.

Many international researchers contend that companies can successfully mail a survey to over 100 countries in English. In Europe, however, there is no lingua franca. While English and French are generally considered the business languages of Europe, many business executives also speak German. In fact, over 200 million people in Europe (both East and West) consider German their primary or secondary tongue. German is one of the official languages in Germany, Austria, Switzerland, Luxembourg, Liechtenstein, and Belgium. Table 18.3 gives the percentage of English proficiency among adults.

The English language is also received differently in many European countries. For example, when mailing into France, it is generally recommended translating materials into French; however, it may be acceptable to mail in English to the Netherlands and Germany. Also, the translated copy may take more space on a page than the English copy. For example, the same message requires 20% more space in French, 30% more space in German, and up to 40% more space in Finnish. It is important to not cut corners when it comes to retaining translation services. It is a necessary cost of doing business and the price should not be the sole criterion for choosing one firm over another; rather, the quality of translation must be the focus.

TABLE 18.3
Top 10 Countries with English Proficiency[13]

Rank	Country	Percentage of Adults Proficient in English
1	Sweden	68.91
2	Denmark	67.96
3	Netherlands	66.32
4	Finland	64.37
5	Norway	63.22
6	Belgium	62.46
7	Austria	62.14
8	Hungary	60.39
9	Germany	60.07
10	Poland	59.08

---

[13] Adapted from EF EPI, "EF English Proficiency Index 2012." Accessed on August 18, 2013 from http://www.ef.com/__/~/media/efcom/epi/2012/full_reports/ef-epi-2012-report-master-lr-2

MAILING LISTS

The type of list being utilized also affects the translation decision. When an internationally compiled list is used for targeting affluent consumers throughout the region, it may be acceptable to mail in English. On the other hand, if mass mailing is done based on a domestically compiled list, then translating the copy is advised. In this regard, talking to list brokers about the language issue can be valuable in administering the mailers.

In recent years, the European Commission has strengthened data protection legislation. Since there is a high probability of using the data collected in one EU country in another EU country, the European Commission brought in unified data protection laws across all EU nations to avoid any conflicting laws in different countries. According to this, personal data can only be collected for legitimate purposes, and agencies that collect data are bound by EU laws to protect data from being misused and are obliged to respect the rights of data owners.[14] Domestic and B2B lists are available for various countries in Europe. The price for a consumer list/business list is anywhere from €288 to in excess of €5,000. The prices are based on specifications such as number of consumers to be reached, criteria of the listings, and other considerations.[15]

COMPUTERIZED INFORMATION AND SERVICES

As a result of advances in the IT field, a number of market research resources are now available through electronic media. This greatly facilitates keeping the information up to date and disseminating the information to the business community. Some of these sources are listed in Exhibit 18.4.

Exhibit 18.4

Electronic Information Sources on the EU

Currently, there are many online resources available for reference regarding the European market. Following are some of the sources from which one can obtain information about trade, policies, and other related information.

Information Collected and Provided by European Organizations
- European Documentation Center (EDC): EDC was established in 1976 and is a repository of all official publications in the EU and can be accessed at http://www.eui.eu/Research/Library/ResearchGuides/EuropeanInformation/EuropeanDocumentationCentreatEUI.aspx
- EU Online: Information about most of the EU activities can be retrieved from http://www.eui.eu/Research/Library/ResearchGuides/EuropeanInformation/EuropeanUnionOnline.aspx

---

[14] European Commission, "Protection of Personal Data," http://ec.europa.eu/justice/data-protection/index_en.htm (Retrieved on August 13, 2013).

[15] CEBUS, "Where New Business Starts," http://www.cebus.net/en/ (Retrieved on August 13, 2013).

- Eurostat: Contains all statistical details regarding EU and can be accessed from http://epp.eurostat.ec.europa.eu/portal/page/portal/eurostat/home
- Europa.eu: This is a valuable source of information regarding all aspects of life in EU. Europa can be accessed from http://europa.eu/index_en.htm
- EBU: This is a resourceful organization for the blind. Here, we can find much information about EU for the visually challenged people which can be accessed from http://www.euroblind.org/resources/guidelines/nr/88

Information Collected and Provided by Non-European Organizations

- The US government provides valuable information and guidance regarding exporting to other countries and the prevailing regulations for US exporters, and this can be obtained from http://export.gov/index.asp
- US Department of State publishes the background of each and every country in the world. They also publish a fact sheet which has details about the relationship between the country and US, which can be accessed from http://www.state.gov/r/pa/ei/bgn/2798.htm
- US Commercial Service publishes global marketing research information on all countries that can be accessed from http://www.buyusainfo.net/adsearch.cfm?search_type=int&loadnav=no
- US Census Bureau publishes information regarding US trade details with other countries and can be referred at http://www.census.gov/foreign-trade/about/index.html.
- World Trade Organization also publishes reports regarding US trade with other countries that can be retrieved from http://wto.org/english/res_e/publications_e/wtr13_e.htm

FRANCE

Country Characteristics[16]

Population: 66,259,012 (July 2014 est.)
Land Area: 643,801 sq. km
Language: French
Literacy Rate: 99%
Religion: Roman Catholic 83–88%, Protestant 2%, Jewish 1%, Muslim 5–10%, and unaffiliated 4%
GDP—Purchasing Power Parity: $2.273 trillion (2013 est.)
GDP per Capita—Purchasing Power Parity: $35,700 (2013 est.)
GDP—Real Growth Rate: 0.2% (2013 est.)
Inflation Rate—Consumer Price Index: 1.1% (2013 est.)

---

[16] "France," in *CIA World Factbook*, https://www.cia.gov/library/publications/the-world-factbook/geos/fr.html (Retrieved August 13, 2013).

Doing Business in France

The French believe in status and often do not mingle between the groups. For instance, the upper bourgeoisie will not attempt to mix with the upper-middle or the middle income classes. Educational qualification and intelligence are the most important selling points in France.

While conversing with the French, it is necessary to be able to distinguish their sardonic comments from humor. French are less likely to use humor in business conversations. Most French are interested in discussions where there are no points of agreement, and as the arguments grow more heated, they tend to enjoy them better. This is seen to be reflective of a person's character and feelings, as well as their thought processes. It would be better to direct the conversation away from personal topics into more general subjects like politics and art as French like to keep their family life private.

The French attitude to work ethics in the public sector is that there is little motivation to strive for excelling in their field. The strength of the union helps in ensuring that these workers maintain their jobs despite lax performance levels; however, in smaller companies, there is significant emphasis placed on quality and performance. Also, as an incentive to the workers, there are significant opportunities to scale up the ladder and gain the respect of the fellow workers.

The French management is rather centralized in structure, with a significant amount of emphasis placed on decision making by CEO in the company. Most of the senior management in French companies are well educated, and they approach leadership with unusual degree of academic precision; hence, management is considered an intellectual task. Decisions are made by senior management passed on to employees for implementation.

Time consciousness is still important at business meetings since it reflects pride to conduct business with the French in most part of France. The French tend to take pride in purchasing products made locally.[17]

Market Research in France

France has a very established and updated infrastructure system that supports its direct marketing ventures. French direct mail market in one of the largest and growing market in Europe. There are close to 13 million families (consumer list) included in the marketing list.[18] In 2010, the direct marketing industry in France was valued at $47 billion, and is expected to grow five times by 2020.[19] However, direct mail order sales have declined. This is mainly due to the increased use of other mediums of communication like telephone and Internet.

---

[17] World Business Culture, "Business Culture in France," http://www.worldbusinessculture.com/French-Business-Negotiation.html (Retrieved on August 14, 2013).

[18] SNA, "National Address Management Service," http://www.laposte.fr/sna/rubrique.php3?id_rubrique=12 (Retrieved on August 15, 2013).

[19] US Commercial Service, "Doing Business in France: 2012 Country Commercial Guide for US Companies," http://www.kallman.com/pdfs/2012-Doing-Business-In-France-Country-Commercial-Guide-for-US-Companies.pdf (Retrieved on August 15, 2013).

Telemarketing is considered a better way to reach consumers because of the convenience and ease of use. With 100% mobile density rate as of 2010, it is easy to reach consumers over phone.[20] Also, e-commerce has been gaining prominence in France with almost 80% of people having access to the Internet. Nearly 12% of Internet users in France visit online shopping websites daily.[21] Telecommunication and IT sectors play a central role in French economy. Excellent telecommunication infrastructure in France has paved more ways to researchers to reach consumers effectively.

It is ideal to conduct primary research by reviewing individual segments of the French population. This is because there are several differences between the classes in the society, and this affects the purchasing pattern per household. The French value their personal time at home and often are not receptive to questions being posed. It is recommended that mall intercepts be used since they are more relaxed in such a social setting and will be more willing to offer their perspectives. It is important, however, to note that the French are rather idealistic in their vision of current lifestyles, and often skew their responses to reflect a better state rather than an actual state. The researcher should discount this bias in response and weigh the relevance of the answers.

GERMANY

The Germany of today is a united market, immersed in the democratic system. The cultural characteristics reflect the commonality between the East and West Germany of yesteryears. This is in line with the thought that regardless of political influence, culture pervades the society and is slower to change and adapt.

Country Characteristics[22]

Population: 80,996,685 (July 2014 est.)
Land Area: 357,022 sq. km
Language: German
Literacy Rate: 99%
Religion: Protestant 34%, Roman Catholic 34%, Muslim 3.7%, unaffiliated or other 28.3%
GDP—Purchasing Power Parity: $3.227 trillion (2013 est.)
GDP per Capita—Purchasing Power Parity: $39,500 (2013 est.)
GDP—Real Growth Rate: 0.5% (2013 est.)
Inflation Rate—Consumer Price Index: 1.6% (2012 est.)

---

[20] "Telecoms and Technology: France," Industry Report, 2012.
[21] US Commercial Service, "Doing Business in France."
[22] "Germany," in *CIA World Factbook*, https://www.cia.gov/library/publications/the-world-factbook/geos/gm.html (Retrieved August 13, 2013).

General Characteristics[23]

Germans are considered to be precision-oriented with immense emphasis on the exactness of the job. This translates into their working behavior, which is meticulous and driven toward goal-oriented philosophies (where efficiency is the primary prerogative). The Germans are not spontaneous in their dealings with people, tending toward being private in their approach. Their company dealings are based upon the etiquette demanded of a position held. It is often that business dealings do not stretch beyond the office working hours and recreation is almost strictly spent in personal endeavors.

Business Characteristics

German managers are experts in their fields and expected to lead others by exhibiting strong and clear leadership skills. Their concept of business dealings involves formal interaction with the clientele where it would be advantageous to the client to be well prepared for the meeting, as Germans generally come well prepared for their meetings. Most often, personal life is never discussed as part of a business meeting. The individual never mentions his achievements or offers insight into his personal matters. In Germany, it is important that the dealings are made specific, either in writing or verbally. This is specifically because Germans pay attention to detail, and anything that is not specified will be considered in breach of trust.[24]

Germans tend to prefer the formal form of addressing people, and the use of first names should be avoided. A good option would be the use of *herr* or *frau*. English is taught in German schools and most people are aware of the nuances of the English language. The younger generation will not mind conducting business in English while the older generation will.[25] The German perception of time is an aspect to note. They value punctuality to be an essential work ethic and do not take very well to clients who fail to show up on time for meetings or who do not specify a timeline for a certain project to be completed.

For the Germans, greeting is almost always a firm handshake. This is regardless of the meeting being for personal or business reasons. There is significant emphasis placed on the seniority of one employee over another, and this inadvertently also relates to the formality of relationships within the company. Some of the aspects of conducting negotiations with Germans are listed in Exhibit 18.5.

Market Research in Germany

The availability of good secondary research information enables a thorough analysis of the consumer perspectives. Germans are intensely private and tend to keep their opinions to themselves. In particular, the northern part of Germany tends to be a rather difficult area to

---

[23] Philip R. Harris and Robert T. Moran, *Managing Cultural Differences* (Houston, TX: Gulf Publishing Company, 1996), pp. 321–325, 4th edition.

[24] World Business Culture, "Business Culture in Germany," http://www.worldbusinessculture.com/German-Business-Structures.html (Retrieved on August 14, 2013).

[25] Internations, "German Business Culture," http://www.internations.org/germany-expats/guide/15987-jobs-business/german-business-culture-15990 (Retrieved on August 14, 2013).

Exhibit 18.5

Conducting Negotiations with Germans[26]

In order to talk to the German representative, it is better to meet him or her in person rather than engage in a discussion over the phone. The primary purpose of the first meeting is to get to know each other and to evaluate whether the other party is trustworthy and whether the relationship would be beneficial. The following points need to be considered for conducting healthy negotiations:

- Germans tend to be direct in sharing their thoughts. This should not be taken personally.
- All claims have to be backed up with appropriate data, as Germans dislike hype and exaggeration.
- Germans require time to establish close business relationships. Their apparent coldness at the beginning will vanish over time. Once they get to know you, Germans are very friendly and loyal.
- Even if German executives speak your language, they appreciate receiving all promotional materials and instruction manuals in German.
- When a problem arises, it would help to explain it clearly, unemotionally, in detail, and in writing if possible.

elicit responses. There is a reasonable amount of resistance to responding to surveys at malls or in answering queries over the telephone. Direct marketing is on the decline in Germany as Internet marketing is on the rise. The number of Germans who prefer online to regular marketing is on the increase. This increasing population that is more inclined toward Web-based solution includes older generation of Germans too. However, Germans are very concerned about the trustworthiness of the websites and the authentication procedures the websites follow.[27] In order to elicit responses, it would be useful to consider providing incentives to the public such as a discount (coupon) on purchases or anything in *kind*.

One misunderstanding that marketers have in targeting consumers in Germany is in assuming that most of them live in urban areas. There is a strong difference in perception as well as lifestyles between rural and urban Germany. Evidence proves that it would be beneficial for the marketer to consider different strategies and operationalize such that it caters to the specific region in Germany rather than a homogenization. Exhibit 18.6 explores Internet marketing in Germany.

---

[26] Adapted from "Germany" from eDiplomat, "Germany." Retrieved on August 14, 2013 from http://www.ediplomat.com/np/cultural_etiquette/ce_de.htm, originally based on material from Mary Murray Bosrock "Put Your Best Foot Forward— Europe: A Fearless Guide to International Communication and Behavior," *International Education Systems*, 1995.; *Doing Business in Europe* (Georgia Department of Economic Development), 2007, http://www.georgia.org/SiteCollectionDocuments/Business/International/GC_trade_DoingBiz_Europe.pdf (Retrieved on August 14, 2013).

[27] Ponemon Institute, "Moving Beyond Passwords: Consumer Attitudes on Online Authentication," http://www.ponemon.org/local/upload/file/NokNokWP_FINAL_3.pdf (Retrieved on August 14, 2013).

Exhibit 18.6

Internet Marketing in Germany[28]

As of 2011, Germany had an Internet penetration of 83% and mobile density of 141.3%.[29] Though there is a considerable level of Internet censorship in Germany, it is aimed at maintaining law and order than any other ideological purposes. For example, child pornography sites are banned in Germany. Germany has been far ahead in terms of downloading speed with an average of 17.5 mbps. With this kind of Internet/mobile density rates and Internet speeds, Germany would be an ideal market for video marketing. Mobile apps are very popular in Germany and this paves the way for social book-marking as a means of marketing through mobile apps. Increasingly, Germans are using their smart-phones to access the Internet. This trend suggests that marketers need to design their campaigns such that they attract the mobile Internet users as well.

GREAT BRITAIN

Country Characteristics[30]

Population: 63,742,977 (July 2014 est.)
Land Area: 243,610 sq. km
Language: English
Literacy Rate: 99%
Religion: Christian (Anglican, Roman Catholic, Presbyterian, Methodist) 71.6%, Muslim 2.7%, Hindu 1%, other 1.6%, unspecified or none 23.1% (2001 census)
GDP—Purchasing Power Parity: $2.378 trillion (2013 est.)
GDP per Capita—Purchasing Power Parity: $37,300 (2013 est.)
GDP—Real Growth Rate: 1.4% (2013 est.)
Inflation Rate—Consumer Price Index: 2.7% (2013 est.)

Conducting Business in the UK

Although the entire UK can be classified as being proud of their heritage, the English, Welsh, and Scottish cannot be confused to be from the same *land*. Although British is preferred, it is ideal that one's *region* in the country is known prior to any generalized remark.

As in Germany, a good handshake establishes confidence in the other party and a will-ingness to conduct business. While it is improper to end a meeting without an affirmative

---

[28] Adapted from MVF Global, "Lead Generation and Internet Marketing in Germany." Retrieved on August 14, 2013 from http://www.mvfglobal.com/germany

[29] "Telecoms and Technology —Germany."

[30] "United Kingdom," in *CIA World Factbook*, https://www.cia.gov/library/publications/the-world-factbook/geos/uk.html (Retrieved August 13, 2013).

handshake, it is ideal to follow the cue of the British counterpart. The concept of time in the UK is valued. Punctuality is seen as a virtue, as an awareness of how important the company or relationship is perceived by the client. Whereas people from the older generation prefer to do business with people they know well, the younger generation has a more open approach to conducting business.[31]

It is essential to adhere to the strict line between friendship and business relations. Very seldom do the British intrude upon the personal life of the client. In fact, it is rarely that the British counterpart would refer to the foreign representative by his first name, unless stated. Exhibit 18.7 provides some tips for conducting negotiations with the British.

Exhibit 18.7

Conducting Negotiations with the British[32]

Business in the UK is now generally quite informal, and approaches can be made directly to senior executives without any necessity for third parties. Frequently, business people will move to first names during a first meeting or when telephoning or e-mailing. The following points need to be considered for conducting healthy negotiations:

- Expect meetings to be polite and reasonably casual. Declining refreshment offered at the start of the meeting is acceptable and will not cause a problem. Small talk about family/personal details is welcomed, as the British like to understand the background and interests of those they meet with.
- Unlike the Germans, British do not like to be too direct at the start or end of meetings.
- It is better to avoid controversial topics such as politics or religion, and not discuss comparative work ethics.
- The British traditionally underplay dangerous situations. Similarly, they refrain from extravagant claims about products or plans.
- In negotiations, it is better to avoid the hard sell approach, and rushing the British into making a decision.
- It would be wise to send senior executives to the UK, as they may be received with more respect and are usually more restrained in conduct.
- While the British are often self-critical, it is better to only listen and not join in any of the criticisms. Similarly, when complaints are shared, it is better if visitors do not participate.
- The British apologize often, for even small inconveniences. They also have a habit of adding a question to the end of a sentence; for example: "It's a lovely day, don't you think?"

The British are very aware of the language differences within their own country as well as with the US; however, the fact that English is a common turf for conducting marketing ventures is a trap that one should refrain from falling into. Not only are the connotations different for several words, as well as differences in usage, it is necessary to refer to the kind of cues that

---

[31] Kwintessential, "Doing Business in UK," http://www.kwintessential.co.uk/etiquette/doing-business-uk.html (Retrieved on August 14, 2013).

[32] *Doing Business in Europe* (Georgia: Department of Economic Development).

would stir the consumer in the British. This impacts the manner in which advertising would have to be constructed as well as the way in which the British consumer would be addressed. Also, it is important to note the differences in nonverbal communication which affect the interpretation of attitudes.

Conducting Market Research in UK

There are several detailed sources of secondary data available for conducting preliminary research in Great Britain. The UK National Statistics website (http://www.statistics.gov.uk/hub/index.html) published by the Government Statistical Service offers detailed data that is very useful in secondary research. The Central Statistical Office website is also a good source for secondary research. This website is a good source of information about the economy, people, business sector, labor market, and the environment. Some of the other sources include:

- *Annual Abstract of Statistics:* Provides information on population, housing, manufactured goods, and so on
- *Scotland Statistics:* Statistics for Scotland
- *Welsh Government Statistics:* Statistics for Wales
- *Social Trends:* Collection of key social statistics covering demographic trends, income and wealth, education, employment, households and families, leisure, and so on
- *Financial Statistics:* Key UK monetary and financial statistics
- *Family Expenditure Survey:* Annual detailed report presenting income and expenditure by type of household for the UK

There are several non-official sources of data available for the UK. For example, Euromonitor publishes various kinds of market research reports on business and trade in UK.

The UK is a highly diverse country, which makes it a very complex country to understand despite its sometimes homogeneous *appearance*. The British have not been responsive to the opportunities posed to the European Community in general. In terms of responsiveness to purchase or participate in international market research activities, the UK lags behind countries like Finland, Denmark, France, and Italy.

Telemarketing

Telemarketing in the UK has been a popular media for market research in the past; however, the charm of telemarketing is dying as telephone surveys are seen as intrusive when compared to online surveys in the UK. Being creative is the key for the future of telemarketing in the UK. Selection of respondents needs to be based on relevance and not purely on data available.[33] Only when respondents see the relevance of the call would they be willing to participate in telemarketing calls. Exhibit 18.8 talks about selecting samples in the UK.

---

[33] *Marketing Magazine*, "Creativity Is the Key to the Future of Telemarketing," June 5, 2006, http://www.marketingmagazine.co.uk/article/562686/creativity-key-future-telemarketing (Retrieved on August 14, 2003).

Exhibit 18.8

Selecting the Sample[34]

When attempting to obtain a random sample, it is important for marketers to have a firm understanding of the consumers who choose to participate in the study. Customers are often classified in a geo-demographic manner, which associates them with the particular regional area they live in. Increasing sample sizes gives greater power to detect differences. Certain tendencies are noticeable when analyzing a large sample of consumers, with postal codes often serving as indicators of geo-demographics. Using CAMEO, MOSAIC, and ACORN, marketers are able to obtain an understanding of the individuals who chose to participate in the study.

Direct Mailing

Direct mailing was the most effective tool in the past in the UK. With the recent explosion of digital channels, direct mails have been relegated to one of the many options available to marketers. An ideal mix of e-mail, mobile, TV, and printed media communication have to be determined for a product. Different businesses feel differently about using direct mailing as a form of communication. For example, Virgin Media uses direct mailing extensively while British Gas feels that direct mailing does not contribute to sales as much as it used to in the past.[35] With many lists available, researchers need to spend time in selecting the target respondents to ensure they get meaningful and relevant responses. Exhibit 18.9 explains the tools for catalog marketing.

Exhibit 18.9

Targeting Strategies for Catalogs[36]

When marketing products through the use of catalogs, it is essential to consider multiple strategies that will boost profits, such as:

- Have a clear sense of your market and what customer you are trying to lure.
- Catalog must contain direct response copywriting.
- Inclusion of arts and graphics to attract the readers and encourage subscription.
- Ensure that your catalogue has its own personality and appeal.
- Organize products in a manner that can carry the reader throughout the catalog.

---

[34] Adapted as on May 6, 2014 from http://www.select-statistics.co.uk/article/blog-post/the-importance-and-effect-of-sample-size

[35] *Marketing Magazine*, "Direct Marketing," Special Report, July 20, 2012, http://www.marketingmagazine.co.uk/article/1141352/special-report-direct-marketing (Retrieved on April 14, 2013).

[36] Adapted from "Creative Direct Marketing Group, Inc." at http://www.cdmginc.com/direct-response-articles/article.aspx?cid=110 (Retrieved on May 9, 2014).

One of the major aspects to think about in terms of addresses of consumers is that most of the houses have names rather than street numbers or house numbers. A large number of the houses are termed as *Mansfield Manor* as opposed to addresses we are used to as a means to sectionalize the population.

While the usual response of international marketers is that the British are reserved and secretive of their actual purchase need, the scenario is not much different to the lack of responsiveness that one gets in the US. One benefit of conducting research in the UK is that the distribution system is similar to the US and approachability to the consumer is equally effective.

Online Marketing

As of 2010, Internet penetration in the UK was 78% and mobile density was 134.9%. More and more people are accessing the Internet through their smartphones. According to a recent survey about e-mail marketing in the UK, 43% of consumers are signing up for 10 or more brand communications and feel that the e-mails are more relevant and of interest to them. Consumers are more welcoming to e-communications from different brands. Though as per the survey not many consumers are using the mobile phones to access Internet, consumers are going to use their smartphones more extensively in the near future. Hence, reaching consumers through mobile is not going to take time. Marketers need to gear up to reach consumers effectively through mobile phones as well.

SUMMARY

This chapter deals with marketing research in Europe. With the diverse political and economic conditions, it is not always feasible to see Europe as a homogeneous entity. Rather, it would be advisable to distinguish different regions needs and cater to them separately. This is discussed in detail in this chapter. The chapter also deals specifically with France, Germany, and the UK. Relevant statistics, business characteristics, and cultural norms have been provided for each of these countries.

19

Latin America

INTRODUCTION

The varied cultural influences that have impacted the 12 countries in Latin America have resulted in varied business patterns and strategies to be taken by the foreign concern. Not only do the differences in language (Spanish or Portuguese) affect the degree to which the company has to adapt to the local climate, other factors such as the diversity in ethnicity and religion would be applicable too.

CONDUCTING RESEARCH IN LATIN AMERICA

The main concern for marketing researchers in Latin America is the limited resources from which to conduct research. The access to data is a major hindrance as researches often do not know enough about the market and do not have the appropriate contacts in the market. There is also a lack of reliable secondary data available in Latin America.[1]

Attitude Toward Research

In the US, consumers are more experienced, and with the high amount of exposure, tend to be critical of market research. People in Latin America, however, do not view market research in that light. Rather, it is an area that is new to them, which attends to their needs and desires, and serves as a means to evaluate their opinions.

In trying to obtain information from the Latin American consumer, it is important to note their candor and eagerness to respond. Latin Americans are typically friendly and open to communicating with researchers. In addition, researchers do not have to deal with the privacy issues often encountered in other regions (i.e., Europe). In this regard, consumers view research favorably and are often willing to participate freely.[2] They believe that their opinions should be given because they were asked to respond. Compensation toward participation is

---

[1] F. Fastoso and J. Whitelock, "Why Is So Little Marketing Research on Latin America Published in High Quality Journals and What Can We Do About It? Lessons from a Delphi Study of Authors Who Have Succeeded," *International Marketing Review* 28, no. 4 (2011): 435. (Publisher provided full text searching file, Ipswich, MA. Accessed August 5, 2013).

[2] Ibid.

normal and paying in kind or *cariñito* (a small token of appreciation) is not uncommon. In some cases, a cash offering may offend respondents and could turn an otherwise informal and pleasant arrangement into a transaction.[3] Latin Americans place a great deal of importance on personal relations and the will and desire to help someone they know. Exhibit 19.1 discusses the challenges faced when conducting research with companies in Latin America.

Exhibit 19.1

Challenges in Conducting Research with Companies in Latin America[4]

Conducting research in Latin America is faced with two main challenges: lack of research networks for data collection, and problems related to gathering data. Although conducting research with consumers can be relatively easy, it can be challenging to obtain company support for research initiatives. Conducting research with managers can prove to be difficult and often result in low response rates. Scheduling interviews with managers can be elusive due to differences in time perceptions or a general avoidance to be interviewed. The competitive nature of the industry in Latin America also hinders research with companies. Companies place a high level of confidentiality on their operations and anything related to the company. As such, asking questions about the company can be met with skepticism.

Culture and History

Latin American countries share a common culture and history due to their origins. Most of their cultures represent a unique blend of European, indigenous Amerindian, and African influences. Despite many similarities resulting from a shared culture and history, Latin American countries are very diverse and differ from each other in their composition and demographics. Each country has its own cultural identity that varies based on its heritage, customs, and social norms.

The relative location and economic influences of each country play a role in the consumer behavior exhibited by its inhabitants. Countries like Argentina and Chile have strong European influences and look up to Europe, while inhabitants of Mexico and Central America tend to be influenced by the consumer culture in the US. Exhibit 19.2 examines cultural differences across Latin American countries in a business setting.

Language Nuances

Most of the Latin American countries use Spanish as the predominant language, except for Brazil where they speak Portuguese. Beyond this understanding, the variations that exist in

---

[3] Adapted from Strategy Research Corporation, *Household Buying Power Report*, 1996

[4] Adapted from Fastoso and Whitelock, "Why Is So Little Marketing Research on Latin America Published in High Quality Journals and What Can We Do About It?."

the Spanish language across countries must be addressed in order to conduct market research in Latin America.

It is necessary for the translator or the speaker to be aware of the specific nuances that exist within regions. The different dialects, word usage, and idiosyncrasies are aspects to look out for, so that the lack of awareness of the language should not be an impediment to the success of the market research venture. For example, in Argentina, the usage of Spanish is interspersed with Italian. In countries like Guatemala and Paraguay, where there is a larger Amerindian population, most of the inhabitants will speak an indigenous language, in addition to Spanish. The same word can also have different meanings in each country. The word used to describe a retail outlet in Mexico would be understood as an electrical outlet in Venezuela.[5] In addition, different words can be used to describe the same thing. In most countries, a jacket is called *chaqueta*; however, in Argentina, it is called *campera*. Furthermore, methods of addressing people vastly differ between countries, with *usted* being a common form in Colombia, while *tú* is widely used in several countries.

Exhibit 19.2

Culture in Business[6]

Latin America represents a unique dichotomy of homogeneity of culture mixed with significant heterogeneity across countries. In a study of multinational firms operating in Latin America, the differences in employee behavior are analyzed across seven dimensions of culture in Argentina, Brazil, Chile, Colombia, and Mexico.

For example, Argentina and Chile place a higher value on status and display more overt gender bias, whereas in Brazil, Colombia, and Mexico, more value is placed on the achievements of self-made individuals, and gender lines are blurred. Argentines and Chileans also tend to be more traditional and prefer organizations to have a clearly defined hierarchy. In contrast, Brazilians and Colombians do not value power distances across hierarchical lines and prefer more flexible environments for upward mobility. Mexicans tend to oscillate between the two extremes of hierarchy and status. The employees in each country demonstrate varying degrees of response to the cultural dimensions confirming that effective management practices must take into consideration the individual cultural differences within a country.

Clothing Codes of Conduct

The codes of conduct can vary greatly across the countries in Latin America. From how someone should speak to what one should wear, the appropriate behavior in social and business settings is important for the researcher to understand.

---

[5] Cateora and Graham, *International Marketing*, 13th edition.

[6] Adapted from P. Friedrich, L. Mesquita, and A. Hatum, "The Meaning of Difference: Beyond Cultural and Managerial Homogeneity Stereotypes of Latin America," *Management Research: The Journal of the Iberoamerican Academy of Management* 4, no. 1 (2006): 53.

The choice of clothing is important for making a good impression in Latin America. On a spectrum, Argentina would probably rank as the most formal with Brazil as the least formal in terms of the attire to be worn. In order to conduct a B2B focus group in Argentina, for example, it is necessary to maintain a formal setting. It is also important for the moderator to adhere to a formal dress code. When addressing the head of household in Bogotá, Colombia, as well as Brazil, it is important to note the differences. In Brazil, dressing is more casual, while in Bogotá, significant emphasis is placed on the kind of clothes.

Middle Class in Latin America[7]

The middle class represents 30% of the population in Latin America. In large part, due to job creation, education, and social programs, the middle class in Latin America has grown 50% over the past decade. In addition, women have joined the labor force in increasing numbers. The Latin American middle class earns income of $10–$50 per capita per day. Table 19.1 explains the income levels across countries.

TABLE 19.1
POPULATION DISTRIBUTION BY CLASS IN LATIN AMERICA (2009)[8]

	Upper Class (%)	Middle Class (%)	Vulnerable (%)	Poor (%)
Argentina	3	47	34	16
Bolivia	1	17	35	47
Brazil	3	31	40	26
Chile	5	43	40	12
Colombia	3	30	37	30
Costa Rica	4	37	40	19
Dominican Republic	2	21	43	34
Ecuador	2	20	42	36
El Salvador	1	16	41	42
Honduras	1	16	30	53
Mexico	2	26	45	27
Panama	3	29	39	29
Paraguay	2	23	41	34

(Table 19.1 Contd.)

[7] *Economic Mobility and the Rise of the Latin American Middle Class* (Washington, DC: International Bank for Reconstruction and Development/The World Bank, 2013).
[8] Adapted from *Economic Mobility and the Rise of the Latin American Middle Class.*

(Table 19.1 Contd.)

	Upper Class (%)	Middle Class (%)	Vulnerable (%)	Poor (%)
Peru	2	24	39	35
Uruguay	5	56	32	7

Note: Data from SEDLAC (Socio-Economic Database for Latin America and the Caribbean). Class composition in Bolivia is for 2008 and in Mexico is for 2010.
Poor = Individuals with a per capita daily income lower than $4.
Vulnerable = Individuals with a per capita daily income of $4–$10.
Middle class = Individuals with a per capita daily income of $10–$50.
Upper class = Individuals with a per capita daily income exceeding $50.
Poverty lines and incomes are expressed in 2005 US$ PPP per day. PPP = Purchasing Power Parity.

The motivation to advance economically varies in each country. Brazil's middle class experienced the fastest growth at over 40%. Other Latin American countries experiencing substantial growth in the middle class include Colombia, Costa Rica, Chile, and Peru. Mexico's middle class has steadily increased with close to 17% growth from 2000 to 2010. The growing middle class in these countries creates a new consumer base for brands to target. Exhibit 19.3 discusses the changes in Latin America's demographics.

Exhibit 19.3

Changing Demographics in Latin America[9]

Latin America is experiencing a drastic change in its demographics due to decreases in the fertility rate and increases in the working age population. These factors ultimately create a demographic dividend.

For example, Brazil, Chile, and Mexico have fertility rates below the replacement rate of 2.1. The decrease in births is important to note as households with fewer children are able to have more discretionary income and mothers are more likely to pursue employment outside of the home.

The working age population in Latin America is projected to grow by 41 million people by 2020, increasing from 42% to 53% since 2000. As such, the demand for discretionary spending items like computers, cars, and travel will increase. These increases will position Latin America to enter an era of consumption.

Conducting Research: Dos and Don'ts

There are several things that must be considered when conducting research in Latin America. Most interviews are still conducted on a face-to-face basis. Telecommunications in Latin America is steadily improving but there are still areas where there is lack in the infrastructure

---

[9] Adapted from J. Price, "Latin America's Brave New Demographics," *Latin Trade (English)* 21, no. 3 (2013): 12.

and network coverage to effectively reach consumers. However, advances have been made in telecommunications in Latin America in the past decade. Mobile phone penetration has reached upwards of 100% in Latin America due to subscribers in urban areas having multiple lines; however, in rural areas, penetration can fall to 60% or lower. In raw numbers, about 70% of Latin Americans have access to a mobile phone.[10]

Recruiting for focus groups in Latin America can tend to be misleading. When asking respondents if they would be interested, the cultural stigma in saying "no" often stifles them to refuse the offer. The best means is to offer transportation for them such that the respondents would feel more obliged to attend.[11]

It is also necessary to have a good concept regarding the timeline to project completion. It takes a lot of time to conduct personal interviews and also to exercise a tremendous level of flexibility when dealing with Latin American partners. It is vital to note the seasonal differences that exist between the Latin American countries and much of the rest of the world. With some countries in the Southern hemisphere, the vacation time tends to fall in January or February and this would cause problems in trying to conduct research.

Direct Marketing

The direct marketing industry in Latin America is growing rapidly as a means to communicate directly with the consumer via traditional methods such as postal mail and outdoor, and new media such as SMS text, e-mail, and online. The infrastructure in Latin America has a major impact on direct marketing capabilities and varies greatly from country to country. The different levels of direct marketing infrastructure can pose a challenge to the marketer who would have to take into account the resources available in a particular country. For example, Brazil has a very updated and sophisticated direct marketing infrastructure in comparison to other Latin American nations. The once prevalent need to compensate for often lax systems in database management has decreased in Latin America as advances have been made in the telecommunications, Internet, and mail infrastructures in several of the countries. Exhibit 19.4 discusses the postal service infrastructure in Latin America.

Over the years, many advances have been made in direct marketing in Latin America. Several countries now have associations dedicated to managing and promoting direct marketing. In 1999, the Federation of the Associations of Direct and Interactive Marketing in Latin America (ALMADI: *Federación de las Asociaciones de Marketing Directo e Interactivo de América Latina*) was founded. Argentina, Brazil, Chile, Mexico, Peru, Venezuela, and Colombia are represented in the federation, which aims to promote the growth of direct marketing in Latin America.

Direct marketing places emphasis on the customer and encourages customer interaction. Ultimately, it is crucial for the direct marketing effort to be designed to fit the appropriate country specifications for language nuances and cultural appropriateness in order to capture the consumer's attention and garner the desired reaction.

---

[10] Informa Telecoms and Media, http://www.informa.com/Media-centre/Press-releases--news/Latest-News/Latin-America-reaches-100-mobile-penetration-says-Telecoms--Media/

[11] "Research International Revelations," *Marketing News*, no. 6, 1994.

Exhibit 19.4

Postal Service in Latin America[12]

Latin America has an unofficial liberalization of post in which there is a free market and competition in the postal service industry. There is no mail monopoly, which allows for the potential for innovation through the development of new technologies and the improvement of products and services.

The mail in Latin America is mostly privatized with about 60% of mail being carried by private postal operators. Some of these companies have organized themselves into the Latin American Association of Private Mail and Postal Providers (ALACOPP: *Asociación Latinoamericana de Correos y Operadores Postales Privados*) within the countries of Argentina, Brazil, Colombia, Mexico, Chile, and Uruguay. This presents an interesting dynamic when implementing direct marketing efforts through the mail in Latin American countries.

The Use of the Internet

The use of the Internet in Latin America has changed drastically in the past decade. Latin America was once a continent grossly underserved by the Internet. Although there is still room for much improvement in comparison to other nations, Latin American countries have seen advances in Internet use with it becoming more available to consumers. The presence of mobile and social media is transforming Internet usage in Latin America with 37% of Latin Americans having access to the Internet.[13] Table 19.2 shows the Internet penetration in the Latin American countries.

The majority of Internet content is in English. However, foreign language content has increased exponentially in recent years. As shown in Table 19.3, Spanish and Portuguese are represented among the top content languages on the Internet. Yet, Spanish and Portuguese content is still underrepresented, making it an area to be considered for further development.

If a general survey is conducted via the Internet, biases may occur given the composition of the users. A majority of the Internet content is in the English language, and this makes it all the more crucial of an area to be considered for development. The translation services currently available help Web surfers to better understand the content of the website, immaterial of whether it is in Spanish or Portuguese.

The problem in implementing any system in Latin America is in encountering the political framework that has the potential to impose restrictive communication policies. This can significantly limit the accessibility to the Internet for the Latin Americans. Argentina, Chile,

---

[12] Adapted from "Quantum Leaps and Baby Steps: How Postal Platforms are Evolving Worldwide," Global Address Data Association, May 15, 2012, http://www.globaladdress.org/wp-content/uploads/downloads/2012/05/Quantum-leaps-and-baby-steps-Publication.pdf. To learn more, visit http://noticias.am-pm.com.mx/ALACOPP_ComiteConsultivoUPU.html

[13] Tendencias Digitales, http://www.tendenciasdigitales.com/wp-content/uploads/2012/02/Tendencias-Digitales-Ingles-01.jpg

TABLE 19.2
INTERNET PENETRATION IN LATIN AMERICA[14]

Country	Population	Internet Penetration (%)
Bolivia	10,426,154	12
Brazil	200,019,467	38
Chile	17,295,000	58
Colombia	49,665,343	50
Costa Rica	4,694,854	47
Dominican Republic	10,026,000	41
Ecuador	14,204,900	23
El Salvador	7,440,662	14
Guatemala	14,729,000	17
Honduras	8,202,681	13
Mexico	112,890,633	34
Nicaragua	6,050,373	12
Peru	29,957,804	35
Puerto Rico	4,032,707	55
Uruguay	3,565,825	58
Venezuela	29,499,000	37

TABLE 19.3
TOP 10 CONTENT LANGUAGES ON THE INTERNET[15]

	Language	Website Content (%)
1	English	56.2
2	Russian	6.0
3	German	5.9
4	Japanese	4.9
5	Spanish, Castilian	4.5
6	Chinese	3.9
7	French	3.2
8	Portuguese	2.2
9	Polish	1.8
10	Italian	1.7

Note: A website may use more than one content language.

---

[14] Adapted from Tendencias Digitales.

[15] Adapted from W3Techs, http://w3techs.com/technologies/overview/content_language/all (Retrieved in August 2013). Represents percentage of websites using various content languages.

and Brazil have achieved some degree of political stability, which has helped in fostering a positive climate for the growth of telecommunications.[16]

Several companies target the markets in Argentina, Brazil, Chile, and Colombia, which accounts for over 50% of the overall population of approximately 600 million. This is also because these countries have reflected a growing trend in telecommunications development as well as an increase in home computer purchases. The biggest challenge that faces Latin America is in trying to increase the relevance of content channels as well as boosting advertising online.

Mobile Technology[17]

In addition to the increase in Internet usage, the ability to engage consumers through mobile devices and social media is gradually changing the scope of research in Latin America. Latin America is leading the world in the growth of mobile technology with 98% of the Latin American population having access to a mobile cell signal and 84% of households being subscribed to some type of mobile service. Argentina, Chile, Mexico, and Venezuela take the lead in mobile subscriptions in Latin America.

From farmers to pharmacists, mobile connectivity in Latin America is far-reaching and making a major impact. Although the majority of mobile usage is to use the phone as a phone, SMS texting and Internet usage is on the rise. Approximately one-fourth of subscribers in Venezuela and Mexico have mobile Internet. In Chile, mobile phones are being used by farmers to receive market updates via SMS messages from the Chilean government to help increase productivity. Along with improvements in infrastructure, the decreasing cost of handsets has made the benefits of mobile technology a reality for many Latin Americans.

THE MERCOSUR

The benefit of conducting business in Latin America is boosted by the MERCOSUR, which is a common market formed by Argentina, Brazil, Paraguay, Uruguay, and Venezuela. Since its establishment in 1991 and inauguration in 1995, this free trade zone has been successful in increasing international business activity and in the process enabling the markets to be reasonably stabilized. Table 19.4 compares selected geographic data of the MERCOSUR countries.

TABLE 19.4
MERCOSUR—BASIC DATA (2011)[18]

Country	GDP–PPP (billions of US$)	Land Area (millions of sq. km)	Population (millions)
Argentina	755.3	2.7	42.6
Brazil	2,394.0	8.5	201.0

(Table 19.4 Contd.)

[16] C. Ryder, "Internet Opportunity," *Computer World*, September 29, 1997.
[17] World Bank, "Latin America Leads Global Mobile Growth," July 18, 2012.
[18] *CIA World Factbook*, 2013, https://www.cia.gov/library/publications/the-world-factbook/

(Table 19.4 Contd.)

Country	GDP–PPP (billions of US$)	Land Area (millions of sq. km)	Population (millions)
Paraguay	41.6	0.4	6.6
Uruguay	54.7	0.2	3.3
Venezuela	408.5	0.9	28.5
Total	3,654.1	12.7	282.0

LATIN AMERICAN RELATIONS WITH ASIA[19]

The paradox that describes Latin American trade with Asia is that while the current economic crisis has affected the level of relations, it has also prompted several Latin American countries to source and be sourced for investments. Latin America now has five investment-grade countries: Brazil, Peru, Panama, Mexico, and Chile. This rating positions these countries to be able to attract investors and reduce financing costs. Exhibit 19.5 explains the economic influence in Latin American.

Exhibit 19.5

Economic Influence in Latin America[20]

There are two types of economies in Latin America—those that will be impacted by their relations with the US and those that will do much of their business with countries other than the US.

Central American countries and Mexico will continue to gravitate toward the US with their already established economic ties. These countries comprise the first category of Latin American economies that send about half of their exports to the US. Many of these countries are the recipients of US economic assistance. In the case of Mexico, its relationship with the US is the most deeply rooted with the majority of its exports going to the US

The second category of Latin American economies includes the countries of Brazil, Argentina, Chile, and Peru. In addition to the US and other Latin American countries, these countries trade heavily with the EU and Asia. In particular, these countries are among Latin America's top exporters to China.

Toward the end of the 20th century, the Latin American economies grew, especially due to the growth rates in Argentina, Chile, and Mexico. Further, Latin American countries aggressively pursued their trade opportunities and took advantage of their economic growth, as well

---

[19] Joachim Bamrud, "Latin America's Decade," *Latin Trade*, March 30, 2011, http://latintrade.com/2011/03/latin-america%E2%80%99s-decade

[20] Adapted from L. Martinez-Diaz, "Latin America: Coming of Age," *World Policy Journal* 25, no. 3 (Fall 2008): 221–227.

as declining inflation levels. Coupled with the decline in demand for products in the Asian domestic markets, this prompted several companies to consider the Latin American region.

In recent years, Latin America's performance has been boosted by high demand from Asian countries. Asia is now one of Latin America's largest trade partners, second to the EU. For example, China has become the top export market for several Latin American countries. China's demand for natural resources from countries like Brazil, Chile, Peru, and Argentina has helped offset falling demand from traditional markets like the US and Europe. Table 19.5 provides a merchandise trade comparison of exports from Latin American countries to the EU, the US, and China.

The fact that this market poses a growth potential implies that it is worth investing in market research to better understand the consumers' requirements. As trade increases, this prompts a simultaneous requirement to have global marketing research in order to capture the nuances of the individual markets.

ARGENTINA

Argentina is a severe clash between European and Latin American Indian cultures; however, it is one of the most accessible of Latin American countries because its diversity has European overtones, which make it *homely* to American and European visitors.

TABLE 19.5
MERCHANDISE TRADE COMPARISON—EXPORTS FROM LATIN AMERICAN COUNTIES TO THE EU, THE US, AND CHINA[21]

	Total Exports ($ million)	Exports to the EU (%)	Exports to USA (%)	Exports to China (%)
Argentina	83,950	16.9	5.1	7.4
Brazil	256,039	20.7	10.1	17.3
Chile	81,411	17.7	11.2	22.8
Colombia	57,420	15.6	38.5	3.5
Costa Rica	10,408	17.2	38.3	5.1
Dominican Republic	8,612	8.0	54.5	5.4
Mexico	349,569	5.5	78.7	1.7
Peru	46,268	18.2	13.3	15.3
Venezuela	94,811	0.6	0.5	0.5

Country Characteristics[22]

Population: 43,024,374 (July 2014 est.)
Land Area: 2,736,690 sq. km

---

[21] Adapted from "World Trade Organization Trade Profiles," April 2013.
[22] CIA World Factbook 2013

Language: Spanish (official), Italian, English, German, French, Indigenous (Mapudungun, Quechua)
Literacy Rate: 98.1%
Religion: Nominally Roman Catholic (92%—less than 20% practicing), Protestant (2%), Jewish (2%), other (4%)
GDP—Purchasing Power Parity: $771 billion (2013 est.)
GDP per Capita—Purchasing Power Parity: $18,600 (2013 est.)
GDP—Real Growth Rate: 3.5% (2013 est.)
Inflation Rate—Consumer Price Index: 20.8% (2013 est.)

Cultural Characteristics

The Argentines emphasize the individual's role in society and view the individual who is independent as capable. This affects the business culture, since the Argentines perceive one who takes orders from another as weak and inadequate. Exhibiting *guachadas*, or acts of generosity which manifest in helping someone in need, is considered an exercise of free will. The difference between the residents of Buenos Aires and the rest of the country is also an aspect of culture that should be noted.

When dealing with an Argentine, it is important to note their frankness in voicing out their opinions, though they take extreme care in being diplomatic. Their warm nature and friendliness is seen in situations when they try to establish a personal relationship prior to business dealing.

It is also important to note the concept of space and time in dealing in this Latin American country. Most Argentines maintain little physical distance between speakers and tend to broach personal issues pertaining to the family in their conversation. Time is considered to be an asset to be enjoyed rather than utilized, and most Argentines take this to be useful to establish relationships and to clarify situations better.

The role of the family in Argentine life is to be emphasized. Family is deemed central to the life of the average citizen, and filial piety and bonds to elders are cherished; however, one of the main perils with working in Argentina would be in dealing with nepotism. Most positions are filled with family members first, and while there are specific rules which limit such incidents, this occurrence is significantly less than in other Latin American countries.

Similar to other Latin American countries, it is not considered appropriate to give respondents cash in reciprocation to their participation in surveys or focus groups. Most often, a small gift (i.e., anything in kind) is far more appreciated, because money slights their intention to voice their opinions, making it more of a transaction than an informal exchange of their sentiments.

Business Characteristics

Argentine business people tend to differ from the stereotypical model of Latin Americans in the way they conduct business. They are seen as resourceful, highly educated, and motivated to form business networks and to boost the exchange between Argentina and the rest of the world.

Business style in Argentina is colored by the mixed heritage that it has. Generally, they are intensely competitive, and this has been one of the redeeming factors that have increased the internationalization of its markets. Most often, the atmosphere at work is friendly and informal, though the attire is formal, as is the attitude to work. There is a lot of emphasis given to specific aspects of any contract, and most Argentines would be interested in getting their queries sorted out prior to furthering the business topic. It is ideal that the foreign party be aware of the Argentine culture as well as business environment before engaging in a conversation. The usual tactic is to analyze the person in terms of his attitudes and to learn more about their culture before assessing their knowledge of Argentina.

It is also crucial to note that the practice of paying *propinas* (tips) and *coimas* (bribes) is part of the Argentine business culture. It is a rather delicate situation for a foreigner but a must-know if the ultimate goal is to function effectively in the country. They believe that while this expedites the process, periodic anti-corruption campaigns also coexist, which make the business culture even more complex to function in. The business etiquette of Argentina is illustrated in Exhibit 19.6.

Exhibit 19.6

Business Etiquette in Argentina[23]

When meeting someone for the first time, handshakes are the most common form of greeting, with emphasis placed on eye contact. Appropriate dress attire goes a long way in establishing credibility, with men wearing a suit and tie, and women wearing a blouse and suit with a skirt. It is important to greet someone with the appropriate title such as Senor or Senora.

One must be aware of whom they are doing business with, and proper respect must be given to those of superior power. Work hours in Argentina can be quite excessive, with the workday often stretching past 10 p.m.

It is important to be punctual for meetings, but be willing to stay for a long time as the pace tends to be slow in comparison to other countries. Appropriate body language must be displayed while in a meeting, as the importance of a personal relationship is necessary prior to business relations being established.

It is extremely important to recognize the power or status of the person with whom the company is dealing. The higher the person is in the organizational structure, the more likely he or she is to delay in keeping appointments. Regardless of the hierarchy, it is extremely important to establish closure for the business deal since Argentines tend to discuss the *appropriate* aspects, which may be for your benefit at the time of the dealing.

Market Research in Argentina[24]

Argentina is one of the most developed countries in Latin America. As such, there are more reliable avenues to conduct market research.

Telephone

Since opening its telecommunications market to competition in 1998, Argentina has experienced substantial growth. At about 10 million lines, there are an estimated 39 lines per 100 people in Buenos Aires and other major metropolitan areas; however, penetration in rural areas

---

[23] Adapted from Fundacion Invertir Argentina, *Argentina Business: The Portable Encyclopedia for Doing Business with Argentina* (World Trade Press, 1995); and "Argentine Business Etiquette & Culture," http://www.internationalbusinesscenter.org/ (Retrieved on May 6, 2014).

[24] "Telecoms and Technology Industry Report: Argentina," *Telecoms Industry Report: Argentina* 4, no. 2 (2012): 1–15.

is still low at only 7 lines per 100 people. Ranked first in Latin America in terms of fixed-line and mobile subscription, Argentina has seen modest growth in fixed-line penetration in contrast to many of the other Latin American countries. Like other Latin America countries, Argentina's telecommunications growth is coming from advances in mobile availability and access.

Mobile

There has been major expansion in mobile phone penetration in Argentina in recent years. In addition to the private sector, the government is positioned to promote the continued expansion of mobile technology to more rural areas. As of 2012, there are 142 mobile subscriptions per 100 people in Argentina. Three companies dominate the market—Claro, Telecom Personal, and Movistar—to provide mobile service to approximately 59 million Argentines. In the years to come, mobile data and broadband services will drive the growth in mobile technology.

Internet

Internet access in Argentina has increased in recent years due to increased government programs and initiatives to improve access. The Argentine government supplies free broadband and digital TV access to rural, underdeveloped areas through a program called "Conectada." There is also strong competition in the Internet market in Argentina, which keeps subscription fees low and service quality high. In addition, inexpensive PCs and high household incomes made it possible for Internet penetration to reach 56% in 2012. Argentina now outperforms the region in Internet access including broadband, which represents 90% of subscriptions.

Mail

There are over 5,000 post offices available nationwide in Argentina, making it one of the most developed in Latin America. About 800 million package units are delivered annually in Argentina via the national service, Correo Argentino, and the other private mail carriers. Despite the availability and reliability of Argentine post, there is still a lack of popularity in mail-order marketing in Argentina, and prices for mail distribution are high.[25]

BOLIVIA

Bordered by Argentina, Brazil, Chile, Paraguay, and Peru, Bolivia ranks near the bottom among Latin American countries in terms of socioeconomic development.

Country Characteristics[26]

Population: 10,631,486 (July 2014 est.)
Land Area: 1,083,301 sq. km
Language: Spanish (official), Quecha (official), Aymara (official)

---

[25] US and Foreign Commercial Service and US Department of State, "Doing Business in Argentina: 2013 Country Commercial Guide for U.S. Companies," http://export.gov/argentina/doingbusinessin argentina/argentinacountrycommercialguide/index.asp. All rights reserved outside of the US. International Copyright.

[26] *CIA World Factbook 2013*.

Literacy Rate: 86.7%
Religion: Roman Catholic (95%), Protestant–Evangelical Methodist (5%)
GDP—Purchasing Power Parity: $58.34 billion (2013 est.)
GDP per Capita—Purchasing Power Parity: $5,500 (2013 est.)
GDP—Real Growth Rate: 6.5% (2013 est.)
Inflation Rate—Consumer Price Index: 5.9% (2012 est.)

Cultural Characteristics

Bolivian culture is heavily influenced by the indigenous cultures as well as popular Latin American culture. The principle ethnic groups in Bolivia are Quechua and Aymara Indians, who make up an estimated 55% of the total population, Mestizo or mixed white and Amerindian (30%), and white (15%). Most of the population is concentrated in the 10% of Bolivia located on the cold and bleak Altiplano, which has been the center of Indian life since pre-Inca days. About half of the population lives in rural areas, mostly by subsistence farming. As one of the poorest Latin American countries, the majority of Bolivia's population lives in poverty. Exhibit 19.7 explains the education expenditures of Bolivian families and its impact on poverty.

Exhibit 19.7

Bolivian Household Expenditures on Education[27]

Education is highly valued in Bolivia. In recent years, public spending on education has represented a significant percentage of the country's GDP. Approximately 80% of education cost is financed by the State, with the remaining 20% being contributed by households.

Bolivian families spend the majority of their household income on food (53%), followed by housing and basic services (18%), and then education (6.5%). Household spending on education is more than that of clothing and healthcare combined. Although educational expenses are contrasted across socioeconomic lines with upper-class households spending more on education than poor households, and urban households spending twice as much as rural households, major efforts are being made to improve primary and secondary education across the country in order to close the educational divide.

The impact of education and its ability to create employment opportunities and raise the population from poverty to middle class is paramount in a developing nation such as Bolivia.

Business Characteristics[28]

The Bolivian government is eager to attract foreign investment. Most members of Bolivia's private sector are experienced businesspersons with ample direct exposure to US and West European customs and procedures. The local representative is a vital component in the successful operation of foreign-based firms.

---

[27] Adapted from Economic and Social Policy Analysis Unit (UDAPE) and the United Nations Children's Fund (UNICEF), "Bolivia—Household Spending on Education," 2006, http://www.unicef.org/bolivia/resumen_gasto_hogares_educacion_ENG.pdf

[28] US Department of Commerce, "Marketing in Bolivia—Overseas Business Reports," January 1989.

With regard to product promotion and distribution, Bolivia's small market requires that most agents represent more than one line of merchandise. The amount of effort given to promoting a particular product line is determined in part by the interest and support expressed by the supplier, as well as the agent's ability and interest.

After a firm business relationship has been established, local distributors and agents generally expect to be extended an offer to visit the foreign company's plant facilities and head offices in order to become more familiar with the company's personnel and operating techniques.

Spanish is considered to be the official language of Bolivia, as well as the language of commerce. English is widely spoken among business and public officials, but most prefer to speak Spanish.

Market Research in Bolivia

Bolivia is a country still very much in the development stage, which can present several challenges when conducting market research.

Telephone

Although fixed telephone coverage has steadily improved, most telephones are concentrated in urban areas such as La Paz and Santa Cruz. As of 2011, Bolivia had only 879,000 fixed telephone lines for a population of approximately 10 million.[29] Given this condition, companies attempting to conduct research would have to take into consideration the reach of the targeted segment. Also, the cost consideration of convenience sampling would have to be taken into account, despite the problems in terms of accuracy and reliability of the segment. As such, companies should investigate the use of alternative methods to reach the consumer.

Mobile

In contrast to fixed telephone lines, mobile phone density in Bolivia reached about 80 per 100 persons in 2011.[30] Like other countries in Latin America, the trend is toward mobile subscriptions with the presence of mobile phones being ten times more than fixed lines. However, after Cuba, Haiti, and Nicaragua, Bolivia has the lowest telecom indicators in the region. Even in larger cities, there may be issues with slow connectivity and network congestion. Due to the country's high poverty levels and lack of mobile bandwidth, growth is far below that of other Latin American counties.[31]

Internet

Bolivia's broadband prices are the most expensive in Latin America, making access difficult for the majority of its population. As of 2012, there are 1.4 million Internet connections coving 30% of the population. However, only 2 out of 100 inhabitants have broadband access. Most of the connectivity (82.5%) is concentrated in La Paz, Santa Cruz, and Cochabamba.[32]

---

[29] CIA World Factbook 2013

[30] Ibid.

[31] "Research and Markets: Bolivia—Telecoms, Mobile and Broadband," *Business Wire* (English).

[32] *Informe de Milenio sobre la Economía, Gestión 2012, No. 34, Fundación Milenio* (Germany: Konrad-Audenaur-Stiftung, 2012).

Mail

Postal service in Bolivia is still under development. Advancements have been made in recent years; however, there is still room for improvement in consistent and timely mail delivery to homes and businesses.

BRAZIL

Brazil is the largest and most industrialized nation of the Latin American countries with a vast size and diversity, which often tempts marketers.

Country Characteristics[33]

Population: 202,656,788 (July 2014 est.)
Land Area: 8,459,417 sq. km
Language: Portuguese (official), Spanish, English, and French
Literacy Rate: 88.6%
Religion: Nominally Roman Catholic (73.6%), Protestant (15.4%), Spiritualist (1.3%), Bantu/Voodoo (0.3%)
GDP—Purchasing Power Parity: $2.422 trillion (2013 est.)
GDP per Capita—Purchasing Power Parity: $12,100 (2013 est.)
GDP—Real Growth Rate: 2.5% (2012 est.)
Inflation Rate—Consumer Price Index: 6.2% (2013 est.)

Cultural Characteristics

The Brazilian culture is one of the world's most varied and diverse cultures. It is derived from influences from Portuguese, African, indigenous, and other European cultures. The family structure and values are very important in Brazil, with large, extended families being the norm. Brazilians tend to be affectionate, tactile people with a smaller sense of personal space. There is a level of informality in how Brazilians greet and address each other. Shaking hands, hugs, and kisses on the cheek are common greetings though women tend to touch more and greet with kisses. Brazilians usually address teachers, doctors, priests, and other professionals using their title followed by their first name—Presidente Dilma. Body language and terms of address also vary with an individual's social standing.[34]

Brazilian culture has class distinctions based on one's socioeconomic status and ethnic background. The tremendous problems with inflation in the late 1990s reduced the purchasing power by about 50% among the working and lower-middle class, and caused a major polarization of income.[35] Brazil's poverty and income inequality levels remain high despite improvements in the 2000s, and continue to disproportionately affect populations in different regions and classes.

---

[33] *CIA World Factbook 2013.*
[34] http://www.brazil.org.za/brazil-culture.html
[35] USDOC International Trade Administration, Brazil—Country Marketing Plan, Market Research Report, 1994.

Business Characteristics

Most of the businesses in Brazil are operated via an agent or distributor. This is partly explained by the market peculiarities with which they are familiar, such as inflationary tendencies. Brazil's business community is highly educated, and a significant portion of the population is well versed in English as well as another foreign business language.

The expectation when conducting business in Brazil is to deal with the individual first, not the company. A relationship will need to be established, as Brazilians prefer to take their time to get to know one another before committing to a contract. Punctuality to events and dinners is expected. In addition, formal dress is the norm within the business setting. When in doubt, it is considered better to over-dress than to appear too casual in appearance.[36]

Market Research in Brazil

In a snapshot of the available telecommunication services in Brazil, this country has the largest telecommunications sector in all of Latin America. As such, Brazil is a prime market for research.

Telephone[37]

The Brazilian government has a monopoly in the provision of telephone, telegraph, data transmission, and other public services. Brazil has seen major improvements in its telecommunications system. Brazil at present has an installed base of 43 million fixed telephones. With a rate of 20 fixed telephones for every 100 inhabitants, Brazil is ranked sixth in the world. Brazil's well-developed and reliable telephone system also makes the use of faxing a viable means to send questionnaires to businesses.

Mobile[38]

In terms of mobile access, about 120 mobile phones exist for every 100 inhabitants. There are over 244 million mobile devices in use in Brazil with service provided by seven providers. The high usage of mobile phones is driven by the relatively easy access for persons with lower income. As such, reaching consumers via mobile is becoming an increasingly more feasible option.

Internet[39]

Brazil ranks fourth in the world with 76 million Internet users as of 2009.[40] In addition, Brazil has a well-developed Internet traffic exchange infrastructure, which allows for improved performance for customers and applications. There are over 2,500 broadband providers in Brazil; however, 95% of the market is held by five providers: Oi, NET Servicos (Embratel), Telefónica Brazil, Universo Online (UOL), and GVT. Although access to the Internet via PCs and laptops

---

[36] http://www.brazil.org.za/brazil-culture.html

[37] *CIA World Factbook 2013.*

[38] Ibid.

[39] Mike Jensen, *Broadband in Brazil: A Multipronged Public Sector Approach to Digital Inclusion* (Washington, DC: infoDev/World Bank, 2011), http://www.broadband-toolkit.org

[40] Ibid.

is present in many Brazilian households, mobile devices are the primary means for accessing the Internet. Access to the Internet via mobile is very prevalent, with 83% of smartphone users using their phones to go online.

Mail

Brazil's postal service is one of the best in Latin America. As the growth of mail order catalogs (with companies like Sears Roebuck and JCPenney) indicated, the use of mail as a good survey tool has improved. The reliability of the mail service in terms of reach, as well as the number of undelivered or lost mail, is crucial to the effectiveness of this method of data collection. Brazil's advancements in its postal service have allowed its direct marketing industry to become the most advanced in Latin America. Exhibit 19.8 discusses direct marketing in Brazil.

Exhibit 19.8

Direct Marketing in Brazil[41]

Brazil's direct marketing industry is growing rapidly. For the past decade, Brazil's direct marketing industry has experienced growth of about 13% annually with revenues of $15 billion in 2011. Brazilian consumers receive about 9.3 pieces of direct mail each month with 74% of those consumers having a preference for receiving direct mail.

Due to its reliable postal service, large consumer base, and growing economy, Brazil touts a validated database of 20 million unique opt-in users segmented by their demographics and psychographics via ABEMD. The Brazilian Association of Direct Marketing (ABEMD—*Associação Brasileira de Marketing Direto*) is an organization dedicated to developing and promoting direct marketing in the country by bringing together agencies that render the services and companies that use direct marketing strategies. As such, direct marketing in Brazil is a viable option for companies interested in entering the market. More information about ABEMD can be found at http://www.abemd.com.br/english.php.

VENEZUELA

Bordering the Caribbean Sea between Colombia and Guyana in the northern part of South America, Venezuela (which means *Little Venice*—a reflection of early European connections) is a land of abundant resources, both natural and human.

---

[41] Adapted from US and Foreign Commercial Service and US Department of State, "Doing Business in Brazil: 2013 Country Commercial Guide for US Companies," http://export.gov/brazil/build/groups/public/@eg_br/documents/webcontent/eg_br_034878.pdf

Country Characteristics[42]

Population: 28,459,085 (July 2013 est.)
Land Area: 882,050 sq. km
Language: Spanish (official), native dialects
Literacy Rate: 93%
Religion: Nominally Roman Catholic (96%), Protestant (2%)
GDP—Purchasing Power Parity: $408.5 billion (2012 est.)
GDP per Capita—Purchasing Power Parity: $13,800 (2012 est.)
GDP—Real Growth Rate: 5.5% (2012 est.)
Inflation Rate—Consumer Price Index: 21.1% (2012 est.)

Cultural Characteristics[43]

Venezuela is a country comprised of diverse people often characterized by their outgoing and friendly nature. This can be seen in how they greet each other and their body language. Venezuelans are known to stand in close proximity and to use hand gestures, even touching, when in conversation. Greeting with two kisses to the check is common for both men and women, although men only kiss women. Men typically greet each other with a firm hand-shake and in some cases a hug depending on the status of the p erson.

Venezuela is a patriarchal society that displays machismo, the notion of masculine superiority. As a result, there are distinct differences between the social expectations and the treatment of men and women in society. The belief in traditional gender roles is still prevalent; however, the ideal of machismo is being confronted as more women continue to join the workforce and North American culture penetrates.

Venezuela has a strongly defined socioeconomic class structure that is often divided along gender and ethnicity. The large middle class that developed in the 20th century was significantly affected by the social crisis of the 1990s. Although poverty in Venezuela has declined, dropping from nearly 50% in 1999 to about 27% in 2011, it remains high. Caracas, the capital of Venezuela, is a fairly large metropolitan city, yet only a small portion of the population has high purchasing power. In addition, a large proportion of the Venezuelan population is young, which has a significant impact on the social and economic structure of the country. When taking a cross-section of the Venezuelan population, 30% are less than 14 years old and just 6% are aged 65 or older.

Business Characteristics[44]

The Venezuelan business style is casual, with most of the address being informal. The manner in which they address each other in business is *tú*, which loosely translated as *you*. Their greeting and saying goodbye to an acquaintance with a kiss is another cultural aspect to consider; however, in the first-time business meeting, in order to gauge the other side's responses, most Venezuelans would assume a more formal stance. The offer of coffee is considered normal practice and not an indication of the atmosphere becoming more lax. The first meeting may end in expression of interest, which may be more for the sake of politeness. The Venezuelans

---

[42] *CIA World Factbook 2013.*
[43] http://www.everyculture.com/To-Z/Venezuela.html#ixzz2aenm068z
[44] International Trade Administration, "Market Research Reports—USDOC," 1992.

have a strong sense of independence and do not feel compelled to abide by the rules at all times. Overall, their laid-back attitude translates into the business environment.

Venezuelans have a great difficulty in saying "no." It would be to the advantage of the corporation if the conditions were not demanded or imposed. As the Venezuelans are coerced into a certain position, they would not want to compromise. It is important that the American businessman be patient and probe to gain information on what the Venezuelan wants and how best to adapt to those needs.

It is interesting to note that retail outlets and other businesses are operated at the employees' convenience, rather than that of the shoppers. This reflects the attitude that the Venezuelans take toward service provision to their customers. The concept of refunds is usually unheard of and exchanging of garments as well as products with which the customer is unsatisfied is virtually impossible. Time consciousness is another area that Venezuelans differ vastly from their American counterparts. Arriving at an appointment late does not carry with it the stigma that exists in the US.

Patriotism toward their country is what most Venezuelans feel; however, most Venezuelans feel that the foreigners are not in the country to boost the growth of the nation or appeal to US–Venezuelan friendship.

Drawing up contracts in Venezuela is never a reciprocal situation. Most of them are reluctant to commit things to writing, yet would appreciate it greatly if the information that they receive is specified.

Market Research in Venezuela

Ranking fourth behind Brazil, Mexico, and Argentina, Venezuela has one of Latin America's largest telecommunications and IT markets.

Telephone[45]

The telephone system in Venezuela has modernized and expanded its bandwidth. In the past years, making telephone calls required several attempts, which made research time-consuming and difficult to compile over a period of time. In addition, the lack of infrastructure meant that the telephone was not a dependable mode to conduct survey research. However, today Venezuela has seen major improvements in its telephone service, particularly in rural areas. Combined fixed and mobile telephone penetration is at 130 phones per 100 persons in the country.

With the improvements in the telecommunications infrastructure, the use of facsimile (fax) has also increased as a reliable option. Faxing is one of the more common tools used by businesses in order to get an expedient as well as detailed response to their questionnaires. However, as is the case in most Latin American countries, personal interviews are still prevalent. Exhibit 19.9 discusses the process of conducting personal interviews in Venezuela.

Mobile[46]

Venezuela was an early adopter of mobile technology in Latin America. There are three main mobile service providers, Movilnet, Movistar, and Digitel, which sustain the high penetration

---

[45] *CIA World Factbook 2013.*

[46] Industry Report, "Telecoms and Technology: Venezuela," 2012, Telecoms Industry Report: Venezuela, issue 1, pp. 1–12.

rates in the country. As of 2012, there were 29 million mobile phones in use in Venezuela at a penetration rate of 100% as a result of subscribers having multiple numbers. Due to political instability, mobile growth has slowed, with some consumers having to cancel their contracts. However, demand will continue as more subscribers add data capabilities to their plans.

Internet[47]

Internet penetration in Venezuela is increasing rapidly. Penetration is estimated at 44% with almost 13 million users in 2012, up from 7 million in 2008. PC ownership is low in Venezuela; however, Internet use is driven by access to mobile devices, cybercafés, and publically funded *infocentros*. Moving forward, broadband and mobile data subscriptions will drive the growth in the Venezuelan telecommunications market. Currently, broadband penetration is very low, at about 1%. Mobile Internet accounts for 24% of all mobile subscriptions in Venezuela.[48]

Mail

The biggest problem in the reliability of the mail service is delivering the questionnaires to the specific sample homes. Most of the questionnaires are lost, with many never reaching the destination, and this may significantly affect the data collection. There are several private companies that address this problem by having the questionnaires delivered to major collection points.

Exhibit 19.9

Personal Interviews in Venezuela

When conducting personal interviews in Venezuela, the problem was that there is no private time at home. In a society where the involvement of the family extends to every realm, obtaining an individual response to a questionnaire or a product satisfaction query is virtually impossible.

As for business interviews, the working hours in most offices are from 9 a.m. to 1 p.m. and from 3 p.m. to 7 p.m. during the weekdays and some Saturdays. It is generally easier to obtain respondents amongst the business folk, mainly due to the fact that the work ethic is flexible. As for interviews in malls or on streets, this is not commonly practiced, primarily due to the irregular setup.

SUMMARY

This chapter discusses Latin America from a marketing research perspective. It provides data about trade, culture, history, and the languages of Latin American countries in general. Special attention is paid to Argentina, Bolivia, Brazil, and Venezuela. The cultural norms, business habits, infrastructure, and data sources for these countries are discussed in detail.

---

[47] Industry Report, "Telecoms and Technology: Venezuela," 2012, pp. 1–12.
[48] "Latin America Leads Global Mobile Growth," World Bank, July 18, 2012.

20

CHAPTER _____

Middle East and Africa

The Middle East and Africa are plagued with problems regarding inconsistent infrastructure and poor transportation. The biggest benefit for the countries is that their oil-rich sources boost their economies. Countries such as Saudi Arabia, Israel, and Lebanon have had immense improvements made to enhance their telecommunication systems and to modernize the current framework. The market research industry is relatively new to the Arab world, and in some countries, the concept had not taken off to its maximum level until the 1990s.[1]

CONDUCTING MARKET RESEARCH IN THE MIDDLE EAST AND NORTH AFRICA

The contrast between the levels of importance given to the role of market research by local companies as opposed to foreign companies is extreme. Most local companies assume that they would have full awareness of the home market—the current trends in lifestyles and incomes. As such, they do not believe in investing in intensive field research.

Primary Research

Conducting primary research has been mainly through observation and sample surveys. These can be seen as effective ways to gather information, especially regarding the psychographic profile of the average Arab. The method of observational research is through installing cameras and setting up consumer panels that will help gain some insight into consumer behavior; however, this has to be sanctioned first by the authorities and, of course, elicit a positive response from the consumers. Most often, they consider this to be an invasion of privacy and that the information regarding preference should be derived more from sales levels.

When having focus groups, the biggest disadvantage is that people are apprehensive of answering personal questions. It is necessary to ensure that the context or frame references are specified within the Middle Eastern countries, in order to avoid cultural misunderstanding. Door-to-door interviews tend to be a problem since people are not receptive to the idea and tend to become suspicious of the intent behind the information sought. Also, interviewing women is considered to be difficult, and this skews the results since the actual decision

---

[1] Some sections in this chapter were developed with the information provided by G. Subramaniam of Dubai, UAE.

maker for consumer goods does not reflect upon the purchasing process. This problem has been circumvented to a degree by employing women to ask the questions. Women respond well to female interviewers, and the recommendations and ideas have been positive. Also, it is necessary to note that many Arabs are resistant to answering any queries over the phone and the response rate to mail surveys can be low.

Secondary Research

The problem in conducting or gathering secondary research in the Middle East is that there is immense inaccuracy and most of the information is dated. It is also difficult to inculcate the culture of conducting market research. In addition, infiltrating the barriers of religion and social constructs to win respondents' trust (especially when it comes to Arab women) can be a major obstacle. This is also compounded by the government hesitating to release consumer information to the marketers (local as well as multinationals).

Beyond the government, there are other secondary sources that can be used to gather information about the markets in the Middle East. A description of the sources of secondary market information is provided in this section.

Government Publications

The main secondary source in this region for a researcher is the publications from the local governments. Governments publish economic and demographic data as well as industrial and trade data including exports, imports, and re-exports statistics annually. Though these publications prove to be reliable, some reports could contain information that is lagged by one to two years. In addition, the government publications from many countries in the region do not follow unified codes in presenting the trade statistics. Even within the UAE, the foreign trade statistics published by Dubai, Abu Dhabi, and Sharjah emirates followed different SITC and HS codes prior to being updated. Further, these statistics are available in hardcopy only. Electronic databases are not common in this region. Some of the publications from the local government are statistical yearbook, foreign trade statistics, chambers of commerce.

Commercial Databases

Although the presence of commercial databases in this region is limited, research companies such as Nielsen, Dun and Bradstreet, and Business Monitor International routinely study the Middle East markets and compile databases that can be used by companies. These reports are designed to help senior executives, analysts, and researchers assess and better manage operating risks, and exploit business opportunities.

Nongovernment Agencies

A number of associations and special interest groups operating in the Middle East region offer valuable information. A partial list of the agencies/associations available in the region is given below.

1. Arab Air Carriers' Organization (AACO)
2. Arab Authority for Agricultural Investment and Development (AAAID)
3. Arab Bureau of Education for the Gulf States
4. Arab Federation of Petroleum, Mining, and Chemicals Workers
5. Arab Federation of Textile Workers

6. Arab Federation of Transport Workers
7. Arab Fund for Economic and Social Development (AFESD)
8. Arab Gulf Program of the United Nations Development Organizations (AGFUND)
9. Arab Iron and Steel Union (AISU)
10. Arab League
11. Arab Monetary Fund
12. Arab Organization for Human Rights (AOHR)
13. Arab Organization of Mineral Resources
14. Arab Society of Certified Accountants
15. Arab Sports Confederation
16. Arab Towns Organization
17. Arab Union of Railways
18. Association of Arab Historians
19. Association of Arab Universities
20. Islamic Economics Institute
21. Center for Social Science Research and Documentation for the Arab Region
22. Gulf Cooperation Council (GCC)
23. Council of Arab Economic Unity
24. Federation of Arab Engineers
25. Federation of Arab Scientific Research Councils
26. General Union of Chambers of Commerce, Industry, and Agriculture for Arab Countries
27. Gulf Organization for Industrial Consulting (GOIC)
28. International Association of Islamic Banks
29. International Confederation of Arab Trade Unions (ACATU)
30. International Planned Parenthood Federation
31. Islamic Development Bank
32. Muslim World League
33. Organization of Arab Oil Exporting Countries (OAPEC)
34. Organization of the Islamic Cooperation (OIC)
35. Organization of the Petroleum Exporting Countries (OPEC)
36. OPEC Fund for International Development
37. Parliamentary Association for Euro-Arab Cooperation
38. Arab Maghreb Union (AMU)
39. Union of Arab Jurists
40. Union of Arab Stock Exchanges

Overseas Sources

Information on the Middle East markets can also be obtained from a number of sources published from outside the region, such as: (a) export.gov, the US government's trade portal that provides information to assist American businesses in planning their international sales strategies, (b) US reports on GCC: trade policies, import policies, and so on, (c) the CIA World Fact Book, (d) the European Community, (e) the United Nations Trade Database, and (f) the global financial organizations such as the International Monetary Fund and the World Bank.

Universities and Research Institutions

Other potential sources of secondary market data for Middle East include universities and research agencies operating within the region as well as outside. A partial list of such universities and agencies is provided in Table 20.1.

TABLE 20.1

UNIVERSITIES AND RESEARCH INSTITUTIONS

Organization	Description
Interuniversity Consortium of Arab and Middle Eastern Studies (ICAMES)	ICAMES is a collaborative project of McGill University, the Université de Montréal, and Concordia University, along with associated researchers from other institutions that promotes and facilitates research on the contemporary Middle East (http://www.mcgill.ca/icames/)
Institute for National Security Studies (INSS)	INSS is an independent academic institute that studies issues relating to Israel's national security and Middle East affairs (http://www.inss.org.il/)
Amman University	http://www.ammanu.edu.jo/
The University of Jordan	http://www.ju.edu.jo/
Birzeit University	Maintains a regularly updated chronicle of events in Palestine and hosts a Palestine Archive (http://birzeit.edu/)
United Arab Emirates University College of Food and Agriculture	Center for research and knowledge development covering all aspects of food, agriculture and natural resources of the UAE (http://ffa.uaeu.ac.ae/cfa_research/ffa_research_grad.shtml)
The Middle East Institute at Columbia University	Directories for Middle East and access to the Muslim organizations and organizations for Middle East and Islamic studies (http://library.columbia.edu/locations/global/mideast.html)
Center for Contemporary Arab Studies at Georgetown University	Focuses on IT and electronic communications in the Middle East (http://ccas.georgetown.edu/)
Tel Aviv University	Nearly 130 pioneering research centers and institutes at Tel Aviv University (http://english.tau.ac.il/research_institutes)

Newspapers and Trade Magazines

A number of English and Arabic newspapers and magazines provide information on the Middle East market. A partial list of newspapers available on the Internet is provided in Table 20.2.

TABLE 20.2

NEWSPAPERS AND TRADE MAGAZINES

Publication	Description
Al Arabiya	One of the top Middle East broadcaster and news site based in Dubai (http://english.alarabiya.net/)
Al-Hayat	Beirut-based pan-Arabian newspaper providing in-depth reporting on the Middle East and the Arab world (http://english.daralhayat.com/)
Al-Jadid	US-based cultural magazine featuring original articles along with many translations of essays and interviews by Arab writers, journalists, scholars, and poets (http://www.aljadid.com/)
Arabian Business	Provides Middle East business news, gulf financials, and industry events and information (http://www.arabianbusiness.com/)

(Table 20.2 Contd.)

(Table 20.2 Contd.)

Publication	Description
Middle East Economic Digest (MEED)	Weekly magazine providing business news, analysis, and comment on the North African and Middle East regions. Free registration is required (http://www.meed.com/)
Middle East Monitor	Independent media research institution based in London, aiming to foster accurate coverage of Middle Eastern issues in the Western media (http://www.middleeastmonitor.com/)
Middle East Research and Information Project (MERIP)	Washington-based publisher of the Middle East Report Magazine providing in-depth analysis of events and developments in the region (http://www.merip.org/)
Mosaic News	Daily compilation of television news reports from the Middle East including Egypt, Lebanon, Israel, Syria, the Palestinian Authority, Iraq, and Iran (http://www.linktv.org/mosaic)
Trade Arabia	Portal for business news and information covering the Middle East and Arabian Gulf countries (http://www.tradearabia.com/)
Your Middle East	Independent digital newspaper that provides news, analysis, and in-depth reporting on a range of issues relating to the Middle East (http://www.yourmiddleeast.com/)

Miscellaneous Sources

A partial list of additional secondary data sources that can be used for the Middle East is provided in Table 20.3.

TABLE 20.3
MISCELLANEOUS SOURCES

Source	Description
LookLex	Norway-based media house presenting North Africa and the Middle East to a mainly western audience through encyclopedias, traveler guides, and basic language courses in Arabic (http://looklex.com/e.o/index.htm)
Middle East Review of International Affairs (MERIA)	Published by Israel-based Global Research in International Affairs (GLORIA) Center and includes several analytical publications and research guides (http://www.gloria-center.org/about-meria/)
Middle East Online	Features news articles about the Middle East from various media outlets (http://www.middle-east-online.com/english/)
The Jordanian General Intelligence Department	http://www.gid.gov.jo/en/home.html
The Israel Defense Forces	The Israel Defense Forces blog providing news from the field, ground-breaking technology, and stories from the men and women fighting to defend Israel (http://www.idfblog.com/)
Palestine Central Bureau of Statistics	The Palestinian National Authority collects and publishes demographic, economic, and census data (http://www.pcbs.gov.ps/default.aspx)

Culture and Religion

The countries in the Middle East share several cultural similarities due to their historical ties. When taking into consideration the expansion of Arab culture, the countries of the Middle East are often joined by the countries of North Africa to form the MENA (Middle East and North Africa). MENA represents a vast region extending from Morocco to Iran including the Levant and the Arabian Peninsula. Although the countries can vary drastically across bounders, they are linked together by two prominent cultural components—the Arabic language and the Islamic religion. These two components dictate much of the behavior and attitudes of people in the Middle East. Exhibit 20.1 explains some of the cultural traits typical of Middle Eastern countries.

Exhibit 20.1

Cultural *Dos* and *Don'ts* in the Middle East[2]

- Handshakes are common greetings, which can last for longer periods of time. Traditional Islamic greeting is "As-salaam Alaikum" which means "Peace be with you."
- Very common to address people by their first names.
- Excessive interaction between males and females is not approved. Men must not shake hands with a woman unless she reaches her hand out first.
- It is best not to admire the possessions of one's host. They feel obligated to give the items to you.
- Meetings also do not carry a formal structure or agenda, so it is important for one to be patient.
- Significant importance placed on one's word, as opposed to a written agreement.
- Though Arabs enjoy negotiating, important not to use high-pressure tactics, as this will not be productive.

There is a strong relationship between culture and religion that must be taken into consideration when conducting business in the Middle East. The overwhelming majority, nearly 91%, of the population in the Arab Middle East is Muslim. The remaining 9% is made up of Christians, Jews, and other religion groups.[3] As such, the Islamic religion plays a significant role in politics and public life in the Middle East. Exhibit 20.2 discusses the role religion plays in consumer behavior in the Middle East.

When conducting business in the Middle East, religious holidays such as the Ramadan in the Arab countries, and the Rosh Hashanah and Yom Kippur in Israel can have a significant impact. Everyday life is affected by these holidays, including office hours and business

---

[2] Adapted from "Doing Business in the Middle East," http://www.kwintessential.co.uk/etiquette/doing-business-middle-east.html (Retrieved on May 6, 2014).

[3] S. A. Zahra, "Doing Research in the (New) Middle East: Sailing with the Wind," *Academy Of Management Perspectives* 25, no. 4 (2011): 6–21, doi:org/10.5465/amp.2011.0128

Exhibit 20.2

Islam and Consumer Behavior[4]

Arab consumers represent a quintessential dichotomy. Although progress and modernization is welcomed, they are not interested in letting go of their culture, including religion. Consumers are open to trying new products; however, they must not conflict with their religious values.

As a central component of life in the Middle East, the pillars of Islam dictate much of the consumer behavior and impact the practices of every business. As such, it is vital for a business to understand not only the basic principles of the religion but the undertones as well. For example, the interpretation or *hadith* of the Islamic faith can vary from region to region leading to differences in practices by its followers. Companies must understand these nuances and tailor their communications accordingly.

Although Islam is engrained in all facets of life, there is a line of separation that most consumers observe. Arab consumers have a preference for businesses that make a clear delineation between business and religion. The key is to develop an understanding of the religion and to show respect for their culture, but not to focus on religious messages.

dynamics. As such, it is often best not to conduct business during the time between the Jewish holidays of Rosh Hashanah and Yom Kippur. Conducting business during the Muslim holiday of Ramadan can also present a challenge as people may be affected by the fasting and late night social gatherings observed during the holiday.[5]

Language Nuances

The Arabic language is a central force in the Middle East; however, one major aspect to note is the subtle dialects that exist due to a class structure (dictated by economic status). This has been identified as a major barrier by marketing researchers. Dialects can vary so greatly that speakers in one country can find it difficult to communicate with speakers in another country.

In addition, when dealing with the Arab population, a lot can be lost in the translation process. Arabic is a very rich language with words having numerous synonyms. This is particularly important to note when conducting qualitative research. For example, personification—where the researcher asks the respondent to pretend that a particular brand name is a person—may not be effective. Translating the verbal as well as nonverbal communication elements requires expertise and familiarity with the Arab countries and the inherent culture(s).

---

[4] Adapted from V. Mahajan, "Understanding the Arab Consumer," *Harvard Business Review* 91, no. 5 (2013): 128–133.

[5] US and Foreign Commercial Service and US Department of State, "Doing Business in the Middle East and North Africa 2005," http://export.gov/middleeast/Doing%20Business%20in%20the%20Middle%20East.pdf. All rights reserved outside of the United States. International Copyright.

Income Differences[6]

There are drastic differences in the economic conditions of the countries across MENA. Saudi Arabia and Qatar are among the countries with the highest standard of living. In contrast, countries such as Somalia and Comoros lead the way as those with the lowest per capita income. The poorer countries are plagued by unemployment, especially among young people. Unemployment averages 23% among young people in the region due to limited job prospects.[7] Despite the disadvantages in the poorer countries, the region is experiencing a shift in wealth as the middle class continues to grow. Collectively, the MENA represents 6% of the global middle class.[8] Table 20.4 shows the distribution of the middle class in the MENA countries.

TABLE 20.4
THE ARAB MIDDLE CLASS[9]

Country	Top of the Pyramid (in %)	Middle Class (in %)	Bottom of the Pyramid (in %)
Algeria	17	55	28
Bahrain	7	60	33
Egypt	13	34	53
Jordan	20	41	39
Kuwait	22	57	21
Lebanon	10	60	30
Libya	15	35	50
Mauritania	3	30	67
Morocco	13	32	55
Oman	6	63	31
Qatar	8	70	22
Saudi Arabia	13	65	22
Sudan	8	46	46
Syria	3	57	40
Tunisia	22	52	26
UAE	11	60	29
Yemen	4	60	36

[6] Zahra, "Doing Research in the (New) Middle East."

[7] Ibid.

[8] David Rohde, "The Swelling Middle," *Reuters*, 2012, http://www.reuters.com/middle-class-infographic

[9] Adapted from V. Mahajan, "Understanding the Arab Consumer," *Harvard Business Review* 91, no. 5 (2013): 128–133. Population data are from IMF's World Economic Outlook Database and World Bank's World Development Indicators database (accessed January 2013).

Expatriates in the Middle East

One of the most unique features of the Arab region is the number of expatriates in the different countries, particularly in the GCC. This complicates the nature of the market, and this multi-cultural characteristic makes conducting market research even more difficult. It would involve significant cost in trying to get a representative sample from the entire market. For instance, in the UAE, a cross-section of the population reflects a composition of 30% locals and the rest expatriates. It would be crucial for a company to analyze the degree of difference in consumer culture, level of affordability, and accessibility to a select sample.

Technological Infrastructure

The infrastructure in the Middle East has improved significantly in the past decade; however, the region is still behind other areas of the world in terms of its technology preparedness. Outside of the more wealthy Arab Gulf countries, the technology infrastructure is well below international standards in these countries.[10]

Telecommunications

Liberalization of telecommunications in the MENA is still underway, with services being modernized and expanded. There has been significant growth in the infrastructure in recent years; however, there are still cases in which telephone service is restricted to the metropolitan areas. Given the nomadic characteristics of some of the population, fixed lines would be extremely unreliable. Also, the infrastructure in some of these countries does not support such a means of data collection. This translates to the fact that perhaps only more developed countries such as Saudi Arabia would be a *good* market to conduct the research via telephone.

In terms of mobile, touch-screen phone penetration is at 46% in the MENA region. The majority of consumers still own first-generation devices, used for making calls and sending SMS texts, and second-generation Nokia- and Blackberry-based devices, used for e-mail and instant messaging. However, decreasing costs are making it more possible for consumers to adopt third-generation mobile devices and services to include data capabilities for accessing the Internet.

Mobile phone usage varies greatly across the region due to market differences. Saudi Arabia and the UAE lead the way in smartphone penetration with two mobile phones for every inhabitant. In comparison, 72% of Saudis read their e-mails via their phones while only 7% of Egyptians do so. In addition, location-based services in conjunction with social media are popular in the region with 34% of consumers using them. Despite these advances in mobile subscription and usage, high prices and lack of Internet access in many areas still present obstacles to mobile expansion in the region.[11] Table 20.5 provides details of the telecommunications infrastructure in some Middle Eastern countries. This will be helpful in deciding the research methodology to be adopted in each of these countries.

---

[10] Zahra, "Doing Research in the (New) Middle East."
[11] A. Webster, "MENA Mobile," *Middle East* 433 (2012): 40.

TABLE 20.5

TELECOMMUNICATIONS INFRASTRUCTURE IN THE MIDDLE EAST[12]

Country	Population (in million)	Telephones (in million)		Internet Users (in million)
		Fixed	Mobile	
Syria	22.5	4.3	13.1	4.5
Lebanon	4.1	0.9	3.4	1.0
Iran	79.9	27.8	56.0	8.2
Saudi Arabia	26.9	4.6	53.7	9.8
Israel	7.7	3.5	9.2	4.5

Internet[13]

Internet access in the Middle East is expanding rapidly. Access is being spurred by increasing availability at various public locations throughout the region such as bars and cafes. As of 2011, 29% of the population in the Middle East had used the Internet. Globally, Arab-speakers represent 5% of Internet users; yet only 2% of Web content is in Arabic. This number is expected to increase as more businesses continue to invest in the region.

Women and youth are playing a significant role in the growth of the Internet in the Middle East. In particular, wealthy Arab women are expected to increase e-commerce. For the younger generation, the Internet and social media will serve as a means to start businesses, create jobs, and participate in activism. Two-thirds of the population in the MENA is under the age of 30, making this region the fastest growing for Internet access. However, there are still major limitations to access in the region.

In addition to economic and infrastructure restrictions, government control of Internet access is a factor that must be considered in the region. MENA is one of the most censored regions in the world. Governments often have strict regulations for Internet access and online content with emphasis put on censoring content that opposes or conflicts with the government or the Islamic religion. For example, Jordan, which is often called *Silicon Wadi* for its advancements in technology in the region, has tightened its press and publication laws to include restrictions on website and social media content that requires sites to be registered with authorities before going live. Many Arab countries have also introduced measures to monitor Internet activities in public places such as Internet cafes. Table 20.6 talks about the Internet penetration of countries in MENA.

---

[12] Adapted from *World Factbook 2013* (Accessed as of December 2013).
[13] P. Smith, "MENA's Huge Internet Promise," *Middle East* 438 (2012): 44.

TABLE 20.6
INTERNET USAGE IN THE MIDDLE EAST[14]

Middle East	Population (2012 est.)	Penetration (in %)
Bahrain	1,248,348	77.0
Iran	78,868,711	53.3
Iraq	31,129,225	7.1
Israel	7,590,758	70.0
Jordan	6,508,887	38.1
Kuwait	2,646,314	74.2
Lebanon	4,140,289	52.0
Oman	3,090,150	68.8
Palestine (West Bk)	2,622,544	57.7
Qatar	1,951,591	86.2
Saudi Arabia	26,534,504	49.0
Syria	22,530,746	22.5
UAE	8,264,070	70.9
Yemen	24,771,809	14.9

Mail[15]

There are nearly 20,000 post offices in the MENA, with one post office for every 13,000 inhabitants. In comparison to other networks in the region, it is relatively well advanced. In addition to postal services, the carriers offer financial services, with approximately 25% of the MENA population having postal savings or *giro* accounts. There is also future consideration for further diversification of postal services to include government services and communication centers. By using post offices as tele-centers and Internet cafés, access to the Internet can be increased in the region.

However, there are variations that exist across the region in terms of postal reliability. The problem with mail service is that although the current system in Saudi Arabia is reliable, however, that cannot be applied across all of the Middle Eastern nations. Mail is supposed to be delivered to households at least once a month; however, more often than not, the mail does not get delivered on time and it must be picked up from the post office by the receiver.

---

[14] *Source*: Adapted from Internet World Stats, http://www.internetworldstats.com/stats5.htm (Retrieved on May 6, 2014).

[15] "The Role of Postal Networks in Expanding Access to Financial Services: Middle East and North Africa Region," The World Bank Group—Global Information and Communication Technology Postbank Advisory, ING Bank Postal Policy, 2004, http://www-wds.worldbank.org/external/default/WDSContentServer/WDSP/IB/2012/06/05/000426104_20120605142535/Rendered/PDF/694640ESW0P08500PUBLIC00P0853960MNA.pdf

Mail volume can also have an impact on reliability. In Syria, a low of 150 items are processed per day. A high of 700 items per day are processed in Morocco.

The distance from a post office can also vary greatly. For example, the average distance in Egypt, Tunisia, Jordan, and Morocco is less than 15 kilometers. In contrast, the average in Iraq, Iran, and Libya is more than 40 kilometers. The degree of reach can reduce the sample size, and limit sampling to just the cities. Also, the difference in literacy and economic classes across both the individual country and the regions makes mail a rather difficult method, though cost-effective, to implement.

THE GULF COOPERATION COUNCIL

The GCC is a political and economic union of Arab countries along the Persian Gulf. These countries include Bahrain, Kuwait, Oman, Qatar, Saudi Arabia, and the UAE. Although small in population at 45 million, the GCC is a wealthy region in comparison to the rest of MENA with a GDP per capita similar to Europe.[16] Table 20.7 explains the demographic and economic profile of the GCC.

TABLE 20.7
DEMOGRAPHIC AND ECONOMIC PROFILE OF THE GCC[17]

Demographic Profile of GCC		Economic Profile of GCC	
Total Population	44.6 million	GDP	$1.38 trillion
Average Age	27 years	GDP per Capita	$231,633
Age Dynamics (% of population):		GDP PPP	$38,606
Less than 15 Years	22.0	Inflation	4.6%
Over 65 Years	2.0	Trade Balance	$303.8 billion
Expatriates	53.0		
Unemployment	12.1		

[16] "GCC Demographic Shift: Intergenerational Risk-Transfer at Play," Markaz Research—Kuwait Financial Centre, June 2012, http://www.markaz.com/MARKAZ/media/Markaz/Documents/Business%20Activities/DemographicsResearch-MarkazResearch-June-2012.pdf (Accessed on August 18, 2013).

[17] Adapted from "GCC Demographic Shift: Intergenerational Risk-Transfer at Play," Markaz Research—Kuwait Financial Centre, June 2012, http://www.markaz.com/DesktopModules/CRD/Attachments/DemographicsResearch-MarkazResearch-June%202012.pdf (Accessed on August 18, 2013); "The GCC Economic and Trade Overview," National Council on US–Arab Relations, 2012, http://ncusar.org/publications/Publications/GCC-Trade-Facts-Figures.pdf (Accessed on August 18, 2013).

SAUDI ARABIA

Country Characteristics[18]

Population: 26,939,583 (July 2013 est.)
Land Area: 2,149,690 sq. km
Language: Arabic (official)
Literacy Rate: 86.6%
Religion: Muslim (official)
GDP—Purchasing Power Parity: $921.7 billion (2012 est.)
GDP per Capita—Purchasing Power Parity: $31,800 (2012 est.)
GDP—Real Growth Rate: 6.8% (2012 est.)
Inflation Rate—Consumer Price Index: 4% (2012 est.)

Cultural Characteristics

The majority of the population in Saudi Arabia (75%) is native to the country, with foreigners from the Middle East, Africa, and other countries comprising the remainder. Most of the population, including the traditionally nomadic population, has settled in the major cities throughout the country. One-fourth of the population has origins from the Bedouin people, the majority of nomadic population in the region, who hold a prominent position in the society.

Saudi Arabia, as defined by Saudi law, is a Muslim nation, with Islam being the only recognized religion. The majority of residents, about 90%, are Sunni Muslims who follow the Salafism Islamic code, and 5% of the population are Shia Muslims.[19] Beyond the stereotyping that all Arabs are Muslim, what is essential to note is that the religion complements the Arab way of life. Arab means pertaining to Arabia, and carries with it the cultural connotation and not the religious association.[20] As such, Saudi Arabians are Arab by culture and Muslim by faith. Exhibit 20.3 discusses the curious mix of religion and cosmopolitanism among Saudi Arabian youth.

Business Characteristics

Saudi Arabians tend to perceive business to be a means to gain understanding of the Middle Eastern methods of management. Often, in order to succeed, these following pointers are useful.

- Time is a major commodity, but patience is virtue. It is beneficial for the foreign party to spend time in getting accustomed to the Arab culture. Time is considered to be decided upon by God. It is important not to stipulate rigid time frames without giving allowance for the concept of God's will. Saudi Arabians are also fatalistic; they believe in fate and the *hand of God*. Hence, planning for contingencies is not something they frequently indulge in

---

[18] *CIA World Factbook*, 2013.
[19] Exhibit 20.3 discusses the curious mix of religion and cosmopolitanism among Saudi Arabian youth.
[20] Harris and Moran, *Managing Cultural Differences*, 4th edition, p. 347.

Exhibit 20.3

Saudi Arabian Youth[21]

Millennials or Generation Y make up the majority of Saudi Arabia's population. Sixty-four percent of Saudi Arabians are under the age of 30. Demonstrating the behavior of most youth of this generation, Saudi youth are highly connected. Usage of the Internet and social media has skyrocketed, allowing them to become more connected to the outside world. In 2012, YouTube use alone increased by 260% in Saudi Arabia compared to 50% internationally.

As a result of this exposure, the Saudi youth are beginning to think critically about the state of affairs in their country. They are exercising the freedom to express themselves via social media. For example, Twitter is being used by Saudi youth to openly discuss religion, politics, gender relations, and other once-taboo topics. Although this generation is expressing themselves more, they are not interested in drastically cutting all ties with tradition. Instead, they have a preference for gradual change that will still allow for financial stability and connection to the Islamic faith. Saudi youth seek more tolerance for their religious beliefs in terms of the acceptance of differences among Muslims and more tolerance in the treatment of women. They are also interested in a government that is less ruled by religion and more by law.

- Arabs are considered to be people of great emotional depth who believe in expressing their loyalty and friendship as key to an ongoing relationship. In conducting business, they tend to be warm, hospitable, and when the party becomes more aware of the nuances of the culture, makes it a very easy-going discussion. It is necessary to note that the dealings are with the person and not the company, so the role of fostering relations is emphasized
- The concept of the individual is very important in Arab culture. One cannot afford to lose face or ruin his family's name in the process of dealing with others. There is a hierarchy in the society, whether stipulated or otherwise, and an individual who has been shamed loses his status in the eyes of the group
- Negotiating is considered to be part of the average business deal and one should ideally expect that it would take time for an unanimous decision to be reached
- Nonverbal communication is especially complicated in Saudi Arabia. Most Arabs express themselves with a multiplicity of gestures that the foreigner should be able to recognize. This is particularly important when conducting market research in this country
- When targeting all of the countries in the Middle East region, one falls into the stereotypical thought that all Arabs in that part of the world conduct business alike. Saudi Arabia has raced ahead in its modernization attempts, while countries like Syria and Iran are catching up, slowly
- The role of women in business was considered to be secondary; however, with women becoming more educated, their presence in the business front has become significantly prominent. The foreign party, however, has to be conscious of the physical distance that should be maintained with an Arab woman when conducting business

---

[21] Adapted from Isobel Coleman, "Youth, Change, and the Future of Saudi Arabia," March 20, 2013. Retrieved from http://middleeastvoices.voanews.com/2013/03/insight-youth-change-and-the-future-of-saudi-arabia-23098/#ixzz2cAh5NYCD on January 25, 2014.

Market Research in Saudi Arabia[22]

Saudi Arabia is one of the most advanced countries in the MENA region. As such, conducting research can be accomplished if proper consideration is taken for cultural and business characteristics.

Telephone

The telecommunications system in Saudi Arabia is modernized with about 90% of households being covered by a fixed line telephone. As of 2011, there were 4.6 million fixed lines in use in Saudi Arabia. Since the fixed line monopoly ended in 2007, several consortia have entered the Saudi market including Verizon (US), PCCW (Hong Kong), and the Bahrain Telecommunications Company (Batelco). As such, fixed line penetration has increased in recent years due to a decrease in prices and an increase in broadband services. In addition, Internet telephony for free international calling is driven by the large expatriate population in Saudi Arabia.

Mobile

Mobile phone penetration is far above fixed line penetration in Saudi Arabia. There are three mobile phone operators in the country—STC, Mobily, and Zain Saudi Arabia. Due to increased competition and lower prices, there were 53.7 million mobile phones in use in Saudi Arabia in 2011. Many Saudis have more than one mobile device leading to the extremely high penetration rates of almost 200%. With the market saturation of mobile devices, the demand for the next generation of mobile phones will be prompted by high income levels and the large youth population in Saudi Arabia. Smartphone adoption will continue to increase with growth in mobile commerce and social networking sites increasing in popularity.

Internet

Despite lagging behind the region, Internet penetration has reached 53% in Saudi Arabia as of 2012. Access to broadband has grown to 6.23 million subscribers with 2.25 million being fixed line subscriptions and the remainder being mobile subscriptions. As of 2012, mobile broadband penetration was at 40%. Like several other Arab nations, there is heavy censorship of the Internet, which puts limitations on growth.

Mail

Saudi Arabia has an efficient postal infrastructure. Headquartered in Riyadh, Saudi Post has elevated its services, making it one of the most sophisticated in the world. With the majority of the country being addressed, mail is delivered via a GPS grid system with each address coordinating to a unique coordinate. Saudi Post also offers smart mailboxes. In addition, Saudi Post provides every citizen with a postal-specific e-mail address by which opt-in mail can be delivered.[23]

---

[22] "Industry Report: Telecoms and Technology: Saudi Arabia," *Telecoms Industry Report: Saudi Arabia* 1 (2013): 1–12.

[23] "Saudi Post: Connecting All the Dots," *Foreign Affairs* 87, no. 3 (2008): 15.

CONDUCTING MARKET RESEARCH IN SUB-SAHARAN AFRICA

The most reliable sources of information on this continent and in South Africa are from data-bases already constructed by the multinational corporations and international organizations. The problem, however, is that the information is dated and cannot be relied upon to provide an accurate estimate of the demographic constitution of the country or region. The availability of newspapers, as well as other media, tends to be inconsistent, with Cape Town being the sole exception.

Economy

Africa's economic activities can be characterized by a redundant dynamic environment with a great deal of promise for the future. Often, African countries have been dismissed as difficult or unviable markets owing to insufficient infrastructure, limited talent pool, political turmoil, severe economic hardships, and poor health conditions. For these reasons, companies have preferred to look toward Asian economies, unmindful of the hidden potential in the African consumer markets. The economic progress posted by the African nations in recent years has belied such notions and indicated a consistent growth in the future. Table 20.8 presents the African economic situation now and as predicted in the future.

TABLE 20.8
AFRICA—TODAY AND TOMORROW[24]

Africa Today	Africa Tomorrow
Collective GDP of $1.6 trillion (2008)	Collective GDP of $2.6 trillion (2020)
Combined consumer spending of $860 billion (2008)	Combined consumer spending of USD 1.4 trillion (2020)
316 million new mobile phone subscribers since 2000	1.1 billion Africans of working age (2040)
60% of world's total uncultivated, arable land	128 million households with discretionary income (2020)
52 cities with more than 1 million people	50% of Africans living in cities by 2030
20 companies with revenues of at least $3 billion	

In the wake of such economic progress, several sectors, such as retailing, telecommunications, and financial services, are beginning to show much promise to companies. Multinational corporations such as Nokia and Coca-Cola already have distribution networks in nearly every African country. Other foreign companies to have a presence in Africa include Unilever (20 countries), Nestlé (19 countries), Société Générale (15 countries), Standard Chartered Bank

---

[24] Adapted from Charles Roxburgh, Norbert Dorr, Acha Leke, Amine Tazi-Riffi, Arend van Wamelen, Susan Lund, Mutsa Chironga, Charles Atkins, Nadia Terfous, and Till Zelno-Mahmalat (2010). Lions on the Move: The Progress and Potential of African Economies. McKinsey Global Institute.

(14 countries), and Barclays (12 countries). Even African companies are beginning to expand their operations past their origin country into other African nations.

The reasons for the recent African growth story and its projected future prosperity can be attributed to three key issues.[25] First, several African nations such as Angola and Mozambique have taken appropriate measures in fostering political stability necessary for growth, as evidenced by the decrease in the number of political strife. The number of serious conflicts in Africa that led to deaths in excess of 1,000 people a year declined from an average of 4.8 a year in the 1990s to 2.6 in the 2000s. Second, financial austerity measures by way of lower budgets deficits (from 4.6% of GDP to 1.8% since 2000) and decreased foreign debt (82% of GDP to 59% since 2000) have led to lower inflation (from 22% to 8% since 2000). Finally, the adoption of market-friendly policies such as privatization of state-owned enterprises, reduction in trade barriers, removal of corporate taxes, and strengthening of regulatory and legal systems have immensely helped boost Africa's growth rates. For instance, Nigeria privatized more than 116 enterprises between 1999 and 2006; Morocco and Egypt struck free-trade agreements with their main export partners; and Rwanda established courts to settle business disputes.

Given the 50-plus nations and their varying growth rates, companies can have a difficult time deciding their presence among these nations. Each of these nations is characterized by their own set of policies and attitudes toward multinational companies, as well as languages, customs, currency, and traditions. In a recent classification of the African nations based on the levels of exports and economic diversification, the countries can be grouped under four main categories: diversified economies, oil exporters, transition economies, and pre-transition economies.[26] Table 20.9 presents the classification that companies can use.

Culture and Language

Conducting research in Africa requires a thorough analysis of the reach into the continent's several countries. The actual research, analysis, and interpretation as well as applicability becomes difficult for the market researcher due to the extreme polarization that exists within the continent. From Tunisia to South Africa, Sudan to Ethiopia, the researcher needs to take on a country-by-country approach to targeting within Africa as compared to a standardized strategy.

When attempting to conduct primary research, it would be beneficial to note that interviewing the respondents may not necessarily represent the entire consumer base. A significant portion of the population lives in the rural areas, though in relation to the consumption levels, it is rather miniscule. While it would help to isolate the respondents to a specific income level, it may defeat the purpose of asking questions.

Conducting personal interviews with probes as well as focus groups may be a better option when dealing with such a diverse population. The biggest problem would be in terms of the cultural differences, the languages, as well as habits which tend to differ from region to region, across classes, and races. The construct should be able to reflect an insight across the board rather than minute subtleties.

---

[25] Mutsa Chironga, Acha Leke, Susan Lund, and Arend van Wamelen, "Cracking the Next Growth Market: Africa," *Harvard Business Review*, May 2011, pp. 117–122.

[26] Ibid.

TABLE 20.9

OPPORTUNITIES IN THE AFRICAN NATIONS[27]

	Diversified Economies	Oil Exporters	Transition Economies	Pre-transition Economies
Typical Countries	• Egypt • Morocco • South Africa • Tunisia	• Algeria • Angola • Nigeria	• Ghana • Kenya • Uganda • Senegal	• Congo • Ethiopia • Mali
Main Characteristics	• Mainly manufacturing and services industries such as banking, telecom, and retailing • High per capita income • More stable GDP growth	• Mainly oil exports • Least diversified economy • Growing services industry • Highest per capital income	• Lower per capita income • Growing rapidly, on average 7% p.a.	• Poor economies • Lowest GDP per capita • Lack the basics such as stable governments, strong public institutions, and sustainable agricultural development
Market Opportunities	• Largest consumer markets—90% of household have discretionary income • Ideal for consumer-facing businesses to anchor their operations	• Attractive markets for high-end goods and services	• Attractive opportunities in banking, telecom and modern retailing • Expected growth in commodity exports leading to turbo charging growth	• Limited, but growing
Challenges	• Higher labor costs than China or India • Struggling to compete even in low-value manufacturing industries • Need to build a skilled workforce, and better infrastructure	• Working toward maintaining political stability • Reducing the economic vulnerability on commodity price	• Products offered in these markets have to be tailored to poorer customers	• Multinational companies must track these economies, only those that can handle the risks should enter them

[27] Adapted from Mutsa Chironga, Acha Leke, Susan Lund, and Arend van Wamelen, "Cracking the Next Growth Market: Africa," *Harvard Business Review*, May 2011, pp. 117–122.

Technological Infrastructure

The telephone is an effective but costly and unreliable means to obtain consumer response. The problem becomes more complex due to inconsistency and poor infrastructure across the continent. In South Africa, telephone interviewing is considered to be appropriate, though the main problem is that there is significant ethnic bias. Mobile technology is increasingly present in many of the countries at much higher rates than fixed line telephones. However, most of the countries severely lag behind international standards. In order to have a better representation, it is recommended that focus groups or personal interviews be used.[28]

Mail is intrinsically linked with the literacy rate which varies from region to region. The mailing system in Africa is also not reliable and does not always extend beyond the usual cities into the rural areas.

While the use of the Internet is relatively higher in other regions, Africa lags behind due to poor infrastructure facilities, regulations, and cost of Internet connection. Although the majority of the countries are low on the development curve, the Republic of South Africa is in striking contrast.[29] Table 20.10 illustrates the telecommunications density in several African countries.

TABLE 20.10

TELECOMMUNICATIONS DENSITY IN AFRICA (IN MILLIONS)[30]

Country	Population	Telephone	Mobile	Internet
Angola	18.6	0.3	9.5	0.6
Botswana	2.1	0.2	2.9	0.1
Cameroon	20.5	0.7	10.5	0.8
Ethiopia	93.9	0.8	14.1	0.5
Ghana	25.2	0.3	21.2	1.3
Kenya	44.0	0.3	28.1	4.0
Mozambique	24.1	0.1	7.9	0.6
Namibia	2.2	0.1	2.2	0.1
Nigeria	174.5	0.7	95.2	44.0
Senegal	13.3	0.4	9.4	1.8
Tanzania	48.3	0.2	25.7	0.7
Uganda	34.8	0.5	16.7	3.2
Zimbabwe	13.2	0.4	9.2	1.4

[28] J. Rice, "The 1994 South African Election—The Research Experience," 23rd MRSA (Marketing Research Society of Australia) Conference, 1994.

[29] Randy Barrett, "Off the Beaten Track: Unexpected Net Hot Spots," *Inter@ctive Week* 5, no. 47 (1998): 44.

[30] CIA World Factbook.

SOUTH AFRICA

Country Characteristics[31]

Population: 48,601,098 (July 2013 est.)
Land Area: 1,214,470 sq. km
Language: 11 official languages including Afrikaans, English, isiNdebele, Sepedi, Sesotho, siSwazi, Xitsonga, Setswana, Tshivenda, IsiXhosa, and IsiZulu
Literacy Rate: 86.4%
Religion: Protestant 36.6% (Zionist Christian, Pentecostal/Charismatic, Methodist, Dutch Reformed, Anglican), Catholic 7.1%, Muslim 1.5%, other Christian 36%, other 2.3%, unspecified 1.4%, none 15.1%
GDP—Purchasing Power Parity: $592 billion (2012 est.)
GDP per Capita—Purchasing Power Parity: $11,600 (2012 est.)
GDP—Real Growth Rate: 2.5% (2012 est.)
Inflation Rate—Consumer Price Index: 5.7% (2012 est.)

Cultural Characteristics

South Africa is a county with a very diverse culture rich in ethnic and language differences among the population. The majority of the population is comprised of the white, colored, Asian/Indian, and Native African ethnic groups. Exhibit 20.4 explores the cultural similarities and dissimilarities between whites and blacks in South Africa.

Exhibit 20.4

Cultural Aspects[32]

- Country is commonly characterized by severe levels of inequality regarding wealth, status, power, and education.
- Greater levels of privilege and entitlement for white families in comparison to blacks, which results from historical exploitation and inequality.
- Black community possesses large levels of togetherness and respect for each other. Togetherness is based largely on the inequality that they endure.
- The lifestyle of those in the white community parallels that of the average European and American, regarding professional opportunities and social privileges.
- In comparison to black family structure, white families are much more stable, united, and privileged.

In terms of language, there are 11 official languages spoken, and these tend to be vernacular or dialects. In order for there to be some consistency, the researcher would have to fix the

---

[31] *CIA World Factbook*, 2013.

[32] Adapted from "South Africa: Culture and Conflict," http://www.sahistory.org.za/archive/chapter-3-south-africa-culture-and-conflict (Retrieved on May 6, 2014).

conceptual aspect and then adjust it in order to be able to convey the same idea and try to eliminate bias induced in translations.

Also when targeting the South African population, it would be necessary to consider the rural–urban settlements. This would determine both the standard of living as well as provide a cross-section of the racial mix of South Africa. There has been a sudden surge in the income levels in South Africa, which has improved the consumer goods industry's feasibility of operations. South Africa surely represents the first world among the rest of the countries in the African continent.

The concept of elders and their status in the society is also to be emphasized. Concepts like seniority play a big role, and it is important to adhere to the word of the oldest member of the host party. Known as *ubuntu*, these concepts are based on the oneness and connectivity between individuals. Exhibit 20.5 discusses the concept of ubuntu.

Exhibit 20.5

Ubuntu: The Human Relationship[33]

The concept of ubuntu is a traditional notion of South African culture. Originating from Bantu culture, it is believed that "a person is only a person through others." Ubuntu relays the qualities of tolerance, compassion, and respect for others, particularly the elderly, those less advantaged, and persons in positions of authority. Deriving from the necessity of a collectivist society, the concept of Ubuntu embraces the relatedness that one person has to another so as to establish peace and harmony within the community. The characteristics of courtesy, loyalty, generosity, and honesty are highly valued.

Business Characteristics

Conducting business dealings in South Africa is rather tedious. Most Africans do not stand on formality, and though that connotes a relaxed attitude, they do not fall into that category either. Personal matters are kept separate from business dealings. Similarly, it is considered impolite to discuss business at home.

Some of the informality can be seen in the way people are most commonly addressed by their first name in business settings. Also, prefixes such as Mr and Mrs and professional titles such as Dr are not commonly used. Most business is conducted in English; however, special note must be taken of the accent and undertones of speech. For instance, the use of overly diplomatic language by a foreigner may be interpreted as a lack of commitment or dishonesty. As such, it is preferred to speak plainly and directly in many instances. It is also preferred that hard selling not be used as a tactic. Such behavior would be perceived negatively. Instead, a friendlier approach that focuses on the relationship would allow for better negotiations.

In terms of gestures, handshaking and backslapping are the norm when greeting or doing introductions. South Africa is a conservative society and dress should be formal and appropriate for the occasion, particularly business meetings.[34]

---

[33] Adapted from J. Nel, V. Valchev, S. Rothmann, F. van de Vijver, D. Meiring, and G. de Bruin, "Exploring the Personality Structure in the 11 Languages of South Africa," *Journal of Personality* 80, no. 4 (2012): 915–948.

[34] http://www.worldbusinessculture.com/Business-in-South-Africa.html

Market Research in South Africa[35]

As one of the wealthiest countries in Africa, South Africa has the infrastructure to allow for the successful conducting of market research. However, for research to be done successfully, consideration must be taken for the different cultural dynamics as well as the ability to reach the population via country's framework.

Telephone

As of 2011, there were 4.1 million fixed lines in South Africa. At 7.3 lines per 100 people, fixed line telephone penetration in South Africa is below international standards for comparable high- and middle-income countries. Even with reduced prices and improved infrastructure, fixed line penetration has decreased in recent years. As such, fixed line access is not a prominent means for reaching the South African consumer.

Mobile

In contrast to fixed line telephones, mobile phones are in high demand. There were 64 million mobile phones in use in South Africa in 2011. At 100% penetration, further growth in the market will be driven by the Black population joining the middle- and high-income segments in the country. The demand for data services will also increase.

Internet

Although Internet usage has increased in South Africa in recent years, penetration is very low for a developed country. Internet penetration in 2011 was at 21%, making it the highest for mainland Africa; however, only 1.9 per 100 people have a broadband subscription. Access to the Internet will be expanded by the increase in mobile services versus personal computers. Fifty percent of broadband connectivity is via a mobile device in South Africa.

Mail

The South Africa Post Office (SAPO) is the national postal service of South Africa. There are almost 1,600 post office locations across the country with an additional 1,000 mail centers and post agencies. In addition to mail, SAPO offers logistics, banking, and digital services.[36]

SUMMARY

This chapter deals with Middle East and Africa. Data about these regions in general and tips on conducting marketing research in the Middle East and Africa are provided. Country information is provided about Saudi Arabia and South Africa. Some relevant statistics and sources of information such as journals and websites are also mentioned.

---

[35] "Telecoms Industry Report: South Africa," *Telecoms Industry Report* 4, no. 2 (2012): 1–12.

[36] South Africa Post Office Annual Report 2012, http://www.postoffice.co.za/group/aboutus/annualreport/PostOfficeannualreport2012.pdf

21

CHAPTER

North America

INTRODUCTION

As a continent, North America consists of Canada, the US, Mexico, and the republics of Central America and the Caribbean. North America can be subdivided into many regions based on cultural, economic, and geographic standards. One of the most common divisions is the cultural separation of the US, Canada, Belize, and the English-speaking Caribbean Islands as Anglo-America and Mexico, and the countries of Central America being designated with Latin America. Another common classification is in terms of the trade bloc between the US, Canada, and Mexico known as the NAFTA.

CONDUCTING MARKET RESEARCH IN NORTH AMERICA

Conducting market research in North America is a common activity of many companies. Most large corporations have budgets for administering research studies to gather consumer insights, competitive intelligence, and industry trends. Within that framework, market segmentation is often a consideration due to the cultural diversity that exists in North America. Exhibit 21.1 discusses the market research industry in the US, Canada, and Mexico.

Exhibit 21.1

Market Research Industry in the US, Canada, and Mexico[1]

The global market research industry generates about $50 billion in revenue annually. The US and the EU account for the majority of the revenue generated in the industry. Outside of the US, research in the rest of North America is largely conducted in Canada and Mexico. According to ESOMAR, North America represents 30% of global market research revenue, second to the EU at 45%. Countries in the Asia/Pacific region account for 15% of revenue. As more countries experience growth in their middle class populations, market research services will grow in those regions.

---

[1] Adapted from Market Research and Polling Services, Hoovers.

The US market research industry generates combined annual revenue of $15 billion across 4,800 companies. The top 50 companies generate about 55% of the marketing research industry revenue in the US. In addition, the majority of expenditure is driven by corporations seeking insights on consumers, competitors, and industries. Market research firms can be found all throughout the US with many having officers in large cities such as New York, Los Angeles, or Chicago. The Marketing Research Association is the professional organization established in the US to promote and develop the market research industry in the US.

Even though the Canadian marketing research industry feels familiar to the US, it is important to address Canada as a distinct market with different potential for growth and development. Through panels at retail stores, as well as TAM systems installed and gauged at Toronto, Vancouver, and Montreal, the Canadian marketing research industry is an important component meeting consumer demands. In terms of breadth, over 50% of market research in Canada is conducted in Ontario—its most populated province. The Marketing Research and Intelligence Association is the representative organization for consumer and market intelligence in Canada.

Still in development, the Mexican marketing research industry has potential for immense growth. Research is often concentrated in three or four markets: Matamoros, Monterrey, Guadalajara, and Mexico City. In 1993, several research firms formed the Asociación Mexicana de Agencias de Investigación de Mercados y Opinion Pública (AMAI) which serves to establish quality and standard methods for conducting research in Mexico.

Culture and Language

The US, Canada, and Mexico represent the most developed countries in North America. Due to its history, North America is very culturally diverse with many ethnicities and racial groups inhabiting the continent. The cultures of Canada and the US have similarities as the result of a shared history from British colonialism; however, there are important differences to be noted between the nationalities. Mexico, due to its proximity to the US, is connected economically and, in some instances, culturally to the US due to the large Hispanic population living in the US.

The most prevalent languages in North America are English, Spanish, and French. The English spoken in the US is different from that spoken in the UK and Australia. The Spanish spoken in Mexico is not the same as that used in Spain and the other countries of Latin America. In France, natives speak French differently from Canadians. In Quebec, Canada, many residents speak English, but French is the official language. Product descriptions, labels, and warranties must be in French. If a Canada-wide mailing includes addresses in Quebec, the materials should be in both English and French. Exhibit 21.2 lists some of the cultural peculiarities of North America.

NORTH AMERICAN FREE TRADE AGREEMENT

In 1988, the governments of the US and Canada agreed to enter into a free trade agreement, which went into effect on January 1, 1989. The goal of the agreement was to eliminate all tariffs on bilateral trade between Canada and the US by 1998. This was followed in 1991 by talks

Exhibit 21.2

Cultural *Dos* and *Don'ts* in North America[2]

- It is important to shake hands firmly and make eye contact when greeting someone for the first time.
- The manner in which one dresses can go a long way in establishing a strong first impression. In a business setting, wearing appropriate business attire establishes confidence and reliability with prospective partner. For men, added value is placed on being clean-shaven.
- When performing business in Canada, it is important to remember that it is not part of the US. Canadians place significant importance on this distinction.
- Men and women are legally and socially required to be viewed as equals.
- In a business setting, it is not necessary to establish a personal relationship before working together.
- Avoid dismissive gestures like rolling eyes heavenwards and walking away.
- Meetings are arranged beforehand and punctuality is important. North Americans expect business cards to be exchanged during meetings.
- Avoid smoking. North Americans are very particular about smoke-free public places.
- It is important to be respectful and to treat people of different ages and races in a polite manner.

among the US, Canada, and Mexico aimed at establishing the NAFTA. The talks concluded in August 1992 with an agreement in principle. The agreement became law on January 1, 1994. It contains the following actions:

- Abolishes within 10 years tariffs on 99% of the goods traded between Mexico, Canada, and the US.
- Removes most barriers on the cross-border flow of services, allowing financial institutions, for example, unrestricted access to the Mexican market by 2010.
- Protects intellectual property rights.
- Removes most restrictions on foreign direct investments between the three member countries, although special treatment (protection) will be given to Mexican energy and railway industries, American airline and radio communications industries, and Canadian culture.
- Allows each country to apply its own environmental standards, provided such standards have scientific basis—lowering standards to lure investment is described as being inappropriate.

NAFTA establishes the principle of national treatment to ensure that NAFTA countries will treat NAFTA-origin products in the same manner as similar domestic products. Service providers of the member nation will receive equal treatment. To protect foreign investors in the free trade area, NAFTA has established five principles: (1) non-discriminatory treatment,

---

[2] Adapted from Angelena Boden, *The Cultural Gaffes Pocketbook* (Management Pocketbooks, 1997). Reprinted by permission of Management Pocketbooks. "American Business Etiquette," http://nyintl.net/story/american_business_etiquette (Retrieved on May 6, 2014).

(2) freedom from performance requirements, (3) free transference of funds related to an investment, (4) expropriation only in conformity with international law, and (5) the right to seek international arbitration for a violation of the agreement's protections.

NAFTA, with more than 467 million consumers from three countries, is the world's largest free trade area. Second only to the EU with its 28 participating countries in terms of population, NAFTA's combined output surpasses the EU with $17 trillion of goods and services produced. The two-way trade for goods between the US and the other NAFTA countries totaled $918 billion in 2010—$412 billion in exports and $506 billion in imports—resulting in a goods trade deficit of $95 billion. Trade in services totaled $99 billion with a trade surplus of $28.3 billion as of 2009.[3]

US and Canada Trade

Canada's focus of economic activity has always been along the US border, which stretches some 4,000 miles. It is not too surprising that the natural axis of trade has always been from north to south rather than east to west. Canada is the largest single market for US exports as well as the largest market for American manufacturers. As a result, US exports to Canada reached $248.2 billion in 2010. Further, Canada–US trade has continued to grow, and the total import of goods from Canada to the US reached $276.5 billion in 2010.[4]

US and Mexico Trade

The US is Mexico's most important trading partner, absorbing over three-fourths of total Mexican exports worldwide. On the other hand, Mexico is the third largest US trading partner, ranking after Japan and Canada. Approximately 50% of all Mexico's imports come from the US.[5] In 2010, US trade in goods with Mexico totaled $393 billion—$163.3 billion in exports and $229.7 billion in imports.[6] Mexico is purchasing most of the durable goods and industrial materials from the US. Not surprisingly, Mexico is the fastest growing major US export market. By far, Mexico is the largest US trading partner in Latin America, accounting for about three-fifths of US exports to and imports from the region. In 2009, Mexico accounted for 11.7% of total US merchandise trade. In comparison, the rest of Latin America combined made up 8.3% of total US merchandise trade.[7]

---

[3] Office of the United States Trade Representative, http://www.ustr.gov/trade-agreements/free-trade-agreements/north-american-free-trade-agreement-nafta

[4] Ibid.

[5] World Trade Organization Trade Profiles, April 2013.

[6] Office of the United States Trade Representative, http://www.ustr.gov/trade-agreements/free-trade-agreements/north-american-free-trade-agreement-nafta

[7] J. F. Hornbeck, "US–Latin America Trade: Recent Trends and Policy Issues," Congressional Research Service, 2011, http://www.fas.org/sgp/crs/row/98-840.pdf

THE UNITED STATES OF AMERICA

Country Characteristics[8]

Population: 316,668,567 (July 2013 est.)
Land Area: 9,161,966 sq. km
Language: English, Spanish (no official language)
Literacy Rate: 99%
Religion: Protestant (51.3%), Roman Catholic (23.9%), Jewish (1.7%), Mormon (1.7%), other Christian (1.6%), Muslim (0.6%), Buddhist (0.7%), unaffiliated (12.1%), other (2.5%), none (4%),
GDP—Purchasing Power Parity: $ 15.94 trillion (2012 est.)
GDP per Capita—Purchasing Power Parity: $50,700 (2012 est.)
GDP—Real Growth Rate: 2.2% (2012 est.)
Inflation Rate—Consumer Price Index: 2.1% (2012 est.)

Cultural Characteristics

The cultural diversity present in the US makes it a very unique market in terms of market research. Outside of the unifying American culture, there are different segments in the population based on demographic and psychographic parameters. The US has inhabitants with origins from all parts of the world with the majority of the population being of European descent. Hispanics (Latinos) and African Americans (Black) constitute the largest minority populations in the country. Table 21.1 illustrates the ethnic diversity in the Unites States.

TABLE 21.1
ETHNIC DIVERSITY IN THE US—2010 CENSUS[9]

	% of Population	% Change Since Census 2000
Hispanic/Latino	16.3	43.0
Not Hispanic/Latino	83.7	4.9
White	72.4	5.7
African American/Black	12.6	12.3
Asian	4.8	43.3
American Indian and Alaska Native	0.9	18.4
Native Hawaiian and Pacific Islander	0.2	35.4
Other	6.2	24.4
Two or More	2.9	32.0

Note: Person of Hispanic/Latino origin can be of any race.

---

[8] *CIA World Factbook*, 2012.
[9] US Census 2010.

In terms of geography, the majority of the population in the US lives in urban areas with many of those being in suburban areas. There are also several regional differences that exist in the US in terms of dialect and colloquial behavior. There are four regions in the US and 50 states, with each having its own nuances and social norms. Often subtle, the differences between a Northern and a Southern can have an impact on what is communicated and considered appropriate behavior.

When conducting research in the US, it is important to clearly define the segment of the population that is being targeted for the study. The ethnic, socioeconomic, and regional differences that can exist amongst the population can lead to varying interpretations of the same message. Due to its large immigrant population, the concept of acculturation must also be considered. Whether the inhabitants have acculturated to the US way of life or still exhibit many traits of their COO is important to understand.

Business Characteristics

For almost all cultures, it is important to understand how executives view power and authority. Many US managers are highly individualistic, time-conscious, goal-oriented people. In most cases, the manager is accountable for all decision-making that they are responsible for. In contrast to more compromise-oriented cultures, decisions may include input from subordinates, but the final call and consequences of decision lie with the manager. As such, the concept of individual merit and accomplishments is highly linked to success and reward.

Open dialogue is often welcomed in regard to debate and discussing business matters. In addition, communication can be very direct and to the point in order to move business along. The primary purpose of communication is to exchange information, facts, and opinions. Establishment of a personal relationship is not as important in US business culture. Instead, forming company relationships are deemed more important. However, the act of networking, or building relationships for future opportunities, is often viewed as a vital component to individual advancement.

Meetings tend to be formal, with the aim being to solidify a business deal versus cultivating a personal connection. Although cordial exchanges, politeness, and small talk upon introduction are common, these should be viewed as protocol. Other business protocols include adhering to meeting times and deadlines, obeying organization structure and hierarchy, and following company policies.[10]

Market Research in the US[11]

Market research in the US is a well-developed industry. Consumers in the US are very familiar with market research activities and many have previously participated in some way. From focus groups to online surveys, the capabilities of market research in the US are numerous. Methodologies for primary research can be tailored to segment specifications and customized to try innovative techniques. In addition, access to secondary data is readily available from government, academic, and private organizations.

---

[10] "Doing Business in the United States | US Social and Business Culture," Communicaid, http://www.communicaid.com/access/pdf/library/culture/doing-business-in/Doing%20Business%20in%20the%20USA.pdf

[11] "Telecoms and Technology Industry Report: United States of America," *Telecoms Industry Report: USA* 4 (2012): 1–12.

The US is the world's largest consumer of information and technology. As such, reaching consumers through the available infrastructure can be easily accomplished as long as consumer privacy and protection laws are adhered to. Exhibit 21.3 discusses consumer data privacy and protection in the US.

Exhibit 21.3

Consumer Privacy and Protection in the US[12]

The protection of privacy is valued by most citizens in the US. Privacy protection laws have existed for many years for postal mail, telephone, computer, and e-mail communications. As technology continues to evolve, protection has been extended to address new modes of communication through the Internet and smartphones.

Privacy protections are critical to maintaining consumer trust in the US. As such, a safeguard known as the Consumer Privacy Bill of Rights is instituted, which allows consumers to control the type and amount of personal data that is made available to and retained by companies. Consumers are also afforded the right to access and correct personal data when necessary. In addition, the bill ensures the rights to transparency, security, accuracy, and accountability in the collection of consumer data. The collection, use, and disclosure of consumer data must also be used for the means for which it was provided. For example, companies will make statements affirming that the consumer's data will not be sold to third parties in order to assure consumers of context protection. The Consumer Privacy Bill of Rights aims to provide consumers with clear guidance for their expectations of those who handle their personal information as well as set guidelines for the companies which solicit and use the personal data of consumers.

Telecommunications

The number of fixed line telephones has steadily decreased over the years in the US. As of 2011, there were 146 million fixed lines in use in the country accounting for 32 lines per 100 inhabitants. In contrast, there were 209.3 million mobile phones in use in 2011. Consumers are adopting other means of communication, including VoIP and mobile phones. VoIP is popular for making international calls, and many households are forgoing house connection all together in favor of mobile devices.

Mobile phone penetration in the US reached 115 per 100 people in 2012 as many consumers own multiple subscriptions. Data and Internet service demands for smartphones, as well as tablets, are the driving force behind mobile usage. In addition, 4G LTE (fourth-generation long-term evolution) networks are increasing data capabilities. Competition among mobile providers is a major component in the development of the network and services made available to consumers. The primary players in the US market are AT&T, Verizon, T-Mobile, and Sprint Nextel.

---

[12] Adapted from "Consumer Data Privacy in a Networked World: A Framework for Protecting Privacy and Promoting Innovation in the Global Digital Economy," US Intellectual Property Enforcement Coordinator Annual Report on Intellectual Property Enforcement, February 2012. Retrieved from http://www.whitehouse.gov/sites/default/files/privacy-final.pdf on January 28, 2014.

Internet

Internet penetration in the US reached 82% in 2012. There are 31 Internet subscribers for every 100 people, with the majority of those being broadband connections via cable modem versus DSL. The US government has a National Broadband Plan to connect 100 million households with high-speed access by 2020. With increases in mobile demands, access to the Internet via smartphones and tablets is increasingly popular. Consumers in the US are using their mobile devices to complete everyday life activities such as shopping, banking, and entertainment in addition to checking e-mails, searching, and social networking.

Mail

Mail in the US is very reliable. The USPS is the sole independent federal agency responsible for delivering mail in the country. In 2012, the USPS had a mail volume of almost 160,000 delivering to more than 152 million residential and business addresses through more than 24,000 delivery units. Direct marketing through the mail is commonplace in the US market. The USPS offers a service known as Every Door Direct Mail for businesses to use for their messages. Services are easily accessible online and can be targeted to reach specified residences.[13]

MEXICO

Country Characteristics[14]

Population: 116,220,947 (July 2013 est.)
Land Area: 1,943,945 sq. km
Language: Spanish, Indigenous languages (various Mayan, Nahuatl, and other regional languages)
Literacy Rate: 93.5%
Religion: Roman Catholic (82.7%), Protestant (1.6%), Jehovah's Witness (1.4%), other Evangelical Churches (5%), other (1.9%), none (4.7%), unspecified (2.7%)
GDP—Purchasing Power Parity: $1.788 trillion (2012 est.)
GDP per Capita—Purchasing Power Parity: $15,600 (2012 est.)
GDP—Real Growth Rate: 3.9% (2012 est.)
Inflation Rate—Consumer Price Index: 4.1% (2012 est.)

Cultural Characteristics[15]

It is important to note that Mexico has been undergoing significant changes in terms of its literacy rate, which has increased to 94%, as well as urbanization, which has been boosted to 78%. The Mexicans are seen to be a hospitable and warm group of people. Mexican attitude and behavior tend to be a combination of both European and Native American influences.

---

[13] "United States Postal Service Annual Report to Congress 2012," http://about.usps.com/publications/annual-report-comprehensive-statement-2012/annual-report-comprehensive-statement-2012.pdf

[14] *CIA World Factbook*, 2012.

[15] Harris and Moran, *Managing Cultural Differences*, 4th edition, pp. 226–231.

To the Mexican, the uniqueness of the individual should be recognized. Comparisons to the ways that others accomplish a task or in particular the way it is done in the US may be perceived as an insult. It is in this light that the Mexican society pays significant attention and respect to those who have had personal accomplishments in the industry or in the arts.[16]

The family plays a chief role in an average Mexican's life, and emphasis is placed on knowing one's family ties and connections prior to conducting business with them. Family relationships tend to be the basis upon which bonds are established and fostered. It is necessary for the foreign company to understand that questions posed regarding family are a means of ascertaining the well-being rather than as intrusion into privacy.[17]

Communication style is markedly different from that in the US. Most Mexicans speak in a circulatory manner and often avoid any direct references or conversations. In order to ensure that there is a pleasant atmosphere, Mexicans will tell their counterparts what they would want to hear, rather than mention anything harsh. This is not to say that they knowingly flatter in order to get their work done; the purpose is often to please the other party and to make them feel at home. Exhibit 21.4 points out some common Mexican gestures.

Exhibit 21.4

Mexican Gestures[18]

1. Longer handshakes and head bows (with women) are common when meeting someone for the first time.
2. The distance between individuals tends to be minimal, with excessive distance between two people being indicative of a sign of rudeness.
3. Arriving to corporate meetings on time is not of significant importance. In Mexico, arriving within 30 minutes is considered punctual.
4. It is considered impolite to talk with one's hands in the pockets, and if one places his/her hands on the hip that is perceived as a form of challenge.
5. It is important to be patient and respectful when conducting business. Many times, it is important to establish personal relationships before professional ones.

Business Characteristics

When approaching the organizational structure, it is important to note the hierarchy within the company. The top-down system is very much in effect and seniority is considered to be a discriminating factor between levels. It is advisable for the foreign concern to be aware of the ranking of officials and alter its decision-making style based on the hierarchical differentiation.

One major aspect to note is machismo—the concept of masculinity that infiltrates into business dealings as well. Though women are represented in several managerial positions, it is

---

[16] Peggy Kenna and Sondra Lucy, *Business Mexico: A Practical Guide to Understanding Mexican Business Culture* (Chicago, IL: Passport Books, 1994), pp. 18–23.

[17] Ibid.

[18] Adapted from "Mexico—Cultural Etiquette," http://www.ediplomat.com/np/cultural_etiquette/ce_mx.htm (Retrieved on May 6, 2014).

believed that only a man should earn the respect from society and demonstrate strong leadership qualities. This affects the manner in which business is conducted; assuming a woman represents the foreign concern, it would take a significant amount of coaxing before she is treated on equal terms to the male counterparts in the host country. Though this scenario is changing, the concept of machismo affects the manner in which market research is to be conducted.

Tangibility in presenting the results of a certain business deal is important to the Mexican. The style of the presentation is seen to be equal to that of the content. Contradicting their opinion on flexibility, Mexicans prefer to see their presentations in terms of visual aids and heavy word play. This becomes central to the market researcher in their effort to help understand or interpret Mexican interests and viewpoints.

Despite such emphasis on presentation, Mexicans prefer to give time in order to make a decision. When conducting business, it would be beneficial to have some time to talk to the Mexican counterparts and establish a personal relationship. Formality of agendas tends to suggest that the other party is not concerned over the overall well-being of the other. A business relationship to the Mexican is to be seen as an extension of the personal friendship that is to be formed prior to the deal. Time to them becomes a crucial element in order to establish that bond. Also, in order for them to avoid *losing face*, they may avoid immediate commitment or direct conversation. This stems from the fact that Mexicans tend to be fatalistic and try to attribute emphasis on the *right time* to conduct business. Time is perceived as relative and flexible to the Mexicans and the concept of *mañana*, which means *tomorrow*, filters into every aspect of business. This is not a means of procrastinating, but a way of evading a deadline or specific time.

Market Research in Mexico

When conducting research in Mexico, it would benefit the foreign company to select translators who would effectively communicate with the consumers and help analyze their reactions. This would be vital when conducting qualitative tests (such as focus groups), where reactions of the respondent form a significant aspect of the questioning process. It is also beneficial to have some support from a local representative who is well versed in Spanish and can address the several dialects in Mexico.

As with other Latin American countries, Mexicans tend to view the interviewing process as one where they can express their ideas and contribute. Rather than paying them the equivalent of what would be given in the US, it would be appropriate to contact a local representative to determine the ideal incentive. Providing the respondents with gifts is often seen to be more appealing as compared to paying money, which may be perceived as for services rendered.

As for secondary data, information regarding the 32 states and close to 2,403 municipalities are available. This would be data on age composition, income, housing, education, and sex, as well as information on specific industries including manufacturing, commerce, and financial services. One of the main sources of this information would be the National Institute of Statistics and Geography (*Insitituto Naciónal de Estadistica Geografía e Informatica*—INEGI).

In terms of infrastructure, Mexico is the second-largest information and communication technologies market in Latin America; however, telecommunications penetration rates are low in comparison to other developed nations. The deficiency in infrastructure and access is attributed to a lack of competition in the market and only moderate growth in real income.

Telecommunications[19]

There is one key player in Mexico's telecommunications market—Telmex, that accounts for 76% of the market share. As a result of the telecommunications monopoly in Mexico, growth in penetration rates will be driven by the decreasing cost of handsets and subscriptions as opposed to innovation. The telecommunications system in Mexico is considered to be developing at a moderate rate. There were 19.7 million fixed lines and 94.6 million mobile phones in use in 2011. This would imply that for the market researcher, contacting potential respondents over telephone or fax would not be too much of a problem; however, there are several impediments to this method of research.

Although there is adequate service availability for businesses and government, there is immense inconsistency between the degrees of growth between major cities in Mexico. While the population of Mexico is concentrated around the cities, there are a significant number of people who live in smaller towns and areas with vastly different incomes, purchasing capacities, and culture. As such, fixed line penetration in 2012 covered only 14% of the population.

In terms of mobile, penetration reached 89% in 2012. This is in stark contrast to other middle-income countries which have penetration rates nearing 200%. More growth is anticipated in the future as competition increases in the market. Subscriptions to include VoIP, mobile data, and Internet capabilities will lead the way as the 3G networks expand and 4G and LTE networks are introduced.

Internet

Internet usage and computer ownership has increased tremendously in Mexico in recent years. Increases in income and credit availability have made it possible for more people to acquire devices and services; however, access is still behind other comparable nations. As of 2012, Internet penetration is at 45%, with broadband connections accounting for 86% of connections.

Mail

The postal system in Mexico is not considered to be effective. This would hamper the use of mail surveys that would be a cost-efficient way to conduct market research. This suggests that the best possible way to conduct surveys in Mexico would be personal interviews or mall intercepts. This allows the required reach to the consumers, and at the same time provides one-to-one interaction, which is extremely important in a country where nonverbal communication is high.

CANADA

Country Characteristics[20]

Population: 34,568,211 (July 2013 est.)
Land Area: 9,093,507 sq. km

---

[19] "Industry Report Telecoms and Technology: Mexico," *Telecoms Industry Report: Mexico* 4, no. 3 (2012): 1–13.
[20] *CIA World Factbook*, 2012.

Language: English (official), French (official)
Literacy Rate: 99%
Religion: Roman Catholic (42.6%), United Church (9.5%), Anglican (6.8%), Baptist (2.4%), Lutheran (2%), other Christian (4.4%), Muslim (1.9%), other (11.8%), none (16%)
GDP—Purchasing Power Parity: $1.513 trillion (2012 est.)
GDP per Capita—Purchasing Power Parity: $43,400 (2012 est.)
GDP—Real Growth Rate: 1.8% (2012 est.)
Inflation Rate—Consumer Price Index: 1.5% (2012 est.)

Cultural Characteristics

Canada is composed of 12 provinces and territories that are extremely diverse. It is interesting to note that most of the major cities are located at the border of the US and Canada. Despite the physical proximity, there are several differences that make the Canadian market distinct from the US, and Canadians have undertaken measures to ensure that distinction. Among them are the protectionism laws implemented by the Canadian government which aim to prevent the erosion of Canadian culture and promote the production of Canadian cultural products, particularly publishing, film, and music. Exhibit 21.5 talks about the role of Canadian cultural protectionism in the digital age.

Exhibit 21.5

Does Canadian Culture Still Need Protection?[21]

Efforts in Canadian cultural protectionism have undergone major changes. Culture has become global and gone digital. Like other developed nations, the majority of Canadians essentially have the world at their fingertips through their computers and mobile devices. The Internet has made cultural products more accessible, but much harder to protect and control. As such, Canadians have access to a broad range of music, publications, and other types of entertainment via the World Wide Web. It is, therefore, inevitable that popular culture in Canada will be influenced by what is happening globally.

Due to the digital availability of many products, protectionism laws are slowly being relaxed to allow for businesses to enter the Canadian market. Many of the regulations that were instituted more than two decades ago no longer make sense in today's economy of digital consumption. For example, Target, a large retailer, was recently given permission to sell Canadian cultural products—bypassing a rule which states that all cultural products must be Canadian-controlled. The ruling suggests that Canada will be developing new cultural investment rules that will allow foreign companies to establish and operate cultural industries in the country.

Many believe that Canadian culture still needs protection from outside influence. In many cases, it is advisable and necessary to protect Canadian content. However, moving forward, the aim will be to preserve the culture but remove all-inclusive prohibitive rulings which put limitations on foreign ownership and ultimately hinder economic development.

---

[21] Adapted from "Canadian Culture Protection Rules Set for Update: Target Ruling Sets Stage for Reworking of Outdated Rules," July 17, 2012. Retrieved from http://www.marketwatch.com/story/canadian-culture-protection-rules-set-for-update-2012-07-17 on February 6, 2014.

Business Characteristics

Canadians do not take very well to comparisons made between the US and Canada. When considering business ties with Canada, it would be advisable to view it as a separate country rather than assume it to be a replica of the US. Also, it would be beneficial to note the differences between the English-speaking Canadian and the French regions, such as Quebec. For instance, this manifests in the manner in which they negotiate.[22] While the English Canadians adopt a more cooperative strategy in complying with the foreign party and business partner, the French Canadians compete in order to obtain the best possible strategy. These differences are represented in the Table 21.2.

The Canadians are more formal as compared to the Americans. It is necessary for the foreign company to understand the patterns of communication and take note of the hierarchy within the Canadian concern. The business culture thrives on establishing ties with the rest of the industry. It takes time to foster ties and this aspect becomes essential for a partner to note. Canadians tend to value relationships in business and take time when choosing a business partner or deciding upon a strategy that will optimize industry relations.[23]

The culture in Canada is so markedly influenced by European norms that it becomes imperative for the marketer to address the regions separately. For example, direct marketing efforts for the French-speaking population should be different, not only in language but also in size and color.

TABLE 21.2
INTERNAL VARIATIONS IN CANADA[24]

	English Canadians	French Canadians
Timing	Emphasis on punctuality	Laid-back approach
Body Language	Minimal movement	Expressive
Negotiation Concept	Abstract arguments	Instrumental arguments
Demeanor	Reserved	Demonstrative
Language Usage	Low-context	Nonverbal emphasis
Selection of Negotiators	Differentiation based on tangible aspects such as age and social class	Differentiation given less emphasis—more tolerance to inequality
Bargaining Strategy	Cooperation	Competition
Protocol Awareness	Not much attention paid	High concern
Trust	Tend to trust those willing to communicate	Evaluate the level of trust to place on information

---

[22] Harris and Moran, *Managing Cultural Differences*, 4th edition, p. 217.

[23] United States Postal Service, *International Marketing Resource Guide*, ed. William A. Delphos (Washington, DC: Braddock Communications, 1994), p. 85.

[24] Adapted from Harris and Moran, *Managing Cultural Differences*, 4th edition. "Canada Business Etiquette and Culture," http://international-business-etiquette.com/besite/canada.htm (Retrieved on May 6, 2014).

Market Research in Canada

Because of common language and long-standing ties between American and Canadian research firms, it is easier to conduct research in Canada than in Mexico.[25] Conducting focus groups as well as personal interviews is feasible if compensation (monetary or otherwise) is offered to the respondent. Most often, qualitative interviews help the researcher to arrive at a more specific niche in such a diverse market to target. In order to translate consumers' opinions more effectively, it would be helpful if a translator were available. A significant number of people speak English in Canada, yet certain terms or jargon, which may add color to the perspective of the respondent, should be duly noted.

The infrastructure in Canada is well developed and capable of effectively reaching consumers to conduct market research. Due to the diversity in the Canadian market, penetration rates of telecommunications can vary; however, improvements in services are being made to meet consumer demands.

Telecommunications[26]

Telecommunications infrastructure in Canada is considered to be extremely advanced, and conducting surveys over telephone, fax, or the Internet is relatively expedient and accurate. Perhaps one of the main problems that several companies face is that consumer groups complain regarding the invasion of privacy. Telemarketers and catalogs tend to aggravate consumers when researchers face low response rates from a select sample and try to inflate it to a larger figure to get a better representation.

In terms of telecommunications coverage, fixed line and mobile phones penetration were 46% and 78% in 2012, respectively. In recent years, fixed line usage has decreased as consumers switch to wireless services and VoIP. Mobile density rates are below those of other similarly developed nations in Europe and Asia due to many subscribers having only one line. In addition, there are users reluctant to navigate to wireless service in several areas and low competition in the market with three main providers.

Internet

Internet penetration reached 84% in 2012 with over 29 million Canadian users. In contrast to mobile, there is heavy competition in the Internet market, which leads to increases in bandwidth capacity and access. Broadband represents the majority of subscriptions, with there being an even split between cable and DSL. As with mobile, there are still pockets of the population that are resistant to adopting Internet services.

Mail

Mail delivery in Canada is performed by the government-owned Canada Post Corporation which provides reliable service throughout the country through its 7,000 retail locations. In 2011, Canada Post employed about 69,000 people; however, frequent labor issues have caused

[25] Jack Honomichl, "Research Cultures are Different in Mexico, Canada," *Marketing News* 27, no. 10 (1993): 12–13.

[26] "Telecoms and Technology Industry Report: Canada," *Telecoms Industry Report: Canada* 2 (2012): 1–12.

disruptions to the company's operations. Labor strikes and lookouts in recent years have threatened productivity and service suspensions.[27]

SUMMARY

This chapter deals with the practical aspects of conducting marketing research in North America—the US, Mexico, and Canada.[28] The three countries are geographically very close to one another and there is a lot of cross-border movement of goods, services, and personnel. Despite this, it would be a fallacy to assume that these countries are similar and the methods that work in one country will be just as effective in the other two. This chapter also presents some of the possible secondary data sources and the cultural peculiarities for these three countries.

---

[27] "Canada Post Corporation SWOT Analysis," 2012, *Canada Post Corporation SWOT Analysis*, pp. 1–9.
[28] For information on marketing research in the US, please refer to Aaker et al., *Marketing Research*, 6th edition; Kumar et al., *Essentials of Marketing Research*.

Section V

Future Directions in
Global Marketing Research

22 | The Future of Global Marketing Research   481

22

The Future of Global Marketing Research

INTRODUCTION

The nature of business today is truly global. Competitive convergence is driven by competitive necessity. The need to battle stronger and stronger global competitors, which are likely to emerge from larger and larger free markets, does not permit firms to ignore global trade customs and practices. At the same time, fewer trade barriers mean that those who do not rapidly adopt global best practices find fewer *safe* or *home* markets. The impact of one country on others has not been more significant ever before. The world economy today is highly interdependent. We see the effect of an economic downturn in one country affecting many more companies with the increased global outreach. The interest of the general public in day-to-day workings of the country and businesses has increased greatly in recent years. Consumers increasingly want more information about their products, how and where is the product manufactured, how the workers are treated in the factory, how well are the workers compensated, etc. There is a growing homogeneity of values among the youth across countries. Global products make the consumers even more connected to one another. Social media has changed the way consumers talk to one another over the Web. Along with the health of the global economy, the technological, social, and political factors seem to have an impact on global business today. As marketers and researchers, these factors play a vital role in the decision-making process; hence, one should be cognizant of these factors.

Given these developments and changes, a few trends and pointers emerge that will be important to note and follow. Some of them are presented here.

- Firms will be clearer in their information needs given the high cost of failure. Therefore, precise and relevant information is a necessity.
- There will be increased focus on geocentric orientation than ethnocentric orientation. As a result, products and services will be developed with global consumers in mind, and hence, the need for assessing their preferences.
- Given the multiple avenues for information flow, the benefits of an innovation can be communicated with little difficulty, and, therefore, the increased demand for the products.
- The ever-expanding realm of the Internet will transform the collection of secondary data.

- Potential sources of biases in data collection and responses will become common knowledge to experienced researchers and measures will be taken to generate more reliable data.
- With the data explosion, more sophisticated data analysis will be requested by clients sponsoring the research studies. However, this will also give rise to misuse of information.
- Global marketing research firms will increasingly be under pressure to reduce the costs of conducting global marketing research and yet preserve the usefulness of the research. Consequently, the need for constantly innovative solutions for each and every study will become the norm.
- The need for global marketing researchers will rise significantly every year as the world becomes one nation.

The world economic scene is constantly changing. Businesses need to be cognizant of these changes in the world that can possibly impact their business. The US witnessed a long period of steady growth and low inflation; however, the economic downturn of the economy in 2008 changed that story, as a result, affecting all major countries in the world. The BRICS (i.e., Brazil, Russia, India, China, and South Africa) attracted a lot of attention from developed economies for their massive growth potential; however, the recent economic slowdown in some of these countries is making the investors skeptical of their investments in these developing economies. Such information is extremely critical as it provides an important perspective while conducting business in these countries.

GLOBAL MARKETING RESEARCH: THE ROAD AHEAD

Global marketing research has grown in popularity and need over the last 20 years. However, it has taken a tremendous leap in the recent past, and growth in global marketing research is expected for a foreseeable future. This is because of the fact that as the world economy continues to grow, more countries are privatizing, new innovations keep occurring at a rapid pace, competitive pressures are increasing for firms, and more countries would like to export their products/services to seek surplus in trade or minimize the gap in trade activities. Technological advances offer more promise for the Internet and World Wide Web. Some important trends to look out for in various global marketing research activities are provided here.

Big Data

Big data has presented a plethora of opportunities for marketing companies today. *Big data* is the term used to describe how advancing trends in technology will change how information is delivered to businesses.[1] Big data helps companies seek market intelligence from the data and use this intelligence to get a business advantage.[2] The knowledge of customers and their preferences allows companies to better design their product/service offerings and make informed business decisions. Big data is characterized by the following three aspects:

---

[1] D. Liebenson, "Big Data: Opportunity or Threat for Market Research?," March 21, 2012, http://www.greenbookblog.org/2012/03/21/big-data-opportunity-or-threat-for-market-research/ (Retrieved on August 22, 2013).

[2] "Ideastorm," http://www.ideastorm.com/ (Retrieved on August 22, 2013).

Volume

The volume of data being collected today is incredible. As of 2012, around 2.5 exabytes of data, that is, 1 billion gigabytes of data, was created each day, and the number was expected to double every 40 minutes. The pace at which technology is changing our lives and thereby the way we collect, store, and interpret data is incredible. Wal-Mart handles more than a million customer transactions each hour and imports those into databases estimated to contain more than 2.5 petabytes of data.[3]

Velocity

It is about the pace, too. The speed of data creation and recording gives companies an edge over their competition. For example, Alex *Sandy* Pentland and his group at the MIT Media Lab used the location data from mobile phones of customers to deduce the number of people in Macy's parking lots on Black Friday, that is, the start of the Christmas shopping season in the US. The analysis of this information made it possible for them to estimate the retailer's sales on this critical day even before Macy's itself had recorded those sales.[4]

Variety

It is observed that around 85% of a firm's data is unstructured and not in numeric format. However, these are still an integral part of the analysis and the decision-making process.[5] This involves messages, status updates on social networking websites, images uploaded on such websites, location-based data from cell phones, etc. Technology changes are revolutionizing things quickly. Social networks, smartphones are all recent additions to our lives, yet they have become ubiquitous. Companies now track consumer-to-consumer portals to understand and measure reviews and opinions that consumers share with each other.

Big data is a recent development in the business world, and as such, many firms are still trying to understand how to get the most out of the plethora of information that is available. The biggest advantage of big data is the ability to alter choices for consumers based on their preference captured in real time. Companies are using big data to not only improve predictions but also to drive sales, and aid in better decision making, and improved customer solutions. However, unprecedented amounts of data also present managerial challenges. For instance, most often, big data needs advanced technology and software to process the information and glean insights. This could present a problem for firms that do not have the infrastructure to mine big data or are unable to meet the costs of the advanced software. With big data still in its nascent stage of development, it is expected that advancements in technology can bring about changes in its usage and implementation that will benefit companies.

Cloud Computing

As discussed earlier, there is a lot of data being generated today and that brings in the discussion about storage capacity in a firm. The cloud is revolutionizing how computing power is consumed by companies today. Forrester Research forecasts that channel partners will increase

---

[3] "Big Data Meets Big Data Analytics," SAS White Paper (Retrieved on August 21, 2013).

[4] A. McAfee and E. Brynjolfsson, "Big Data: The Management Revolution," *Harvard Business Review* 90, no. 10 (2012): 60–66.

[5] "Big Data Meets Big Data Analytics," SAS White Paper.

their reliance on cloud software and services from 22% to 27% from 2013 to 2014.[6] The basic concept of cloud computing works as follows—instead of companies buying their own computing capacity and storing it on-premise, they rent the required space from vendors. Vendors provide maintenance and troubleshooting assistance when needed. Consumers all over the world have used cloud computing in some form even though they might not actually know it. For example, using a Web-based third party e-mail service provider like Yahoo or Google Mail to send e-mails is the most basic form of cloud computing.

Cloud computing allows companies to focus on their core business and react to market conditions quicker. Cloud is extensively used for the purpose of storing, computing, and retrieving data. Cloud enables the client company and its users to access data remotely and also in real time to keep up with the dynamic nature of business today. Another critical use of cloud is the adaptability and customization feature that it brings in the system. This allows the users to access desired information on a point-and-click interface that is adapted to the user requirements and preferences. The automated and customizable platform has enabled companies to function more efficiently.

In addition, cloud computing is scalable. That is, the client company can scale up or down the capacity and service as per the demand, making it easy and cost-efficient for companies. For large and small companies alike, renting rather than owning computing resources seems to be the trend of the future, providing flexibility, customization, and cost savings. Some of the current companies who are cloud computing market leaders are Amazon (Amazon Web Services), Google, Microsoft, Salesforce.com, IBM, Rackspace, etc. However, not all companies have adopted the cloud-based systems whole-heartedly. Some are concerned about integration, data security, reliability, and effective cost savings.[7] Exhibit 22.1 provides some interesting statistics about cloud computing.

Exhibit 22.1

Cloud Computing Facts[8]

- 65% of the US companies shifted to cloud in 2011.
- 80% of the companies have experienced immense progress just within half year, that is, six months after moving to cloud.
- Microsoft spent 90% of its budget of Microsoft 2011 R&D on cloud computer products and strategies.
- Europe will likely be the first region of the world to unleash the true power of the Microsoft cloud, as an estimated 95% of all businesses in Europe are small- and medium-sized businesses (SMBs).

---

[6] "Roundup of Small and Medium Business Cloud Computing Forecasts and Market Estimates," 2013, http://www.forbes.com/sites/louiscolumbus/2013/07/30/roundup-of-small-medium-business-cloud-computing-forecasts-and-market-estimates-2013/ (Retrieved on August 21, 2013).

[7] A. McAfee, "What Every CEO Needs to Know About the Cloud," *Harvard Business Review* 89, no. 11 (2011): 124–132.

[8] Adapted from L. Johnson, "Cloud Computing: Fast Facts," *Business2Community*, January 23, 2013. Retrieved as on August 21, 2013 from http://www.business2community.com/tech-gadgets/cloud-computing-fast-facts-0386816

- 41% of the head executives and employees claim to be using some kind of cloud in their company.
- 64% of the companies have reduced waste and have low energy consumption levels after shifting to cloud computing.
- One of the most rapid expansions to the cloud came in September 2009, when Amazon was able to launch over 50,000 virtual machine instances within 24 hours—all in the same region.
- Google entered the enterprise cloud marketplace late when they launched Google Apps Premier Edition in early 2007.

The above-mentioned aspects of cloud computing can be applied easily and are economical, without any infrastructure or maintenance obstacles. In today's age, business software must be readily adaptable for accessing and processing data in relation to market changes and increasing profits. Being able to familiarize employees quicker with the newest apps grants them the ability to focus more on the work itself: helping, understanding, and serving customers.

The implementation of cloud computing has been growing at an exponential rate, with IDC research forecasting a threefold increase in cloud-related expenditures by 2013 (for a total of $44.2 billion). This industry, expected to surpass $140 billion by 2014, is growing across company boundaries, with midsize companies beginning to embrace these strategies in addition to the major multinational corporations already profiting from the cloud's customer relationship management (CRM) solutions.[9]

Sources of Data Collection

With nearly every business activity of companies and consumers being monitored and studied, it has been predicted that a zettabyte of data will be available on the Internet. In size, a zettabyte equals 1 billion terabytes of data, and is roughly equivalent to the information contained in 100 million libraries of Congress.[10] In fact, a recent research study by IDC indicates that we have already crossed the zettabyte threshold. The study also predicts that global data volume will increase by 29 times over the next 10 years.[11] A significant contributor to the data explosion has been the burgeoning of the Internet. With the emergence of peer-to-peer networks, conversations no longer have boundaries and limitations. These networks are increasingly influencing how customers interact with each other the world over, and how businesses use the social media tools to manage customer relationships. And more importantly, all these communications are data that have immense business value when mined appropriately.

Chapter 6 discussed the revolution Internet has brought about in marketing research. Online interactions and discussions among customers changed the way businesses look at information. Rich information was now available about the customer's behavior in the online world. In 2009 alone, more data was generated by individuals than in the entire history of

---

[9] J. Modavi, "CRM Consulting in the Age of Cloud Computing," 2010, AllThingsCRM.com (Retrieved August 23, 2013).

[10] David Kiron and Rebecca Shockley, "Creating Business Value with Analytics," *MIT Sloan Management Review* 53, no. 1 (2011): 57–63.

[11] "The 2011 IDC Digital Universe Study," June 2011, www.emc.com

mankind through 2008.[12] The information customers share with friends and relatives about themselves, their product purchases, and preferences empower companies operating today. For instance, purchasing a book through an online store not only gave the company information on which book the customer purchased but also information regarding other books that he/she considered before making that purchase.[13] Such type of information was not available earlier.

Customer engagement with each other and the firms have given rise to the abundance of information that is available for marketers today. The increase in online consumer interactions among each other has given companies a peek into personal information about consumers and their choices that are discussed in the online forum. Consumers' level of engagement varies from discussing about a brand among each other to actually engaging with the firm to provide feedback or suggestion to fully engaging in creation and contribution of content for the firm. Consumers not only exchange their thoughts and ideas with each other but also participate in co-creation activities with the firm. They engage with the firm to provide them with new ideas about possible improvements and suggest feedbacks.

Another level of engagement is crowd-sourcing where consumers are creating content and making decisions as against employees of a firm. An example of crowd-sourcing would be Samsung's Open Innovation program that involves participation in global consortia, forging links between the industry and top universities, cooperation with vendors, and operation of successful overseas research centers in order to seek flexible open innovative solutions for its technological and electronic products.[14] In 2013, Samsung partnered with a crowd-sourcing company, Marblar, to use NASA patents to innovate a range of new-tech projects.[15] Waze, a community-based traffic and navigation application, is a company that connects drivers who share real-time traffic and road information. Dell computers' Ideastorm is another website which encourages its users to submit their ideas, where over 19,000 ideas had been submitted as on August 2013.[16]

It is becoming clear that in this new digital age, the expansion and popularity of social media is not only increasing the engagement level of consumers, but also reducing the communication gap between consumers and companies in the B2C, B2B, and consumer-to-consumer (C2C) markets. These social interactions are becoming critical to business operations as formal marketing communication methods are slowly being reconsidered, and novel social media approaches are receiving constant attention.

Research Analysis and Techniques

As mentioned earlier, 85% of data a company deals with is unstructured, and non-numeric. New research techniques are devised to deal with the variety of data that is being generated.

---

[12] A. Weigend, "The Social Data Revolution(s), *Harvard Business Review* (2009). Retrieved from https://hbr.org/2009/05/the-social-data-revolution on March 5, 2014.

[13] McAfee and Brynjolfsson, Big Data: The Management Revolution."

[14] "Open Innovation Is a Samsung Initiative to Identify and Grow the Technologies and Infrastructure of the Future," http://www.samsung.com/global/business/semiconductor/aboutus/business/open-innovation/overview (Retrieved October 31, 2014).

[15] Steve O'Hear, "Marblar Wants You to Create Samsung's Next NASA-Powered Product and Get Paid", October 23, 2013, http://techcrunch.com/2013/10/23/marblar-samsung/ (Retrieved October 31, 2014).

[16] "Ideastorm," Retrieved on August 22, 2013 from http://www.ideastorm.com/

FIGURE 22.1

ILLUSTRATION OF WORLD CLOUD FOR THE WEBSITE WWW.DRVKUMAR.COM

Note: For illustration purpose only.

Text analysis has been around for some time; however, social media has changed the game completely. The conversations are a lot more informal, with slangs and jargons being used extensively. Also, the amount of information being shared is huge today. Researchers and technology experts are developing better and more sophisticated algorithms to measure all of the unstructured data that is available. Some of these are discussed in the following paragraphs.

Word Cloud or Tag Cloud

Techniques like Word Cloud or Tag Cloud allows users to visually depict the word content of the site. An example of a word cloud for a website is shown in Figure 22.1. In essence, Word Cloud quantifies the text that is chosen, wherein often-used words are represented in larger font. Word cloud is helpful in finding the main idea of the text selected or the most frequently used words and depicting all this is an easy-to-consume style for the reader.

Sentiment Analysis or Opinion Mining

Social media analytics is basically gathering data from blogs, websites, and social networking sites to aid in the decision-making process. Majority of the data being non-numeric, there is a need for analyzing the sentiments behind the discussions that are carried on online. Therefore, sentiment analysis is increasingly gaining popularity. The sentiment analysis process actually involves text analytics, linguistics, and accepted language processing to determine and dig subjective information from source materials.[17] To appropriately identify the meaning of the information shared by the consumers, companies are now using sentiment analysis to help them uncover the intended meaning behind consumer opinions and reviews. Companies such as Best Buy, Viacom, Paramount Pictures, Cisco Systems, and Intuit are using sentiment analysis to improve CRM strategies and provide more targeted offerings.

---

[17] A. Aspili, "Who Benefits from Sentiment Analysis?" *Social Media Today*, January 23, 2013. Retrieved as on August 22, 2013 from http://socialmediatoday.com/aspilialleli/1180346/who-benefits-sentiment-analysis

With consumers clearly wanting to be heard, social tools such as blogs, micro blogs, social networking sites, and review portals have gained significant traction. Twitter, for example, enables companies to sort information shared by demography, topic of interest, or any other preferred criterion. For businesses, sentiment analysis immediately lets them know the tone of the conversations about their product or service in social media and find the talking points about their brands—Are the conversations primarily positive or negative or neutral?

A tool that is being increasingly used is text analytics. This tool collects text data on consumer insights not only from Web platforms such as the social media, but also from news articles or information databases. The text analytics provides an objective summary of consumer reactions and responses to a particular company, product, or service. The market for text analytics is expected to double from $499 million in 2011 to almost $1 billion in 2014, according to a report by Forrester Research.[18]

Apart from this, there are several tools available online for analyzing sentiments. Sentiment140 is one such free tool that allows users to discover the sentiment of a brand, product, or topic on Twitter. An illustration of the sentiment analysis for the word "twitter" on Sentiment140 is shown in Figure 22.2.

FIGURE 22.2
SENTIMENT ANALYSIS FOR TWITTER USING SENTIMENT140[19]

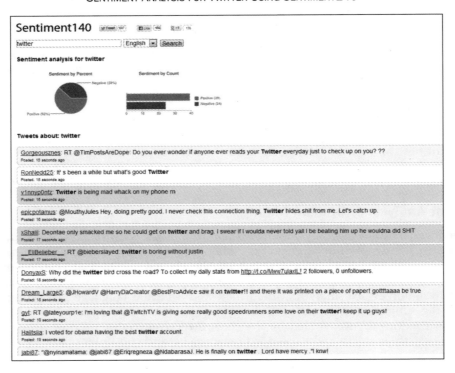

[18] R. King, "Sentiment Analysis Gives Companies Insight into Consumer Opinion," 2011. Retrieved August 23, 2013, from www.businessweek.com
[19] "Sentiment140 Tool." Retrieved as on August 22, 2013 from http://www.sentiment140.com/search?query=twitter&hl=en

Privacy

As companies continue to expand into international markets, the need to collect and use data about their current and potential customers to improve their business performance and marketing initiatives becomes imperative. By obtaining information on customers' transactions and behaviors, as well as their sociodemographic profiles, companies can better understand their customers' preferences and desires. However, companies are also finding a growing reluctance among customers, who prefer not to disclose their personal information or allow tracking of their behaviors out of their concerns for privacy.[20] This concern stems from the data theft or data leaks that continue to occur with considerable periodicity. One such example is the ChoicePoint's sale of 169,000 records in 2005 to inadequately vetted bogus businesses.[21] Such incidents and its related concerns have resulted in growing governmental regulations related to the gathering and use of personal information. These regulations are also raising new obstacles for companies. Privacy concerns can arise from different sources, such as the collection of information, the control over the collected data, errors in using and representing information, the improper access to information, and government regulations in collecting and using data.[22]

Collection of Information

The collection of information refers to "the degree to which a person is concerned about the amount of individual specific data possessed by others relative to the value of benefits received." In other words, if a consumer volunteers to share their information with a company, it is important to know the rules that will regulate the nature of how that information is shared across multiple companies, and in some cases across multiple countries also. Therefore, collection comprises customer concerns about the amount of and the way in which personal information is collected.

Control Over Information

Control refers to a person's degree of "control over personal information as manifested by the existence of voice (i.e., approval, modification) or exit (i.e., opt-out)."[23] This pertains to the approval, modification, and the rights to opt-in and opt-out of sharing information that customers have over their personal data. With increasing information and business operations across country borders, clear indications regarding opt-in and opt-out clauses are essential for ethical usage of data. Table 22.1 provides the opt-in/opt-out rules for various direct marketing channels in Ireland.

---

[20] J. Wirtz and M. O. Lwin, "Regulatory Focus Theory, Trust, and Privacy Concerns," *Journal of Service Research* 12, no. 2 (2009): 190–207.

[21] Bob Sullivan, "ChoicePoint to Pay $15 Million over Data Breach," January 26, 2006. Accessed on August 23, 2013 from http://www.nbcnews.com/id/11030692/ns/technology_and_science-security/t/choicepoint-pay-million-over-data-breach/#.Uhs_kD_9X1Z

[22] V. Kumar and Werner Reinartz, *Customer Relationship Management: Concept, Strategy, and Tools* (Berlin: Springer-Verlag, 2012).

[23] N. K. Malhotra, S. S. Kim, and J. Agarwal, "Internet Users' Information Privacy Concerns (IUIPC): The Construct, the Scale, and a Causal Model," *Information Systems Research* 15, no. 4 (2004): 336–355.

TABLE 22.1

OPT-IN/OPT-OUT RULES FOR DIRECT MARKETING CHANNELS IN IRELAND[24]

	Postal Marketing	Text/E-mail Marketing	Phone Marketing to Landlines	Fax Marketing	Phone Marketing to Mobile Phones
Individual Customer	Opt-out	Opt-out (provided similar product or service)	Opt-out	Opt-out	Opt-out
Individual Non-Customer	Opt-out	Opt-in	Opt-in if on NDD, Opt-out otherwise	Opt-in	Opt-in
Business Contacts (Customer and Non-Customer)	Opt-out	Opt-out	Opt-in if on NDD, Opt-out otherwise	Opt-in if on NDD, Opt-out otherwise	Opt-in

Notes: (1) NDD refers to the National Directory Database that contains telephone listing of landline subscribers, and also operates as a form of national telemarketing opt-out register.

(2) *Opt-in* indicates that an individual can be marketed to only if they have provided explicit consent to do so.

(3) *Opt-out* indicates that an individual can be marketed to provided they have been given the option not to receive such marketing and they have not availed of this option.

Errors in the Information

Errors denote concerns that "protections against both deliberate and accidental errors in the data are not adequate."[25] The errors could range from data entry errors to duplication entries to incomplete user information to the more damaging more errors such as loss of records. Recently, the Australian bank ANZ bank lost thousands of customer records containing tax file numbers during a routine system upgrade. As a result, thousands were charged tax in error.[26] To prevent such errors from occurring, it is important that all personal information in computer databases be double-checked for accuracy. In this regard, companies should undertake necessary efforts to ensure data accuracy. Further, relevant provisions and procedures to identify and correct errors in databases must be in place for better data management.

Improper Access to Information

This aspect relates to the "concerns that data are readily available to parties not authorized to use it."[27] The unauthorized usage of information, also known as data leakage, could be

---

[24] *Direct Marketing—A General Guide For Data Controllers*, Office of the Data Protection Commissioner, Ireland. Accessed on August 23, 2013 from http://www.dataprotection.ie/viewdoc.asp?DocID=905

[25] M. H. Harris, G. Van Hoye, and F. Lievens, "Privacy and Attitudes Towards Internet Based Selection Systems: A Cross Cultural Comparison," *International Journal of Selection and Assessment* 11, no. 2–3 (2003): 230–236.

[26] Charis Palmer, "ANZ Customer Data Lost During System Upgrade," June 3, 2013. Accessed on August 23, 2013 from http://www.itnews.com.au/News/345317,anz-customer-data-lost-during-system-upgrade.aspx

[27] Harris et al., "Privacy and Attitudes Towards Internet Based Selection Systems."

intentional or unintentional in nature. Nevertheless, the repercussions of a data leak are always bad for the organizations and harrowing for their customers. In recent times, several such instances have occurred. Notable among them are the Epsilon data breach wherein the world's largest permission-based e-mail marketing provider lost a massive amount of customer data belonging to nearly 50 of their 2,500 clients;[28] the Sony data leak from their online gaming website that exposed more than 100 million customer records including direct debit records for customers in Austria, Germany, the Netherlands, and Spain;[29] the Verizon Wireless data leak of 300,000 customers containing information such as serial numbers, names, addresses, date of customer enrolment, passwords, and phone numbers;[30] and the data leak of the Australian telecommunications firm Telstra that lost spreadsheets containing customer information and they showed up on search engines.[31] To prevent such occurrences, companies must devote more resources to safeguard personal information by curbing such unauthorized access. Further, companies must secure personal data by making sure unauthorized personnel from within the company do not get access to such information.

Government Regulations

The presence or absence of government regulations regarding data privacy has important consequences. Whereas the presence of a strong government data privacy policy provides a sense of security and support for users in sharing information with the companies, a lack thereof is likely to scare people from sharing information. Further, it has been shown that a perceived lack of business policy or governmental regulation results in greater privacy concerns,[32] and that the differences in privacy regulations highlight cross-national differences in privacy concerns. For instance, Great Britain maintains a closed-circuit television surveillance system in public and private sectors and extensive government and commercial databases, without the permission of the people. Similarly, the USA Patriot Act endows significant surveillance and investigative powers to law enforcement agencies that include permission to search telephone, e-mail communications, and the medical, financial, and other records of US citizens without their consent.[33]

These approaches represent the differences in their cultural and societal values and, thus, their different perceptions of customer privacy. In the German context, it is believed that the threat to personal information such as name and image is primarily from the media, while

---

[28] Mike Lennon, "Massive Breach at Epsilon Compromises Customer Lists of Major Brands," April 2, 2011. Accessed on August 23, 2013 from http://www.securityweek.com/massive-breach-epsilon-compromises-customer-lists-major-brands

[29] Charles Arthur, "Sony Suffers Second Data Breach with Theft of 25m More User Details," May 3, 2011. Accessed on August 23, 2013 from http://www.theguardian.com/technology/blog/2011/may/03/sony-data-breach-online-entertainment

[30] Emil Protalinski, "After Hacker Disappears from Twitter, Verizon Reveals Customer Data Was Leaked by a Marketing Firm," December 23, 2012. Accessed on August 23, 2013 from http://thenextweb.com/insider/2012/12/23/after-hacker-disappears-from-twitter-verizon-reveals-customer-data-was-leaked-by-a-marketing-firm/

[31] Michael Lee, "Telstra Apologetic After Old Customer Data Leaks Online," May 16, 2013. Accessed on August 23, 2013 from http://www.zdnet.com/au/telstra-apologetic-after-old-customer-data-leaks-online-7000015474/

[32] J. Wirtz, M. O. Lwin, and J. D. Williams, "Causes and Consequences of Consumer Online Privacy Concern," *International Journal of Service Industry Management* 18, no. 4 (2007): 326–348.

[33] EPIC "US Patriot Act," 2011. Accessed on August 23, 2013 from http://epic.org/privacy/terrorism/usapatriot/#introduction

in the US context, the threat is viewed to be arising from the government. Such differences find their origin in the countries' histories, wherein the German outlook can be viewed as an outcome to fascism and the societal structures, and the American outlook stems from the concept of minimal governmental intervention in personal liberty.[34] In this light, Table 22.2 presents customer privacy regulations in the US and Germany.

Given these diverse regulations, companies (especially those operating in multiple countries) must constantly update themselves of the different legal requirements and the changes that occur. This is because when customer privacy laws are not adhered to, companies not only have to face the legal consequences, but also lose credibility in the foreign market(s). Further, with increased international trade and online trade, this area is a cause for serious consideration for companies as international laws and regulations have to be followed for market access.

Although the above-mentioned trends are not exhaustive, they provide a flavor and indication of the areas that warrant attention in the future. The information provided in this book should assist the readers to be better prepared for conducting global marketing research in the 21st century.

TABLE 22.2
CUSTOMER PRIVACY REGULATIONS IN THE US AND GERMANY[35]

	US	Germany
Cold calling (i.e., contacting prospective clients or customers with unexpected telephone calls)	Allowed (if not on Robinson List)	Forbidden
Unsolicited commercial e-mails (i.e., commercial electronic messages, typically sent out in bulk without any prior request or consent given by the consumer)	Forbidden	Forbidden
Cross-country data transfer (US to Germany and vice-versa) (i.e., transfer of customer-related data to a different country than where it has been collected, such as when consumers make online purchases from sellers located in a different country)	Allowed	Only allowed with Safe Harbor compliance
Data transfer to third parties (without consent) (i.e., provision of personal data to other companies, such as marketing service providers, without notifying the customer)	Allowed	Forbidden
Right to opt out from data collection (i.e., upon providing their personal information, customers are able to deny any further use of their data)	Not given	Given

---

[34] J. Q. Whitman, "The Two Western Cultures of Privacy: Dignity Versus Liberty," *Yale Law Journal* 113, no. 6 (2004): 1151–1221.

[35] V. Kumar and Werner Reinartz, *Customer Relationship Management: Concept, Strategy, and Tools* (Berlin: Springer-Verlag, 2012).

Case Studies*

Case I	Starbucks—Going to the Source	495
Case II	Tesla's Trademark Troubles	500
Case III	Segmenting Indian Households	507
Case IV	Subaru—A Problem of Plenty	509
Case V	Millennials at Work	514

* These cases were prepared by V. Kumar and Bharath Rajan for the purpose of classroom discussion.

Case I: Starbucks— Going to the Source

Starbucks is a premium coffee chain that sells specialty coffee in 60 countries around the world. Along with coffee, the company also sells other beverages and a variety of fresh food items, through company-operated stores and licensed outlets. In addition to the flagship Starbucks brand, the company also sells a range of coffee and tea products, and licenses their trademarks to other key accounts. Referred to as the Channel Development segment, this portfolio includes whole bean and ground coffees, premium Tazo® teas, Starbucks VIA® Ready Brew, Starbucks® coffee and Tazo® tea K-Cup® portion packs, a variety of ready-to-drink beverages, such as Starbucks Refreshers™ beverages, and other branded products sold worldwide through channels such as grocery stores, warehouse clubs, convenience stores, and US food-service accounts. Table CSI.1 presents the number of Starbucks outlets across the world over a five-year period.

BREWING SUCCESS

The key to Starbucks' success is largely in the sourcing of its coffee beans. The company purchases green coffee beans from multiple coffee-producing regions around the world and custom roast them to suit many blends and single-origin coffees. The company works closely with coffee producers, outside trading companies, and exporters for the supply of green coffee. As part of giving back to the community, Starbucks operates Farmer Support Centers in six countries that are staffed with agricultural experts who work with coffee farming communities to promote best practices in coffee production. In the markets that Starbucks operates in, they primarily compete against quick-service restaurants, the ready-to-drink beverage market, and specialty coffee shops. Table CSI.2 provides the revenue mix of Starbucks from around the world and the growth rate for the past five years.

This business setup has been rewarding for Starbucks with the 2012 financial year turning out to be a resounding success. Their total net revenues increased 14% to $13.3 billion, significantly contributed by global comparable store sales growth of 7% and a 50% increase in Channel Development segment revenue. This commendable growth produced higher operating margins and net earnings compared to previous years, apart from securing them from higher commodity costs, mostly coffee. Table CSI.3 presents the financial position of Starbucks.

TABLE CSI.1

STARBUCKS STORES AROUND THE WORLD[1]

	2012		2011		2010		2009		2008	
	Number	YOY Growth (%)	Number	YOY Growth (%)	Number	YOY Growth (%)	Number	YOY Growth (%)	Number	YOY Growth
Americas										
Company-Owned	7,857	3	7,623	1	7,580	0	7,613	–5	8,030	NA
Licensed Stores	5,046	6	4,776	–5	5,044	2	4,933	2	4,832	NA
Europe, Middle East and Africa (EMEA)										
Company-Owned	882	1	872	3	847	–7	911	2	891	NA
Licensed Stores	987	11	886	10	807	14	707	16	609	NA
China and Asia-Pacific (CAP)										
Company-Owned	666	30	512	17	439	7	409	6	385	NA
Licensed Stores	2,628	13	2,334	9	2,141	4	2,062	7	1,933	NA
Total	18,066	6	17,003	1	16,858	1	16,635	0	16,680	NA

[1] Compiled from company annual reports.

TABLE CSI.2
REVENUE MIX AND GROWTH OF STARBUCKS[2]

	Beverage	Food	Packaged and Single Serve Coffee	Others	Total
2012					
Total revenues ($ million)	7,838	2,092	2,001	1,366	13,299
Revenue share in total (%)	59	16	15	10	100
YOY growth (%)	9	4	38	33	14
2011					
Total revenues ($ million)	7,217	2,008	1,451	1,024	11,700
Revenue share in total (%)	62	17	12	9	100
YOY growth (%)	7	7	28	8	9
2010					
Total revenues ($ million)	6,750	1,878	1,131	947	10,707
Revenue share in total (%)	63	18	11	9	100
YOY growth (%)	8	12	17	6	10
2009					
Total revenues ($ million)	6,238	1,680	965	890	9,774
Revenue share in total (%)	64	17	10	9	100
YOY growth (%)	(–6)	11	(–2)	(–27)	(–6)
2008					
Total revenues ($ million)	6,663	1,511	987	1,220	10,383
Revenue share in total (%)	64	15	10	12	100
YOY growth (%)	11	13	8	7	10

Note: Others include royalty and licensing revenues, beverage-related ingredients, packaging, and other merchandise.

TABLE CSI.3
STARBUCKS FINANCIAL INFORMATION[3]

(in millions)	2012	2011	2010	2009	2008
Americas					
Total net revenues	9,936	9,065	7,560	7,061	*7,491
Operating income/(loss)	2,074	1,842	1,291	530	454

(Table CSI.3 Contd)

[2] Compiled from company annual reports.
[3] Ibid.

(Table CSI.3 Contd)

(in millions)	2012	2011	2010	2009	2008
International					
Total net revenues	1,862	1,598	2,288	1,914	2,099
Operating income/(loss)	263	233	225	91	108
Channel Development					
Total net revenues	1,292	860	707	674	680
Operating income/(loss)	348	287	261	281	269
Others					
Total net revenues	208	175	150	124	111
Operating income/(loss)	(689)	(635)	(358)	(341)	(328)
Total					
Total net revenues	13,299	11,700	10,707	9,774	10,383
Operating income/(loss)	1,997	1,728	1,419	562	503

HOLA COLOMBIA!

The company that has been slow and cautious in its international expansion is now planning its entry into Colombia. The company recently announced plans to open their first Colombian store in the capital city of Bogota and hopes to open at least 50 more outlets around the country over the next five years.

The premium coffee chain's first store in Latin America was in Puerto Rico in September 2002. Soon after, they entered other countries in the region that included Peru, Chile, Costa Rica, Brazil, Argentina, Guatemala, and El Salvador, among others. Despite the slow expansion in Latin America, the company now looks poised to make up for lost time. At last count, the company operates nearly 650 stores in the Latin American region.

WHY COLOMBIA NOW?

Starbucks' entry into Colombia is an important development with respect to their international expansions efforts, as the company has exported coffee beans from Colombia for more than four decades. This move by Starbucks comes in the wake of other significant marketplace developments. First, the announcement comes at a time of ongoing strike by Colombian coffee farmers demanding more subsidies from the government due to low global prices. Between 2011 and 2012, the prices of coffee beans fell nearly 40%. Second, since Colombia exports most of its coffee beans, local consumers complain that coffee available in local coffee stores are from other countries, such as Ecuador, and not homegrown. The desire to have homegrown coffee is discernible among the Colombian consumers. Finally, a military crackdown on drug-funded rebel groups has made Colombia more attractive to foreign firms as an investment destination.

THE GO-TO-MARKET STRATEGY

Starbucks' new coffee shops will be run by a joint venture between Alsea, a Mexican restaurant company that operates Starbucks stores in Latin America, and Colcafe, a subsidiary of Grupo Nutresa, a Colombian food company. This move to involve local companies to manage the coffee shops is expected to prepare Starbucks in addressing the local needs and consumer requirements better. In terms of local competition, Starbucks will be up against local chains such as Oma and Juan Valdez. A significant competitor would also be the street vendors who sell inexpensive, sweet coffee drinks.

As a preparatory step in tackling the competition, Starbucks has decided to offer Colombian customers locally sourced and roasted espresso, drip, and packaged coffee. According to the company's Chief Executive Howard Schultz, "We knew going in that when we opened in Colombia we would roast coffee there. It would be disrespectful, given the long history of farming in Colombia, to send coffee back to America to be roasted." While the premium-charging coffee company did not reveal its pricing structure in Colombia, Schultz said that Starbucks would not undercut the country's farmer-owned Juan Valdez chain and is likely to charge a little more to create Starbucks *home-from-home* lounge environment. He also emphasized that the company wanted to make a *respectful* entry into a country that has been a key coffee supplier for many years.

QUESTIONS FOR DISCUSSION

1. As Starbucks prepares to enter Colombia, what are the issues that it should address to make the entry smooth and successful?
2. What kind of information is needed to obtain the issues identified in Question 1? What are the possible sources of the required information?
3. In your opinion, what other Latin American countries are prime markets that Starbucks should target? Provide reasons for your choices.

SOURCES

1. Company annual reports.
2. Atossa Araxia Abrahamian, "Starbucks to Sell Home-Grown Coffee to the Colombians," *Reuters*, August 26, 2013.
3. Julie Jargon and Dan Molinski, "Starbucks to Serve Locally Grown Coffee in Colombia," *Wall Street Journal*, August 26, 2013.

Case II:
Tesla's Trademark Troubles

Tesla Motors Inc. is an automobile company that designs, manufactures, and sells electric cars and electric vehicle powertrain components. Maker of successful models such as the Roadster (the first fully electric sports car), the Model S (fully electric luxury sedan), and the Model X (fully electric crossover utility vehicle), the company prides itself in pioneering the concept of electric cars and aspires to bringing it within the reach of the average consumer. In addition to producing electric cars, Tesla also markets electric powertrain components, including lithium-ion battery packs to other automakers, and have supplied components to companies such as Daimler, Toyota, and Panasonic.

REVVING IT UP

The company has been clocking a steady performance since launching their first car in 2008. As of December 2012, the company had realized total revenues of $413.3 million, representing an increase of 102% over the previous year. Their revenue is derived from two sources—automotive sales and development services. Their automotive sales revenue in 2012 amounted to $385.7 million, an increase of nearly 160% over 2011. The reason for this surge was the continued sale of Model S in North America, and the international sales of the Roadster. However, the company did experience lower revenues from their development services arm owing to the completion of the Daimler and Toyota projects.

Despite the consecutive losses posted by the company, the company's market capitalization has skyrocketed. It is currently valued at $20 billion, or one-third of Ford's current value. The company's share has gone up by nearly 390% in 2013, and is worth more than other companies such as Suzuki, Mazda, and Fiat. The market optimism is so high that even Tesla's CEO Elon Musk admitted to this recently. He said,

> I actually think that the value of Tesla right now is… I mean the market's being very generous, and they're obviously giving us a lot of credit for future execution, so we'll do our best to honor the faith the market has placed in us…. But I really feel like the valuation we've gotten, that we have right now, is more than, is more than we have any right to deserve, honestly.[1]

Tesla's financial performance is provided in Table CSII.1.

---

[1] Zachary Shahan. Shocker: Elon Musk Humble About Tesla Stock (video). EVObsession, August 28, 2013. Retrieved from http://evobsession.com/shocker-elon-musk-humble-tesla-stock-video/ on April 7, 2014.

TABLE CSII.1

SELECTED FINANCIAL INFORMATION OF TESLA[2]

(in $ Thousands)	2012	2011	2010	2009	2008
Revenues					
Automotive Sales	385,699	148,568	97,078	111,943	14,742
Development Services	27,557	55,674	19,666	–	–
Total Revenues	413,256	204,242	116,744	111,943	14,742
Cost of Revenues					
Automotive Sales	371,658	115,482	79,982	102,408	15,883
Development Services	11,531	27,165	6,031	–	–
Total Cost of Revenues	383,189	142,647	30,731	9,535	(1,141)
Operating Expenses					
R&D Expenses	273,978	208,981	92,996	19,282	53,714
SG&A Expenses	150,372	104,102	84,573	42,150	23,649
Total Expenses	424,350	313,083	177,569	61,432	77,363
Net loss after taxes	(396,213)	(254,411)	(154,328)	(55,740)	(82,782)

MARKETING APPROACH

The company markets and sells cars directly to consumers through an international network of company-owned stores and galleries located at major metro cities around the world. At present, the company operates a network of stores and galleries in North America, Europe, and Asia, and plans to open more such outlets in the future. Most of these stores also provide car service along with retail sales. However, in the coming years, the company intends to build separate sales and service locations in several markets they operate in.

The company believes that owning and operating their stores offers them advantages by way of providing superior customer experience, achieving operational efficiencies, and capturing sales and service revenues. Further, the company believes that such a distribution setup enables them to better control costs of inventory, manage warranty service and pricing, maintain and strengthen the Tesla brand, and obtain rapid customer feedback. Additionally, the company is of the opinion that owning a sales network will avoid the conflict of interest in the traditional dealership structure, and will help them acquire the revenue from the service, and sale of warranty parts and repairs by a dealer, which is a key source of revenue and profit for the dealer.

The company hopes that their focused marketing strategy will help them achieve their primary marketing goals that comprise of: (a) generating demand for the vehicles and driving leads to the sales teams; (b) building long-term brand awareness and managing corporate

---

[2] Compiled from company annual reports.

reputation; (c) managing the existing customer base to create loyalty and customer referrals; and (d) incorporating customer inputs into the product development process.

With such strong business fundamentals and clear agendas, the company hopes to continue receiving media attention about their company and their cars. Tesla has realized that the media coverage and positive word-of-mouth have been the primary drivers of their sales leads and have helped them achieve sales without traditional advertising and at relatively low marketing costs. In addition to the judicious use of media and viral marketing efforts, the company also uses traditional means of advertising including product placement in a variety of media outlets and pay-per-click advertisements on websites and applications relevant to the target demographics.

Given the high levels of competition in the automotive industry, Tesla believes that the impact of stringent safety and regulatory requirements and vehicle emissions norms, technological advances in powertrain and consumer electronics components, and changing customer needs and expectations will continue to grow stronger and will direct the industry in the direction of electric-based vehicles.

COMPETITIVE LANDSCAPE

The electric vehicle segment consists of three major powertrain electrification categories:

- *Electric vehicles* that are powered only by a single on-board energy storage system such as a battery pack or fuel cell, which is refueled directly from a power source. For example, Tesla Roadster and Model S.
- *Plug-in hybrid vehicles* that are powered by both a battery pack and an internal combustion engine with refueling options that include traditional petroleum fuels for the engine and electricity for the battery pack. The internal combustion engine can either work alongside the electric motor to power the wheels, or be used only to recharge the battery. For example, Chevrolet Volt.
- *Hybrid electric vehicles* that are powered by both a battery pack and an internal combustion engine with only the traditional petroleum fuels as the refueling option. The battery pack is charged via regenerative braking. For example, Toyota Prius.

Tesla has realized that nearly all leading automobile companies possess significantly greater financial, technical, manufacturing, and marketing resources than them, and are constantly identifying ways to devote greater amount of resources to the design, development, manufacturing, distribution, promotion, sale, and support of their cars. In addition to a stronger brand name and a longer market presence, the competitors of Tesla typically possess the wherewithal to respond quickly to issues regarding competitive market actions, the emergence of new technologies, making changes or amendments to their vehicles through recalls, vehicle design and development, and overall marketing initiatives.

In light of this complex market structure and composition, Tesla has chosen to rely exclusively on the design and development of electric vehicles and electric vehicle components as the basis of competition in the global marketplace. To help them in maintain this focus, Tesla has chosen to devote more resources on R&D to help them build better and superior vehicles.

BETTING BIG ON RESEARCH & DEVELOPMENT (R&D)

Tesla spends a significant amount of resources on its R&D initiatives. The R&D expenses for 2012 were $274.0 million, representing a 31% increase over 2011. Activities included under R&D included manufacturing readiness, process validation, prototype generation, and product testing at various conditions simulating the various country markets.

Through the company's R&D efforts, the primary focus is on powertrain and vehicle engineering. In fact, Tesla's core intellectual property is contained within the electric powertrain and its constituents, such as the battery pack, the power electronics, the motor, the gearbox, and the software that unifies it into a system. All these were designed in-house and were incorporated in the vastly successful Roadster and Model S. The company also plans to incorporate these designs in their future vehicle developments. The ingenuity in design is evident from the modular design of their powertrain that is very compact and contains far fewer moving parts than the internal combustion powertrain. These features enable us to adapt it for a variety of applications, and have contributed significantly to the success of their vehicles. In addition to this core focus, Tesla also has in-house capabilities to design and engineer bodies, chassis, interiors, heating and cooling, and low-voltage electrical systems, along with computer-aided design and crash test simulations. This has significantly added to Tesla's engineering prowess and has reduced the product development time of their models.

From the level of investments the company has made on R&D efforts, it is understandable that such efforts are protected as their intellectual property. To a large extent, the company has also succeeded in doing so. Tesla has a combination of patents, patent applications, and trade secrets, including know-how, employee and third-party non-disclosure agreements, copyright laws, trademarks, intellectual property licenses, and other contractual rights to establish and protect their proprietary rights in their technology. As of 2012, Tesla had 117 issued patents and more than 258 pending patent applications with the US Patent and Trademark Office and internationally in a broad range of areas. With the company's intention to continue its investments in R&D efforts, it becomes evident that the intellectual property is imperative to their successful presence in the marketplace.

TO THE "T"

Tesla's entry into the Far East began with their launch of the Roadster in Japan in 2010. Since then, the company has increased their presence by entering neighboring markets such as Hong Kong and China. While they seem to have found viable growth markets in the Far East nations, it is not without challenges.

When Tesla made their announcement to enter China, they soon found that their trademark logo and T-shaped badge icon had already been taken by Zhan Baosheng, a young Chinese businessman who claims to be a legitimate electric-car entrepreneur seeking to make and market a *Tesla* electric sedan in China. In 2006, Zhan filed claims to the use of the word *Tesla* in English, the phonetic translation of *Tesla* in Chinese characters, Tesla Motors' T-shaped badge, and Tesla's company logo that includes the badge, the words *Tesla Motors* and the word *Tesla* in the company's distinctive font. Now, Tesla has filed claims in the Chinese court to seek rights to use the name and the logo.

While one might think Tesla can expect a straightforward victory, the reality is far from it. Too often, when Western companies set up operations in China, they encounter such issues. Legal experts opine that such problems constantly arise when companies venture into international markets only to come across people or companies seeking to cash in on foreign brand identities by securing local commercial rights to their logos and names. With respect to China's trademark regime, the case is all too different. It is usually a contest to see who secures the right of use from the Chinese Trademark Office, with the first person/company to get the approval emerging as the winner. When a company fails to get the rights registered, it has two recourses—albeit expensive ones. Take the claim to the court and wage a prolonged legal battle, or settle out of court by buying the trademark rights from the owner.

Apple Inc. had to go through these options in China when they found that the *iPad* had already been registered, nearly a decade before they launched their first iPad. To secure the rights, the company had to shell out $60 million to settle a lawsuit brought on by the local company that owned the rights. Even Ferrari SpA went through these legal hassles when they lost a decade-long trademark battle in 2007. They filed a claim against a Chinese department store that used a *prancing horse* similar to that of Ferrari's. Despite valuable time and resources spent by Ferrari, the company lost; the Chinese court ruled that Ferrari was not sufficiently well-known in China. This also explains why companies such as Coca-Cola (with their red and white effervescent logo), McDonald's (with their golden arches), Disney (with their characters such as Mickey Mouse and Donald Duck), and the Ford (with their discernible blue oval) enjoy significant trademark protection in China as their brands are too well known to be used by another person or company.

CIVIL CODE VERSUS COMMON LAW

The problem primarily rests with the legal framework in operation within China. China is a country that has a civil code. This indicates that laws are dictated by statutes and can be revised or amended only by executive or legislative powers. On the contrary, in countries that have a common-law system, changes or amendments to laws can occur through the court system by establishing legal precedents, and drawing on past rulings to establish new ones. This type of system is largely present in Britain and its former colonies, including the US. Given such a setup, experts feel that Tesla winning this case is not going to be easy, as in civil code countries, the first to file usually wins. Further, for Tesla to win in the Chinese court, it would not be enough to prove that the trademark is well known. They would have to go beyond that and show that the trademark is well known in China.

Another angle to this may include Tesla proving that Zhan is trying to extort money through these alleged claims. This is not going to be easy, as the Chinese trademark law places a high burden of proof on a company trying to prove that the owner of a trademark is acting in bad faith. To prove this angle, Tesla must provide evidence that Zhan was connected with the company in the past and had prior information of Tesla's proposed entry into China. This is easier said, as experts feel that it will be relatively easy for Zhan to show that he had no previous connection with Tesla.

A sliver of hope that Tesla has is the Paris Convention for the Protection of Industrial Property. This globally recognized accord protects *well-known marks*, and even prevails over local statutes if companies can establish that their trademarks are well known. While most countries in the world abide by the convention, they reserve the right to determine if a mark is well known locally. This is where Tesla could run into problems in this case. In effect, Tesla will also have to show that the brand was well known in China at the time Zhan registered the trademark. And going by the company developments, it seems like Zhan can convincingly show that in 2006 (when he registered the trademark), the brand was not well known in China.

In such a complex case and with a relatively new company such as Tesla, one might feel that it would be better to settle out of court. In fact, the company also tried it in 2009, only to fail in the talks. Tesla's CEO Elon Musk offered Zhan about $300,000 in exchange for the trademarks. However, Zhan put forth a counter offer to Musk of the opportunity to be a co-investor in his company for more than $3 million. Yet another approach that Tesla can consider would be show that Zhan attempted to grab trademarks for at least three other companies in recent years. However, the Chinese courts are likely to throw out that argument citing insufficient evidence to prove bad faith.

LEGAL CHANGES TO THE RESCUE

After years of deliberations, China has taken measures to revise the trademark law in the legislature that will help curb infringements and ensure a fair market for trademark holders. The new law raised the compensation ceiling for a trademark infringement to 3 million Yuan ($500,000), from a meager 500,000 Yuan ($82,000). The new law also included the provision that trademark agencies are not allowed to assign the trademarks if they know or should know that the filer is conducting a malicious registration or infringing on the trademark rights of others. Any violation of this inclusion would attract fines and a bad credit record filed by industrial and commercial authorities, and in severe cases, even the suspension of their businesses. The new law also offers protection for renowned trademarks, giving owners the right to ban others from registering their trademarks or using similar ones—even if such brand names are not registered.

While the legal changes do promise hope for Tesla and other companies that could get caught in such cases, Tesla still has an uphill battle to fight. This is because they still have to show that their brand is a renowned trademark in China, not just in the West or in the US. Therefore, there is a lot of skepticism about the new changes and the benefits to Tesla. At the moment, all the new law indicates is that China is becoming more proactive in trying to address its bad reputation as the world's largest patent and trademark infringer.

QUESTIONS FOR DISCUSSION

1. You are hired by Tesla to help them ascertain their brand reputation in China. Design a questionnaire that will help Tesla prove this in a court of law.
2. Tesla previously had a presence in Singapore from July 2010 to February 2011. They chose to leave the country as they did not receive any tax exemptions from the Singaporean government. Do you think Tesla should also leave China, given such complex legal framework? Provide reasons to justify your answer.
3. India and Indonesia are high growth markets for automobiles. Do you think Tesla can consider entering into those markets as their next steps? What legal and regulatory challenges would Tesla likely face in those countries?

SOURCES

1. Company annual reports
2. Angelo Young, "Tesla Motors' (TSLA) Trademark Problem in China: What Multinational Companies Can Learn from Tesla About Securing a Trademark on the Mainland," *International Business Times*, August 30, 2013. Accessed on August 30, 2013 from http://www.ibtimes.com/tesla-motors-tsla-trademark-problem-china-what-multinational-companies-can-learn-tesla-about-1401973
3. "China Passes New Trademark Law," *China Daily USA*, August 30, 2013. Accessed on August 31, 2013 from http://usa.chinadaily.com.cn/business/2013-08/30/content_16932794.htm
4. Zachary Shahan, "Tesla Motors Worth $20 Billion (About 42% GM's Worth), & the One Reason Why," *Clean Technica*, August 29, 2013. Accessed on August 30, 2013 from http://cleantechnica.com/2013/08/29/tesla-motors-worth-20-billion-about-42-gms-worth-the-one-reason-why/
5. Roben Farzad, "Tesla Is Now Worth $20 Billion," *Bloomberg Businessweek*, August 27, 2013. Accessed on August 30, 2013 from http://www.businessweek.com/articles/2013-08-27/tesla-is-now-worth-20-billion
6. Angelo Young, "'Trademark Troll' Zhan Baosheng Tried to Take Other Company Names; Will This Help Electric Carmaker Win Its Trademark Case?" *International Business Times*, August 20, 2013. Accessed on August 30, 2013, from http://www.ibtimes.com/trademark-troll-zhan-baosheng-tried-take-other-company-names-will-help-electric-carmaker-win-its

Case III: Segmenting Indian Households

A report published by McKinsey and Co. divided Indian households into the following five economic classes based on real annual disposable income.

- *Deprived:* This group has an income less than ₹90,000 or $1,969, and is the poorest group. Many people belonging to this group live under the poverty line as determined by the Indian government (2,400 calories per capita per day in rural areas, and 2,100 calories per capita per day in urban areas).[1] People belonging to this segment typically are unskilled and are engaged in seasonal or part-time employment.
- *Aspirers:* This group has an income between ₹90,000 and ₹200,000 or $1,969–$4,376, and mainly consists of people who are low-skilled wage earners and small-time vendors. These people strive to live a comfortable life, typically spending a large portion of their income on basic necessities.
- *Seekers:* This group has an income between ₹200,000 and ₹500,000 or $4,376–$10,941. This segment has the most diverse mix of households ranging from young college graduates to working professionals, businesspeople, government employees, and self-employed individuals. They also differ on demographic and psychographic factors such as age, attitudes, education, and employment, among others.
- *Strivers:* This group has an income between ₹500,000 and ₹1,000,000 or $10,941–$21,882 and comprises of successful businesspeople, industrialists, professionals, senior bureaucrats, government officials, and rich farmers in small towns and villages. This segment has stable financial resources and a significant level of savings to their credit. People in this income band and upwards are considered successful in the Indian society.
- *Global Indians:* This is the crème-de-la-crème of the Indian society in terms of income, and earns in excess of ₹1,000,000 or $21,882. People belonging to this group include C-suite executives in major corporations, owners of large businesses, politicians, and owners of vast agricultural lands. An upcoming group of people into this category includes the young, successful, mid-level executives or graduates from India's top educational institutions who are offered top positions in various multinational companies and command a high salary. These people have a taste for the finer things in life and spend a lot on luxury and lifestyle needs.

Table CSIII.1 provides the changing dynamics in these income groups over the years.

---

[1] This definition was later changed by the Indian government in 2012 as anyone with daily consumption expenditure less than ₹28.35 in urban areas and ₹22.42 in rural areas as being below the poverty line.

TABLE CSIII.1

CHANGING FACE OF PROSPERITY IN INDIA

Income Group	Annual Household Disposable Income (in Thousands)	1995–1996	2001–2002	2005–2006	2009–2010
Deprived	Less than 90	131,176	135,378	132,249	114,394
Aspirers	91–200	28,901	41,262	53,276	75,304
Seekers	201–500	3,881	9,034	13,183	22,268
Strivers	501–1,000	651	1,712	3,212	6,173
Global Indians	1,001–2,000	189	546	1,122	2,373
	2,001–5,000	63	201	454	1,037
	5,001–10,000	11	40	103	255
	More than 10,001	5	20	52	141

QUESTIONS FOR DISCUSSION

1. Develop a questionnaire to identify the segments that would be the ideal candidates to market a fully automatic washing machine.
2. In your opinion, which group will be most likely to recycle the products that they use? Provide reasons to justify your answer.

SOURCE

Jonathan Ablett, Aadarsh Baijal, Eric Beinhocker, Anupam Bose, Diana Farrell, Ulrich Gersch, Erza Greenberg, Shishir Gupta, and Sumit Gupta, "The 'Bird of Gold': The Rise of India's Consumer Market," McKinsey Global Institute, May 2007.

Case IV: Subaru—
A Problem of Plenty

In these troubled economic times, Subaru is having a dream run. Going by the 27% surge in sales it notched up in the US in only the first seven months of 2013, the Japanese automaker could well be in line for another year of sales increase, one of the few automakers to do so. Table CSIV.1 provides a snapshot of Subaru's business performance for the past eight years.

For the month of July 2013, the company reported a 43% increase over July 2012, and its year-to-date sales were 27% higher than the same period in 2012. Based on July 2013 sales, the carmaker could sell its entire US inventory in just 27 days—less than half the auto industry average. What's more, they have witnessed a five-fold increase in their stock price since the beginning of 2012. These impressive numbers are the result of a calculated marketing endeavor.

THE POWER OF NICHE MARKETING

A subsidiary of Fuji Heavy Industries (FHI), Subaru faced challenges early on in facing market giants such as Honda, Toyota, and General Motors, among others. Further, Toyota owning 16.5% of FHI made it difficult for Subaru to compete in the crowded front-wheel drive segment dominated by Toyota and Honda. The competition had what Subaru did not have—financial cushion, higher sales volume, and well-known brands. This enabled them to compete on price, an aspect not within the reach of Subaru. As a result, Subaru started looking at areas overlooked by the competition in order to survive. The company was quick to identify that the market did not have too many all-wheel drive options and started betting big on this niche segment. Add to this a hardware feature—the boxer engine, where the pistons move side to side instead of up and down—and Subaru had a unique combination, ideally suited to counter the snowy and hilly terrains.

Their niche focus was ably supported by several marketing decisions. Despite the potential selling benefits that accrue via lower price points typically offered by the front-wheel drive cars, Subaru has conscientiously stayed away from developing such cars and stuck to the all-wheel drive format. In fact, the newly launched BRZ is their only model to have a rear-wheel drive, a clear departure from their core focus. The company substantiates this move by offering that it is important for sport cars to have such a design for superior functionality and core to an effective product design.

Further, their marketing playbook included a carefully chosen pricing structure, providing standard features in their cars long before competition did, focusing more on advertising and promotion efforts rather than offering discounts and financial incentives to enhance their market presence, and allocating marketing resources to cultivate loyalty among existing Subaru buyers among drivers in the northern parts of the US. The combination of good content, affordable pricing, and all-wheel drive represented a good value proposition for the Subaru models. This attractive combination resulted in increased used-car values for used

TABLE CSIV.1
SUBARU'S BUSINESS PERFORMANCE[1]

	Qtr 1/ 2013–14	Consolidated FY 2012–2013	Consolidated FY 2011–2012	Consolidated FY 2010–2011	Consolidated FY 2009–2010	Consolidated FY 2008–2009	Consolidated FY 2007–2008	Consolidated FY 2006–2007	Consolidated FY 2005–2006
Production (in Thousands)									
Japan	153	583	468	459	453	474	490	484	466
US	44	181	171	165	104	92	109	103	121
Total	197	764	639	624	557	566	599	587	587
Sales—Passenger and Mini cars (in Thousands)									
Japan	41	163	172	158	171	179	209	227	230
US	116	390	309	307	250	207	210	207	210
Others	34	171	159	192	142	169	178	144	132
Total	191	724	640	657	563	555	597	578	572
Net Sales Income Worldwide (in billion Yen)	513.3	1,779.0	1,389.1	1,452.2	1,294.5	1,316.3	1,421.2	1,339.3	1,332.8
Operating Income Worldwide (in billion Yen)	64.9	111.0	39.4	80.4	21.7	(9.2)	37.1	37.8	51.6
Exchange Rate (JPY to $)	98/$	82/$	79/$	86/$	93/$	102/$	116/$	117/$	112/$

[1] Compiled from company annual reports.

Subarus, which further provided Subaru the advantage to offer attractive lease prices, at a time when some competitors were cutting back on leasing.

While all this has taken some years, the concentrated marketing initiative has paid off handsomely. The company has been clocking up incremental sales steadily over the past couple of years, and they breached the 500,000 sales figure in the US in 2014. In fact, Subaru is even benefitting from the least expected quarters—the Cash for Clunkers program. Even though many Subaru cars were not eligible through the exchange program, the company managed to sell nearly 17,000 cars. According to the program spokesman Michael McHale, they were virtually all first-time Subaru buyers. This is a clear indication of the success of the brand.

AWARDS GALORE

The sway Subaru holds over the consumers is not without reason. The more recent models are sweeping various awards for their exemplary engineering and design. The 2012 Japanese New Car Assessment Program (JNCAP) gave 5-star (highest rating) to Impreza G4 (4-door Sedan) / Sport (5-door) series. The other awards received by Subaru from JNCAP include the 2007 JNCAP Grand Prix Award for the Impreza, the 2008 JNCAP Excellent Car Awards for the Forester and Exiga 7-seater (awarded individually), and the 2009 JNCAP Grand Prix Award as well as 2011 Five Star Award for the Legacy. The Subaru was also bestowed with similar awards from the European New Car Assessment program (Euro NCAP). The awards from Euro NCAP include the 5-star (highest rating) to Legacy in 2009, and the 5-star (highest rating) to XV and Forester in 2012.

Further, the 2013 Subaru BRZ recently received the "All Star" award by the Automobile Magazine for its superior driving style and racing performance. Similarly, the new 2014 Forester SUV is the first vehicle to excel in every aspect of the challenging small overlap front crash test conducted by the Insurance Institute for Highway Safety (IIHS) to qualify for the Institute's recently inaugurated top honor, 2013 Top Safety Pick+ (TSP+). This is the third TSP+ award for Subaru vehicles following the last year's first win of 2013 Legacy and Outback. This makes Subaru the only carmaker to be recognized by IIHS for four consecutive years with a TSP winner in all its lineup models (Subaru Legacy, Subaru Outback, Subaru Forester, Subaru Tribeca, Subaru Impreza, Subaru XV Crosstrek, and Subaru BRZ) currently sold in the North American region. With such impressive awards and car safety features, it is easy to see why the car is doing well in the marketplace.

TOO BIG FOR COMFORT

With so much working in favor of Subaru, one would think that the top management must be rejoicing. Not quite so. The reason for their restrained celebrations is because they are selling too much, and they are fast approaching their full capacity. And part of the problem is the typically conservative sales forecasts that were not too helpful in preparing them for the sales surge. In fact, the conservative forecasts were so off-track that Subaru of America Chairman Takeshi Tachimori found himself apologizing instead of complaining to production officials for the shortages. While Subaru has benefitted immensely from the popularity of their new models and the weakening of the Yen, and reaped soaring profits and sales compared to most Japanese carmakers, the success is leading President Yasuyuki Yoshinaga to worry whether their niche positioning is getting too big.

To add to their woes, they are facing shortages of their latest models that have won consumers and critics over. The waiting list for their cars keeps growing. For instance, the year-to-date sales of the BRZ as of July 2013 increased 200% over the same period last year. This model that was jointly developed with Toyota was so popular it once had an eight-month waiting list in the US.

To meet the rising demand, Subaru is planning to add more capacity at their two Japanese plants that are already running at full capacity. Back in the US, the company is also planning to expand the factory at Lafayette, IN, by investing about $400 million to increase output by 76% to 300,000 vehicles by 2016.

THE WAY FORWARD

Based on the current developments, one would be inclined to suggest that a new factory would solve Subaru's supply problems. However, adding a factory that can build 200,000 vehicles a year, usually the amount required to substantiate the setting up of a new plant, will not make much financial sense unless Subaru is prepared to churn out another 200,000 cars. To identify a solution, company executives are discussing various options that include expanding Subaru's lineup of cars, making a push for cheaper vehicles for markets such as India, focusing on the products the company sells well, increasing prices, and making rearrangements in their Indiana factory that they share with Toyota, whereby they alter the production cycle to reassign the production levels of Subaru and Toyota cars. While all these suggestions seem plausible, a closer look into them reveals the intricacies involved.

Expanding the lineup of cars is a possibility that Subaru can consider. In fact, the company launched its first gasoline-electric vehicle in the US—the XV Crosstrek Hybrid—in 2013. But given the recent developments, experts are expressing concern regarding the extent to which the company can support the technology. Further, the company is late to the hybrid market and still does not have a full-electric or plug-in hybrid that meets California emissions rules that go into effect in 2016.

Another alternative is to produce cars for the mass market and for countries like India and Indonesia that are witnessing a massive growth in the number of cars. However, the company president wonders if this is really the right direction for Subaru. According to Yoshinaga, "We're not a carmaker that can grow as big as Toyota. And even if we could, reaching that sort of scale would mean we'd stop being Subaru."

Some experts believe that Subaru is better off small. Owing to its niche product positioning, and a stable partner in Toyota, it is likely that Subaru would do well by focusing on its core competency—its all-wheel drive and boxer engine combination. Any deviation from this would be a gamble for Subaru that may not pay off as expected. This idea of focusing only on the niche strategy and playing it safe would also go well with the relatively conservative approach of their business.

The straightforward suggestion of controlling excess demand, from a microeconomic perspective, would be to raise prices. This would not only boost the company's margins, but also create a strong buffer zone from an inventory management viewpoint. Evidence from other companies also suggests that raising prices might even buff the brand a bit, and lend a *premium* status for the brand. However, their approach thus far has not focused on financial incentives, but only on advertising and promotion. A move such as this could hurt their image and might remove them from the consideration set of consumer shopping lists.

In terms of production patterns, it is true that Toyota churns out much more cars than Subaru and, therefore, can be expected to lend a helping hand to Subaru by providing their assembly lines. However, Toyota spokesman Steven Curtis offered, "While Toyota has announced 10 manufacturing expansions in North America in the past 20 months, resulting in $2 billion in additional investments and more than 4,000 new jobs, we are not working with Subaru on any expansions." Though this is an arrangement that can be reconsidered by Toyota given the faster sales growth rate posted by Subaru over Toyota, it is unlikely that this setup will change owing to the deep company ties between the two corporations.

Even as everything else seems to be working Subaru's way, they seem to be at a fork in the road where they have to make some tough decisions about charting their future course. As the company ponders over the right course, a silver lining that Subaru can look up to is that a problem of plenty is a good problem to have.

QUESTIONS FOR DISCUSSION

1. In identifying the best option, what would you suggest Subaru do to counter their supply side problems? In doing this, what information would you need to arrive at this solution? How would you go about collecting such information?
2. Was Subaru justified in choosing a niche positioning in a foreign market, rather than a general and mass-market positioning? Explain.

SOURCES

1. Annual reports of Fuji Heavy Industries.
2. Kyle Stock, "Two Ways to Fix Subaru's Supply Problem," *Bloomberg Businessweek*, August 28, 2013. Accessed on August 28, 2013 from http://www.businessweek.com/articles/2013-08-28/two-ways-to-fix-subarus-supply-problem#r=nav-fs
3. Yoshio Takahashi and Yoree Koh, "Subaru's Got a Big Problem: It's Selling Too Many Cars," *Wall Street Journal*, August 19, 2013. Accessed on August 27, 2013 from http://online.wsj.com/article/SB10001424127887323838204579002400970446352.html
4. Ma Jie and Yuki Hagiwara, "Subaru's 412% Surge Leads Carmaker to Debate Niche Status," *Bloomberg*, August 9, 2013. Accessed on August 27, 2013 from http://www.bloomberg.com/news/2013-08-08/subaru-s-412-surge-leads-carmaker-to-debate-niche-status-cars.html
5. "All-New Subaru Forester Awarded 2013 'IIHS TOP SAFETY PICK +'," *Automotive World* (news release), May 20, 2013. Accessed on August 27, 2013 from http://www.automotiveworld.com/news-releases/all-new-subaru-forester-awarded-2013-iihs-top-safety-pick/
6. Jim Henry, "Detroit Auto Show: Subaru VP Tom Doll on U.S. Sales Gains with Lower Incentives," *CBS Money Watch*, January 12, 2009. Accessed on August 27, 2013 from http://www.cbsnews.com/8301-505123_162-42940343/detroit-auto-show-subaru-vp-tom-doll-on-us-sales-gains-with-lower-incentives/?tag=bnetdomain
7. Jim Henry, "Subaru Passes 200,000 in U.S.; Next Up 300,000," *CBS Money Watch*, December 9, 2009. Accessed on August 27, 2013 from http://www.cbsnews.com/8301-505123_162-42940913/subaru-passes-200000-in-us-next-up-300000/?tag=bnetdomain
8. Jim Henry, "Subaru's Slim Product Line Drives Record Sales," *CBS Money Watch*, February 22, 2010. Accessed on August 27, 2013 from http://www.cbsnews.com/8301-505123_162-42941057/subarus-slim-product-line-drives-record-sales/

Case V: Millennials at Work

The Pew Research Center characterizes the Millennial generation as a category of people born after 1980, and the first generation to come of age in the new millennium.

THE FACE OF THE MILLENNIALS

In a Pew Research conducted in 2010, Millennials were asked about the features that make them unique among the other segments such as the Generation-X-ers, Baby Boomers, and the Silent Generation. Table CSV.1 provides the results of the survey.

TABLE CSV.1
WHAT DISTINGUISHES THE MILLENNIALS FROM THE OTHER SEGMENTS?[1]

Millennials (n = 527)	Gen-X (n = 173)	Boomers (n = 283)	Silent (n = 205)
Technology use (24%)	Technology use (12%)	Work ethic (17%)	WW II, Depression (14%)
Music/pop culture (11%)	Work ethic (11%)	Respectful (14%)	Smarter (13%)
Liberal/Tolerant (7%)	Conservative/ Traditional (7%)	Values/Morals (8%)	Honest (12%)
Smarter (6%)	Smarter (6%)	*Baby Boomers* (6%)	Values/Morals (10%)
Clothes (5%)	Respectful (5%)	Smarter (5%)	Work ethic (10%)

As indicated by Table CSV.1, nearly 24% of Millennials provided that their use of technology makes them feel distinctive. While Gen-X-ers also cite technology as their generation's biggest source of distinctiveness, the numbers are far fewer (12%) than the Millennials. The Baby Boomers contend that their work ethic is the prime character that distinguishes (17%), while the Silents say that the shared experience of the Depression and World War II characterizes them the best (14%).

MILLENNIALS AND EDUCATION

In education, Millennials have not yet matched the achievements of Gen-X-ers. However, according to the Pew Research Center Survey, over time they are expected to emerge as the

---

[1] "Millennials: A Portrait of Generation Next," February 2010, Pew Research Center.

most educated generation ever. Currently only 19% are still in college, with an additional 26% currently in school and intending to graduate from college, and an additional 30% who expect to pursue a college degree. In comparison, only half of Gen-X-ers are college graduates or plan to get their degree sometime in the future. Further, the share of 18–24-year-olds attending US colleges has hit an all-time high. Additionally, US Census Bureau surveys find that 54% of Millennials already have attended some college or have graduated, compared with 49% of Gen-X-ers.

Many Millennials also undertake employment alongside education. The survey found that 24% of 18–29-year-olds are employed and enrolled in school, about 10% of Millennials study and work full time, and an additional 14% study and hold part-time jobs. Table CSV.2 provides information on Millennials involved in work and education concurrently.

TABLE CSV.2
STUDYING AND WORKING MILLENNIALS[2]

% of Millennials Who...	All Millennials	18–24 Years	25–29 Years
Work full time, do not go to school	31	19	48
Work full time, go to school	10	9	10
Work part time, do not go to school	10	11	9
Work part time, go to school	14	20	5
Do not work, go to school	13	20	4

MILLENNIALS AND EMPLOYMENT

The survey also studied the employment characteristics of Millennials and found that 65% of all Millennials have full- or part-time jobs. Further, as a group, they are less likely to be working than Gen-X-ers (75%) and about as likely to be employed as Baby Boomers (68%). However, 13% of all Millennials are full-time students and do not work for pay, compared with only 1% of Gen-X-ers and even fewer Baby Boomers. When this is factored in the employment aspect, all three groups looked similar. Nearly the same amount of people among Millennials and Gen-X-ers are employed or attending school (80% and 78%, respectively). However, a lesser amount of people among the Baby Boomers were working (68%), considering that nearly 13% of them have already retired.

OPTIMISTIC ABOUT WORK

In a recent phone survey conducted by GfK's OMNITEL and Monster.com, it has been found that Millennials are more upbeat about the idea of a steady career than Baby Boomers. Table CSV.3 provides the results from the survey.

---

[2] "Millennials: A Portrait of Generation Next," February 2010, Pew Research Center.

TABLE CSV.3

PERCEPTION ABOUT CAREERS[3]

% of Each Group That Believes...	Millennials		Baby Boomers	
	Myth	Reality	Myth	Reality
The concept of career to be old-fashioned	62	37	48	45
A career requires college education and training	33	65	39	55
A career means work in one type of job for many years	30	67	37	57

As shown in Table CSV.3, out of a representative sample size of over 1,000, nearly 62% of the Millennials said that they still considered a career very much a part of reality. On the contrary, only 48% of the Baby Boomers felt the same. Furthermore, 37% of Millennials felt that a career could provide a sense of accomplishment, against only 26% of Baby Boomers.

Despite the tough economic times and strained economies, Millennials are found to have a great deal of optimism with regard to their careers. In a 2012 research by the Pew Center among people aged 18–34, a staggering 88% said they had enough money or would have enough in the future to meet their long-term financial goals. Even among the unemployed and financially stressed, nearly 75% believed they would achieve their goals in life, or already had. In contrast, according to a Gallup poll, nearly 54% of Americans over the age of 55 thought young people today were unlikely to have a better life than their parents, compared with 42% of those aged 18–34.

WATCHING THE EXPENSES

Since the onslaught of the financial recession, almost 55% of 18–29-year-olds say they are closely monitoring their expenses. This number is up from 43% of the same age group who shared their view in 2006. Further, adults under age 30 continue to worry that they are not saving or investing enough (72% in 2006 versus 77% in 2010). That is about equal to the percentage of those aged 30–45 (78%) who say they are concerned about growing their nest eggs.

An important factor for the financial vulnerability of Millennials is the low insurance coverage rate. About 61% of all Millennials say they are covered by some form of health plan, compared with 73% of Gen-X-ers, 83% of Baby Boomers and 95% of the Silent generation (eligible for Medicare or receiving health benefits through their retirement plans). Among the Millennials, the Hispanics are more likely to be one serious injury or illness away from financial disaster. Only about 42% of Latinos between ages 18 and 29 have health insurance, compared with 64% of blacks and 67% of whites.

---

[3] Sydney Brownstone, "Millennials Are Actually Optimistic About the Prospect of Careers," *Fast Company*, August 29, 2013.

QUESTIONS FOR DISCUSSION

1. You are the Executive Director at the Career Management Center of a leading business school. How would you position the academic courses at the business school to target the Millennials?
2. What inputs can you provide to the Academic Program Coordinator regarding the design of the academic courses that would better prepare the Millennials for the future?
3. In preparing to invite companies to campus recruitment drives, what type of companies would you invite, and how would you position the business school to the recruiters?

SOURCES

1. "Millennials: A Portrait of Generation Next," February 2010, Pew Research Center.
2. Sydney Brownstone, "Millennials Are Actually Optimistic About the Prospect of Careers," *Fast Company*, August 29, 2013. Accessed on August 31, 2013 from http://www.fastcoexist.com/3016572/millennials-are-actually-optimistic-about-the-prospect-of-careers
3. Emily Alpert, "Millennial Generation Is Persistently Optimistic," *Los Angeles Times*, July 07, 2013. Accessed on August 31, 2013 from http://articles.latimes.com/2013/jul/07/local/la-me-millennial-optimism-20130708
4. Richard Fry, "College Enrollment Hits All-Time High, Fueled by Community College Surge," *Pew Research Center Report*, Oct. 29, 2009. Accessed on August 31, 2013 from http://pewsocialtrends.org/pubs/747/college-enrollment-hits-all-time-high-fueled-by-community-college-surge

INDEX

Acer, 127
AC Nielsen, 121
Adobe, 31
advertising on television, 58–59
alternative hypothesis, 307–316
altruists, 22
Amazon, 151
analysis equivalence, 177–178
analysis of variance (ANOVA). *See also* correlation
    analysis; regression analysis
    F-ratio or *F*-statistic, 326
    measuring the strength of association, 326–327
    one-factor, 323
    p-value, 326
    variation among country of origin, 323–324
    variation within country of origin, 324–325
Apple, 89
Argentina
    business characteristics, 430–431
    country characteristics, 429–430
    cultural characteristics, 430
    market research in, 431–432
Asia-Pacific region
    culture, 377–378
    e-commerce potential, 376
    language and translation issues, 380
    major holidays and seasons, 378–379
    mobile internet marketing, 380
    regional characteristics, 375–377
    secondary sources of information, 380–381
associative scaling, 236
attitudes, 228–229
    measurement, 240–243
Audi, 89, 105
Australia
    business characteristics, 382
    country characteristics, 381–382
    market research in, 382–383
automatic call distribution systems, 36
Avant-Gardians, 197

Backer Spielvogel Bates Worldwide, 195
Barnard, Philip, 42
behavior recording devices, 188–189
benefit chain, 195

biases
    cultural, 171
    in experimental designs, 166–167
    interviewer, 168
    in qualitative and observational research,
        192–193
    in surveys, 223–225
Big Data technologies, 151–153, 369, 482–483
blogs, 150
Bloomerce Access Panels, 121
Bolivia
    business charac teristics, 433–434
    country characteristics, 432–433
    cultural characteristics, 433
    market research in, 434–435
Brazil
    business characteristics, 436
    country characteristics, 435
    cultural characteristics, 435
    direct marketing industry, 437
    market research in, 436–437
Britannia, 83
BSN, 44
business intelligence (BI) system, 129
business-to-business (B2B) market, 146

calibration equivalence, 238–239
Campbell Soup Company, 4
Canada
    business characteristics, 475
    country characteristics, 473–474
    cultural characteristics, 474
    Internet penetration, 476
    market research in, 476–477
    telecommunications in, 476
casual research, 160
categorizing a product, 83
category equivalence, 264–265
causal research, 74
Chameleons, 197
China
    attitudes of workers in, 386
    business characteristics, 384
    country characteristics, 383
    economic data, 131

marketing and consumer behavior, 383–384
market research in, 386–387
methods of data collection in, 387–388
product pricing and positioning strategies, 384–386
sampling techniques in, 388
chi-square test, 318, 320
Cisco, 3
close-ended questions, 255–257
cloud computing, 483–485
cluster analysis, 352–355
cluster sampling, 278
Coca-Cola, 44, 69, 78–79, 100, 200, 222
collectivism, 18
comparability, 24–26
comparative research, 22–24
comparative scale, 232
conceptual equivalence, 264
concurrent validity, 240
conjoint analysis, 359–364
constant-sum scales, 233
construct equivalence, 176, 263–265
construct validity, 240–241
consumer-generated marketing, 32–33
consumption patterns, 13, 81–82
buying characteristics, 145–146
lifestyle segments, 197
content analysis, 188
content communities, 150
contrived observation, 188
convenience sampling, 280
convergent validity, 240
coordinating research work, 61–64, 83–86
Coors, 27
corollary data method, 128
correlation analysis
partial correlation coefficient, 328–329
Pearson correlation coefficient, 327–329
simple, 327–328
Spearman rank correlation coefficient, 329–331
Cossacks, 197
cost of conducting marketing research, 48–50
countries, similarities and differences of
actual and potential target groups, 14
climate, 11
consumption patterns, 13
culture, 10–11
economic differences, 12
historical differences, 13
languages, 14
marketing conditions, 13
race, 11

religion, 12
creatives, 22
criterion validity, 240
cultures and cultural values, 10–11, 16–20
Argentina, 430
Asian countries, 21, 377–378
Bolivia, 433
Brazil, 435
classification, 21–22
contrast between individualism and collectivism, 18
Europe, 405–406
India, 390
and information processing, 17
Japan, 395
Latin America, 423–424
long-term orientation, 19–20
masculinity *vs* femininity, 19
Mediterranean countries, 21
Mexico, 470–471
Middle East and North Africa (MENA), 446–447
Middle Eastern cultures, 22
need to understand, 16–17
North America, 464
North American and Northwestern/Central European cultural groups, 21
power distance dimension, 17–18
questionnaires, 262–263
sampling, 294–295
Saudi Arabia, 453
in scale development, 246–247
South Africa, 460–461
Sub-Saharan Africa, 457–458
and surveys, 223–224
tolerance for uncertainty and ambiguity, 19
Venezuela, 438
customer database, 118–119
customer feedback, 118

data analysis, 306–307. *See also* analysis of variance (ANOVA); correlation analysis; regression analysis
statistical techniques, 307–320
database sample, 281
data collection methods, 54–55
data preparation
coding of data, 304–305
data transformation and adjustments, 305–306
editing data, 304
logging the data, 303
data privacy laws, 38
data visualization, 369

decentralized marketing approach, 44
decision alternatives, 68–69
Dell, 127
demand estimation, 127–128
dependence techniques
    conjoint analysis, 359–364
    discriminant analysis, 358–359
descriptive research, 22–24, 74, 159–160
devouts, 22
direct data method, 127
direct observation, 187
direct questions, 257
discriminant analysis, 358–359
discriminant validity, 240
door-to-door interviewing, 206
DuPont, 68, 198

electrodermal analysis, 244–245
electronic point of sale (EPoS) scanning data, 126–127
e-mail surveys, 147
employment, 55
entering a foreign market, 98–102
    contract manufacturing, 100
    determining factors, 99
    exporting, 99–100
    franchising, 100–101
    joint ventures, 101
    licensing, 100–101
    wholly owned subsidiaries, 101–102
E-Rewards.com, 121
escorted browsing, 36
ESOMAR Global Market Research report, 157–158
ethics in research, 37–38
    in online research, 38
    respondents' rights, 37
    sponsors' rights, 37
ethnocentric, polycentric, regiocentric, or geocentric orientation (EPRG) framework, 106–107
Euro Disney Theme Park, 84
EuroMOSAIC, 122–125
Europe
    computerized information and services, 408–409
    consumer list/business list, 408
    cultural *dos* and *don'ts* in, 406
    culture, 405–406
    EU or European Economic Community (EEC), 404–405
    language issues, 406–407
    major holidays and seasons, 406
    regional characteristics, 400–403
    secondary data sources, 403–404
Eveready Industries, 87
executive interviewing, 207
expansion strategy, 104–105
experimental designs, 160–161
    biases in, 166–167
    pre-, 161–163
    problems in, 165–166
    quasi, 165
    true, 163–164
experiments, 61
exploratory research, 74, 159
eye movement analysis, 243–244

Facebook, 151
facial muscle activity, 246
facial recognition technology, 202–203
fact-finding, 42
factor analysis, 346–352
femininity, 19
focus groups, 169
    advantages and disadvantages, 189–190
    discussions, 60, 183–186
    skills of moderator and assistant moderator, 185
forecasting, qualitative and quantitative approaches to, 102–103
France
    business characteristics, 410
    Consumer Rights Bill in, 82
    country characteristics, 409
    market research in, 410–411
F-ratio or *F*-statistic, 326
functional equivalence, 263–264
fun seekers, 22
future of global marketing research, 481–492
    access to information, 490–491
    Big Data technologies, 482–483
    cloud computing, application of, 483–485
    collection and control over information, 489–490
    data collection sources, 485–486
    government regulations, 491–492
    privacy concerns, 489–492
    research analysis and techniques, 486–488

General Mills Inc., 33, 43
genetic algorithm (GA), 338–339
geodemographic classifications of group consumers, 122–125
Germany
    business characteristics, 412

conducting negotiations with Germans, 413
country characteristics, 411
Internet marketing in, 414
market research in, 412–413
GfK Group, 54
Gillette, 78
Global Consumer Survey, 22
globalization process, 97–103
   diffusion process of a new product/service, 103
   market selection, 97
   mode of entry, 98–102
   qualitative and quantitative approaches to forecasting, 102–103
global marketing research
   approaches to, 59–61
   behavioral and relationship orientation of, 47
   benefits, 6
   challenges, 29–30
   classification of, 26–29
   comparability of data, 24–26
   complexity of, 44, 46–48
   defined, 5
   environmental variables influencing, 45
   firms engaged in, 52–54
   fragmentation of departments, 44–45
   future of, 481–492
   improvement in product features and benefits, 88–89
   indicators for assessing risks and opportunities, 43
   industry, 52
   initiatives, 8
   issues specific to, 43–45
   need for, 78–89
   opportunity analysis, 68
   pitfalls to avoid during, 15–16
   in practice, 38, 64, 90, 110–115, 134–135, 153, 178–179, 203, 225–226, 247–248, 269–270, 296–299
   product development cycle and, 86–88
   purpose of, 7
   significance, 5
   speed and actionability, 45
   understanding, 7
   users, 69
   vs domestic marketing research, 8–14
global or pan-cultural scales, 237–238
global penetration of the Internet, 31–32
global social consumer, 34–36
global spending on marketing research, 42
Glocer, Tom, 32–33
Google, 83, 133

Great Britain
   conducting business in, 414–416
   country characteristics, 414
   direct mailing, 417–418
   negotiating with British, 415
   online marketing in, 418
   telemarketing in, 416
Gulf Cooperation Council (GCC), 452

Hadoop, 151, 153
hard data, 52
Harris Interactive, 121, 148
Helene Curtis, 4
Hero Motors, 101
hidden-issue questioning, 182
Hierarchical Bayes (HB) models, 340–342
hierarchical clustering, 354
Honda, 101
HP, 127
HTC One, 86
humanistic inquiry, 188
hypothesis testing, 307–316
   of differences in means for independent samples with a known population variance, 314
   of differences in means for related samples, 314–316
   of single mean with a known population variance, 309–312
   of single mean with a unknown population variance, 312–313

IBM, 79, 101
idiosyncrasies of different regions, 8–9
imposing research programs, 62
IMS Health Holdings Inc., 54
independent multi-country research, 28–29
India
   business characteristics, 389
   challenges facing market research in, 393–394
   consumer market in, 392–393
   country characteristics, 389
   cultural *dos* and *don'ts* in, 390
   market research in, 390
   methods of data collection, 391–392
Indian households, segmenting, 507–508
Indian transistor, 87
indirect questions, 257
individualism, 18
information needs in marketing research, 111–114
information requirement for research, 69–70, 95
Information Resources Inc., 121

interactive media forms, 147
interdependence techniques
    cluster analysis, 352–355
    factor analysis, 346–352
    multidimensional scaling, 356–358
international researcher
    conducting research, 23
    skills important to, 24
Internet
    Big Data technologies, 151–153
    current trends in, 139–142
    marketing research surveys using, 225
    primary research on, 146–149
    secondary research on, 143–146
    social media, 149–151
    as a source of information, 120–121
    then and now, 137–138
    as a tool in research, 138
interval scale, 76
interviews, 75, 168, 181–183
    advantages and disadvantages, 189
    door-to-door interviewing, 206
    executive interviewing, 207
    personal, 205
    telephone, 208–213
intimates, 22
Ipsos, 54
itemized-category scale, 231

Japan
    business characteristics, 395
    characteristics of the Japanese culture and way
      of conducting business, 396–397
    country characteristics, 394–395
    cultural characteristics, 395
    cultural *dos* and *don'ts* in, 398
    market research in, 397
    methods of data collection, 397–399
    source of marketing-related information, 398
    tips for marketing in, 396
judgmental sampling, 278

Kantar, 54, 56
Kellogg's, 155–156
KFC, 3–4

laddering, 182
Latin America
    attitude towards research, 419–420
    codes of conduct, 421–422
    cultural *dos* and *don'ts* in, 423–424
    culture and history, 420

    direct marketing industry in, 424
    economic influence in, 428
    languages, 420–421
    middle class in, 422–423
    mobile connectivity in, 427
    postal service in, 425
    trade with Asia, 428–429
    use of the Internet in, 425–427
Lenovo, 127
Leo Burnett, 195
lifestyle segmentation schemes, 193–194
Likert scale, 234, 236
list sample, 281
long-term orientation, 19–20
L'Oreal, 44

macro-level units, 71
mail surveys, 213–215
    advantages and disadvantages, 219–220
mall intercept surveys, 207
Manwani, Harish, 149
market complexity, 78–80
marketing communication, 80–82
marketing landscape, trends, 31
marketing research
    use of, 63
marketing research, defined, 4
marketing researcher of the 21st century, 30–37
marketing strategy decisions, role of research in,
    41–43, 81
market selection, 97
Markov chain for the model, 342
Marks & Spencer, 44
Mars, 44
masculinity, 19
matched control group design, 162–163
McDonald's, 23, 44, 80, 89, 391
measurement, 229. *See also* scale development
    attitudes, 240–243
    of equivalence, 238–240
measurement equivalence, 176–177
Mercedes Benz, 89
MERCOSUR, 427–428
mergers and acquisitions (M&A), 55
metric equivalence, 239
Mexico
    business characteristics, 471–472
    country characteristics, 470
    cultural characteristics, 470–471
    Internet penetration, 473
    market research in, 472–473
    telecommunications in, 473

micro-level units, 71
Middle East and North Africa (MENA)
    conducting or gathering secondary research, 442–445
    conducting primary research, 441–442
    consumer behavior, 447
    cultural *dos* and *don'ts* in, 446
    culture and religion, 446–447
    expatriates in, 449
    Gulf Cooperation Council (GCC), 452
    income differences, 448
    Internet access, 450–451
    language, 447
    technology infrastructure, 449–451
    telecommunications in, 449–450
Millennial generation, conducting research with, 514–516
mobile marketing, 33–36
mobile phone tracking technology, 201–202
mongoDB, 153
MOSAIC, 122–125
Motorola, 198
multi-country survey, 23
multidimensional scaling, 356–358
multi-stage sampling, 278
multivariate techniques, 307
National Technical Information Service (NTIS), 381
Nestlé, 198
neuromarketing, 199–201
niche marketing, 44
Nielsen, 52–54, 56–57, 120
Nike, 27
nominal scale, 76
nondirective interviews, 182
non-hierarchical clustering, 354
non-matched control group design, 162
non-probability sampling, 278–281
non-sampling error, 273
nonverbal questions, 258
Nordstrom, 201–202
North America
    cultural *dos* and *don'ts* in, 465
    culture and language, 464
    market research industry in, 463–464
    US and Canada trade, 466
    US and Mexico trade, 466
North American Free Trade Agreement, 464–466
North American Free Trade Agreement (NAFTA), 108
null hypothesis, 307–316
NW Ayer, 195

observational methods, 75–76, 187–189
    advantages and disadvantages, 190–191
observational research, 60
observational techniques, 169
odds ratio, 341
Ogilvy and Mather, 195
omnibus surveys, 170, 208
one group, after-only design, 161–162
one group, before–after design, 163
online focus groups, 148
online panels, 148, 282
online questionnaire, 266–269
online research, 54
online surveys, 215–216
    advantages and disadvantages, 220
open-ended questions, 255–257
operational database, 118
Opinion Outpost, 121
opportunity analysis, 68
ordinal scale, 76
Ordinary Least Squares (OLS) procedure, 335

pan-global research studies, 61–64
Pearson correlation coefficient, 327–329
Pentaho, 153
People Meter, 57
Pepsi, 27, 200
PepsiCo, 71
personal interviews, 205
    advantages and disadvantages, 216–217
personnel resources for conducting research, 52
P&G, 69, 71, 101, 169
Philips, 89
Photosort, 194
physical trace measures, 188
pictorial scales, 233
Pig language, 153
Pontificators, 197
pooled time-series cross-sectional analysis, 335–337
population, defined, 272
positioning the products, 88–89
power distance index, 17–18
predictive validity, 240
pre-experimental designs, 161–163
primary data
    accessibility of, 172
    advantages, 175
    confidentiality of, 173
    data collection, 156
    disadvantages, 175
    EMIC *vs* ETIC Dilemma, 167–168

establishing equivalence in international marketing research, 175–178
expenses in collection of, 174
issues in data collection, 167–168
language and cultural issues with, 171–172
need for, 155
operational difficulties in collection, 174–175
problem of analysis and communication of results, 173
problem of identification, 172
problems with collection of, 171–175
sources, 168–170
technological requirements for collection of, 174
timing of collecting, 173–174
primary data collection, 75
primary research, 159–167
primary research on Internet, 146–149
   e-mail surveys, 147
   interactive media forms, 147
   online focus groups, 148
   online panels, 148
   user-generated reviews, 148–149
problem orientation, 107–108
product development cycle, 86–88
product positioning, 4
projective techniques, 75, 186–187
   advantages and disadvantages, 190
proposing research programs, 62
protocol method, 187
   advantages and disadvantages, 190
psychographic research, 195–197
published data, 119–120
Puma, 27
pupillary response, 245
purchase intercept technique, 207–208
p-value, 326

QR codes, 126
Q-sort scaling, 232
qualitative and observational research
   advantages and disadvantages of, 189–191
   biases in, 192–193
   cultural influences, 191–192
   focus group discussion, 183–186
   frequency and ease of use, 191
   interviews, 181–183
   landmark developments, 193–203
   need for, 180–181
   observational methods, 187–189
   projective techniques, 186–187
   protocol method, 187

qualitative data collection methods, 75–76
quantitative research, 54
quasi-experimental designs, 165
questionnaires. *See also* surveys
   construct equivalence, 263–265
   cultural issues, 262–263
   data organization of, 253
   definition, 250
   development, 252–262
   direct *vs* indirect questions, 257
   format, 255
   language considerations, 260–261
   online, design for, 266–269
   open *vs* close-ended questions, 255–257
   sequence of steps to design, 251–252
   tips for design, 261
   uses, 251
   verbal *vs* nonverbal questions, 258
   wording and translation, 258–260
quota sampling, 280–281, 284

radio frequency identification (RFID) tags, 126
random digit dialing (RDD) method, 209–210
rank-order scale, 232
ratio scale, 77
regression analysis, 331–335
   assumptions in, 331
   computation of regression coefficients, 332
   interpretation of regression model parameters, 333–335
   testing the significance of the independent variable, 333–335
research firm, selecting a, 61
research objective, 66–68
research organizations, 55
research process, 67
   data analysis, 77
   data availability for, 73–74
   decision alternatives and, 68–69
   evaluating the value of research, 131–133
   globalization process, 97–103
   information requirement for, 69–70, 95
   interpretation and presentation, 78
   market orientation, 96–103
   primary data collection, 75
   problem orientation, 107–108
   qualitative data collection methods, 75–76
   research design, 74–75
   sampling, 77
   strategic orientation, 103–107
   surveys, 76–77
   unit of analysis, 71–73, 108–110

result presentation
    integrating new technology and, 369
    oral presentation, 368
    using tablets and mobile devices, 370–371
    validity, reliability, and generalizability in presentations, 368–369
    written report, 366–368

sample and population proportions, testing of, 316–317
sample correlation coefficient, 327–328
sample covariance, 327
sample standard deviation, 288–291
sampling
    advantages and disadvantages, 283–286
    cluster, 278
    convenience, 280
    cost–benefit analysis, 293
    cultural issues, 294–295
    determination of target population, 274
    in developing countries, 295–296
    frame, 274
    judgmental, 278
    methods for determining sample size, 286–293
    multi-stage, 278
    non-probability, 278–281
    online, 281–282
    probability, 276–278
    process, 273–275
    proportions, 291–293
    quota, 280–281, 284
    simple random, 276
    snowball, 280
    statistical basis for, 272–273
    stratified random, 277
    systematic random, 277
sampling equivalence, 177, 294
sampling error, 293
Samsung, 83
Saudi Arabia
    business characteristics, 453–454
    country characteristics, 453
    cultural characteristics, 453
    market research in, 455
    Saudi youth, 454
scale development. *See also* measurement
    attitudes, 228–229
    in cross-national research, 236–237
    cultural issues, 246–247
    generalizability of a scale, 242
    global or pan-cultural scales, 237–238

    interval scale, 230
    multiple-item scales, 234–236
    nominal scale, 229
    ordinal scale, 229–230
    psychophysiological approaches to, 243–246
    ratio scale, 230
    relevance of a scale, 243
    reliability of a scale, 241–242
    sensitivity of a scale, 242
    single-item scales, 231–234
    validity of a scale, 240–241
scale transformation, 306
scaling, 76–77, 229–230
scanner data, 125
secondary data
    advantages of, 129
    disadvantages of, 129–130
    electronic point of sale (EPoS) scanning data, 126–127
    external sources, 119–121
    guidelines for effective online, 133–134
    internal sources, 117–119
    problems in collecting, 130–131
    syndicated data, 121–125
    uses of, 127–129
secondary data in global marketing research, 74
secondary data research on Internet
    agents, 143–144
    buyer behavior, 145–146
    buying characteristics, 145–146
    competitive intelligence analysis, 144–145
    custom search services, 143
    industry analysis, 145
    search engines, 144
segmentation, 128–129, 297–298
    of Indian households, 507–508
    and social responsibility, 196
self-administered questionnaires, 207–208
self-reference criterion (SRC), 20, 107–108
semantic differential scales, 235–236
semantics, 197–198
semi-structured or focused individual interviews, 182
sequential multi-country research, 29
Shell, 44
simple random sampling, 276
simultaneous multi-country research, 29
single-country research, 23, 27–28
Skelly, Florence, 193
snowball sampling, 280
social coupons, 151

socializing, 149
social media, 149–151
    facts, figures, and statistics for 2013, 152
social media marketing, 33–36
social networks, 150
soft data, 52
Solomon Four-Group design, 165
South Africa
    business characteristics, 461
    country characteristics, 460
    cultural characteristics, 460–461
    market research in, 462
Spearman rank correlation coefficient, 329–331
SpliceMachine, 153
sprinkler strategy, 104
standardization or adaptation of a product,
    105–106
standardized sources of marketing information,
    120
standards in research, 49–51
stapel scales, 236
Starbucks, 68, 105, 495–499
statistical adjustment, 306
statistical independence, 318
statistical inference, 355
Stengel, Jim, 32
Stop & Shop, 126–127
strategic orientation, 103–107
stratified random sampling, 277
strivers, 22
Subaru, 509–513
Sub-Saharan Africa
    culture and language, 457–458
    economy, 456–457
    technological infrastructure, 459
subset problem, 274–275
Subway, 105
superset problem, 274–275
surveys, 61, 170. *See also* questionnaires
    advantages and disadvantages, 216–220
    applicability, 222
    basic requirements, 221–222
    cultural influences, 222–223
    door-to-door interviewing, 206
    executive interviewing, 207
    frequency and ease of use, 220–221
    mail, 213–215
    mall intercept, 207
    on mobile, 226
    new approaches to, 225
    omnibus, 208

online, 215–216
personal interviews, 205
problems with, 223
purchase intercept technique, 207–208
self-administered questionnaires, 207–208
sources of bias in, 223–225
telephone interviews, 208–213
Survey Sampling International (SSI), 121, 209
symbolic analysis, 182–183
Synovate Consumer Opinion Panel, 121, 148
systematic random digit dialing (SRD), 210–211
systematic random sampling, 277

targeting, 128–129
T-distribution, 312–314
technological resources for conducting research,
    51
technology-based marketing, 36–37
technology companies, 3
telegram, 87
telephone interviews, 208–213
    advantages and disadvantages, 217–219
telephone prenotification method, 211–213
telephone surveys and group discussions, 54
television advertisement measurement, 55–59
Tesla Motors Inc., 500–505
test of goodness of fit, 320
test of independence, 318–319
text chat, 36
Thematic Apperception Test, 194
theoretical research, 22
Thurstone scales, 235
TNS, 121
translation equivalence, 239
TV penetration, 56–58
two-group, after–only design, 163–164
two-group, before–after design, 164
two sample proportions, testing of, 317–318
type I and II error, 309

uncertainty avoidance, 19
Unibic, 83
Unilever, 44
United States of America
    business characteristics, 468
    consumer privacy and protection, 469
    country characteristics, 467
    cultural characteristics, 467–468
    Internet penetration in, 470
    market research in, 468–470
    telecommunications, 469

unit of analysis, 71–73, 108–110
univariate testing, 307
urban, definitions, 72–73
US Department of Commerce, 380
user-generated reviews, 148–149

Values, Attitudes, and Lifestyles (VALS) program, 193–194, 197
variable re-specification, 306
Venezuela
    business characteristics, 438–439
    country characteristics, 438
    cultural characteristics, 438
    market research in, 439–440
verbal questions, 258
virtual conferencing, 36

voice over Internet, 36
Volkswagen, 199

Wal-Mart, 105, 125
    issues faced in India, 5
waterfall strategy, 104–105
web-screened samples, 281
weighting, 306
Whirlpool, 44
written report, 366–368

Yankelovich, Daniel, 193
Yankelovich Lifestyle Monitor, 194

Zaltman Metaphor Elicitation Technique (ZMET), 198–199